Custom Textbook for CSEC 630

University of Maryland University College

WILEY Custom
LEARNING SOLUTIONS

To order books or for customer service, please call 1(800)-CALL-WILEY (225-5945).

Printed in the United States of America.

ISBN 978-0-470-92441-9

Printed and Bound by EPAC Technologies, Inc.

10 9 8 7 6 5 4 3 2 1

Contents

HANDBOOK
— OF —
INFORMATION SECURITY

Key Concepts, Infrastructure, Standards, and Protocols

Volume 1

Hossein Bidgoli
Editor-in-Chief
California State University
Bakersfield, California

John Wiley & Sons, Inc.

Library of Congress Cataloging-in-Publication Data:

The handbook of information security / edited by Hossein Bidgoli.
    p. cm.
  Includes bibliographical references and index.
    ISBN-13: 978-0-471-64830-7, ISBN-10: 0-471-64830-2 (CLOTH VOL 1 : alk. paper)
    ISBN-13: 978-0-471-64831-4, ISBN-10: 0-471-64831-0 (CLOTH VOL 2 : alk. paper)
    ISBN-13: 978-0-471-64832-1, ISBN-10: 0-471-64832-9 (CLOTH VOL 3 : alk. paper)
    ISBN-13: 978-0-471-22201-9, ISBN-10: 0-471-22201-1 (CLOTH SET : alk. paper)
    1. Internet–Encyclopedias.   I. Bidgoli, Hossein.
TK5105.875.I57I5466   2003
004.67′8′03–dc21

2002155552

Printed in the United States of America

10 9 8 7 6 5 4 3 2 1

HANDBOOK
—OF—
INFORMATION
SECURITY

Information Warfare; Social, Legal, and International Issues; and Security Foundations

Volume 2

Hossein Bidgoli
Editor-in-Chief
California State University
Bakersfield, California

WILEY

John Wiley & Sons, Inc.

Wiley also publishes its books in a variety of electronic formats. Some content that appears in print may not be available in electronic books. For more information about Wiley products, visit our web site at www.Wiley.com.

Library of Congress Cataloging-in-Publication Data:

The handbook of information security / edited by Hossein Bidgoli.
    p. cm.
  Includes bibliographical references and index.
    ISBN-13: 978-0-471-64830-7, ISBN-10: 0-471-64830-2 (CLOTH VOL 1 : alk. paper)
    ISBN-13: 978-0-471-64831-4, ISBN-10: 0-471-64831-0 (CLOTH VOL 2 : alk. paper)
    ISBN-13: 978-0-471-64832-1, ISBN-10: 0-471-64832-9 (CLOTH VOL 3 : alk. paper)
    ISBN-13: 978-0-471-22201-9, ISBN-10: 0-471-22201-1 (CLOTH SET : alk. paper)
    1. Internet–Encyclopedias.   I. Bidgoli, Hossein.
TK5105.875.I57I5466   2003
004.67′8′03–dc21
                                        2002155552

Printed in the United States of America

10 9 8 7 6 5 4 3 2 1

HANDBOOK
OF
INFORMATION
SECURITY

**Threats, Vulnerabilities, Prevention,
Detection, and Management**

Volume 3

Hossein Bidgoli
Editor-in-Chief
California State University
Bakersfield, California

WILEY

John Wiley & Sons, Inc.

Firewall Basics

James E. Goldman, *Purdue University*

INTRODUCTION

When an organization or individual links to the Internet, a two-way access point out of and into their information systems is created. To prevent unauthorized activities between the Internet and the private network, a specialized hardware, software, or software–hardware combination known as a firewall is often deployed.

Overall Firewall Functionality

Firewall software often runs on a dedicated server between the Internet and the protected network. Firmware-based firewalls and single-purpose dedicated firewall appliances are situated in a similar location on a network and provide similar functionality to the software-based firewall. All network traffic entering the firewall is examined, and possibly filtered, to ensure that only authorized activities take place. This process may be limited to verifying authorized access requested files or services, or it may delve more deeply into content, location, time, date, day of week, participants, or other criteria of interest. Firewalls usually provide a layer of isolation between the inside, sometimes referred to as the "clean" network, and the outside or "dirty" network. They are also used, although less frequently, to separate multiple subnetworks so as to control interactions between them. Figure 1 illustrates a typical installation of a firewall in a perimeter security configuration.

A common underlying assumption in such a design scenario is that all of the threats come from the outside network or the Internet, but many modern firewalls provide protection against insiders acting inappropriately and against accidental harm that could result from internal configuration errors, viruses, or experimental implementations. Research consistently indicates that 70–80% of malicious activity originates from insiders who would normally have access to systems both inside and outside

of the firewall. In addition, outside threats may be able to circumvent the firewall entirely if dial-up modem access remains uncontrolled or unmonitored, if radiolocal area networks or similar wireless technology is used, or if other methods can be used to co-opt an insider, to subvert the integrity of systems within the firewall, or to otherwise bypass the firewall as a route for communications. Incorrectly implemented firewalls can exacerbate this situation by creating new, and sometimes undetected, security holes or by creating such an impediment to legitimate uses that insiders subvert its mechanisms intentionally. It is often said that an incorrectly configured and maintained firewall is worse than no firewall at all because it gives a false sense of security.

The advantages of firewalls are as follows:

1. When properly configured and monitored, firewalls can be an effective way to protect network and information resources.
2. Firewalls are often used to reduce the costs associated with protecting larger numbers of computers that are located inside it.
3. Firewalls provide a control point that can be used for other protective purposes.

The disadvantages of firewalls are as follows:

1. Firewalls can be complex devices with complicated rule sets.
2. Firewalls must be configured, managed, and monitored by properly trained personnel.
3. A misconfigured firewall gives the illusion of security.
4. Even a properly configured firewall is not sufficient or complete as a perimeter security solution. A total security solution typically also includes intrusion detection/prevention systems, vulnerability assessment

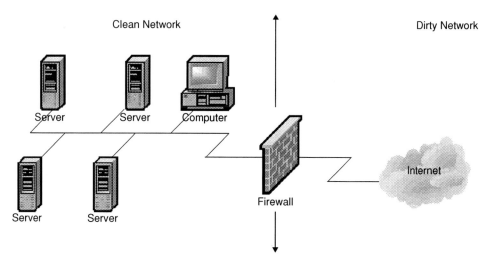

Figure 1: Typical installation of a firewall in a perimeter security configuration.

technology, and antivirus technology. According to the Computer Security Institute, 80% of successful network attacks either penetrate or avoid firewall security.

5. The processing of packets by a firewall inevitably introduces latency that, in some cases, can be significant.

6. Firewalls often interfere with network applications that may expect direct connections to end user workstations such as voice-over-Internet protocol (IP) phones and virtual private networks (VPNs) as well as some collaborative tools such as instant messenger and video and audio conferencing software.

7. The level to which firewalls inspect the data contained with packets varies widely. Although some firewalls only filter packets based on source and destination addresses, other firewalls perform much more comprehensive packet inspection on the contents of those packets.

8. Firewalls cannot prevent vulnerabilities introduced directly at client computers such as malicious code,

e-mail attacks, and Web-based Trojans. Such Trojan programs can then launch attacks within the internal network, undetected by the perimeter-based firewall.

FIREWALL FUNCTIONALITY
Background

Network communication between computers, whether or not that communication is through a firewall, is most often organized into layers according to the open systems interconnect (OSI) model. Figure 2 illustrates basic firewall functionality and technology categories in terms of the OSI model.

Firewalls were initially introduced as application level programs running over standard operating systems. As a result, these firewall programs were easily bypassed by directly attacking the vulnerabilities of the underlying TCP/IP stack and native operating system. Such operating

OSI Model Layer	Firewall Functionality	Firewall Technology	
7 Application	Application level proxies forward and reverse proxies	Proxy Servers	Switched Firewalls Air Gap Technology
6 Presentation		Firewall Appliances	
5 Session	Stateful firewall		
4 Transport TCP/UDP	Port filtering circuit level proxy		
3 Network IP	Packet filtering address filtering packet filtering firewall	Router	
2 Data link			
1 Physical			

Figure 2: Basic firewall functionality and technology versus the OSI model.

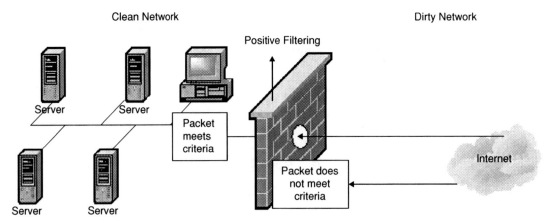

Figure 3: Positive filtering.

systems were sometimes referred to as nonhardened operating systems. Firewalls conforming to this type of configuration are sometimes referred to as first-generation firewalls.

Today, most firewalls use hardened operating systems and are run as single programs on a dedicated computing device or hardware firewall appliance. As a result, it is more difficult to attack firewalls through the underlying vulnerabilities of operating systems and network protocols. Firewalls conforming to this architecture are sometimes referred to as second-generation firewalls.

Firewalls basically act as filters. They either allow or disallow a given packet based on rules contained in a filter table. At the highest level, filtering is either positive or negative. Positive filters allow traffic to pass through the firewall if those packets meet the criteria listed in the filter table and block all traffic that does not. Negative filters prevent any traffic that meets criteria on filter tables from passing through the firewall and allows all traffic to pass that does not. Firewall rules are processed in a serial fashion. Initially, the first rule in a firewall is generally to block all traffic, followed by exception rules allowing those packets specified in the filter table (positive filtering). Conversely, the first rule could be to allow all traffic to pass through the firewall followed by exception rules in a filter table specifying which traffic must be blocked (negative filtering). Filters can be applied as easily to traffic going

from internal (secure) networks to the Internet (nonsecure) as they can be from the Internet into the secure internal networks. Which packets get allowed and disallowed in either direction can vary based on the order in which the firewall rules are processed. As a result, firewall rule logic can be extremely complicated and must be tested carefully. Figure 3 illustrates positive and Figure 4 illustrates negative filtering.

A given firewall may, but does not necessarily, offer any or all of the following functions.

Bad Packet Filtering

The first type of filtering normally done is to remove bad packets, sometimes also referred to as misshapen packets. Such abnormal packets are often used to look for vulnerabilities or to launch attacks such as denial of service attacks or distributed denial of service attacks. Bad packet filtering can be, and often is, implemented in a router, sometimes referred to as a filtering router, that faces the dirty network. However, it is highlighted here as an initial firewall function to assure that it is not overlooked. More specific examples of bad packets are packet fragments, packets with abnormally set flags, time-to-live (TTL) fields, abnormal packet length, or Internet control message protocol (ICMP) packets. The overall purpose in removing such "trash" initially is that the processing

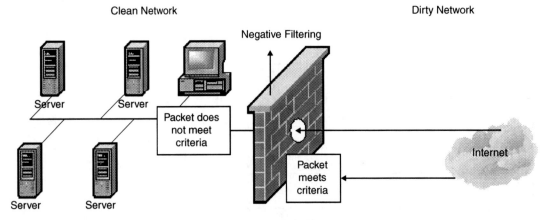

Figure 4: Negative filtering.

intensive firewall can spend its time only looking at legitimate (although not necessarily authorized) packets.

Address Filtering

This function can, and perhaps should, be performed by a device other than the firewall, such as a border router. Based on address filter tables containing allowed or disallowed individual or groups (subnets) or addresses, address filtering blocks all traffic that contains either disallowed source or destination addresses. Address filtering by itself may not provide adequate protection because it is too large a granularity for some protective requirements.

Port Filtering

Port filtering goes beyond address filtering, examining to which function or program a given packet applies. For example, file transfer protocol (FTP) typically uses ports 20 and 21, inbound electronic mail (simple mail transfer protocol; SMTP) typically uses port 25, and inbound nonencrypted Web traffic (hypertext transfer protocol; HTTP) typically uses port 80. Attacks are often targeted and designed for specific ports. Port filtering can be used to ensure that all ports are disabled except those that must remain open and active to support programs and protocols required by the owners of the inside network. Static port filtering leaves authorized ports open to all traffic all the time, whereas dynamic port filtering opens and closes portions of protocols associated with authorized ports over time as required for the specifics of the protocols.

Domain Filtering

Domain filtering applies to outbound traffic headed through the firewall to the Internet. Domain filtering can block traffic with domains that are not authorized for communications or can be designed to permit exchanges only with authorized "outside" domains.

Network Address Translation

When organizations connect to the Internet, the addresses they send out must be globally unique. In most cases, an organization's Internet service provider specifies these globally unique addresses. Most organizations have relatively few globally unique public addresses compared with the actual number of network nodes on their entire network.

The Internet Assigned Numbers Authority has set aside the following private address ranges for use by private networks: 10.0.0.0 to 10.255.255.255, 172.16.0.0 to 172.31.255.255, and 192.168.0.0 to 192.168.255.255.

Traffic using any of these "private" addresses must remain on the organization's private network to interoperate properly with the rest of the Internet. Because anyone is welcome to use these address ranges, they are not globally unique and therefore cannot be used reliably over the Internet. Computers on a network using the private IP address space can still send and receive traffic to and from the Internet by using network address translation (NAT). An added benefit of NAT is that the organization's private network is not as readily visible from the Internet.

All of the work stations on a private network can share a single or small number of globally unique assigned public IP address(es) because NAT mechanism maintains a table that provides for translation between internal addresses and ports and external addresses and ports. These addresses and port numbers are generally configured so as not to conflict with commonly assigned transmission control protocol (TCP) port numbers. The combination of the shared public IP address and a port number that is translated into internal address and port numbers via the translation table allows computers on the private network to communicate with the Internet through the firewall. NAT can also run on routers, dedicated servers, or other similar devices, and "gateway" computers often provide a similar function.

Dynamic NAT entries are created automatically in the NAT table as the firewall or router receives packets that require NAT translation. Dynamic NAT entries are purged after a preset period. For mapping addresses on a more permanent basis through the firewall, static NAT entries can be manually entered into the NAT table and must be manually removed as well. Most firewalls provide some type of NAT functionality as illustrated in Figure 5.

Data Inspection

The primary role of many firewalls is to inspect the data passing through it using a set of rules that define what is and is not allowed through the firewall and then to act appropriately on packets that meet required criteria. The various types of firewalls, described in the next section, differ primarily in what portions of the overall data packet are inspected, the types of inspections that can be done, and what sorts of actions are taken with respect to those data. Among the data elements that are commonly inspected are the following:

- IP address
- TCP port number
- User datagram protocol port number
- Data field contents

Contents of specific protocol payloads, such as HTTP, to filter out certain classes of traffic (e.g., streaming video, voice, and music), access requests to restricted Web sites, information with specific markings (e.g., proprietary information), and content with certain words or page names.

Virus Scanning and Intrusion Detection

Some firewalls also offer functionality such as virus scanning and intrusion detection. Advantages of such firewalls include the following:

- "One-stop shopping" for a wide range of requirements
- Reduced overhead from centralization of services
- Reduced training and maintenance

Disadvantages include the following:

- Increased processing load requirements
- Single point of failure for security devices

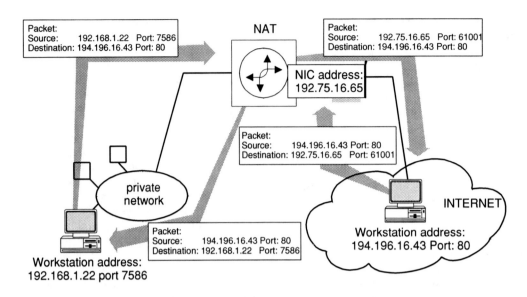

NAT Source/Destination Table

Private Source IP Address	Private Source Assigned Port ID
192.168.1.22	61001
192.168.1.23	61002
192.168.1.24	61003
192.168.1.25	61004
..and so on..	..and so on..

GOLDMAN & RAWLES: ADC3e
FIG. 09-13

Figure 5: NAT functionality.

• Increased device complexity
• Potential for reduced performance over customized sub-solutions

Other Functions

Some firewalls also offer such functions as the following:

• Virtual Private Networks (VPN): VPN functionality, allowing secure communication over the Internet, was typically provided by separate, dedicated devices (VPN traffic would have to be decrypted from the VPN tunnel and then passed through a separate firewall for filtering. By combining the VPN functionality with the firewall functionality on a single box, the process is somewhat simplified)

• Usage monitoring, traffic monitoring, and traffic logging: these functions provide usage statistics that can be valuable for capacity planning and also provide information to troubleshoot problems or spot potential abuse

• Protection against some forms of IP address spoofing

• Protection against denial of service attacks

FIREWALL TYPES

Another difficulty with firewalls is that there are no standards for firewall types, configuration, or interoperability. As a result, users must often be aware of how firewalls work to use them, and owners must be aware of these issues to evaluate potential firewall technology purchases. Many different devices can all be called firewalls, but that does not imply that these devices provide identical or even similar functionality. Firewall types and configuration are explained in the next few sections.

Bastion Host

Many firewalls, whether software or hardware based, include a bastion host—a specially hardened server or a trusted system designed so that the functionality of the device cannot be compromised by attacking vulnerabilities in the underlying operating system or software over which its software runs. Specifically, the bastion host employs a secure version of the operating system with the most recent patches, security updates, and minimum number of applications to avoid known and unknown vulnerabilities. A bastion host is nothing more than the platform on which the firewall software is installed, configured, and executed. Once configured with firewall software, the

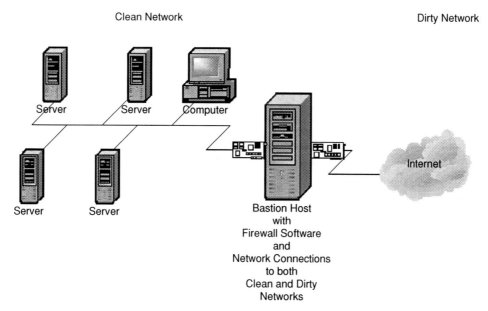

Clean Network   Dirty Network

Server   Server   Computer

Server   Server

Bastion Host
with
Firewall Software
and
Network Connections
to both
Clean and Dirty
Networks

Internet

Figure 6: Bastion host.

bastion host sits between clean and dirty networks providing a perimeter defense as illustrated in Figure 6.

Packet Filtering Firewalls

Every packet of data on the Internet can be identified by a source address (IP address) normally associated with the computer that issued the message and the destination address (IP address) normally associated with the computer to which the message is bound. These addresses are included in a portion of the packet called the header.

A packet filter can be used to examine the source and destination address of every packet. Network access devices known as routers are among the commonly used devices capable of filtering data packets. Filter tables are lists of addresses with data packets and embedded messages that are either allowed or prohibited from proceeding through the firewall. Filter tables may also limit the access of certain IP addresses to certain services and subservices. This is how anonymous FTP users are restricted to only certain information resources. It takes time for a firewall server to examine the addresses of each packet and compare those addresses to filter table entries. This filtering time introduces latency to the overall transmission time and may create a bottleneck to high volumes of traffic. Hardware implementations of such filters are often used to provide low latency and high throughput.

A filtering program that only examines source and destination addresses and determines access based on the entries in a filter table is known as a network-level filter or packet filter. The term network level or network layer in this case refers to the network layer or Layer 3 of the OSI Model (see Figure 2) where IP addresses reside in the TCP/IP protocol stack.

Packet filter gateways can be implemented on routers. This means that an existing piece of technology can be used for dual purposes. Maintaining filter tables and access rules on multiple routers is not a simple task and

packet filtering of this sort is limited in what it can accomplish because it only examines certain areas of each packet. Dedicated packet-filtering firewalls are usually easier to configure and require less in-depth knowledge of protocols to be filtered or examined. One easy way that many packet filters can be defeated by attackers is a technique known as IP spoofing. Because these simple packet filters make all filtering decisions based on IP source and destination addresses, an attacker can often create a packet designed to appear to come from an authorized or trusted IP address, which will then pass through such a firewall unimpeded.

Packet filtering is illustrated in Figure 7.

Circuit-Level Gateways and Proxies

Circuit-level proxies or circuit-level gateways provide proxy services for transport layer (Layer 4) protocols such as TCP. Socks, an example of such a proxy server, creates proxy data channels to application servers on behalf of the application client. Socks uniquely identifies and keeps track of individual connections between the client and server ends of an application communication over a network. Like other proxy servers, both a client and server portion of the Socks proxy are required to create the Socks tunnel. Some Web browsers have the client portion of Socks included, whereas the server portion can be added as an additional application to a server functioning as a proxy server. The Socks server would be located inside an organization's firewall and can block or allow connection requests, based on the requested Internet destination, TCP port ID, or user identification. Once Socks approves and establishes the connection through the proxy server, it does not care which protocols flow through the established connection. This is in contrast to other more protocol-specific proxies such as Web proxy, which only allows HTTP to be transported, or WinSock Proxy, which only allows Windows application protocols to be transported.

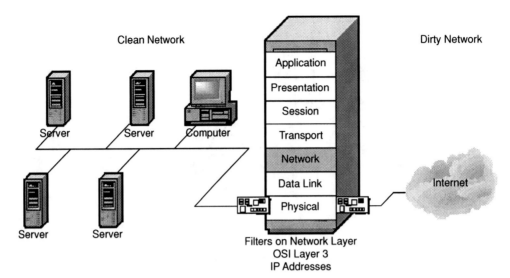

Figure 7: Packet filtering firewall.

Because all data go through Socks, it can audit, screen, and filter all traffic in between the application client and server. Socks can control traffic by disabling or enabling communication according to TCP port numbers. Socks4 allowed outgoing firewall applications, whereas Socks5 supports both incoming and outgoing firewall applications, as well as authentication.

The key negative characteristic of Socks is that applications must be "socksified" to communicate with the Socks protocol and server. In the case of Socks4, this meant that local applications had to be recompiled using a Socks library that replaced its normal library functions. However, with Socks5, a launcher is employed that avoids "socksification" and recompilation of client programs that in most cases do not natively support Socks. Socks5 also uses a private routing table and hides internal network addresses from outside networks. Figure 8 illustrates Circuit level gateways and proxies.

Application Gateways

Application gateways are concerned with what services or applications a message is requesting in addition to who is making that request. Connections between requesting clients and service providing servers are created only after the application gateway is satisfied as to the legitimacy of the request. Even once the legitimacy of the request has been established, only proxy clients and servers actually communicate with each other. A gateway firewall does not allow actual internal IP addresses or names to be transported to the external nonsecure network, except as this information is contained within content that the proxy does not control. To the external network, the proxy application on the firewall appears to be the actual source or destination, as the case may be.

Application-level filters, sometimes called assured pipelines, application gateways, or proxy servers, go beyond port-level filters in their attempts to control packet

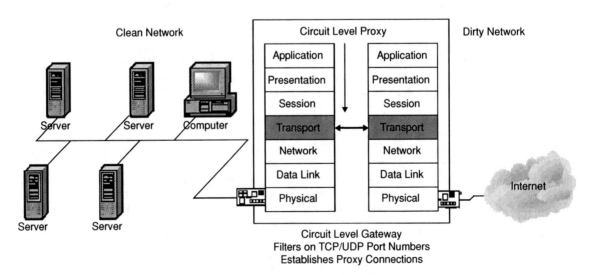

Figure 8: Circuit-level gateways and proxies.

flows. Whereas port-level filters determine the legitimacy of the IP addresses and ports within packets, application-level filters are intended to provide increased assurance of the validity of packet content in context. Application-level filters typically examine the entire request for data rather than just the source and destination addresses. This ability to examine the entire contents of a data packet in the context of its intended application is sometimes referred to as deep packet inspection. Controlled files can be marked as such, and application-level filters can be designed to prevent those files from being transferred, even within packets authorized by port-level filters. Of course, this increased level of scrutiny comes at the cost of a slower or more expensive firewall.

Proxies are also capable of approving or denying connections based on directionality. Users may be allowed to upload but not download files. Some application-level gateways have the ability to encrypt communications over these established connections. The level of difficulty associated with configuring application-level gateways versus router-based packet filters is debatable. Router-based gateways tend to require a more intimate knowledge of protocol behavior, whereas application-level gateways deal predominantly at the application layer of the protocol stack. Proxies tend to introduce increased latency compared with port-level filtering. The key weaknesses of an application-level gateway is their inability to detect embedded malicious code such as Trojan horse programs or macro viruses and the requirement of more complex and resource intensive operation than lower level filters.

Certain application-level protocols commands that are typically used for probing or attacking systems can be identified, trapped, and removed. For example, SMTP is an e-mail interoperability protocol that is a member of the TCP/IP family and used widely over the Internet. It is often used to mask attacks or intrusions. Multipurpose internet mail extension (MIME) is another method that is often used to hide or encapsulate malicious code such as Java applets or ActiveX components. Other application

protocols that may require monitoring include but are not limited to World Wide Web protocols such as HTTP, telnet, ftp, gopher, and Real Audio. Each of these application protocols may require its own proxy, and each application-specific proxy must be designed to be intimately familiar with the commands within each application that will need to be trapped and examined. For example an SMTP proxy should be able to filter SMTP packets according to e-mail content, message length, and type of attachments. A given application gateway may not include proxies for all potential application layer protocols. Figure 9 illustrates application gateway functionality.

Trusted Gateway

A trusted gateway or trusted application gateway seeks to relieve all the reliance on the application gateway for all communication, both inbound and outbound. In a trusted gateway, certain applications are identified as trusted and are able to bypass the application gateway entirely and are able to establish connections directly rather than be executed by proxy. In this way, outside users can access information servers and Web servers without tying up the proxy applications on the application gateway. These servers are typically placed in a demilitarized zone (DMZ) so that any failures in the application servers will grant only limited additional access to other systems. Figure 10 illustrates a trusted gateway only. See the chapter on firewall architectures for further discussion on DMZs.

Stateful Firewalls

Rather than simply examining packets individually without the context of previously transmitted packets from the same source, stateful firewalls, sometimes referred to as stateful multiplayer inspection firewalls, store information about past activities and use this information to test future packets attempting to pass through. Stateful firewalls typically review the same packet information as normal simple packet filtering firewalls such as

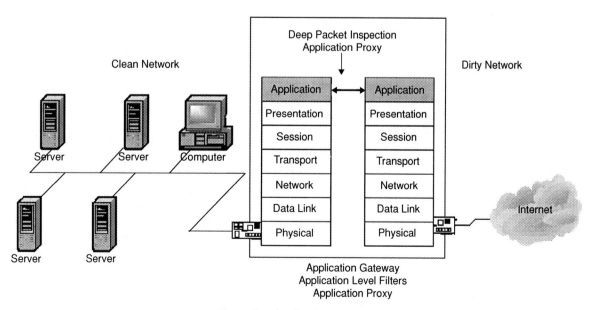

Figure 9: Application gateway.

9

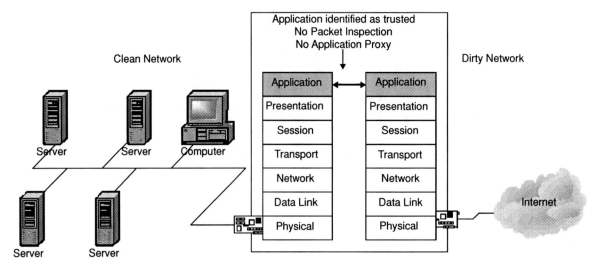

Figure 10: Trusted gateway.

source address, destination address, protocol, port, and flags; however, they also record this information in a connection state table, also referred to as a dynamic state table, before sending the packet on. This table will have an entry for each valid connection established over a particular reference frame. The multiplayer aspect of their functionality refers to the fact that they filter packets at the network, transport, session (connection), and application layers. Although stateful firewalls filter applications and evaluate application packet contents, they do not provide application specific proxies. They combine the functionality of network packet filters, circuit level gateways, and application level gateways while adding the connection oriented stateful inspection.

Some stateful firewalls keep sequence number information to validate packets even further, so as to protect against some session hijacking attacks. As each packet arrives to a stateful firewall, it is checked against the connection table to determine whether it is part of an existing connection. The source address, destination address, source port, and destination port of the new packet must match the table entry. If the communication has already been authorized, there is no need to authorize it again and the packet is passed. If a packet can be confirmed to belong to an established connection, it is much less costly to send it on its way based on the connection table rather than re-examine the entire firewall rule set. This makes a stateful firewall faster then a simple packet filtering firewall for certain types of traffic patterns, because the packet filtering firewall treats each connection as a new connection. Additionally, because there is a "history" in the state tables, flags can be analyzed to ensure the proper sequence as in the TCP connection handshake, and the stateful firewall can drop or return packets that are clearly not a genuine response to a request.

As a result, stateful firewalls are better able to prevent some sorts of session hijacking and man-in-the-middle attacks. Session hijacking is very similar to IP spoofing, described earlier, except that it hijacks the session by sending forged acknowledgment (ACK) packets so that the victimized computer still thinks it is talking to the legitimate intended recipient of the session. A man-in-the-middle attack could be seen as two simultaneous session hijackings. In this scenario, the hacker hijacks both sides of the session and keeps both sides active and appearing to talk directly to each other when, in fact, the man-in-the middle is examining and potentially modifying any packet that flows in either direction of the session. Figure 11 illustrates the basic functionality of a stateful firewall.

Internal Firewalls

Not all threats to a network are perpetrated from the Internet by anonymous attackers, and firewalls are not a stand-alone, technology-based quick fix for network security. In response to the reality that most losses because of computer crime involve someone with inside access, internal firewalls have been applied with increasing frequency. Internal firewalls include filters that work on the data link, network, and application layers to examine communications that occur only within internal networks. Internal firewalls also act as access control mechanisms, denying access to applications for which a user does not have specific access approval. To ensure the confidentiality and integrity of private information, encryption and authentication may also be supported by firewalls, even during internal communications.

Virtual Firewalls and Network-Based Firewall Services

Virtual firewalls, also known as virtual firewall systems, provide a single, centralized point of control over multiple distributed firewalls. As enterprise networks have grown in both scale and complexity, it has become more difficult to manage increasing numbers of firewalls on an individual basis. As a result, centralized firewall management systems have been developed. Each individual firewall is able to be configured uniquely with its own policies and rule sets. The area of protection provided by each firewall is referred to as its security domain or risk domain. All

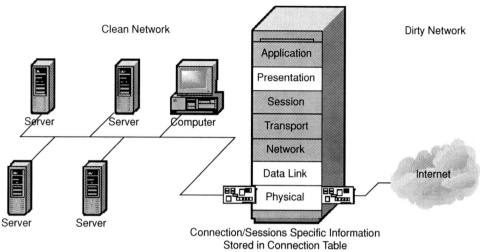

Clean Network   Dirty Network

Application
Presentation
Session
Transport
Network
Data Link
Physical

Server   Server   Computer

Server   Server

Internet

Connection/Sessions Specific Information
Stored in Connection Table
Each packet verified for appropriateness given connection history or state
Filtering takes place on network, transport, and application

Figure 11: Stateful firewall.

of the configuration for the distributed firewalls can be done from a single, centralized location. A third party service provider, such as an Internet VPN provider, may provide virtual firewall services, otherwise known as network-based firewall services.

Switched Firewalls—Air Gap Technology

Some vendors try to assert the strength of their protection by using widely known terms such as switched firewalls and *air gap* to characterize their protective mechanisms. One example of such a technology provides the same separation of the clean and dirty networks as firewalls. A hardware-based network switch is at the heart of this technology. The premise of creating a physical disconnection between the clean or secure network (Intranet) and the nonsecure or dirty network (Internet) is accomplished by connecting a server on the Internet connection that will receive all incoming requests. This server will connect to an electronic switch that strips the TCP headers and stores the packet in a memory bank, and then the switch disconnects from the external server and connects with the internal server. Once the connection is made, the internal server recreates the TCP header and transmits the packet to the intended server. Responses are made in the reverse order. The physical separation of the networks and the stripping of the TCP headers remove many of the vulnerabilities in the TCP connection-oriented protocol. Of course this provides little additional protection over other firewalls at the content level because content-level attacks are passed through the so-called air gap and responses are returned.

By utilizing high speed switches for the rule checking and packet forwarding, switched firewalls, also known as switch-accelerated firewalls, are able to filter and forward packets at multigigabit speeds. In some switched firewall architectures, separate dedicated devices sometimes referred to as switched firewall directors perform firewall control functions such as policy and session management, connection table management, and packet handling rules

specification, thus freeing the dedicated separate switched firewall to perform only rule checking and packing forwarding. In some cases, applications specific filtering is provided on the air gap technology. Such devices may be referred to as application firewall appliances or air gap application firewalls. Figure 12 illustrates air gap functionality.

There is a protective device that is highly effective at limiting information flow to one direction. The so-called digital diode technology is applied in situations in which the sole requirement is that no information be permitted to leak from one area to the other while information is permitted to flow in the other direction. An example would be the requirement for weather information to be available to military planning computers without the military plans being leaked to the weather stations. This sort of protection typically uses a physical technology such as a fiber optic device with only a transmitter on one end and receiver on the other end to provide high assurance of traffic directionality.

Small Office Home Office Firewalls

As telecommuting has boomed and independent consultants have set up shop in home offices, the need for firewalls for the small office home office (SOHO) market has grown as well. These devices are often integrated with integrated services digital network-based multiprotocol routers that supply bandwidth on demand capabilities for Internet access. Some of these SOHO firewalls offer sophisticated features such as support for virtual private networks at a reasonable price. The most expensive of these costs less than $3,000 and some simpler filtering firewalls cost as little as $100. Some of these devices combine additional functionality such as network address translation, built in hub and switch ports, and load balancing in a combined hardware–software device known as a security appliance. Often digital subscriber line (DSL) or cable modems include firewall functionality because of their "always on" connection status.

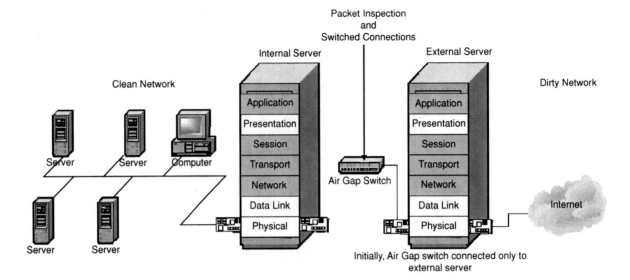

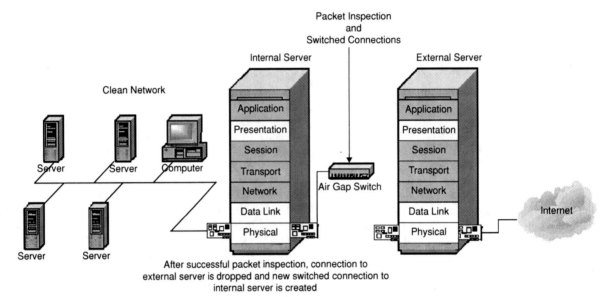

Figure 12: Air gap functionality.

Software-only solutions are also available. These products are installed on every computer and provide firewall-like functionality to each work station, thereby effectively eliminating client-side vulnerabilities that may bypass server-based or perimeter firewalls. Additional benefits are that each workstation has an extremely inexpensive solution and that protection can be customized at the system level. The problem is that this requires all users to be firewall administrators for their computers, losing the economy of scale that was one of the original benefits associated with firewalls.

FIREWALL FUNCTIONALITY AND TECHNOLOGY ANALYSIS

Commercially available firewalls usually employ either packet filtering or proxies as firewall architecture and add an easy-to-use graphical user interface (GUI) to ease the configuration and implementation tasks. Some firewalls even use industry standard Web browsers as their GUIs. Several certifying bodies and internationally accepted criteria are available to certify various aspects of firewall technology. Common Criteria Evaluation Assurance Level (EAL) 4 has been certified on some firewalls. These evaluation criteria are officially known as "Common Criteria for Information Technology Security Evaluation" ISO/IEC 15408 (2000). In addition ICSA (International Computer Security Association) Labs, a division of TruSecure Corporation, offers certification of a variety of security technology including firewalls.

In general, certification seeks to assure the following:

• That firewalls meet the minimum requirements for reliable protection
• That firewalls perform as advertised
• That Internet applications perform as expected through the firewall

Table 1 summarizes some of the key functional characteristics of firewall technology.

Table 1 Sample Functional Characteristics of Firewall Technology.

Firewall functional characteristic	Explanation/importance
Encryption	Allows secure communication through firewall. Encryption schemes supported: DES, 3DES, and AES Encryption key length supported: 40, 56, 128, 168, 256 bits
Virtual Private Network (VPN) support	Allows secure communication over the Internet in a virtual private network topology VPN Security protocols supported: IPSEC and SSL
Application proxies supported	How many application proxies are supported? Internet application protocols (HTTP, SMTP, FTP, telnet, NNTP, WAIS, SNMP, rlogin, ping traceroute)? Real Audio? How many controls or commands are supported for each application?
Proxy isolation	In some cases, proxies are executed in their own protected domains to prevent penetration of other proxies or the firewall operating system should a given proxy be breached.
Operating systems supported	Unix and varieties; Windows NT, 2000, and XP
Virus scanning included	Because many viruses enter through Internet connections, the firewall is a logical place to scan for viruses.
Web tracking	To ensure compliance with corporate policy regarding use of the World Wide Web, some firewalls provide Web tracking software. The placement of the software in the firewall makes sense because all Web access must pass through the firewall. Access to certain uniform resource locators (URLs) can be filtered.
Violation notification	How does the firewall react when access violations are detected? Options include SNMP traps, e-mail, pop-up windows, pagers, reports.
Authentication supported	As a major network access point, the firewall must support popular authentication protocols and technology.
Network interfaces supported	Which network interfaces and associated data link layer protocols are supported?
System monitoring	Are graphical systems monitoring utilities available to display such statistics as disk usage or network activity by interface?
Auditing and logging	Is auditing and logging supporting? How many different types of events can be logged? Are user-defined events supported? Can logged events be sent to SNMP managers?
Attack protection	Following is a sample of the types of attacks that a firewall should be able to guard against: TCP denial of service attack, TCP sequence number prediction, source routing and RIP attacks, EGP infiltration and ICMP attacks, authentication server attacks, finger access, PCMAIL access, DNS access, FTP authentication attacks, anonymous FTP access, SNMP access remote access remote booting from outside networks; IP, MAC, and ARP spoofing and broadcast storms; trivial FTP and filter to and from the firewall, reserved port attacks, TCP wrappers, gopher spoofing, and MIME spoofing.
Attack retaliation/counterattack	Some firewalls can launch specific counterattacks or investigative actions if the firewall detects specific types of intrusions.
Administration interface	Is the administration interface graphical in nature? Is it forms based?

Abbreviations: ARP = address resolution protocol; DNS = domain name server; EGP = exterior gateway protocol; DES = data encryption standard; FTP = file transfer protocol; HTTP = hypertext transfer protocol; ICMP = Internet control message protocol; IP = Internet protocol; MAC = media access control; MIME = multipurpose Internet mail extension; NNTP = network news transfer protocol; RIP = routing information protocol; SMTP = simple mail transfer protocol; SNMP = simple network management protocol; TCP = transmission control protocol; WAIS = wide area information services.

CONCLUSION

Firewalls are an essential and basic element of many organizations' security architecture. Nonetheless, technology must be chosen carefully to ensure that it offers the required functionality, and firewalls must be arranged into properly designed enterprise firewall architectures and properly configured, maintained, and monitored. Even in the best circumstances, firewalls should be seen as a relatively small solution within the overall information protection challenge and should not be considered sufficient on their own.

GLOSSARY

Address Filtering A firewall's ability to block or allow packets based on Internet protocol addresses.

Air Gap Technology Switched connections established to connect external and internal networks that are not otherwise physically connected.

Application-Level Gateway Application-level filters examine the entire request for data rather than only the source and destination addresses.

Bastion Host Hardened server with trusted operating system that serves as the basis of the firewall.

Circuit-Level Proxies Proxy servers that work at the circuit level by proxying such protocols as file transfer protocol.

Demilitarized Zone (DMZ) A neutral zone between firewalls or between a packet filtering router and a firewall in which mail and Web servers are often located.

Domain Filtering A firewall's ability to block outbound access to restricted sites.

Dual-Homed Host A host firewall with two or more network interface cards with direct access to two or more networks.

Firewall A network device capable of filtering unwanted traffic from a connection between networks.

Internal Firewall Firewalls that include filters that work on the data link, network, and application layers to examine communications that occur only on an organization's internal network, inside the reach of traditional firewalls.

Multitiered DMZ A DMZ that segments access areas with multiple layers of firewalls.

Network Address Translation A firewall's ability to translate between private and public globally unique Internet protocol addresses.

Packet Filtering Gateway A firewall that allows or blocks packet transmission based on source and destination Internet protocol addresses.

Port Filtering A firewall's ability to block or allow packets based on transmission control protocol port number.

Proxy Server Servers that break direct connections between clients and servers and offer application and circuit layer specific proxy services to inspect and control such communications.

Screened Subnet Enterprise firewall architecture that creates a DMZ.

Stateful Firewall A firewall that monitors connections and records packet information in state tables to make forwarding decisions in the context of previous transmitted packets over a given connection.

Trusted Gateway In a trusted gateway, certain applications are identified as trusted, are able to bypass the application gateway entirely, and are able to establish connections directly rather than by proxy.

CROSS REFERENCES

See *Firewall Architectures; Packet Filtering and Stateful Firewalls; Proxy Firewalls.*

FURTHER READING

Canavan, J. E. (2001). *Fundamentals of network security.* Boston: Artech House.

CERT Coordination Center. (1999, July 1). *Design the firewall system.* Retrieved January 1, 2004, from http://www.cert.org/security-improvement/practices/p053.html

Check Point Software Technologies. (1999, June 22). *Stateful inspection firewall technology tech note.* Retrieved June 2, 2004, from http://www.checkpoint.com/products/downloads/Stateful_Inspection.pdf

Edwards, J. (2001, May 1). Unplugging cybercrime. *CIO Magazine.* Retrieved March 1, 2004, from http://www.cio.com/archive/050100/development.html

Enterprise Technology. (2001, October). *Keeping a safe distance.* Retrieved January 2, 2004, from http://www.avcom.com/et/online/2001/oct/keeping.html

Goldman, J. E., & Rawles, P. T. (2001). *Applied data communications: A business oriented approach* (3rd ed.). New York: John Wiley & Sons.

Hurley, M. (2001, April 4). *Network air gaps—Drawbridge to the backend office.* Retrieved January 2, 2004, from http://rr.sans.org/firewall/gaps.php

NetGap. (n.d.). *SpearHead Security Web site.* Retrieved January 2, 2004, from http://www.spearheadsecurity.com/products.shtml

Scheer, S. (2001, January 10). *Israeli start-up may thwart Internet hackers.* Retrieved January 2, 2004, from http://staging.infoworld.com/articles/hn/xml/01/01/10/010110hnthwart.xml?Tem

Senner, L. (2001, May 9). *Anatomy of a stateful firewall.* Retrieved January 2, 2003, from http://rr.sans.org/firewall/anatomy.php

Whale Communications. *Air gap technology.* Retrieved January 2, 2004, from http://www.whalecommunications.com/fr_0300.htm

Firewall Architectures

James E. Goldman, *Purdue University*

INTRODUCTION

When an organization or individual links to the Internet, it creates a two-way access point in and out of their information systems. To prevent unauthorized activities between the Internet and the private network, a specialized hardware, software, or software–hardware combination known as a firewall is often deployed.

Brief Review of Firewall Functionality

Firewall software often runs on a dedicated server between the Internet and the protected network. Firmware-based firewalls and single-purpose dedicated firewall appliances are situated in a similar location on a network and provide similar functionality to the software-based firewall. All network traffic entering the firewall is examined, and possibly filtered, to ensure that only authorized activities take place. This process may be limited to verifying authorized access to requested files or services, or it may delve more deeply into content, location, time, date, day of week, participants, or other criteria of interest. Firewalls usually provide a layer of isolation between the inside, sometimes referred to as the "clean" network, and the outside or "dirty" network. They are also used, although less frequently, to separate multiple subnetworks so as to control interactions among them. Figure 1 illustrates a typical installation of a firewall in a perimeter security configuration.

A common underlying assumption in such a design scenario is that all of the threats come from the outside network or the Internet, but many modern firewalls provide protection against insiders acting inappropriately and against accidental harm that could result from internal configuration errors, viruses, or experimental implementations. Research consistently indicates that 70–80% of malicious activity originates from insiders who would normally have access to systems both inside and outside of the firewall. In addition, outside threats may be able to circumvent the firewall entirely if dial-up modem access remains uncontrolled or unmonitored or wireless local area networks (LANs) or similar wireless technology are used. Other methods can be used to co-opt an insider, subvert the integrity of systems within the firewall, or otherwise bypass the firewall as a route for communications.

Incorrectly implemented firewalls can exacerbate this situation by creating new, and sometimes undetected, security holes or by creating such an impediment to legitimate uses that insiders subvert its mechanisms intentionally. It is often said that an incorrectly configured and maintained firewall is worse than no firewall at all because it gives a false sense of security.

Advantages of firewalls include the following:

1. When properly configured and monitored, firewalls can be an effective way to protect network and information resources.
2. Firewalls are often used to reduce the costs associated with protecting larger numbers of computers that are located inside it.
3. Firewalls provide a control point that can be used for other protective purposes.

Disadvantages of firewalls include the following:

1. Firewalls can be complex devices with complicated rule sets.
2. Firewalls must be configured, managed, and monitored by properly trained personnel. Distributed or network-based firewalls are more comprehensive in terms of detection ability but far more complex in terms of configuration and systems administration.

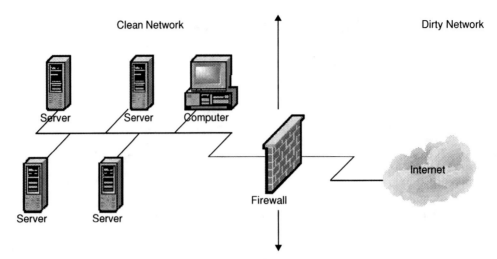

Figure 1: Typical installation of a firewall in a perimeter security configuration.

3. A misconfigured firewall gives the illusion of security.
4. Even a properly configured firewall is not sufficient or complete as a perimeter security solution. A total security solution typically also includes intrusion detection/prevention systems, vulnerability assessment technology, and antivirus technology. According to the Computer Security Institute, 80% of successful network attacks either penetrate or avoid firewall security.
5. The processing of packets by a firewall inevitably introduces latency that, in some cases, can be significant.
6. Firewalls often interfere with network applications that may expect direct connections to end user work stations such as voice-over-Internet protocol (IP) phones and some VPNs (virtual private networks) as well as some collaborative tools such as instant messenger and video and audio conferencing software.
7. The level to which firewalls inspect the data contained within packets varies widely. Whereas some firewalls only filter packets based on source and destination addresses, other firewalls perform much more comprehensive packet inspection on the contents of those packets. This could perhaps more properly be classified as a choice in level of capability as opposed to being considered strictly as a disadvantage. Stateful firewalls can add this deep packet inspection capability. More and more protocols are embedded within or tunnel over port 80 (HTTP) as accessed via a Web browser. Deep packet inspection or content inspection is required to peer within the outer protocol to examine packet contents. Data streams are often encrypted, preventing the firewall from thoroughly inspecting them.
8. Firewalls do not necessarily prevent vulnerabilities introduced directly at client computers such as malicious code, e-mail attacks, and Web-based Trojans. Such Trojan programs can then launch attacks within the internal network, undetected by the perimeter-based firewall. Prevention of such vulnerabilities is typically handled by packet filters or routers that set rules to deny certain types of internal and egress communications. For instance, a rule can be set to disallow outbound ICMP, spoofed source addresses, out-of-range internal addresses, and so on.

REQUIREMENTS ANALYSIS FOR FIREWALL ARCHITECTURES
Importance of Understanding Security Requirements

The term firewall architecture refers to the physical and logical arrangement of firewalls in relation to each other, to the information assets (usually servers) they are protecting, and to other security-related devices such as intrusion detection systems.

Which firewall architecture is correct for a given scenario depends on the unique security requirements of that scenario. Although security requirements analysis is beyond the scope of this chapter, the bulleted list below gives a high-level view of the kinds of issues that must be thoroughly understood before a particular firewall architecture can be chosen.

- Asset identification—what are you trying to protect? Where is the information to be protected stored?
- Vulnerability analysis—how might the information be accessed by unauthorized parties?
- Threat analysis—who might want to potentially use the information in an unauthorized manner? Where are these individuals located? Internally? Known external locations? Unknown external locations?
- Risk analysis—what is the likelihood that a given threat will attack a given asset via a given vulnerability?
- Protective measures analysis—what can be done to mitigate a given risk? Is the cost of the protective measure justifiable given the value of the asset?
- Cost—how much will alternative choices in firewall architectures cost? How much functionality/security is gained for a given increase in cost among alternative firewall architecture choices?

16

Clean Networks and Dirty Networks

Security requirements analysis often uses terms such as clean networks and dirty networks to define the scenarios into which firewalls are deployed. To assure the proper placement of firewalls, or to assure the proper selection of a firewall architecture, one must first understand where the boundaries of clean and dirty networks exist, as this is where firewalls and other security devices must be placed. The terms clean and dirty networks might lead one to believe that there are only two polarized categories of risk: clean, or totally secure and trusted, and dirty, totally nonsecure and untrusted. In fact there can be many interim categories of risk environments in between these two poles.

Risk Domains

Risk domains, also known as security domains or security zones, consist of a unique group of networked systems sharing common elements of exposure/risk and often also sharing common business functions as well. These common business functions and risks are identified during initial risk analysis or assessment. Risk domains are differentiated or isolated from each other based on the differences in risks associated with each risk domain. Because each risk domain has unique business functions and risks, it would stand to reason that each should have a uniquely designed set of security policies, security control processes, and security technology to offer the required level of security for that particular risk domain. Risk domains are important to security analysts because of their use as a means to determine security strategies and technology. Firewall placement will depend largely on the boundaries of an enterprise's risk domains. As a result, risk domain identification is directly related to the selection of the preferred firewall architecture.

Requirements versus Firewall Functionality

Once security requirements have been determined and risk domains have been defined, these requirements must be matched against available firewall functionality. Not all firewalls offer identical functionality. In some cases, additional security technology such as intrusion detection systems or VPN servers might be deployed. However, the list below summarizes typical security functionality offered by firewalls.

Bad Packet Filtering

The first type of filtering normally done is to remove bad packets, sometimes also referred to as misshapen packets. Such abnormal packets are often used to look for vulnerabilities or to launch attacks such as denial of service attacks or distributed denial of service attacks. Bad packet filtering can be, and often is, implemented in a router, sometimes referred to as a filtering router, that faces the dirty network. However, it is highlighted here as an initial firewall function to assure that it is not overlooked. More specific examples of bad packets are packet fragments, packets with abnormally set flags, time-to-live (TTL) fields, abnormal packet length, or Internet control message protocol (ICMP) packets. The overall purpose in removing such "trash" initially is that the processing intensive firewall can spend its time only looking at legitimate (although not necessarily authorized) packets.

Address Filtering

This function can, and perhaps should, be performed by a device other than the firewall, such as a border router. Based on address filter tables containing allowed or disallowed individual or groups (subnets) of addresses, address filtering blocks all traffic that contains either disallowed source or destination addresses. Address filtering by itself may not provide adequate protection because it is too large a granularity for some protective requirements.

Port Filtering

Port filtering goes beyond address filtering, examining to which function or program a given packet applies. For example, file transfer protocol (FTP) typically uses ports 20 and 21, inbound electronic mail (simple mail transfer protocol; SMTP) typically uses port 25, and inbound nonencrypted Web traffic (hypertext transfer protocol; HTTP) typically uses port 80. Attacks are often targeted and designed for specific ports. Port filtering can be used to ensure that all ports are disabled except those that must remain open and active to support programs and protocols required by the owners of the inside network. Static port filtering leaves authorized ports open to all traffic all the time, whereas dynamic port filtering opens and closes portions of protocols associated with authorized ports over time as required for the specifics of the protocols.

Ephemeral ports are port numbers that are temporarily assigned by the computer's IP protocol stack to client-side connections from a predetermined range of available port numbers. Ephemeral port numbers are reused, so a given client will not always have the same ephemeral port number. These are typically assigned to the client-side connection when that client initiates an outbound connection for a remote service. BSD Unix uses ports 1024 to 4999 and Windows uses 1024 to 5000 as their default ephemeral port allocation. The implication for firewall port filtering of ephemeral ports is that when the requested remote service attempts to respond to the requesting client behind the firewall, that firewall must enable or leave open that ephemeral port number so that the return traffic can reach the requesting client. Whereas ephemeral port ranges are not typically service port addresses, they are often blocked or disabled by firewalls.

Domain Filtering

Domain filtering applies to outbound traffic headed through the firewall to the Internet. Domain filtering can block traffic with domains that are not authorized for communications or can be designed to permit exchanges only with authorized "outside" domains.

Network Address Translation

When organizations connect to the Internet, the addresses they send out must be globally unique. In most cases, an organization's Internet service provider specifies these globally unique addresses. Most organizations have relatively few globally unique public addresses compared with the actual number of network nodes on their entire network.

The Internet Assigned Numbers Authority has set aside the following private address ranges for use by private networks: 10.0.0.0 to 10.255.255.255, 172.16.0.0 to 172. 31.255.255, and 192.168.0.0 to 192.168.255.255. Traffic using any of these "private" addresses must remain on the organization's private network to interoperate properly with the rest of the Internet. Because anyone is welcome to use these address ranges, they are not globally unique and therefore cannot be used reliably over the Internet. Computers on a network using the private IP address space can still send and receive traffic to and from the Internet by using network address translation (NAT). An added benefit of NAT is that the organization's private network is not as readily visible from the Internet.

All of the work stations on a private network can share a single or small number of globally unique assigned public IP address(es) because NAT mechanism maintains a table that provides for translation between internal addresses and ports and external addresses and ports. These addresses and port numbers are generally configured so as to not to conflict with commonly assigned transmission control protocol (TCP) port numbers. The combination of the shared public IP address and a port number that is translated into internal address and port numbers via the translation table allows computers on the private network to communicate with the Internet through the firewall. NAT can also run on routers, dedicated servers, or other similar devices, and "gateway" computers often provide a similar function.

Dynamic NAT entries are created automatically in the NAT table as the firewall or router receives packets that require NAT translation. Dynamic NAT entries are purged after a preset period. For mapping addresses on a more permanent basis through the firewall, static NAT entries can be manually entered into the NAT table and must be manually removed as well. Most firewalls provide some type of NAT functionality.

Data Inspection

The primary role of many firewalls is to inspect the data passing through it using a set of rules that define what is and is not allowed through the firewall and then to act appropriately on packets that meet required criteria. The various types of firewalls, described under "Virus Scanning and Intrusion Detection," differ primarily in what portions of the overall data packet are inspected, the types of inspections that can be done, and what sorts of actions are taken with respect to that data. Among the data elements that are commonly inspected are the following:

- IP address,
- TCP port number,
- user datagram protocol port number,
- data field contents, and
- contents of specific protocol payloads, such as HTTP, to filter out certain classes of traffic (e.g., streaming video, voice, and music), access requests to restricted Web sites, information with specific markings (e.g., proprietary information), and content with certain words or page names.

Virus Scanning and Intrusion Detection

Some firewalls also offer functionality such as virus scanning and intrusion detection. Advantages of such firewalls include the following:

- "one-stop shopping" for a wide range of requirements,
- reduced overhead from centralization of services, and
- reduced training and maintenance.

Disadvantages include the following:

- increased processing load requirements,
- single point of failure for security devices,
- increased device complexity, and
- potential for reduced performance over customized subsolutions.

Other Functions

Some firewalls also offer such functions as the following:

- Virtual private networks (VPN)—VPN functionality, allowing secure communication over the Internet, was typically provided by separate, dedicated devices. VPN traffic would have to be decrypted from the VPN tunnel (or secure, encrypted end-to-end connection) and then passed through a separate firewall for filtering. By combining the VPN functionality with the firewall functionality on a single box, the process is somewhat simplified.
- Usage monitoring, traffic monitoring, and traffic logging—these functions provide usage statistics that can be valuable for capacity planning and also provide information to troubleshoot problems or spot potential abuse.
- Protection against some forms of IP address spoofing.
- Protection against denial of service attacks.

ENTERPRISE FIREWALL ARCHITECTURES
Conceptual Design Options of Firewall Architectures

Firewalls, or any security technology for that matter, are virtually useless without associated security policies and the requisite education and communication that are associated with those policies. Before considering alternative enterprise firewall architectures, the information security analyst must be sure that the policies to be implemented on that enterprise firewall architecture are clearly understood and rigorously enforced.

Before the correct physical firewall architecture for a given situation can be determined, alternative conceptual design options for firewall architectures must be analyzed. At a high level, there are really two alternative conceptual philosophies to firewall architecture design: defense in depth security and perimeter security.

Defense in Depth

A defense in depth design philosophy proposes multiple levels of security devices such as firewalls and intrusion detection devices. The greater the value of the information assets within a given risk domain, the greater the number of layers of security technology must be penetrated to reach those information assets. Such a philosophy would seem to assume that intrusion or attack is as likely to come from someone inside a corporate network as from outside that network. Defense in depth at its extreme would propose server-specific firewalls protecting individual servers. In a physical or building security metaphor, defense in depth would propose biometric locks on every door throughout a building not just on the outside doors.

Perimeter Security

A perimeter security design philosophy draws an imaginary line, or moat, around the perimeter of the risk domain it is seeking to protect. An underlying design assumption in perimeter security is that threats to the information assets within the protected risk domain are only likely to come from outside that risk domain. Individual servers within a risk domain are typically not specifically or individually protected. All of the emphasis is on building impenetrable perimeter security architecture. In a physical or building security metaphor, perimeter security would have biometric access to the outside doors or armed guards protecting the entrance to the building, but no further security within the building.

Firewall Architecture Design Elements

Once an overall security or firewall philosophy has been determined, key decisions remain to be made regarding the number and location of these firewalls in relation to the Internet and a corporation's public and private information resources. Each of the alternative enterprise firewall architectures explored in this section attempt to segregate three distinct networks or risk domains:

1. The Internet or other "dirty" networks: contains legitimate customers and business partners as well as hackers.

2. The DMZ(s), otherwise known as the screened subnet, neutral zone, or external private network: contains Web servers and mail servers among other information assets.

3. The internal private network, otherwise known as the secure network or intranet: contains most valuable corporate information.

The firewall architectures described in the following sections represent generalized designs or approaches to firewall architecture design. They are not necessarily mutually exclusive. Elements of various firewall architectures described below may be combined to properly meet the security requirements of a particular risk domain. For example, packet-filtering routers could easily, and correctly, be added to any of the other firewall architectures described. Likewise, server- or host-specific firewalls could easily be added to other firewall architectures as well.

PACKET-FILTERING ROUTERS
Functionality

Packet-filtering routers or border routers are often the first devices that face the Internet or dirty network from an organization network perspective. These packet-filtering routers first remove all types of traffic that should not even be passed to the firewalls. This process is typically fast and inexpensive because it involves only simple processes that are implemented in relatively low-cost hardware. Examples of removed packets include packet fragments, packets with abnormally set flags, TTL, abnormal packet length, or ICMP packets, all of which could potentially be used for attacks or to exploit known vulnerabilities, and packets from or to unauthorized addresses and ports. Figure 2 illustrates a packet-filtering router architecture.

Advantages of packet-filtering routers are as follows:

• Perimeter routers can easily perform this task.
• Fast processing.
• No additional expense or specialized equipment.
• Filter tables listing bad packets to remove are relatively static; not a lot of maintenance involved.

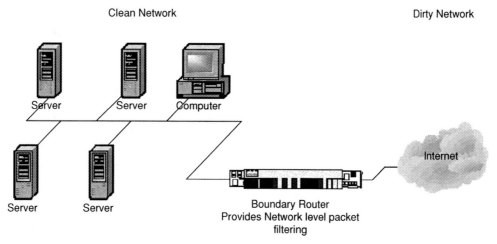

Figure 2: Packet-filtering router architecture.

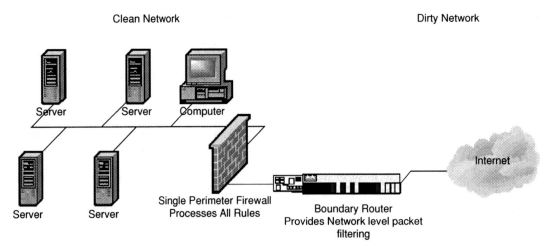

Figure 3: Perimeter firewall architecture.

Disadvantages of packet-filtering routers are as follows:

- Should not be mistaken as a replacement for a firewall.
- Processor speed and memory on the router must be properly sized to handle required throughput.
- Filter tables must be manually maintained.

PERIMETER FIREWALL ARCHITECTURE
Functionality

The perimeter firewall architecture represents the physical implementation of the perimeter security conceptual design described previously. It was, and in some cases still is, the most commonly implemented firewall architecture. All rules processing and packet filtering is performed on the perimeter firewall. It is very important that firewall rules are carefully configured and tested because there is no additional security provided once past the perimeter firewall. A perimeter firewall architecture implies that all information assets within a risk domain protected in this manner are of equal value and face equal risk. Figure 3 illustrates a perimeter firewall architecture.

One advantage of perimeter firewall architecture is that it is relatively simple to configure and manage and disadvantages include the following: a single point of security implies a single point of failure, and all information assets within risk domain are at risk if perimeter security is breached.

SERVER/HOST FIREWALL ARCHITECTURE
Functionality

The server/host firewall architecture is also known as a screened host architecture. This architecture can be used in combination with other architectures such as the perimeter, DMZ, and multitiered DMZ. A server/host firewall is often software based and resides/executes on the application server that it is protecting. It is sort of a personal bodyguard for the application server within an otherwise secure environment.

TCPWrapper is just one example of a Unix-based program that could be considered a limited function server/host firewall software program. It is a utility that can intercept and log any requests for TCP services. It could be considered a "shim" program, much like a proxy server that sits between the computer connection requesting the service and the actual service itself on the server computer. Server/host firewall software programs such as TCPWrapper may provide some or all of the following functionality:

- Attempts to detect IP address spoofing by performing what is known as a double-reverse lookup of the IP address to ensure that the IP address and hostname match the domain name service (DNS) entry. DNS is a service that translates between commonly remembered names such as www.wiley.com and an IP address such as 128.210.114.39.
- Performs address and service filtering to be sure that the requested connection is allowed or authorized.
- Logs the connection.
- Completes the connection to the requested service.

Server/host firewalls such as TCPWrapper often run directly on application servers. Microsoft's ISA (Internet Security & Acceleration) server, formerly known as Microsoft Proxy Server, is another example of a software-based firewall package that can run on an application server. This makes them distinct from other software-based firewalls that require a dedicated server. Checkpoint would be an example of such a software-based dedicated server firewall. Figure 4 illustrates a server/host firewall architecture.

Advantages of server/host firewall architecture include the following:

- Relatively easy to install and configure.
- Adds server-specific incremental protection to other firewall architectures.

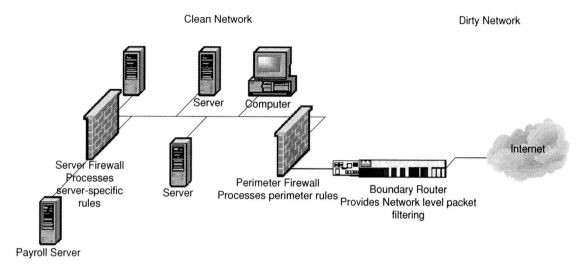

Figure 4: Server/host firewall architecture.

Disadvantages of server/host firewall architecture include the following:

• Ongoing maintenance/management can become difficult as the numbers of individual server/host firewalls are installed unless some type of centralized firewall management system is utilized.

SCREENED SUBNET FIREWALL ARCHITECTURE
Functionality

Rather than using only the packet-filtering router as the front door to the DMZ, a second firewall is added behind the packet-filtering router to further inspect all traffic bound to or from the DMZ. The initial application gateway or firewall still protects the perimeter between the DMZ and the intranet or secure internal network.

A DMZ is considered a neutral or safe zone. Outbound communications from the clean network to the Internet can go through proxy servers in the DMZ. The general public accessing this network from the Internet would only be able to access servers located in the DMZ. The DMZ contains mail, Web, and often e-commerce servers. Servers located behind the DMZ firewall on the clean network would not be accessible by the general public from the Internet. Figure 5 illustrates a screened subnet (DMZ) firewall architecture. Although this logical diagram would suggest that multiple distinct firewalls are required to establish a DMZ, this is actually not the case. Numerous vendors sell "multilegged" (multiple interface) firewalls that allow both DMZ or Internet-accessible networks as well as clean or protected networks to be physically attached to a single firewall device.

Advantages of DMZ firewalls include the following:

• Provides flexibility especially for Internet based applications such as e-mail, Web services, and e-commerce.
• Allows servers that must be accessible to the Internet while still protecting back office services on the secure internal network or Intranet.

Disadvantages of DMZ firewall include the following:

• More complicated rule configuration means more likelihood of errors.

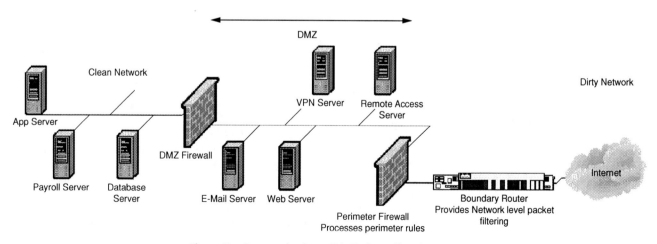

Figure 5: Screened subnet (DMZ) firewall architecture.

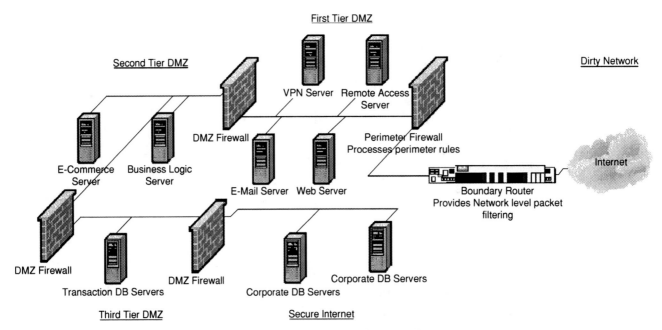

Figure 6: Multitiered/distributed DMZ architecture.

- Applications running in DMZ may still need access to servers/resources in the secure internal network.
- Once through the server between the DMZ and the internal network, there is no further protection or differentiated levels of security.

MULTITIERED/DISTRIBUTED DMZ ARCHITECTURE
Functionality

As e-commerce and e-business have proliferated, the need for e-commerce servers to access more and more secure information from database and transaction servers within the secure intranet has increased proportionately. As a result, the number of connections allowed through firewalls into the most secure areas of corporate networks has increased dramatically. In response to this phenomenon, the model of a multitiered DMZ has developed. Such a scenario really builds on the DMZ architecture by adding additional tiers to the DMZ, each protected from other tiers by additional firewalls. Typically, the first tier of the DMZ closest to the Internet would contain only the presentation or Web portion of the e-commerce application running on Web servers.

A firewall would separate that first tier of the DMZ from the second tier that would house the business logic and application portions of the e-commerce application typically running on transaction servers. This firewall would have rules defined to only allow packets from certain applications on certain servers with certain types of requests through from the first-tier DMZ to the second-tier DMZ. The third (most secure) tier of the DMZ is similarly protected from the second tier by a separate firewall. The servers in the third-tier DMZ would be database servers and should contain only the data necessary to complete requested e-commerce transactions. Finally, as

in the screened subnet firewall architecture, a firewall would separate the third-tier DMZ from the intranet, or most secure corporate network. Figure 6 illustrates the multitiered/distributed firewall architecture.

Advantages of multitiered/distributed firewall architecture include the following:

- When combined with screened host/server specific firewalls, a multitiered DMZ firewall architecture provides good protection for back office systems such as payroll and inventory servers.
- A multitiered DMZ system provides the greatest level of flexibility and highest number of risk domains thus providing ability for optimal placement of information resources.

Disadvantages of multitiered/distributed firewall architecture include the following:

- Each additional level of firewalls adds a level of complexity in terms of rule configuration and opportunity for configuration errors that can lead to security breaches.
- There is obviously a proportional increase in expense for each level of security/DMZ added.

AIR GAP ARCHITECTURE
Functionality

A hardware-based network switch is at the heart of the air gap architecture. The premise of creating a physical disconnection between the clean or secure network (intranet) and the nonsecure or dirty network (Internet) is accomplished by connecting a server on the Internet connection that will receive all incoming requests. This server will connect to an electronic switch that strips the TCP headers and stores the packet in a memory bank, and then the switch disconnects from the external server and connects with the internal server. Once the connection is made, the internal server recreates the TCP header and transmits the packet to the intended server. Responses are made in the reverse order. The physical separation of the networks and the stripping of the TCP headers remove many of the vulnerabilities in the TCP connection-oriented protocol. Of course this provides little additional protection over other firewalls at the content level because content-level attacks are passed through the so-called air gap and responses are returned.

By utilizing high-speed switches for the rule checking and packet forwarding, switched firewalls, also known as switch-accelerated firewalls, are able to filter and forward packets at multigigabit speeds. In some switched firewall architectures, separate dedicated devices sometimes referred to as switched firewall directors perform firewall control functions such as policy and session management, connection table management, and packet handling rules specification, thus freeing the dedicated separate switched firewall to perform only rule checking and packing forwarding. In some cases, application-specific filtering is provided on the air gap technology. Such devices may be referred to as application firewall appliances or air gap application firewalls. Figure 7 illustrates an air gap architecture.

Advantages of air gap architecture include the following:

• Provides switched connections between clean and dirty networks, thereby creating a physical gap or moat between the two.
• High-speed network switches at the heart of the air gap architecture provide high throughput.

Disadvantages of air gap architecture include the following:

• Effectiveness of the architecture is still dependent on the effectiveness of the packet filtering rules within the air gap device.
• Deep packet inspection or content/application specific inspection cannot be assumed.
• Vendors loosely interpret the term *air gap technology*. Specific functionality of any given device should not be assumed.

CONCLUSION

There is no single firewall architecture that is the correct choice for all security scenarios. Firewall architectures

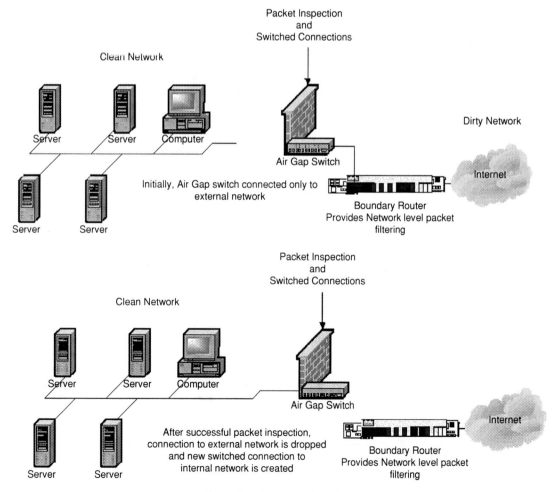

Figure 7: Air gap architecture.

vary primarily in the number of firewalls employed and the placement of those firewalls relative to each other, the information resources they are trying to protect, and the dirty networks or threats they are trying to protect the information resources from. A thorough security requirements analysis is prerequisite to firewall architecture choice. Such a security requirements analysis must start with a detailed understanding of the applications that must be secured. Firewalls, and their arrangement in a particular architecture, are just one piece of the overall security framework puzzle.

GLOSSARY

Address Filtering   A firewall's ability to block or allow packets based on Internet protocol addresses.
Air Gap Technology   Switched connections established to connect external and internal networks that are not otherwise physically connected.
Application-Level Gateway   Application-level filters examine the entire request for data rather than only the source and destination addresses.
Bastion Host   Hardened server with trusted operating system that serves as the basis of the firewall.
Circuit-Level Proxies   Proxy servers that work at the circuit level by proxying such protocols as File Transfer Protocol.
Demilitarized Zone (DMZ)   A neutral zone between firewalls or between a packet filtering router and a firewall in which mail and Web servers are often located.
Domain Filtering   A firewall's ability to block outbound access to restricted sites.
Dual-Homed Host   A host firewall with two or more network interface cards with direct access to two or more networks.
Ephemeral Ports   Port numbers that are temporarily assigned to client-side connections from a predetermined range of available port numbers.
Firewall   A network device capable of filtering unwanted traffic from a connection between networks.
Internal Firewall   Firewalls that include filters that work on the data-link, network, and application layers to examine communications that occur only on an organization's internal network, inside the reach of traditional firewalls.
Multitiered DMZ   A DMZ that segments access areas with multiple layers of firewalls.
Network Address Translation   A firewall's ability to translate between private and public globally unique Internet Protocol addresses.
Packet-Filtering Gateway   A firewall that allows or blocks packet transmission based on source and destination Internet Protocol addresses.
Port Filtering   A firewall's ability to block or allow packets based on Transmission Control Protocol port number.
Proxy Server   Servers that break direct connections between clients and servers and offer application and circuit layer specific proxy services to inspect and control such communications.
Screened Subnet   Enterprise firewall architecture that creates a DMZ.

Stateful Firewall   A firewall that monitors connections and records packet information in state tables to make forwarding decisions in the context of previous transmitted packets over a given connection.
Trusted Gateway   In a trusted gateway, certain applications are identified as trusted, are able to bypass the application gateway entirely, and are able to establish connections directly rather than by proxy.

CROSS REFERENCES

See *Firewall Basics; Packet Filtering and Stateful Firewalls; Proxy Firewalls.*

FURTHER READING

Bittard, C. (2003, April). *Security infrastructure technology overview*. Retrieved January 2, 2003, from http://www.evidian.com
Canavan, J. E. (2001). *Fundamentals of network security.* Boston: Artech House.
CERT Coordination Center. (1999, July 1). *Design the firewall system.* Retrieved January 2, 2004, from http://www.cert.org/security-improvement/practices/p053.html
Check Point Software Technologies. (1999, June 22). *Stateful inspection firewall technology tech note.* Retrieved January 2, 2004, from http://www. checkpoint. com/products/downloads/Stateful_Inspection.pdf
Cisco Systems. (2003). *PIX 500 series firewalls.* Retrieved January 2, 2003, from http://www.cisco.com
Dubrawsky, I. (2003, July). *Firewall evolution—Deep packet inspection* Retrieved January 2, 2004, from http://www.securityfocus.com/infocus/1716
Edwards, J. (2001, May 1). *Unplugging cybercrime.* Retrieved January 2, 2003, from http://www.cio.com/archive/050100/development.html
Garfinkel, S., & Spafford, G. (2003). *Practical Unix and Internet security* (3rd ed.). Sebastapol, CA: O'Reilly.
Goldman, J. E., & Rawles, P. T. (2004). *Applied data communications*: *A business oriented approach* (4th ed.). New York: John Wiley & Sons.
Hurley, M. (2001, April 4). Network air gaps—Drawbridge to the backend office. Retrieved January 2, 2003, from http://rr.sans.org/firewall/gaps.php
Intoto, Inc. (2002). *Virtual firewalls white paper.* Retrieved January 2, 2003, from http://www.intotoinc.com
Keeping a safe distance. (2001, October). *Enterprise Technology.* Retrieved January 2, 2004, from http://www.avcom.com/et/online/2001/oct/keeping.html
Mercadet, R. (2003, February). *From DMZ to DdMZ.* Retrieved January 2, 2004, from http://www.evidian.com
NASA. (2003, September). *Wireless firewall gateway white paper.* Retrieved January 2, 2003, from http://www.nas.nasa.gov
NetGap. (n.d.). *SpearHead Security Web site.* Retrieved January 2, 2004, from http://www.spearheadsecurity.com/products.shtml
Nortel Networks. (2001). Alteon switched firewall. Retrieved January 2, 2004, from www.nortelnetworks.com

Poynter, I., & Doctor, B. (2003, January). *Beyond the firewall: The next level of network security*. Retrieved January 3, 2004, from http://www.stillsecure.com

Qwest. (2001, June). *Leveraging network based firewall services in your next generation wide area network solution*. Retrieved January 2, 2004, from http://www.qwest.com

Ramsey, J. (2003, July). *Client-side vulnerabilities: Meet your network's weakest link*. Retrieved January 2, 2003, from http://www.secureworks.com

Scheer, S. (2001, January 10). *Israeli start-up may thwart Internet hackers*. Retrieved January 2, 2003, from http://staging.infoworld.com/articles/hn/xml/01/01/10/010110hnthwart.xml?Tem

Senner, L. (2001, May 9). *Anatomy of a stateful firewall*. Retrieved January 2, 2002, from http://rr.sans.org/firewall/anatomy.php

Trlokom. (2003). *Beyond perimeter firewalls and intrusion detection systems*. Retrieved January 2, 2004, from http://www.trlokom.com/white_paper/distributed_firewall. php

Whale Communications. *Air gap technology*. Retrieved January 2, 2004, from http://www.whalecommunications.com/fr_0300.htm

Whale Communications. (2003, January). *E-gap application firewall appliance: A technical overview*. Retrieved January 2, 2004, from http://www.whalecommunications.com

Proxy Firewalls

John D. McLaren, *Murray State University*

INTRODUCTION

As network security issues continue to dominate the world of networking, new devices and software are constantly surfacing. Proxy firewalls are just one of the players that are receiving more attention lately. Proxies have been around for a long while, but their primary purpose historically has been to serve as Web accelerators.

The endless variety of the application layer contents make it ripe for potential security vulnerabilities; there is a need for more detailed traffic analysis. Things such as viruses and spam cannot be discovered using simple packet-filtering firewalls. The solution to issues such as these is application layer and proxy firewalls.

Like most hot subjects, proxies are often misunderstood. There is considerable variation in the definition of firewalls that work at the application layer. Proxy firewalls not only provide the capability to examine the application data in detail, making decisions in terms of whether to drop or accept a packet, but they also are able to modify the packet. Proxy firewalls stand between the client and the server, providing a totally separate connection.

PROXY TERMINOLOGY

In the modern telecommunications world of technobabble, there are many terms that are used in a variety of connotations. *Proxy* is one of these terms. Before we begin a discussion of what might be considered a proxy firewall, it might be a good idea to clear the air on the potential contexts that will be involved. This section attempts to define some of the key terms, and later sections further distinguish proxy firewall functions through examples.

Houston, We Have a Proxy

In August 2003, Russian cosmonaut Yuri Malenchenko married Ekaterina Dmitriev. However, it was an uncon-

ventional wedding. Yuri was on board the International Space Station, and said his "I dos" via videolink. The wedding was a modern example of a proxy marriage—a wedding ceremony where a third party stands in for one or the other of the principals.

Using a video link-up between the station and the wedding hall, Malenchenko, with his best man, fellow astronaut Ed Lu, appeared in his formal flight uniform. Following Texas' proxy marriage law, the marriage ceremony proceeded with one of Yuri's friends, a Russian flight surgeon, standing in for him in Houston. There was even a life-size cutout of the groom placed at the reception to great the guests.

Throughout history, proxies have stood in for their counterparts. In the 18th and early 19th centuries, when duels were fairly common, it was traditional to select someone to act as a proxy for one of the principals. In the case that one of principals was rendered incapable of performing their part, the proxy would stand in. The practice of proxy weddings was quite common in WWI, when soldiers returned to combat after a short leave only to discover that their loved one was with child. A proxy wedding helped save the bride's reputation. Napoleon married Marie Louise, his second wife, by proxy in 1810 and Italian immigrants to Australia were marrying girls back in Italy by proxy until as late as 1976.

What does all this have to do with proxy firewalls? Not a lot. However, with today's confusion about telecommunication and networking terminology, it is good to have one definition that we can depend on. The term *proxy* is used in a variety of connotations, and its definition changes almost daily. Proxy is in the same nebulous position as terms such as *firewall* and *gateway*. New software and new appliances are appearing regularly that use the term *proxy* when describing their functions—such as proxy firewall.

Topics such as state firewalls can be accurately described in terms of their functions. The topic of proxy firewalls will encompass a much wider range of definitions. Therefore, this chapter spends some considerable time providing the user with a set of terms used to help distinguish one proxy firewall from another.

One key characteristic distinguishes a proxy from any other firewall. Like the stand-in groom from the Malenchenko wedding, the proxy *stands in* for one of the parties. In our connotation, the parties are the client and the server. The proxy will be between them so that there is never any direct communications between the client and the server. *This is a very important distinction. Whenever the term proxy is used, it should at least imply that the system being discussed can serve as an intermediary between client and server. Throughout the rest of the chapter, this characteristic is referred to as the SiG (Stand-in Groom).*

Definition of Firewall

Because the topic of this chapter is proxy firewalls, let us also define *firewall*. It is generally accepted that a firewall is a system that sits between two networks—one assumed to be trusted and the other untrusted. The system monitors traffic passing between the two networks. In this context, firewalls are choke points—a place in a network topology through which traffic is forced to pass. This allows the traffic to be analyzed and manipulated, based on the analysis. Certainly, if a proxy has the SiG characteristic that we have defined previously, it must also be a choke point. Therefore, any proxy is also a firewall by definition. As shown, it may not be a choke point for *all* traffic between two networks, but certainly it will serve that function for *some* traffic.

The Application Layer Gateway

In some sources, we find an application layer gateway defined as a machine that is surrounded by a firewall on either side, and neither of the firewalls will forward any packets unless those packets are to or from the gateway. For example, to transfer a file from inside to outside, the file must first be transferred to the gateway machine, at which point the file is accessible to be read by the outside. To access any machine on the outside, you must first log into the gateway. In this scenario, the application is ultimately performed by the gateway, so the gateway can be said to be working at the application layer. However, the gateway is *not* performing as a real-time SiG—so some may not refer to it as a proxy. An SMTP server falls into this category, performing a store-and-forward type operation.

The Application Layer Firewall

An application layer firewall is simply a firewall that has the capabilities to look into the application layer of a packet. This is often a characteristic that is associated with proxies by default. Because a proxy is a SiG, it must evaluate the application request by the client and translate that request into its own application request to the server.

Many firewalls have the capability to analyze application-layer information. Even iptables has the ability to associate related FTP data connections, which requires at least partial analysis of the FTP control application data. So, in itself, application-layer analysis does not identify a proxy, and an application-layer firewall will not necessarily be a proxy.

The NAT-ing Firewall

A NAT-ing firewall (network address translation) will substitute its IP for the client's IP (Layer 3). A PAT-ing firewall (port address translation) will do the same for ports (Layer 4). Because a proxy is creating an entirely new conversation with the server on behalf of the client, the source IP address must obviously be changed. It is most likely that the source port will be replaced as well. Therefore, a proxy server performs NAT functions by default. Actually, the proxy takes this process one step further because it creates an entirely new connection (e.g., new three-way handshake). In most cases, this means entirely new header contents for Layers 3 and up.

In summary then, let us go forth with the following understanding: A proxy is a SiG. Because the proxy is relaying application requests, it must work at the application layer, and it must be a choke point (firewall) for at least *some types* of traffic. In the next section, we look at more specific characteristics of proxies and then take a look at the different categories.

WHY AND WHEN TO USE A PROXY
Goals of a Proxy Firewall

A proxy is an application that accesses a server *for* the client. It serves to isolate a client from a server. One of the primary goals of using a proxy server is that both parties (client and server) avoid a peer-to-peer connection. Strictly speaking, a proxy server is both a server *and* a client.

The process is fairly simple:

1. The client accesses the proxy with a request that is to be forwarded to the server.
2. The proxy then forwards the request to the server, making changes to the request as specified by the proxy configuration.
3. The server responds to the request by sending information back to the proxy.
4. The proxy then forwards that reply on to the client, again making changes to the response as specified by the proxy rule set.

To the user, it appears that he or she is talking directly to the real server. To the server, it appears that he or she is talking to the proxy and has no knowledge of the real user.

Proxy servers are often bundled with firewalls, creating a bit of confusion as to which does what. The primary differences can be summarized in the layers at which each works. A packet-filtering firewall operates at the network and transport layers of the OSI model, whereas proxy servers work at the application layer.

Each layer of a packet adds complexity to the packet. The more layers a packet has, the more permutations that are possible and the more complex the software that analyzes it must be. The Layer 3 and Layer 4 headers are very predictable and have only a finite set of possible permutations. Application-layer protocols have considerably more possible entries, and these entries can often be extended in an indefinite fashion. Once the application layer is involved, the possible permutations grow extremely large, and analyzing the information therein can become quite involved and consume considerable processor time.

Packet filters check each packet against a set of filtering rules based on information contained in Layers 3 and 4. For example, it is an easy matter for a packet-filtering firewall to block traffic based on source or destination IP or the service involved. Packet-filtering firewalls have the advantage of speed when compared to a proxy firewall. One situation that should definitely be avoided is using a proxy firewall when a packet-filtering or stateful firewall could accomplish the same task.

Proxy servers are different from a packet-filtering or stateful firewall in that they break the direct link between client and server. They start by performing network address translation, mapping the client's IP address to the address of the proxy. They continue to analyze the client's requests embedded in the application layer, as well as the server's responses. Because they operate at the application layer of the OSI model, proxy servers are capable of much more detailed analysis. A given proxy will be a specialist in a single application protocol such as HTTP, FTP, SMTP/POP, NNTP, and so on. The degree to which a proxy can be configured is only limited to the same extent as the potential application layer content.

Advantages of Proxy Firewalls

Before considering the use of a proxy firewall, one should review a proxy's potential capabilities versus the needs of the network in terms of both security and functionality. The following is a list of functions that proxies are most often used to accomplish.

Conceal Internal Clients

Because the proxy creates a new connection for the client, the client's identity is concealed. This type of function resembles NAT. However, proxies go beyond simply remapping IP addresses. The headers in the packets coming from a proxy are totally rebuilt based on the proxy's TCP stack. Using proxies will help reduce the threat from hackers who monitor network traffic in an attempt to gather information about computers on internal networks. NAT and PAT firewalls are simpler systems and can accomplish this task rather well. Therefore, if this is the *only* reason you are considering a proxy firewall, you should probably rethink your plan.

Block URLs

This is one of the conceived uses of Web proxy servers. The goal is to block users from visiting certain URLs, which are specified as either IP addresses or DNS names. However, this function is very unreliable unless the administrator is diligent. He or she must keep up with domain name changes and their IP counterparts. Just entering domain names in a "forbidden list" will still allow users to enter IP addresses directly into their browser. A packet-filtering firewall can block access to given IPs or domain names.

Unless you need to be able to look at the exact complete URL being accessed, a packet-filtering firewall would be a more efficient solution.

Block and Filter Content

In terms of internal network security, it is important to prevent malicious content from entering. This is an application firewall function. Proxy firewalls can be configured to scan for potential damaging payloads, such as Java applets, ActiveX controls, or any executables. This filtering can be extended to spam as well (although spam is much harder to define and fingerprint).

Improve Security

With proxies, security policies can be much more powerful and flexible because of all of the information in the packets can be used to write the rules that determine how packets are handled by the gateway. A variety of time-based access rules is available with most proxies.

Authenticate Users

Most modern proxy products provide at least some form of user authentication. The simplest provision might utilize the operating system's authentication capabilities, but most today will provide alternate, standardized choices. Many firewalls (and even some routers) can provide user authentication services as well.

Perform More Advanced Logging

Because proxy servers examine application-layer data, they are privy to more information—and any combination of this additional information can be logged. This additional logging can help identify and isolate new security problems, such as application-level attacks. Some proxy systems even provide a degree of intrusion detection system (IDS)—notifying the administrator when a particular signature is discovered.

Improve Performance

Actually, proxy servers were originally developed as a way to speed up communications on the Web by storing a site's most popular pages in cache. Proxies can be used as intermediate caching servers and as load-balancing systems—providing controlled access to a server bank. Caching proxies can also work in "clusters" to provide more efficient Web content delivery throughout areas of the Internet. Under this same category, a proxy firewall can actually be used to improve network throughput when properly coupled with a packet-filtering firewall. The firewall can simply route the packets that have to do with a given application directly to the proxy. This will allow the firewall filters to be less complex. The total number of rules does not decrease, but the load is distributed.

Disadvantages of Proxy Firewalls

Let us now take a look at the other side of the coin—what negative issues are normally associated with proxy firewalls?

Reduced Performance

If throughput is already an issue, you probably do not want to put a proxy in the path of all traffic. Proxies can severely reduce performance. Newer technologies have helped to reduce this issue considerably, but it is still a basic fact that proxies must evaluate a lot of information—requiring more system resources than a packet-filtering firewall.

A Proxy for Each Application

An application-layer proxy firewall is typically written around a single application. In general, you will need a different proxy for each application you intend to proxy (although they can run on the same machine). There will be some lag time between when a new application appears and when a proxy server is available for that application.

Not Immune to OS Problems

A proxy server runs on an existing platform (e.g., Linux and Microsoft). Therefore, it is dependent on that operating system's strength and vulnerable to its weaknesses. If the system needs to be patched, the proxy will have to go down. Some specialized proxies are starting to appear as appliances.

Complex

Proxy firewalls are inherently more complex than their packet-filtering and even stateful counterparts. Most proxies can be set up and running easily in their default configuration, but to use them in a more advanced configuration often introduces a considerable level of complexity. If you employ a proxy to serve your clients, you will also need to configure the clients.

Single Point of Failure

If your proxy firewall is situated such that all traffic is routed through it, it will obviously be a key point of failure. Most often, a proxy is set up to handle traffic for only a specific application or set of applications. We look at several topological arrangements under "System Configuration."

Inability to Handle Encryption

A proxy cannot handle authentication and encryption because the keys are held by the end nodes.

PROXY CHARACTERISTICS AND CAPABILITIES

Building a Proxy

To better understand the characteristics of a proxy, it might help to examine the functions that are desirable in a proxylike system. Keep in mind our key characteristic of a proxy (SiG): the proxy is an intermediary between the client and the server. The intermediary will fashion the client's requests into a format that is satisfactory to the proxy.

Proxy Firewall Characteristics

Let us begin by dividing the desired capabilities into two categories—those that are fairly easy to incorporate and those that are more complex.

Those capabilities that are easily realized are as follows:

- User authentication: our system more than likely will require some sort of user authentication whenever they log in. We could customize this in a variety of ways—selecting the encryption technique and setting requirements in terms of password characteristics.
- User account control: it may be that we would like to control the available applications based on individual users. This is a standard control in any multiuser system. Users can be restricted in terms of which programs they are allowed to launch, what times and days they are allowed to use the system, and what percentage of the system resources they can consume.
- Logging: standard system logging can be employed, allowing us to record the applications run by each user, time of day, and length of time they spend using each application, as well as nonapproved operations that they may be attempting.
- Encryption: if we employ a system such as Secure Shell for users logging in, we will have encryption on the local network to prevent advantages that might be obtained from sniffing and session hijacking. Externally, we can employ a variety of systems, such as Secure Sockets Layer or even VPNs in selected situations.

All of these capabilities are fairly easy to implement in a system such as Linux. PAM modules can be customized to provide authentication and account control. The standard syslog system can be set up to provide adequate logging, and SSH can provide our local encryption.

Those capabilities *not* so easily realized are as follows:

- Better logging: when we analyze the system's built-in logging capabilities, we realize that we can easily determine when a user is running a particular application—such as a browser. However, the basic logging does not provide the facility for actually determining *what or where* the user is browsing. In other words, there is no built-in, easy-to-use logging facility that allows us to log application-layer information. Most browser clients keep a browse history, which is stored in the user's home directory by default. The administrator could customize this setting, making the browse history either accessible only by the admin or at least copied to a file that is only accessible to admin. This allows us to determine and log the destination IPs and URLs but still no detailed application data.
- More granular restrictions: restricting access to particular sites means that our system will probably have to include firewall capabilities of some sort. In a Linux system, this might be accomplished through ipchains or iptables. The addition of firewall functionality will further increase our logging capabilities as well.
- Log management: the result of all this logging will obviously generate a mass of disjunctive logs that must be somehow assimilated chronologically as well as divided by user. A set of customized scripts could undoubtedly accomplish this for the administrator but at the expense of time and effort.
- User interface: providing a seamless user interface would not be so simple. The user may not be familiar

with the pseudoproxy system at all, and the tools available for Internet access may be as foreign as well. To overcome this problem and make the connection seamless would require custom applications. For example, a custom browser would be written that performed automatic login and automatic startup of the browser application on the pseudoproxy and then received and displayed the returning information. The custom application would be designed to look and act just like the browser application to which the user was accustomed. (There would *still* be an obvious delay, however.)

- Application-layer filtering: with all of these enhancements to our pseudoproxy, there is still one major difference. There is no application-layer analysis. We have *control* over the application, who can run it, how it is run, and when it is run but no real analysis of the actual application-layer data. For example, in the case of Web browsing, we may wish to monitor and control the sites visited as well as the types of material retrieved. Adding a packet-filtering or stateful firewall (e.g., iptables) could monitor, and control Web access based on site identity (i.e., domain names and IP addresses) but could not provide controls based on specific content at the application layer.

All of these characteristics are typical of the capabilities of a proxy firewall. Some of the same characteristics are available without using specific proxy application software, but many are not. In addition, the system designed from the beginning as a proxy will integrate these functions in a more efficient fashion.

One other note: we are demanding much more of the system when its set up as this pseudoproxy because it must actually run the application for each user as well as deliver the full content (including graphics) to the user. With a standard proxy server, the application is run on the user's system and only the connection is managed by the proxy.

Summary of Capabilities

- Those capabilities that are also achievable with a packet filter are as follows:
  - Source/destination IP address
  - Current day/time
  - Destination port
  - Protocol (FTP, HTTP, SSL)
- Those achievable with only application-layer information are as follows:
  - Source/destination domain
  - Regular expression match of requested domain
  - Words in the requested URL
  - Words in the source or destination domain
  - Command/method (e.g., FTP PORT, HTTP GET, or HTTP POST)
  - Client/browser type
- Those achievable through OS capabilities or additional applications are as follows:
  - Identification of user (e.g., use of the Ident protocol)
  - Username/password pair

This last category is mostly about identification and authentication—typically an important characteristic of a proxy system. A proxy server should never be used in a public environment (e.g., an ISP) without a sophisticated access control system. Ideally, the proxy server should not be used in *any* environment without some kind of basic authentication system. It is amazing how fast other Internet users will find your proxy and use it to relay requests through your cache or disguise their real identity.

The source IP address of a request that originates from a multiuser system will only identify the system itself, not the user specifically. To solve this problem, the *ident* protocol was created. The Ident protocol is a mechanism that can be used on any multiuser system to more positively identify the source of an incoming request. When the proxy accepts a connection, it can connect back to the multiuser system and find out which user just connected.

If you want to track Internet usage, it is best to get users to log into the proxy server whenever they want to access the Internet. You can then use a statistics program to generate per-user reports, no matter which machine on your network a person is using. User authentication can be custom code that is part of the proxy software, or it can utilize the operating system's user authentication tools or third-party modules could be used (PAM modules, for example). Any proxy administrator should inquire as to the type of authentication available on a proxy package that is being considered for use.

Proxy Protocols

Because different Internet services require different protocols, the proxy application must be able to converse in the appropriate protocol(s). A proxy server may run only a single protocol to handle a single service, or it may run a variety of service protocols.

Each layer of a packet adds complexity to the packet. The more layers a packet has, the more permutations that are possible, and the more complex the software that analyzes it must be. If the application layer is involved, the possible permutations grow extremely large.

The Layer 3 and Layer 4 headers are very predictable and have only a very finite set of possibilities. The application-layer protocols have considerably more possible entries, and these entries can often be extended in an indefinite fashion. Therefore, the software that analyzes application-level protocols must be, by nature, considerably more complex.

The appearance of new application-layer protocols is quite commonplace. Notable examples recently include protocols for music, video, conferencing, and file sharing. The appearance of new applications provides a serious challenge for the proxy administrator that is endeavoring to keep his users satisfied while maintaining a given level of security. In many cases, there is not a proxy server available for a new application and the administrator has a limited set of choices:

- Write his/her own proxy server for the new application
- Do not permit the new application
- Permit the new application to run *around* the proxy

Off-the-shelf proxy systems are typically designed with a particular set of application protocols in mind (the minimum usually includes HTTP and FTP). It is important that any administrator entertaining the use of a proxy become aware of the restrictions that any given product might impose. Determine your application needs and then choose a proxy that will provide the necessary capabilities and flexibility.

TYPES OF PROXIES

In this section, we continue our definitions by looking into current terminology concerning *types* of proxies. The following proxy-related systems are discussed:

- Store-and-forward
- Application-level proxy
- Circuit-level proxy
- Forward proxy
- Reverse proxy
- Proxy firewalls
- Caching/Web-caching proxy
- Proxy appliances/application filters

Store-and-Forward Servers

Some services, such as SMTP, NNTP, and NTP, provide proxylike functions by default. These services are all designed so that messages (e-mail messages for SMTP, Usenet news postings for NNTP, and clock settings for NTP) are received by a server and then stored until they can be forwarded. In SMTP, the e-mail messages are forwarded directly to the e-mail message's destination. For NNTP and NTP, the messages are forwarded to all neighbor servers. Obviously, each of these servers creates a new connection, acting as a proxy for the original sender or server.

The primary difference between a store-and-forward server and a conventional proxy server is that one works in real time. The proxy server performs SiG services as they are requested. A store-and-forward server performs the requested services at its own convenience and the convenience of the recipient.

Application versus Circuit-Level Proxies

An application-level proxy is one that is aware of the particular application and makes decisions based on the contents of the application layer. The circuit-level proxy completes the connection independent of the contents of the application layer.

At one end of the spectrum, an SMTP server that performs store-and-forward must be totally aware of the contents of the application data to deliver the e-mail. At the other end, a circuit-level proxy such as SOCKS will be concerned only with IP addresses and port numbers.

A circuit-level proxy is often referred to as a gateway. It is slightly more complex than a state firewall in that it *monitors* the sessions as they progress. A simple state firewall will add a session to its state table and then allow or reject future packets based on whether they match one of the entries. A circuit-level proxy will continue to monitor the traffic within an established state (circuit) to verify the transmission of additional packets.

Remember, even though the circuit-level proxy is *like* a state firewall, it is *still a proxy*. This means that

as a proxy, it will *stand between* the client and server (i.e., there is no direct connection between client and server).

Beyond this, there is a lot of disparity in exactly how deep into the packet the circuit-level proxy will venture. For example, WinGate 3.0 (which is based on SOCKS) is considered to be a circuit-level proxy; it uses only packet information from Layers 3 and 4 (source and destination ports indicating the application), whereas flags and sequence numbers are used to indicate the connection. Conversely, the Cisco series of PIX firewalls can (and often do) look into the application layer to maintain complex connections, such as FTP and H.323.

Circuit-level proxies are popular because once they are configured, they can be used to proxy most Internet protocols, such as IMAP, LDAP, POP3, SMTP, FTP, and HTTP. They can even be used to proxy Internet protocols secured with SSL.

Whereas SOCKS attempts to provide a single, general proxy, a system such as Trusted Information Systems Firewall Toolkit (TIS FWTK) provides individual proxies for the most common Internet services. The philosophy behind such a system is to use small separate programs for each application but at the same time employ a common configuration file.

TIS FWTK uses the destination port and the source address of the connection as an indicator of where the new connection should be sent. This means that the only way a client can specify a different destination is to connect to a different port on the proxy. Obviously, this makes *plug-gw* inappropriate for many types of services.

In general, the two terms (i.e., circuit level, application level) are really related to the *depth* to which a program looks into the packets. The term *proxy* can be applied to a variety of systems that typically scrutinize traffic more extensively than packet-filtering or state firewalls. Circuit-level proxies would be considered to be at the simplistic end of the range, and application-level proxies would be further up the chain of complexity.

Circuit-level proxies will not provide the level of monitoring and control of an application-level proxy, but they can be beneficial in many ways, as follows:

- Secures addresses from exposure: remember that even circuit-level proxies are *proxies* (i.e., they have the SiG characteristic). There is no direct connection between an application client and an application server. Proxy servers hide the address structure of the network and make it difficult to access confidential information.

- Offers a high degree of flexibility: because circuit-level proxies communicate at the session layer, they support a multiprotocol environment. As new Internet services are added, circuit-level proxies automatically support them. Also, configuring clients to work with circuit-level proxies is much simpler than application-level proxies. Client software no longer needs to be configured on a case-by-case basis. With Microsoft's Proxy Server, for example, once WinSock Proxy software has been installed onto a client computer, client software such as the Windows media player, Internet relay chat (IRC), or telnet will perform just as if it were directly connected to the Internet.

• Ease of configuration: although application-level proxies are considered highly secure, they do require a high degree of technical configuration and support. Circuit-level proxies were developed to resolve this problem.

Forward versus Reverse Proxies

These two terms are used to describe whether the proxy is set up to protect the client or the server. If the proxy is set up to protect the client, it is said to be a *forward proxy*. The idea of the forward proxy began to appear with the infusion of firewalls as choke points between private trusted networks and the Internet. The proxies provided safe Internet access to inside users.

If the proxy is set up to protect the *server*, it is a *reverse proxy*. A reverse proxy is typically set up outside the firewall to represent a secure content server to clients on the Internet (or at least outside the trusted network). This will prevent unnecessary direct connections to the server's data. The reverse proxy can also improve performance by caching often-accessed information and by performing load balancing.

Proxies can be set up to provide both forward and reverse functions. However, physical placement of a proxy machine in terms of a company's firewall could dictate its use.

Application Firewalls

Security threats on the Internet are constantly becoming more specialized. The Layer 3 and layer 4 vulnerabilities are finite. At this point, the vulnerabilities in these layers have been well published. Modern firewalls and educated administrators have evolved to defend against this finite set of possibilities. Now the attackers are turning to the packet's payload and new application-layer protocols—providing them with an almost infinite set of possibilities.

This attack specialization has spawned a variety of new products (both software and hardware) designed to deal with a particular category of attacks.

One example of specialized protection is in the area of viruses being delivered as part of the application payload—e-mail and Web content are two primary cases. Numerous software products have appeared over the last few years that can be integrated with an SMTP's functions. The payloads that are destined to be processed by an SMTP can be preexamined by one of these products to remove malicious content. In some circles, a product such as this is considered a specialized proxy firewall. As we have already discussed, an SMTP server is in itself a proxy and a choke point of sorts. Adding this new type of capability to the SMTP server certainly promotes it to application firewall level.

Caching Proxies/Web-Caching Proxies

A Web cache sits between Web servers and the client(s). It monitors requests for Web objects (e.g., HTML pages, images, scripts). When the Web server responds with the object, the caching proxy saves a copy locally. Whenever another request arrives for the same object, the caching proxy will deliver the local copy, saving the time and bandwidth of an additional connection to the server. The advantages of a caching proxy are obvious: the client will realize a reduced latency, there will be less traffic generated, and the proxy will have fewer connections to create and maintain.

An organization might use a caching on a reverse proxy to help speed access to its own Web servers and as a type of load balancing. On a forward proxy, caching might be used to speed up access for local users as well as reduce bandwidth needs on the connection to the Internet.

PROXY CONFIGURATIONS

As we have seen, proxy servers can provide a considerable level of security. However, these capabilities do not come easily. Proxy firewalls are among the most difficult systems to configure properly and, once configured, they cannot be left to run without constant attention. There are several configuration topics that must be carefully considered. This section breaks these topics into two categories: system configuration and network configuration.

System Configuration

A proxy server will typically be installed on a dual-homed machine that has been thoroughly hardened. The machine will be connected in such a way that it is available on one side for the clients and the other side for the servers (more on the placement of the proxy in the next section). The proxy server evaluates requests from the client, deciding which of these to forward. Assuming a request is approved, the proxy will then communicate with the real server, forwarding the client's requests and then relaying the server's replies back to the client. In the situation where the proxy is the only machine communicating with the Internet, it is the only machine that requires a public IP address. Therefore, it is natural to use private address ranges for the internal machines.

Proxy servers are based entirely on software—no special hardware is required. Obviously, the speed of the system and its interfaces will ultimately determine how much traffic it can handle and how many connections it can proxy simultaneously. Sophisticated proxy systems avoid user frustration and their shortcomings when dealing with an unknown operating system. The user has the illusion of dealing directly with the server with a minimum of interaction with the proxy itself. The proxy server and proxy client software are exactly what makes this possible. There are a number of issues that will influence the selection, configuration, and topological placement of a proxy system.

Scalability

Proxy servers must grow with network needs. Additional network clients will require additional bandwidth and more proxy connections. Multiple "parallel" proxies can be configured to handle increased load. Alternately, the administrator can configure individual proxies for different network segments, and these can be customized to support the particular segment's needs. Additionally, proxy servers can be divided according to the applications that they serve.

New Applications

New network applications will require new proxy plug-ins or custom coding. Keep in mind that application-level proxies are configured to work on an application-by-application basis. When an application arises that is not supported by your proxy server, there are a few options, as follows:

- Disallow the service
- Upgrade the proxy (either through an available plugin or through custom coding)
- Route the service around the proxy (i.e., do not proxy that service)
- Use a circuit-level proxy for that service

Client Configuration

Remember that application-level proxies will typically have two components—the proxy server component and the client component. The client software must know how to contact the proxy server rather than the designated server. Some applications come with this capability built in (e.g., CERN compatible browsers). However, most do not, particularly new applications. Alternately, a circuit-level proxy can be used (e.g., SOCKS), and a one-time client configuration will satisfy future applications.

The problem of client configuration is one of volume. Typically, the client component for a proxy aware application is simple to install and, once running, works without incident. However, installing the client component companywide might be a daunting task. Some proxy systems provide an automatic delivery mechanism to handle this task—typically through the client's browser.

Because of the considerable time requirement that client configuration entails, the administrator should evaluate prospective proxy packages with this task in mind.

Caching Service

If your proxy is functioning as a reverse proxy for your own set of Web servers, or if you want to speed up Web responses for your clients, you will undoubtedly want to configure caching service. There are numerous considerations involved with caching.

Most proxy server packages provide an easy initial caching setup. As long as there are no problems, this default caching configuration may be satisfactory. If problems do arise, however, it can be extremely difficult to troubleshoot. To effectively judge the performance impact of proxy caches, one needs to take into consideration the interactions among HTTP, TCP, and the network environment. (Before attempting to configure and fine-tune a Web caching system, the administrator should review the work done in proxy cache testing by Cáceres, Douglis, Feldmann, Glass, and Rabinovich at the AT&T research labs.)

Another often-overlooked concern of caching is the legal aspects—caching copyrighted material. At this point in time, there is a lot of uncertainty regarding the rights of the Web page owners and those engaged in caching. Undoubtedly, there will be cases in the future that address this issue.

Building the Firewall

Just as with any firewall, a proxy firewall will have a rule set—commonly referred to as the access control. Most of the proxy systems have some form of GUI for setting up the most common rules, such as URL filtering, but setting up detailed custom rule sets will typically be as complex as configuring any firewall. The more filtering that can be done *before* the packet reaches the proxy, the easier it will be to build the proxy's access-control rule set. Layers 3 and 4 filtering will be done more efficiently with a packet or stateful firewall.

Filtering application-layer information is considerably more difficult than filtering Layer 3 or 4 information because of the almost limitless range of possible content. Rules written with one intention in mind can often lead to unpredictable results. Only thorough testing can provide some degree of confidence in a particular rule set. As with packet-filtering firewalls, always start with the "deny all, accept by exception" philosophy. It will be far better to open new doors based on friendly user requests than to discover you have exploitable holes from unfriendly attackers.

Proxy Vulnerabilities

In addition to the configuration considerations listed herein, the proxy administrator needs to be aware of the specialized vulnerabilities introduced through the use of *any* proxy system.

Whenever you have a proxy system that is a choke point for all traffic in and out of your network, you are setting up a single point of failure. If your proxy crashes, your network could be totally cut off from the Internet.

One might argue that such a problem exists with *any* choke point—such as a router or packet-filtering firewall. However, failover with these devices is a fairly common utility, built into the system by design. Proxy-server failover is typically a responsibility designated to the administrator. There are a number of ways to implement proxy failover:

- Provide multiple proxies working in parallel. This will also provide a degree of load-sharing capabilities
- Alternate routes can be provided that are enabled only when the proxy fails. This type of functionality would typically be realized by allowing the router to make the decision based on the "availability" of the proxy.
- Fix it. Both of the previous solutions obviously reduce the security of your network. If the proxy is considered to be an important security cornerstone in your network, then any time you allow traffic to go around it you are compromising your security intentions. Having a spare proxy, ready to come online (either automatically or manually) would be the best choice. Redundancy is an excellent solution on paper but often is economically unfeasible.

The proxy server stands to protect, but what protects the proxy server? As we have already mentioned, a proxy server should be installed on only the most robust and hardened system. Nonetheless, proxy servers can still fall victim to any number of problems that typically afflict

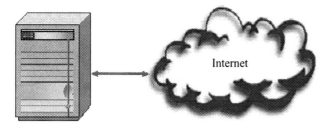

Figure 1: Single-homed proxy.

any complex application software. The most common of these today is the buffer overflow. The impact of a buffer overflow can vary from server malfunctioning to server crash to providing an attacker with a command line. As with all key systems and servers, the administrator must stay informed as to the latest vulnerabilities and apply all security patches.

Ideally, a single host would be used for each proxy service. This would make it easier to administer and control the service in question. Advancements in computer speed and storage have led to systems that provide multiple services on a single machine, however, and this has become the normal approach. Keep in mind the old adage about keeping all of your eggs in one basket. Putting a number of proxy services on a single host creates a single point of failure.

Network Configuration

A proxy server can work with a single network connection (as in Figure 1). However, in the case of the single connection, traffic is not *forced* to go through the proxy. In some circles, such a setup would probably not qualify as a proxy *firewall*.

A common example of a proxy with a single network connection could be an SMTP server. The user sends a composed e-mail message to the SMTP server. The SMTP server then transfers the message to the appropriate destination SMTP server, which then passes the message to the recipient user. In this case, the SMTP servers at both ends are acting as proxy servers. Because they handle the e-mail messages, they can be used to perform filtering operations—shielding the recipient from dangerous or unwanted contents (malicious code or spam).

Alternately, a similar situation is shown in Figure 2. In this case, the proxy is probably multihomed (alternatively, it could have a single interface with two IP addresses), but both of its interfaces are connected to the Internet. Such a proxy can serve as what is typically referred to as an *anonymous proxy*. It provides a SiG for Internet users who would like to conceal their machine specifics, such as IP address, operating system, browser, and so on.

Because anonymous proxy servers are an SiG and create an entirely new connection on behalf of the user, they hide the user's IP address and other OS fingerprinting information. Most anonymous proxy servers can be used for any kind of services that are normally accessed through a browser, such as Web mail, Web chat rooms, FTP archives, and so on.

One might question why anonymous proxies even exist—what is the economical advantage? Following are some of the reasons such a service might be provided:

- As part of an ISP's service (helps to reduce their traffic as well, because of caching)
- As part of "bundled services," for example, with an e-mail account
- A way to deliver advertising or spam

The anonymous proxy service is also available as a charged service—anonymous proxying offered with a monthly fee—playing strong on the "anonymous" and "private" functions. There is even software that will do the work of finding an appropriate anonymous proxy server and then connecting to it automatically whenever one uses their browser.

Any user intending to use an anonymous proxy should be aware of one important issue—whether or not the proxy is truly anonymous. Though the proxy may create an entirely new connection, it may also include the user's IP in the payload of new packets. For example, in the following proxy connection where the proxy is forwarding a request to a Web site from a user, we see that part of the content is the user's IP (192.168.1.2 in this case):

```
X-Forwarded-For: 192.168.1.2..
```

Obviously, this type of service is not totally anonymous.

If the proxy is set up on a dual-homed machine, the machine may also be set to either provide IP forwarding (i.e., as a router). For example, in Figure 3, a dual-homed proxy is set up as the *only* path between a local network and the Internet. If the proxy does not allow IP forwarding, then the proxy software must process *all* packets, rebuild them, and deliver them. If IP forwarding is allowed (as illustrated in Figure 4), the packets can be *selectively* processed. The routing process occur first, and then packets are either routed *around* the proxy or *through* the proxy.

Finally, the proxy could be a separate machine that has packets selectively routed to it by a router or dual-homed bastion host, as shown in Figure 5. Functionally, this setup is the same as that shown in Figure 4, but now the functions are provided by individual machines, and the routing function will likely be provided by an appliance. Obviously, this arrangement could help alleviate the "single point of failure" issue discussed earlier.

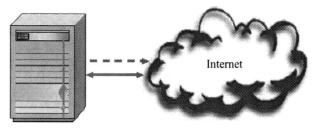

Figure 2: Anonymous proxy.

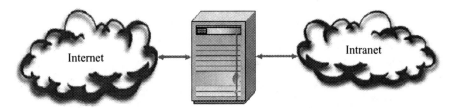

Figure 3: Dual-homed proxy without IP forwarding.

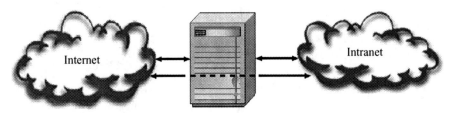

Figure 4: Dual-homed proxy with IP forwarding.

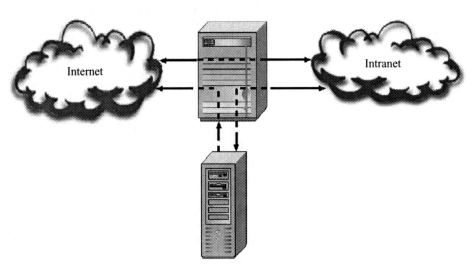

Figure 5: Separate proxy.

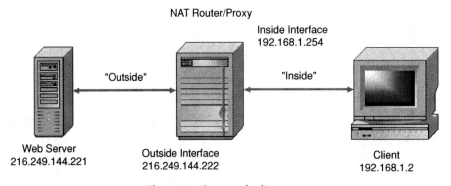

Figure 6: Case-study diagram.

Table 1. NAT-Only Inside Traffic

#	Source IP	Destination IP	Size	Protocol	Sequence #
1	192.168.1.2	216.249.144.221	78	TCP HTTP	S=1531784746
2	216.249.144.221	192.168.1.2	82	TCP HTTP	S=2805436594
3	192.168.1.2	216.249.144.221	70	TCP HTTP	S=1531784747
4	192.168.1.2	216.249.144.221	449	TCP HTTP	S=1531784747
5	216.249.144.221	192.168.1.2	1494	TCP HTTP	S=2805436595
6	192.168.1.2	216.249.144.221	70	TCP HTTP	S=1531785126
7	192.168.1.2	216.249.144.221	78	TCP HTTP	S=1542623850
8	216.249.144.221	192.168.1.2	82	TCP HTTP	S=2805611041
9	192.168.1.2	216.249.144.221	70	TCP HTTP	S=1542623851
10	192.168.1.2	216.249.144.221	601	TCP HTTP	S=1542623851
11	216.249.144.221	192.168.1.2	1518	TCP HTTP	S=2805611042
12	192.168.1.2	216.249.144.221	70	TCP HTTP	S=1542624382
13	216.249.144.221	192.168.1.2	1518	TCP HTTP	S=2805612490
14	192.168.1.2	216.249.144.221	70	TCP HTTP	S=1542624382
15	216.249.144.221	192.168.1.2	206	TCP HTTP	S=2805613938
16	192.168.1.2	216.249.144.221	70	TCP HTTP	S=1542624382

CASE STUDY: TRAFFIC ANALYSIS OF A PROXY OPERATION

This analysis compares a NAT-only connection with a connection through a proxy. The network layout is shown in Figure 6. In the first set of captures (Tables 1 and 2), the middle machine is serving as a NAT router. In the second set of captures (Tables 3 and 4), the middle machine is serving as a proxy. The operation performed is the same in both cases—the client is accessing a Web page on the server and then a cookie is transferred.

First let us analyze the general traffic pattern. The operation performed by the client was identical in both cases—a browser was used to open a single page on the server and a cookie was transferred. In the first set of captures, there is a NAT-ing router between the client and the server. In the second set, there is a proxy between the client and the server.

In both cases, the client's IP address is replaced by the router/proxy's IP address. The client is 192.168.1.2 and the Web server is 216.249.144.221. The outside IP address of the router/proxy is 216.249.144.222, and the inside address is 192.168.1.254. So, as the client's traffic is relayed onto the outside network, the 192.168.1.2 address is replaced by the 216.249.144.222 address. In both cases, the outside conversation is between .221 and .222.

The inside conversation varies, however. In the NAT-only scenario, the client uses the specific IP address of the server as the destination. When the proxy is involved, however, the client speaks directly to the proxy. This indicates that the client must be configured to translate any given set of browser requests into requests directed to the proxy. This is done in the browser settings.

The next thing that is quite obvious from the NAT-only scenario to the proxy scenario is the difference in the inside traffic. In the case of the proxy, there is considerably

Table 2. NAT-Only Outside Traffic

#	Source IP	Destination IP	Size	Protocol	Sequence #
1	216.249.144.223	216.249.144.221	78	TCP HTTP	S=1531784746
2	216.249.144.221	216.249.144.223	82	TCP HTTP	S=2805436594
3	216.249.144.223	216.249.144.221	70	TCP HTTP	S=1531784747
4	216.249.144.223	216.249.144.221	449	TCP HTTP	S=1531784747
5	216.249.144.221	216.249.144.223	1494	TCP HTTP	S=2805436595
6	216.249.144.223	216.249.144.221	70	TCP HTTP	S=1531785126
7	216.249.144.223	216.249.144.221	78	TCP HTTP	S=1542623850
8	216.249.144.221	216.249.144.223	82	TCP HTTP	S=2805611041
9	216.249.144.223	216.249.144.221	70	TCP HTTP	S=1542623851
10	216.249.144.223	216.249.144.221	601	TCP HTTP	S=1542623851
11	216.249.144.221	216.249.144.223	1518	TCP HTTP	S=2805611042
12	216.249.144.221	216.249.144.223	1518	TCP HTTP	S=2805612490
13	216.249.144.223	216.249.144.221	70	TCP HTTP	S=1542624382
14	216.249.144.221	216.249.144.223	206	TCP HTTP	S=2805613938
15	216.249.144.223	216.249.144.221	70	TCP HTTP	S=1542624382
16	216.249.144.223	216.249.144.221	70	TCP HTTP	S=1542624382

Table 3. Proxy Inside Traffic

#	Source IP	Destination IP	Size	Protocol	Sequence #
Packets 1-3: Handshake between client and proxy					
1	192.168.1.2	192.168.1.254	78	IP TCP	S=2555300348
2	192.168.1.254	192.168.1.2	78	IP TCP	S=2132876752
3	192.168.1.2	192.168.1.254	70	IP TCP	S=2555300349
Packets 4 and 5: Client request and proxy ACK					
4	192.168.1.2	192.168.1.254	474	IP TCP	S=2555300349
5	192.168.1.254	192.168.1.2	70	IP TCP	S=2132876753
Packets 6 and 7: Proxy response and client ACK					
6	192.168.1.254	192.168.1.2	1518	IP TCP	S=2132876753
7	192.168.1.2	192.168.1.254	70	IP TCP	S=2555300753
Packets 8-10: FIN Sequence					
8	192.168.1.254	192.168.1.2	104	IP TCP	S=2132878201
9	192.168.1.2	192.168.1.254	70	IP TCP	S=2555300753
10	192.168.1.2	192.168.1.254	70	IP TCP	S=2555300753
Packets 11-13: Handshake between client and proxy for next connection					
This second connection is to transfer a cookie. Follows the same general pattern.					
11	192.168.1.254	192.168.1.2	70	IP TCP	S=2132878235
12	192.168.1.2	192.168.1.254	70	IP TCP	S=2555300754
13	192.168.1.2	192.168.1.254	78	IP TCP	S=2560783519
14	192.168.1.254	192.168.1.2	78	IP TCP	S=2132834458
15	192.168.1.2	192.168.1.254	70	IP TCP	S=2560783520
16	192.168.1.2	192.168.1.254	626	IP TCP	S=2560783520
17	192.168.1.254	192.168.1.2	70	IP TCP	S=2132834459
18	192.168.1.254	192.168.1.2	1518	IP TCP	S=2132834459
19	192.168.1.2	192.168.1.254	70	IP TCP	S=2560784076
20	192.168.1.254	192.168.1.2	104	IP TCP	S=2132835907
21	192.168.1.2	192.168.1.254	70	IP TCP	S=2560784076
22	192.168.1.254	192.168.1.2	1518	IP TCP	S=2132835941
23	192.168.1.2	192.168.1.254	70	IP TCP	S=2560784076
24	192.168.1.254	192.168.1.2	230	IP TCP	S=2132837389
25	192.168.1.2	192.168.1.254	70	IP TCP	S=2560784076
26	192.168.1.2	192.168.1.254	70	IP TCP	S=2560784076
27	192.168.1.254	192.168.1.2	70	IP TCP	S=2132837549
28	192.168.1.2	192.168.1.254	70	IP TCP	S=2560784077

Table 4. Proxy Outside Traffic

#	Source IP	Destination IP	Size	Protocol	Sequence #
Packets 1-3: Proxy Handshake with Web server					
1	216.249.144.222	216.249.144.221	78	TCP HTTP	S=2125937178
2	216.249.144.221	216.249.144.222	82	TCP HTTP	S=3048224752
3	216.249.144.222	216.249.144.221	70	TCP HTTP	S=2125937179
Packet 4: Proxy relays client request to Web server					
4	216.249.144.222	216.249.144.221	538	TCP HTTP	S=2125937179
Packets 5-8: Web server responds with data and proxy ACK's					
5	216.249.144.221	216.249.144.222	1518	TCP HTTP	S=3048224753
6	216.249.144.221	216.249.144.222	94	TCP HTTP	S=3048226201
7	216.249.144.222	216.249.144.221	70	TCP HTTP	S=2125937647
8	216.249.144.222	216.249.144.221	70	TCP HTTP	S=2125937647
Proxy relaying second request from client					
Connection continues and transfers cookie					
9	216.249.144.222	216.249.144.221	690	TCP HTTP	S=2125937647
10	216.249.144.221	216.249.144.222	1518	TCP HTTP	S=3048226225
11	216.249.144.221	216.249.144.222	1518	TCP HTTP	S=3048227673
12	216.249.144.221	216.249.144.222	230	TCP HTTP	S=3048229121
13	216.249.144.222	216.249.144.221	70	TCP HTTP	S=2125938267
14	216.249.144.222	216.249.144.221	70	TCP HTTP	S=2125938267
15	216.249.144.222	216.249.144.221	70	TCP HTTP	S=2125938267

more traffic. Also note the protocol. Despite the fact that the operation is intended to be HTTP (Web browser), the protocol in use is simply TCP. All data transferred between the client and the proxy is considered to be TCP payload. The extra traffic is primarily because of the fact that each request and response requires a new connection (and handshake), and there must be additional acknowledgments.

If you look at the NAT-only connection, you will see that the traffic on the outside connection precisely mirrors the traffic on the inside connection—right down to the packet sizes. The only thing changed about the packets is the source IP address. (Of course, the TTL is decremented and the data link layer information is modified.)

Details on the Proxy Scenario

Packets 1–5 are used to connect to the proxy and send the request. The reader will note that the protocol listed on the inside traffic is just TCP. This is because the proxy is listening on Port 3128 rather than Port 80, and the protocol analyzer does not associate Port 3128 with HTTP protocol. However, the application-layer data in the packets from the client to the proxy are *identical* to those that would have been sent directly to the server.

Notice that the request from the proxy to the server (Packet 4) is 474 bytes. The same request in the NAT situation is 449 bytes. The difference is because of the fact that the destination-machine information must be included in the payload rather in the header.

The first part of the request in the NAT-only scenario is as follows:

```
GET / HTTP/1.1..
Connection: Keep-Alive
User-Agent: Mozilla/5.0 (compatible; Konqueror/2.2-11; Linux)
```

The first part of the request in the proxy scenario is as follows:

```
GET / http://216.249.144.221:80/ HTTP/1.1
Connection: Keep-Alive
User-Agent: Mozilla/5.0  (compatible; Konqueror/2.2-11; Linux)
```

The additional information is indicated in bold and totals 25 bytes (474–449).

After this initial request to the proxy server, the proxy server relays that request onto the Web server. This can be seen in the outside traffic, Packets 1–4. Packet 5 is then the response (which is too large to fit in one packet, so is extended to Packet 6).

Note also that as the request gets relayed from the proxy to the Web server, the request packet grows in size from 474 to 538 bytes. This difference is because of the fact that the proxy includes the client's IP address in the payload. Compare the original request to the relayed request as follows:

Inside (only the tail shown)
```
... ALJLJ
```
Outside (only the tail shown)
```
  ALJLJ
Via: 1.1 Inside1:3128 (Squid/2.4.STABLE1)
X-Forwarded-For: 192.168.1.2
Host: 216.249.144.221
Cache-Control: no-cache,  max-age=259200
Connection: keep-alive
```

All of the portion in bold is added by the proxy. The portion that is not bolded was part of the original request, but the proxy moved it to this position. The total additional bytes are 89. However, the additional 25 bytes that were part of the original request can now be removed, because the proxy is talking directly to the server. This leaves $89 - 25 = 64$ additional bytes ($538 - 474 = 64$).

This response received by the proxy is then passed onto the client. This traffic can be seen on this inside listing and is represented by Packets 6–9. Packets 6 and 8 are the actual data corresponding to Packets 5 and 6 of the outside traffic, and Packets 7 and 9 are the client's acknowledgements to the proxy. Note again the change in the size of the packets. The proxy received a 1,518-byte packet and a

---

94-byte packet, but it passed on a 1,518-byte packet and a 104-byte packet. This difference is because of a number of changes and additions the proxy makes to the packet. An example of one addition is shown below in the packet that is relayed (showing that the proxy is indicating that the information is *not* cached):

```
Cache-Control: p  43 61 63 68 65 2D 43 6F 6E 74 72 6F 6C 3A 20 70
rivate..X-Cache:  72 69 76 61 74 65 0D 0A 58 2D 43 61 63 68 65 3A
 MISS from Insid  20 4D 49 53 53 20 66 72 6F 6D 20 49 6E 73 69 64
e1..Proxy-Connec  65 31 0D 0A 50 72 6F 78 79 2D 43 6F 6E 6E 65 63
tion: keep-alive  74 69 6F 6E 3A 20 6B 65 65 70 2D 61 6C 69 76 65
......<!--... W   0D 0A 0D 0A 0D 0A 3C 21 2D 2D 0D 0A 09 20 20 57
```

The next transfer follows the same general procedure. One key issue to note, however, is that the proxy–client connection is closed in the interim. Packets 10–12 on the inside traffic represent the FIN handshake sequence. Packets 13–15 represent the three-way handshake for the next connection (cookie transfer). Note that the connection remains persistent on the outside traffic, never closing until Packets 13–15.

One last lesson that this capture can verify is the complete reconstruction of the connection. It is obvious that the source IP address is changed (in both the NAT-only and in the proxy scenarios), but note that the sequence numbers are also changed in the proxy scenario but remain the same in the NAT-only scenario.

CONCLUSION

A proxy firewall is first and foremost a *proxy*. It serves as a SiG, standing between the server and the client. Because it establishes a new connection with the server on behalf of the client, the connection parameters (e.g., source IP and port) are replaced with its own. By default, the proxy performs a type of network address and port address translation (NAT and PAT).

Second, a proxy firewall is a firewall. Because certain types of traffic are funneled through the proxy, it is a choke point. It also makes decisions concerning clients' requests and servers' responses based on a rule set (i.e., access-control list).

A proxy should probably be considered if you need:

• More advanced control over client access to the Internet: use a forward proxy
• More advanced control over access to your servers: use a reverse proxy
• To improve performance: use a caching proxy
  • Better service for your clients when accessing outside servers
  • Better service for your customers accessing your servers
  • Reduced traffic

A proxy should probably *not* be considered if you just need:

• To shield internal machine information (e.g., IPs): consider a NAT-ing firewall
• To limit Internet access to clients based on the client identity, protocol, or time of day. These things can all be done more efficiently with packet-filtering and stateful firewalls.

When considering a proxy, there are some key issues of which you should be aware:

• Proxies are generally designed for a single application, and each new application will require a new proxy. Alternatively, you can use a circuit-level proxy, but it will not provide the same degree of control.
• Clients must be configured. No matter what type of proxy you use to protect your clients, the client machines will almost invariably need to be modified in some way. Be sure to examine the client needs before committing to a particular proxy and include the time needed for setting up the clients in your implementation estimation.
• Logs can get out of hand and rule sets can get quite complex. For simple operations, default proxy settings will suffice, but when advanced functions are needed, defining rule sets can become intimidating and resultant logs can quickly become overwhelming.
• Caching issues can further complicate matters. If one of the reasons for using a proxy is performance, you will undoubtedly be caching. Like rule sets, default caching can be simple. However, advanced caching techniques are new and many aspects yet undocumented. Additionally, one should be aware of the legal ramifications involved.

In conclusion, before considering a proxy firewall, be sure your security needs warrant the additional effort and cost involved with such a decision. Do not underestimate the time necessary for both setup and maintenance. Finally, always check for the latest products available. There may be an application-layer firewall appliance specifically designed for your need.

GLOSSARY

Application-Layer Firewall Any firewall that has the capability to examine application-layer data.

Application-Level Proxy A proxy that is designed around a particular application and has the capabilities to analyze traffic involved with that application.

Caching Proxy A proxy that caches client requests. When identical requests occur, the proxy will provide the reply from its own cache.

Circuit-Level Proxy A proxy that is not concerned with the application but simply creates an intermediate connection—separating client from server.

Firewall A system that has the capability to analyze traffic passing through it, make decisions based on a set of rules that determine whether the traffic should be passed, dropped, or modified.

Forward Proxy A proxy that is installed to protect the client.

Network Address Translation Changing the source and/or destination IP address of a packet.

Port Address Translation Changing the source and/or destination port of a packet.

Proxy A system the stands between the client and a server, creating a new connection on behalf of the client.

Proxy Appliance A proxy that is built as its own box. These are fairly new to the market and primarily supplement SMTP servers to check for viruses.

Reverse Proxy A proxy that is installed to protect the server.

Store-and-Forward Server A type of proxy that does not necessarily operate in real time, such as an SMTP server.

Web Accelerator A proxy that is installed to provide improved Web performance, primarily by caching Web content.

CROSS REFERENCES

See *Firewall Architectures; Firewall Basics; Packet-Filtering and Stateful Firewalls.*

FURTHER READING

Chappell, L. A., & Tittel, E. D. (2002). *Guide to TCP/IP.* Course Technology.

Forouzan, B. A. (2003). *TCP/IP protocol suite.* New York: McGraw-Hill.

Holden, G. (2004). *Guide to Firewalls and Network Security.* Course Technology.

Kaufman, Perlman, & Speciner (1995). *Network Security.* Prentice Hall.

Larson, E. (2000). *Web Servers, Security, and Maintenance.* Prentice Hall.

Northcutt, Zeltser, Winters, Frederick, & Ritchey (2003). *Inside Network Perimeter Security.* New Riders.

Sheldon & Cox (2001). *Windows 2000 Security Handbook.* Osborne/McGraw-Hill.

Shinder, T. W., & Shinder, D. L. (2001). *ISA Server 2000.* Syngress.

Tipton & Krause (2000). *Information Security Management Handbook.* Auerbach.

Zeigler, R. L. (2002). *Linux Firewalls.* New Riders.

Zwicky, Cooper, & Chapman (2000). *Building Internet Firewalls.* Sebastopol, CA: O'Reilly.

Online Material
(all online sources were last accessed by this author in October 2003)
General Information:
http://wp.netscape.com/proxy/v3.5/evalguide/criteria.html
http://service.real.com/help/library/whitepapers/rproxy/htmfiles/proxy22.htm
http://www.novell.com/info/collateral/docs/4621235.02/4621235.html
http://www.ctlinc.com/Pages/News_CTL.html
http://www.winproxy.com/english/products/AVStripper/pd_avstripper_en.asp

Installing and setting up the Linux proxy firewall:
http://new.linuxnow.com/docs/content/Firewall-HOWTO-html/Firewall-HOWTO-12.html

Shareware and Freeware Proxies:
http://www.hairy.beasts.org/fk/competition.html
http://www.solsoft.org/nsm/
http://www.obtuse.com/juniper/
http://www.opensourcefirewall.com/trex.html
http://www.delegate.org/delegate/

SOCKS:
http://www.socks.permeo.com/
http://www.inet.no/dante/

Squid was the proxy used to generate the captures included in this paper. For more information on setting up your own Squid proxy:
General Page:
http://www.squid-cache.org/

Programmer's Guide:
http://www.squid-cache.org/Doc/Prog-Guide/prog-guide.html
Used as a reverse proxy:
http://secinf.net/unix_security/Linux_Administrators_Security_Guide/Linux_Administrators_Security_Guide_Proxy_software.html

TIS FWTK Home Site:
http://fwtk.intrusion.org/fwtk/
Anonymous/Public Proxy Servers:
http://www.publicproxyservers.com/index.html
http://www.inetprivacy.com/a4proxy/anonymous-proxy-faq.htm
http://www.anonymous-surfing-web.com/
Automatic Public Proxy Software:
http://www.winnowsoft.com/anonymous-proxy.htm
http://www.publicproxyservers.com/index.html

Web Caching:
http://www.cs.wisc.edu/~cao/WISP98/html-versions/anja/proxim_wisp/index.html

Legal Considerations:
http://www.mnot.net/cache_docs/

The Houston Proxy Marriage
MSNBC:
http://www.msnbc.com/news/950579.asp

Digital Certificates

Albert Levi, *Sabanci University, Turkey*

INTRODUCTION

Public key cryptography has become popular in information and telecommunication security. Algorithms in this family use two different, but related, keys. One of them is kept private by the key owner, and the other is made public. The private key is used to decrypt messages as well as to sign digital information. The corresponding public key is used to encrypt messages and to verify digital signatures. Because these latter operations can be done by anyone, public keys need to be made public. Although public keys are widely known, it is not computationally feasible to obtain a private key using the corresponding public key.

Public key distribution is not an easy task. Public keys can be distributed through global directories or servers, but the key must be bound to the holder's identity. Without binding, the key holders could use any name they wanted. For example, suppose *Charlie* creates a key pair and publishes the public key as if he is *Bob*. Later *Alice* wants to obtain the *Bob's* correct public key. She queries the server and obtains the public key that seemingly belongs to *Bob*, but was actually uploaded by *Charlie*. In this way, *Charlie* can masquerade as *Bob*. This method of cheating is called *name spoofing*. The possible dangers of name spoofing are the following:

- Suppose *Charlie* has intercepted the encrypted messages from *Alice* to *Bob*. *Alice* has encrypted these messages using the fake public key of *Bob*, which actually belongs to *Charlie*. Because *Charlie* also knows the corresponding private key, he is now capable of decrypting these messages.
- Suppose *Bob* has digitally signed a message using his private key and sent it to *Alice*. Because the public key that *Alice* has for *Bob* is in fact incorrect, she cannot verify the signature on the message, even if it is legitimate.

There are some methods proposed in the literature to overcome the name-spoofing problem. When public key cryptography was first proposed by Diffie and Hellman (1976), the proposed method for public key distribution was a "public file" where the public keys and the corresponding owners were listed. The write access was limited to authorized users, but the read access was not limited. This idea would have been useful for small communities where there was no need to update the public file very often, but it was never realized because the demand was to provide for larger communities. Later, centralized online mechanisms were proposed to distribute public keys on demand (Popek & Kline, 1979), but such a service was never widely implemented mainly because of the dependency on online servers.

The concept of *certificate* was first proposed by Kohnfelder (1978) as a distributed public key distribution mechanism that did not need online servers. The idea was to employ trusted entities that would validate and endorse the *public-key-to-owner* binding with a digital signature.

A public key certificate (or identity certificate) is a digital binding between the identity and the public key of a user. Sometimes certificates are used to bind a credential or a permit to a public key without using the identity of the owner. This type of certificate is called an *attribute certificate* (or *authorization certificate*). The binding in a certificate is digitally signed by a trusted *certification authority* (*CA*). Anyone who wants to find a legitimate public key verifies the CA signature on the certificate. The verifier must trust that the CA has correctly bound the public key to the holder. The CA is responsible for verifying the holder's identity before issuing the certificate.

Obtaining legitimate public keys via certificate verification allows encrypted and authentic communication between two parties. Moreover, the signer cannot later deny sending a signed message, because his public key has been certified by a trusted CA. Nonrepudiation is very important in e-commerce and e-banking.

An example certificate issuance model is depicted in Figure 1. In this model, first, the user applies to a CA by providing his or her public key and some proof of identity. The CA verifies the identity and makes sure that the public key really belongs to the user. After that, the CA creates a certificate by digitally signing the necessary information. This certificate is stored in some public servers or databases.

Figure 1: Example certificate issuance model.

A simple signed document verification scenario is depicted in Figure 2. Suppose the signer (not shown in the figure) previously signed a document using his or her private key. The verifier needs the correct public key of the signer for verification of this signature. To do so, first, the verifier obtains the signer's certificate from the public key server or database. Then, the signer verifies the signature of the CA on this certificate. This verification yields the correct public key of the signer. Using this public key and the signed document, the verifier verifies the signature on the document.

In this simple scenario, verification of the signer's certificate requires knowing the CA's public key and we assume that this public key is known to the verifier. However, in most cases, a series of certificates might be verified in a chain to reach the signer's certificate. This mechanism, called *certificate path*, is explained in a subsequent section.

As the public key cryptosystems and their applications become more widespread, the need for a secure public key distribution method became more and more important. At this point, the industry took up Kohnfelder's idea and practicalized the concept of certificates for commercial use. Since then, several standards have been issued and several secure applications have either adopted a standard or defined their own certification mechanism. Today digital certificates offer a promising market and are an enabler technology in Internet security for a wide range of applications from e-commerce to e-mail.

CERTIFICATE STRUCTURE

Attempts to standardize certificates were started in the late 1980s. The first standard was published by ITU-T (International Telecommunications Union) in 1988 as the X.509 recommendation (ITU-T, 1988). The same standard was also published by ISO/IEC (International Organization for Standardization/International Electrotechnical Commission) as International Standard 9495–8.

Other than X.509 certificates that bind an identity to a public key, there are other relatively less common certificate types. These are detailed in this section. First we start with classical X.509 identity certificates.

X.509v3 Certificate Characteristics and Structure

The X.509 recommendation was revised three times: in 1993, 1997, and 2000 (ITU-T, 1993, 1997, 2000). The certificate structure of the original 1988 recommendation is named version 1 (v1). Version 2 (v2) is the structure defined in the 1993 edition. X.509v2 is not so different than v1 (the details are given later in this subsection). The X.509 version 3 (v3) certificate structure is defined in the third edition of X.509 in 1997. The main distinguishing feature of the X.509v3 certificate structure is the extension fields, which are explained in the subsequent section in detail. The X.509 recommendation was revised once

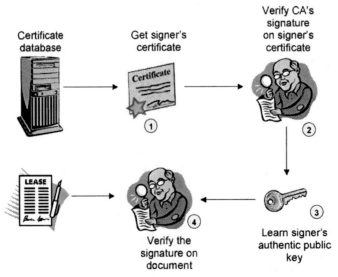

Figure 2: Simple signed document verification scenario.

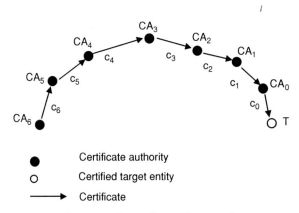

Figure 3: Example certificate path.

more in 2000, but the certificate structure was not updated in this revision.

The X.509v3 certificate structure includes identification and public key information for the *subject* (the entity for which the certificate has been issued) and identification for the *issuer* (authority who signed the certificate). In addition, the certificate structure includes some managerial fields such as serial number, version, and so forth.

A certificate is signed by a CA with a digital signature covering all applicable certificate fields. The signature algorithm and its parameters are included in a header to facilitate the verification process. The digital signature, which is a binary stream, is appended to the certificate.

Certificates are processed as a chain known as the *certificate path*, as exemplified in Figure 3. The last certificate of this path (c_0) is the certificate of the end user (T) whose public key is sought. Other certificates are CA certificates, that is, certificates issued by CAs to other CAs. The verifying agent starts the verification process with the first CA (CA_6) certificate (c_6). Generally, the first CA certificates are known as root CAs and their certificates are *self-signed* certificates, that is, both issuer and subject entities are the same. If such a self-signed certificate of a root CA is deemed trustworthy by the verifying agent, then the verification process can safely start with it. Such a root CA is called the *trust anchor* of the verification process. Verification of a self-signed certificate yields the verified public key of the root CA, which in turn is used to verify the next CA certificate. Verification of the next CA certificate yields its public key, and so on. Verifications continue until the last certificate on the path—which is for the end user—is verified and the end user's public key is found. In the example in Figure 3, once the verifier verifies c_6, he or she finds the public key of CA_5 and then, using this public key, verifies c_5. Verification of c_5 yields the public key of CA_4, and the chain goes on until c_0 is verified to find the public key of T.

In X.509, there is a clear distinction between CA certificates and end-user certificates. CA certificates, as the name suggests, are used for CAs, and CAs can issue certificates for other CAs. End-user certificates are issued for ordinary clients; end users can never issue certificates for other entities.

The certificates that are described in this subsection are identity certificates. Identity certificates are used to bind a public key to an owner who is explicitly identified

in the certificate. The public key certificate framework defined in the X.509 specification mainly addresses identity certificates. This type of certificate is a critical component of a public key infrastructure (PKI). However, X.509 does not define a PKI in its entirety.

Names of the certificate issuer and subject are specified in X.509 using the X.500 family's distinguished name (DN) structure. A DN is simply a set of attribute and value pairs that uniquely identify a person or entity. It is a tree-based naming structure with a root at the top and a naming authority at every node. Assuming that each node ensures the uniqueness of the names that it assigns, the overall DN structure will yield globally unique entity names.

X.509 uses abstract syntax notation 1 (ASN.1) notation to describe certificates and related structures, and the ASN.1 *distinguished encoding rules* (DER) to encode these objects for sending.

The details of the X.509 certificate fields are given here and depicted in Figure 4. First we start with the fields included in the X.509v1 certificate structure and then continue with the additional fields of X.509v2 and v3.

Version: this determines the version of the certificate. Currently this value could be 1 (default value), 2, or 3.

Serial number: an integer value identifying the certificate. This value should be unique for each CA, but global uniqueness is not required. Thus, there is no need to have an authority for the distribution of certificate serial numbers.

Signature algorithm: the algorithm identifier for the algorithm and hash function used by the CA in signing the certificate.

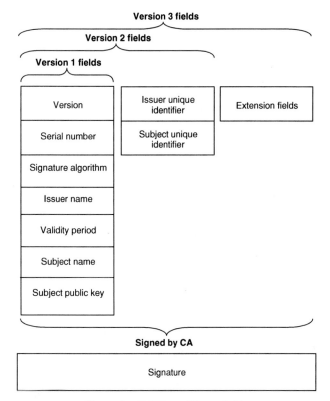

Figure 4: X.509 certificate fields.

Issuer name: DN of the CA that issued the certificate. This field identifies the CA but not necessarily in a unique way.

Validity: this specifies the time period during which the certificate is valid and the CA warrants that it will maintain information about the status of the certificate. This field contains two date and time values that determine the starting and the ending date and time.

Subject name: this identifies the owner of the certificate using the DN structure.

Subject public key information: the public key of the subject (owner of the certificate). Actually, the binding between this value and subject name fields are endorsed by the CA. This field also contains the algorithm corresponding to the key.

These fields exist in all three versions of X.509 and are the core fields of the certificates. In X.509v2 two more optional fields are added:

Issuer unique identifier and **subject unique identifier:** these fields are needed in case the subject and/or issuer DNs are assigned to two or more different users.

During the preparation of the third edition of X.509, it became apparent that more fields were needed. The X.509 committee put forward the concept of extension fields as a way to continue the expansion of the standard into the future. Because these extension fields were generic, it was possible to make use of them for different purposes without changing the certificate structure. Several extension fields were defined in the third edition of X.509 recommendation, where the extension fields were first included in the certificate structure (X.509v3). Later, some other extension fields were added in the fourth edition, but the certificate structure remained the same.

X.509v3 Extension Fields

An extension field consists of a unique extension identifier, a criticality flag, and the data part of the extension. Extensions are optional. The criticality flag determines how the verifier of the certificate reacts if it does not recognize the extension (this is possible when the particular extension is not implemented by the verification system). If the criticality flag is TRUE, then the certificate is treated as invalid. In contrast, if the flag is FALSE, then the extension is ignored.

In the third and fourth editions of the X.509 recommendation, several extensions were defined. These can be grouped in five categories, as listed:

1. Basic certificate revocation list (CRL) extensions
2. CRL distribution points and delta CRLs
3. Key and policy information
4. Subject and issuer attributes
5. Certification path constraints

The first two groups of extensions, which deal with CRLs, are discussed briefly in a subsequent section. The third and the fourth groups of extensions can be applied both to public key certificates and to CRLs. The last group is only for public key certificates. The latter three groups are briefly explained in the following sections.

Key and Policy Information

Additional information about the keys involved, including key identifiers for subject and issuer keys, indicators of intended or restricted key usage, and indicators of certificate policy, are contained in this group of extensions.

The **certificate policies** extension specifies the policies applied by the CA during the creation of the subject certificate. Each policy is identified by unique policy identifiers. In practice, policies map to certification practice statements (CPS) declared by the CAs. The verifying entity may put restrictions on certificate policies and, as a result, may not accept some certificates even if the signature is valid. This mechanism is a way to circumvent the blind trust that was inherent in the first two versions of the X.509 recommendation.

The **authority key identifier** extension is used to identify the public key of the CA that issued the certificate or CRL. One could argue that the issuer-unique-identifier field added to X.509v2 could solve the identification problem for the authority. However, because a CA could have more than one key pair, key-based identification was needed, and it was provided by this extension.

The **subject key identifier** extension is used to identify the public key of the subject to whom the certificate has been issued. This feature is useful when a subject has more than one public key and certificate.

The **key usage extension** limits the use of the public key to some certain cryptographic tasks such as digital signatures, key agreement, encipherment, and so forth.

The **extended key usage** extension is one of the visionary extensions. If the use of the key is not one of the basic usages described in the key usage extension field, this extension is used to specify a usage for the key. Such an extended usage is identified by an object identifier value that has to be formally registered according to ITU-T and ISO regulations.

The **private key usage period** extension is used to assign a different lifetime to the private key corresponding to the certified public key. Without this extension, the lifetimes of the public and private keys are the same. However, this is generally not the case in practice. Take, for example, the case of a digital signature application where the validity of the public key could be longer than the private key because the signed documents may have been verified after the private key expires. This extension is a mechanism that allows such flexibility. However, to utilize this extension, the signed documents should bear a time stamp that shows when the document was signed using the private key. Otherwise, it would be impossible for the verifier to check the expiration status of the private key used in the signature.

Subject and Issuer Attributes

The native naming mechanism of X.509 is the DN structure. The DN structure was specialized to the global distributed directory concept standardized by X.500 family of recommendations. This special structure did not meet the requirements of other applications that use X.509 certificates because each application needs a different naming mechanism. For example, a secure e-mail application needs e-mail addresses; a secure WWW application needs URLs as names. Because the requirements of these types of applications were so urgent, a temporary solution was found: the common name (CN) field of the DN structure was used to include such application-specific names. Although this temporary solution is still in use, a special extension field was added to X.509v3 to support alternative names for certificate issuer and subject. Alternative names can be in a variety of forms including an e-mail address, a URL, an IP address, and so forth. Moreover, a special form of name can also be defined via the *other name* option.

Certificate Path Constraints

These certificate extensions allow constraint specifications to be included in CA certificates (certificates for CAs issued by other CAs) to facilitate the automated processing of certificate paths. The constraints may restrict the types of certificates that can be issued by the subject CA or that may occur subsequently in a certification path. In this way, trust processing can be customized according to different needs. Although these extensions are included in CA certificates, processing and interpreting these extensions is mostly the task of the certificate path verification entity, that is, an end user. Four extensions are defined in this context: *basic constraints*, *name constraints*, *policy constraints*, and *inhibit any policy*.

The **basic constraints extension** indicates whether the subject may act as a CA or not. If so, a *certification path length* constraint may also be specified. If the length of the path exceeds the specified value, then the end-entity certificate is automatically disqualified.

The **name constraints extension** indicates a name space within which all subject names in subsequent certificates in a certification path are to be located. The idea behind this extension is to be able to implement policies based on trusted and distrusted CAs known by name.

The **policy constraints extension** specifies constraints that may require explicit certificate policy identification for the remainder of the certification path. If such policy identifiers are present in a certificate, then the forthcoming certificates on the path must bear the required or equivalent policy identifiers in order for the certificate path to be validated.

Normally, a CA may assert *any-policy* identifier in certificate policies extensions to trust a certificate for all possible policies. The **inhibit any-policy extension** specifies a constraint that indicates *any-policy* is not considered as an explicit match. This rule applies for all certificates in the certification path starting with the certificate that bears this extension. In this way, explicit identification for policies is enforced.

Other Types of Certificates

Other than X.509v3 identity certificates, there are some alternative certificate structures. One issue behind developing alternatives is to address the requirements of access control in certificates. Another issue is the unsuitability of lengthy formats for restricted applications such as WAP (wireless access protocol). Yet another issue is the belief that X.509 is not good at addressing the trust management requirements of liberal applications mainly because of the strict distinction between the concepts of CA and end users. Alternative certificate structures are discussed in this section.

Attribute Certificate Framework of X.509
Classical identity certificates (i.e., public key certificates) are used to assign a valid public key to an entity. The privileges of this entity are to be managed separately by the verifying system. This approach is criticized by the access control community, which believes that the two-step approach enforced by identity certificates is impractical. In the fourth edition of the X.509 recommendation, these concerns are addressed by the attribute certificate framework.

X.509 attribute certificates have a structure that is different than classical identity certificates. Although the identification of the certificate holder is still possible in attribute certificates, it is optional. The actual task of an attribute certificate is the binding of a privilege to an entity. After the verifying agent verifies the attribute certificate of an entity and authenticates it successfully, it gives access to the resources allowed within the certificate.

The certificate path concept is also valid for attribute certificates. However, there are some differences in terminology and roles as compared with identity certificates and PKI, because attribute certificates are used to implement PMI (privilege management infrastructure) rather than PKI. PMI defines the rules and the general concepts about using attribute certificates as a system for managing access control. Although the X.509 recommendation defines some critical components of a PMI, it does not define a PMI in its entirety.

In PMI, the root CA becomes the SOA (source of authority), which issues attribute certificates to AAs (attribute authorities). AAs, which are analogous to CAs in PKI, issue attribute certificates to end entities.

The fields of attribute certificates are briefly described as follows:

Version differentiates between the different versions of the attribute certificates.

Holder is an optional field that conveys the identity of the attribute certificate's holder.

Issuer conveys the identity of the AA that issued the certificate.

Signature identifies the cryptographic algorithm used to digitally sign the attribute certificate.

Serial number is the number that uniquely identifies the attribute certificate. The uniqueness is within the scope of the certificate issuer.

Validity period conveys the time period during which the attribute certificate is considered as valid.

Attributes contains a list of attributes (or privileges) associated with the certificate holder.

Issuer unique ID is an optional field that is used to uniquely identify the issuer of the attribute certificate when such an identification is necessary.

Similar to identity certificates, the structure of the attribute certificate allows some extension fields.

SPKI/SDSI Certificates

The simple public key infrastructure (SPKI; Ellison, 1999b; Ellison et al., 1999) was designed by an Internet Engineering Task Force (IETF) working group (Simple Public Key Infrastructure Charter, n.d.) led by Ellison (this working group is currently inactive). The SPKI certificates contain authorization information and bind the keys to that information. Thus, SPKI certificates are also called *authorization certificates*. The primary purpose of SPKI authorization certificates is to grant permissions. They also include the ability to delegate permissions to other entities. In that respect, it can be deduced that the basic aim of SPKI is quite similar to the X.509 attribute certificate framework, but the SPKI initiative started much earlier, in 1996.

Rivest and Lampson (1996) proposed simple distributed security infrastructure (SDSI). SDSI combines a simple PKI design with a means of defining groups and issuing group membership certificates. SDSI's groups provide simple, clear terminology for defining access control lists and security policies. The designs of SDSI and SPKI have merged in the SDSI 2.0 version.

Proponents of SPKI/SDSI have had two basic arguments against X.509 certificates:

- The X.509 certificate format is complicated and bulky.
- The concept of a globally unique identity (such as X.500's DN structure) will never be realized. Ellison (1999a) and Adams and Lloyd (1999) discuss some difficulties in dealing with globally unique names and DN. The main point here is the fact that globally unique names are not so meaningful without local significance. For example, "John Smith, from XYZ Co., NYC" may be unique, but does not help you to figure out that he is the person that you met on vacation unless you locally store the extra information "from the Canary Islands" in your address book.

SPKI certificates used public keys as the identities. Later, SPKI inherited the local name concept from SDSI. SDSI allows each user to define his or her own local name space and issue his or own certificates in that name space. SPKI associated SDSI local names with the keys. In this way, the SPKI/SDSI initiative avoided using global names in certificates.

The SPKI specifications developed by the IETF working group (Ellison, 1999b; Ellison et al., 1999) discuss concepts and provide detailed certificate formats, signature formats, and associated protocols. SPKI RFCs use S-expressions, a LISP-like parenthesized expression, as the standard format for certificates and define a canonical form for those S-expressions.

An SPKI authorization certificate has a number of fields similar to X.509 certificates, such as issuer, subject, and validity. However, the syntax and, most of the time, the semantics are different. Moreover, SPKI has a number of fields for access control and delegation. The structure of these fields is not strictly defined in the specifications. This is done deliberately to provide enough flexibility to applications that proliferate SPKI certificates.

The SPKI working group of the IETF (Simple Public Key Infrastructure Charter, n.d.) mentions "the key certificate format and associated protocols are to be simple to understand, implement, and use." However, according to Adams and Lloyd (1999), the sophisticated certificate structure of SPKI has diminished the intended simplicity.

The IETF work on SPKI was completed in 1999. Some libraries and prototype implementations have been developed (Ellison, n.d.). However, it is very hard to say that there is an important demand for SPKI certificates in the market (Adams & Lloyd, 1999).

WTLS Certificates

WAP (wireless access protocol; WAP Forum, 2001b) is a framework for developing applications to run over wireless networks. WAP, which was developed by an international industrywide organization called the WAP Forum, has a layered structure. WTLS (wireless transport layer security; WAP Forum, 2001a) is the security protocol of the WAP protocol suite. WTLS operates over the transport layer and provides end-to-end security, where one end is the mobile client and the other end is the WAP gateway. The WAP gateway acts as a proxy for the mobile client to access an application server, which is hosted somewhere on the Internet. The handicaps of the wireless environment are basically the limited processing power of mobile clients and the limited data transfer rate of the mobile communication environment. Thus, classical X.509 certificates are not so feasible for WTLS because of their lengthy format.

The WTLS standard (WAP Forum, 2001a) defines a special certificate structure, so-called WTLS certificates, that can be used in this restricted environment. In essence, a WTLS certificate is the light version of a X.509 certificate. The infrastructural rules of WTLS certificates are more or less the same as X.509, but some fields are either removed or simplified. WTLS certificate fields are explained in the following:

Certificate version determines the version of the certificate. Currently it is 1.

Signature algorithm describes the public key algorithm used for signing the WTLS certificate.

Issuer defines the CA who signed the certificate. Several name formats are available including the DN format employed by classical X.509 certificates.

Subject identifies the owner of the WTLS certificate. As with the issuer field, several name formats can be used.

Not valid before, not valid after: these fields determine the validity period of the WTLS certificate.

Public key type, parameters, public key: these three fields determine the public key to be certified along with its type and parameters.

WTLS certificates do not include any extension fields.

The use of elliptic curve cryptosystems (ECC; Menezes, 1993) is encouraged because of smaller key and signature sizes as compared to the RSA cryptosystem. Moreover, ECC implementations are known to be faster than those of its rivals.

PGP Key Signatures (Certificates)

Although PGP (Pretty Good Privacy) is known as an e-mail security software, its unique public key management offers a new certificate-like structure (although it is not 100% correct to name this structure *certificate*, we do so for the sake of consistency in terminology). The philosophy of PGP is to allow the utmost freedom to its users in selecting their trust anchors and trust policy. In such a system, there is no distinction between the CA and the end user. Indeed, in PGP, every end user can also be an authority resulting in a mesh-like certificate graph, known as a **web of trust**.

Actually, PGP's liberal approach has changed over time. Together with the commercialization of the software, commercial concerns have impaired the original liberal approach. This section highlights the original approach of version 2.6.

In PGP, every user, as verifier, determines his or her trusted entities and accepts certificates issued by them. A particular entity may be trusted by one user, but may not be trusted by another one. Moreover, this trust is not binary; the verifier may partially trust an entity as an authority. To deem a public key P belonging a user X as valid, the verifier should either (a) know X and issue the certificate for P or (b) obtain valid certificates for P issued by entities trusted by the verifier. In the latter case, the verifier should obtain one such certificate if the issuer is fully trusted or two such certificates if the issuers are partially trusted.

A PGP public key is stored together with all of the certificates issued for it. That is why obtaining a certificate is quite straightforward.

The structure is explained as follows:

Time stamp: the time stamp indicates the date and time that the key was generated. This is not lifetime. Original PGP does not grant lifetimes for keys and certificates. See the Certificate Revocation section for more details.

Key ID: key ID is an identifier for the key. This is actually the least significant 64 bits of the public key.

Public key: the public key of the owner together with necessary parameters.

User ID: this identifies the owner of the key. This field generally contains a textual name and an e-mail address.

Signatures: the digital signatures over this public key. These are issued by several people. Each signature entry also includes the identification of the signer.

Apart from these data that can be downloaded from public key servers, each user (verifier) adds some more information after storing a public key and its signatures into his or her local public key ring file. These are explained as follows:

Owner trust: this indicates how much the verifier trusts the owner of the public key as a certificate issuer for other people.

Signature trust: there is a signature trust field for each signature over a public key. This field indicates how much the verifier trusts the issuer of the signature. This field's value is copied from the owner trust value of the entry for the public key of the signature issuer.

Key legitimacy: this is a computed value that indicates whether the subject public key is deemed to be legitimate or not. It is computed by the PGP software using other fields of the public key entry in the key ring file and parameters set by the verifier.

ISSUES AND DISCUSSIONS

Apart from the structure and basic characteristics of certificates, there are several other issues that must be addressed. These issues are discussed in this section.

Certificate Revocation

X.509-based certificates have specific validity periods and a certificate is valid only within this period. However, various circumstances may cause a certificate to become invalid prior to the expiration of the validity period. Such circumstances might include change of name, change of association between the certificate owner and CA, and compromise or suspected compromise of the corresponding private key. Under such circumstances, the CA or the certificate owner needs to revoke the certificate.

The method for certificate revocation in X.509 is to employ the certificate revocation list (CRL) concept. A CRL is a signed list of unexpired but revoked certificates. The CRL structure includes serial numbers and the revocation dates of the revoked certificates. This list is signed by the corresponding CA. CRLs are issued periodically by the CAs. Each CRL invalidates the previous CRL. The certificate entries in a CRL are removed when the expiration dates of the revoked certificates are reached. A certificate, for which the validity period has not yet expired, should not appear in the most recent CRL of the issued CA to be verified successfully.

A supplementary approach to the CRL is the delta-CRL approach where the idea is to transfer incremental information when the revocation lists are updated and not to repeat the previously sent revocation information. This is done to save both time and bandwidth.

In addition to the base CRL message structure, two extension groups are dedicated for CRLs as well. These are *basic CRL extensions* and *CRL distribution points and delta-CRLs*.

Basic CRL extensions allow a CRL to

- Include indications of the reason for revocation.
- Include the date when the authority posted the revocation (for each revoked certificate).
- Provide flexibility for temporary suspension of a certificate.
- Include the scope of certificates covered by that list.
- Include CRL issue sequence numbers for each CRL issue to help certificate users to detect missing CRLs.

CRL distribution points and delta-CRLs extensions allow the complete set of revocation information from one CA to be partitioned into separate CRLs and allow revocation information from multiple CAs to be combined in one CRL. These extensions also support the use of delta CRLs described previously.

Online certificate status protocol (OCSP) is published as an RFC (Myers et al., 1999). It is a simple request/response protocol that requires online servers, so-called OCSP responders, to distribute the certificate status on demand. Each CA must run its own OCSP responder, unless several CAs collaborate on this issue. The main advantage of using OCSP is that the most up-to-date certificate status information, which is stored in the OCSP responder system, is returned because of the real-time response feature of the OCSP. However, in the CRL approach, there is latency between a particular revocation time and the next CRL or delta CRL issuance time. It should also be noted that the promptness of the response in the OCSP is only as good as the source of the revocation information. Here there might be some delays in storing the revocation data in the OCSP responder system, but this delay is not as large as in the CRL case.

Kocher (1998) has proposed certificate revocation trees (CRTs). CRTs are used to compile the revocation information on a single hash tree. CRTs provide an efficient and scalable mechanism to distribute revocation information. As Kocher mentions, CRTs are gaining increased use worldwide for several reasons. They can be used with existing protocols and certificates, and they enable the secure, reliable, scalable, and inexpensive validation of certificates (as well as digital signatures and other data). The main disadvantage of CRTs is that any change in the set of revoked certificates results in recomputation of the entire CRT.

PGP (Zimmermann, 1994) public keys and certificates may optionally have validity periods, but it is more common not to have them and to make them nonexpiring. Therefore, PGP public keys and certificates are valid until they are revoked. PGP public keys can be revoked only by the public key owner and by issuing a key revocation certificate. Similarly, certificates can be revoked by revocation certificates issued by the certificate signers. These revocation certificates invalidate the public keys/certificates; however, the revoked objects do not disappear. Moreover, there is no revocation list concept in PGP. Revocation certificates are distributed like the public keys and certificates. The most common approach is to use public key servers. The revocation certificates are kept in the public key servers together with the keys and certificates. If a key or certificate has a revocation certificate, then the verifier understands that this key or certificate is invalid.

Yet another and extreme approach to certificate revocation is not to have the revocation concept at all as in the SDSI (Rivest & Lampson, 1996) and SPKI (Ellison et al., 1999) systems. There is no CRL in these systems. Instead, each certificate is assigned an appropriate validity period. The certificate times out after this period and needs revalidation. Revalidations are performed either by the certificate issuers or by specific revalidation authorities.

To revalidate a certificate, the certificate issuer re-signs the certificate content with a new time stamp. In contrast, revalidation authorities sign the whole certificate content and the original signature on it to revalidate a certificate.

A similar approach is also used for WTLS certificates. Because of the significant cost of existing revocation schemes in mobile environments, Verisign, Inc., a leading WTLS certificate provider, has chosen to issue short-lived certificates and reissue them within short intervals (say one day). In this way, the servers update their certificates every so often, but the mobile clients need not download anything for revocation control.

Certificate Distribution

The problem of certificate distribution is mostly addressed by the applications that use the certificates. In most cases, applications exchange necessary certificates at the beginning of the interaction or when needed; they do not rely on some other mechanism for the procurement of certificates. Some of these applications are discussed in the next section.

When the X.509 certificates were first proposed, the main idea was to make use of X.500 distributed directories for certificate distribution. The CAs would serve as directory servers, or they would publish the certificates that they issued to other directory servers. The verifier would query the directory to get the certificates on a certificate path to verify the public key of a specific end user. Although it is not exactly the same as the X.500 directories, DNSSEC (domain name system security extensions; Eastlake, 1999) also assumes a distributed approach. It may be too early to comment on the DNSSEC approach, but it is fairly clear that the X.500 directory approach is unlikely ever to come to fruition, as discussed by Ellison (n.d.). The main reason Ellison put forward is that collections of directory entries (such as employee lists, customer lists, contact lists, etc.) are considered valuable or even confidential by their owners and are not likely to be released to the world.

As described, PGP makes use of centralized databases (public key servers) for the distribution of keys and certificates. There are numerous PGP key servers all over the world. They are synchronized and keep the same information. Thus, it is sufficient to communicate with one of them for public key transfers. To see an example key server, readers may refer to http://www.keyserver.net, which currently holds more than 1.6 million PGP public keys. The main disadvantage of these key servers is that they keep the keys and certificates without any control and verification of authenticity; users should therefore verify the authenticity of these public keys on their own. As an alternative, PGP Corp. has recently announced a verified key service, called PGP Global Directory (PGP Corp., n.d.). The PGP Global Directory is a verified directory of PGP keys. Unlike previous servers that stored PGP keys indiscriminately, the PGP Global Directory allows users to upload and manage their keys in a verified manner. When uploading a key or performing other key management features, PGP Global Directory verifies a key by requiring a response to a verification e-mail sent to each e-mail address specified on the key. Because this is not a 100% secure authentication mechanism, there is always a risk that the verified key in the PGP Global Directory is not actually owned by the person who appears to own it. Thus, the PGP Global Directory should not be considered as a replacement for the PGP web of trust, but as an additional mechanism.

Peer-to-peer certificate transfer is another mechanism that should not be underestimated. Here the basic idea is the transfer of the certificate from one peer to another via an online/offline link such as an e-mail attachment or on a CD.

Certificates as Electronic IDs

One of the marketing strategies of certificates is to promote them as electronic versions of IDs. This analogy is intuitively appealing. There are, indeed, similarities between IDs and certificates: both are endorsed by authorities, both bear the name of the owner, both are small. However, a detailed analysis of certificates shows that there is a difference between certificates and IDs in terms of the participation of the holder in subsequent authentication and authorization transactions. The verification of an ID via the picture on it and the recognition of the authority's endorsement are sufficient for the owner to obtain privileges; the person holding the ID need not do anything extra. However, the verification of a certificate via the verification of the CA signature on it is not sufficient to make sure that the owner is really the person he or she claims to be. Certificate verification only helps the verifier confirm the public key of the certificate holder. The certificate holder should also show that he or she knows the private key corresponding to the public key in the certificate to prove his or her identity. This requires an extra protocol run embedded in applications, and the certificate holder should actively participate in this protocol.

Privacy Concerns

Identity certificates are not designed to provide privacy-enhanced transactions. An identity certificate contains personal information, such as name, addresses, date of birth, affiliation, and so forth, about its owner. Because certificates are stored in public registers, as explained previously, and certificates are in cleartext, the personal information stored in them may be obtained by anyone. This encourages identity theft. Moreover, whenever an identity certificate is used in an application, the privacy of the certificate owner can no longer be maintained. Most people would object to having to identify themselves in every transaction and interaction they undertake. Assuming that these applications use OCSP to check certificate validity, the activities of the certificate owner can be tracked using central OCSP logs. In this way, all of an individual's actions can be linked and traced automatically and instantaneously by various parties.

This discussion points to a significant privacy problem in using certificates. Attribute certificates may be considered as a primitive step to achieving privacy because they may not include the owner's identity. However, because these certificates are not issued in anonymously (at least the AA knows to whom it issued the certificate), we cannot say that attribute certificates address all of the concerns of privacy advocates.

In this regard, Stefan Brands' contributions to anonymity and privacy-enhancing techniques in certificates are worth mentioning. Brands (2000, 2002) proposed a different conception and implementation of digital certificates, called *digital credentials*, such that privacy is protected and anonymity is provided without sacrificing security. The validity of digital credentials and their contents can be checked, but the identity of the holder cannot be extracted, and different actions by the same person cannot be linked. Holders of digital credentials have control over the information to be disclosed to other parties.

Brands' book (2000) is a very good source of information on privacy-related discussions regarding certificates and other privacy-enhancing techniques.

PKIX and X.509

PKIX (X.509-based PKI) is a working group of the IETF established in 1995 (Public-Key Infrastructure, X.509, PKIX, n.d.). The initial role of this working group was to develop Internet standards needed to support an X.509-based PKI. The scope of PKIX has since expanded, and some new protocols have been developed that are related to the use of X.509-based PKIs on the Internet.

Although it seems that PKIX is only a user of X.509, the progress of X.509 has been extensively influenced by the PKIX working group because the X.509 standard was not sufficient to address the PKI issues of the Internet.

The PKIX working group has published several RFCs. A full list of these RFCs can be obtained at the charter Web site (Public-Key Infrastructure, X.509, PKIX, n.d.). Some of them that are directly related to certificate structure and processing are listed here:

- Algorithms and Identifiers for the Internet X.509 Public Key Infrastructure Certificate and CRI Profile (RFC 3279).
- An Internet Attribute Certificate Profile for Authorization (RFC 3281).
- Internet X.509 Certificate Request Message Format (RFC 2511).
- Internet X.509 Public Key Infrastructure Certificate and CRL Profile (RFC 3280).
- Internet X.509 Public Key Infrastructure Certificate Management Protocols (RFC 2510).
- Internet X.509 Public Key Infrastructure Certificate Policy and Certification Practices Framework (RFC 3647).
- Internet X.509 Public Key Infrastructure Data Validation and Certification Server Protocols (RFC 3029).
- Internet X.509 Public Key Infrastructure Proxy Certificate Profile (RFC 3820).
- Internet X.509 Public Key Infrastructure: Qualified Certificates Profile (RFC 3739).

APPLICATION PROTOCOLS BASED ON X.509 CERTIFICATES

The development of the PKIX standards and X.509 certificates encouraged several TCP/IP-based applications to provide security mechanisms featuring certificates. In this section, some of these applications are overviewed with some detail on how they utilize certificates.

PEM (privacy-enhanced mail) was one of the first protocols to utilize X.509. PEM provides encryption and authentication features to e-mails utilizing a variety of cryptographic primitives. RFCs 1421–1424 define PEM; RFC 1422 explains the certificate-based key management employed in PEM.

Because PEM was defined during the period when X.509v1 was the only certificate structure available, it was based on X.509v1. Consequently, it did not support any custom-defined policies and end-user-centric trust management. The PKI model of PEM was a strictly hierarchical one. The verifiers could not practice their own trust policies; thus, they had to blindly trust all authorities in this hierarchy in order to participate in the system. These strict regulations discouraged people from using PEM. Thus, PEM never reached a significant population. This experience showed that the certificate structure should be flexible to be able to implement different policies and user-centric trust management. This conclusion made the X.509 designers think about a flexible certificate structure that eventually yielded X.509v3.

SSL (secure sockets layer) is the most widely used certificate-based TCP/IP security mechanism. The aim is to create an upper-TCP security sublayer that can be used for several client–server applications such as HTTP (hypertext transfer protocol), FTP (file transfer protocol), POP3 (post office protocol version 3), SMTP (simple mail transfer protocol), IMAP (Internet mail access protocol), and so forth. SSL works in a session manner. Before the data connection, the end parties create a session key and forthcoming traffic is authenticated and encrypted using this session key. Session key generation requires some public key operations. Necessary public keys are distributed via X.509 certificates at the beginning of the protocol.

There is no enforced PKI model for SSL. Generally each CA generates a local hierarchy for the certificates issued by itself. Thus, there is no global PKI for SSL. Necessary root CA certificates are predistributed within client software such as MS Windows and Netscape.

The reason behind the success of SSL is mainly due to its flexibility in PKI topology and support given by key players in the industry. This industry support has come not only with root CA certificate predistributions, but also with integration of the protocol in key products such as operating systems, browsers, and other client applications. Thus, clients do not need to make any configurations to use SSL. Moreover, SSL is a protocol such that all necessary steps that are taken are transparent to the client. This is another reason behind the success of SSL.

S/MIME (secure/multipart Internet mail extensions) is the security enhancement on top of MIME, the Internet e-mail format standard. MIME describes content types for various types of attachments to e-mail messages.

S/MIME defines secure content types for encrypted and signed e-mail messages that are to be sent peer to peer. The security functionality provided by S/MIME is not so different from its predecessor, PEM. The difference is in certificate and key management features: S/MIME uses X.509v3 certificates; a particular PKI is not assumed as in SSL; necessary root-CA certificates come with the e-mail client programs.

Although S/MIME follows the successful certificate and key management strategy of SSL, it has not achieved a significant user population. The main reason for this is that in e-mail applications, both end points are clients and they need to use certificates. Individuals generally refrain from spending time, money, and effort on such add-on utilities. This is exactly what has happened in the case of S/MIME, and the use of S/MIME has not been very significant. In contrast, the use of SSL is mostly in the form of server authentication where only the server uses certificate; clients rarely use certificates to authenticate themselves. It is quite reasonable for an organization to spend time, money, and effort to obtain certificates to secure its servers.

To improve the use of this important technology, e-mail vendors need to find a mechanism to make the system transparent to the clients so that they do not need certificates. One alternative, as in the DomainKeys proposal by Yahoo (Delany, n.d.), could be using S/MIME not end to end but between e-mail gateways (sender and receiver SMTP servers), and providing another solution (e.g., using SSL over POP3 or IMAP) in the local area. In this way, only e-mail gateways need to use certificates; clients do not. One disadvantage of this mechanism, however, is that end-to-end security is not provided.

Another e-mail security solution, which uses certificates among the servers but not for the clients, is proposed by Levi and Ozcan (2004). In this system, called PractiSES (practical and secure e-mail system), clients register to their domain servers free of cost. Once registered, they can send and accept signed/encrypted e-mails without dealing with the complexity of public key transfers. Domain servers arrange the necessary public key transfers in a collaborative way without putting an extra burden on the client side. Unlike DomainKeys, PractiSES provides end-to-end security.

SSH (secure shell) can also be considered as a secure version of telnet, that is, secure remote terminal application. In SSH, public key agreement techniques are utilized before the username/password transfer. When a common key is established, encryption is performed to ensure the confidentiality of the transferred data. In SSH, certificates may be used to facilitate public key transfers between the client and the server. When client certificates are used, authentication of the client can be performed using public key techniques rather than the classical username/password mechanism. In contrast, server certificates are used to initiate the initial key agreement and to establish server authentication to the client.

Although it may seem that at least a server certificate is necessary for an authenticated key agreement between the client and the server, this is not essential. SSH allows the transfer of the server public key to the client in cleartext form. The client checks the fingerprint of the key and accepts this public key as valid for all subsequent communications. To make sure that the key is correct, the client should double-check its fingerprint against a known source. This may not be feasible in a large distributed client–server system, but in the case of SSH this check may be performed because the number of servers is manageable.

IPSec (IP security) is the IP (Internet protocol) layer security architecture that has been standardized by an IETF working group (IP Security Protocol Charter, n.d.). IPSec architecture contains a set of concepts and protocols for authenticity, integrity, confidentiality, and key exchange/management at the IP layer. The IKE (Internet key exchange) protocol (Harkins & Carrel, 1998) of IPSec provides authenticated key exchange using a specific profile of X.509 certificates.

Use of Certificates in the Financial Services Industry

Certificates are being used by several applications operated by the financial services industry. Nowadays, e-banking applications targeted at individual customers are mostly SSL/TLS-based because such an approach requires minimal maintenance at the client end and, thus, makes the system scalable. However, financial institutions are keen to develop and/or obtain application-specific solutions for their corporate customers. Such applications use certificate-based solutions for key exchange and management.

With regard to e-payment, SET (SET Secure Electronic Transaction LLC; n.d.) defines protocols for certificate issuance and processing in the context of credit card payments via the Internet.

In 1998, NACHA (National Automated Clearing House Association) sponsored a successful pilot for CA interoperability for the Web shopping experience. Several banks and CAs participated in this pilot. Lessons learned from this pilot activity were published by NACHA (Prince & Foster, 1999).

The ANSI (American National Standards Institute) committee X9F (Accredited Standards Committee X9, n.d.) and ISO (International Organization for Standardization) Technical Committee 68 (TC68; ISO/TC68 Financial Services, n.d.) have developed some standards to profile X.509 certificates and CRL structures to provide for the particular needs of the financial services industry.

KEY PLAYERS IN THE INDUSTRY AND THEIR CERTIFICATION PRACTICES

The CAs that issue X.509v3 certificates for different applications follow a set of rules in their certification practices. These CAs, such as Verisign, Entrust, Baltimore, Globalsign, and so forth, follow slightly different approaches; however, the main idea is generally the same. The certification practice of each CA is declared on its Web site.

Certificate Classes

Certification practices propose different levels of identity verification in different classes of certificates. In this section, a general picture of these classes is given.

Class 1 certificates: The name of the subject entity is not checked. Only an e-mail address control is performed by sending an authentication string to the mailbox address that the subject entity provides in the certificate application. To complete the certificate issuance process, the subject entity should use this authentication string. That naively proves the ability of the subject entity's access to a mailbox. That mailbox address appears in the certificate. Some CAs also include the name of the subject entity in the certificate, specifying that the name is not validated. However, the appropriate action would be not to include a name in class 1 certificates, as some other CAs do. Class 1 certificate issuance is an online process. Class 1 certificates are mostly used for S/MIME.

Class 2 certificates: Name and some other information (such as address) of the subject entity are checked against a third-party database. Mailbox access control as in the class 1 certificates is also processed. The whole process is online.

Class 3 certificates: In addition to the mailbox access control, the subject entity should personally present an identity document to a registration authority. The level of assurance in identification is the highest of all the classes, but the process is offline and it may take several days to obtain the certificate. SSL server certificates are issued in this class. CAs also perform DNS control to make sure that the certified URL really belongs to the organization that claims to have it.

As can be seen, class 1 certificates provide the lowest degree of identity assurance but are the easiest to issue, whereas class 3 certificates provide the highest degree of identity assurance but are the most difficult to issue. Having said this, it should be mentioned that the certificate issuance process is not always fail-proof even for class 3 certificates because of the human factor involved in the certificate issuance process. An example of such an incident was reported by CERT® (Computer Emergency Response Team; CERT® Advisory CA-2001-04, 2001). The overview part of this report is quoted below with no comments.

> On January 29 and 30, 2001, VeriSign, Inc. issued two certificates to an individual fraudulently claiming to be an employee of Microsoft Corporation. Any code signed by these certificates will appear to be legitimately signed by Microsoft when, in fact, it is not. Although users who try to run code signed with these certificates will generally be presented with a warning dialog, there will not be any obvious reason to believe that the certificate is not authentic.

PKCS Standards Related to Certificates

The PKCS standards are specifications produced by RSA Laboratories in cooperation with secure systems developers worldwide for the purpose of accelerating the deployment of public key cryptography. Some of those standards, namely PKCS #6 (extended certificate syntax standard), PKCS #10 (certification request syntax standard), and PKCS #15 (cryptographic token information format standard), are related to certificates. These PKCS standards, except PKCS #6, mostly deal with implementation issues rather than defining new certificate types.

PKCS #6 standard, which was issued in 1993, describes the syntax for extended certificates. An extended certificate consists of an X.509v1 public key certificate and a set of attributes, collectively signed by the issuer of the X.509v1 public key certificate. These additional attributes were needed at that time because the X.509v1 certificate structure was rather limited. With the addition of extensions to X.509v3 certificates, PKCS #6 became redundant and RSA Laboratories started to withdraw their support for PKCS #6.

PKCS #10 is an important standard that describes syntax for certification requests. A certification request consists of a distinguished name, a public key, and optionally a set of attributes, collectively signed by the entity requesting certification. Certification requests are sent to a certification authority, which transforms the request into an X.509 public key certificate.

PKCS #15 is the cryptographic token information format standard. This standard aims at using cryptographic tokens as identification devices. To do so it defines different structures for the storage of different types of certificates, such as X.509, PGP, and WTLS certificates, in tokens.

SUMMARY AND CONCLUSION

This chapter has discussed different types of certificates together with some issues and standards associated with them. There is an important trend of certificate use in security applications. Classical client–server or peer-to-peer applications have been utilizing certificates for about a decade. Apart from these conventional applications, certificates have started to be included in smart cards as well. In this way, not only electronic and mobile commerce but also conventional card-based payment and identification schemes would utilize certificates. This wide range of applications makes certificates an important market where several companies are currently competing. These companies are mostly CA companies that issue certificates for end users and organizations.

Expiration of the RSA patent has created an opportunity for generating key pairs without paying royalties. However, CA companies have not reflected these savings in the cost of certificates. To improve the attractiveness of certificate-based solutions at the client end, CA companies need to revise their revenue models to attract more clients. Moreover, certificate-based solutions should be designed such that they provide flexibility and transparency for the clients.

GLOSSARY

Attribute Authority An authority that issues attribute certificates. In this way, the authority assigns privileges to certificate holders.
Attribute Certificates A data structure signed by an attribute authority for the binding of a privilege to an entity.
Certificate (or Digital Certificate) A data structure endorsed by an authority that binds an entity to an identity, attribute, characteristic, or privilege.
Certificate Path An ordered sequence of certificates, which is processed to obtain the public key of the last object on the path.
Certification Practice Statement (CPS) A document that describes (in detail) how a CA issues certificates and the policies observed by that CA.
Certificate Revocation List (CRL) A signed list indicating a set of certificates that are no longer considered valid by the certificate issuer.
Certificate Verification Verification of the signature on the certificate. In this way, the binding endorsed by the authority is assumed to be legitimate.
Certification Authority (CA) A well-known and trusted entity that issues public key certificates.
Delta CRL A partial certificate revocation list (CRL) that only contains entries for certificates that have had their revocation status changed since the issuance of the base CRL.
Digital Signature Digital information obtained by the application of a private key on a message.
Privilege Management Infrastructure (PMI) The infrastructure that is able to support the management of privileges in support of a comprehensive authorization service and in relationship with a public key infrastructure.
Public Key (Identity) Certificate A data structure signed by a certification authority for the binding of a public key to an entity whose identity is provided.
Public Key Infrastructure (PKI) The infrastructure for the management of public keys in support of authentication, encryption, integrity, or nonrepudiation services.
Root CA A top-level certification authority in hierarchical PKI.
S-Expression The data format chosen for SPKI/SDSI. This is a LISP-like parenthesized expression.
Self-Signed Certificate A certificate where the issuer and the subject are the same CA. Generally root CA certificates are of this type.
Subject The entity for which the certificate has been issued.
Trust Anchor An authority that is deemed trustworthy by a user.

CROSS REFERENCES

See *Digital Signatures and Electronic Signatures; IPsec: IKE (Internet Key Exchange); PGP (Pretty Good Privacy); PKCS (Public-Key Cryptography Standards); PKI (Public Key Infrastructure); Public Key Algorithms; S/MIME (Secure MIME); Public Key Standards: Secure Shell (SSH); Secure Sockets Layer (SSL); Security and the Wireless Application Protocol (WAP).*

REFERENCES

Accredited Standards Committee X9. (n.d.). *Financial industry standards.* Retrieved January 9, 2005, from http://www.x9.org/

Adams, C., & Lloyd, D. (1999). *Understanding public key infrastructures*. Indianapolis, IN: New Riders.

Brands, S. (2002). *A technical overview of digital credentials*. Retrieved December 16, 2004, from http://www.credentica.com/technology/overview.pdf

Brands, S. A. (2000). *Rethinking public key infrastructures and digital certificates: Building in privacy*. Cambridge, MA: MIT Press.

CERT. (2001). *Unauthentic "Microsoft Corporation" certificates* (Advisory CA-2001-04). Retrieved April 12, 2001, from http://www.cert.org/advisories/CA-2001-04.html

Delany, M. (n.d.). *Domain-based email authentication using public-keys advertised in the DNS (DomainKeys)* (Internet Draft). Retrieved December 27, 2004, from http://antispam.yahoo.com/domainkeys/draft-delany-domainkeys-base-01.txt

Diffie, W., & Hellman, M. E. (1976, November). New directions in cryptography. *IEEE Transactions on Information Theory, IT-22*(6), 644–654.

Eastlake, D. (1999). *Domain name system security extensions* (RFC 2535). Retrieved February 26, 2003, from http://www.ietf.org/rfc/rfc2535.txt

Ellison, C. (1999a, April). The nature of a usable PKI. *Computer Networks, 31*(9), 823–830.

Ellison, C. (1999b, September). *SPKI requirements* (RFC 2692). Retrieved December 23, 2004, from http://www.ietf.org/rfc/rfc2692.txt

Ellison, C. (n.d.). *SPKI/SDSI certificate documentation*. Retrieved December 23, 2004, from http://world.std.com/~cme/html/spki.html

Ellison, C., Frantz, B., Lampson, B., Rivest, R., Thomas, B., & Ylonen, T. (1999). *SPKI certificate theory* (RFC 2693). Retrieved December 23, 2004, from http://www.ietf.org/rfc/rfc2693.txt

Harkins, D., & Carrel, D. (1998). *The Internet key exchange (IKE)* (RFC 2409). Retrieved May 29, 1999 from http://www.ietf.org/rfc/rfc2409.txt

IP security protocol (IPsec) charter. (n.d.). Retrieved January 9, 2005, from http://www.ietf.org/html.charters/ipsec-charter.html

ISO/TC68 Financial Services. (n.d.). Retrieved January 9, 2005, from http://www.tc68.org/

ITU-T. (1988). *Information technology—Open systems interconnection—The directory: Authentication framework* (1st ed.). Recommendation X.509, ISO/IEC 9594-8. Geneva, Switzerland: Author.

ITU-T. (1993). *Information technology—Open systems interconnection—The directory: Authentication framework* (2nd ed.). Recommendation X.509, ISO/IEC 9594-8. Geneva, Switzerland: Author.

ITU-T. (1997). *Information technology—Open systems interconnection—The directory: Authentication framework* (3rd ed.). Recommendation X.509, ISO/IEC 9594-8. Geneva, Switzerland: Author.

ITU-T. (2000). *Information technology—Open systems interconnection—The directory: Public-key and attribute certificate frameworks* (4th ed.). Recommendation X.509, ISO/IEC 9594-8. Geneva, Switzerland: Author.

Kocher, P. (1998, February). On certificate revocation and validation. In *Proceedings of Financial Cryptography 98* (LNCS 1465; pp. 172–177). Berlin, Germany: Springer-Verlag.

Kohnfelder, L. M. (1978). *Towards a practical public-key cryptosystem*. Unpublished bachelor's thesis, Massachusetts Institute of Technology.

Levi, A., & Ozcan, M. (2004). Practical and secure e-mail system (PractiSES). *In Advances in Information Systems: ADVIS 2004—Third Biennial International Conference on Advances in Information Systems* (LNCS 3261; pp. 410–419). Berlin, Germany: Springer-Verlag.

Menezes, A. (1993). *Elliptic curve public key cryptosystems*. Norwell, MA: Kluwer Academic.

Myers, M., Ankney, R., Malpani, A., Galperin, S., & Adams, C. (1999). *X.509 Internet public key infrastructure on-line certificate status protocol—OCSP* (RFC 2560). Retrieved January 21, 2000, from http://www.ietf.org/rfc/rfc2560.txt

PGP Corp. (n.d.). *PGP global directory—Key verification policy*. Retrieved April 14, 2005, from https://keyserver-beta.pgp.com/vkd/VKDVerificationPGPCom.html

Popek, G., & Kline, C. (1979). Encryption and secure computer networks. *ACM Computing Surveys, 11*(4), 331–356.

Prince, N., & Foster, J. (1999). *Certification authority interoperability: From concept to reality*. Herndon, VA: NACHA.

Public-key infrastructure (X.509) (PKIX). (n.d.). Retrieved January 9, 2005, from http://www.ietf.org/html.charters/pkix-charter.html

Rivest, R., & Lampson, B. (1996). *SDSI—A simple distributed security infrastructure*. Retrieved December 23, 2004, from http://theory.lcs.mit.edu/~cis/sdsi.html

SET Secure Electronic Transaction LLC. (n.d.). Retrieved April 13, 2005, from http://web.archive.org/web/20020930024644/http://www.setco.org/

Simple public key infrastructure (SPKI) charter. (n.d.). Retrieved December 23, 2004, from http://www.ietf.org/html.charters/spki-charter.html

WAP Forum. (2001a, April 6). *Wireless transport layer security specification*. WAP-261-WTLS-20010406-a. Retrieved February 25, 2002, from http://www.wapforum.com

WAP Forum. (2001b, July 12). *Wireless application protocol architecture specification*. WAP-210-WAPArch-200100712-a. Retrieved April 4, 2002, from http://www.wapforum.com

Zimmermann, P. (1994). *PGP user's guide, Vol. 1: Essential topics; Vol. 2: Special topics*. Retrieved January 9, 2005, from http://www.pgpi.org/doc/guide/2.6.3i/en/

PKI (Public Key Infrastructure)

Radia Perlman, *Sun Microsystems Laboratories*

INTRODUCTION

PKI is an acronym for "public key infrastructure." This chapter discusses what that means and the challenges associated with providing this functionality.

If Bob believes Alice's public key is pub_A, and Alice knows the private key associated with pub_A, then Bob can use pub_A to encrypt a message for Alice, or Alice can use the associated private key to prove to Bob that she is Alice (i.e., she can *authenticate* to Bob). The purpose of a PKI is to provide a convenient and secure method for obtaining the public key associated with some principal.

The basic idea is to have a trusted authority known as a CA (certification authority) digitally sign a message known as a *certificate*, thereby vouching that a particular key goes with a particular name. If Alice has been certified by the CA, Bob knows the CA's public key, Bob trusts that CA, and Bob receives Alice's certificate, then he can validate the CA's signature on that certificate and know Alice's public key. In the chapter about digital certificates in this volume, some examples of certificate formats that have been deployed are discussed. In this chapter, we concentrate on the concepts and ignore the formats.

There is not universal agreement on the definition of a PKI, the minimal functionality that one must provide to be credibly called a PKI, nor the limits of functions that might be provided by a PKI. Besides providing a secure mapping between a name and a key, other functions of a PKI are to provide timely revocation of certificates (such as if a private key were stolen), to enable users to obtain their own private key, and to provide certification of attributes or privileges.

Authentication

Authentication is generally assumed to mean proving one's identity, but like most words in the field, there is no universally agreed-upon definition. For instance, there might be a shared key for a group, and for purposes of access to some resource it might be enough to prove knowledge of the shared key. Some might consider this authentication, although this would definitely not be proving an identity, because proving knowledge of a key shared by a set of individuals does not distinguish between individuals. It just proves that you are one of the individuals in the set.

For most cases, however, the PKI will link an identity's name with a public key, and authentication will be done by proving knowledge of the associated private key.

Authorization

Authorization is the right to do something. A common method of specifying authorization is through an *access control list* associated with a resource, which specifies the identities authorized to access the resource, together with what access rights they have. For instance, for a file, some members might have read-only access, whereas others might have read and write access.

Usually authorization involves authentication because it is often convenient to specify authorization as a set of identity or rights pairs.

In contrast, another model of authorization is "credentials based," where possession of a credential implies authorization. In the real world, this might be a door key or the combination to a safe. In the network security world, sometimes knowledge of a key is thought of as a credential. The key might not be associated with any named identity, but it might be used to assure someone that two messages originated from the same source. In that case, one might claim that authentication has taken place and that the identity is "the holder of that private key."

We will discuss more issues associated with identity, authentication, and authorization later in this chapter.

Security without Public Key Cryptography

At first glance, security appears similar whether it is based on secret keys (symmetric keys) or public keys. Authentication, encryption, and integrity protection all

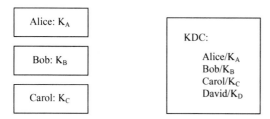

Figure 1: KDC knows one secret for each principal.

are possible. However, there are important functional differences.

One important aspect of public key cryptography is the ability to verify a signature without knowing the private value. In contrast, with secret key cryptography, the same secret that was used to generate the integrity check must be known by the verifier to verify the signature. This means that with secret keys, it is hard for Bob to prove to a third party that a message came from Alice. If only Bob and Alice know the secret, then if Alice sends a message to Bob using an integrity check based on their shared secret, Bob can know it came from Alice, but he cannot prove to anyone else that Alice generated the message because Bob could have created the same message. Also, with secret key cryptography, if Alice needs to send a message to multiple recipients and she has a different key she shares with each recipient, she has to generate an integrity check separately for each recipient, using the key she shares with that recipient. In contrast, with public key cryptography, Alice can sign the message using her private key and anyone can verify it using her public key.

Because it would be impractical to separately configure a key between every pair of entities that might want to communicate [an $O(n^2)$ solution], the usual solution is to use a key distribution center (KDC), as is done in Kerberos. The KDC stores a secret for each individual, and each individual only needs to store a single secret (the one the individual shares with the KDC). A diagram is shown in Figure 1.

If Alice wants to talk to Bob, she requests that the KDC introduce them. The KDC invents a new secret, K_{AB}, and prepares a message for Alice, encrypted with K_A (the secret the KDC shares with Alice), that tells her to use K_{AB} to talk to Bob. It also prepares a message for Bob, encrypted with K_B, that tells him to use K_{AB} to talk to Alice. See Figure 2 for an illustration.

FUNCTIONAL COMPARISON BETWEEN PUBLIC KEY– AND SECRET KEY–BASED SYSTEMS

If Alice and Bob each know their own private key, they each know the CA's public key, and they each have a certificate from the CA, then they can talk by exchanging certificates, without needing to talk to a third party. See Figure 3.

The functional differences between a PKI-based solution (one based on public keys) and a KDC-based solution (one based on secret keys) are described in the next few sections.

Security

The KDC-based solution will be less secure. The KDC has a highly sensitive database (secrets for all its clients). In contrast, a CA does not need to know anyone's private keys. It only certifies public keys and therefore does not have access to any secrets (other than its own private key).

A KDC must be online because it is needed to facilitate all conversations. This makes it an attractive target for network-based attacks. In contrast, the CA does not need to be online. It signs certificates once, and the certificate can be made accessible on the network, but the CA does not need to be accessible.

Because the KDC must be available to facilitate conversations, it must be replicated (because having it be down would be intolerable). Each replica needs to be physically secured. In contrast, it would not be a problem if the CA were down for some period of time. New users might not be able to be certified, but communication between existing clients would not be hindered (except possibly for revocation, although a revocation server could be different from the CA and have a different key—see the section on revocation in this chapter). Physically securing the CA is easy because it need not be accessible to the network.

The KDC needs to be a complicated system, capable of simultaneously communicating via the network to many clients simultaneously. This makes it likely that it will have security vulnerabilities. In contrast, the CA is a simple system. All it needs to do is sign certificates, a much simpler problem than communicating via a network. Plus, the CA need not be online, so if physical security is enforced, even if the CA had security vulnerabilities, they would not be exploitable. On the other hand, a real security flaw for any system is the involved humans, so if the CA operator can

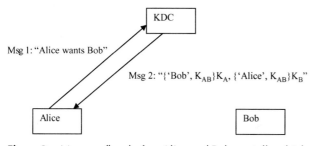

Figure 2: Message flow before Alice and Bob can talk, which uses secret keys.

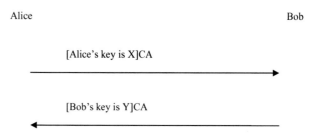

Figure 3: With certificates, Alice and Bob can immediately communicate.

be bribed or tricked or threatened, it would be possible to forge certificates.

Cost

The KDC solution will be more expensive, because the KDC is a complex, performance-sensitive, replicated system. A CA does not have these properties.

When Kerberos was designed, licensing of public key technology was prohibitively expensive, so the Kerberos designers needed to avoid public key technology. Once the RSA patent expired, a public key–based system became less expensive.

Performance

Public key cryptography is a lot slower than secret key cryptography. However, the performance of the mathematics is counteracted by the necessity, in KDC-based systems, of having additional round trips before connection setup in order to communicate with the KDC. Once a conversation is facilitated, whether with PKI or with KDC, a secret key is established between the parties, so performance is only an issue on conversation startup.

Interorganizational Communication

It is common for organizations to communicate with the outside world through a firewall. Because the KDC is the most security-sensitive box in the network, it is likely that the firewall administrator would want to block access to the KDC from outside the network. This would preclude setting up a conversation between parties in different organizations. In contrast, with a public key–based system, Alice and Bob can e-mail their certificates. Thus, a PKI-based system is more likely to work between organizations.

Issues with Public Key Infrastructure

Although on the surface a PKI-based system seems straightforward, there are many deeper issues, which we explore in the remainder of this chapter. If Alice knows her own private key, Bob knows the CA's public key, and Alice has a certificate signed by the CA that Bob trusts, then Bob can, for instance, send an encrypted message to Alice. However, how does Alice know her own private key? How does Bob know the CA's public key? How can Alice get securely certified? How can Bob obtain Alice's certificate?

PKI MODELS

In this section, we explore various ways of building the PKI. Who should be the initially trusted CAs? How does a principal obtain the CA's key? If Alice is not directly certified by a CA that Bob knows and trusts, how can Bob (or Alice) find a chain of certificates linking Alice's name with a CA that Bob trusts?

The public key(s) that Bob trusts a priori, and which are somehow securely known to Bob (e.g., by being installed on his system) are known as Bob's *trust anchors*.

Monopoly

In this model, the world chooses one organization, universally trusted by all countries, companies, organizations, and individuals, and configures that organization's public key into all software and all hardware. In other words, that key is everyone's trust anchor. Everyone obtains certificates from this one organization. This model is simple to understand and implement. However, there are problems:

- There is no such thing as a universally trusted organization.
- Even if everyone agreed to trust one organization, the entire security of the world would depend on that one organization never having an employee that could be tricked, bribed, or threatened into misusing the CA's private key.
- This model grants an eternal monopoly to one organization. Once widely deployed, it would be impractical to switch organizations if that organization started charging too much money or being careless about creating certificates, because it would mean reconfiguring everything and perhaps even changing hardware.
- The configured key can never be changed. If it ever was stolen, or if advances in cryptography warranted changing to a different algorithm or a different key size, it would be prohibitively expensive to change that key.

Oligarchy

In this model, instead of choosing a single organization, each piece of software (and perhaps hardware) comes preconfigured with several CA public keys. In some cases, users are allowed to edit that list. This eliminates the monopoly issue, but there are still problems:

- The default keys (the ones that come preconfigured) are those trusted by the software or hardware vendor, not necessarily the user.
- In the previous model, security depended on one organization never having a corruptible employee. Now there are more organizations, and a breach of an employee at any of those organizations will compromise the security of the world.
- Even if all the CAs in the default list are trustworthy, if the list is modifiable, a user can be tricked into using a platform with bad CA keys inserted. This can be because the user is using a platform in a public place (like at an Internet café) or because the user visited some site that presented a certificate signed by an unknown CA, the user was presented with a pop-up box with an obscure message about "unknown CA," and the user agreed to trust this CA forever.
- It would be impractical for even a sophisticated user to examine the list of configured CA keys to see if they are all legitimate. It is not enough to look at the organization names. It would be necessary to examine hashes of the keys.

Anarchy

In the previous models, there are no certificate chains. Alice must be directly certified by one of Bob's trust anchors. In this model, we allow chains of certificates.

In this model, users each configure their own trust anchors, based on who they have personally met, trust, and for whom they have securely received a public key. If Bob wants to find Alice's public key and Alice is not one of Bob's trust anchors, then Bob must somehow find an external source of certificates and search through them to try to find a path from one of his trust anchors to Alice's name.

This is the model used by PGP ("pretty good privacy"), a secure e-mail product. Often when there is a gathering of technical people, there is an event called a "PGP key signing party," in which people distribute their public keys and publicly announce their names and digests of their keys. Anyone who believes a person's identity and that the person has securely obtained his or her key can sign a certificate for that person. There are public databases of certificates to which anyone can contribute. Thus, if Bob wants Alice's key, and her key is not one of his trust anchors, he can search through a public database of certificates to see if he can find a path from one of his trust anchors to her name.

The problems with this model are these:

• This will not scale. If this was the model for Internet authentication, there are potentially billions of users, and if each signed, say, 10 certificates on average, the database of certificates would be on the order of 10s of billions. It would be unwieldy to search through such a database to try to find a mathematically valid sequence of certificates that would lead to Alice's name.

• Even if a path is found that mathematically works out (X1 is a trust anchor, X1 vouches for X2, X2 vouches for X3, X3 vouches for Alice), it does not mean that this path should be trusted. In a relatively small community of honest people, this scheme will seem to work, but once the community is infiltrated by people motivated to poison the database with incorrect information, there is no feasible way to securely find the key of someone several certificate hops away. Revocation is yet another issue. If someone's private key were stolen, how would they know everyone that needed to be notified?

Revocation is an interesting issue with this model. The designers of PGP suggest that to revoke your public key, you sign a revocation certificate (with the private key you want to revoke), stating "please stop using this public key for me because it has been compromised." If you knew all the certificate repositories in which anyone would be looking, you could then store the revocation certificate in each of them. That you would know all the repositories is a fairly major assumption. It also assumes that you can create such a revocation certificate (you need to know the compromised private key to create the certificate). In case the private key is on a smart card that got stolen, you would have needed to create the revocation certificate in advance, while you had control of the private key, and store it someplace for safekeeping so that it could be retrieved and distributed after the key was compromised.

As for all the users that might have your public key as one of their trust anchors, in order for revocation to work at all for them, they would have to periodically check the public certificate repositories to see if you have posted a revocation certificate.

Name-Based Trust

This is an important concept that says that instead of trust in a CA being a binary decision (the CA is either "trusted" or "not trusted"), a CA is trusted for certifying only certain name and key pairs. For this model, we assume a hierarchical name (such as a domain name server– style name). Each node in the namespace (say, "example.com") is represented by a CA, who is responsible for certifying names below it in the hierarchy. Thus, example.com might certify its child node "labs.example.com," which in turn might certify "alice.labs.example.com."

This trust policy is rather natural. The name by which an object is known implies who is trusted to certify its key. A person might be known by the name JohnDoe. Smalltown.Alaska.us, in which case it might be the town clerk of Smalltown, Alaska, USA, that would be trusted to certify their key. That person might also have an identity JD9975.RandomISP.com, in which case RandomISP would be trusted to certify the mapping between that identity and a key. Or, the person might be JohnD.Company.com, in which case Company would be trusted to certify the key of that identity. Or, the person might be agent99.freedomfighters.org, in which case freedomfighters.org would certify the mapping. It is in an organization's interest to take care to manage the key/name mappings of its members. These different identities may or may not use the same public key pair, and it is irrelevant that they might all map to the same human being. Each name is a different identity.

Top-Down, Name-Based

In this model, there is a root CA (representing the root of the namespace), each node in the namespace is represented by a CA, and each CA signs the key of each of its children. This model is scalable, and it is clear what path to take to lead to a node (follow the namespace). There are problems, however. The root must be configured to be everyone's trust anchor. If compromised, it can impersonate the world, because all certificate chains start with the root. It also gives the organization holding the root key a monopoly. We fix these problems in the next model.

Bottom-Up, Name-Based

We modify the previous model by also having each child in the namespace certify the parent. That way, the trust anchor need not be the root. With a tree, and links in both directions, one can start anywhere and navigate to anywhere else. The rule is that some principal in the namespace, probably a leaf node (say, AliceSmith.labs.Company.com) that wants the key of JohnD.Company.com, starts with its trust anchor (which could be anywhere, but the most elegant place is its own key). Starting at that place, the rule is that if you are already at an ancestor of the target name, then just follow the namespace down.

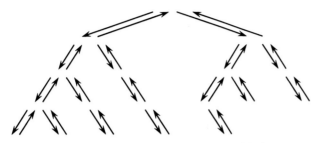

Figure 4:   Name tree with bidirectional links.

Otherwise, go up as far as necessary to get to a least common ancestor (in this case it would be Company.com), and then go down from there. See Figure 4 for an example.

An additional important feature is the notion of a *cross link*. A cross link is where any node in the namespace can certify the key of any other node. Cross links are important for several reasons:

- They connect organizations before a global interconnected PKI exists.
- They bypass untrusted CAs higher in the hierarchy.

This might seem like it would lead to the anarchy model, but the rule is that only one cross link would be followed on any path. The rule is that one starts at the trust anchor, and if you are at an ancestor of the target, you go down. Otherwise, you look to see if there is a cross link from that point to an ancestor, in which case you follow it. If there is not, you go up a level and continue until you get either to the least common ancestor (in which case you go down) or to a cross link to an ancestor of the target (in which case you go down). See Figure 5 for an illustration.

The assumption is that PKIs would grow from the bottom. Each organization would grow its own PKI, and organizations would then link them together with cross links. Then, there would be a business case for providing root service. "We offer interorganizational certification. If you certify us, and let us certify you, you will have a path to the following *n* organizations that have already joined. This is how much we charge. This is how much liability we assume. This is how careful we are about checking before we certify keys."

There could be multiple roots in parallel, and different organizations might use a different subset of the roots. If there were many roots, it might be hard to find a common root, and there might be pairs of organizations that did not have a connected chain of certificates to each other.

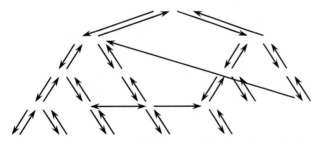

Figure 5:   Name tree with bidirectional links and cross links.

The advantages of this model are these:

- To deploy public–key–based authentication and authorization within your organization, there is no need to get certificates from any outside organization.
- Certificate chain paths are easy to find.
- The policy is something that will make sense to people, without them needing to understand it, and be sufficiently flexible.
- Security of what are presumably the most security-sensitive operations, authentication between things in your own organization, is entirely in your hands. This is because chains of trust between two identities within your namespace never leave your namespace. Each of the certificates in the chain of certificates will have been issued by a CA within your organization.
- No single compromised key requires massive configuration.
- Configuration is minimal: a user's own private key can be her only trust anchor, and starting with one's own public key is the minimal configuration necessary.

Bridge Model

A model known as the bridge model had been adopted for the U.S. federal PKI. It is the same as the bottom-up model, except that the trust anchor is the root of the user's organization. This is practical in organizations in which all the workstations are centrally managed, so that in case the organization's root key changes, a central administrator can reconfigure all the machines.

To find a target's public key, start at the root of your own organization (say fbi.gov), and, if you are at an ancestor of the target, go down from there to the target's name. If not, then go up a level to what is called the "bridge CA," and then go down from there.

USING PKI

Regardless of what model is used for the trust anchors and certificate paths, there is also the problem of gathering the relevant certificates. Suppose Bob needs to know Alice's public key. There are various possibilities for gathering the chain:

- Alice could gather the chain and give them to Bob, for instance, in a real-time protocol, such as IPsec or SSL, or e-mail.
- Bob could gather the chain from some online certificate storage system.
- A helper node whose job it was to gather certificate chains could be queried, and it would gather the chain to be presented to Bob.
- The helper node might gather and verify the chain, and then sign an assertion that it has securely discovered that Alice's public key = P.

What does it mean to have a chain by which Bob will know Alice's public key? The chain must start with a trust anchor of Bob's and terminate with Alice's name. How could Alice or the helper node know what Bob's trust anchors are? The real-time protocols such as IPsec and SSL provide a method for Bob to inform Alice of his trust anchors. In PEM (privacy enhanced email, RFC 1422), the model is assumed to be the monopoly model, with the single root trust anchor configured into everything.

In the case of a helper node gathering and verifying the chain and asserting Alice's key to Bob, the helper node is completely trusted by Bob, and the trust anchor for the chain, and the legal chains, would be determined by the helper node.

In the case of Bob finding the certificate chain, it is clear what model the X.509 community had in mind because of the terminology. To them, building a chain from the target name to a trust anchor is known as building in the "forward direction," whereas building from a trust anchor to the target name is known as building in the "reverse direction." However, building from the target name is more suited to the monopoly model or perhaps the oligarchy model with very few roots.

Certificate Revocation

If a private key is stolen, it is important that the certificate vouching for the mapping between the compromised public key and the name no longer be honored. Certificates have expiration dates, but because it is expensive to issue certificates, the certificate is generally valid for a relatively long time (such as a year). It is unacceptable for someone who has stolen a private key to be able to impersonate a valid principal until the certificate expires. Therefore, there needs to be some method for more timely revocation.

There are two models in the real world for revoking credit cards when a card is reported stolen. One model is where a list of all the revoked but unexpired credit card numbers is distributed to all merchants, a model that was common several years ago. Today, instead, credit card revocation is done by having the merchant check, on each transaction, about the revocation status of a particular card.

In the PKI world, the first model is implemented through use of a CRL (certificate revocation list), periodically issued and signed by the CA or by a public key that the CA certifies as authorized to sign the CRL. The CRL contains a list of unexpired, revoked certificates. It must be issued periodically even if nothing changes, because otherwise there is no way to know whether an old CRL (before the relevant certificate was posted) was substituted for the most recent CRL. The period with which it needs to be posted must be no longer than the maximum amount of time it is acceptable for revocation to take effect.

It is possible for the CRL to get very large. In this case, it would be expensive for every principal that must verify certificates to download the latest CRL every period. In this case, an optimization to the CRL mechanism can be used that is known as a "delta CRL." A delta CRL contains a reference to the last full CRL, and it only states the changes that have occurred since that last full CRL. So, in many cases, the delta CRL will have no information

(other than a pointer to the last full CRL). Only when the delta CRL starts to become large would it be necessary to issue a new full CRL, in which case the subsequent delta CRLs would be small again.

The other model for revocation is what is currently done in the credit card world. An online service accepts queries about specific certificates and responds with the revocation status of those certificates. Typically, this is done by the verifier.

CONCLUSION

PKI is very successfully deployed in the Web environment, but primarily in order for the server to authenticate to the client. Although some PKI-based email standards are in use, their wide adoption has been slow because of the difficulty in use of existing products. However, the basic concepts are sound, the advantages of having a widely deployed PKI are profound, and there is hope that sometime in the future PKI will be more widely deployed.

GLOSSARY

Authentication Showing proof of identity.
Authorization The right to access a resource or perform an action.
Certificate A signed assertion, usually the mapping between a name and a key.
Certification Authority A party that creates certificates.
KDC (Key Distribution Center) The server, in a secret key–based authentication system, that holds a key for every principal and allows secure introduction between principals.
PKI (Public Key Infrastructure) The databases, data structures, and protocols whereby public keys can be securely obtained.
Revocation Invalidation of a certificate.

CROSS REFERENCES

See *Computer and Network Authentication; Digital Certificates; Digital Signatures and Electronic Signatures; IPsec: IKE (Internet Key Exchange); PKCS (Public-Key Cryptography Standards); Public-Key Algorithms; S/MIME (Secure MIME); Secure Shell (SSH); Secure Sockets Layer (SSL).*

FURTHER READING

Adams, C., & Farrell, S. (1999). *Internet X.509 public key infrastructure certificate management protocols* (RFC 2510).
Boeyen, S., Howes, T., & Richard, P. (1999a). *Internet X.509 public key infrastructure LDAPv2 schema* (RFC 2587).
Boeyen, S., Howes, T., & Richard, P. (1999b). *Internet X.509 public key infrastructure operational protocols— LDAPv2* (RFC 2559).
Housley, R., Ford, W., Polk, W., & Solo, D. (1999). *Internet X.509 public key infrastructure certificate and CRL profile* (RFC 2459).

Housley, R., Polk, W., Ford, W., & Solo, D. (2002). *Internet X.509 public key infrastructure certificate and certificate revocation list (CRL) profile* (RFC 3280).

ISO/IEC 9594-8/ITU-T Recommendation X.509. (1997). *Information technology: Open systems interconnection: The directory: Authentication framework.*

Kaufman, C., Perlman, R., & Speciner, M. (2002). *Network security: Private communication in a public world* (2nd ed.). Englewood Cliffs, NJ: Prentice-Hall.

Myers, M., Adams, C., Solo, D., & Kemp, D. (1999). *Internet X.509 certificate request message format* (RFC 2511).

Myers, M., Ankney, R., Malpani, A., Galperin, S., & Adams, C. (1999). *X.509 Internet public key infrastructure online certificate status protocol—OCSP* (RFC 2560).

Pinchas, D., & Housley, R. (2002). *Delegated path validation and delegated path discovery protocol requirements* (RFC 3379).

Secure Sockets Layer (SSL)

Robert J. Boncella, *Washburn University*

SECURE COMMUNICATION CHANNELS
Overview

This chapter provides an overview of how the SSL protocol and its variant the TLS protocol are used to establish and operate a secure communication channel. It is assumed that the readers of this chapter are nontechnical in their academic background. As a result some space will be spent in explaining the background concepts necessary for a full understanding of SSL and TLS. If the reader requires more technical detail (Boncella, 2000) is suggested.

This chapter has five major sections. First is a discussion of the need for and history of secure channels. Second is an overview of the internetworking concepts necessary to appreciate the details of SSL and TLS protocols. Third is a brief review of cryptographic concepts used in SSL and TLS. Fourth is a detailed exposition of SSL and TLS. The chapter concludes with a discussion of SSL and TLS protocol's status—its strengths and weakness and threats and possible alternatives to it.

The Internet can be used to provide a number of communication services. A user can take advantage of e-mail, news posting services, and information gathering services through Web browsing to name a few of its uses. Under certain conditions the user's expectation is that the service to be provided is legitimate, safe, and private—legitimate in the sense that the providers of the service are who they say they are, safe in the sense that the services or information being provided will not contain computer viruses or content that will allow the user's computer system to be used for malicious purposes, and finally, private in the sense that the provider of the requested information or services will not record or distribute any information the user may have sent to the provider in order to request information or services. The server's expectation is that the requestor of the information or service is legitimate and responsible—legitimate in the sense the user has been accurately identified, and responsible in that the user will not attempt to access restricted documents, crash the server, or use the server computing system as a means of gaining illegal access to another computer system. Both the server and the user have an expectation that their communications will be free from eavesdropping and reliable—meaning that their transmissions will not be modified by a third party. The purpose of Internet security is to meet the security expectations of users and providers. To that end, Internet security is concerned with client-side security, server-side security, and secure transmission of information.

Client-side security is concerned with the techniques and practices that protect a user's privacy and the integrity of the user's computing system. The purpose of client security is to prevent malicious destruction of a user's computer systems (e.g., by a virus that might format a user's fixed disk drive) and to prevent unauthorized use of a user's private information (e.g., use of a user's credit card number for fraudulent purposes).

Server-side security is concerned with the techniques and practices that protect the server software and its associated hardware from break-ins, server site vandalism, and denial-of-service attacks. The purpose of server-side security is to prevent modification of a site's contents; to prevent use of the server's hardware, software, or databases for malicious purposes; and to ensure reasonable access to a server's services (i.e., to avoid or minimize denial-of-service attacks).

Secure transmission is concerned with the techniques and practices that will guarantee protection from eavesdropping and intentional message modification. The purpose of these security measures is to maintain the confidentiality and integrity of user and server information as it is exchanged through the communication channel. This chapter focuses on a solution to the requirement for a secure channel.

Secure Channels

The Internet can be used for electronic communication. Those who use the Internet for this purpose, on occasion, have the need for that communication to be secure. Secure communication can be ensured by the use of a secure channel. A secure channel will provide three things for the user: authentication of those involved in the communication, confidentiality of the information exchanged in a communication, and integrity of the information exchanged in the communication.

SSL and its variant TLS are protocols that can be used to establish and use a secure communication channel between two applications exchanging information. For example, a secure channel may be required between a user's Web browser and the Web server the user has accessed. The paradigm example is the transfer of the user's credit card information to a Web site for payment of an online purchase. Another example would be an employee using the Web to send his or her check routing information to her employer for use in a direct deposit payroll request.

In addition to Web services, other services that might be in need of a secure channel would be e-mail, file transfer, and news posting. A discussion of how these services utilize a secure channel is presented at the end of the SSL Architecture section.

History of Secure Channels—SSLv1 to v3, PCT, TLS, STLP, and WTLS

SSL is a computer networking protocol that provides authentication of, confidentiality of, and integrity of information exchanged by means of a computer network. Netscape Communications designed SSL in 1994 when it realized that users of its browser needed secure communications. SSL version 1 was used internally by Netscape and proved unsatisfactory for use in its browsers. SSL version 2 was developed and incorporated into Netscape Navigator versions 1.0 through 2.X. This SSLv2 had weaknesses (Stein, 1998) that required a new version of SSL. During that time—1995—Microsoft was developing PCT (private communications technology) in response to the weaknesses of SSLv2. In response, Netscape developed SSL version 3, solving the weakness of SSLv2 and adding a number of features not found in PCT.

In May 1996, the Internet Engineering Task Force (IETF) authorized the TLS working group to standardize a SSL-type protocol. The strategy was to combine Netscape's and Microsoft's approaches to securing channels. At this time, Microsoft developed its secure transport layer protocol, which was a modification of SSLv3 and added support for UDP (datagrams) in addition to TCP support.

In 2002, the WAP Forum (wireless access protocol) adopted and adapted TLS for use in secure wireless communications with its release of WAP 2.0 Protocol Stack. This protocol provides for end-to-end security over wireless or combined wireless and wired connections (Boncella, 2002; WAP Forum, 2002).

An in-depth understanding of secure channels in general and SSL and TLS in particular requires familiarity with two sets of concepts. The first is how the client–server computing paradigm is implemented using the transmission control/Internet protocols (TCP/IP). The second set of concepts deals with cryptography. In particular, one needs to be familiar with the concepts of encryption, both symmetric and asymmetric (public key encryption), key sharing, message digests, and certification authorities.

The first set of concepts, clients and servers using TCP/IP, is discussed in the following section, and the cryptography concepts are reviewed following TCP/IP discussion.

INTERNETWORKING CONCEPTS
Clients and Servers

The Internet is implemented by means of interconnection of networks of computer systems. This interconnection provides information and services to users of the Internet. Computer systems in this interconnection of networks that provide services and information to users of computer systems are called servers. Services are provided by programs running on those computer systems. Computer systems that request services and information use software referred to as client software or simply clients. The communication channel between the client and server may be provided by an Internet service provider (ISP) that allows access to the communication channel for both the server and client. The communication of the client with a server follows a request–response paradigm. The client, via the communication channel, makes a request to a server and the server responds to that request via a communication channel.

The Web may be viewed as a two-way network composed of three components:

1. Clients
2. Servers
3. Communication path connecting the servers and clients

The devices that implement requests and services both are called hosts because these devices are "hosts" to the processes (computer programs) that implement the requests and services.

Communication Paths

The communication path between a server and a client can be classified in three ways:

1. An internet
2. An intranet
3. An extranet

An internet is an interconnection of networks of computers. However, the Internet (with an upper case I) refers to a specific set of interconnected computer networks that allows public access. An intranet is a set of interconnected computer networks belonging to an organization and is accessible only by the organization's employees or members. Access to an intranet is controlled. An extranet uses the Internet to connect private computer networks or intranets. The networks connected together may be owned by one organization or several. At some point, communication between hosts in an extranet will use a communication path that allows public access.

For a request or response message to travel through a communication path, an agreed-on method for message creation and transmission is used. This method is referred to as a protocol. The de facto protocol of the Internet is the TCP/IP protocol. An understanding of the client–server request–response paradigm requires an overview of the TCP/IP protocol. The TCP/IP protocol can best be understood in terms of the open system interconnection (OSI) model for data communication.

The OSI Model and TCP/IP

The open system interconnection model defined by the International Standards Organization (ISO) is a seven-layer model that specifies how a message is to be constructed for it to be delivered through a computer network communication channel. This model is idealized. In practice, few communication protocols follow this design. Figure 1 provides a general description of each layer of the model. The sender of the message, either a request or a response message, provides input to the application layer.

The application layer processes sender input and converts it to output to be used as input for the presentation layer. The presentation layer, in turn, processes this input to provide output to the session layer, which uses that output as input, and so on, until what emerges from the physical layer is a signal that can be transmitted through the communication channel to the intended receiver of the message. The receiver's physical layer processes the signal to provide output to its data link layer, which uses

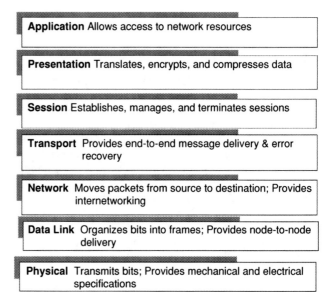

Figure 1: Open system interconnection (OSI) model.

that output as input and processes it to provide output to the receiver's network layer, and so on, until that message is accepted by the receiver.

This process is depicted in Figure 2. Figure 2 also illustrates the signal (message) being relayed through the communication channel by means of intermediate nodes. An intermediate node is a host that provides a specific service with the purpose of routing a signal (message) efficiently to its intended destination.

Figure 3 depicts the TCP/IP protocol on the OSI model. For our purposes the TCP/IP protocol is made up of four layers. What follows is a brief overview of the TCP/IP protocol. For an introduction to the details of TCP/IP, consult Forouzan (2000).

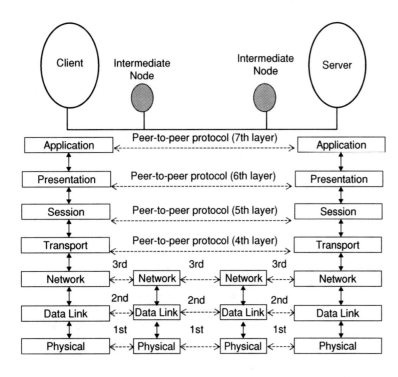

Figure 2: Messaging delivery using open system interconnection (OSI) model.

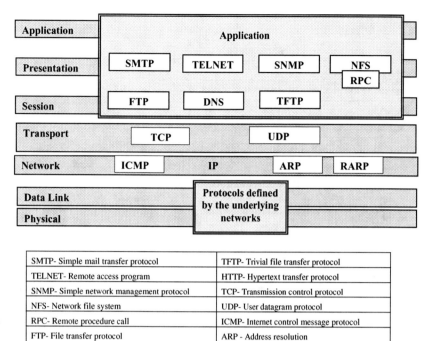

Figure 3: The open system interconnection (OSI) model and the transmission control/Internet protocol (TCP/IP).

SMTP- Simple mail transfer protocol	TFTP- Trivial file transfer protocol
TELNET- Remote access program	HTTP- Hypertext transfer protocol
SNMP- Simple network management protocol	TCP- Transmission control protocol
NFS- Network file system	UDP- User datagram protocol
RPC- Remote procedure call	ICMP- Internet control message protocol
FTP- File transfer protocol	ARP - Address resolution

The application layer contains a number of applications that a user may use as client processes to request a service from a host. The client processes are said to run on a local host. In most cases, the requested service will be provided by a remote host. In many cases, there will be a similarly named application on the remote host that will provide the service. For example, the user may open a Web browser and request HTTP (hyper text transfer protocol) service from a remote host to copy an HTML (hypertext markup language) formatted file into the user's Web browser. If the receiving host provides HTTP service, it will have a process running, often named HTTPD, that will provide a response to the client's request. Note that users need to specify the host by some naming method and the service they desire from that host. This is taken care of by the use of a universal resource locator (URL; e.g., http://www.washburn.edu). The application Layer produces a message that will be processed by the transport layer.

The client's request will pass through the local host's transport layer. The responsibility of the transport layer is to establish a connection with the process on the remote host that will provide the requested service. This client-process-to-server-process connection is implemented by means of port numbers. A port number is used to identify a process (program in execution) uniquely. Unique identification is necessary because local hosts and remote hosts may be involved in a number of simultaneous request–response transactions. The hosts' local operating systems, in concert with the TCP/IP protocol concept of port numbers, can keep track of which of several responses corresponds to the correct client process request on that local host and which request corresponds to the correct service on the remote host.

The transport layer will cut the message into units that are suitable for network transport. In addition to the port numbers, the transport layer adds information that will allow the message to be reconstructed in the receiver's transport layer. Other information is added to these units that allows flow control and error correction. The output from the transport layer is called a segment. The segment is composed of the data unit and a header containing the information described earlier. Figure 4 shows this process.

The output of the transportation layer, a segment, is sent to the network or IP layer. The responsibilities of the IP layer include providing the Internet or IP address of the source (requesting) host and destination (response) host of the segment. One important part of the IP address is a specification of the network to which the host is attached. Depending on the underlying physical network, the segments may need to be fragmented into smaller data units. The information from the segment header is duplicated in each of these fragments as well as the header information provided by the network or IP layer.

The output of the IP layer is called a datagram. The datagram is passed to the lowest layer, where the physical addresses associated with the source and destination hosts' IP addresses are added. The physical address of a host uniquely identifies the host on a network. It corresponds to a unique number of the network interface card (NIC) installed in the host. An example is the 48-bit-long Ethernet address provided by the manufacturer of an Ethernet card. When the TCP/IP protocol is installed on a host, that host's physical address is associated with an IP address. The physical address allows a particular host to be independent of an IP address.

To understand Internet security, we need to be aware of three concepts associated with the TCP/IP protocol:

1. Port address
2. IP addresses
3. Physical addresses

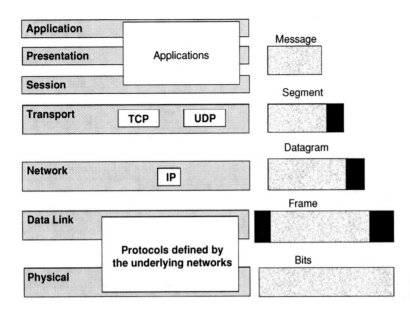

Figure 4: Transmission control/Internet protocol (TCP/IP) message delivery.

These concepts allow the request–response message to be exchanged by the intended processes (as specified by port numbers.). Those processes are running on hosts attached to the intended networks (as specified by the IP addresses) and, finally, running on the intended hosts (as specified by physical addresses). Figure 5 depicts these address assignments and the layers responsible for their assignments.

CRYPTOGRAPHIC CONCEPTS USED IN SSL AND TLS

The following is a brief review of these concepts. The details of each are provided elsewhere in the *Handbook of Information Security*. Volume 2, Part 3, will contain the details of most of these ideas.

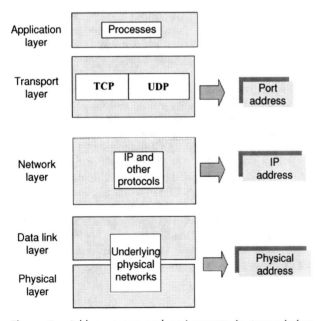

Figure 5: Address types and assignments in transmission control/Internet protocol (TCP/IP).

Encryption

Encryption is the process of converting plaintext (readable text) into ciphertext (unreadable text). Decryption is the process of converting ciphertext into plaintext. Usually this is done by means of a publicly known algorithm and a shared key. Encryption is vital in providing message confidentiality, client–server authentication, and message integrity. There are two methods of encryption: symmetric or secret key and asymmetric or public/private-key pair. Each method of encryption has its particular use. Symmetric encryption is used for encryption of the messages exchanged between a client and a server, whereas asymmetric encryption is used to exchange the common keys used by clients and servers in their symmetric encryption process. Asymmetric encryption may also be used for the encryption of messages.

Symmetric Encryption

There are two main types of symmetric encryption: stream ciphers and block ciphers. Stream ciphers combine 1 byte of the key with 1 byte of the plaintext to create the ciphertext in a byte-after-byte process. Block ciphers process plaintext in blocks of bytes, generally 8 or 16 bytes in length, into blocks of ciphertext.

RC4 is a widely used stream cipher. There are a number of block ciphers, including Data Encryption Standard (DES), Triple DES (3DES), and Rivest Cipher #2 (RC2). AES is another block cipher that is an improvement over DES in that it uses variable block sizes and has longer key lengths—128-, 192-, or 1256-bit keys. The specifics of these ciphers are discussed elsewhere in this volume.

Symmetric encryption requires the sender and receiver to share a secret key. This secret key exchange is a drawback of symmetric systems that is typically overcome by asymmetric or PKI systems.

Asymmetric Encryption

In asymmetric encryption a pair of keys, a public key and a private key, are used to carry out the encryption process. If the private key is used to create the ciphertext, then only the corresponding public key can be used to decrypt that ciphertext and vice versa. Asymmetric (or public/private-key) encryption can be used for key sharing, encryption, and digital signatures.

Key Sharing

There are two means to carry out key sharing. One is "key exchange" in which one side of the message exchange pair generates a symmetric key and encrypts it with the public key of the private–public key pair of the other side. The other technique of key sharing is "key agreement." In this technique each side of the message exchange pair cooperate to generate the same key that will be used for symmetric encryption. The RSA (named for its creators, Rivest, Shamir, Adelman) public key algorithm can be used for the key exchange technique. The Diffie–Hellman public key algorithm can be used for the key agreement technique. The details of these algorithms are discussed elsewhere in this text.

Message Digest Algorithms

Message digest algorithms are used to generate a "digest" of a message. A message digest algorithm computes a value based on the message content. The same algorithm and message content will generate the same value. If a shared secret key is included with the message before the digest is computed, then when the digest is computed the result is a message authentication code (MAC). If the client and server are sharing this secret key and know each other's message digest algorithms, they can verify the integrity of the message exchange.

Two commonly used message digest algorithms are Message Digest #5 (MD5), which computes a 16-byte value (128 bits), and Secure Hash Algorithm 1 (SHA-1), which computes a 20-byte value (160 bits).

Digital Signatures

Digital signatures are used for nonrepudiation. Public-key algorithms can be used for digital signatures. RSA is a means of providing a digital signature by the sender encrypting a known pass phrase with his or her private key. This pass phrase is generally a message digest of the message being sent. Only the corresponding public key will decrypt the ciphertext of the pass phrase to the correct plaintext. It should be noted that not all public–private key systems are "reversible" like RSA. The digital signature algorithm (DSS) is another algorithm that can be used for this purpose.

Certification Authorities

A certification authority (CA) is a trusted third party that is responsible for the distribution of the public key of a public–private key pair. The CA does this by issuing (and revoking) public key certificates. A standard for these certificates is X.509v3. This standard defines the fields contained in the certificate. This is a widely accepted standard and is used by most CAs.

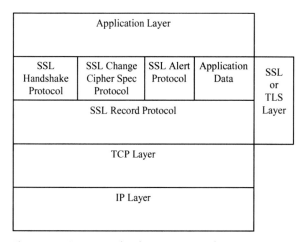

Figure 6: Secure socket layers (SSL) within transmission control/Internet protocol (TCP/IP).

SSL ARCHITECTURE
Overview

SSL is composed of four protocols. Three of the four, SSL handshake protocol, SSL change cipher spec protocol, and SSL alert protocol, are used to set up and manage secure communication channels. The remaining protocol, the SSL record protocol, provides the security service required by applications. The SSL lies between the application layer and the TCP layer of the TCP/IP protocols. This architecture is represented in Figure 6.

Once a secure channel has been established the SSL takes messages to be transmitted, fragments the message into manageable blocks, optionally compresses the data, applies a message authentication code (MAC), encrypts, prefixes the SSL record header, and sends the result to the TCP layer. Ultimately these data blocks are received and the data are decrypted, verified, decompressed, reassembled in the receiver's SSL layer, and then delivered to higher level clients. The technical details of these protocols are discussed in a number of places. The primary document is the Web page http://wp.netscape.com/eng/ssl3/ssl-toc.html.

A number of excellent secondary sources provide more background information as well as the specifications of the protocols. The interested reader is directed to Rescorla (2001) and Stallings (2003). The protocols used to establish a secure channel give SSL its flexibility for client–server communication.

SSL is flexible in the choice of which symmetric encryption, message digest, and authentication algorithms can be used. When an SSL client makes contact with an SSL server, they agree on the strongest encryption methods they have in common. Also, SSL provides built-in data compression. Data compression must be done before encryption.

For example, when an SSL connection is established for an SSL-protected HTTP connection, client-to-server and server-to-client communication is encrypted. Encryption includes the following:

URL of requested document
Contents of the document

Contents of browser forms

Cookies sent from browser to server

Cookies sent from server to browser

Contents of HTTP header, but not particular browser to particular server

In particular, socket addresses—IP address and port number—are not encrypted; however, a proxy server can be used if this type of privacy is required.

Connection Process Preview

The connection process is shown in Figure 7. Figure 7 and the following narrative serve as an overview of this process. To establish an SSL connection, the client (browser) opens a connection to a server port. The browser sends a "client hello" message—Step 1. A client hello message contains the version number of SSL that the browser uses, the ciphers and data compression methods it supports, and a random number to be used as input to the key generation process.

The server responds with a "server hello" message (Step 2). The server hello message contains a session ID and the chosen versions for ciphers and data compression methods the client and server have in common. The server sends its digital certificate (Step 3) which is used to authenticate the server to the client and contains the server's public key (Step 4). Optionally, the server may request a client to authenticate. If requested, the client will send a signed piece of data unique to this handshake and known to both the client and server as the client's means of authentication (Step 5). If the client cannot be authenticated, then connection failure results. Assuming a successful connection, the client sends a "ClientKey Exchange" message (Step 6). This message is a digital envelope created using the server's public key and contains the session key chosen by the client. Optionally, if client authentication is used, the client will send a certificate verify message (Step 7). The server and client send a "Change-CipherSpec" message (Step 8) indicating they are ready to begin encrypted transmission with the newly established parameters The client and server send finished messages to each other (Step 9). The finished messages are MACs of their entire conversation up to this point. (Recall: a MAC, message authentication code, is a key-dependent one-way hash function. It has the same properties as the one-way hash functions called message digests, but they have a key. Only someone with the identical key can verify the hash value derived from the message.) Accordingly, if the MACs match, then messages were exchanged without interference, and hence the connection is legitimate. Once the secure channel is established, application-level data

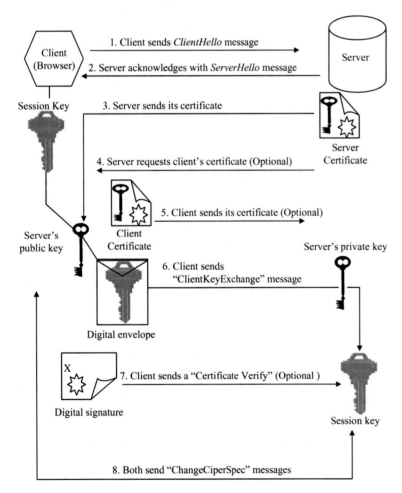

Figure 7: Secure socket layers (SSL) connection process.

1. Client sends *ClientHello* message

2. Server acknowledges with *ServerHello* message

3. Server sends its certificate

4. Server requests client's certificate (Optional)

5. Client sends its certificate (Optional)

6. Client sends "ClientKeyExchange" message

7. Client sends a "Certificate Verify" (Optional)

8. Both send "ChangeCiperSpec" messages

9. Both send "Finished" messages

Client (Browser)

Server

Session Key

Server's public key

Server Certificate

Client Certificate

Digital envelope

Server's private key

Digital signature

Session key

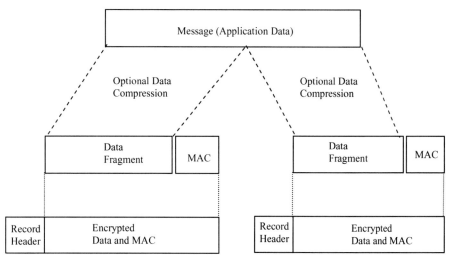

Figure 8: Secure socket layers (SSL) message protocol.

can be transmitted between the client and server using the SSL record protocol.

Record Protocol

The SSL record protocol provides two of the three essential requirements for secure transmission of data: confidentiality and message integrity. Confidentiality is provided by symmetric encryption that uses the shared session key exchanged between the client and server during the handshake protocol. This handshake protocol also defines a shared secret key that can be used to create a MAC, which can be used to ensure message integrity. The third requirement, authentication, is provided by the handshake protocol in its requirement of at least a server's certificate.

The record protocol processes a message by first breaking the message into fragments of equal fixed size, padding the last fragment as needed. The next step is optional compression of each fragment. Once the compression is completed, a MAC is computed for each fragment and appended to the fragment. The result is then encrypted using the key and algorithm agreed on by the client and server. An SSL record header is appended. Then this segment is passed to the TCP layer for processing. The received data are processed by the receiving protocol in the reverse process: data are decrypted, verified by means of the MAC, and decompressed if necessary, then the fragments are reassembled, and the result is passed on to the destination application. This process is depicted in Figure 8.

TLS—Transport Layer Security

TLS is an attempt by the IETF to specify an Internet standard version for SSL. The current proposed standard for TLS is defined in RFC 2246 (2002). The proposed TLS standard is very similar to SSLv3. The TLS record format is identical to the SSL record format. There are a few differences between SSL and TLS. Some of these are how MAC computations are carried out, how pseudorandom functions are used, including additional alert codes and client certificate types, and how certificate verification and

finished message are carried out. The details of these differences are discussed in Stallings (2003).

SSL and TLS Protocols: Details

The preceding sections provide an overview of how a secure channel is set up and used. A better understanding of this process is obtained when a detailed examination of this process is presented. It is informative to work through each step of Figure 7 and detail how the protocols work to set up the secure channel. The following is an adaptation of information that may be found in specification documents for SSL (Netscape Communications, 1996, 1998).

Handshake Protocol

Of the four protocols that make up SSL and TLS, the handshake protocol is the most critical. This protocol is responsible for setting up the connection. It uses a sequence of messages that allows the client and server to authenticate each other and agree on encryption and MAC algorithms and their associated keys, as well as the key exchange algorithms to be used.

The format of the handshake protocol is simple, as depicted in Figure 9. The type field of the handshake protocol indicates 1 of 10 messages listed in Table 1. Length is the length of the message in bytes. Content is the parameters associated with the message type (cf. Table 1).

Step 1 of Figure 7 is the *ClientHello* message. Its parameters are as follows:

version The version of the SSL protocol by which the client wishes to communicate during this session. This should be the most recent version supported by the client.

random A client-generated random structure. This is a value 32 bytes long. The first four bytes are the time

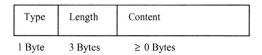

Type	Length	Content
1 Byte	3 Bytes	≥ 0 Bytes

Figure 9: Handshake protocol layout.

Table 1 Handshake Protocol Messages

Message Type	Parameters
HelloRequest	Null
ClientHello	Version, random, session_id, cipher_suite, compression_method
Serverhello	Version, random, session_id, cipher_suite, compression_method
Certificate	Chain of X.509v3 certificates
ServerKeyExchange	Parameters, signatures
CertificateRequest	Type, authorities
ServerDone	Null
CertificateVerify	Signature
ClientKeyExchange	Parameters, signatures
Finished	Hash_value

of day the message was generated, and the remaining 28 bytes are created using a secure random number generator. This 32-byte value will be used as one of the inputs to the key generation procedure. The time stamp (first 4 bytes) prevents a possible "man in the middle" attack as well as protecting against reply attacks.

session_id The ID of a session the client wishes to use for this connection. This parameter will be *empty* if no session_id is available or the client wishes to generate new security parameters.

cipher_suites A list of the cryptographic options supported by the client, sorted descending preferences. If the session_id field is not *empty* (implying a session resumption request) this vector must include at least the cipher_suite from that session.

compression_methods A list of the compression methods supported by the client, sorted by client preference. If the session_id field is not *empty* (implying a session resumption request), this vector must include at least the compression method from that session. All implementations must support a null compression method (i.e., no data compression is used).

After sending the **client hello** message, the client waits for a **server hello** message. Any other handshake message returned by the server except for a **hello request** is treated as a fatal error.

Step 2 is the **server hello** message. The server processes the **client hello** message and responds with either a handshake_failure **alert** or a **server hello** message. The *ServerHello* message parameters are as follows:

server_version This field will contain the lower of that suggested by the client in the *ClientHello* message and the highest supported by the server.

random This structure is generated by the server and *must* be different from (and independent of) the *ClientHello* random structure.

session_id This is the identity of the session corresponding to this connection. If the *ClientHello* message session_id parameter was nonempty, the server will look in its session cache for a match. If a match is found and the server is willing to establish the new connection using the specified session state, the server will

respond with the same value as was supplied by the client. This indicates a *resumed* session and dictates that the parties *must* proceed directly to the *finished* messages. Otherwise this field will contain a different value identifying the new session. The server may return an *empty* session_id to indicate that the session will not be cached and therefore cannot be resumed.

cipher_suite The single cipher suite selected by the server from the list in the *ClientHello* message cipher_suites parameter. For *resumed* sessions, this field is the value from the state of the session being resumed.

compression_method The single compression algorithm selected by the server from the list in the *ClientHello* message compression_methods parameter. For *resumed* sessions, this field is the value from the resumed session state.

Step 3 is the *Certificate* message. If the server is to be authenticated (which is generally the case), the server sends its certificate immediately following the *ServerHello* message. The certificate type must be appropriate for the selected cipher suite's key exchange algorithm and is generally an X.509.v3 certificate. The same message type is also used for the client's response to a server's *CertificateRequest* message.

If the server has no certificate or if a key exchange technique other than RSA or fixed Diffie–Hellman is used, the server will send *ServerKeyExchange* message. In this case, the parameters for this message will contain the values appropriate for the key exchange technique (see Stallings, 2003, for details).

In **Step 4** (optional), a nonanonymous server can optionally request a certificate from the client, if appropriate for the selected cipher suite. The *CertificateRequest* message has two parameters:

types A list of the types of certificates requested, sorted in order of the server's preference.

authorities A list of the distinguished names of acceptable certificate authorities.

After **Step 3** (or optional **Step 4**), the server will send a *ServerHelloDone* message to indicate that the server has sent all the handshake messages necessary for the server hello phase. After sending this message, the server will wait for a client response. When the client receives the *ServerHelloDone* message, the client will determine the validity of the server's certificate and the acceptability of the *ServerHello* message parameters. If the parameters and certificate are valid, the client will receive one or two messages.

Step 5 (optional) is the *Certificate* message. This is the first message the client can send after receiving a *ServerHelloDone* message. This message is only sent if the server requests a certificate. If no suitable certificate is available, the client should send a *NoCertificate* alert instead. This error is only a warning; however, the server may respond with a *FatalHandshakeFailure* alert if client authentication is required.

Step 6 is the *ClientKeyExchange* message. The content of the message will be based on the type of key exchange negotiated during the first phase of the handshaking process. The key exchange method is determined by the cipher suite selected and server certificate type. For example, if the client and server agree on the RSA key exchange method, the client generates a 48-byte *premaster_secret* and encrypts it with the public key from the server's certificate or uses the temporary public key from the server's *ServerKeyExchange* message.

If the server has requested a client certificate and it requires verification, the client will send a *CertificateVerify* message to provide explicit verification of its client certificate.

In **Step 8,** the client sends a *ChangeCipherSpec* message that indicates the client has switched to the negotiated cipher suit. All subsequent messages will be sent using those encryption algorithms and appropriate keys. It should be noted that the *ChangeCipherSpec* message is a separate protocol and not part of the handshake protocol. The purpose of this is to make SSL and TLS more efficient. The *ChangeCipherSpec* message consists of only 1 byte.

In **Step 9,** the client sends the handshake message *Finish*. The message is a concatenation of two message digest values. Each value is computed using a different message digest algorithm—MD5 and SHA—on the same data. The data are the master secret (described later) and the set of handshake messages sent up to this point.

In response to these two client messages, the server sends its version of the *ChangeCipherSpec* and a *Finished* message computer using that same data as the client. If this *Finished* message value differs from the *Finished* message value sent by the client then this indicates that the handshake has been modified and a secure channel may not be set up. When the client receives the *finish* message from the server, it does a comparison with its locally computed *finish* message value. If they match, then all is well; otherwise the secure channel may not be established.

Cipher Suites and Master Secrets

There are two more concepts that need to be presented to complete this discussion. In Step 1, the client sends a list of cipher suites to the server that the client is able to use. In Step 6, the client sends a pre_master_secret that will be used to compute the master secret. This master secret is then used to compute the key_block. This key_block is used to derive the keys that will be used with the algorithms

specified in the cipher suites. The details of each of these need to presented.

Cipher Suites

The **cipher_suite** parameter of the *ClientHello* message provides a set of key exchange techniques, server authentication algorithms, bulk encryption algorithms, and message digest algorithms that the client can support. The client lists these sets in order of the client's preference. For example, one of the entries of this set may be

TLS_DHE_RSA_WITH_3DES_EDE_CBC_SHA

In this example, the key exchange technique is DHE, where DHE denotes ephemeral Diffie–Hellman. The Diffie–Hellman parameters are signed either by DSS or RSA. The signing algorithm used is specified after the DHE parameter. In this case, the signing algorithm is the RSA algorithm.

The bulk encryption and message digest algorithms follow the WITH delimiter, in which the bulk encryption is performed by 3DES_EDE_CBC, where 3DES_EDE_CBC denotes 3DES encryption using the encrypt–decrypt–encrypt mode in the cipher block chaining mode, and the message digest algorithm is SHA, where SHA denotes the secure hash algorithm.

Master Secret

The master secret creation is the vital component in setting up the secure channel. The master secret is used to compute the key_block. Once the key_block computed, it is partitioned into six keys that are used by the client and server in their communications. The computation of the key_block is as follows.

The *ClientKeyExchange* message provides the server with the pre_master_secret when using RSA. Otherwise this message contains the client's Diffie–Hellman parameters. The client and server use this 48-byte value along with the *ClientHello* random parameter value and *ServerHello* random parameter value (they both have copies of these) to create a hash value by using the MD5 and SHA algorithms in the same sequence on this common set of values. They will both compute the identical hash value. This value is the master secret that is shared (computed) by both. A similar process is used to compute the key_block, but instead of using the pre_master_secret in the computation, the master_secret is used. This results in a key_block that is "shared," computed independently but to the same value, by the client and server.

The size of the key_block is determined by the cipher specifications. These specifications give the number of bytes required for the bulk encryption keys (i.e., one for the client to use and one for the server to use), MAC keys, and, if necessary, initialization vector keys. Initialization vectors (IV) are necessary if a bulk encryption algorithm will be using the cipher block chaining mode.

This "shared" key_block is partitioned in the same sequence by the client and server. The first set of bytes is used in the client MAC secret. The second set is used for the server MAC secret. The third set is used for the client bulk encryption key. The fourth set is used for the server bulk encryption key. The fifth set of bytes is used for the

Table 2 Secure Internet Services and Their Associated Port Numbers

Keyword	Secure Port Number	Function
https	443/tcp	SSL/TLS Protected HTTP
ssmtp	465/tcp	SSL/TLS Protected SMTP mail sending
spop3	995/tcp	SSL/TLS Protected POP3 mail receiving
imaps	993/tcp	SSL/TLS Protected IMAP mail server
ftps-data	989/tcp	SSL/TLS Protected FTP data sending
ftps	990/tcp	SSL/TLS Protected FTP control
nntps (snews)	563/tcp	SSL/TLS Protected Usenet News
ssl-ldap	636/tcp	SSL/TLS Protected LDAP

client initialization vector. Finally, the last set of bytes is used as the server's initialization vector.

Secure Internet Services Implemented Using SSL

Many services using the Internet run over TCP. It is a simple task to convert these services to run over SSL. In particular, Web browsing services, e-mail services, and network news posting services have been converted to use SSL when appropriate. Table 2 contains the key word of each service and the ports they are assigned when using SSL.

STATUS OF SSL
SSLv3 and TLS 1.0 and Commercial Use

SSL and TLS primarily function to protect Web traffic using HTTP. For this to work, both the client and the server need to be SSL or TLS enabled. All major Web browsers, including Netscape Navigator and Microsoft Internet Explorer, support SSL and TLS. These browsers allow the user to configure how SSL or TLS will be used. In Netscape Navigator 6.0, the user may consult the Security Preferences panel and open the SSL option under the Privacy and Security selection. In Internet Explorer, the user may consult the Security entry in the Advanced Tab on the Internet Options selection in the drop down menu item for Tools. An interesting option in both browsers is the choice of whether to save the downloaded page to the local cache. The downloaded page is no longer encrypted

and if it is saved to local storage it will be in plaintext. If the local machine is compromised or stolen (e.g., a laptop), that document is readable by any user.

When a secure channel has been established, these browsers will inform the user by means of a small padlock icon at the bottom of the browser. This indicates the page was downloaded using SSL or TLS. The URL of the Web page indicates if SSL is required on the part of the Web browser. A URL that begins with HTTPS indicates that SSL should be used by the browser. A number of Web servers support SSL and TLS. A sample of such programs is displayed in Table 3.

The details of what is required to install and set up an SSL/TLS Web server can be found in various of places. For a detailed overview, the reader is directed to Garfinkel and Spafford (2002) and to Stein (1998). For a technical discussion of what is required, the reader should consult Rescorla (2001).

Advantages, Disadvantages, Threats, and Alternatives to SSL/TLS

SSL and TLS provide server authentication, encryption of messages, and message integrity. This design has several advantages, disadvantages, threats, and alternatives.

Advantages
An important advantage of both SSL and TLS is they provide a generic solution to establishing and using a secure channel. This solution lies between the application and

Table 3 Web Servers That Support the SSL Protocol

Package	Creator	Obtain From
OpenSSL	OpenSSL Development Team	www.openssl.org
Apache mod_ssl (requires OpenSSL)	Apache Software Foundation	www.apache.org
Microsoft IIS	Microsoft Coporation	Bundled with WINNT, WIN2000 and WINXP
Netscape Enterprise and Suitspot	Netscape Communications	www.netscape.com
Covalent SSL (SSL Acclerator)	Covalent Technologies, Inc.	www.covalent.net
Apache Stronghold (commercial Apache)	C2Net	www.c2.net

TCP layers of the TCP/IP protocol suit. As illustrated in Table 2, this implies that any protocol that can be carried over TCP (e.g., ftp, nntp) can be guaranteed security using SSL or TLS.

Another advantage is that SSL's and TLS's designs are publicly available. Because of this, a large number of SSL and TLS implementations are available both as freeware and as commercial products. Furthermore, these implementations are designed as Application Programming Interfaces (APIs) that are similar to networking APIs. In a C/C++-based implementation, the SSL APIs emulate Berkeley sockets; in Java they emulate they Java socket class. As a result, it is a simple matter to convert a non-secure application into a secure application using SSL or TLS.

Disadvantages

When using SSL/TLS for security, it must be remembered that the packets that make up the message are encrypted at the TCP layer. As a result, the IP information will be in clear text. Anyone monitoring the communication will be able to determine the source and destination address of the messages. This kind of traffic analysis could lead to information that ought to remain confidential.

In e-commerce, the application of SSL and TLS has several disadvantages. Both protocols are able to solve the problem of transmitting a credit card number securely, but they are not designed to help with other aspects of that type of transaction. In particular, they are not designed to verify the credit card number, communicate and request authorization for the transaction from the consumer's bank, and ultimately process the transaction. In addition, they are not designed to carry out additional credit card services (e.g., refunds, back order processing, debit card transactions).

An additional disadvantage of SSL/TLS is security of a credit card information on the server. In particular, if the credit card number is cached on the server, it will be stored in plaintext. If the server becomes compromised, that number would be available in plaintext.

Finally, SSL/TLS is not a global solution. In the United States, systems that use strong encryption cannot be exported.

Threats to SSL/TLS

SSL/TLS are vulnerable to the "man in the middle" attack. Such an attack takes place when a malicious host is able to intercept the transmission to and from a client requesting an Internet service and the server providing the Internet service. The malicious host carries out an SSL/TLS exchange with both the client and the server. The result is that the malicious host appears to be a server for the client and also appears to be the client to the server. In fact, the malicious host is really an intermediary between them and will have access to the information being exchanged between the client and server. In particular, the malicious host will set up session keys for use with the client and another set of session keys for use with the server. This threat can be dealt with by the client's use of server certificates issued by a trusted certification authority (CA). For additional details, see Ellison and Schneier (2000).

Alternatives to SSL/TLS

In the area of e-commerce, an alternative to SSL that does not have the disadvantages just cited is SET (secure electronic transaction). SET is a cryptographic protocol developed by Visa, Mastercard, Netscape, and Microsoft. It is used for credit card transactions on the Web and provides the following:

Authentication: All parties to a transaction are identified.

Confidentiality: A transaction is encrypted to foil eavesdroppers.

Message integrity: It is not possible to alter an account number or transaction amount.

Linkage: Attachments can only be read by a third party if necessary.

In addition, the SET protocol supports all features of a credit card system: cardholder registration, merchant registration, purchase requests, payment authorizations, funds transfer (payment capture), chargebacks (refunds), credits, credit reversals, and debit card transactions. Furthermore, SET can manage real-time and batch transactions and installment payments. In addition, because SET is used for financial transactions only, it can be exported and hence can be a global solution for e-commerce. The details of SET are discussed in another chapter.

In the area of providing a secure channel for messages, there are alternatives to SSL/TLS. One is IPSec (IP security), which is a set of open standards designed by IETF and specified in RFC 2401 (2002). IPSec provides for end-to-end encryption and authentication at the IP layer. IPSec is supported in Ipv4 and mandatory in Ipv6. Another alternative to SSL/TLS is SSH (secure shell). SSH is an application and protocol suite that allows a secure connection to be established between two computers that are using a public network. The SSH protocol architecture has three components:

1. Transport layer protocol, which provides server authentication, confidentiality, and data integrity

2. Authentication protocol, which provides user authentication

3. Connection protocol, which provides multiple data channels in a single encrypted tunnel

These protocols run on top of the TCP layer in the TCP/IP protocol suite, which is similar to SSL and TLS.

GLOSSARY

Advanced Encryption Standard (AES) A cipher that encrypts blocks of data of a variable size. In addition, it uses keys of 128, 192, or 256 bits.

Asymmetric Encryption A cryptographic algorithm that uses separate but related keys for encryption and decryption. If one key of the pair is used for encryption, the other key of the pair must be used for decryption. This is sometimes referred to as a public-key algorithm.

Authentication The process of verifying that a particular client or server is who it claims to be.

Block Cipher A cipher that encrypts blocks of data of a fixed size.

Certificate, Public Key A specified, formatted block of data that contains the name of the owner of a public key as well as the public key. In addition, the certificate contains the digital signature of a CA. This digital signature authenticates the CA.

Certification Authority (CA) A trusted entity that signs public key certificates.

Ciphertext The result of encrypting plaintext.

Confidentiality A condition in which information exchanged between a client and server is disclosed only to those intended to receive it.

Data Encryption Standard (DES) A widely commercially used block cipher.

Diffie–Hellman (DH) An asymmetric algorithm that generates a secret shared between a client and server on the basis of some shared, public, and randomly generated data.

Digital Envelope Used to send a symmetric key to recipient for use in future communications. It is created by the sender encrypting the symmetric key using the recipient's public key.

Digital Signature A data value computed using a public key algorithm. A data block is encrypted with the sender's private key. This ciphertext is not confidential but the message cannot be altered without using the sender's private key.

Digital Signature Standard (DSS) A digital signature algorithm developed by the National Security Agency (NSA) and endorsed by the National Institute of Standards and Technology.

Hash Function A function that maps a variable-length message into a value of a specified bit length. This value is the hash code. There is no known method that will produce the original message using the hash value of the message. There is no known way of creating two messages that hash to the same value.

Integrity Being able to ensure that data are transmitted from source to destination without unauthorized modification.

Internet Protocol A protocol that allows packets of data to be sent between hosts in a network or hosts in connected networks.

Message Digest #5 (MD5) A one-way hash algorithm.

Nonrepudiation Being able to ensure the receiver that the sender of a message did indeed send that message even if the sender denies sending it.

Rivest Cipher #2 (RC2) A block cipher sold by RSA data security. This is a 40-bit key cipher.

Rivest Cipher #4 (RC4) A stream cipher used in commercial products

Rivest, Shamir, Adelman (RSA) An asymmetric cipher (public-key cipher) that can encrypt and decrypt. It is also used to create digital signatures.

Secret Key A cryptographic key that is used with a symmetric algorithm.

Session Key A secret key that is used for a limited period of time. This time period covers the length of time there is communication between a client and a server.

Symmetric Algorithm A cipher that requires one shared key for both encryption and decryption. This shared key is a secret key, and the strength of the ciphertext depends on keeping the shared key secret.

Transmission Control Protocol (TCP) The Internet protocol that provides reliable communication between client and a server.

Triple DES (3DES) A cipher that uses DES three times with either two or three DES keys.

X.509 A public-key certificate standard.

CROSS REFERENCES

See *Digital Certificates; Digital Signatures and Electronic Signatures; Encryption Basics; Key Management; Secure Shell (SSH).*

REFERENCES

Boncella, R. J. (2000). Web security for e-commerce. *Communications of the AIS, 4,* Article 10. Retrieved October 1, 2002, from http://cais.isworld.org/

Boncella, R. J. (2002). Wireless security: An overview. *Communications of the AIS, 9,* Article 15. Retrieved March 5, 2003, from http://cais.isworld.org/

Ellison, C., & Schneier, B. (2000). Ten risks of PKI: What you're not being told about public key infrastructure. *Computer Security Journal, 16,* 1–7, Retrieved April 8, 2004, from http://www.schneier.com/paper-pki.html

Forouzan, B. A. (2000). *TCP/IP protocol suite.* Boston: McGraw-Hill.

Garfinkel, S., & Spafford, G. (2001). *Web security, privacy & commerce* (2nd ed.). Cambridge, MA: O'Reilly and Associates.

Netscape Communications. (1996). *SSL 3.0 specification.* Retrieved October 1, 2002, from http://wp.netscape.com/eng/ssl3/ssl-toc.html

Netscape Communications. (1998). Introduction to SSL. Retrieved October 1, 2002, from http://developer.netscape.com/docs/manuals/security/sslin/contents.htm

Rescorla, E. (2001). *SSL and TLS: Designing and building secure systems.* Boston: Addison-Wesley.

RFC 2246 (2002). *The TLS protocol version 1.0.* Retrieved October 1, 2002, from www.ietf.org/rfc/rfc2246.txt

RFC 2401 (2002). *Security architecture for the Internet protocol.* Retrieved October 1, 2002, from http://www.ietf.org/rfc/rfc2401.txt

Stallings, W. (2003). *Network security essentials: Applications and standards* (2nd ed.). Upper Saddle River, NJ: Prentice-Hall.

Stein, L. D. (1998). *Web security: A step-by-step reference guide.* Reading, MA: Addison-Wesley.

WAP Forum. (2002). *Wireless application protocol WAP 2.0.* WAP Forum Technical White Paper. Retrieved October 1, 2002, from http://www.wapforum.org/what /WAP-White_Paper1.pdf

FURTHER READING

Gast, M. (2002). *802.11 wireless networks: The definitive guide.* Cambridge, MA: O'Reilly and Associates.

National Institute of Standards and Technology. *Guidelines on securing public web Servers* (NIST Special

Publication 800-44). Retrieved April 8, 2004, from http:// csrc.nist.gov/publications/nistpubs/800-44/sp800-44.pdf. September 2002

Netscape Communications. (1999). How SSL works. Retrieved October 1, 2002, fromhttp://developer.netscape.com/tech/security/ssl/howitworks.html

Schneier, B. (1996). *Applied cryptography* (2nd ed.). New York: Wiley.

Schneier, B. (2000). *Secrets and lies: Digital security in a networked world*. New York: Wiley.

Smith, R. E. (1997). *Internet cryptography*. Reading, MA: Addison-Wesley.

Stallings, W. (2003). *Cryptography and network security: Principles and practice* (3rd ed.), Upper Saddle River, NJ: Prentice-Hall.

Thomas, S. (2001). *SSL and TLS essentials*. New York: Wiley.

Viega, J., Messier, M., and Chandra, P. (2000). *Network security with OpenSSL*. Cambridge, MA: O'Reilly and Associates.

Biometric Basics and Biometric Authentication

James L. Wayman, *San Jose State University*

INTRODUCTION

Biometric authentication is the automatic recognition of individual persons based on distinguishing biological (usually anatomical) and behavioral traits. The field is a subset of the broader field of human identification science. Example technologies include, among others, fingerprinting, face recognition, hand geometry, speaker recognition, and iris recognition. At the current level of technology, DNA analysis is a laboratory technique not fully automated and requiring human processing, so it not considered biometric authentication under this definition. Some techniques (such as iris recognition) are more biologically based, some (such as signature recognition) are more behaviorally based, but all techniques are influenced by both behavioral and biological elements.

Biometric authentication is frequently referred to as simply biometrics, although this latter word has historically been associated with the statistical analysis of general biological data. The word *biometrics*, like *genetics*, is usually treated as singular. It first appeared around 1980 in the vocabulary of physical and information security as a substitute for the earlier descriptor, *automatic personal identification*, which was in use in the 1970s. Biometric systems recognize "persons" by recognizing "bodies." The distinction between person and body is subtle but is of key importance in understanding the inherent capabilities and limitations of these technologies. In our context, biometrics deals with computer recognition of patterns created by human behaviors and biological structures and is usually associated more with the field of computer engineering and statistical pattern analysis than with the behavioral or biological sciences.

Today, biometrics is being used to recognize individuals in a wide variety of contexts, such as computer and physical access control, law enforcement, voting, border crossing, social benefit programs, and driver licensing.

FUNDAMENTAL CONCEPTS

It has been recognized since 1970 that the three pillars of personal identification are as follows: "What you have (keys and tokens), what you know (PINS and passwords), and what you are (biometrics)" (IBM, 1970). Biometric technology, this last pillar, can be used alone, but is generally combined in access control systems with the other forms of identification (PINs, passwords, or physical tokens). Physical access control applications using biometrics can currently be found at airports, amusement parks, consumer banking kiosks, international ports of entry, universities, office buildings and secured government facilities. When used to control access to information systems, biometrics becomes a technology important to the field of information security.

The perfect biometric measure for all applications would be distinctive (different across users), repeatable (similar across time for each user), accessible (easily displayed to a sensor), acceptable (not objectionable to display by users), and universal (possessed and observable on all people). Unfortunately, no biometric measure has all of the above properties; there are great similarities among different individuals, measures change over time, some physical limitations prevent display, "acceptability" is in the mind of the user, and not all people have all characteristics. Practical biometric technologies must compromise on every point. Consequently, the challenge of biometric deployments is to develop robust systems to deal with the vagaries and variations of human beings.

Biometric systems verify claims (test hypotheses) regarding the source of a biometric pattern in the database. The claim can be made by the person presenting a biometric sample (e.g., "I am the source of a biometric data record in the database") or about the source by another actor in the system (e.g., "She is the source of a biometric data record in the database"). The claims can be positive (e.g., "I am the source of a biometric record in the database") or negative (e.g., "He is not the source of a

459

biometric record in the database"). Claims can be specific (e.g., "I am the source of biometric record A in the database") or unspecific (e.g., "I am not the source of any biometric record in the database"). Any combination of specific or unspecific, positive or negative, or first or third person is possible in a claim.

Systems requiring a positive user claim to a specific enrollment record treat the biometric pattern as an attribute of the record. These systems "verify" that the biometric attribute in the claimed enrollment record matches the sample submitted by the user and are called "verification" systems. Some systems, such as those for social service and driver's licensing, verify negative user claims of no biometric pattern already in the database by treating the biometric pattern as a record identifier or pointer. These systems search the database of biometric pointers to find one matching the submitted sample and are called "identification" systems. However, the act of finding an identifier (or pointer) in a list of identifiers also verifies an unspecific claim of enrollment in the database, and not finding a pointer verifies a negative claim of enrollment. Consequently, the differentiation between "identification" and "verification" systems is not always clear and these terms are not mutually exclusive.

In the simplest systems, "verification" of a positive claim to a specific enrollment record might require the comparison of submitted samples to only the biometric attributes in the single claimed record. For example, a user might claim to be the source of the hand geometry record stored on an immigration card, such as the INSPASS card used by the United States government since 1994 to facilitate airport immigration by frequent air travelers. To prove the claim to being the source of the enrolled identity, the user would insert the card into a card reader that reads the record and then place his/her hand on the hand geometry reading device. The system compares the hand geometry recorded on the card to that of the hand placed on the reader. If the two measures are reasonably close, the system concludes that the user is indeed the source of the record on the card and therefore should be afforded the rights and privileges associated with the card.

Simple "identification" might require the comparison of the submitted biometric samples to all of the biometric identifiers stored in the database. The State of California requires applicants for social service benefits to verify the negative claim of no previously enrolled identity in the system by submitting fingerprints from both index fingers. Depending on the specific automated search strategy, these fingerprints might be searched against the entire database of enrolled benefit recipients to verify that there are no matching fingerprints already in the system. If matching fingerprints are found, the enrollment record pointed to by those fingerprints is returned to the system administrator to confirm the rejection of the applicant's claim of no previous enrollment.

These are examples of the simplest systems. More advanced systems might use comparisons with multiple enrolled records for verification of a claimed identity or only a very limited number of comparisons for identification among all the enrolled records. There is no dependable relationship between verification or identification and the number of comparisons that the system is required to make.

Information security systems generally use biometrics to verify positive user claims to be the source of a specific or unspecific enrollment record in the database. These systems are commonly called verification systems regardless of the search strategy and architecture employed. If a claim to enrollment is verified, authorizations associated with the verified or identified enrollment record can then be applied with confidence to the requested activities, such as computer logon. Although hybrid systems—verifying at the time of enrollment the negative claim that a subject is not already in the database and then verifying in later encounters positive claims of enrollment—are also possible, they are not currently widespread.

Biometric technologies are playing a growing role in information security systems today to connect users to system authorizations through verification of claims of enrolled identity. The argument can be made that biometric measures more closely link the authentication process to the human user than "what you have" or "what you know." Biometric measures are not as easy to transfer, forget, or steal as PINs, passwords, and tokens and so may increase the security level of systems employing them. Biometrics can be combined with PINs and tokens into "multifactor" systems for added security should the PINs or tokens be stolen or compromised.

A SHORT HISTORY

The science of recognizing people based on physical measurements owes to the French police clerk Alphonse Bertillon, who began his work in the late 1870s (Beavan, 2001; Cole, 2001). The Bertillon system involved multiple measurements, including height, weight, the length and width of the head, width of the cheeks, and the lengths of the trunk, feet, ears, forearms, and middle and little fingers. Categorization of iris color and pattern was also included in the system. By the 1880s, the Bertillon system was in use in France to identify repeat criminal offenders. Use of the system in the United States for the identification of prisoners began shortly thereafter and continued into the 1920s.

Although research on fingerprinting by a British colonial magistrate in India, William Herschel, began in the late 1850s, knowledge of the technique did not become known in the western world until the 1880s (Faulds, 1880; Herschel, 1880), when it was popularized scientifically by Sir Francis Galton (1888) and in literature by Mark Twain (1893). Galton's work also included the identification of persons from profile facial measurements.

By the mid-1920s, fingerprinting had completely replaced the Bertillon system within the U.S. Bureau of Investigation (later to become the Federal Bureau of Investigation). Research on new methods of human identification continued, however, in the scientific world. Handwriting analysis was recognized by 1929 (Osborn, 1929) and retinal identification was suggested in 1935 (Simon & Goldstein, 1935)

None of these techniques are "automatic," however, so none meet the definition of biometric authentication being used in this article. Automatic techniques require automatic computation. Work in automatic speaker recognition can be traced directly to experiments with analog filters done in the 1940s (Potter, Kopp, & Green, 1947) and early 1950s (Chang, Pihl, & Essignmann, 1951). With the computer revolution picking up speed in the 1960s, speaker (Pruzansky, 1963) and fingerprint (Trauring, 1963a) pattern recognition were among the very first applications in automatic signal processing. By 1963, a "wide, diverse market" for automatic fingerprint recognition was identified, with potential applications in "credit systems" and "industrial and military security systems" and for "personal locks" (Trauring, 1963b). Computerized facial recognition research followed (Bledsoe, 1966; Goldstein, Harmon, & Lesk, 1971). In the 1970s, the first operational fingerprint and hand geometry systems were fielded, results from formal biometric system tests were reported (Wegstein, 1970), measures from multiple biometric devices were being combined (Fejfar, 1978; Messner, Cleciwa, Kibbler, & Parlee, 1974), and government testing guidelines were published (National Bureau of Standards, 1977). In the 1980s, fingerprint scanners and speaker recognition systems were being connected to personal computers to control access to stored information. Based on a concept patented in the 1980s (Flom & Safir, 1987), iris recognition systems became available in the mid-1990s (Daugman, 1993). Today there are close to a dozen approaches used in commercially available systems, utilizing hand and finger geometry, iris and

fingerprint patterns, face images, voice and signature dynamics, computer keystroke, and hand vein patterns.

SYSTEM DESCRIPTION
Overview

Given the variety of applications and technologies, it might seem difficult to draw any generalizations about biometric systems. All such systems, however, have many elements in common. Biometric samples are acquired from a person by a sensor. The sensor output is sent to a processor that extracts the distinctive but repeatable measures of the signal (the "features"), discarding all other components. The resulting features can be stored in the database as a template or compared to a specific template, many templates, or all templates already in the database to determine if there is a match. A decision regarding the identity claim is made based on the similarity between the sample features and those of the template or templates compared.

Figure 1 illustrates this information flow, showing a general biometric system consisting of data collection, transmission, signal processing, storage, and decision subsystems. This diagram illustrates both enrollment and operation of systems designed for verifying specific or unspecific, positive or negative claims of enrollment. In the following sections, we go through each of these subsystems in detail.

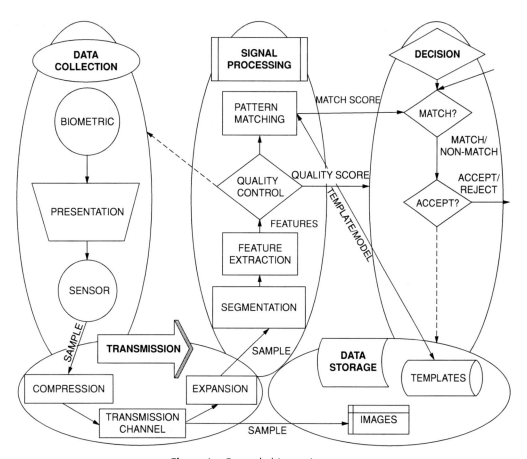

Figure 1: Example biometric system.

Data Collection

Biometric systems begin with the collection of a signal from a behavioral/biological characteristic. As data from a biometric sensor can be one- (speech), two- (fingerprint), or multidimensional (handwriting dynamics), we are not generally dealing with images. To simplify our vocabulary, we refer to raw signals simply as samples.

Key to all systems is the underlying assumption that the signal from the biometric characteristic being observed is both distinctive between individuals and repeatable over time for the same individual. Therefore, it is desirable that there be as much variation between individuals and as little variation within an individual as possible. The challenges of measuring and controlling these variations begin in the data collection subsystem.

The user's characteristic must be observed by a sensor, such as a microphone, CCD-based fingerprint scanning chip, digital camera, or computer keyboard. In systems where a user seeks verification of a positive claim to an enrolled identity, the user can cooperatively present the characteristic to the sensor. The act of presenting a biometric measure to a sensor introduces a behavioral component to every biometric method as the user must interact with the sensor in the collection environment. The output of the sensor is the combination of (1) the biometric measure, (2) the way the measure is presented, and (3) the technical characteristics of the sensor. All measurements and decisions made by the system will be based on this sensor output. Both the repeatability and the distinctiveness of the measurement are negatively impacted by changes in any of these three factors. If a system is to exchange data with other systems, the presentation and sensor characteristics must be standardized to ensure that biometric characteristics collected with one system will match those collected on the same individual by another system.

Transmission

Some biometric systems collect data at one location but process it at another. If a great amount of data is involved, data compression may be required to conserve transmission bandwidth. It is not usual that raw biometric data is stored, but those systems requiring sample storage do so in a compressed format. Figure 1 shows compression and transmission occurring before signal processing or sample storage. The transmitted or stored compressed data must be expanded before further use. The process of compression and expansion generally causes quality loss in the restored signal, with loss increasing with higher compression ratios. An interesting area of research is in finding, for a given biometric technique, compression methods with minimum negative impact on the subsequent signal processing activities. Interestingly, limited compression has been seen in many cases to improve the performance of the pattern recognition software, as information loss in the original signal is generally in the less repeatable high-frequency components.

Signal Processing

The biometrics signal processing subsystem is composed of four modules: segmentation, feature extraction, quality control, and pattern matching. The segmentation module must determine if biometric signals exist in the received data stream (signal detection) and, if so, extract the signal from the surrounding noise. If the segmentation module fails to properly detect or extract a biometric signal, we say that a failure-to-acquire has occurred.

The feature extraction module must process the signal in some way to preserve or enhance the between-individual variation (distinctiveness) while minimizing the within-individual variation (nonrepeatability). The output of this module are numbers that, although called biometric features, may not have direct biological or behavioral interpretation. For example, the numerical values developed by a facial recognition system do not indicate the width of the lips, length of the nose, or the distances between the eyes and the mouth but rather represent the face in a more abstract, mathematically based way.

The quality control module must do a statistical "sanity check" on the extracted features to make sure they are not outside population statistical norms. If the sanity check is not successfully passed, the system may be able to alert the user to resubmit the biometric pattern. If the biometric system is ultimately unable to produce an acceptable feature set from a user, a failure-to-enroll or a failure-to-acquire will be said to have occurred. Failure-to-enroll/acquire may be because of failure of the segmentation algorithm, in which case no feature set will be produced. The quality control module might even impact the decision process, directing the decision subsystem to adopt higher requirements for matching a poor-quality input sample, for instance.

The pattern matching module compares sample feature data with previously enrolled feature data (templates) from the database and produces a numerical comparison score. When both template and features are vectors, the comparison may be as simple as a Euclidean distance. Neural networks or statistical measures, such as likelihood ratios, might be used instead. Regardless of what pattern matching technique is used, templates and features from samples will never exactly match because of the repeatability issues already discussed. Consequently, the matching scores determined by the pattern matching module will have to be interpreted by the decision subsystem.

In more advanced systems, such as speaker verification, the enrollment templates might be models of the feature generation process—very different data structures than the observed features. The pattern matching module determines the consistency of the observed features with the stored model. Some pattern matching modules may even direct the adaptive recomputation of features from the input data to see if better matches might be made through small adjustments to the input data.

Decision

The decision subsystem is considered independently from the pattern matching module. The decision subsystem might make a simple match or no match determination by comparing the output score from the pattern matching module against a predetermined threshold value. The ultimate acceptance or rejection of a user's identity claim might be based on multiple match/no match decisions from multiple measures or from some dynamically determined, user-dependent, or measure-dependent decision criteria. For instance, common decision policies will accept a user transaction if a match occurs in any of three attempts or against any one of several stored templates.

The decision module might also direct operations to the stored database, storing features as templates during enrollment, updating templates in the database after a successful transaction, calling up additional templates for comparison in the pattern matching module, or directing a database search.

Because input samples and stored templates will never exactly match, the decision modules will make mistakes—wrongly rejecting a correctly claimed identity of an enrolled user or wrongly accepting the identity claim of an impostor. Thus, there are two types of errors: false rejection and false acceptance. These errors can be traded off against one another to a limited extent: decreasing false rejections at the cost of increased false acceptances and vice versa. In practice, however, inherent within-individual variation (nonrepeatability) limits the extent to which false rejections can be reduced, short of accepting all comparisons. The decision policies regarding match/no match and the accept/reject criteria are specific to the operational and security requirements of the system and reflect the ultimate cost and likelihood of errors of both types.

Because of the inevitability of false rejections, all biometric systems must have exception handling mechanisms in place. If exception handling mechanisms are not as strong as the basic biometric security system, a vulnerability will result. High numbers of falsely rejected transactions may overload even strong exception handling mechanisms and lower the responsiveness of system management to potential attacks on the system. Consequently, a high false rejection rate can lead not only to user inconvenience and operational delays but to a compromise in system security as well.

The false acceptance rate measures the percentage of "zero effort" impostor transactions that result in access to the system. The false acceptance rate should never be confused with the probability that a successful transaction is actually fraudulent. This latter probability depends on both the false acceptance rate and the percentage of all transaction attempts that are actually by impostors. Depending on the application and how alarms are handled, even a 20% false acceptance rate (which indicates an 80% probability of intercepting an impostor) may be low enough to decrease the frequency of attacks on the biometric system to the point that there are no successful impostor transactions. Truly determined fraudsters might find other entry points, including the exception handling mechanism, more appealing than the biometric portal.

Consequently, the security level provided by a biometric system might be as sensitive to the false rejection rate as to the false acceptance rate. Sound practice would indicate that we not rely on a single biometric safeguard to catch every impostor, not place extreme emphasis on attaining near-zero false acceptance rates, and continue to couple biometrics with other methods, such as PINs and passwords.

Storage

The remaining subsystem to be considered is that of storage. The processed features or the feature generation model of each user will be stored or "enrolled" in a database for future comparison by the pattern matcher to incoming feature samples. Systems for verifying negative claims of identity require a centralized database (or the equivalent, linked decentralized databases) of all enrolled templates to verify a claim that a person is not enrolled in the system. Such systems generally return the records of any previous enrollments found, so are called identification systems as previously discussed. Large-scale identification systems generally partition the database using factors such as gender or age so that not all centrally stored templates need be examined to establish that a person is not in the database. Such systems are sometimes loosely called one-to-N to indicate that a submitted sample must be compared to multiple enrollment templates or models.

For systems only verifying positive claims to a specific identity, the database of templates may be distributed on a magnetic stripe, optically read or smartcards carried by each enrolled user; no centralized database need exist. Such positive verification systems are sometimes loosely called one-to-one to indicate that biometric samples might be compared to the templates or models of only the single claimed identity. However, verification systems based on likelihood estimation techniques compare samples not only to the claimed enrollment templates, but also to the templates of other users or to background models so might not really be one to one.

Although distributed storage is possible, positive claim verification systems might use a centralized, encrypted database to prevent creation of counterfeit cards or to reissue lost cards without re-collecting the biometric measures.

The original biometric measurement, such as a fingerprint pattern, is generally not reconstructable from the stored templates. However, if access can be had to unencrypted templates, it is quite possible for a knowledgeable hacker in possession of an identical system to construct an artifact capable of regenerating the accessed template. Although this artifact will not have the exactly the same visible pattern as the original biometric sample, the biometric system will generate the same template. For this reason, biometric templates must always be protected as sensitive data and will generally require encryption, even when stored on user-controlled cards. The decision to maintain a centralized template database for verification applications should be done with an assessment of the privacy and security risks should the database be compromised.

Biometric templates are created using the proprietary feature extraction algorithms of the system vendor. Consequently, biometric systems are not currently interoperable at the level of the feature vector. To support interoperability (for instance, to allow future use of legacy data), it may be necessary to store raw data, usually in

Table 1 Biometric Template Sizes

Device	Size in Bytes
Fingerprint	200–1,000
Speaker	100–6,000
Finger geometry	14
Hand geometry	9
Face	100–3,500
Iris	512

compressed form. Of course, unauthorized access to raw biometric data can allow for compromise through the construction of artifacts or through replay attacks. Unlike PINs and passwords, however, raw biometric data cannot be changed at the request of the user. Consequently, the storage of raw biometric data presents particular security and liability concerns.

Table 1 shows some example unencrypted template sizes for various biometric devices.

PERFORMANCE TESTING

Biometric devices and systems might be tested in many different ways. Types of testing include the following: technical performance; reliability, availability, and maintainability (RAM); vulnerability; security; user acceptance; human factors; cost/benefit; and privacy regulation compliance.

Technical performance has been the most common form of testing since the mid-1970s. Technical tests are generally conducted with the goal of predicting system performance with a target population in a target environment, but historically, extrapolation of results from a test environment to the real world has been difficult.

Technical tests can be either closed-set or open-set. A closed-set test assumes that all users are enrolled in the system and does not acknowledge the existence of impostors. A closed set test returns the rank of the true comparison when an input sample is compared to all of the enrolled patterns. Closed-set tests measure the probability that the true pattern was found at rank k or better in the search against the database of size N. In any test, the rank k probability is dependent on the database size, decreasing as the database size increases.

An open-set test does not require that all input samples be represented by a pattern in the enrolled database and measures all comparison scores against a score threshold. An open-set test returns, as a function of the threshold, the probability of either missing a true comparison (the false nonmatch rate) or matching a wrong comparison (the false match rate). Open-set measures are independent of the size of the database searched, converging to the correct estimator as the test size increases. Examples of both open-set and closed-set tests are found in the literature, but as most applications must acknowledge the potential for impostors, open-set results are of the greater practical value to the system designer or analyst.

To make test results more predictive of real-world performance, testing best practices are developing (Mansfield & Wayman, 2002). Metrics generally collected in

open-set technical tests are as follows: failure-to-enroll, failure-to-acquire, false match, false non-match, and throughput rates. Failure-to-enroll rate is determined as the percentage of all persons presenting themselves to the system in good faith for enrollment who are unable to do so because of system or human failure. Failure-to-acquire rate is determined as the percentage of "good faith" presentations by all enrolled users that are not acknowledged by the system. The false non-match rate is the percentage of all users whose claim to identity is not accepted by the system. This will include failed enrollments and failed acquisitions, as well as false nonmatches against the user's stored template. The false match rate is the rate at which zero-effort impostors making no attempt at emulation are incorrectly matched to a single, randomly chosen false identity. Because false match/nonmatch rates are competing measures, they can be displayed together on a decision error trade-off (DET) curve.

The throughput rate is the number of persons processed by the system per minute and includes both the human/machine interaction time and the computational processing time of the system.

Types of Technical Tests

Three types of technical tests have been described: technology, scenario, and operational (Philips, Martin, Wilson, & Przybocki, 2000).

Technology Test. The goal of a technology test is to compare competing algorithms from a single technology, such as fingerprinting, against a standardized database collected with a universal sensor. There are competitive, government-sponsored technology tests in speaker verification (National Institute of Standards and Technology, 2003), facial recognition (Philips, Grother, Bone, & Blackburn, 2002), and fingerprinting (Maio, Maltoni, Wayman, & Jain, 2002)

Scenario Test. Although the goal of technology testing is to assess the algorithm, the goal of scenario testing is to assess the performance of the users as they interact with the complete system in an environment that models a real-world application. Each system tested will have its own acquisition sensor and so will receive slightly different data. Scenario testing has been performed by a number of groups, but few results have been published openly (Bouchier, Ahrens, & Wells, 1996; Mansfield, Kelly, Chandler, & Kane, 2000; Rodriguez, Bouchier, & Ruehie, 1993).

Operational Test. The goal of operational testing is to determine the performance of a target population in a specific application environment with a complete biometric system. In general, operational test results will not be repeatable because of unknown and undocumented differences between operational environments. Further, "ground truth" (i.e., who was actually presenting a good faith biometric measure) will be difficult to ascertain. Because of the sensitivity of information regarding error rates of operational systems, few results have been reported in the open literature (Wayman, 2000).

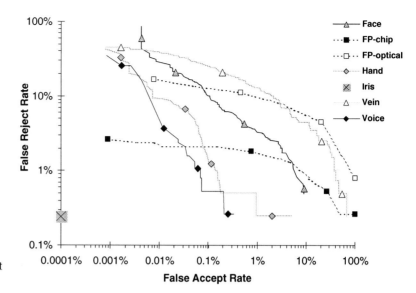

Figure 2: Detection error trade-off curve: best of three attempts.

Regardless of the type of test, all biometric authentication techniques require human interaction with a data collection device, either standing alone (as in technology testing) or as part of an automatic system (as in scenario and operational testing). Consequently, humans are a key component in all system assessments. Error, failure-to-enroll/acquire and throughput rates are determined by the human interaction, which in turn depends on the specifics of the collection environment. Therefore, little in general can be said about the performance of biometric systems or, more accurately, about the performance of the humans as they interact with biometrics systems.

The National Physical Lab Tests

A study by the UK National Physical Laboratory, Mansfield et al. (2000), looked at eight commercially available biometric products in a scenario test designed to emulate access control to computers or physical spaces by scientific professionals in a quiet office environment. A more detailed description of the products, test environment, and volunteer population is available in the original report.

The false accept/false reject DET under a "three-tries" decision policy for this test is shown in Figure 2. The false rejection rate includes failure-to-enroll/acquire rates in its calculation.

Figure 2 allows estimation of the false rejection rate for each of the tested products for any required false acceptance rate but only for this test environment and this set of test subjects. The figure does not show the decision thresholds required to attain those false acceptance rates. The tested products may not be representative of the technology in general and it is not possible to extrapolate these results to any other application environment or set of test subjects. For example, the figure shows that it is possible for National Physical Laboratory users of hand geometry to attain a 1% false rejection rate at a 0.1% false acceptance rate in this environment. A failure-to-enroll was considered as a false rejection in the computation of this figure. These results relate to the average error rates over all users. Individual users may have error rates considerably above or below the averages.

It is also important to note that the National Physical Laboratory results do not tell us about the user error rates with technologies such as PINs and tokens, generally thought to be competitors of biometrics. Determining the strength of biometrics relative to the other mechanisms for personal identification is an unresolved research issue.

The National Physical Laboratory study also established the access control transaction times for these users with the various biometric devices in this office environment, shown as Table 2.

In Table 2, the term *PIN?* indicates whether the transaction time included the manual entry of a four-digit identification number by the user. These times referred only to the use of the biometric device and did not include actually accessing a restricted area.

BIOMETRICS AND INFORMATION SECURITY

Hopefully it is clear by this point that biometrics can have an important role in information security, being much more closely linked to a user and more difficult to forget,

Table 2 Transaction Times in Office Environment

Device	Transaction Time (seconds)			PIN?
	Mean	Median	Minimum	
Face	15	14	10	No
Fingerprint—optical	9	8	2	No
Fingerprint—chip	19	15	9	No
Hand	10	8	4	Yes
Iris	12	10	4	Yes
Vein	18	16	11	Yes
Speaker	12	11	10	No

give away, or lose than a token, a PIN, or a password. Use of biometrics can provide additional evidence that an authorization credential is being presented by the person to whom it was issued. However, biometric technologies do not represent a silver bullet eliminating PINs, passwords, and tokens while resolving all security issues.

In architecting a system for verifying a positive claim to identity, we must decide whether each person's biometric template will be carried by the person themselves on a token or whether the template will be stored centrally in a database linked to the point of service by a communications system. The former approach has positive implications for privacy (Kent & Millett, 2003), but will require some form of key, such as a PIN or a password, to unlock the biometric measure that will be encrypted on the token. Consequently, all the issues regarding data security on tokens, as considered elsewhere in this *Handbook*, still exist.

If biometric templates are stored centrally, several different questions arise:

1. Will the sample be sent to the central system or will the central system pass the template to the point of service for processing? In either case, some strong form of encryption will be required to protect the data during transmission.
2. If the data are sent from the point of service to the central site, will it be in raw form or processed into features? If processed into features prior to transmission, computational power and knowledge of the feature extraction algorithm will be required at each point of service but transmission bandwidth will be reduced.
3. How will the encrypted data be unencrypted when necessary for comparison?
4. How will the user trust the point of service to be legitimate and not to be storing the biometric data after transmission?

Although these issues are not insurmountable, they demonstrate that use of biometrics does not eliminate the usual security issues.

It has been well known since the 1970s that biometric devices can be fooled by forgeries (Lummis & Rosenberg, 1972; National Bureau of Standards, 1977; Raphael & Young, 1974). In a system for verifying positive claims of identity, spoofing is the use of a forgery of another person's biometric measures. In a system for verifying a negative claim, spoofing is an attempt to disguise one's own biometric measure. Forging biometric measures of another person is more difficult than disguising one's own measures but is quite possible nonetheless. Several studies (Blackburn, Bone, Grother, & Phillips, 2000; Matsumoto, Matsumoto, Yamada, & Hoshino, 2002; Thalheim, Krissler, & Ziegler, 2002; van der Putte & Keuning, 2000) discuss ways by which facial, fingerprint, and iris biometrics can be forged. Speaker recognition systems can make forgery difficult by requesting the user to say numbers randomly chosen by computer. However, the current state of technology does not provide reliable "liveness testing" to ensure that the biometric measure is both from a living person *and* not a forgery.

The use of biometrics does not reduce the need to fully vet all applicants for authorizations. A biometric system can neither verify the external truth of the enrolled identity itself nor establish the link automatically to an external identity with complete certainty. Determining a user's "true" identity, if required, is done at the time of enrollment through trusted external documentation, such as a birth certificate or driver's license. The biometric measures link the user to an enrolled identity and associated authorizations that are only as valid as the original determination process.

Not all systems, however, have a requirement to know a user's true name or identity. Biometric measures can be used as anonymous and pseudoanonymous identifiers and consequently have intriguing potential for privacy enhancement of authorization systems.

All biometric measures may change over time, because of aging of the body, injury, or disease. Therefore, reenrollment may be required. If true identity or continuity of identity is required by the system, reenrollment must necessitate presentation of trusted external documentation. Both enrollment and reenrollment also require the physical presence of the enrolling person before the enrolling authority. Otherwise, there is no way to determine that the enrolled biometric measure came from the body of the person presenting it.

EXAMPLE APPLICATIONS

San Jose State University has been using hand geometry readers for around-the-clock, controlled, secure access to the Computer and Telecommunications Center since 1993. About 125 employees are enrolled in the system and log a combined 500 entrance events each day at the three entrances. The system records all events on a central PC, allowing management to audit after-hour access to the Center.

Employees enter a four-digit PIN into the system and place their right hand down on a reflective platen. Infrared light reflects vertically off the platen, but not the skin, allowing a "shadow" of the hand without texture information to be imaged. Additionally, a mirror reflects light horizontally across the top of the hand, supplying a second two-dimensional shadow of the side of the hand. These two, two-dimensional images are reduced using image processing techniques to a 9-byte sample, the values of which cannot be directly related to finger lengths, widths, or other anatomical measures. If the sample is "close enough" in Euclidean distance to the 9-byte template stored at enrollment, the door strike opens and access is permitted. Upon successful use, the system automatically updates the stored template by averaging in the newly acquired sample. The threshold used to determine "close enough" can be set individually, if necessary, to accommodate anyone having unusual difficulty using the system. The entire access process takes just a few seconds and the false rejection of daily (and therefore, habituated) users of the system is exceedingly rare.

Impostors would need both a valid PIN and the correct hand shape to gain access to the system. PIN guessing can be prevented by locking the system or alarming after some number of consecutive access failures.

The hand readers at each door cost about U.S.$1500 in 2005. Some additional items, such as electrically activated door strikes, cabling, and request-to-exit switches must be purchased and installed. The door strikes are controlled and powered directly from the hand reader unit. Although the units can stand alone, a central PC is usually desirable for event logging and for networking multiple units into a single template database. University management has been quite pleased with the cost, efficiency, and security of the system.

We can classify this as an application to verify a positive claim of identity, with trained, habituated users in an unsupervised office environment. The system is used only by employees of the Computer and Telecommunications Center, so is not a "public" application. It serves as a good cost, performance, and procedure model only for proposed applications with these same characteristics.

Since 1997, Purdue Employees Federal Credit Union (PEFCU) in West Lafayette, Indiana, has been using fingerprint verification to replace PINs at nine automatic teller machines (ATMs) kiosks. About 11,500 customers (20% of the PEFCU membership) are enrolled in the system, generating about 28,000 biometrically enabled transactions per month. Customers electing to use fingerprinting can enroll in the system at the central office by presenting any two fingers to an optical scanner. Customers with poor fingerprints because of age or occupation, and customers not wishing to participate, can continue to use traditional PINs at all PEFCU ATMs.

The scanner takes a digital image of the fingerprint, which is converted into a numerical structure based on the patterns in the fingerprint ridges. The numerical structure, but not the original fingerprint image, is stored in a central database. After enrollment, customers can withdraw or deposit cash or apply for loans presenting their ATM card with either enrolled fingerprint to the kiosk scanner. No PIN entry is required. To guide users in the proper placement of the finger, a display screen on the kiosk shows the user the image of the presented fingerprint and an image of an ideally placed finger. The numerical structure extracted from the presented fingerprint is compared to that in the central database stored under the entered user name. Close similarity between the stored and presented structures verifies that the user is the source of the claimed enrollment record and is, therefore, the authorized ATM card holder.

The fingerprinting technology is estimated to represent only a small fraction of the total $70,000 cost of the ATM kiosk. No case of fraud owing to misuse of the fingerprinting system has ever been reported. Incidence of fraud originating from fingerprint-equipped ATMs is currently less than 5% of the fraud rate on other ATMs operated by PEFCU. The credit union is currently expanding the fingerprint system to traditional teller lines to eliminate the need for enrolled users to present photo identification when making withdrawals.

We can classify this use by PEFCU as an application to verify a positive claim of identity, with habituated and nonhabituated users in an unsupervised indoor or outdoor environment. The system is used by a wide cross section of credit union customers, so can be called a public application. Consequently, we would expect the PEFCU

application to be more challenging than the San Jose State University Computer Center application with its more controlled population and environment.

BIOMETRICS AND PRIVACY

The concept *privacy* is highly culturally dependent. Legal definitions vary from country to country and, in the United States, even from state to state (Alderman & Kennedy, 1995). A classic definition is the intrinsic "right to be let alone" (Warren & Brandeis, 1890), but more modern definitions include informational privacy: the right of individuals "to determine for themselves when, how and to what extent information about them is communicated to others" (Westin, 1967). Both types of privacy can be impacted positively or negatively by biometric technology.

Intrinsic (or Physical) Privacy

Some people see the use of biometric devices as an intrusion on intrinsic privacy. Touching a publicly used biometric device, such as a fingerprint or hand geometry reader, may seem physically intrusive, even though there is no evidence that disease can spread any more easily by these devices than by door handles. People may also object to being asked to look into cameras or to stand still while giving an iris or facial image.

Not all biometric methods require physical contact. A biometric application that replaced the use of a keypad with the imaging of an iris, for instance, might be seen as enhancing of physical privacy.

If biometrics are used to limit access to private spaces, then biometrics can be more enhancing to intrinsic privacy than other forms of access control, such as keys, which are not as closely linked to the holder

There are people who object to use of biometrics on religious grounds: Some Muslim women object to displaying their face to a camera and some Christians object to hand biometrics as the Biblical "the sign of the beast." In response, it has been noted (Seildarz, 1998) that a theistic interpretation would more properly consider biometric patterns to be marks given by God.

It can be argued (Locke, 1690; Baker, 2000) that a physical body is not identical to the person that inhabits it. Whereas PINs and passwords identify persons, biometrics identifies the body. Some people are uncomfortable with biometrics because of this connection to the physical level of human identity, the possibility of nonconsensual collection, and the impossibility of changing biometric measures if stolen. Biometric measures could allow linking of the various "persons" or psychological identities that each of us choose to manifest in our separate dealings within our social structures. Biometrics, if universally collected without adequate controls, could aid in linking employment records to health history and church membership, for example. This leads us to the concept of "informational privacy."

Informational Privacy

With notably minor qualifications, biometric features contain no personal information whatsoever about the user. This includes no information about health status, age, nationality, ethnicity, or gender. Consequently, this also limits the power of biometrics to prevent underage access to pornography on the Internet or to detect voting registration by noncitizens.

No single biometric measure has been demonstrated to be distinctive or repeatable enough to allow the selection of a single person out of a very large database. However, when aggregated with other data, such as name, telephone area code, or other even weakly identifying attributes, biometric measures can lead to *unique* identification within a large population. For this reason, databases of biometric information must be treated as personally identifiable information and protected accordingly.

Biometrics can be directly used to enhance informational privacy. Use to control access to and promote accountability with databases containing personal and personally identifiable data can enhance informational privacy. The use of biometric measures, in place of name or social security number, to anonymize personal data, is privacy enhancing.

SUGGESTED RULES FOR SECURE USE OF BIOMETRICS

From what has been discussed thus far, we can develop some reasonable rules for the use of biometrics for logical and physical access control and similar applications.

1. Never participate in a biometric system that allows either remote enrollment or reenrollment. Such systems have no way of connecting a user with the enrolled biometric data, so the purpose of using biometrics to connect the user more closely to the authentication mechanism is lost.
2. Biometric measures can reveal your identity only if they are linked at enrollment to your name, social security number, or other closely identifying information. Without that linkage, your biometric measures are anonymous.
3. Remember that biometric measures cannot be reissued if stolen or sold. Do not enroll in a nonanonymous system unless you have complete trust in the system administration.
4. All biometric access control systems must have "exception handling" mechanisms for those that either cannot enroll or cannot reliably use the system. If you are uncomfortable with enrolling in a biometric system for verifying positive claims of identity, insist on routinely using the "exception handling" mechanism instead.
5. The most privacy enhancing biometric systems are those in which each user controls his/her own template.
6. Because biometric measures are not perfectly repeatable, are not completely distinctive, and require specialized data collection hardware, biometric systems are not useful for tracking people within large populations. Anyone who really wants to physically track the movements of a person in a large population will use credit card, phone records, or cell phone emanations instead. But over a small population, biometric measures are distinctive and repeatable enough to provide

accountability for activities such as accessing stored information. Consequently, the technology itself should not be feared. In the proper applications, biometrics can be used as a strongly privacy enhancing technology.

CONCLUSIONS

Automated methods for human identification have a history predating the digital computer age. For decades, mass adoption of biometric technologies has appeared to be just a few years away (Raphael & Young, 1974), yet even today, difficulties remain in establishing a strong business case, in motivating consumer demand, and in creating a single system usable by all sizes and shapes of persons. Nonetheless, the biometric industry has grown at a steady pace as consumers, industry, and government have found appropriate applications for these technologies. Although the privacy implications continue to be debated, biometrics can be used in privacy enhancing applications. Only time will tell if biometric technologies will receive widespread application in the area of information security.

GLOSSARY

Biometrics The automatic recognition of living persons based on distinguishing traits.
Decision A determination of probable validity of a subject's claim to an identity or no identity in the system.
Enrollment A subject presenting (or being presented) to a biometric system for the first time, creating an identity within the system, and submitting biometric samples for the creation of biometric measures to be stored with that identity.
Failure-to-Acquire rate The percentage of transactions for which the system cannot obtain a usable biometric sample.
Failure-to-Enroll rate The percentage of a population for which the system cannot create a usable template.
False Acceptance Rate The expected proportion of transactions with wrongful claims of identity (in a positive ID system) or nonidentity (in a negative ID system) that are incorrectly confirmed. In applications to verify positive claims, the FAR will be dependent upon the false match rate and the system policy specifying how many attempts will be allowed to prove the claimed identity. In negative identification systems, the FAR may include the failure-to-acquire rate and the false nonmatch rate.
False Match Rate The false match rate is the expected probability that an acquired sample will be falsely declared to match to a single, randomly-selected, non-self template or model.
False Nonmatch Rate (FNMR) The false nonmatch rate is the expected probability that an acquired sample will be falsely declared not to match a template or model from the same user.
False Rejection Rate (FRR) The expected proportion of transactions with truthful claims of identity (in a positive ID system) or nonidentity (in a negative ID system) that are incorrectly denied. In positive

identification systems, the FRR will include the failure-to-enroll and the failure-to-acquire rates, as well as the false nonmatch rate.

Features A mathematical representation of the information extracted from the presented sample by the signal processing subsystem that will be used to construct or compare against enrolment templates. Biometric features generally have no direct anatomical meaning.

Identifier An identity pointer, such as a biometric measure, a PIN (personal identification number), or a name.

Identity An information record about a person, perhaps including attributes or authorizations, or other pointers, such as names or identifying numbers.

Matching Score A measure of similarity or dissimilarity between a presented sample and a stored template or model.

Models Mathematical representation of the generating process for biometric measures.

Negative Claim of Identity The claim that a subject is not known to or enrolled in the system. As an example, social service systems open only to those not already enrolled require all applicants to make negative claims to any existing identity in the system.

Positive Claim of Identity The claim that a subject is enrolled in or known to the system. A specific positive claim of identity will be accompanied by an identifier in the form of a name, PIN, or identification number. Common access control systems are an example. An unspecific positive claim of identity will not require any identifier be given other than the biometric sample. "PIN-less" verification systems are an example.

Sample A biometric signal presented by the subject and captured by the data collection subsystem. (E.g., voice signals, fingerprints, and face images are samples)

Template A subject's stored reference measure based on features extracted from samples.

Transaction An attempt by a subject to prove a claim of identity or nonidentity by consecutively submitting one or more samples, as allowed by the system policy.

Verification Proving as truthful a subject's claim to an identity in the system.

Zero-Effort Impostor a fraudulent or opportunistic user who submits their own biometric measure without alteration in an attempt to make a positive claim to another, randomly chosen identity.

CROSS REFERENCES

See *Computer and Network Authentication; Issues and Concerns in Biometric IT Security; Password Authentication.*

REFERENCES

Alderman, E., & Kennedy, C. (1995). *The right to privacy.* New York: Vintage.

Baker, L. R. (2000). *Persons and bodies: A constitution view.* Cambridge, UK: Cambridge University Press.

Beavan, C. (2001). *Fingerprints.* New York: Hyperion.

Blackburn, D., Bone, M., Grother, P., & Phillips, P. J. (2001). *Facial recognition vendor test 2000: Evaluation report.* Retrieved January 25, 2004, from http:/www.frvt.org

Bledsoe, W. W. (1966). *Man–machine facial recognition: Report on a large-scale experiment.* Palo Alto, CA: Panoramic Research, Inc.

Bouchier, F., Ahrens, J., & Wells, G. (1996). *Laboratory evaluation of the IriScan Prototype Biometric Identifier.* Retrieved July 11, 2004, from at http://infoserve.library.sandia.gov/sand_doc/1996/961033.pdf

Chang, S. H., Pihl, G. E., & Essignmann, M. W (1951). Representations of speech sounds and some of their statistical properties. *Proceedings of the Institute of Electrical and Electronic Engineers,* IRE, New York, NY:147–153.

Cole, S. (2001). *Suspect identities.* Cambridge, MA: Harvard University Press.

Daugman, J. (1993). High confidence visual recognition of persons by a test of statistical independence. *Transactions on Pattern Analysis and Machine Intelligence, 15,* 1148–1161. [Retrieved July 1, 2004, from http://www.cl.cam.ac.uk/users/jgd1000/PAMI93.pdf]

Faulds, H. (1880). On the skin furrows of the hand. *Nature, 22,* 605. [Retrieved July 11, 2004, from http://www.scafo.org/library/100101.html]

Fejfar, A. (1978, May). *Combining techniques to improve security in automated entry control.* Paper presented at Carnahan Conference on Crime Countermeasures, Mitre Corp. MTP-191, University of Kentucky.

Fejfar, A., & Myers, J. W. (1977, July). The testing of three automatic identity verification techniques. In *Proceedings of the International Conference on Crime Countermeasures,* Oxford, UK.

Flom, L., & Safir, A. (1987). Iris recognition system, U.S. Patent 4,641,349.

Galton, F. (1888). On personal identification and description. *Nature, 21/28,* 201–202. [Retrieved July 11, 2004, from http://www.scafo.org/library/100801.html]

Goldstein, A. J., Harmon, L. D., & Lesk, A. B. (1971). Identification of human faces. *Proceedings of the Institute of Electrical and Electronic Engineers, 59,* 748–760.

Herschel, W. J. (1880). Skin furrows of the hand. *Nature, 23,* 76.

IBM. (1970). *The considerations of data security in a computer environment* (Report G520-2169). White Plains, NY: Author.

Kent, S. T., & Millett, L. I. (2003). *Who goes there? Authentication through the lens of privacy.* Washington, DC: National Academies Press. [Retrieved July 11, 2004, from http://books.nap.edu/html/whogoes/]

Locke, J. (1690). *An essay concerning human understanding* (Book 2, Chapter 27). [Retrieved July 11, 2004, from http://www.ilt.columbia.edu/publications/locke_understanding.html]

Lummis, R. C., & Rosenberg, A. (1972). Test of an ASV method with intensively trained professional mimics. *Journal of the Acoustical Society of America, 51,* 131.

Maio, D., Maltoni, D., Wayman, J., & Jain, A. (2002). FVC2000: Fingerprint verification competition. *Transactions on Pattern Analysis and Machine Intelligence, 24,* 402–411.

Mansfield, A. J., Kelly, G., Chandler, D., & Kane, J. (2000). *Biometric product testing final report.* Retrieved

July 11, 2004, from http://www.cesg.gov.uk/site/ast/ biometrics/media/BiometricTestReportpt1.pdf

Mansfield, A. J., & Wayman, J. L. (2002). *Best practices for testing and reporting biometric device performance, issue 2.0.* U.K. Biometrics Working Group. Retrieved July 11, 2004, from http://www. cesg.gov. uk/site/ast/biometrics/media/BestPractice.pdf

Matsumoto, T., Matsumoto, H., Yamada, K., & Hoshino, S. (2002, January). *Impact of artificial 'gummy' fingers on fingerprint systems.* In Proceedings of SPIE, 4677, San Jose, CA.

Messner, W. K., Cleciwa, C. A., Kibbler, G. O. T. H., & Parlee, W. L. (1974). Research and development of personal identify verification systems. In *Proceedings 1974 Carnahan and International Crime Countermeasures Conference,* University of Kentucky, Laxington, KY.

Osborn, S. (1929). *Questioned documents.* Chicago: Nelson-Hall.

National Bureau of Standards. (1977). *Guidelines for evaluation of techniques for automated personal identification.* (Federal Information Processing Standard Publication 48). Washington, DC: Author.

National Institute of Standards and Technology. (2003). *Speaker recognition evaluation.* Retrieved July 11, 2004, from http://www.nist.gov/speech/tests/spk/2003/ index.htm

Philips, P. J., Grother, P., Bone, M., & Blackburn, D. (2002). Facial recognition vendor test 2002. Retrieved July 11, 2004, from http://www.frvt.org/DLs/ FRVT_2002_Evaluation_Report.pdf

Phillips, P. J., Martin, A., Wilson, C. L., & Przybocki, M. (2000). An introduction to evaluating biometric systems. *Computer, 33,* 56–63. Retrieved July 11, 2004, from www.frvt.org/DLs/FERET7.pdf

Potter, R. K., Kopp, G. A., & Green, H. C. (1947). *Visible speech.* New York: van Nostrand Co.

Pruzansky, S. (1963). Pattern-matching procedure for automatic talker recognition. *Journal of the Acoustical Society of America, 26,* 403–406.

Raphael, D. E., & Young, J.R. (1974). *Automated personal identification.* Palo Alto, CA: SRI International.

Rodriguez, J. R., Bouchier, F., & Ruehie, M. (1993). *Performance evaluation of biometric identification devices.* Albuquerque: Sandia National Laboratory Report SAND93-1930.

Seildarz, J. (1998, April 6). [Letter to the editor]. *Philadelphia Inquirer.*

Simon, C., & Goldstein, I. (1935). A new scientific method of identification. *New York State Journal of Medicine, 35,* 901–906.

Thalheim, L., Krissler, J., & Ziegler, P. (2002). Biometric access protection devices and their programs put to the test. *C T Magazine, 11,* 114. Retrieved July 11, 2004, from www.heise.de/ct/english/02/11/114.

Trauring, M. (1963a). On the automatic comparison of finger ridge patterns. *Nature, 197,* 938–940.

Trauring, M. (1963b). Automatic comparison of finger ridge patterns. *Hughes Research Laboratory Report,* 190.

Twain, M. (1893). Pudd'nhead Wilson. In *The Century,* serialized *47(2)–48(2).* New York: The Century Company.

van der Putte, T., & Keuning, J. (2000). Biometrical fingerprint recognition: Don't get your fingers burned. In *IFIP TC8/WG.8., Fourth Working Group Conference on Smart Card Research and Advanced Applications* (pp. 289–303). Retrieved July 11, 2004, from http:// www.keuning.com/biometry/Biometrical_Fingerprint_ Recognition.pdf

Warren, S., & Brandeis, L. (1890). The right of privacy. *Harvard Law Review, 4,* 193. Retrieved July 11, 2004, from www.louisville.edu/library/law/brandeis/privacy. html.

Wayman, J. L. (2000). Evaluation of the INSPASS hand geometry data. In J. L. Wayman (Ed.), *U.S. National Biometric Test Center Collected Works: 1997–2000.* San Jose: San Jose State University.

Wegstein, J. (1970). Automated fingerprint identification. *National Bureau of Standards Technical Note,* Gaithersburg, MD. 538.

Westin, A. (1967). *Privacy and freedom.* Boston: Atheneum.

The Common Criteria

J. McDermott, *Center for High Assurance Computer Systems, Naval Research Laboratory*

INTRODUCTION

The Common Criteria is a framework for comparing the technical security of as-built products. The term *product* is used in a general way, to include any information technology component that might be constructed, not just those that may be for sale. Products are expected to be primarily software but the Common Criteria is not limited to software. By long-established convention, the Common Criteria is referred to as though it were a single document rather than a plural collection of criteria.

The Common Criteria framework (Common Criteria Project Sponsoring Organizations, 2000a, 2000b, 2000c) is used to define a set of criteria for measuring a single product. Different products that satisfy various requirements from the Common Criteria may then be compared against the criteria they have in common. The Common Criteria framework is essentially hierarchical so that it allows ordered comparisons, when used properly. The Common Criteria refers to the process of measuring a specific information technology product as *evaluation* (Common Criteria Project Sponsoring Organizations, 2000d).

The Common Criteria captures the important idea that security is defined in terms of both features and *assurance*. In the Common Criteria, the term *assurance* means the confidence we have that a product's features work as claimed. The best possible features provide little security if their implementation is flawed. Likewise, a high-assurance implementation of the wrong features provides no protection against the actual threats faced by an information technology product. So the requirements defined by the Common Criteria framework contain both *functional* and *assurance* requirements [as shown in Figure 1].

The Common Criteria is focused on measurement of completed products but is not limited to that. The framework also includes criteria for software development processes. The security of a product can only be defined in terms of the as-built product itself, not by the process that was used to build it. On the other hand, as-built quality depends on the process used. For this reason, the development process components of the Common Criteria framework are assurance components associated with higher levels of assurance.

The Common Criteria is useful to many kinds of people. Information technology consumers or procurement officials can use it to choose and describe their security requirements. The Common Criteria can help users decide whether to trust their data to an information technology product. Information technology vendors can use the Common Criteria to communicate the security features and quality of their product. Developers can use the Common Criteria to understand and interpret the security requirements they must satisfy. Evaluators, certifiers, and accreditors can use it to assess the security of an information technology product. (I explain the terms *certifier* and *accreditor* shortly.) Finally, students can use validated sets of Common Criteria requirements to see how security functional and assurance requirements are properly related.

The Common Criteria is not a cookbook for security. It is complex and easily misused. It assumes a firm understanding of general information technology, security features, and assurance techniques. For these reasons, it is best to look at several validated sets of Common Criteria requirements as well as the criteria themselves.

The Common Criteria does not address all issues of security. It has no criteria for physical, operational, or personnel security even though all three of those disciplines have an impact on practical security. It does not explain how technical security evaluations are to be performed but only the necessary relationships between the work products it requires. It does not describe the follow-on use of Common Criteria evaluations in accreditation or certification activities. Even though the Common Criteria is mutually recognized by a number of countries, this recognition is not addressed by the criteria. Finally, the Common Criteria does not explain the administrative, economic, political, or legal context under

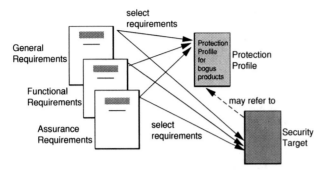

Figure 1: Structure of the Common Criteria.

which it is used. Ross Anderson's (2001) book on security engineering is a good treatment of these and other pertinent nontechnical issues not covered by the Common Criteria

The Common Criteria is a multipart standard that is structured into three volumes:

- Part 1: Introduction and General Model
- Part 2: Security Functional Requirements
- Part 3: Security Assurance Requirements

Part 1 defines the structure and application of the Common Criteria including the rules for building well-formed sets of security comparison criteria; parts 2 and 3 contain the framework of criteria. A well-formed collection of security features and assurance requirements can be either a *Protection Profile* or a *Security Target*, depending on the intended target of the collection.

If you are interested in using the Common Criteria to build an evaluated product, you should first get a copy of one of the Security Targets listed under Further Reading at the end of this chapter. A good one to look at initially is the Security Target for Netscape Certificate Management System 6.1. A Security Target is a kind of document produced using the Common Criteria. Have a brief look at it before continuing.

Essential Terminology

The Common Criteria uses very precise terminology that can seem pedantic but is necessary for some of its applications. Because the sets of criteria defined by the Common Criteria framework may be used in contractual situations, precise language is necessary. Precise language is also needed for the evaluation process, to avoid problems caused by misunderstandings between the developers and the evaluators. Finally, it is also needed for fair comparison of different products.

Before we go any further, it is best to look at some of this terminology. The following terms are the most basic definitions used in the Common Criteria:

Target of Evaluation: More frequently seen as the abbreviation TOE. The product to be evaluated. This includes all developer and user documentation as well as the actual product. The notion of TOE is for a very specific instance of a product, as in Linux Kernel 2.4. 21-9.0.1.EL rather than just *Linux*. This is because

small changes to a product can introduce significant new security vulnerabilities.

Protection Profile: Frequently seen as the abbreviation PP. A product-independent set of security criteria for a class of products. A (fictitious) example might be the high-assurance firewall protection profile. A Protection Profile is a document derived from the Common Criteria.

Security Target: Frequently seen as the abbreviation ST. A document that includes a product-specific set of security criteria. Security targets include a specification of a TOE and describe the assurance measures that were actually applied to it. Security targets also include an abbreviated assurance argument that explains why the specified security features and applied assurance measures satisfy the criteria. A security target for a TOE that falls into a general class of products, for example, high-assurance firewalls, may refer to the applicable PP. A security target may be written without an associated PP, if the TOE is a one-of-a-kind product. A security target is a document derived from the Common Criteria.

TOE Security Functions: Most frequently seen abbreviated as TSF. The collection of all the software, hardware, and firmware that must be relied on for the correct enforcement of the TOE security policy.

TOE Security Policy: Frequently seen abbreviated as TSP. The set of rules that define how resources or assets are managed and protected by the TOE.

TSF Scope of Control: Most frequently seen abbreviated as TSC. The set of all interactions (both allowed and illegal) that can with a TOE. These interactions are constrained by the rules of the TSP.

Evaluation: The assessment of a TOE, a protection profile, or a security target, against criteria chosen from the Common Criteria framework.

Evaluation Authority: An oversight body that applies the Common Criteria for a specific community. An evaluation authority usually does not conduct actual evaluations but sets standards, provides interpretations, and oversees the quality and consistency of evaluations. The rules and procedures used by an evaluation authority are referred to as an evaluation scheme.

Evaluation Scheme: The regulatory and administrative framework used by an evaluation authority to implement the Common Criteria.

History

The Common Criteria grew out of work on similar national standards for several North American and European countries. It is an international standard, ISO (International Standards Organization) 15408, developed by a group of agencies known as the Common Criteria Project Sponsoring Organizations.

The USA's Trusted Computer System Evaluation Criteria (TCSEC or Orange Book) was the first initiative for standardized security evaluation of information technology products that led to the Common Criteria. It was published in 1985 by the NSA. In 1991, the European Commission published the Information Technology

Security Evaluation Criteria (ITSEC) as the outcome of a joint project involving the United Kingdom, Germany, France, and the Netherlands. In 1993, Canada published the Canadian Trusted Computer Product Evaluation Criteria (CTCPEC), which combined the TCSEC and ITSEC schemes. At the same time, a draft Federal Criteria for Information Technology Security (FC) was developed in the United States. In 1993, the sponsors of the CTCPEC, FC, TCSEC, and ITSEC began a joint project, the Common Criteria Project, that ultimately lead to the ISO standard.

National Schemes

Eight countries are now part of the Common Criteria Recognition Agreement (CCRA) that supports mutual recognition of Common Criteria evaluation results under each country's evaluation scheme. This mutual recognition increases the number of evaluated security products available to each country and increases the uniformity of evaluations across national boundaries. Member countries share evaluation knowledge and work together to improve the evaluation process and the quality of the results. Other countries that do not have their own evaluation schemes have agreed to recognize CCRA evaluation results. This increases the size of the potential market for vendors who build information technology to the Common Criteria standard.

At the time of this writing, CCRA mutual recognition applies to evaluations at EAL 4 and below. Higher EAL evaluations are not mutually recognized because they are used for national security systems, and it is not clear that evaluation results would be shared for such products. Table 1 lists the members of the CCRA that have their own schemes.

STRUCTURE

The organization of the Common Criteria is related to the *hierarchical definition of security* as shown in Figure 2. Security in an information system is a complex property that depends on the usage of the system and the assets it handles and the specific protection its users expect. The protection users should expect depends on the threats present in the system's environment. Although the full

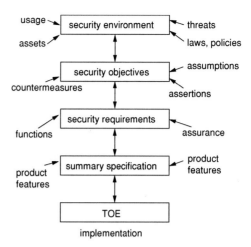

Figure 2: Hierarchical definition of security.

range of threats includes a variety of problems, security emphasizes (primarily malicious) human-sponsored actions. These human actions cause damage or loss to the assets. From a computer science perspective, damage may be characterized as loss of confidentiality, loss of integrity, or loss of availability. The loss of availability refers primarily to features of the information system itself that may be destroyed or disabled. Risk is a measure of the degree of exposure to loss; generally it is a product of likelihood and asset value. For example, a threat with high likelihood presents high risk to assets of almost any value. On the other hand, low likelihood threats can still present a significant risk, if the value of the assets is sufficiently high. The Common Criteria framework supports the specification of countermeasures to specific threats, coupled with a level of confidence that the countermeasures reduce the risk by an acceptable amount, hence the need for assurance requirements in the third part of the criteria.

Information technology products and systems are also subject to laws and regulations established by governments, for example, regulations concerning medical information. These laws or regulations may require the presence of specific countermeasures or the enforcement of specific security policies.

Table 1 Mutual Recognition of Evaluation Schemes of the Common Criteria Recognition Agreement (CCRA)

CCRA Scheme	Country
Australian Information Security Evaluation Program (AISEP) Defense Signals Directorate	Australia
Communications Security Establishment	Canada
Bundesamt für Sicherheit in der Informationstechnik	Germany
Service Central de la Sécurité des Systèmes d'Information	France
Japan Information Technology Security Evaluation and Certification Scheme (JISEC)	Japan
Government Communications Security Bureau	New Zealand
Communications-Electronics Security Group and Department of Trade and Industry	United Kingdom
National Information Assurance Partnership (NIAP) Common Criteria Evaluation and Validation Scheme (CCEVS)	United States of America

In either case, the Common Criteria framework requires an explicit discussion and analysis of the usage, assets, threats, and security policies that define the *security environment* of an information technology product. A description and analysis of the security environment is required for either protection profiles or security targets.

A security environment forms the top level of a hierarchical definition of security. Below this level, the Common Criteria requires the notion of *security objectives*. The Common Criteria uses the term *security objectives* to mean the most abstract security requirements for a product or system. These abstract requirements are derived from the stated security environment. The security objectives identify the countermeasures needed to address the threats, risk, and assets identified in the security environment. A critical part of the security objectives is the separation of abstract requirements into *assertions* (called security objectives for the TOE) and *assumptions* (called security objectives for the environment). Some countermeasures to threats are based on procedures and practices carried out in the environment of an information technology product. The product itself is not expected to provide these countermeasures. Other countermeasures are technical mechanisms that the information technology product provides to mitigate or reduce risk. The statement of security objectives should contain an argument that the abstract security requirements cover all of the threats from the security environment, in an appropriate manner. Explicit definition and analysis of security objectives is required for any well-formed set of Common Criteria requirements.

The Common Criteria security requirements form the next level of the hierarchy. These requirements are taken from the criteria, following a set of rules for constructing well-formed protection profiles or security targets. These functional and assurance requirements are shown to be a refinement of the security objectives.

The next level in the hierarchical definition of security is called the TOE Summary Specification. The TOE Summary Specification is an abstract description of the TOE itself (i.e., the interface of the product or system itself). The concrete TOE proper is the lowest level of the hierarchical definition of security. The logic of this hierarchical definition is that the final product provides the right kind of security, in the environment described in the applicable protection profile or security target.

Nothing in this definition implies a particular process or life-cycle model. (At the highest assurance levels, the chosen process or life-cycle model must be documented and the chosen model must have some community acceptance.) The relationship between levels is one of forward design refinement and backward correspondence analysis. This hierarchical relationship is continued in the assurance requirements, as discussed shortly.

The three parts of the criteria define a modular framework for constructing well-formed sets of security requirements, as either protection profiles or security targets. The first part, *Introduction and General Model*, defines the framework and gives rules for constructing well-formed sets of requirements. The two parts *Security Functional Requirements* and *Security Assurance Requirements* contain the functional and assurance requirements, respectively.

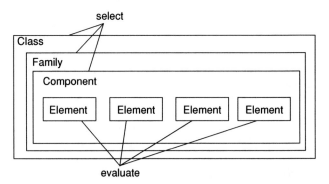

Figure 3: Organization of Common Criteria requirements.

The requirements in Parts 2 and 3 are organized into *classes*, which contain *families*, which contain *components*, as shown in Figure 3. A component is the smallest unit of security requirement selection. Components are broken down into *elements*. Elements are the smallest unit of security requirement evaluation.

A well-formed set of security requirements may be selected from the classes of Parts 2 and 3 by applying four operations: *iteration, assignment, selection, refinement*. Iteration allows a component to be used more than once; assignment allows specification of values for component parameters (e.g., allowable covert channel capacity); selection allows choice from a list inside a component, to narrow the scope of an element; refinement is the process of adding details to a component, to restrict the allowable implementations. Refinements may not extend the scope of requirements or alter the dependencies that one requirement may place on another. The Common Criteria requirements include specific dependencies between requirements when components are not self-sufficient. These dependencies must be included in any well-formed set of security requirements.

EVALUATIONS, CERTIFICATIONS, AND ACCREDITATIONS

In the Common Criteria and in documents associated with it, you will encounter the terms *evaluation, certification,* and *accreditation*. The term evaluation is usually applied in only one way and its meaning is clear, as given earlier. (Recall that protection profiles and security targets must be evaluated.) The other two terms may be used in more than one way, and it is worthwhile to understand each usage.

The system, hardware, and software engineering activities of measuring an information technology product are referred to as evaluation, certification, or accreditation depending on the purpose of the activity. Evaluation looks at a single information technology product, with respect to its Security Target, and confirms that the product meets both the security and assurance requirements in the Security Target.

If several products are to be integrated into a single larger system, then another measurement of security and assurance requirements should be performed. Although the Common Criteria uses the term *certification* to refer to the validation of the results of an evaluation, I also use the term to refer to the measurement of an integrated collection of information technology products. The context will make it clear which kind of certification is meant. Notice that this second kind of measurement may be required when only one of the products to be integrated has security features. The presence or application of the other products may influence the security of the overall system. Common Criteria documents may use the term accreditation to mean either an official decision to operate a system with sensitive production data or it may use it to mean the vetting of an evaluation vendor to perform Common Criteria evaluations under a certain evaluation scheme. Accreditation in the first sense uses the evidence produced during the evaluation or certification (for integration of security products) activities.

Evaluations

The Common Criteria contains both *evaluator notes*, in Part 2, and *evaluator actions*, in Part 3. The evaluator notes serve as commentary on specific security requirements. Evaluator notes are used to provide clarifications, interpretation guidance, and warnings to evaluators. Evaluator actions cover two kinds of evaluation: validation of a PP/ST and verification that a TOE satisfies its PP/ST. Evaluator actions explain specific steps to be taken by evaluators to validate or verify. For example, the term *confirm* is used to indicate to the evaluator that he or she needs to review someone else's work in detail and independently assess the sufficiency of that work. In contrast, the term *determine* is used to refer to independent analysis in contrast to review of a developers work. There are many other such terms defined in Section 2.4 of Part 3 of the Common Criteria.

The success of an evaluation depends on the general independence of the evaluator from the developer. Conflicts of interest can arise in many ways. One form of conflict that is difficult to avoid is financial. Someone must pay for each evaluation, but then the one who pays usually has an expectation of success. So evaluations that are paid for directly by the developer are less credible than evaluations by an independent-funded organization. Also, it is best if the organizations that perform evaluations do not sell or build security products. This creates a tension because the evaluators themselves should be persons who have significant experience in building information technology products with security. In fact it is preferable that at least one member of the evaluation team have some experience in building a similar product or at least a product that involves similar construction technology. Evaluators also need to understand general independent verification and validation concepts, project management, and analytical thinking, as well as mathematics, computer science and engineering. Maintaining skilled evaluation teams is difficult because the personnel with the necessary skills and qualifications can become burned out very quickly. The first or second evaluation such a person performs is interesting and challenging, but the appeal begins to fade rapidly after that. This suggests that the best strategy is to have the evaluation be a short-term responsibility, with rotation to other forms of work after two or three years.

Evaluation results are stated as pass/fail. For a protection profile or a security target, the results mean that the set of requirements is complete, consistent, and technically sound. If a protection profile passes its evaluation by the relevant evaluation scheme authority, it is usually entered into a registry for that authority. When a TOE is evaluated, the results mean that the evidence supplied with the TOE gives the specified level of confidence that the TOE meets its security requirements. A TOE evaluation results also explains what set of security requirements it met, as either *conformant* or *extended*. Conformant means that the TOE met the associated requirements and extended means that the TOE met the associated requirement and other requirements not in the Common Criteria or the relevant protection profile or security target. A result of extended can be misleading because it only requires a small difference to qualify as extended.

Certifications

The Common Criteria provides little guidance on certification, for either sense of the word. The Common Criteria uses certification as a means of increasing the uniformity of evaluation. Because evaluation is a technical assessment based on specialist expertise, the results are somewhat subjective. If each assessment is validated by a common authority, the likelihood of individual bias is reduced.

For certification as validation of evaluation results, the chief difficulty is dealing with interpretations of the requirements. An evaluation of a product may raise a question about the application or meaning of a Common Criteria requirement. The question may be raised by the product developer or by the evaluation team. The resolution of the question may be applicable only to the evaluation where the question was raised. This can be handled by the evaluation scheme authorities. It may be necessary to incorporate the interpretation into the Common Criteria, however. This is done by consultation with members of the Common Criteria Recognition Agreement, and a final decision is made by the Common Criteria Interpretations Management Board.

When the term certification is used to mean evaluation of an integrated collection of information technology products that have each been evaluated separately, there are two issues:

1. Integrated systems are usually built under a contract that is not how products are built
2. The process of evaluating an integrated system is less understood.

When the context of integrated system construction includes contracts, those contracts can help or hinder application of the Common Criteria. It is difficult to meet contract schedules when the certification (evaluation) process is not part of the contract. On the other hand, it is difficult to believe a certification (evaluation) that is paid for by the contract performer. A further complication is the approach to certifying a system that integrates several evaluated products or subsystems. If the complete results of evaluation are available for each product, the approach to integrating the products would seem to trivial. If, however, the assumptions about the threats and usage of a product in the integrated system differ from those made for its evaluation as a product, then certification can be problematic. It may be necessary to repeat the entire process for each product. A further complication can arise if the evaluation results for a product are not made public and are thus not available for the certification effort. This is particularly difficult when a flaw is discovered in a product but not reported as part of the evaluation results. Because the Common Criteria results are essentially pass/fail against a stated protection profile or security target, it is possible for an evaluation authority to withhold this information and still comply with the Common Criteria.

Accreditations

Assuming no problems with the individual product evaluations or system certification (evaluations) the process of accreditation can be quite straightforward. The essential challenge is to understand the risk that entails from actual use of the product. The key to understanding this is to analyze the differences between the various security environments and security objectives from the protection profiles and security targets that apply. If the risk is too great because of differences in threat levels or characteristics then the accreditation authority must identify measures to reduce the remaining risk. A less obvious source of excessive risk is a difference in asset value from that assumed by a product's protection profile. If the assets in the deployed system have significantly more value than the product's evaluators assumed then the risk may be too high, even though the threats and usage match. An example of this would be using a product to protect national security information when it had not been designed with this in mind.

PROTECTION PROFILES

The most frequently seen collection of Common Criteria requirements is the protection profile. A protection profile defines an implementation-independent set of security requirements, both functional and assurance. It is used when there is a class of similar information technology products or systems produced by different vendors. The difference between a protection profile and a security target is that the latter includes a description of a specific product but the former does not. Security targets that claim *conformance* to protection profile do not repeat the security requirements but include them by reference to the protection profile.

A protection profile can be written by either a producer of information technology or by a consumer. In the latter case, the consumer writes the protection profile and then seeks developers who will try to meet it. Instead of writing a profile, a consumer may search for an existing profile that meets its needs. Because the existing protection profile may already have been certified and entered into an evaluation scheme's registry, the consumer can reduce risk as well as save time and money.

Construction of protection profile can be a delicate matter. It is clear from both plain reason and the Common Criteria's own requirements for protection profile evaluation that the resulting document must be complete, consistent, and technically sound. An important aspect of this not found in other technical documents is *balance*. As the beginning of this chapter pointed out, the Common Criteria framework defines security in terms of both function and assurance. This is where balance is needed. Not only must the functional and assurance requirements of the protection profile be matched to the security objectives but also the assurance requirements must be balanced with the functional requirements. Special security expertise is required to ensure this.

Some security mechanisms or functions are intrinsically weak, no matter how flawless their implementation. An example that is easy to see is encryption for confidentiality with a small key, say, 16 bits. For assurance of this hypothetical security function, we could formally analyze the cryptographic protocols that use this key and expend significant engineering effort in construction of flawless software to implement the verified protocols. This level of assurance would be unbalanced and excessive because the key is too small; the cryptosystem can be broken with brute force methods no matter what the assurance. The most frequently seen imbalance lies the other way. A strong security mechanism or function is chosen, but the assurance requirements are set too low. If a product is to provide strong security protections for high-value assets in a high-threat environment, then the level of assurance used to build it must correspond. Choice of a correct assurance level is not just a technical matter but depends on the value of the resources presumed and the threats defined for the product.

The impact of unbalance on a protection profile can be serious. If the assurance requirements are too strong, no vendors will develop products to match the profile. On the other hand, if the protection profile is unbalanced because of weak assurance requirements, then many vendors could supply inadequate products that fail in actual use. Consumers will be mislead in to expecting sufficient protection when it is not there.

The best approach to constructing a complete, consistent, technically sound but also balanced protection profile is to follow the Common Criteria's hierarchical definition of security. Begin with an analysis of the intended use, planned asset characteristics and values, and the applicable laws or regulations the protection profile will support. Follow this with an analysis of the threats to be countered by the product. Threat analysis requires specialist security expertise corresponding to the anticipated asset values; that is, high-asset values require more experience in defining the threats. (Security expertise is primarily knowledge of threats and the effectiveness of possible countermeasures.)

Once the security environment for the protection profile has been defined, we should move on to analysis of the security objectives. The security objectives analysis matches countermeasures to threats based on a division of responsibility between the product (assumptions) and its environment (assumptions). Trade-offs can be made between countermeasures, assumptions, and assertions. Specialist security expertise is needed in both the analysis and trade-off studies.

The third step in the process is composing a set of functional and assurance requirements from the Common Criteria. The selected functions and assurance measures must be mapped back to the security objectives. The completed protection profile must also supply a rationale for its choice of requirements. This rationale captures all of the analysis that led to the requirements and justifies them against the security objectives and environment. The rationale is a defense of the completeness, technical soundness, and balance of the protection profile.

Writing a good rationale can be difficult. There is a tendency to reduce it to a tabular mapping or listing of requirements because this is a necessary part of the rationale. However, the rationale as whole must constitute a valid argument for the protection profile's completeness, technical soundness, and balance. Some validated protection profiles have indifferent rationales in this respect, so they do not serve as good examples. Rationales for protection profiles with higher evaluation assurance levels tend to have better rationales and are thus more likely to be good examples.

We can compensate for lack of specialist security expertise during protection profile construction by using an extremely precise fine-grained model of the intruder. Intruder models should define both the initial knowledge of an intruder and the intruder's capabilities. Persons with appropriate general backgrounds in mathematics, computer science, and computer engineering can approximate security specialist expertise by looking at the implications of this intruder model.

It is also possible to construct protection profiles by survey and analysis of a collection of existing security products to summarize their functions and assurance measures. In some sense, this also compensates for a lack of security specialist expertise but does not remove the need for it. Expertise is needed in choosing the products or systems to be included in the collection. Expertise is also needed in analyzing the shortfalls or weaknesses of the particular products. On the other hand, if a set union approach is taken to constructing a protection profile by analysis and summary of existing products (i.e., take the sum of all functions and all assurance measures), then there is a risk that the result will be too difficult to satisfy.

SECURITY TARGETS

Protection profiles are the most important sets of criteria defined by the Common Criteria framework because most information technology products are members of a family of similar products. Nevertheless, all Common Criteria evaluations are performed against a security target not a protection profile. The security target forms the basis for TOE evaluation, for each product. It may be thought of as an instantiation of a protection profile.

Security targets must contain everything that appears in a protection profile and more. The additional contents are

- Common Criteria conformance claim
- Qualification of uncompleted protection profile requirements operations

- Summary specification of the TOE
- Statement of assurance measures
- Protection profile conformance claims

The Common Criteria conformance claim is simply an evaluable statement of the specific version of the Common Criteria that applies to the security target and whether the evaluation results are supposed to be "conformant" or "extended." It is a necessary part of establishing the context for the actual security evaluation.

The security target may also claim conformance to a protection profile as the source of its requirements specifications. If the protection profile states all of its requirements in complete form, the security target need not restate those requirements. However, some protection profile requirements may be unfinished, with some parts to be filled in for specific products. In Common Criteria terminology, the requirements operations are not completed. In this case, the security target will complete those requirements. In other instances, the security target will contain refinements of protection profile requirements. In all three cases—no change, completion, or refinement—there must be an explicit claim of protection profile conformance. Any differences or additions must be pointed out and justified in a protection profile claims rationale.

The two most significant differences between a security target and a protection profile are the *summary specification* and the *statement* of *assurance measures*. The summary specification for the TOE is just that, an abstract description of the product features. The summary specification is used to demonstrate how the product (TOE) meets its claimed functional security requirements of the security target. The statement of assurance measures is a summary of the specific tools, techniques, and procedures used to meet the claimed assurance requirements of the security target. The statement of assurance measures is used to demonstrate how the assurance measures will be applied to the development of the TOE. Both the summary specification and the statement of assurance measures are justified and mapped to the security target requirements by a separate rationale. This rationale is critically important.

First of all, the evaluators will study this rationale statement to decide whether the TOE is a suitable candidate for evaluation. Evaluation is a labor intensive process that requires security (and evaluation) specialist expertise, expertise that is currently in short supply. For this reason, evaluation organizations must be careful not to commit time and expertise to an evaluation that is not likely to succeed. To accomplish this, the Common Criteria provides a rationale for the summary specification and the statement of assurance measures. A complete, consistent, technically sound, and balanced security target will represent a product that has a good chance of passing its evaluation.

A second reason this rationale can be important is that it serves as a description of the product's features and quality. In this role, the rationale gives the prospective user or consumer of the information technology product a detailed explanation of the product's benefits.

Some information technology products are evaluated under the Common Criteria without a protection profile. If a product or subsystem is unique and there is little chance of it leading to a class or family of products, there is no benefit from an implementation-independent set of criteria. For these products, a security target is constructed directly from the criteria. Constructing a security target directly from the Common Criteria is the same as constructing a protection profile except that there is no need to provide for a general class of products.

It is also possible to use a Common Criteria security target structure as a (security) development plan for a product or system. The security target provides organization of requirements and relationships between work products in a convenient form. When a security target is used this way, it is constructed as a guide to developers, to show what work products are needed and how they relate. Use of a security target in this way does not require use of a particular life-cycle model or approach. Furthermore, using a security target as a development plan does not imply that the developers intend to have the resulting product evaluated.

SECURITY FUNCTIONAL REQUIREMENTS

Part 2 of the Common Criteria contains the collection of security features that a protection profile or security target developer chooses from to create a well-formed set of security requirements. The 11 classes of functional security requirements are listed in Table 2.

The functional requirements of the Common Criteria are subject to revision although not frequently. New technology introduces new security requirements. Research, development, and experience improve security for existing technology. Researchers and security experts propose, analyze, and discuss possible additions or interpretations. An example of this process is the privacy functional requirements (FPR) that were not part of earlier versions of the Common Criteria but were added after various groups pointed out the growing need for these kinds of features in some information technology products. Now I briefly summarize each of the 11 classes of functional security requirements that a protection profile or security target from which designer can choose.

Class FAU: Security Audit—This class contains six families of requirements. Each family of the class defines requirements for auditing security-relevant events. Two (FAU-SAA and FAU-ARP) are concerned with recognizing and responding to events; two (FAU-GEN and FAU-SEL) are concerned with recognizing events; one (FAU-STG) is about storing and protecting event data; and one (FAU-SAR) is about review and analysis of events.

Class FCO: Communication—The two families of this class (FCO-NRO and FCO-NRR) are concerned with proof of origin or receipt, respectively, of transmitted data.

Class FCS: Cryptographic Support—The two families of this class (FCS-CKM and FCS-COP) provide requirements for cryptographic key management and cryptographic operation, respectively.

Table 2 Security Functional Requirement Classes of Part 2 of the Common Criteria

Class	Identifier	Scope
Security audit	FAU	Capture, storage, and analysis of security events
Communications	FCO	Confirming identities during data exchange
Cryptographic support	FCS	Key management and cryptographic operations
User data protection	FDP	Access control, information flow, integrity, import–export, and recovery
Identification and authentication	FIA	Verifying user identity, authorization, association
Security management	FMT	Management of security data, roles, and attributes
Privacy	FPR	Anonymity, pseudonymity, unlinkability, and unobservability
Protection of the TSF	FPT	Self-protection requirements
Resource utilization	FRU	Denial of service, quality of service, and fault tolerance
TOE access	FTA	Session management
trusted path	FTP	Trusted communication between human users and the TOE

Class FDP: User Data Protection—This large class contains the Common Criteria requirements for protecting end user resources, the ultimate reason for providing security. It includes families of requirements for security policies, user data protection mechanisms, import and export of user data, and transfer of data between the TOE and other security products.

Class FIA: Identification and Authentication—This class provides requirements for identifying authorized users and assigning them the correct identity, group, role, session, or set of security privileges associated with their user identity. It includes requirements for dealing with authentication failures and handling secrets associated with authentication and identification.

Class FMT: Security Management—This class provides a collection of incomplete (i.e., the requirements must be completed by assignment, selection, or refinement). All of the requirements cover security management, so there are requirements for protecting and restricting management functions, assigning and revoking privileges or security attributes, and defining security management roles for the TOE.

Class FPR: Privacy—This class provides a means for selecting anonymity, pseudonymity, unlinkability, or unobservability. By proper selection and refinement of these requirements a protection profile designer can specify protection against a wide range of identity misuse.

Class FPT: Protection of the TSF—This class specifies self-protection requirements for the TSF of the TOE; that is, requirements that the product protect its security functions from tampering and bypass. The families in this class form a list of generic ways of tampering with or bypassing a security mechanism. They include confidentiality, integrity, and availability of TSF data that has left the TOE scope of control; fail safe and trusted recovery; safe internal movement of TSF data; resistance to physical tampering; replay detection; and consistency of distributed TSF components.

Class FRU: Resource Utilization—Requirements from this class can be used to specify fault tolerance, quality of service, or resource management functions for a TOE.

Class FTA: TOE Access—This class specifies a set of session management requirements. Each interaction of a user with the TOE constitutes a session. The user is identified and authenticated, negotiates any selectable security attributes for the session, and does some work using the TOE. When the session is terminated, the user is no longer able to use the resources that were available. Specific requirements include limitations on concurrent sessions, initiating a session, session locking, session history, user-visible session labels or banners.

Class FTP: Trusted Path—Trusted path requirements are available for specifying trusted path or trusted channel functions in the TOE. These functions are used to protect human users from spoofing attacks that present a deceptive interface to the user. A trusted path provides a means for a human user to confirm that he or she is communicating with the TSF and not some masquerading unauthorized process.

A reader wanting deeper understanding of the functional security requirements should consult Part 2 of the Common Criteria.

ASSURANCE REQUIREMENTS

The assurance requirements in Part 3 are perhaps the least understood aspect of the Common Criteria. The seven classes of security assurance requirements are listed in Table 3. It is clear that security-relevant product functions should be developed carefully to avoid the introduction of security flaws, thus the popularity of books on "secure programming." What is less clear is the relationship between various system or software development activities on one hand and assurance per se on the other. Some activities advance the design and implementation of the developing product but do not significantly increase the assurance we have in the information technology product's security. In fact, many software practitioners, researchers, and others do not have a clear understanding of assurance. This is reflected in the fact that the U.S. government has adopted the term *information assurance* to mean "measures that protect and defend information and information systems" (Committee on National Security Systems, 2003) that is, security functions. Many have confused the notion of security functions with assurance.

It is important to understand the issue of balance between assurance and the strength of the security mechanisms used in the TOE. Some security weaknesses are inherent in the mechanism itself. For example, so-called discretionary access controls on resources that can be set by the user or owner of a resource are weaker than mandatory access controls that cannot be set by the user or owner. No matter how flawlessly they function, discretionary access controls can be turned off or otherwise changed by malicious software, even though the controls themselves are not compromised. Because of this, the highest assurance levels do not balance with discretionary access controls. For the same reason, higher assurance levels do not balance with weak cryptographic protocols. For example, at the time of this writing, the wired equivalent privacy (WEP) protocol had been shown to contain fundamental flaws. No matter how well this protocol could be implemented in hardware or software, it would still be vulnerable because of its design flaws. So higher assurance would not balance with a product that used the WEP protocol.

CLASS ACM: CONFIGURATION MANAGEMENT

This class of assurance requirements describes how to monitor and track changes, including refinement, made to the various work products. Full use of all of these requirements would also ensure the integrity of the TOE and increase our confidence that we can trace each implementation artifact back to a function security requirement. This tracing not only improves attempts to simplify and minimize the implementation but also helps prevent the introduction of malicious code. Without effective configuration management, the tracing is not believable.

Requirements in this class include not only automated configuration management but also plans and procedures for using the configuration management tools. The required automation includes protecting the work products and implementation from unauthorized modification, deletion, or addition of components or evidence.

CLASS ADO: DELIVERY AND OPERATION

Assurance requirements for distribution of the TOE describe the measures that must be taken to protect it during distribution. The specific protection that must be provided is for the threats described in the security environment of the applicable security target or protection profile. These protections might include detecting bogus copies of a TOE; preventing substitution of the wrong version of a TOE; and preventing an end user from replicating the distribution service. The protections not only address delivery or distribution of a TOE but also include

Table 3 Security Assurance Requirement Classes of Part 3 of the Common Criteria

Class	Identifier	Scope
Configuration management	ACM	Procedures and tools for tracking changes to work products
Delivery and operation	ADO	Measures for protecting the distribution of a product
Development	ADV	Defines requirements for system and software engineering work products needed for assurance
Guidance documents	ADG	Administrator and user guidance
Life-cycle support	ALC	Requirements for securing the development process itself and for suitable development processes
Testing	ATE	Demonstration of functional requirements
Vulnerability assessment	ADV	Independent adversarial analysis and testing

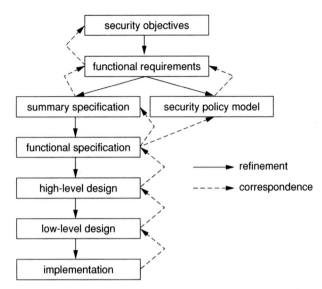

Figure 4: Target of evaluation representations from class ADV.

mechanisms or procedures to protect the installation, generation, and startup of a TOE once it has been distributed.

CLASS ADV: DEVELOPMENT

This class comprises the requirements targeted at the work products needed for high-assurance software. It requires a collection of descriptions or specifications of the TOE that provide different levels of abstraction. A mapping from the more abstract to the less abstract description is required to show correspondence, demonstrate the absence of malicious code, and justify the residual complexity of the implementation. This mapping must be produced for each pair of required specification documents, using the same degree of rigor as the target specifications. Figure 4 shows the full set of required TOE representations. (These documents may be thought of as a fine-grained refinement of the hierarchical definition of security shown in Figure 2, inserted between the summary specification and the TOE.)

This class includes requirements for modularity, explicitly justified simplicity, and high-level architecture beyond modularity. The more rigorous requirements call for the TOE software modules to contain only security-relevant code, with an explanation of why the code in

each module is security-relevant. The most rigorous requirements also specify that the TOE software must be organized into layered abstract virtual machines, such that each abstract machine can be evaluated separately.

The more rigorous requirements call for the use of formal methods for the more abstract specifications. Levels of assurance are increased by requiring formal methods for the less-abstract descriptions.

The explicit abstraction and refinement required by this class may be misunderstood to call for a particular development approach, such as the much-maligned waterfall model. That would be a misunderstanding; what is required is a final set of documents and an explicitly justified refinement from the abstract to the concrete. The author asked the builders of one of the highest assurance software products that has ever been built what life cycle model they used. "Crazed rat," was the reply. Nevertheless, the work products associated with the product had essentially flawless justified refinement from the abstract models to the concrete concrete code.

The existence of the ALC life-cycle support assurance requirements indicates the importance of development processes in the Common Criteria model, but no particular life-cycle model is required. The choice of development approach can be critical to the final security of a product, so it should be addressed in higher-assurance protection profiles and security targets. Which development approach should be chosen is outside the scope of the Common Criteria. The chapter "Software Development and Quality Assurance" should provide more information on development approaches for security.

CLASS ADG: GUIDANCE DOCUMENTS

The ADG requirements specify the documentation that should be provided for the security administration of the TOE. Not only should this guidance cover installation, configuration, and management but also the meaning of all warnings, reports, or exceptional operating states. The administrator guidance should also describe appropriate or recommended management actions to be taken in response to each security-relevant event.

The ADG requirements also call for user documentation that explains any nonadministrative interfaces for the TOE. This might include programming as well as user-supplied security settings. In particular, the user guidance should clarify the kind of protection supplied and what assumptions must be satisfied by the users for the TOE to provide the expected protection. An indication of the importance of this is built into the Common Criteria. During an evaluation, vulnerability assessment required by class AVA will check both user and administrative guidance to see if any inconsistencies or ambiguities can be exploited to defeat the security of the product.

The brevity of this section can be misleading. Human factors and usability are vital to security. Few products can provide security if they are misused; on the other hand, if the product is difficult to operate, then users may put their high-value assets and resources into a system that is not secure but easy to operate.

CLASS ALC: LIFE-CYCLE SUPPORT

This assurance requirements class calls out the measures that should be used to provide security for development work products, bug fixes and flaw removal, and tool support for the development process. The most rigorous assurance requires that development work products must not only be managed but also protected from tampering or the insertion of malicious code. Development security must address operational and physical security measures coordinated with the protection features of the configuration management tools. Flaw removal requires procedures for fixing vulnerabilities discovered after product release. It also requires that user or administrator guidance explain how to report vulnerabilities and how to receive vulnerability reports. Procedures for checking the proposed fix must also be in place along with a method of distributing the corrected software. This class also sets out requirements for programming languages, development tools, use of generally accepted notations and consistency in use of these tools and techniques. Requirements for libraries and third-party software are also defined.

Finally, at the highest degree of rigor, class ALC contains requirements for use of life-cycle models. Not only must the development follow an explicitly defined process, as for lower degrees of rigor, but also it must use a generally accepted process or life-cycle model. This highest degree of rigor also requires the use of metrics to establish the quality of the work products produced by the process.

CLASS ATE: TESTING

The goal of the testing required by this class is demonstration that the TOE meets its functional security requirements. It include both confirmation of correct function and checks for undesirable behavior that violates the requirements. It does not include penetration testing or related activities, as described in the next subsection, AVA Vulnerability Assessment.

This class separates requirements for *test coverage* and *test depth*. Test coverage has the usual meaning and includes requirements for analysis of coverage, to varying degrees of rigor. The term test depth is used to refer to the use of the various TOE representations as a basis for the test cases. Shallow testing uses only the most abstract TOE representations, such as the functional requirements or the summary specification, as the basis. The deepest testing will include the abstract representations and all the refinements, including the implementation representation.

Class ATE also provides for independent (evaluator) testing. The evaluators will design and conduct their own functional tests under these assurance requirements. The evaluators will also repeat some or all of the developer's functional testing, depending on the specified level of assurance.

CLASS AVA: VULNERABILITY ASSESSMENT

Like the development requirements, vulnerability assessment requirements are also poorly understood. Vulnerability assessment is based on an adversarial analysis of the TOE and its requirements. This adversarial analysis seeks to locate vulnerabilities in the TOE that could be exploited to violate the security policy. It provides some measure of understanding about the residual risk of insider attacks on the TOE.

The vulnerability assessment class is organized into four families

- Covert channel analysis
- Misuse
- Strength of function
- Vulnerability analysis

Covert channels are unwanted artifacts in the TOE implementation that can be exploited, usually by malicious software, to signal information contrary to the security policy of the TOE. Covert channel analysis is covered by the chapter "Information Leakage" of this *Handbook*. Covert channel analysis requirements of increasing rigor are defined in terms of the approach used and the basis for the analysis. The most rigorous requirement is for analysis that is justified as exhaustive and is based on complete detailed specifications.

The term misuse is interpreted to mean accidental misuse of the TOE due to problems with its usability, or with the guidance documents provided according to class ADG. In higher levels of this family, the developer is required to conduct human factors analysis of the guidance documentation (and, by implication, the interfaces used by humans) to discover and remove inconsistencies or other failings such as omission of a warning or unreasonable expectation. At the highest level of assurance, the evaluators independently try to misuse the TOE and put it into an insecure state or operating mode.

Class AVA also includes requirements for assessing the strength of proposed security mechanisms. Conventionally, strength of function is only applied to mechanisms that depend on stochastic properties, such as passwords and encryption. Strength of function is also an issue for other security mechanisms, however, such as access control, virtual machine monitors, and integrity lock architectures. Protection profile writers have been careful to avoid strength of function for these latter, more problematic mechanisms.

Finally, the Common Criteria uses the term vulnerability analysis to refer to what is more commonly called *penetration testing*. The term *vulnerability analysis* is probably a better term; the best penetration testing does not involve much testing per se. The small amount of testing that is done is directed toward showing the impact of a vulnerability discovered through analysis. The lowest level of assurance is that the developer will perform a vulnerability analysis. Higher levels require independent and systematic vulnerability analysis and independent penetration testing to confirm the developer's results. The highest levels of assurance require that the TOE be found to have a certain level of resistance to penetration.

EVALUATION ASSURANCE LEVELS

Because assurance is less well understood, the Common Criteria provides seven predefined Evaluation Assurance Levels (EALs). An EAL is a predefined collection of assurance requirements that is consistent and addresses all dependencies. The EALs constitute a hierarchy of assurance, with EALs Level 1 being the lowest. That is, EAL 1 has the least rigor and scope for assurance evidence and EAL 7 has the most (Table 4). The degree of difficulty does not increase in a linear way. The first four levels are intended to approximate various levels of commercial development practice. Only the highest of these levels, EAL 4, requires any source code analysis and then only examination of "sample" selected by the developer rather than the evaluator. The logic for this is sound because these lower levels do not require extensive modeling and specification of security, internal structuring, architectural arrangement, and life-cycle restrictions. Without these measures, source code analysis is not particularly effective (Anderson, 2001). On the other hand, these same assurance measures are either too costly or specialized for application to large products.

The remaining three levels, EAL 5 through 7, are essentially aimed at products that will be developed using security specialists and security-specific approaches. At present, CCRA mutual recognition does not extend to these higher levels. The rigor of these levels is increased not only because of the use of formal methods but also internal structuring, architectural, and life-cycle requirements.

The predefined EALs do not use all of the possible Common Criteria assurance requirements. It is possible to *augment* an EAL by adding assurance requirements or substituting a more rigorous requirement (as in EAL 5 +). The Common Criteria does not allow definition or use of a "minus" EAL (as in EAL 5 −), where one or more requirements are omitted from an EAL. If such a collection of assurance requirements is needed, it should be defined by augmenting the next lower level to contain all of the necessary requirements.

Level EAL 1 is for environments where security threats are not considered serious. It involves independent testing of the product with no input from its developers. EAL 2 increases the assurance provided by including review of a high-level design provided by the product developer. It also includes a requirement that the developer conduct a vulnerability analysis for well-known flaws. There is no independent vulnerability analysis at EAL 2. The original intent was to provide an EAL that could apply to legacy systems that had some security features. The next higher level, EAL 3, increases assurance by requiring some security measures be used in the development environment and independent assessment of the security test coverage. Although it does not require more modeling and specification than EAL 2, it does require that the design separate security-relevant components from those that are not. It also requires the design models or specifications to describe how the security is enforced. That is, the design document must support detailed analysis for design flaws in the security mechanisms. Finally, it requires testing to be based on both the interface and high-level design of the product, that is gray-box testing as opposed to black-box testing. EAL3 does not require independent vulnerability analysis.

EAL 4 requires a significant step up in developer effort but not one that is considered beyond best commercial practice. In addition to a security-enforcing high-level design, EAL 4 also requires a low-level design. Assurance is also increased by requiring that the interface specification of the product be complete, a nontrivial requirement. EAL 4 also introduces a requirement for an explicit security model, that is, an abstract model that defines security for the product. Finally, EAL 4 also includes a (low-attack-potential) independent vulnerability analysis.

EALs 5 through 6 are for products developed using security specialists and security-specific design and development. Although the Common Criteria has defined these levels, there is no common acceptance of evaluations at these higher levels. There is also no corresponding common understanding of what measures and approaches satisfy each level. Readers interested learning about these higher levels or in developing products for these levels should contact the appropriate national evaluation scheme authorities or a consultant specializing in these matters.

Table 4 Common Criteria Evaluation Assurance Levels

EAL	1	Functionally tested
EAL	2	Structurally tested
EAL	3	Methodically tested
EAL	4	Methodically designed, tested, and reviewed
EAL	5	Semiformally designed and tested
EAL	6	Semiformally verified design and tested
EAL	7	Formally verified design and tested

CONCLUSIONS

The Common Criteria has potential to provide good, balanced sets of security requirements. It captures the central idea that security is a matter of assurance as much as function and that assurance should balance function. Application of the Common Criteria has been hampered by its national security sponsorship and the politics of government regulation. In such an environment, it is difficult to proceed rapidly or make painful decisions. This is particularly true when one of the stakeholders in a protection profile, security target, or evaluation has motives other than ultimate protection of user resources. Despite this, the Common Criteria can be useful if it is employed with consideration of the latest security technology and threats, by stakeholders who mean to produce security technology that meets the user's needs.

There are two other assurance-related standards for safety in information technology systems that might be of interest. The first is the avionics related DO-178B standard, (Radio Technical Commission for Aeronautics, 1992) for software in aircraft and aviation technology. The second, IEC 61508 (International Electrotechnical Commission, n.d.), is a more general international standard for electrical and electronic systems with safety requirements. The reader who is interested in issues of assurance and certification should investigate these standards.

GLOSSARY

This glossary complements the essential terminology of provided in the second section of this chapter.

Assurance   Grounds for confidence that an entity meets it security objectives. This definition is taken directly from the Common Criteria. It is sufficient for many uses but could be improved. For example, security objectives are not granular and might be met by a system that did not have the desired security functions. Also, the definition does not distinguish assurance evidence, that is, the engineering work products, from the degree or level of confidence that the evidence provides.

Assurance Argument   An organization or arrangement of assurance evidence into a logical structure that shows how the evidence is (a) interrelated and (b) gives confidence that the security objectives are met. The Common Criteria does not use this concept but instead employs a more simple tabular arrangement in the rationale parts of protection profiles and security targets.

Attack Potential   The perceived potential for success of an attack, expressed in terms of an attacker's expertise, resources, and motivation.

Formal   Expressed in a restricted syntax language with defined semantics based on well-established mathematical concepts. Under this definition, most UML is not formal.

Product   A package of information technology software, firmware, or hardware that provides functionality. This definition omits the Common Criteria's additional qualification, "designed for use or incorporation within a multiplicity of systems" as unnecessarily restrictive.

Security Objective   A statement of intent to counter identified threats or to satisfy identified organization security policies and assumptions.

Security Function   A part (or parts) of the target of evaluation (TOE) that has to be relied on for enforcing a closely related subset of the rules from the TOE security policy.

CROSS REFERENCES

See *Software Development and Quality Assurance; Standards for Product Security Assessment.*

REFERENCES

Anderson, R. (2001). *Security engineering: A guide to building dependable distributed systems*. New York: Wiley.

Committee on National Security Systems. *National information assurance glossary*.

Common Criteria Project Sponsoring Organizations (Ed.). (2004a). *Common criteria for information technology security evaluation: Part 1. Introduction and general model Version 2.2.*

Common Criteria Project Sponsoring Organizations. (Ed.). (2004b). *Common criteria for information technology security evaluation: Part 2. Security functional requirements*. Version 2.2 in rev. 256.

Common Criteria Project Sponsoring Organizations. (Ed.). (2004c). *Common Criteria for Information Technology Security Evaluation: Part 3. Security assurance requirements Version 2.2.*

Common Criteria Project Sponsoring Organizations. (Ed.). (2004d). *Common Methodology for Information Technology Security Evaluation Version 2.2.*

International Electrotechnical Commisssion (n.d.). *IEC 61508 Safety Standard for Safety Instrumented Systems(SIS).*

Radio Technical Commission for Aeronautics. (1992, December). *DO-178B Software Considerations in Airborne Systems and Equipment Certification.*

FURTHER READING

There are many research issues regarding the Common Criteria. Most of them arise in practical or research projects that target the highest levels of assurance (Alves-Foss, Rinker, & Taylor, n.d.; Ross, 2001).

Application of the Common Criteria is a complex topic that can fill a whole book. Fortunately, there is such a book, one that provides examples that make the Common Criteria requirements more concrete:

Herrmann, D. S. (2002). *Using the Common Criteria for IT security evaluation*. Auerbach.

For technical issues regarding security engineering and assurance, Ross Anderson's (2001) book is recommended.

The study of actual protection profiles and security targets is still one of the best ways to understand practical application of the Common Criteria. Presentation of a complete protection profile and its corresponding security target would take more room than this entire chapter, even for a relatively simple product. There is also a wide variation in details and approach, depending on the target of evaluation. Ultimately, the best understanding comes from looking at examples for several kinds of products.

The protection profiles and security targets listed here are not flawless. The protection profiles tend to be of much higher quality because they undergo more review. On the other hand, a protection profile does not refer to a specific product and lacks the concrete relation to a product that may be found in a security target. Security targets are working documents; they are formal and of relatively good quality, but they have not undergone as much internal and external review as a well-used protection profile. The following protection profiles and security targets were available from the U.S. Common Criteria Evaluation and Validation Scheme, as of October 2004, from the corresponding Web site: http://niap.nist.gov/cc-scheme.

- EAL 4 Augmented Security Target for *Netscape Certificate Management System 6.1 Service Pack 1.* This security target is a good one to study and has a corresponding Protection Profilewhich is listed next. The Security Target shows how the requirements of a Protection Profile may be augmented to achieve a higher EAL.
- EAL 3 Augmented Protection Profile for *Certificate Issuing and Management Components (CIMC), Security Level 3.*
- EAL 3 Security Target for *Marimba Desktop/Mobile Management and Server Change Management.*
- EAL 4 Augmented Security Target for *XTS-400/STOP 6.0E.*
- EAL 3 Protection Profile for *Controlled Access Protection Profile.* This protection profile addresses basic host operating system security, for nonhostile environments where attempts to breach security are casual or inadvertent.
- EAL 4 protection profile for *Single-Level Operating Systems in Environments Requiring Medium Robustness.*

The following three documents were available from the United Kingdom Communications Electronic Security Group Web site: http://cesg.gov.uk in October 2004. The first two are security targets for database systems. The third document is the corresponding DBMS protection profile that can be obtained from the same site. It is interesting to see how the discrepancy in EALs is resolved:

- EAL 4 augmented security target for *Oracle 9i Release 9.1.0.1.0.* This security target refers to the database management system (DBMS) protection profile listed last.
- EAL 4 augmented security target for *Oracle 9i Label Security.* This security target also refers to the DBMS protection profile.
- EAL 3 Protection Profile for *Database Management System, ver. 2.1,* May 2000.

Readers that are interested in protection profiles and security targets for higher EALs should contact the applicable national scheme authorities and request examples. This exercise itself should provide additional enlightenment.

Alves-Foss, J., Rinker, B., & Taylor. C. (n.d.). Towards Common Criteria certification for DO-178B compliant airborne software systems. Retrieved October 27, 2004 from http://www.cs.uidaho.edu/jimaf/docs/compare02b.htm

Greve, D., Wilding, M., & Vanfleet, W. M. (2003, July). A separation kernel formal security policy. Presented at the Fourth International Workshop on the ACL2 Prover, Boulder, Colorado.

Irvine, C., Levin, T., & Dinolt, G. (2002, September). Diamond high assurance security program: Trusted computing exemplar (technical report). Monterey, CA: U.S. Naval Postgraduate School.

National Computer Security Center. (1985, December). *DoD 5200.28-STD Trusted Computer System Evaluation Criteria.* Washington, DC: Department of Defense.

National Computer Security Center. (1987, July). *NCSC-TG-005 Trusted Network Interpretation.* Washington, DC: Department of Defense.

National Computer Security Center. (2001, April). *NCSC-TG-021 Trusted Database Management System Interpretation.* Washington, DC: Department of Defense.

National Computer Security Center. (1993, July). *NCSC-TG-023 A Guide to Understanding, Security Testing and Test Documentation.* Washington, DC: Department of Defense.

National Computer Security Center. (1994, July). *NCSC-TG-029 Introduction to Certification and Accreditation.* Washington, DC: Department of Defense, January 1994.

U.S. NIAP Interpretations Board. (n.d.). The public interpretations database. Retrieved October 27, 2004, from http://niap.nist.gov/cc-scheme/PUBLIC

U.S. NIAP Validation Body. (n.d.). CCEVS scheme policy letters. Retrieved October 27, 2004, from http://niap.nist.gov/cc-scheme/policy/ccevs/policy-ltrs.html

Software Development and Quality Assurance

Pascal Meunier, *Purdue University*

INTRODUCTION

This chapter, which has for its title the subject of many books, focuses on current observations, practices, consideration, and techniques that appear most effective in producing secure and trustworthy software. This chapter does not address related software engineering issues, such as obtaining predictions of release readiness, software quality metrics and quality models, or modularization and layer models. With reference to the common criteria EALs (evaluation assurance levels), the content is appropriate for low- and medium-assurance software projects (EALs 1–4). Because commercial, off-the-shelf software (COTS) rarely reaches EAL 4, this chapter is relevant for most COTS projects. Another chapter in this handbook focuses on high-assurance efforts (EALs 5–7).

The current state of COTS is grim. The ICAT (http://icat.nist.gov) vulnerability database contains more than 6,600 vulnerability entries (as of May 2004). Crackers think that they are clever for finding them and releasing exploits. Spam e-mail marketing, after getting banned and pursed away from legitimate hosts, uses hosts compromised on a large scale by worms and viruses, for which they pay crackers (Leyden, 2004). Patches are issued at a pace that leaves system administrators dazed and breathless. Patches break previous patches, sometimes in unclear circumstances, and other patches are issued to fix the problems introduced by previous patches. Sometimes patches attempt to block an exploitation path to a vulnerability, without fixing the coding or design errors that enable the vulnerability itself. However, a new exploitation path is found later, which results in a new set of patches. What is wrong with our current software development processes, and why are we flooded with such vulnerable software?

Some business-models value time to market highly. The ability to deliver patches "easily" over the Internet favors a quality debt attitude stated as "deliver now, fix later." As a result, patching is now the nightmare of the information technology world. Often repeated mistakes have become noticeable in vulnerability databases. Can these often-repeated mistakes be avoided without significantly impacting time to market?

The market for COTS software has changed enormously over the past 10 years, with an increasing emphasis being put on security. Vendors have an increasing awareness that vulnerabilities cost money, reputation, and customers. The same development methods that produced faulty software cannot be expected now to produce correct software and patches. Which development methods are appropriate to these changing requirements? How are security requirements captured, validated, and verified? Are formal methods too theoretical? Can better programming languages help? What have we learned about secure programming?

Whereas the importance of the development and quality assurance methods may be easy to grasp, choosing the correct or near-optimal ones to produce good, reliable, secure software in a timely and cheap manner remains a conundrum. Bad choices can compound because being late may prompt programmers to hurry and work while tired, thus creating more flaws that take longer to fix or result in more patches.

METAISSUES IN SOFTWARE DEVELOPMENT

Software development traditionally is concerned with delivering software that meets customer needs as defined and "captured" by software requirements. This delivery has a number of constraints, such as time, cost, reliability, low number of faults, maintainability, and functionality. There are three types of metaissues of importance that help address these constraints and manage development activities. The first type is development models, such as the waterfall, the spiral, and the agile class of development models; these define practices, processes, and activities carried out during development. The second type is capability maturity models, such as the system security engineering capability maturity model (SSE-CMM), which provide a framework for the assessment of the presence, quality, and improvement of the practices and processes used during development. The third type is postdelivery certifications, such as the common criteria, which assess security assurance and security features of the produced software artifacts. It is theoretically correct to select any one construct for each type because they are separate dimensions of the software development process. However, the particularities of development models can affect the usability of the other constructs (discussed later).

Software Development Models

Software development models define processes, activities, and methods or at least provide an ordered framework for their definition. There are a large number of models available, from the classical waterfall model, spiral development models (Boehm, 1988), and the more recent "lightweight" or "agile" models (Cohen, Lindvall, & Costa 2003). Some models apply at different organizational levels; the Software Engineering Institute's Team Software Process (TSP, Humphrey, 1999) and the Personal Software Process (PSP) apply respectively at the team and personal levels (Humphrey, 2002), as their name suggests. Interesting questions are how the choice of a model may affect the number and severity of security defects (including vulnerabilities) and whether vulnerabilities were enabled during requirement and design or coding phases. Reports on the performance of these models typically do not differentiate security flaws from other flaws. Nevertheless, several observations can be made.

The Waterfall Model

In the waterfall model, a development phase is fully completed before another is started. These phases consist of requirements definition and analysis, design, implementation and unit testing, integration and system testing, and operation and maintenance. Requirements and design are stated in documents before coding starts and therefore do not benefit from the insight into problems that coding sometimes yields. These steps can also be seen as brittle because if requirements change, time has been wasted working on them. If requirements change faster than the time needed to produce the matching design documents, then code never gets written. The documents may also need to change not because of a change in the problem space but because of customers' or the software development team's improved understanding or improved communications between the two. The frustration experienced in these situations has led to the development of "lighter" (the spiral) and "lightweight" (agile) development methods (see the following sections). Therefore, the waterfall model is appropriate and should be used for projects where the following assumptions of the model are true (Boehm, 2000):

1. The requirements are knowable in advance of implementation.

2. The requirements have no unresolved, high-risk implications, such as risks due to COTS choices, cost, schedule, performance, safety, security, user interfaces, and organizational impacts.

3. The nature of the requirements will not change much during either development or evolution.

4. The requirements are compatible with all the key shareholder's expectations, including users, customers, developers, maintainers, and investors.

5. The right architecture for implementing the requirements is well understood.

6. There is enough calendar time to proceed sequentially.

The Spiral Development Model

The spiral development model (Boehm, 1988) holds the middle ground between agile methods and the waterfall model. It was created for use in situations were the assumptions needed for the waterfall model could not be made or were found false. It has six invariants, designed to minimize project risk (Boehm, 2000):

1. Concurrent determination of key artifacts (ops concept, requirements, plans, design, code).

2. Each cycle does objectives, constraints, alternatives, risks, review, and commitment to proceed.

3. Level of effort driven by risk considerations.

4. Degree of detail driven by risk considerations.

5. Use of anchor point milestones (life-cycle objectives, life-cycle architecture, and initial operating capability).

6. Emphasis on system and life-cycle activities and artifacts.

Invariant 1 shows that it does not, contrary to common misconception, comprise many incremental cycles of a miniwaterfall model with sequential phases of requirements, design, implementation, and so on. Invariants 3 and 4 make obvious that its use requires the understanding of the relevant risks, and it may therefore be inappropriate for inexperienced programmers and project managers. Spiral development look-alike models that violate these invariants expose projects to significant risks (Boehm, 2000).

The Agile Programming Movement

Agile software development favors "individuals and interactions over processes and tools; working software over comprehensive documentation; customer collaboration over contract negotiation; and responding to change over following a plan" (Agile Alliance, 2001). Agile methods were reviewed by Cohen et al. (2003). They are particularly appropriate whenever the requirements are difficult to capture (e.g., the customer does not know what is needed), are changing, when the project could be terminated at any time and some partially functioning software is desired, or as soon as possible. Their main weakness is that long-term vision in the architecture and design is necessarily lacking, and correctness is difficult to establish. If possible, it would be interesting to perform a study relating agile programming to secure programming, number of vulnerabilities or security issues. Are agile programming development models favorable to security? Are there fewer or more vulnerabilities in software developed that way?

"Extreme Programming" (Wells, 2003) is the most well-known of the agile development models. It advocates programming in pairs, which has the advantage of providing an instant code review. Pair programming was shown to enhance the learning and increase the quality of code produced by undergraduate students (Williams & Upchurch, 2001). Among its benefits, pair programming can help catch obvious cases of well-known programming errors leading to the most common vulnerabilities (e.g., buffer overflows), provided that at least one in the pair is knowledgeable in this area. However, this author believes that it is not a complete replacement for code reviews because it is not favorable to reflection and the careful consideration of the security implications of some operations or combinations thereof.

In Extreme Programming, the design and requirements are in flux until the last version is released. Focus is on releasing (tested) functionality as early as possible. Design periods are short (ideally 10 minutes), followed by implementation sessions. Therefore, it is unlikely that emerging risks posed by the changing designs, and matching security requirements, will be identified before they are implemented. Correcting security problems after implementation has known security limitations; "products claiming security that are created from previous versions without security cannot achieve high trust because they lack the fundamental and structural concepts required for high assurance" (Sullivan, 2003).

An intriguing aspect of Extreme Programming is the practice of creating unit tests first, as a way of encoding functional requirements. Software is validated by passing all the tests. Therefore, the security of programs depends on whether tests were included for unexpected, malicious inputs and behavior; this practice essentially replaces security requirements and security analyses in other models. Some of the tests are to be provided by the customer, who may not be knowledgeable in the area of security. This software development method can be compared with the two classic ways to test the security of software: black-and white-box (a.k.a. structural) testing. Black-box testing assumes or has no knowledge of the implementation, whereas white-box testing has access to all the information. Writing tests before the implementation (and part of the design) is similar to black-box testing, which is less powerful than white-box testing. Security testing requires broader coverage than normal testing and also focuses particularly on the least used aspects of security functions (Sullivan, 2003) and "what if" malicious scenarios. These are the least likely to be emphasized and captured during test creation before coding. Therefore, establishing the trustworthiness of software artifacts produced using Extreme Programming is more difficult than in other development models and may require separate, additional security testing or code reviews.

These observations are not fatal flaws but are pointed out so that programmers and customers will be aware of the risk factors they pose and knowingly accept or mitigate them with other practices. It should be noted that Extreme Programming also requires complete adoption of all its activities because each activity assumes that the others are performed to cover the risks that each poses individually. As a result, it can be seen as a risky or unstable development model (Stephens & Rosenberg, 2003).

It would be a mistake to form an opinion of all agile development models based solely on this brief analysis of Extreme Programming. Whereas none specifically address security concerns, other models put a greater emphasis on the definition, analysis, and documentation of requirements (Cohen et al., 2003). This author feels that this is preferable to the exploration of security risks and threats and to the generation of security requirements and appropriate, thoughtful changes in the architecture and design. One way to strengthen agile programming development models is to use them in conjunction with the SSE-CMM (discussed later) to provide higher assurance and security, inasmuch as the original software capability maturity model can be seen as compatible with agile methods (Cohen et al., 2003).

Cleanroom

The Cleanroom development model (Mills, Dyer, & Linger, 1987; Linger, 1994) uses incremental development, which bears some similarities with agile methods, but under statistical quality control. Cleanroom is not considered an agile development model because it involves a strict sequence of phases in which code execution comes last; specification must precede design and correctness verification through review precedes code execution. Each increment delivers functionality to the end user.

The Personal Software Process (PSP)

PSP specifies activities and a discipline to be performed by the individual programmer to gather metrics, improve estimation and prediction capabilities, and reduce errors. Its benefits are documented in more than 30 journal publications (not listed here). However, it is not a free and open system. Instructors who are interested in teaching PSP courses to third parties must sign a license agreement with the SEI (see also TSP, which follows).

The Team Software Process (TSP)

TSP (Humphrey, 2000) was created to bridge the gap between the PSP and the SE-CMM and specifies activities that apply at the team level. It has phases similar to those of the waterfall model; requirements, design, implementation, and test. However, phases can and should overlap. Marketing material and reports state impressive reductions in the number of defects (including security defects) and time required (Davis & Mullaney, 2003). However, a disadvantage of the TSP at this time is that it is not a free and open system; licensing is required. Moreover, this author was unable to find publications on TSP independent from the SEI (Software Engineering Institute) except for a few teaching experiments. Training must be done by the SEI, their approved partners, or organizational trainers trained and licensed by the SEI. As it is proprietary, attempts at improvement, or unlicensed teaching, would breach the SEI's intellectual property rights. Nevertheless, the combination of the PSP and TSP deduces results unmatched by other development practices (Davis & Mullaney, 2003) and is most likely (in the absence of independent reports, this author is somewhat cautious) the best available for the development of secure software (in combination with a CMM such as the SSE-CMM).

Correctness by Construction (CbyC)

CbyC focuses on bug prevention or early removal, rather than bug detection in traditional validation and verification efforts, through the careful selection of powerful language tools and analysis methods (Amey, 2002). By using unambiguous languages that support strong static analyses (see SPARK later in the chapter), faults can be prevented or caught very early. This and the use of formal methods at early stages lowers the cost of verification and validation efforts (Hall & Chapman, 2002). This process was compared favorably with TSP (National Cyber Security Partnership Task Force, 2004). The usage of formal methods in CbyC can help certification (discussed later in this section).

Capability Maturity Models

Capability maturity models are frameworks to assess the existence, effectiveness, and maturity of development activities, practices, and processes. These are grouped by areas (domains, a.k.a. process areas, PAs) and levels of maturity (ratings) and are called Base Practiced (BPs). They describe what needs to be done, but not how to do it. They usually require performance measurement and reproducibility in the first levels because a fundamental axiom of CMMs is that without measurements, it is impossible to know if performance has been improved or not through a change or through the use of one development model instead of another. Development environments and models that resist the implementation of measurements as being too "heavyweight" are limiting themselves, from the viewpoint of CMMs, to make anecdotal, qualitative, or unsupported and doubtful quantitative claims of performance. Consequently, this author expects development models that persist in resisting or preventing measurements to face fates similar to those of diet fads or to become closed belief systems ("religions").

The capability Maturity Model Integration (CMMI). The CMMI product suite replaces the older software capability maturity model (SW-CMM). CMMI melds together several CMMs and so links the software development phase to the greater context of systems engineering, configuration, environment, life-cycle management, and more.

SSE-CMM

The SSE-CMM addresses the management of the software development processes, with an emphasis on security practices. The SSE-CMM became an ISO (International Standards Organization) standard in 2002 (ISO/IEC 21827:2002). It used the systems engineering capability maturity model (SE-CMM) as starling point and added to the engineering process area.

INFOSEC Assurance Capability Maturity Model (IA-CMM). IA-CMM applies to providers of Information Security (INFOSEC) assurance services but not directly to the development process. However, it is relevant to this chapter because it is based on SSE-CMM and links software development to information security.

ISO-9001

This international effort bears similarities to CMMs and promotes quality. It specifies both systemic (processes, documentation, etc.) and management (quality policy, quality objectives, customer requirements, and satisfaction) requirements. ISO-9001 certification helps CMM certificiation and vice versa through overlaps (see Paulk, 1994).

Certification

Common Criteria. The Common Criteria for Information Technology Security Evaluation (Common Criteria Project Sponsoring Organizations, 1999) specify functional and assurance requirements of software artifacts (targets of evaluations), which can be matched against desired assurance properties (protection profiles). Common criteria (CC) do not certify that a product is free from defects or vulnerabilities. Rather, CC evaluate the presence, quality and proofs of assurance in the form of architectural decisions, access control mechanisms, development methodology, testing, and other evidence of security assurance and security functionality. These assurance properties provide trust in the software artifact, for example, that requirements were captured, designed, and implemented correctly and that protection mechanisms limit the possible damage should a fault occur or a vulnerability be found. In this manner, CC rate the trustworthiness of the software artifact. CC certification is slow and expensive because it is time consuming to assess, prove, and demonstrate these properties. However, CC are used and recognized internationally (through the signature of the Common Criteria Recognition Arrangement, CCRA) and have supplanted other certifications (for new software). Another chapter of this handbook describes the Common Criteria and high-assurance software engineering in more detail.

REQUIREMENTS AND DESIGN

It is useful to think of security problems as being enabled at three times: design and architecture (including requirements), implementation, and operations (Graff & Van Wyk, 2003). Fixing security bugs with a patch costs 60 times more than catching them at design time (Soo Hoo, Sudbury, & Jaquith, 2001). Because this chapter does not cover operation and configuration issues, this leaves design, covered in this section, and implementation, covered in the next section.

In the general case, the security of a particular design and its implementation are undecidable (Cervesato et al., 1999; Even & Goldreich 1983; Heintze & Tygar 1996) Some security properties can be formally proved, or shown to be broken, under some circumstances (Meadows, 2003). Requirements specification and good design and development processes do not deterministically guarantee secure programs. However, they provide assurance that the systems will be reasonably secure for the intended use, especially when combined with formal methods (see Correctness by Construction earlier in the chapter). The scope of the following considerations is limited to EALs 1–4; another chapter of this handbook focuses on high-assurance software engineering (EALs greater than 4).

Requirements

There are several types and level of requirements; Wiegers (1999) discussed business, user and functional requirements, as well as "other non-functional requirements." Security objectives, policies, and requirements would then fall into the last catchall category and are discussed for less than a page in a 350-page book (Wiegers, 1999). The objective in mentioning this is not to criticize this book, but to provide a typical example of the priority and coverage given to security requirements in the industry. Is this a lack of attention, or does it reflect what we really know about how to specify security requirements? Has academia not come forward with ideas applicable in real situations? Crook et al. (2002) contended that conventional requirements modeling is inadequate to represent the organizational procedures that underpin a security policy. The difficulty in specifying security requirements contributes to the security problems and the nonstop patching environment we are now experiencing. Security requirements define goals and what must be done to secure a system against likely threats and to mitigate risks; without security requirements, your system is already secured by this definition. Possible results are the surprise of finding that your product is vulnerable, that customers were hacked, and that they are now blaming you. We ride from surprise to surprise and patch to patch.

Security requirements are harder to capture than other requirements. Typically the customer has thought about desired features and behavior but not about all the ways things could go wrong in the technology that supports its business model when faced with a malicious, clever user. The concept of antirequirements is that of requirements formulated by crackers, to subvert existing requirements (Crook et al., 2002). However, although it is possible to interview management and end users, it is not possible to interview a panel of crackers and trust the results. Security requirements can be captured based on risk assessments (Brown, 1989). A difficulty with deriving security requirements from risk and hazards assessments is that some unforeseen risks emerge out of particularities of design, implementation and coding choices, and low-level interactions (Berry, 1997), and a failure to foresee inconsistencies. These discoveries may require revisiting earlier development phases.

In quality assurance, requirements comprise security objectives, policies, and security requirements; it is easy to confuse "requirements" and "security requirements." Security objectives help define policies and are higher-level goals than security requirements. An example security objective would be "all money transfers must be legal." A policy specifies whether activities, states, and processes in the system are acceptable or not; one could be that "money transfers can be authorized only by the owner(s) of the account or designated parties." Security requirements prevent, deter, or provide accountability for policy violations; one could be that "the authorization credentials of people authorizing money transfers shall be verified and audited within a reasonable time period." Security requirements can be further divided into security functional requirements and security assurance requirements. Vetterling, Wimmel, and Wisspeintner (2002) provided an illuminating account of the determination of all these for a system designed to be evaluated with the Common Criteria.

Requirements Documentation and Specifications
We wish to formulate security requirements and derive specifications from them with better assurance that the requirements were complete, will be well understood, and that the specifications are correct. The Unified Modeling Language (UML) "use cases" that help capture functional requirements were adapted to provide "abuse cases," which can also be represented in regular UML (McDermott & Fox, 1999). A similar idea is that of "misuse" cases (Sindre & Opdhal, 2000). UML has recently been extended with UMLsec, and mathematical tools can be used to verify UML specifications against formal security requirements (Juerjens, 2004).

Determination of Requirements
Baskerville (1993) identified three categories of methods: checklist, mechanistic engineering, and logical (i.e., formal). Using the SSE-CMM as an inspiration to generate security requirements (Phillips, 2003) is similar to a checklist method. Requirements are greatly influenced by the system's architecture and intended usage contexts. Consideration of how the system must operate inside an organization with a social context shows how responsibility modeling leads to security requirements (Strens & Dobson, 1993). From a theoretical approach, Petri nets are suitable for modeling information flow security requirements in distributed systems (Varadharajan, 1990). Requirements can be statically verified using finite-state techniques (Ahmed & Tripathi, 2003). Example security requirements, and the processes used to derive them, are available for open systems (Kolstad & Bowles, 1991), medical applications (Hamilton, 1992), cooperative work (Ahmed & Tripathi, 2003; Coulouris & Dollimore, 1994), and mobile agents (Reiser & Vogt, 2000). Missing are follow-up studies showing how well these requirements fared in practice several years later and whether the ways they were derived are applicable elsewhere.

Secure Design Principles
There are eight secure design principles, described by Saltzer and Schroeder (1975), that are still relevant and important today.

Least Privilege
A subject should only be given those privileges it needs to complete its task. An example of excessive privileges was Microsoft IIS version 5 and earlier, which ran under the Local System Account (strictly speaking, it was "possible" to create and configure a special account with fewer privileges). Taken to an extreme, this may translate into an access control problem. The complexity of the access control mechanism and its configuration may increase to model the needed privileges (e.g., capabilities).

Fail-Safe Defaults
Unless a subject is given explicit access to an object, it should be denied access to that object. An example using the Apache access control through htaccess files, to deny by default and allow only specific clients, would be:

deny from all
allow from...

This issue is related to the issue of failing "safe" versus failing "functional," as exemplified by network switches that unexpectedly fail "open" and function as hubs when overwhelmed under unusual circumstances. This failure policy in practice removes any security benefit from using switches instead of hubs.

Economy of Mechanism

Security mechanisms should be as simple as possible because complex mechanisms may not be correctly understood, modeled, configured, implemented, and used. Moreover, complex mechanisms may engender partial implementations and compatibility problems between vendors (see the IPSEC-related RFCs; compatibility between IPSEC implementations is a problem).

Complete Mediation

All accesses to objects must be checked to ensure that they are allowed. This is a performance versus security issue; the results of access checks are often cached. Permissions may have changed since the last check; if caching is used, there must be a mechanism to flush or invalidate caches when changes happen. An example vulnerability resulting from a failure to apply this principle was observed in xinetd 2.3.4 (CVE: CAN-2002-0871), which leaked file descriptors for the signal pipe to services it launched. This allowed those services (e.g., if compromised) to attack xinetd.

Open Design

The security of a mechanism should not depend on the secrecy of its design or implementation. This is because if the details of the mechanism are leaked, reverse engineered, or otherwise found, then it produces a catastrophic failure for all users at once. By contrast, if the secrets are abstracted from the mechanism, for example, inside a key, then leakage of a key only affects one user or one group of users. Examples of failures of open design abound, from electronic voting machines to the old days when various word processors and spreadsheets offered to "encrypt" all documents with the same key. Failure to follow this principle also results in insider threats, because insiders may know enough to compromise the mechanism everywhere it is in use (which is especially disturbing in the case of electronic voting machines). Note that this principle does not require the capability to audit the code, nor does it require that designs and implementation details be revealed or made public. However, providing assurance that this principle was followed is difficult without revealing a good part of the design, at least to a trusted party.

Separation of Privilege

A system should not grant permission based on a single condition. This removes a single point of failure and is analogous to the separation of duty principle. By requiring multiple factors, "collusion" (the compromise of several factors) becomes necessary and risks due to bribery or a single vulnerability are reduced.

Least Common Mechanism

Mechanisms used to access resources should not be shared. The idea is to avoid the transference of risks (or data, e.g., covert channels) from one task or service to another. An example is the vulnerability CVE-1999-1148; because under Microsoft NT architecture, the FTP (file transfer protocol) and Web services shared a common thread pool, exploiting a denial-of-service attack in the FTP server (keeping all threads busy) resulted in a loss of Web services.

Psychological Acceptability

Security mechanisms should not make the resource more difficult to access than if the security mechanism were not present. This is to avoid presenting an incentive for users (or help desks) to disable, bypass, or defeat security mechanisms. In practice, difficulty proportionate to the value of the protected assets is accepted. An example is even the mild annoyance of entering passwords many times to access resources. The "rhosts" mechanism can bypass password security checks. However, authentication is then based on Internet protocol (IP) addresses, which can be mapped to a different host through Address Resolution Protocol (ARP) poisoning, so the resources become vulnerable.

Best Practices

Over the years, the repetition of mistakes resulted in the generation of some best practices. Although not as hallowed as the previous eight principles, these can avoid several of the issues listed later in "Quality Assurance in Coding and Testing."

Separate Control From Data

Many problems, from phone "phreaking" to metacharacter and character encoding issues, Structured Query Language (SQL) injection vulnerabilities, cross-site scripting vulnerabilities, and so on, are due to the fact that the same channel is used to transmit both data and code (commands). Whenever databases are queried with a search term provided by a user, chances are that the data (the search term) were simply inserted inside a command string sent to the database engine. The malicious composition of data to contain commands (shell commands, SQL, javascript, etc.) and to trigger a context switch to command interpretation inside the software processing the channel is the class of code injection attacks. Using separate channels will defeat these attacks. A partial example of using separate channels is the use of stored procedures in databases. The commands were sent to the database engine ahead of time and setup as functions, and during execution only the data are sent (with a specification of which function to use). Then, allowing only function calls in the data channel prevents the execution of arbitrary SQL commands injected by attackers into data. This is not entirely safe because attackers could still trigger unwanted executions of functions. However, it shows that even partial compliance to this principle reduces risks. Another example is the use of the exec UNIX family of functions instead of the "system" call; by using separate arguments ("channels"), some interpretations and possibilities for code injection are made impossible.

Use Whitelists Instead of Blacklists

Blacklists of "bad" things are rarely complete. Whether character encodings, escape sequences or globbing (see Glossary) are involved, it is difficult to list all combinations (CERT Coordination Center 1998). The "wrapper" problem is especially difficult, whereas a script or program attempts to sanitize input for an unsafe program. The wrapper has to understand fully and model how the unsafe program will parse and interpret its arguments and keep up-to-date with changes, as well as to use the calling mechanism correctly. Wrappers can be entire programs in their own right, such as the wu-ftpd FTP server. FTP conversion processes files through a program that does the conversion (e.g., tar or uncompress). Wu-ftp allowed an attacker to execute commands via malformed file names, because the conversion program interpreted and parsed differently the command passed to it (CVE-1999-0997). Wrappers should only allow known good commands.

Use Operating System Provided Services

Only the operating system (OS) can provide guarantees about the atomicity of the creation of temporary files with correct permissions and a unique name, and thereby avoid race conditions and symlink vulnerabilities. Random number generation is another problem best solved by the OS. Cryptographically good random number generation is a difficult problem, and it is doubtful that custom solutions will be good unless the programmer is an expert cryptologist. Moreover, only the OS has access to certain sources of entropy that help provide superior random number generation. Use virtual devices such as /dev/urandom to obtain random numbers from the OS.

Manage Trust

The designers and programmers should be aware at all times of which objects, variables, and inputs they can trust. There should be well-defined "trust boundaries" that act like a country's customs. Untrusted inputs should be validated to become trusted. This boundary is formalized in some languages (e.g., Perl's "taint" mode). The custody of data and code affects the trust that can be put in it. There are more than a dozen CVE entries relating to shopping cart applications that stored the price of items in the client browsers, and then trusted the prices given back to them by the client. Likewise, there are numerous software artifacts that trust the integrity of their execution on client computers, such as javascript or Java authentication code. These trust management failures would be similar to unsupervised and unmonitored self-checkout lanes in supermarkets.

Protect Resources

Anonymous, unauthenticated requests should be given minimal or no resources unless it is a policy to serve their requests. The ordering of operations should be such that authentication, followed by permissions and credentials verifications, and any check that might fail should be performed before expensive operations. Sometimes, resources owned by the requester can be used instead.

In transmission control protocol (TCP)/IP networking, a security problem known as "SYN flooding" was due to the consumption of memory to keep track of connections. It was solved by using "SYN cookies," in which local memory was replaced by remote resources through the encryption of data. This effectively traded central processing unit time against memory usage.

Languages

The choice of language has important security ramifications. When programming in a low-level language such as "C," proper checks for safe and proper handling of buffers and string formats are tricky, extremely tedious, and time consuming to get right. As a result, the temptation is great for programmers cut corners and omit some checks whenever they feel they are not needed. The result is that buffer overflows and string format vulnerabilities are common. Even programmers trying their best to avoid these vulnerabilities occasionally get the code wrong with a boundary error (a.k.a. "off-by-one" error) or by forgetting to ensure that strings are terminated correctly in all circumstances. Then follows the call to strlen that produces a segmentation fault, or an exploit that benefits from the effective concatenation of two adjacent buffers (because the last NUL byte was not written, string functions will treat the two buffers as one). Better languages, such as C#, Perl, or Java, and variants of the "C" language (discussed next) prevent these two kinds of vulnerabilities from happening. Coding style can also reduce the probability of software faults (see next section).

Cyclone

The Cyclone programming language is a safer version of C and prevents buffer overflows and string format vulnerabilities while preserving the power of the C language (Jim et al., 2002).

SPARK

The Spade Ada Kernel (SPARK) is an Ada derivative in which some features of Ada were removed and annotations added to allow proving properties of the code. As a result, delta and information-flow static analyses are possible. It is also interesting in that SPARK tools link formal specification and verification (Amey, 2001). "Proof of the absence of pre-defined exceptions offers strong static protection from a large class of security flaws" (Hall & Chapman, 2002). "SPARK code was found to have only 10 percent of the residual errors of full Ada; Ada was found to have only 10 percent of the residual errors of code written in C" (Amey, 2002).

QUALITY ASSURANCE IN CODING AND TESTING

There are a number of security issues that can not be prevented by cryptography or clever requirements. Noticeably, the same mistakes keep being repeated by programmers and fall within well-understood broad categories. Using key-word searches on the description of CVE entries from 2000 to 2002, vulnerabilities related to buffer overflows, directory traversal attacks, format string vulnerabilities, symlink attacks, cross-site scripting vulnerabilities, and shell metacharacter issues represented, respectively, 20%, 11%, 9%, 4%, 4%, and 3% of all vulnerabilities. This means that at least 51% of vulnerabilities are repeated basic mistakes. Whereas it could be argued that some are design issues, they are such simple ideas (in principle; some are extremely tricky to get right in practice) and low-level design issues that we like to think of them as implementation problems (i.e., in the realm of secure coding).

Coding Style

Coding style affects readability, understandability, and maintainability. Obfuscated C code makes it harder to find mistakes and vulnerabilities—for both the original author and others doing a code review or maintenance. On the other hand, some coding styles help the programmer think more clearly and avoid mistakes and make the intent of the programmer easier to understand. MISRA (the United Kingdom's Motor Industry Software Reliability Association) recognized this and established a set of 127 guidelines for the use of C in safety-critical systems (MISRA, 1998). Some guidelines are mandatory and some are advisory, but all are copyrighted and the guidelines are only available from MISRA; nevertheless, they are increasing in popularity because they are effective and make sense.

There is no absolutely wrong or right coding style; however, to reduce the occurrence of bugs, code should be produced to be easily understandable by as many people as possible, as quickly as possible, with the least chance of misunderstandings. Maintaining a consistent coding style throughout a project also speeds up code reviews (discussed later). Coders producing brilliant but indecipherable code are bad coders because they significantly increase the cost of code reviews, maintenance, and the risk that their code contains a vulnerability or be called by others in such a way as to create a vulnerability. Assume as an axiom the following: if the functionality of the code is hard to understand, then the security implications will be obscure.

Coding style is more than indentation; it is also how functions are called and their side effects. Consider this "if" statement:

Typically, the first one takes longer to understand and is more error prone. In this example, there was an assignment, a function called, and a test condition within the "if" statement; moreover, the first branch was on the same line as the if statement, without brackets. Brackets ease the insertion of additional code and make obvious that a branch is happening; they also maintain a consistent usage for semicolons. Bugs happen where brackets would have prevented them. Here is another example of bad style, in PHP:

```
if (!$z || $y =="") {
        s1
        s2
        S3...
}
```

Did the author mean to test against the integer zero, a NULL value possibly indicating an error, or is $z a Boolean, which the "!" operator will all happily convert to something that will pass the "if" test? Additionally, in PHP a NULL value tests true against an empty string, so the test for $y is also ambiguous. The answer can be found by investigating the code, or perhaps the author was thoughtful enough to write a comment about it, but it is better to make it explicit. PHP has a triple equal operator that verifies type as well; it should be used everywhere possible:

```
if ($z === false || $y === NULL) {
        s1
        s2
        s3...
}
```

This is obviously not an exhaustive list but demonstrates how to be aware of unclear or ambiguous code.

Secure Programming

Secure Programming (a.k.a. secure coding) is the awareness and understanding of the security consequences of implementing requirements in various possible ways. Secure programming classes at Purdue University teach students to avoid common mistakes (Meunier, 2002) or teach awareness and how to work around security defects in widely used protocols (Meunier, 2003). Secure programming documents oriented toward UNIX

```
if ((A = fn3(G, H)) == B) myfunc (A, D, E) else{
        s1
        s2
        s3...
}
as opposed to
A = fn3(G,H);    // comment on fn3
if (A == B){ // comment on what it means if they are equal
        myfunc (A, D, E) // comment on myfunc
} else {
        s1
        s2
        s3...
}
```

(Wheeler, 1999), Web programming (Open Web Application Security Project, 2002), and a functionality-oriented book (Viega & Messier, 2003) are available. I describe here the two kinds of vulnerabilities specific to the C language because they are very common and refer the reader to the best practices section and the above citations for other secure programming issues.

Buffer Overflows

Buffer overflows occur when manipulating strings, arrays, and regular buffers. Fixed buffer sizes used to hold inputs from untrusted (or misidentified as trusted) sources are the easiest targets of buffer overflow attacks, but not the only ones. In arrays, they occur when counting from 1 instead of 0, or when the programmer forgets that the index "n" actually refers to the $n + 1$th element. In string manipulation, they occur when or after strings are not null terminated, when strings are concatenated in a buffer that is too small, or when the programmer forgets to count the byte holding the null byte in the total buffer size. Although the concept is obvious, it is in practice tricky to catch all cases, especially when the standard C string functions are not safe and sometimes return strings that are not null terminated. Strings that are not null terminated are not safe to use with C functions, so the standard C functions are not even self-consistent. Using the C functions that take buffer sizes as arguments is a step in the right direction but is insufficient because even those are not self-consistent. Moreover, they sometimes require as argument the remaining available space in the buffer, instead of the original buffer size, which allows the programmer to make arithmetic mistakes. The new strlcpy() and strlcat() functions should be strongly preferred because these guarantee null-termination and avoid unnecessary arithmetic.

Format String Vulnerabilities

Format string vulnerabilities occur in part because of the inability of the C language to know how many arguments were passed to a function. Format strings violate the recommendation to avoid mixing code and data because they contain formatting instructions mixed with characters to display. In addition, format strings under the control of an attacker can specify where to write values almost anywhere in memory. Because a format string that contains only data will simply result in that data being printed, the most common mistake is to use data as a format string. If an attacker can change the data, then perhaps formatting commands can be inserted, with disastrous results. Always make sure that format strings are specified even when only printing a string, that they are constants, and that they cannot fall under the control of an attacker.

Code Reviews

Code reviews are an expensive but effective technique for identifying software quality issues, including vulnerabilities. Code reviews involve having other people read your code and pointing out mistakes, vulnerabilities, and bad practices, or simply asking questions about parts of the code they did not understand and comparing the code to specifications and documentation. Few developers like being the author in a code review because it can be somewhat humiliating when others find stupid mistakes and point them out. On the other hand, the reviewers should be sharp, knowledgeable, and critical people. They should be familiar with the most common secure coding errors and vulnerabilities and with secure programming principles.

Reducing the Cost

The number of people involved in the code review can be as few as one plus the author. Obviously, the more people involved, the greater the assurance provided, but also the more likely that code reviews will be abandoned under time pressure. Code reviews are less time consuming when a coding style standard emphasizing clarity and comments has been adopted. The human mind seems to find mistakes much more easily on printed pages than on computer screens, so most code review processes require printing everything. Numbered lines of code speed up references during discussion. It is essential to perform the reviews individually to enable reviewers to concentrate fully without distractions and then meet to discuss issues. Meeting lengths are shorter if the reviews are performed before the meeting rather than during the meeting ("online"); online meetings proceed at the pace of the slowest reviewer and therefore time is wasted, or the slowest reviewer is hurried and cannot review the code properly, which is another waste of time. Durations depend on the number of issues found, so the duration is somewhat unpredictable. It is also more efficient if someone other than the author takes notes, freeing the author to discuss issues without distractions.

Code Review Goals

The main goal of code reviews is to gain a different perspective and apply a different set of skills to the code. However, it is useful to put emphasis on helping the author with a particularly difficult problem on securing one part of the code against a likely kind of vulnerability, or on providing assurance that the code meets specifications and security requirements. Code reviews also provide signals and warning signs of design flaws. If the review of a section of code requires the reviewers to "jump around" between different files stored in different directories and carry most of the project's code along for reference, it is likely that the organization of the code (modularization or layers) is incorrect.

Testing

Testing is an important and a costly phase of the software development life cycle and is part of validation and verification activities. There are many books on software testing, so the coverage in this section focuses on the security aspects of testing.

Scenario Testing

Scenario testing is used to ensure that requirements capture is complete and consistent. This is a validation effort. At this stage, "abuse cases" (McDermott & Fox, 1999) and "misuse" cases (Sindre & Opdhal, 2000) are particularly relevant.

Specification Testing

There are a variety of specification testing methods, including formal proof and symbolic execution. These attempt to prove the completeness and correctness of the specification, often represented in an intermediate language. This is both validation and primarily verification. An example is the use of mathematical tools to verify

UMLsec specifications against formal security requirements (Juerjens, 2004).

Statistical Testing

Whereas specification-based testing aims at finding as many defects as possible (effectiveness), statistical testing aims at running as few test cases as possible with maintained high-quality efficiency (Olsson, 2002). For security purposes, we find specification testing more attractive because of the emphasis on complete coverage, whereas statistical testing considers complete coverage that is neither possible nor very effective.

Inline Testing

Inline testing (including uses of ASSERT macros, pre- and postconditions, etc., . . .) are a form of execution testing to verify adherence to specifications. These are normally built into the code at the time of development. For security, these should verify that the internal state of the software is an allowed and expected state for the algorithm, is self-consistent, and is consistent with a state approved by policies and requirements.

Unit Testing

Unit testing is performed during construction and is a form of local testing to verify proper behavior of subroutines, functions, modules, libraries, and so on. This stage is appropriate to detect several of the vulnerabilities enumerated at the beginning of section 4, such as buffer overflows, directory traversal, and format string vulnerabilities. However, testing for issues such as symlink vulnerabilities is difficult because race conditions are not reproducible. Moreover, it is unlikely that the testers will think of the metacharacter issues that the coders forgot (especially if they are the same people) and even less likely that random input will produce them.

Integration Testing

Integration testing is when the interfaces and common interfaces of modules are tested during linking and loading. One could argue that the syntactic–semantic checks of arguments in calls is a form of testing at this stage if it is done statically, at link time. Otherwise, it is a form of inline testing. In either case, it is a form of verification. It is at this stage that discrepancies in assumptions and the assignment of responsibilities for various parts of the software can create vulnerabilities. An example would be if Part A makes a call to Part B, relying on Part B to perform access control, whereas Part B assumes that the caller did it. At this stage, security testing should ensure that all operations and requests that should be denied, are denied, and that partial accesses are allowed only what they should.

Final Testing

Final testing is what most people mean when they talk about testing. This is where test cases are developed and run against the entire software artifact. Lots of different methods can apply here, some of which have already been mentioned. Theoretically, testing should exhaustively exercise all the execution paths in a program, with all possible values and kinds of inputs, but this can be rather complicated and time consuming. In its simplest form, random input can be used, such as that generated by the "fuzz" testing program (Miller, Fredriksen, & So, 1990) or IP Stack Integrity Checker (Frantzen, 1999). In large or complex systems, however, the cause of a given malfunction can be difficult to pinpoint even if the random input is replayed. Using binary search to isolate the input responsible for the malfunction ignores accumulated state in the system and can result in contradictory results, such as the "critical input" (which may not exist independently) being in a set of inputs but being absent from both halves of the set. More sophisticated approaches involve creating a grammar describing inputs and testing the running program with various inputs designed to find flaws; this technique has proved powerful but requires significant investment and deep understanding of the program's function to bear fruit (Oulu University Secure Programming Group, 2001). The effectiveness of software testing can also be improved based on partitioning the input domain, which reduces the number of test cases needed (Vagoun, 1996).

Acceptance Testing

Acceptance testing is done for contracts and is a validation step. This is when the customer uses the software to ensure that it meets the needs of the customer in real use. Customers should try to include tests of every threat that can be tested. Interoperability testing may also occur to ensure that the new artifact works with other necessary hardware and software. Of course, these needs should be in the requirements but are often overlooked.

Maintenance Testing

Maintenance testing is done after changes in the system or its platform. This may include regression testing to ensure that no old bugs (or new bugs) are (re-)introduced in the process of fixing a flaw. Vendors have a much bigger maintenance testing load than most hackers understand, and this is one reason it takes so much time to build and release a good patch.

CONCLUSION

Programmer brilliance is not a substitute for security knowledge and discipline. Moreover, coding secure programs is different from producing assurance so that customers or third parties can trust that the programs are reasonably secure. Revealing the entire source code (as in open source) does not in itself produce assurance or increase security; however, it may enable auditing and testing. Auditing and testing are of benefit only if performed by qualified people. Although this chapter did not provide exhaustive coverage of these issues, it is hoped that the discussions and questions asked will inspire the application of these ideas as well as further research.

GLOSSARY

Commercial Off-the-Shelf (COTS) Basic software, as opposed to more expensive special purpose software.

Common Vulnerabilities and Exposures (CVE) A project started by MITRE to identify all vulnerabilities; the project homepage is http://cve.mitre.org

Evaluation Assurance Level (EAL) The Common Criteria standardized evaluations. Note that the use of the Common Criteria is not limited to specifying EALs. The seven EALs are described at http://csrc.nist.gov/cc/Documents/CC%20v2.1%20-%20HTML/PART3/PART36.HTM

Globbing A UNIX term for the shell's process of wild-card filename expansion to develop a list of literal filenames that the shell then passes to a command. The C shell permits the user to disable globbing by default; the Bourne, Korn, and POSIX shells require the user to quote or escape metacharacters in file names if globbing is not desired. (Digital UNIX Documentation Library)

CROSS REFERENCES

See *Standards for Product Security Assessment; The Common Criteria.*

REFERENCES

Agile Alliance. (2001). Principles behind the Agile Manifest. Retrieved from http://agile-manifesto.org/principles.html

Ahmed, T., & Tripathi, A. R. (2003). Static verification of security requirements in role-based CSCW systems. In *Proceedings of the Eighth ACM Symposium on Access Control Models and Technologies, Villa Gallia, Como, Italy* (pp. 196–203). New York: ACM Press.

Amey, P. (2001). A language for systems not just software. 2001 ACM SIGAda Annual International Conference (SIGAda'01), Minneapolis USA.

Amey, P. (2002). Correctness by Construction: Better can also be cheaper. Cross Talk Magazine. *The Journal of Defence Software Engineering, 15*(3), 24–28.

Baskerville, R. (1993). Information-systems security design methods: Implications for information-systems development, *Computing Surveys, 20*, 375–414.

Berry, D. M. (1998). The safety requirements engineering dilemma. In *Proceedigns on the Ninth International Workshop on Software Specification and Design* (pp. 147–149). Los Alamitos, CA: IEEE Computer Society Press.

Boehm, B. (1988). A spiral model of software development and enhancement. *Computer, 21*(5), 61–72.

Boehm, B. (1997). Developing multimedia applications with the win win spiral model. *Lecture Notes in Computer Science, 130*, 20–39.

Boehm, B. (2000). Spiral development: Experience, principles, and refinements. In W. J. Hansen (Ed.), *Spiral Development Workshop*. (CMU/SEI-2000-SR-008). Pittsburgh, PA: Carnegie Mellon University, Software Engineering Institute.

Boehm, B., Egyed. A., Kwan, J., Port, D., & Madachy, R. (1998). Using the win win spiral model: A case study. *Computer, 31*(7), 33–44.

Brown, N. (1989). Assessment of security requirements for sensitive systems. In *Fifth Annual Computer Security Applications Conference* (p. 142). Los Alamitos, CA: IEEE Computer Society Press.

CERT Coordination Center. (1998). How to remove meta-characters from user-supplied data in CGI scripts. Retrieved from http://www.cert.org/tech_tips/cgi_metacharacters.html

Cervesato, I., Durgin, N., Lincoln, P., Mitchell, J., & Scedroy, A. (1999). Ametanotation for protocol analysis. Proceedings of the 12th IEEE Computer Security Foundations Workshop (pp. 55–69).

Cohen, D., Lindvall, M., & Costa, P. (2003). Agile Software Development (Tech Report DACS-SOAR-11). Retrieved from http://fc-md.umd.edu/fcmd/papers/DACS-SOAR-AgileSoftwareDevelopment.pdf

Common Criteria Project Sponsoring Organizations. (1999). Common criteria for information technology security evaluation, version 2.1. Retrieved from NIST's Computer Security Resources Center http://csrc.nist.gov/cc/CC-v2.1.html

Coulouris, G., & Dollimore, J. (1994). Security requirements for cooperative work: a model and its system implications. 6th ACM SIGOPS European Workshop, Dagstuhl.

Crook, R., Ince, D., Lin, L., & Nuseibeh, B. (2002). Security requirements engineering: When anti-requirements hit the fan. In *Proceedings of the IEEE Joint International Conference on Requirements Engineering* (pp. 203–205). Los Alamitos, CA: IEEE Computer Society Press.

Davis, N., & Mullaney, J. (2003). The team software process (TSP) in practice: A summary of recent results (Technical report CMU/SEI-2003-TR-014) Retrieved from http://www.sei.cmu.edu/publications/documents/03.reports/03tr014.html

Even, S., & Goldreich, O. (1983). On the security of multiparty ping-pong protocols. Proceedings of the 24th IEEE Symp. Foundations of Computer Science (pp. 34–39).

Frantzen, M. (1999). ISIC (IP Stack Integrity Checker). Retrieved from http://www.nestonline.com/TrinuxPB/isic.txt

Graff, M. G., & Van Wyk, K. R. (2003). *Secure coding: Principles and practices*. Cambridge, MA: O'Reilly & Associates.

Hall, A., & Chapman, R. (2002). Correctness by construction: Developing a commercial secure system. *IEEE Software, Jan/Feb*, 18–25.

Hamilton, D. L. (1992). Identification and evaluation of the security requirements in medical applications. In *Fifth Annual IEEE Symposium on Computer-Based Medical Systems* (pp. 129–137). Los Alamitos, CA: IEEE Computer Society Press.

Heffley, J., & Meunier, P. C. (2004). Can source code auditing software identify common vulnerabilities and be used to evaluate software security? In *37th Hawaii International Conference on System Sciences (HICSS)*. Los Alamitos, CA: IEEE Computer Society Press.

Heintze, N., & Tygar, J. D. (1996). A model for secure protocols and their composition. *IEEE Transactions on Software Engineering, 22*, 16–30.

Humphrey, W. S. (1999). Pathways to process maturity: The personal software process and team software process. Retrieved from http://interactive.sei.cmu.edu/Features/1999/June/Background/Background.jun99.htm

Humphrey, W. S. (2000). The team software process. (CMU/SEI-2000-TR-023). Retrieved from http://www.sei.cmu.edu/publications/documents/00.reports/00tr023.html

Humphrey, W. S. (2002). Three process perspectives: Organization, teams, and people. *Annals of Software Engineering, 14*(1–4), 39–72.

Jim, T., Morrisett, G., Grossman, D., Hicks, M., Cheney, J., & Wang, Y. (2002). Cyclone: A safe dialect of C.

In *USENIX Annual Technical Conference, Monterey* (pp. 275–288). Berkeley CA: USENIX Association.

Jones, E. L., & Chapman, C. L. (2001). A perspective on teaching software testing. *Journal of Computing in Small Colleges, 16*(3), 92–100.

Juerjens, J. (2004). *Secure systems development with UML.* London: Springer-Verlag.

Kolstad, K. O., & Bowles, J. (1991). Security requirements and models in open systems. In *Proceedings of the Twenty-Third Southeastern Symposium on System Theory, University of South Carolina)* (pp. 518–523). Piscataway, NJ: IEEE.

Leyden, J. (2004). Spam fighters infiltrate spam clubs. Retrieved from http://www.theregister.co.uk/2004/05/14/spam_club/

Linger, R. C. (1994). Cleanroom process model. *IEEE Software, 11*, 50–58.

Meadows, C. (2003). Formal methods for cryptographic protocol analysis: Emerging issues and trends. *IEEE Journal on Selected Areas in Communications, 21*, 44–54.

McDermott, J., & Fox, C. (1999). Using abuse case models for requirements analysis. In *Proceedings of the 15th Annual Computer Security Applications Conference, Phoenix AZ* (pp. 55–64). Los Alamitos, CA: IEEE Computer Society Press.

Meunier, P. C. (2002). CS390S secure programming. Class slides retrieved from http://www.cs.purdue.edu/homes/cs390s/refs.html

Meunier, P. C. (2003). CS490S secure network programming. Class slides retrieved from http://www.cs.purdue.edu/homes/cs490s/refs.html

Miller, B. P., Fredriksen, L., & So, B. (1990). Study of the reliability of UNIX utilities. *Communications of the ACM, 33*, 32–44.

Mills, H., Dyer, M., & Linger, R. (1987). Cleanroom software engineering. *IEEE Software, 4*, 19–25.

Motor Industry Software Reliability Association. (1998). Guidelines for the use of the C language in vehicle based software. Retrieved from http://www.misra.orq.uk/misra-c.htm

National Cyber Security Partnership Task Force. (2004). Security across the software development life cycle. Retrieved from http://www.cyberpartnership.org/init-soft.html

Olsson, T. (2002). Specification-based and statistical testing—A comparison. Lund, Sweden: Lund University, Department of Communication Systems. Retrieved from: http://www.telecom.lth.se/Personal/thomaso/publications/s_and_s_testing.pdf

Open Web Application Security Project. (2002). OWASP guide to building secure Web applications. Retrieved from: http://www.owasp.org/documentation/guide

Oulu University Secure Programming Group. (2001). PROTOS—Security testing of protocol implementations. Retrieved from: http://www.ee.oulu.fi/research/ouspg/protos/index.html

Paulk, M. C. (1994). A comparison of ISO 9001 and the capability maturity model for Software (CMU/SEI-94-TR-12). Software Engineering Institute.

Phillips, M. (2003). Using a capability maturity model to derive security requirements (GSEC practical). SANS Institute GIAC practical repository. (CMU/SEI-94-TR-12).

Reiser, H., & Vogt, G. (2000). Security requirements for management systems using mobile agents. In *Proceedings of the Fifth IEEE Symposium on Computers and Communications, Antibes, Juan Les Pins, France* (pp. 160–165). Los Alamitos, CA: IEEE Computer Society Press.

Saltzer, J. H., & Schroeder, M. D. (1995). Protection of Information in computer systems. *Proceedings of the IEEE, 63*(9) 1278–1308.

Sindre, G., & Opdhal, A. L. (2000) Eliciting security requirements by misuse cases. In B. Henderson-Sellers & B. Meyer (Eds.), *Proceedings of the 37th International Conference on Technology of Object-Oriented Languages and Systems*, Sydney, Australia (pp. 120–131). Los Alamitos, CA: IEEE Computer Society.

Soo Hoo, K., Sudbury, A. W., & Jaquith, A. R. (2001). In *Tangible ROI through Secure Software Engineering.* Secure Business Quarterly, Volume 1, Issue 2, Cambridge: Secure Business Quarterly (publishers, www.sbq.com)

Stephens, M., & Rosenberg, D. (2003). *The Extreme Programming refactored case against XP.* Berlin: A Press.

Strens, R., & Dobson, J. (1993). How responsibility modelling leads to security requirements. In J. B. Michael, V. Ashby, C. Meadows (Eds.), *Proceedings on the 1992–1993 workshop on New Security Paradigms, Little Compton, Rhode Island* (pp. 143–149). Los Alamitos, CA: IEEE Computer Society.

Sullivan, E. (2003). Building systems with assurance. In M. Bishop (Ed.), *Computer security art and science* (pp. 497–544). Boston: Addison-Wesley.

Vagoun, T. (1996). Input domain partitioning in software testing. In *Proceedings of the 29th Hawaii International Conference on System Sciences (HICSS), Volume 2: Decision support and knowledge-based systems (Maui. Hawaii)* (pp. 261–268). Los Alamitos, CA: IEEE Computer Society Press.

Varadharajan, V. (1990). Petri net based modelling of information flow security requirements. In *Proceedings of the Computer Security Foundations Workshop III, Franconia. New Hampshire* (pp. 51–61). Washington, DC: IEEE Computer Society Press.

Vetterling, M., Wimmel, G., & Wisspeintner, A. (2002). Secure systems development based on the common Criteria: The PalME project. *ACM SIGSOFT Software Engineering, 27*, 129–138.

Viega, J., & Messier, M. (2003). Secure programming cookbook for C and C++. Cambridge, MA: O'Reilly & Associates.

Wells, D. (2003). Extreme Programming: A gentle introduction. Retrieved from http://www.extremeprogramming.org/

Wheeler, D. (1999). Secure programming for Linux and Unix howto. Retrieved from http://www.dwheeler.com/secure-programs/

Wiegers, K. E. (1999). Software Requirements. Redmont, Washington: Microsoft Press.

Williams, L., & Upchurch, R. L. (2001). In support of student pair programming. In H. Walker, R. McCauley, J. Gersting, & I. Russell (Eds.), *Proceedings of the Thirty-Second SIGCSE Technical Symposium on Computer Science Education, Charlotte, North Carolina,* (pp. 327–331). New York: ACM Press.

Antivirus Technology

Matthew Schmid, *Cigital, Inc.*

INTRODUCTION

This chapter addresses the technologies and techniques being used in the fight against malicious software. The roots of this battle can be found in software designed to detect and eliminate computer viruses, though as this chapter illustrates, this 1.5 billion dollar industry has progressed far beyond the simple scanning techniques often associated with antivirus products (Gartner, 2002). A constant game of cat-and-mouse between the antivirus industry and malicious software authors has resulted in comprehensive tools designed to protect users from harm and equally sophisticated malicious software that attempts to evade detection and spread voraciously throughout the Internet.

Throughout this chapter the term *antivirus* refers to anything designed to combat a variety of malicious threats, including computer viruses, worms, Trojan horses, spyware, and other digital pests. Detailed information on various types of malicious software can be found elsewhere in this *Handbook*, and the distinctions will be largely ignored in this chapter except when necessary to the discussion (please refer to the chapters on Computer Viruses and Worms, Trojan Horse Programs, and Spyware). Many of the technologies described originated as countermeasures to computer viruses and have since been adapted to protect against new classes of malicious threats. Before delving into the details of how antivirus software works, it is important to understand what this technology is being used to accomplish.

Antivirus Goals

Antivirus technology has the common goal of protecting users from undesired damage, disclosure, or loss of data and computing resources because of the introduction of malicious software. This objective can be further subdivided into goals that address the different stages of a malicious threat. The four subgoals of antivirus software can be expressed as blocking the introduction of malicious software, detecting the presence of malicious software, preventing damage caused by the execution of malicious software, and recovering from an attack.

Blocking Malicious Threats

The first line of defense against malicious software includes tools and approaches that prevent these threats from ever executing on a protected computer system. Because of the growth of the Internet and the connectedness of today's computer systems, the spread of malicious software is no longer limited by geographical bounds. Unlike the early days of computer viruses, when malicious software was spread almost exclusively through the use of floppy disks, today's antivirus software must address numerous points of entry including e-mail, Web browsers, Internet enabled services, and shared file systems.

There are two basic approaches that antivirus software can use to prevent malicious programs from being introduced: they can block programs that are known to be malicious or they can allow only a set of programs that are known to be benign. These practices are respectively known as blacklisting and whitelisting. A more advanced approach to blocking malicious software involves trying to determine whether an unknown program is malicious or benign. This method is further discussed under "Heuristic Virus Detection."

Detecting Malicious Software

The detection and identification of malicious software is essential to both blocking its introduction and cleaning up after an attack. There is an important distinction between detection and identification: detection implies only determining the existence of a malicious threat, whereas identification involves matching the malicious software to a previously known example of this attack. Many modern antivirus products contain techniques capable of both the identification of known malicious threats and the detection of previously unknown malicious software. The accuracy of both identification and detection techniques is a large component of the overall effectiveness of an antivirus product, and improvement in these capabilities is a fertile area for ongoing research. Techniques for the detection and identification of malicious software are described in detail later in this chapter.

Tolerating Malicious Software

Despite the best efforts of antivirus software and practices, some malicious threats slip by these defenses. Virus writers continue to develop new malicious programs that are able to evade existing antivirus software—at least until the vendor is able to distribute updates designed to catch a new threat. The time between the development of a new virus and the release of a corresponding antivirus update is a window of opportunity during which a virus may spread unchecked.

Because the development of new malicious software that evades detection is likely to continue in the near future, antivirus researchers have created defensive measures designed to limit the damage that can be done by malicious software without requiring its detection. Designing protection that does not interfere with the operation of benign software applications is a challenging task.

Recovering from an Attack

In addition to detecting and identifying malicious software, most antivirus tools include mechanisms for helping users to remove threats from their systems and to repair files that may have been damaged. Successful recovery from a malicious software attack is dependent on many factors and may not be possible in all situations. Accurate identification of the malicious threat is important to most recovery approaches. In the case of computer viruses that infect executable programs or documents, it is essential that all traces of the virus be removed to prevent further infection. Maintaining the integrity of the program or document during virus removal can be a difficult process to automate.

ANTIVIRUS TECHNOLOGIES AND TECHNIQUES

Technologies for protecting users from malicious threats have evolved significantly since the mid-1990s. The goal of this section is to provide the reader with a basic idea of how existing antivirus techniques work and thereby facilitate a better understanding of the capabilities of antivirus software and the challenges that are faced by the antivirus industry. Although commercial antivirus products contain proprietary technologies and varying methods for protecting against malicious threats, the goal of this section is to cover the core techniques that are common across many of these solutions.

Signature Scanning

Signature scanning is the most common, accurate, and effective technique currently used in the fight against malicious software. It is the method employed by the earliest antivirus software and it continues to be an important piece of all comprehensive antivirus products. The goal of signature scanning is to examine a *target* for the presence of a *signature* that is used to indicate infection by a malicious program (Computer Knowledge, 2001). The target can be any type of data file, though it is often a program or other executable. The signature is a set of characteristics that can uniquely identify a malicious program.

Early virus signatures were often as simple as a string of bytes taken from a malicious program. The antivirus scanner then searches the target for this string. If the

Table 1 Simple Virus Signature

Virus Name:	W32.Sample.A
Byte Signature:	0A 8E 91 82 86 4C D2

scanner finds the string, then it assumes that the target is infected with the virus. If the string is not found, then the target is assumed to be free of this particular virus. Table 1 shows a fictitious example of a basic virus signature.

Although the process of scanning for virus signatures sounds fairly simple, getting it to work accurately and efficiently in practice is not quite so easy.

The Signature Development Process

The process of building a virus signature begins with the capture of a specimen. The virus specimen can come from any number of sources. Many infected executables are submitted to antivirus companies by customers every day. The antivirus company examines these programs to determine whether they actually are infected with a virus. If they are infected, and the virus is not one that has been seen before, then they may decide to generate a new signature.

The first step is to get the virus to propagate to other hosts. This may be as simple as running the virus (in a controlled environment) and looking to see if any files on the system have changed because of the infection. For viruses that are more particular about which files they will infect and/or when they will propagate it may require manual analysis of the virus to determine how it can be forced to spread under laboratory conditions.

After the virus has propagated to several additional files, the antivirus vendor can begin to look for a suitable signature. The signature must exist across all of the examples of the infected programs, must not exist in any known benign programs, and should serve as a unique identifier for this particular virus (signatures that match more than one virus are often desirable, but they must be augmented with information that can be used to distinguish one match from another). The large and continually growing number of software programs in the world makes finding a valid signature a difficult task. Many antivirus venders evaluate each signature against a huge collection of benign programs to ensure that it is unlikely to show up accidentally.

Once the virus signature has been verified to be unique, it needs to be made available to the antivirus program. Most of today's virus scanners use the Internet to receive signature updates. After receiving the new signature, the antivirus program is ready to protect against this most recent threat. To facilitate updates, modern antivirus software is separated into two main components: the analysis engine and the virus database (Muttik, 2000). The database contains information on how to detect and remove viruses. It may contain both information specific to particular viruses and data that can be used to address families or classes of malicious software. The analysis engine is a software program that knows how to use the information in the virus database to search for and remove malicious software. In many antivirus implementations, the boundary between the analysis engine and the virus database is somewhat blurred because the database may actually contain code modules used for detecting certain viruses. This provides the flexibility to easily extend the antivirus software to handle new threats without directly updating the analysis engine.

To improve efficiency, the antivirus industry has managed to automate a significant portion of the signature development process. Researchers at IBM explored the creation of an antivirus system capable of analyzing viruses and generating signatures with minimal human interaction (Kephart, 1994). This work has since been expanded into Symantec's *Digital Immune System*, which automates the detection, analysis, and response to over 85% of the virus specimens they receive (Symantec, 2001). This level of automation leaves virus analysts with more time to address more complicated threats and reduces the overall amount of time required to release updates that can counter newly discovered malicious software.

Improved Signature Scanning

Scanning an entire file for a sequence of bytes is a time- and processor-intensive operation that is not feasible in many antivirus scenarios. A modern computer system with a typically sized hard drive contains tens of thousands of files. Scanning each of these for all of the signatures in the signature database would take far more time than most people are willing to wait. Fortunately, this level of thoroughness is rarely required. By paring down the number of files that need to be examined and the areas within a file that need to be analyzed, it is possible to greatly reduce the amount of time needed to scan a hard drive effectively. Time is also a key consideration when antivirus software performs on-access scanning (looking for malicious code when a file is accessed or executed) or when antivirus software is deployed as part of a network gateway. Significant performance degradation is unacceptable in these situations.

To reduce the performance cost of signature scanning, antivirus software limits the types of files that are scanned and the areas of these files that are examined (Network Associates, 2002). The signature for a particular virus is expanded to include additional information on where to look for that virus. Viruses that infect executable programs are only searched for in files of an appropriate type. Likewise, macro virus signatures are not applied to executable files. Limiting scanning by file type can greatly reduce the search space with only a small impact on the effectiveness of a scanner.

Even with these reductions, scanning a large file can still be a time-consuming operation. Signature scanning can be refined further by limiting the areas of a file that are examined to those that are most likely to contain the signature. Each signature is tailored to include information that instructs the scanner on where to look for that particular virus. For example, some viruses may only infect the header section of an executable program. Others may be found immediately at the program's entry point (the location in the file where program execution begins). The signature may also restrict the size of the area that is

Table 2 More Sophisticated Virus Signature

Virus Name:	W32.Sample.A
Byte Signature:	0A 8E 91 82 86 4C D2
File Types:	Executable files
Scan Region:	Program entry point
Scan Length:	112 bytes

scanned. Table 2 illustrates how a virus signature can be refined to include additional information.

The efficiency of signature scanning can be greatly increased by using more detailed virus signatures. Unfortunately, this also has the effect of making virus signatures less resilient to small variations in the virus. These variations may be because of the virus itself (in the form of metamorphism), may be the result of a malicious individual making modifications to an existing virus, or may be because of infection by more than one virus. If a virus signature consists of a sequence of instructions at a particular location in an executable file, a slight change to the virus that leaves this sequence intact, but moves the location of the virus by a few bytes, may result in a failure to detect the variant.

Evading Signature Detection

A major goal of virus writers has been to develop malicious software that cannot be detected by the simple, but effective, signature scanning approach favored by the antivirus industry. One of the most common techniques used by viruses is to attempt to avoid detection by hiding their actual code from the antivirus scanner. Polymorphic viruses, which first began to appear in the wild in 1991 (Nachenberg, 1996), vary their appearance with each new host they infect. This is often accomplished through using simple encryption algorithms with variable keys to make signature detection more difficult (Ludwig, 1995). These viruses typically contain a simple symmetric encryption/decryption algorithm that is executed early in the program and used to decrypt the main body of the virus. When the virus infects a new target, it chooses a new key, infects the target, and then encrypts the body of the virus. The result is an obfuscated virus body that contains no recognizable signatures.

A major weakness of polymorphism is that the decryption algorithm itself cannot be encrypted (it must be able to execute). This makes it a good candidate for a virus signature. One way that virus writers have tried to counter this detection technique is by introducing metamorphic viruses. These viruses further disrupt signature scanning by actually altering their own executable code as they infect new hosts (Ször & Ferrie, 2001). Typically, metamorphic viruses modify their own code by adding new instructions that do not have any real effect on the execution of the virus. Table 3 illustrates how a metamorphic engine might alter the instructions in a virus (and disrupt its signature) without actually affecting the semantics of the code. The ineffective instructions are marked as NOP.

A more sophisticated metamorphic program might reorder instructions or substitute equivalent (but different)

Table 3 Metamorphic Virus Example

Original Code	Metamorphic Code	Comments
mov eax, 5	mov eax, 5	
add eax, ebx	push ecx	NOP
call [eax]	pop ecx	NOP
	add eax, ebx	
	swap eax, ebx	NOP
	swap ebx, eax	NOP
	call [eax]	
	nop	NOP

instructions. A metamorphic virus may apply these alterations to its entire body (including the code for performing the metamorphosis), or it may consist of a polymorphic virus that uses metamorphism to disguise only its decryption algorithm. A recent study (Christodorescu & Jha, 2004) found that simple obfuscating transformations were enough to confuse several popular antivirus products. Fortunately for the antivirus industry, the difficulty of writing a robust metamorphic virus has limited their number.

Advanced Scanning Techniques

Addressing the threat of polymorphic and metamorphic viruses required changes to how virus scanning is performed. Simply updating the database of virus signatures would not work against these new attacks. The success of polymorphic viruses led to an increase in the use of polymorphism and to the development of virus writing tools that assisted others in the creation of hard-to-detect malicious software. To deal with these new threats, the antivirus industry turned to a novel antivirus technique that became known as generic decryption (Nachenberg, 1997).

The idea was to allow a program to execute for a short period of time before applying traditional signature scanning to the program's image in memory. If the virus code was executed during this time, it would perform the decryption operation itself, exposing the virus body to the antivirus software. To do this safely required that the program's execution was emulated rather than actually executed on the computer. Although computationally expensive, this improvement to signature scanning was very effective at dealing with polymorphic viruses.

Metamorphic viruses continue to be a dangerous threat even today. Although approaches to detecting them do exist, the methods are often time consuming and failure prone. Inexact string matching algorithms are one technique that can be used to identify metamorphic viruses. A signature based on inexact matching allows for some of the variations introduced by metamorphic viruses and incorporates wildcards in the byte signature (Harley, Slade, & Gattiker, 2001; Kumar & Spafford, 1992). If the sequence of bytes in the signature is A B C, the signature must be able to match the sequence A [bogus instructions] B [bogus instructions] C (as in the example in Table 3). Accounting for this type of inexact match requires a more sophisticated scanning engine and is potentially more prone to false positives. There is also a

significantly greater chance that an inexact signature may inadvertently match a benign program than that an exact signature (with the same number of instructions) will do so. Researchers in both industry and academia continue to search for a solution for effectively detecting metamorphic viruses.

Another improvement made to antivirus scanning engines is the ability to analyze compressed or archive files. Archive files contain collections of other files that are bundled together for easier transport. The problem with archives is that they may contain infected files and analyzing their contents requires the antivirus engine to support multiple extraction algorithms. Most antivirus solutions are able to handle common archive and compression formats, but proprietary formats may prevent analysis, and files that have been encrypted and protected with a password or key cannot be analyzed.

Heuristic Virus Detection

Although signature scanning is an effective approach to detecting known malicious software, it is notoriously poor at detecting novel malicious programs. As previously discussed, virus signatures are designed to accurately identify a particular malicious program. The result is that even minor variations to a virus may result in it slipping by scanners unnoticed. Likewise, there is almost no chance of detecting a newly created malicious program with existing signatures.

Signature scanning forces the antivirus industry to react to each new threat that is discovered. The use of the Internet for malicious code propagation has dramatically reduced the amount of time that it takes for a virus to spread, thereby reducing the amount of time that antivirus companies have to release new signatures. Although the spread of viruses that require human interaction to propagate may still be contained by rapid response to new threats, the growing problem of malicious software that propagates on its own clearly requires a new approach. The recent outbreak of the Sapphire worm spread to over 90% of vulnerable hosts in about 10 minutes (Moore et al., 2003). A reactive approach to defending against these threats is clearly inadequate.

Heuristic virus detection refers to techniques used to detect malicious software based on a set of rules rather than using predefined signatures (Symantec, 1997). The goal is to develop measurements that can be used to indicate whether a program is infected with a virus without needing prior knowledge of that virus. Heuristic scanners look for common characteristics of viruses that have been defined by experts or discovered through machine learning. By applying these rules to an unknown program, the heuristic engine makes an educated guess as to whether the unknown program is infected with a virus.

A heuristic scanning engine may examine a suspicious file for dozens or even hundreds of signs of infection. The exact nature of what today's antivirus software looks for is a closely guarded trade secret and is a major differentiator among antivirus products. A few examples of signs of infection that may be used by heuristic scanners include the following:

- The location of the program's entry point
- The permissions of each section of a program (read, write, and/or execute)
- The presence/absence of certain patterns of instructions
- ASCII strings that may be included in the program

Although none of these rules may be very reliable when used alone, combined they provide a capable method of detecting the presence of malicious software. Although difficult to thoroughly evaluate, antivirus vendors claim that modern heuristics are capable of detecting over 80% of newly emerging threats (Symantec, 1997). As new malicious software is released, heuristic engines may be updated with additional rules based on information from these latest examples.

Advantages

Heuristic virus detection has the potential to greatly improve protection against new and unknown malicious software. A strong heuristic engine would be capable of detecting most threats without requiring frequent updates from the antivirus vendor. This provides a great advantage against fast-spreading viruses that propagate before a detection signature can be distributed to the scanning software. Heuristics may also prove more effective against polymorphic and metamorphic viruses that are designed to thwart signature detection. A heuristic scanning engine may actually look for signs of this behavior. For example, determining that a program is capable of modifying its own code may be viewed as suspicious. When found in conjunction with other unusual properties, this may provide enough information to assume that the program is hostile.

Disadvantages

Several unsolved problems with heuristic virus scanning have kept the technology from playing a more significant role in many antivirus products. Heuristic techniques are generally more likely than signature scanning to falsely determine that a program is malicious. This is because heuristics look for indicators that a program is malicious rather than identifying the presence of a particular virus. Though the designers of heuristic algorithms strive to keep false positives to a minimum, occasionally legitimate programs will appear to contain malicious behavior. For example, a program that automatically decrypts itself when executed may be flagged as suspicious even though it may be perfectly benign. With most heuristic techniques, it is possible to tune the sensitivity of the algorithm to favor increased detection capabilities or a lower false positive rate. Some antivirus products even allow the users to adjust these parameters themselves.

The use of rules rather than signatures also means that heuristic scanners can detect that a program may be malicious, but it cannot identify the threat by name. In some cases, heuristic scanners may be able to determine that a virus appears related to a known family of viruses. Although this may not seem like a significant shortcoming, it is, however, a barrier to user acceptance. Heuristic engines may also face difficulties in removing the virus infections that they detect because they do not have specific enough information about the threat. Without this additional information, the virus scanner risks damaging the file or failing to remove all of the malicious content.

Analyzing a file with a heuristic engine can also be time and processor intensive. Although some heuristics may be relatively easy to calculate, others may require reading and analyzing a significant portion of the program file. The amount of time required for heuristic analysis will affect the acceptance of the solution.

Finally, as in the case with signature scanning, virus writers have the advantage of being able to test their viruses against existing heuristic engines before actually releasing a new malicious program on the Internet. Although a good set of heuristic rules is more difficult to evade than a virus signature, through trial and error a virus writer may be able to produce something that cannot be detected by available heuristic scanners. By not publicizing their heuristic scanning rules, antivirus vendors make the virus writers' task more difficult though not insurmountable.

Future of Heuristics

In a seminal paper on computer viruses, Cohen (1987) showed that it is theoretically impossible to develop an algorithm that can differentiate between viruses and nonviruses based on examination. The author reasons that if we assume the existence of an algorithm for detecting a particular virus, then the virus could use that same algorithm to examine itself and propagate if and only if the algorithm does not identify the program as a virus. The resulting contradiction in logic proves the impossibility of designing such an algorithm: the program will act as a virus when it is not identified as a virus and will fail to exhibit virus behavior when it is identified as a virus. More recent work (Chess & White, 2000) uses a similar argument to prove that there exist viruses for which no error-free detection algorithm can be developed. Although these papers focus on the theoretical limits of virus detection rather than the practical aspects of the problem, they do effectively demonstrate that the perfect virus detection tool can never exist.

For the reasons discussed in this chapter, heuristic virus scanning will not replace signature scanning anytime soon. Antivirus vendors look to heuristics as a technology that can augment traditional signature scanning and can hopefully improve protection against new threats. Reactive approaches to detecting known threats remain the best way of identifying common viruses, and with reductions in the amount of time required to generate and distribute virus signatures, it is an effective solution in most instances. The use of heuristic virus scanners does further raise the bar for virus writers, making it more difficult for a novice virus writer to create a virus that will not be detected by existing antivirus products. It also offers a level of protection against new threats that is otherwise nonexistent.

Integrity Checking and Code Signing

Verifying the integrity of data and program files has been shown to be useful for virus detection and for identifying other malicious activity. The goal is to alert the user to any unusual changes that are made to the file system. Although the contents of data files are changed frequently, most executable files are modified only during software upgrades. Any unauthorized changes to an executable file may indicate infection by a virus.

Integrity verification programs, such as Tripwire (Kim & Spafford, 1994), use cryptographic hashing to establish a baseline for file contents. Files are hashed again either when accessed or at a predetermined time, and the hash values are compared. Any changes to the hash values indicate that a file's contents have been altered. This simple approach is fairly effective at detecting viruses that infect executable files, though it is less useful for detecting viruses that hide in frequently modified data files (as is often the case with macro viruses). To get the most out of an integrity checking program, it is essential that the system is clean from malicious software when the initial hash values are established and that the cause of all integrity violations is determined. Integrity checking can serve as a useful heuristic for detecting and containing malicious software outbreaks before updated signatures can be obtained.

Digital signatures can also be used to verify the integrity and source of software that is downloaded over the Internet. Technology such as Microsoft's Authenticode packages software with a digital signature that can be used to help in deciding whether to trust a particular program (Grimes, 2001). Prior to executing the software, the signing certificate is displayed, and the user is given a choice of whether to proceed. If any changes have been made to the software, then the signature is rendered invalid.

The downside of this approach is that signed code is not necessarily safe. The signature only tells you what certificate was used—it says nothing about the trustworthiness of the signer or the behavior of the signed software. Obtaining a code-signing certificate is easy, and if users are not discriminating in whom they decide to trust, then code signing offers little or no protection.

Scanning on Demand

The scanning techniques described previously can be made more effective and efficient by performing them only when needed. On-access (or on-demand) scanning invokes the antivirus engine at the point when a user accesses a potentially dangerous file. For data files this means prior to being read and for executable files it takes place just prior to execution. Because it is performed while a user is accessing a file, on-access virus scanning must be very fast to minimize the latency that is introduced. If a virus is detected, the scanner can block the user's access to the file, preventing the spread of the virus. Some antivirus products combine integrity checking with on-access scanning to prevent repeating the examination of a file that has not changed.

Behavior Monitoring

The techniques examined so far are based on the static analysis of files and simple processor emulation. Dynamic antivirus technologies differ in that they monitor the behavior of a program while it is executing. It is often easier to determine what a program is doing by observing its interaction with the system rather than trying to predict its behavior by analyzing it statically. Because dynamic approaches are watching program behavior, they are typically heuristic in nature. An example of a heuristic that is sometimes employed is to watch for programs that are writing to other executable files. This unusual behavior may indicate that a virus is infecting a new host—or it may be the benign actions of a programming language compiler. If a program is believed to be a virus, it can be terminated by the antivirus software to prevent further damage.

A different dynamic approach that some antivirus products take is to restrict an application's behavior based on a predefined policy. The objective is to limit a program's access to system resources while still enabling it to execute. This technique, often referred to as running an application in a *sandbox*, can be applied to all programs or only to suspicious applications. The most well-known example of a sandbox is probably that implemented by the Java virtual machine (JVM). Beginning with Java 2, the JVM is capable of enforcing fine-grained policies on all executing Java programs and applets (McGraw & Felten, 1999). The sandbox policy can be used to specify which system resources should be made available to the Java program and how the program can use them.

Although this discussion focused on the Java sandbox, researchers have shown that a similar model can be enforced by the native operating system (Goldberg, Wagner, Thomas, & Brewer, 1996), and sandbox technology is beginning to emerge in commercial tools. A sandbox can be very effective at containing potentially malicious code while enabling it to execute in a safe environment. A significant weakness of using a sandbox is the difficulty in defining an appropriate policy for each target program. If the sandbox policy is too permissive, malicious software can still damage the system; however, if the policy is too restrictive, the program will not be able to access the resources necessary to run. Each application may require its own custom sandbox policy, resulting in an administrative nightmare. Researchers continue to explore effective techniques for implementing this promising technology in a noninvasive manner (Balfanz & Simon, 2000; Weber, Schmid, Geyer, & Schatz, 2002).

Virus Removal and Recovery

In addition to detecting viruses, most antivirus solutions incorporate technology to disinfect files that have been compromised. The goal of disinfection (or cleaning) is to remove any dangerous components of the virus from the infected file and to restore the file to working order. This means repairing infected executables so that they will run correctly and removing viral code from data files without corrupting the file. Virus removal is a valuable feature of antivirus software because otherwise the file must be restored from a backup or may be lost entirely. The ability to clean files is less important in a tool that is being used to block viruses from entering an organization but may be essential when being used to recover from a virus outbreak.

Cleaning or removing viruses is closely tied to virus detection and identification. Cleaning engines are similar to scanning engines in their ability to perform both generic cleaning and virus-specific cleaning. Antivirus companies are able to reduce the size and complexity of their product by designing cleaning techniques that can be applied to large families of viruses rather than requiring a unique approach to cleaning each infection. The balance that companies try to achieve is to cover the vast majority of viruses with a few generic disinfection routines and develop virus-specific techniques only when needed. Modern antivirus scanners are able to use generic methods of disinfection over 50% of the time when dealing with new executable viruses and as often as 90% of the time with new macro viruses (Muttik, 2000).

The process of cleaning data files and executable files is quite different because of the structure of these files and the methods used during infection. In the case of many macro viruses, cleaning is as simple as deleting the macros that contain the malicious code. Cleaning viruses from an executable can be a much more complicated endeavor. All executable viruses alter the infected program's control flow to take control at some point during execution (typically the virus takes control near the beginning of the program). If a cleaning tool were to simply remove or overwrite the virus code, then the executable, though rendered harmless, would fail to run. To make the host program functional again, the disinfection routine must reverse the changes made during the infection process.

Some viruses intentionally make the disinfection process more difficult for antivirus software. These viruses may encrypt or even overwrite portions of the host file that they infect. Removing the virus can result in lost data or a program that will not run. In most cases, it is possible to derive an effective algorithm for removing a virus from an executable by carefully studying how the infection routine works. Preparing and distributing custom disinfection routines is costly, however, and tends only to be done for the most prevalent viruses.

In the worst-case scenario, recovering from a virus infection may require a complete reinstallation of the operating system and may even require hardware replacement. One of the most critical factors in limiting the damage that can be done by malicious code is restricting the privileges granted to the program when it is executed. Most viruses are executed with the same privileges that the user is granted. This means that if a user running as an administrator on a Microsoft Windows NT/2000/XP machine (or *root* on a UNIX-based system) accidentally launches a virus, it can perform all of the actions available to that user. Viruses executed with elevated privileges can make changes to the operating system, can disable antivirus software, and can install stealthy *rootkits* that provide attackers with access to the machine. Particularly dangerous viruses have even been known to install themselves into the persistent RAM found on peripherals such as graphics cards (Hoglund & McGraw, 2004). Fortunately, the damage done by most viruses is fairly limited, and antivirus products are often successful in removing them.

ANTIVIRUS POLICIES AND PRACTICES

The technologies discussed in this chapter are most effective when deployed according to established best practices and placed within the context of an organizational security policy. Defining a policy designed to minimize the threat posed by viruses and malicious software is essential to maintaining a secure environment. Users are very likely to inadvertently introduce viruses into an organization unless proper policies are in place and vigorously enforced. Preventing viral outbreaks in the workplace can be accomplished only through a combination of technical and nontechnical solutions. Home users must also be vigilant in practicing safe Internet behavior. This section will describe key elements of protecting both homes and businesses from computer viruses (for a broader look at security policies, refer to the chapter on Security Policy Guidelines).

Deploying Antivirus Solutions

By now the reader should have a good idea of how existing antivirus solutions can protect them from viruses and other malicious software. Deploying antivirus solutions on all general-purpose computer systems is the best approach to preventing viral infections for both home and business users. In addition to installing antivirus software on desktops, it is also a good practice for organizations to incorporate antivirus solutions at all entry points to the network. Mail servers, FTP servers, and other gateways should all be protected.

Installing solutions from multiple vendors rather than selecting a single antivirus solution for the entire enterprise can improve the odds of detecting and stopping a virus. These solutions should be deployed in a layered fashion to ensure that a virus must make it past several antivirus solutions to succeed. For example, an organization may deploy one company's product at the network gateway and a different company's product on users' computers. Deploying more than one antivirus solution on a particular machine should generally be avoided as it may result in incompatibilities that could render one or both solutions ineffective.

Antivirus solutions that employ signature detection must be kept up to date if they are to detect newly discovered threats. Most antivirus products are able to obtain updates across the Internet. The update schedule may either be periodic or triggered by the vendor's release of new signature information. In either case, it is important to verify that the antivirus solution is able to receive updates and is not blocked by a firewall or other network restriction. Not all antivirus products that include heuristic detection engines have them enabled by default. As discussed previously, heuristics currently offer the best form of protection against unknown viruses and should therefore be enabled when available. Files flagged as potentially malicious by a heuristic engine should be treated as dangerous unless proven otherwise.

Awareness

Most users are aware of the dangers of malicious software because of the high-profile news coverage of computer viruses and worms during the past several years. Unfortunately, merely knowing about these threats is not enough to prevent people from becoming victims. Teaching people the basics of *how* viruses propagate and what they should watch out for can help them to avoid attacks. Deep technical knowledge of how viruses work is not a requirement and providing too much information may be counterproductive.

People are often tricked into opening e-mail attachments because they appear to have been sent by someone they trust. Users can be made less susceptible to these attacks by learning that viruses often use this method of social engineering as a way of spreading across the Internet (Harley et al., 2001). Similarly, the installation of unauthorized software must be actively discouraged. Malicious threats that arrive through Web browsers are particularly dangerous because many people believe that Web browsing is inherently safe. They often do not realize that ActiveX controls and signed Java applets can be every bit as damaging as an e-mail attachment or downloaded program. Improving the awareness of how malicious threats are introduced can reduce the success rate of many common attacks.

Enforceable Security Policies

Whenever possible, users should be prevented from making decisions that impact organizational security. When given the choice between security and interesting functionality, people often make the wrong choice. This is where antivirus technology can provide valuable assistance by enforcing organizational policies. Antivirus software is often capable of quarantining potentially dangerous attachments and preventing users from installing and running unauthorized software. Rather than just telling people not to install ActiveX controls, most Web browsers support the central administration of policies that enforce this guideline. There are analogous methods of addressing macro and script viruses. It is important that this functionality is mandatory and cannot be easily circumvented by the end user.

Updates and Operating Systems

The choice of an operating system will have a significant impact on how susceptible the system is to viruses and other malicious threats. The emphasis on usability and interoperability in the most popular operating systems often opens these systems to attack, as by far the most common family of operating systems, Microsoft Windows and its associated software, has been the victim of numerous high-profile attacks. Although vendors are often quick to respond to significant outbreaks, the rapid spread of malicious software across the Internet can occur long before an appropriate patch becomes available. Selecting a less common operating system such as Mac OS X, Linux, or another UNIX-based operating system may reduce the likelihood of being attacked by viruses or worms, but these systems are certainly not immune to the malicious software problem. In environments where high availability is a requirement, the best solution is often to deploy multiple operating systems with the knowledge that it is unlikely for a single attack to succeed against all.

Ensuring that the operating system and its software are kept up to date with the latest patches, revisions, and service packs is paramount to preventing malicious software attacks. Many widespread viruses and worms enter systems through known vulnerabilities that can be eliminated with freely available vendor-supplied patches. System administrators and home users should keep their computers secure by routinely verifying that they have installed all available updates. To help users with this otherwise time-consuming task, many operating systems and applications are able to determine when updates are available by communicating with the vendor over an Internet connection. For example, Microsoft Windows provides the *Windows Update* service, which can automatically detect, download, and install important operating system upgrades (Thurrott, 2004).

As mentioned previously, performing routine tasks as a user that does not possess administrative or root privileges can prevent viruses from inflicting the most serious damage. Even home users should resist the urge to always run as an administrator as most applications do not require elevated privileges to function. Although antivirus technology can help to prevent attacks from succeeding, it is best to employ a layered system of defenses. If an administrative account is compromised by malicious software, then the possibilities for damage or information theft are endless.

SUMMARY

This chapter has explained the goals of antivirus software and has introduced the technologies and practices that support these goals. Antivirus software is an important countermeasure to dangerous malicious software that can spread rapidly across the Internet. Recent improvements in antivirus technology provide better protection than ever against new or unknown malicious software. By providing an understanding of how antivirus software works, it should be more apparent why viruses and other threats continue to plague today's computer systems. Knowing the strengths and weaknesses of these solutions will enable users to make better informed decisions when choosing an antivirus solution and should provide a context for understanding new technological advances being made in this field. Computer users must also understand that antivirus technology is only one element in the fight against viruses and other malicious threats. The best protection from viruses and other malicious software comes from a combination of technology, policies, and practices. By following the guidelines provided in this chapter and installing strong antivirus solutions, most computer virus infections can be prevented.

GLOSSARY

Executable The compiled binary image of a program that is loaded into memory and executed by the processor.

Heuristic A set of rules or guidelines that can be used to infer the presence or absence of malicious software.

Macro Virus A computer virus that is written in an interpreted application macro language. The host of a macro virus is typically a document rather than a program executable.

Signature　A set of characteristics that can be used to uniquely identify an element of malicious software.

Virus　A program that can "infect" other programs by modifying them to include a possibly evolved copy of itself (Cohen, 1987).

Worm　A self-replicating computer program that typically spreads via computers connected to the Internet. Unlike a virus, a computer worm does not necessarily infect a benign host program.

CROSS REFERENCES

See *Computer Viruses and Worms; Hoax Viruses and Virus Alerts; Hostile Java Applets; Spam and the Legal Counter Attacks; Trojan Horse Programs.*

REFERENCES

Balfanz, D., & Simon, D. (2000). WindowBox: A simple security model for the connected desktop. In *Proceedings of the 4th USENIX Windows System Symposium*, Seattle, WA.

Chess, D., & White, S. (2000). An undetectable computer virus. In *Proceedings of the 2000 Virus Bulletin Conference*, Orlando, FL.

Christodorescu, M., & Jha, S. (2004). Testing malware detectors. In *Proceedings of the 2004 ACM SIGSOFT International Symposium on Software Testing and Analysis*, Boston, MA.

Cohen, F. (1987). Computer viruses: Theory and experiments. *Computers and Security, 6*(1), 22–35.

Computer Knowledge. (2001). *Virus tutorial: Scanning.* Retrieved October 15, 2004, from http://www.cknow.com/vtutor/vtscanning.htm

Gartner. (2002). *Total worldwide security software market revenue forecast by segment.* Gartner Press Room. Retrieved October 21, 2004, from http://www.dataquest.com/press gartner/quickstats/security.html

Goldberg, I., Wagner, D., Thomas, R., & Brewer, E. (1996). A secure environment for untrusted helper applications: Confining the wily hacker. In *Proceedings of the 1996 USENIX Security Symposium*, San Jose, CA.

Grimes, R. (2001). *Malicious mobile code: Virus protection for Windows* (pp. 358–361). Sebastopol, CA: O'Reilly.

Harley, D., Slade, R., & Gattiker, U. (2001). *Viruses revealed: Understand and counter malicious software* (pp. 158–159, 406–410). Los Angeles, CA: McGraw-Hill.

Hoglund, G., & McGraw, G. (2004). *Exploiting software: How to break code* (pp. 408–429). Boston: Addison-Wesley.

Kephart, J. (1994). A biologically inspired immune system for computers. In *Proceedings of the Fourth International Workshop on Synthesis and Simulation of Living Systems* (pp. 130–139). Cambridge, MA: MIT Press.

Kim, G., & Spafford, E. (1994). Writing, supporting, and evaluating Tripwire: A publicly available security tool. In *Proceedings of the 1994 USENIX Applications Development Symposium* (pp. 89–107), Toronto, Canada.

Kumar, S., & Spafford, E. (1992). A generic virus scanner in C++. In *Proceedings of the 8th Computer Security Applications Conference* (pp. 210–219), Los Alamitos, CA.

Ludwig, M. (1995). *The giant black book of computer viruses* (pp. 425–467). Arizona: American Eagle.

McGraw, G., & Felten, E. (1999). *Securing Java: Getting down to business with mobile code* (pp. 95–114). New York: John Wiley & Sons.

Moore, D., Paxson, V., Savage, S., Shannon, C., Staniford, S., & Weaver, N. (2003). *The spread of the Sapphire/Slammer worm.* Technical Report, Cooperative Association for Internet Data Analysis, Berkeley, CA.

Muttik, I. (2000). Stripping down an AV engine. In *Proceedings of the 2000 Virus Bulletin Conference* (pp. 59–68), Orlando, FL.

Nachenberg, C. (1996). Understanding and managing polymorphic viruses. The Symantec Enterprise Papers, Volume XXX.

Nachenberg, C. (1997). Computer virus-antivirus coevolution. *Communications of the ACM, 40*(1), 46–51.

Network Associates. (2002). *Advanced virus detection scan engine and DATs.* Executive White Paper. Retrieved October 15, 2004, from http://www.networkassociates.com/us/local_content/white_papers/wp_scan_engine.pdf

Symantec. (1997). Understanding heuristics: Symantec's bloodhound technology. Symantec White Paper Series, Volume XXXIV.

Symantec (2001). The digital immune system. Technical Brief. Retrieved October 15, 2004, from http://securityresponse.symantec.com/avcenter/reference/dis.tech.brief.pdf

Ször, P., & Ferrie, P. (2001). Hunting for metamorphic. In *Proceedings of the 2001 Virus Bulletin Conference* (pp. 123–144), Prague, Czech Republic.

Thurrott, P. (2004). *What you need to know about Windows update services.* Windows IT Pro, InstantDoc #41969. Retrieved October 20, 2004, from http://www.windowsitpro.com

Weber, M., Schmid, M., Geyer, D., & Schatz, M. (2002). A toolkit for detecting and analyzing malicious software. In *Proceedings of the 2002 Annual Computer Security Applications Conference*, Las Vegas, NV.

Computer Viruses and Worms

Robert Slade, *Vancouver Institute for Research into User Security, Canada*

INTRODUCTION

Computer viruses are unique among the many security problems in that the fact that someone else is infected increases the risk to you. However, viruses also seem to be surrounded by myths and misunderstandings. It is hoped this chapter will help to set the record straight.

History of Computer Viruses and Worms

Many claims have been made for the existence of viruses prior to the 1980s, but, so far, these claims have not been accompanied by proof. The Core Wars programming contests did involve self-replicating code, but usually within a structured and artificial environment.

The general perception of computer viruses, even among security professionals, has concentrated on their existence in personal computers (PCs) and particularly Wintel-type systems. This is despite the fact that Fred Cohen's seminal academic work took place on mainframe and minicomputers in the mid-1980s. The first e-mail virus was spread in 1987. The first virus hoax message (then termed a *metavirus)* was proposed in 1988. Even so, virus and malicious software (malware) research has been neglected, possibly because malware does not fit easily into the traditional access control security models.

There is some evidence that the first viruses were created during the 1980s. At least two Apple II viruses are known to have been created in the early 1980s. However, it was not until the end of the decade (and 1987 in particular) that knowledge of real viruses became widespread, even among security experts. For many years boot sector infectors and file infectors were the only types of common viruses. These programs spread relatively slowly, were primarily distributed on floppy disks, and were thus slow to disseminate geographically. However, these viruses tended to be very long lived.

During the early 1990s, virus writers started experimenting with various functions intended to defeat detection. (Some forms had seen limited trials earlier.) Among these were polymorphism, to change form in order to defeat scanners, and stealth, to attempt to confound any type of detection. None of these virus technologies had a significant impact. Most viruses using these so-called advanced technologies were easier to detect because of a necessary increase in program size.

Although demonstration programs had been created earlier, the mid-1990s saw the introduction of macro and script viruses in the wild. These were initially confined to word processing files, particularly files associated with the Microsoft Office suite. However, the inclusion of programming capabilities eventually led to script viruses in many objects that would normally be considered to contain data only, such as Excel spreadsheets, PowerPoint presentation files, and e-mail messages. This fact led to greatly increased demands for computer resources among antiviral systems, because many more objects had to be tested, and Windows OLE (Object Linking and Embedding) format data files presented substantial complexity to scanners. Macro viruses also increase new variant forms very quickly, because the virus carries its own source code and anyone who obtains a copy can generally modify it and create a new member of the virus family.

E-mail viruses became the major new form in the late 1990s and early 2000s. These viruses may use macro capabilities, scripting, or executable attachments to create e-mail messages or attachments sent out to e-mail addresses harvested from the infected machine. E-mail viruses spread with extreme rapidity, distributing themselves worldwide in a matter of hours. Some versions create so many copies of themselves that corporate and even service provider mail servers are flooded and cease to function. E-mail viruses are very visible and so tend to be identified within a short space of time, but many are macros or scripts, and so generate many variants.

With the strong integration of the Microsoft Windows operating system with its Internet Explorer browser, Outlook mailer, Office suite, and system scripting, recent viruses have started to blur the normal distinctions. A document sent as an e-mail file attachment can make a call to a Web site that starts active content that installs a remote access tool acting as a portal for the client portion of a distributed denial of service network. Indeed, not only are viruses starting to show characteristics that are similar to each other, but functions from completely different types of malware are beginning to be found together in the same programs, leading to a type of malware convergence.

Recently, many security specialists have stated that the virus threat is reducing because, despite the total number of virus infections being seen, the prevalent viruses are now almost universally e-mail viruses and therefore constitute a single threat with a single fix. This ignores the fact that, although almost all major viruses now use e-mail as a distribution and reproduction mechanism, there are a great many variations in the way e-mail is used. For example, many viruses use Microsoft's Outlook mailer to spread and reproduction can be prevented simply by removing Outlook from the system. However, other viruses may make direct calls to the Mail Application Programming Interface (MAPI), which is used by a number of mail user programs, whereas others carry the code for mail server functions within their own body. A number of e-mail viruses distribute themselves to e-mail addresses found in the Microsoft Outlook address book files, whereas others may harvest addresses from anywhere on the computer hard drive or may actually take control of the Internet network connection and collect contact data from any source viewed online.

Because the work has had to deal with detailed analysis of low-level code, virus research has led to significant advances in the field of forensic programming. However, to date computer forensic work has concentrated on file recovery and decryption, so the contributions in this area likely still lie in the future.

Many computer pundits, as well as some security experts, have proposed that computer viruses are a result of the fact that currently popular desktop operating systems have only nominal security provisions. They further suggest that viruses will disappear as security functions are added to operating systems. This thesis ignores the fact, well established by Cohen's research and subsequently confirmed, that viruses use the most basic of computer functions and that a perfect defense against viruses is impossible. This is not to say that an increase in security measures by operating system vendors could not reduce the risk of viruses: the current danger could be drastically reduced with relatively minor modifications to system functions.

It is going too far to say (as some have) that the very existence of viral programs, and the fact that both viral strains and the numbers of individual infections are growing, means that computers are finished. At the present time, the general public is not well informed about the virus threat, and so more copies of viral programs are being produced than are being destroyed.

Indeed, no less an authority than Fred Cohen has championed the idea that viral programs can be used to great effect. An application using a viral form can improve performance in the same way that computer hardware benefits from parallel processors. It is, however, unlikely that viral programs can operate effectively and usefully in the current computer environment without substantial protective measures being built into them. A number of virus and worm programs have been written with the obvious intent of proving that viruses could carry a useful payload, and some have even had a payload that could be said to enhance security. Unfortunately, all such viruses have created serious problems themselves.

Virus Definition

A computer virus is a program written with functions and intent to copy and disperse itself without the knowledge and cooperation of the owner or user of the computer. A final definition has not yet been agreed upon by all researchers. A common definition is, "a program which modifies other programs to contain a possibly altered version of itself." This definition is generally attributed to Fred Cohen from his seminal research in the mid-1980s, although Cohen's actual definition is in mathematical form. Another possible definition is an entity that uses the resources of the host (system or computer) to reproduce itself and spread, without informed operator action.

Cohen is generally held to have defined the term *computer virus* in his thesis (published in 1984). (The suggestion for the use of the term virus is credited to Len Adleman, his seminar advisor.) However, his original definition covers only those sections of code that, when active, attach themselves to other programs. This, however, neglects many of the programs that have been most successful "in the wild." Many researchers still insist on Cohen's definition and use other terms such as *worm* and *bacterium* for those viral programs that do not attack programs. Currently, viruses are generally held to attach themselves to some object, although the object may be a program, disk, document, e-mail message, computer system, or other information entity.

Computer viral programs are not a natural occurrence. Viruses are programs written by programmers. They do not just appear through some kind of electronic evolution. Viral programs are written, deliberately, by people. However, the definition of *program* may include many items not normally thought of in terms of programming, such as disk boot sectors and Microsoft Office documents or data files that also contain macro programming.

Many people have the impression that anything that goes wrong with a computer is caused by a virus. From hardware failures to errors in use, everything is blamed on a virus. A virus is not just any damaging condition. Similarly, it is now popularly believed that any program that may do damage to your data or your access to computing resources is a virus. Viral programs are not simply programs that do damage. Indeed, viral programs are not always damaging, at least not in the sense of being deliberately designed to erase data or disrupt operations. Most viral programs seem to have been designed to be a kind of electronic graffiti: intended to make the writer's mark in the world, if not his or her name. In some cases a name is displayed, on occasion an address, phone number, company name, or political party.

Is My Computer Infected? What Should I Do?

Many books and articles contain lists of symptoms to watch for to determine whether your computer is infected. These signs include things such as running out of memory space, running out of disk space, the computer operating slower than normal, files changing size, and so forth. In fact, many factors will create these same effects, and current viruses seldom do. The best way to determine whether you have been infected by a virus is to get and use an antiviral scanner. In fact, get more than one. With the rapid generation of new viruses these days, it is quite possible for a maker of antivirus software to make mistakes in updating signatures. Therefore, having a second check on a suspected virus is always a good idea.

One scanner for the Wintel platform is F-PROT. It is available in a DOS version, free of charge from www.f-secure.com. (Look under Downloads and Tools.) Although a DOS scanner has some limitations in a Windows environment (particularly with a New Technology File System [NTFS] under Windows XP), it will still be able to identify infected files and is quite good at picking out virus infections within e-mail system files (the files of messages held on your computer).

Another scanner available for free is AVG, from www.grisoft.com. This one also does a good job of scanning and will even update itself automatically (although that feature is problematic on some machines).

The various commercial antiviral producers generally produce trial versions of their software, usually limited in some way. Sophos and Avast have been very good in this regard.

In regard to the suggestion to use more than one scanner, it should be noted that a number of successful software publishers have included functions that conflict with software from other vendors. These products should be avoided, because of the previously noted possibility of failure in a single protection program. The use of free software, and purchase of software from companies that provide such free versions, is recommended, because the existence of these free scanners, and their use by other people, actually reduces your risk, because there will be fewer instances of viruses reproducing and trying to spread.

Readers may be surprised at the recommendation to use free software: there is a general assumption that commercial software must be superior to that provided free of charge. It should be noted that the author of this chapter is a specialist in the evaluation of security and, particularly, antiviral software and has published more reviews of antiviral software than any other individual. The reader can be assured that it can be proven that, in the case of antiviral software, free software is as effective, and in some cases superior to, many very expensive products.

TROJAN HORSES, VIRUSES, WORMS, RATs, AND OTHER BEASTS

Malware is a relatively new term in the security field. It was created to address the need to discuss software or programs that are intentionally designed to include functions for penetrating a system, breaking security policies, or carrying malicious or damaging payloads. Because this type of software has started to develop a bewildering variety of forms, such as backdoors, data diddlers, distributed denial of service (DDoS), hoax warnings, logic bombs, pranks, remote access Trojans (RATs), Trojans, viruses, worms, and zombies, the term malware has come to be used for the collective class of malicious software. The term is, however, often used very loosely simply as a synonym for virus, in the same way that virus is often used simply as a description of any type of computer problem. This chapter will attempt to define the virus and worm problem more accurately, and to do this we need to describe the various other types of malware.

Viruses are the largest class of malware, both in terms of numbers of known entities and in impact in the current computing environment. Viruses, therefore, tend to be synonymous, in the public mind, with all forms of malware.

Programming bugs or errors are generally not included in the definition of malware, although it is sometimes difficult to make a hard and fast distinction between malware and bugs. For example, if a programmer left a buffer overflow in a system and it creates a loophole that can be used as a backdoor or a maintenance hook, did he or she do it deliberately? This question cannot be answered technically, although we might be able to guess at it, given the relative ease of use of a given vulnerability.

In addition, it should be noted that malware is not just a collection of utilities for the attacker. Once launched, malware can continue an attack without reference to the author or user and in some cases will expand the attack to other systems. There is a qualitative difference between malware and the attack tools, kits, or scripts that have to operate under an attacker's control and that are not considered to fall within the definition of malware. There are gray areas in this aspect as well, since RATs and DDoS zombies provide unattended access to systems, but need to be commanded to deliver a payload.

Trojans

Trojans, or Trojan horse programs, are the largest class of malware in terms of numbers of different entities produced. However, the term is subject to much confusion, particularly in relation to computer viruses.

A Trojan is a program that pretends to do one thing while performing another, unwanted action. The extent of the pretense may vary greatly. Many of the early PC Trojans relied merely on the filename and a description on a bulletin board. Login Trojans, popular among university student mainframe users, mimicked the screen display and the prompts of the normal login program and could, in fact, pass the username and password along to the valid login program at the same time as they stole the user data. Some Trojans may contain actual code that does what it is supposed to be doing while performing additional nasty acts that it does not tell you about.

An additional confusion with viruses involves Trojan horse programs that may be spread by e-mail. In years past, a Trojan program had to be posted on an electronic bulletin board system or a file archive site. Because of the static posting, a malicious program would soon be identified and eliminated. More recently, Trojan programs have been distributed by mass e-mail campaigns, by posting on Usenet newsgroup discussion groups, or through automated distribution agents (bots) on Internet relay chat (IRC) channels. Because source identification in these communications channels can be easily hidden, Trojan programs can be redistributed in a number of disguises, and specific identification of a malicious program has become much more difficult.

Some data security writers consider that a virus is simply a specific example of the class of Trojan horse programs. There is some validity to this usage because a virus is an unknown quantity that is hidden and transmitted along with a legitimate disk or program, and any program can be turned into a Trojan by infecting it with a virus. However, the term *virus* more properly refers to the added, infectious code rather than the virus/target combination. Therefore, the term *Trojan* refers to a deliberately misleading or modified program that does not reproduce itself.

A major aspect of Trojan design is the social engineering (fraudulent or deceptive) component. Trojan programs are advertised (in some sense) as having a positive component. The term *positive* can be in dispute, because a great many Trojans promise pornography or access to pornography, and this still seems to be depressingly effective. However, other promises can be made as well. A recent e-mail virus, in generating its messages, carried a list of a huge variety of subject lines, promising pornography, humor, virus information, an antivirus program, and information about abuse of the recipient's e-mail account. Sometimes the message is simply vague, and relies on curiosity.

Social engineering really is nothing more than a fancy name for the type of fraud and confidence games that have existed since snakes started selling apples. Security types tend to prefer a more academic sounding definition, such as the use of nontechnical means to circumvent security policies and procedures. Social engineering can range from simple lying (such as a false description of the function of a file), to bullying and intimidation (to pressure a low-level employee into disclosing information), to association with a trusted source (such as the user name from an infected machine).

Worms

A worm reproduces and spreads, like a virus and unlike other forms of malware. Worms are distinct from viruses, though they may have similar results. Most simply, a worm may be thought of as a virus with the capacity to propagate independently of user action. In other words, they do not rely on (usually) human-initiated transfer of data between systems for propagation, but instead spread across networks of their own accord, primarily by exploiting known vulnerabilities in common software.

Originally, the distinction was made that worms used networks and communications links to spread and that a worm, unlike a virus, did not directly attach to an executable file. In early research into computer viruses, the terms *worm* and *virus* tended to be used synonymously, it being felt that the technical distinction was unimportant to most users. The technical origin of the term *worm program* matched that of modern distributed processing experiments: a program with segments working on different computers, all communicating over a network (Shoch & Hupp, 1982).

The first worm to garner significant attention was the Internet Worm of 1988, discussed in detail later in this chapter. Recently, many of the most prolific virus infections have not been strictly viruses, but have used a combination of viral and worm techniques to spread more rapidly and effectively. LoveLetter was an example of this convergence of reproductive technologies. Although infected e-mail attachments were perhaps the most widely publicized vector of infection, LoveLetter also spread by actively scanning attached network drives, infecting a variety of common file types. This convergence of technologies will be an increasing problem in the future. Code Red and a number of Linux programs (such as Lion) are modern examples of worms. (Nimda is an example of a worm, but it also spreads in a number of other ways, so it could be considered to be an e-mail virus and multipartite as well.)

Viruses

A virus is defined by its ability to reproduce and spread. A virus is not just anything that goes wrong with a computer, and virus is not simply another name for malware. Trojan horse programs and logic bombs do not reproduce themselves.

A worm, which is sometimes seen as a specialized type of virus, is currently distinguished from a virus because a virus generally requires an action on the part of the user to trigger or aid reproduction and spread. The action on the part of the user is generally a common function, and the user generally does not realize the danger of the action or the fact that he or she is assisting the virus.

The only requirement that defines a program as a virus is that it reproduces. There is no necessity that the virus carries a payload, although a number of viruses do. In many cases (in most cases of "successful" viruses), the payload is limited to some kind of message.

A deliberately damaging payload, such as erasure of the disk or system files, usually restricts the ability of the virus to spread because the virus uses the resources of the host system. In some cases, a virus may carry a logic bomb or time bomb that triggers a damaging payload on a certain date or under a specific, often delayed, condition.

Because a virus spreads and uses the resources of the host, it affords a kind of power to software that parallel processors provide to hardware. Therefore, some have theorized that viral programs could be used for beneficial purposes, similar to the experiments in distributed processing that are testing the limits of cryptographic strength. (Various types of network management functions, and updating of system software, are seen as candidates.) However, the fact that viruses change systems and applications is seen as problematic in its own right. Many viruses that carry no overtly damaging payload still create problems with systems. A number of virus and worm programs have been written with the obvious intent of proving that viruses could carry a useful payload and some have even had a payload that could be said to enhance security. Unfortunately, all such viruses have created serious problems themselves. The difficulties of controlling viral programs have been addressed in theory, but the solutions are also known to have faults and loopholes.

Logic Bombs

Logic bombs are software modules set up to run in a quiescent state, but to monitor for a specific condition, or set of conditions, and to activate their payload under those conditions. A logic bomb is generally implanted in or coded as part of an application under development or maintenance. Unlike a RAT or Trojan, it is difficult to implant a logic bomb after the fact. There are numerous examples of this type of activity, usually based upon actions taken by a programmer to deprive a company of needed resources if employment was terminated.

A Trojan or a virus may contain a logic bomb as part of the payload. A logic bomb involves no reproduction and no social engineering.

A persistent legend in regard to logic bombs involves what is known as the salami scam. According to the story, this involves the siphoning off of small amounts of money (in some versions, fractions of a cent) credited to the account of the programmer, over a very large number of transactions. Despite the fact that these stories appear in a number of computer security texts, the author has a standing challenge to anyone to come up with a documented case of such a scam. Over a period of 8 years, the closest anyone has come is a story about a fast food clerk who diddled the display on a drive-through window and collected an extra dime or quarter from most customers.

Other Related Terms

Hoax virus warnings or alerts have an odd double relation to viruses. First, hoaxes are usually warnings about new viruses: new viruses that do not, of course, exist. Second, hoaxes generally carry a directive to the user to forward the warning to all addresses available to them. Thus, these descendants of chain letters form a kind of self-perpetuating spam.

Hoaxes use an odd kind of social engineering, relying on people's naturally gregarious nature and desire to communicate, and on a sense of urgency and importance, using the ambition that people have to be the first to provide important new information.

Hoaxes do, however, have common characteristics that can be used to determine whether their warnings may be valid:

- Hoaxes generally ask the reader to forward the message
- Hoaxes make reference to false authorities such as Microsoft, AOL, IBM, and the FCC (none of which issue virus alerts) or to completely false entities

- Hoaxes do not give specific information about the individual or office responsible for analyzing the virus or issuing the alert
- Hoaxes generally state that the new virus is unknown to authorities or researchers
- Hoaxes often state that there is no means of detecting or removing the virus.
- Many of the original hoax warnings stated only that you should not open a message with a certain phrase in the subject line. (The warning, of course, usually contained that phrase in the subject line. Subject-line filtering is known to be a very poor method of detecting malware.)
- Hoaxes often state that the virus does tremendous damage and is incredibly virulent
- Hoax warnings very often contain A LOT OF CAPITAL LETTER SHOUTING AND EXCLAMATION MARKS!!!!!!!!!!
- Hoaxes often contain technical-sounding nonsense (technobabble), such as references to nonexistent technologies such as nth complexity binary loops

It is wisest, in the current environment, to doubt all virus warnings, unless they come from a known and historically accurate source, such as a vendor with a proven record of providing reliable and accurate virus alert information or preferably an independent researcher or group. It is best to check *any* warnings received against known virus encyclopedia sites. It is also best to check more than one such site: in the initial phases of a fast burner attack, some sites may not have had time to analyze samples to their own satisfaction, and the better sites will not post information they are not sure about. A detailed treatment of hoax warning viruses is found in another chapter in this *Handbook*.

RATs are programs designed to be installed, usually remotely, after systems are installed and working (and not in development, as is the case with logic bombs and backdoors). Their authors would generally like to have the programs referred to as remote administration tools to convey a sense of legitimacy.

When a RAT program has been run on a computer, it will install itself in such a way as to be active every time the computer is started subsequent to the installation. Information is sent back to the controlling computer (sometimes via an anonymous channel such as IRC) noting that the system is active. The user of the command computer is now able to explore the target, escalate access to other resources, and install other software, such as DDoS zombies, if so desired.

DDoS is a modified denial of service (DoS) attack. DoS attacks do not attempt to destroy or corrupt data, but attempt to use up a computing resource to the point at which normal work cannot proceed. The structure of a DDoS attack requires a master computer to control the attack, a target of the attack, and a number of computers in the middle that the master computer uses to generate the attack. These computers between the master and the target are variously called agents or clients, but are usually referred to as running zombie programs. The existence of a large number of agent computers in a DDoS attack acts to multiply the effect of the attack and also helps to hide the identity of the originator of the attack.

There is a lot of controversy over a number of technologies generally described as adware or spyware. Most people would agree that the marketing functions are not specifically malicious, but what one person sees as aggressive selling another will see as an intrusion or invasion of privacy.

Shareware or freeware programs may have advertising for a commercial version or a related product, and users may be asked to provide some personal information for registration or to download the product. For example, an unregistered copy of the WinZip archiving program typically asks the user to register when the program is started, and the free version of the QuickTime video player asks the user to buy the commercial version every time the software is invoked. Adware, however, is generally a separate program installed at the same time as a given utility or package and continues to advertise products, even when the desired program is not running. Spyware is, again, a system distinct from the software the user installed and passes more information than simply a user name and address back to the vendor: often these packages will report on Web sites visited or other software installed on the computer and possibly compile detailed inventories of the interests and activities of a user.

The discussion of spyware often makes reference to cookies or Web bugs. Cookies are small pieces of information in regard to persistent transactions between the user and a Web site, but the information can be greater than the user realizes, for example in the case of a company that provides content, such as banner ads, to a large number of sites. Cookies, limited to text data, are not malware and can have no executable malicious content. Web bugs are links on a Web page or embedded in e-mail messages that contain links to different Web sites. A Web bug therefore passes a call, and information, unknown to the user, to a remote site. Most commonly a Web bug is either invisible or unnoticeable (typically it is 1 pixel in size) to avoid alerting the user to its presence.

There is a persistent chain letter hoax that tells people to forward the message because it is part of a test of an e-mail tracking system. Although all such chain letter reports to date are false, such a system has been implemented and does use Web bug technology. The system is not reliable: Web bugs in e-mail rely on an e-mail system calling a Web browser function, and although this typically happens automatically with systems such as Microsoft's Outlook and Internet Explorer, a mailer such as Pegasus requires the function call to be established by the user and warns the user when it is being invoked. On susceptible systems, however, a good deal of information can be obtained: the mail system noted can frequently obtain the Internet protocol (IP) address of the user, the type and version of browser being used, the operating system of the computer, and the time the message was read.

Pranks are very much a part of the computer culture, so much so that you can now buy commercially produced joke packages that allow you to perform "Stupid Mac (or PC or Windows) Tricks." There are numberless pranks available as shareware. Some make the computer appear to insult the user; some use sound effects or voices; some use special visual effects. A fairly common thread running through most pranks is that the computer is, in some way, nonfunctional. Many pretend to have detected some kind of fault in the computer (and some pretend to rectify such faults, of course making things worse). One entry in the virus field is PARASCAN, the paranoid scanner. It pretends to find large numbers of infected files, although it does not actually check for any infections.

Generally speaking, pranks that create some kind of announcement are not malware: viruses that generate a screen or audio display are actually quite rare. The distinction between jokes and Trojans is harder to make, but pranks are intended for amusement. Joke programs may, of course, result in a denial of service if people find the prank message frightening.

One specific type of joke is the easter egg, a function hidden in a program and generally accessible only by some arcane sequence of commands. These may be seen as harmless, but note that they do consume resources, even if only disk space and also make the task of ensuring program integrity much more difficult.

FIRST GENERATION VIRUSES

Many of the books and articles that are currently available to explain about viruses were written based on the research that was done on the first generation of viruses. Although these programs are still of interest to those who study the internal structures of operating systems, they operated much differently than the current crop of malicious software. First generation viruses tended to spread very slowly, but to hang around in the environment for a long time. Later viruses tended to spread very rapidly, but also to die out relatively quickly.

Boot Sector Viruses

Viruses are generally partly classified by the objects to which they attach. Worms may be seen as a type of virus that attaches to nothing.

Most desktop computer operating systems have some form of boot sector, a specific location on the disk that contains programming to bootstrap the startup of a computer. Boot-sector infectors (BSIs) replace or redirect this programming to have the virus invoked, usually as the first programming running on the computer. Because the minimal built-in programming of the computer simply starts to read and execute material from a specific location on the disk, any code that occupies this location is run. BSIs copy themselves onto this location whenever they encounter any new disk.

Boot-sector infectors would not appear to fit the definition of a virus infecting another program, because BSIs can be spread by disks that do not contain any program files. However, the boot sector of a normal MS-DOS disk, whether or not it is a system or bootable disk, always contains a program (even if it only states that the disk is not bootable), and so it can be said that a BSI is a true virus.

The terminology of BSIs comes from MS-DOS systems, and this leads to some additional confusion. The physical first sector on a hard drive is not the operating-system boot sector. On a hard drive, the boot sector is the first logical sector. The number one position on a hard drive is the master boot record (MBR). Some viral programs, such as the Stoned virus, always attack the physical first sector: the boot sector on floppy disks and the master boot record on hard disks. Thus viral programs that always attack the boot sector might be termed pure BSIs, whereas programs such as Stoned might be referred to as an MBR type of BSI. The term *boot-sector infector* is used for all of them, though, because all of them infect the boot sector on floppy disks.

File Infecting Viruses

A file infector infects program (object) files. System infectors that infect operating system program files (such as COMMAND.COM in DOS) are also file infectors. File infectors can attach to the front of the object file (prependers), attach to the back of the file and create a jump at the front of the file to the virus code (appenders), or overwrite the file or portions of it (overwriters). A classic is Jerusalem. A bug in early versions caused it to add itself over and over again to files, making the increase in file length detectable. (This has given rise to the persistent myth that it is a characteristic of a virus that it will fill up all disk space eventually: by far the majority of file infectors add minimally to file lengths.)

Polymorphic Viruses

Polymorphism (literally many forms) refers to a number of techniques that attempt to change the code string on each generation of a virus. These vary from using modules that can be rearranged to encrypting the virus code itself, leaving only a stub of code that can decrypt the body of the virus program when invoked. Polymorphism is sometimes also known as self-encryption or self-garbling, but these terms are imprecise and not recommended. Examples of viruses using polymorphism are Whale and Tremor. Many polymorphic viruses use standard mutation engines such as MtE. These pieces of code actually aid detection because they have a known signature.

A number of viruses also demonstrate some form of active detection avoidance, which may range from disabling of on-access scanners in memory to deletion of antivirus and other security software (Zonealarm is a favorite target) from the disk.

Virus Creation Kits

The term *kit* usually refers to a program used to produce a virus from a menu or a list of characteristics. Use of a virus kit involves no skill on the part of the user. Fortunately, most virus kits produce easily identifiable code. Packages of antiviral utilities are sometimes referred to as tool kits, occasionally leading to confusion of the terms.

MACRO VIRUSES

A macro virus uses macro programming of an application such as a word processor. (Most known macro viruses use Visual Basic for Applications (VBA) in Microsoft Word: some are able to cross between applications and function in, for example, a PowerPoint presentation and a Word document, but this ability is rare.) Macro viruses

infect data files and tend to remain resident in the application itself by infecting a configuration template such as Microsoft Word's NORMAL.DOT. Although macro viruses infect data files, they are not generally considered to be file infectors: a distinction is generally made between program and data files. Macro viruses can operate across hardware or operating system platforms as long as the required application platform is present. (For example, many Microsoft Word macro viruses can operate on both the Windows and the Macintosh versions of Microsoft Word.) Examples are Concept and CAP. Melissa is also a macro virus, in addition to being an e-mail virus: it mailed itself around as an infected document.

Viruses contained in test or data files had been both theorized and tested prior to the macro viruses that used VBA. DOS batch files had been created that would copy themselves onto other batch files, and self-reproducing code had been created with the macro capabilities of the Lotus 1-2-3 spreadsheet program, but these were primarily academic exercises.

Macro viruses are not currently a major class of malware and are certainly nothing in comparison to e-mail viruses and network worms. However, increasing numbers of applications have macro programming capabilities, and it is possible that macro viruses may become a problem again as the computing environment changes.

What Is a Macro?

As noted above, a macro is a small piece of programming contained in a larger data file. This differentiates it from a script virus that is usually a standalone file that can be executed by an interpreter, such as Microsoft's Windows Script Host (.vbs files). A script virus file can be seen as a data file in that it is generally a simple text file, but it usually does not contain other data and generally has some indicator (such as the .vbs extension) that it is executable. Loveletter is a script virus.

Free Technology to Avoid Macro Viruses

A recommended defense is MacroList, written by A. Padgett Peterson. This is a macro itself, available for both Wintel and Macintosh machines. It will list all the macros in a document. Because most documents should not contain macros, any document that does should either have a really good reason for it or be looked at with suspicion. You can find MacroList at www2.gdi.net\~padgett\index.htm.

E-MAIL VIRUSES

With the addition of programmable functions to a standard e-mail user agent (usually Microsoft's Outlook), it became possible for viruses to spread worldwide in mere hours, as opposed to months.

The Start of E-Mail Viruses: Melissa

Melissa was far from the first e-mail virus. The first e-mail virus to successfully spread in the wild was the CHRISTMA exec, in the fall of 1987. However, Melissa was certainly the first of the fast burner e-mail viruses and the first to come to wide public attention.

The virus, generally referred to as W97M.Melissa, is a Microsoft Word macro virus. The name "Melissa" comes from the class module that contains the virus. The name is also used in the registry flag set by the virus.

The virus is spread, of course, by infected Word documents. What has made it the "bug du jour" is that it spreads *itself* via e-mail. Melissa was originally posted to the alt.sex newsgroup. At that time it was LIST.DOC and purported to be a list of passwords for sex sites.

If you get a message with a Melissa-infected document, do whatever you need to do to invoke the attachment, and have Word on your system as the default program for .doc files, Word starts up, reads in the document, and the macro is ready to start.

Assuming that the macro starts executing, several things happen.

The virus first checks to see if Word 97 (Word 8) or Word 2000 (Word 9) is running. If so, it reduces the level of the security warnings on Word so that you will receive no future warnings. In Word97, the virus disables the Tools/Macro menu commands, the Confirm Conversions option, the Microsoft Word macro virus protection, and the Save Normal Template prompt. It upconverts to Word 2000 quite nicely and there disables the Tools/Macro/Security menu.

Specifically, under Word 97 it blocks access to the Tools|Macro menu item, meaning you cannot check any macros. It also turns off the warnings for conversion, macro detection, and to save modifications to the NORMAL.DOT file. Under Word 2000 it blocks access to the menu item that allows you to raise your security level and sets your macro virus detection to the lowest level, that is, none. Because the access to the macro security menu item is blocked, you must delete the infected NORMAL.DOT file to regain control of your security settings. Note that this will also lose all of your global templates and macros. Word users who make extensive use of macros are advised to keep a separate backup copy of a clean NORMAL.DOT in some safe location to avoid problems with macro virus infections.

After this, the virus checks for the HKEY CURRENT_USER\Software\Microsoft\Office\Melissa?\ registry key with a value of "...by Kwyjibo." (The "kwyjibo" entry seems to be a reference to the "Bart the Genius" episode of the *Simpsons* television program where this word was used to win a Scrabble match.)

If this is the first time you have been infected, then the macro starts up Outlook 98 or higher, in the background, and sends itself as an attachment to the top 50 names in *each* of your address lists. (Melissa will not use Outlook Express. Also, Outlook 97 will not work.) Most people have only one (the default is "Contacts"), but if you have more than one then Outlook will send more than 50 copies of the message. Outlook also sorts address lists such that mailing lists are at the top of the list, so this can get a much wider dispersal than just 50 copies of the message/virus.

Once the messages have been sent, the virus sets the Melissa flag in the registry and looks for it to check whether to send itself out on subsequent infections. If the flag does not persist, then there will be subsequent mass mailings. Because the key is set in HKEY_CURRENT_USER, system administrators may have set permissions

such that changes made are not saved, and thus the key will not persist. In addition, multiple users on the same machine will likely each trigger a separate mailout, and the probability of cross infection on a common machine is very high.

Because it is a macro virus, it will infect your NORMAL.DOT and will infect all documents thereafter. The macro within NORMAL.DOT is "Document_Close()" so that any document that is worked on (or created) will be infected when it is closed. When a document is infected, the macro inserted is "Document_Open()" so that the macro runs when the document is opened.

Note that not using Outlook does not protect you from the virus, it only means that the 50 copies will not be automatically sent out. If you use Word but not Outlook, you will still be infected and may still send out infected documents on your own. Originally the virus would not invoke the mailout on Macintosh systems. However, infected documents would be stored, and, recently, when Outlook became available for Macs, there was a second wave of Melissa mailings.

The message appears to come from the person just infected, of course, since it really is sent from that machine. This means that when you get an infected message, it will probably appear to come from someone you know and deal with. The subject line is "Important Message From: [name of sender]" with the name taken from the registration settings in Word. The text of the body states "Here is that document you asked for...don't show anyone else ;-)." Thus, the message is easily identifiable: that subject line, the very brief message, and an attached Word document (file with a .doc extension to the filename).

However, note that, as with any Microsoft Word macro virus, the source code travels with the infection, and it was very easy for people to create variations of Melissa. Within days of Melissa there was a similar Excel macro virus, called Papa.

One rather important point: the document passed is the active document, not necessarily the original posted on alt.sex. So, for example, if I am infected, prepare some confidential information for you in Word, and send you an attachment with the Word document, containing sensitive information that neither you nor I want made public and you read it in Word, and you have Outlook on your machine, then that document will be mailed out to the top 50 people in your address book, and so forth.

How to Avoid E-Mail Viruses

It really is very simple to avoid e-mail viruses: do not double-click on any attachments that come with your e-mail. We used to say not to run any programs that came from someone you do not know, but many e-mail viruses spread using the identity of the owner of the infected computer, so that is no longer any protection. Do not run anything you receive, unless you know from some separate verification that this person intended to send you something, that it is something you need, and that the person sending it is capable of protecting themselves from infection.

It is also somewhat safer to use a mail program other than Outlook, because some versions of Outlook allowed attachments to run even before the user read the message to which they were attached.

WORMS (FIRST AND THIRD GENERATION)

In autumn 1988, the Internet/UNIX/Morris worm did not actually bring the Internet in general and e-mail in particular to the proverbial grinding halt. It was able to run and propagate only on machines running specific versions of the UNIX operating system on specific hardware platforms. However, given that the machines that are connected to the Internet also comprise the transport mechanism for the Internet, a minority group of server-class machines, thus affected, degraded the performance of the Net as a whole. Indeed, it can be argued that despite the greater volumes of mail generated by Melissa and LoveLetter and the tendency of some types of mail servers to achieve meltdown when faced with the consequent traffic, the Internet as a whole has proved to be somewhat more resilient in recent years.

During the 1988 mailstorm, a sufficient number of machines had been affected to impair e-mail and distribution-list mailings. Some mail was lost, either by mailers that could not handle the large volumes that backed up or by mail queues being dumped in an effort to disinfect systems. Most mail was substantially delayed. In some cases, mail would have been rerouted via a possibly less efficient path after a certain time. In other cases, backbone machines, affected by the problem, were simply much slower at processing mail. In still others, mail routing software would crash or be taken out of service, with a consequent delay in mail delivery. Ironically, electronic mail was the primary means that the various parties attempting to deal with the trouble were trying to use to contact each other.

In many ways, the Internet Worm is the story of data security in miniature. The Worm used trusted links, password cracking, security holes in standard programs, standard and default operations, and, of course, the power of viral replication.

Big Iron mainframes and other multiuser server systems are generally designed to run constantly and execute various types of programs and procedures in the absence of operator intervention. Many hundreds of functions and processes may be running all the time, expressly designed neither to require nor report to an operator. Some such processes cooperate with each other; others run independently. In the UNIX world, such small utility programs are referred to as daemons, after the supposedly subordinate entities that take over mundane tasks and extend the power of the "wizard," or skilled operator. Many of these utility programs deal with the communications between systems. *Mail*, in the network sense, covers much more than the delivery of text messages between users. Network mail between systems may deal with file transfers, the routing of information for reaching remote systems, or even upgrades and patches to system software.

When the Internet Worm was well established on a machine, it would try to infect another. On many systems, this attempt was all too easy, because computers on the

Internet are meant to generate activity on each other, and some had no protection in terms of the type of access and activity allowed.

The finger program is one that allows a user to obtain information about another user. The server program, fingerd, is the daemon that listens for calls from the finger client. The version of fingerd common at the time of the Internet Worm had a minor problem: it did not check how much information it was given. It would take as much as it could hold and leave the rest to overflow. "The rest," unfortunately, could be used to start a process on the computer, and this process was used as part of the attack. This kind of buffer overflow attack continues to be very common, taking advantage of similar weaknesses in a wide range of applications and utilities.

The sendmail program is the engine of most mail-oriented processes on UNIX systems connected to the Internet. In principle, it should only allow data received from another system to be passed to a user address. However, there is a debug mode that allows commands to be passed to the system. Some versions of UNIX were shipped with the debug mode enabled by default. Even worse, the debug mode was often enabled during installation of sendmail for testing and then never turned off.

When the Worm accessed a system, it was fed with the main program from the previously infected site. Two programs were used, one for each infected platform. If neither program could work, the Worm would erase itself. If the new host was suitable, the Worm looked for further hosts and connections.

The program also tried to break into user accounts on the infected machine. It used standard password-cracking techniques such as simple variations on the name of the account and the user. It carried a dictionary of words likely to be used as passwords and would also look for a dictionary on the new machine and attempt to use that as well. If an account was cracked, the Worm would look for accounts that this user had on other computers, using standard UNIX tools.

Following the Internet Worm, and a few similar examples in late 1988 and early 1989, worm examples were very infrequent during the 1990s.

By spring 2001, a number of examples of Linux malware had been seen. Interestingly, although the Windows viruses generally followed the CHRISTMA exec style of having users run the scripts and programs, the new Linux worms were similar to the Internet/Morris/UNIX worm in that they rely primarily on bugs in automatic networking software.

The Ramen worm makes use of security vulnerabilities in default installations of Red Hat Linux 6.2 and 7.0 using specific versions of the wu-ftp, rpc.statd, and LPRng programs. The worm defaces Web servers by replacing index.html and scans for other vulnerable systems. It does this initially by opening an file transfer protocol (FTP) connection and checking the remote system's FTP banner message. If the system is vulnerable, the worm uses one of the exploitable services to create a working directory and then downloads a copy of itself from the local (attacking) system.

Lion uses a buffer overflow vulnerability in the bind program to spread. When it infects, Lion sends a copy of output from the ifconfig command /etc/passwd and /etc/shadow to an e-mail address in the china.com domain. Next the worm adds an entry to etc/inetd.conf and restarts inetd. This entry would allow Lion to download components from a (now closed) Web server located in China. Subsequently, Lion scans random class B subnets in much the same way as Ramen, looking for vulnerable hosts. The worm may install a rootkit onto infected systems. This backdoor disables the syslogd daemon and adds a trojanized ssh (secure shell) daemon.

Code Red uses a known vulnerability to target Microsoft IIS (Internet Information Server) Web servers. Despite the fact that a patch for the loophole had been available for 5 months prior to the release of Code Red, the worm managed to infect 350,000 servers within 9 to 13 hours.

When a host gets infected, it starts to scan for other hosts to infect. It probes random IP addresses but the code is flawed by always using the same seed for the random number generator. Therefore, each infected server starts probing the same addresses that have been done before. (It was this bug that allowed the establishment of such a precise count for the number of infections.)

During a certain period of time the worm only spreads, but then it initiates a DoS attack against www1.whitehouse.gov. However, because this particular machine name was only an overflow server, it was taken offline prior to the attack and no disruptions resulted. The worm changed the front page of an infected server to display certain text and a background color of red, hence the name of the worm.

Code Red definitely became a media virus. Although it infected at least 350,000 machines within hours, it had probably almost exhausted its target population by that time. In spite of this, the Federal Bureau of Investigation held a press conference to warn of the worm.

Code Red seems to have spawned quite a family, each variant improving slightly on the random probing mechanism. In fact, there is considerable evidence that Nimda is a descendent of Code Red.

Nimda variants all use a number of means to spread. Like Code Red, Nimda searches random IP addresses for unpatched Microsoft IIS machines. Nimda will also alter Web pages to download and install itself on computers browsing an infected Web site using a known exploit in Microsoft Internet Explorer's handling of Java. Nimda will also mail itself as a file attachment and will install itself on any computer on which the file attachment is executed. Nimda is normally e-mailed in HTML format and may install automatically when viewed using a known exploit in Microsoft Internet Explorer. Nimda will also create e-mail and news files on network shares and will install itself if these files are opened.

DETECTION TECHNIQUES

All antiviral technologies are based on the three classes outlined by Fred Cohen in his early research. The first type performs an ongoing assessment of the functions taking place in the computer, looking for operations known to be dangerous. The second checks regularly for changes in the computer system where changes should occur only in-

frequently. The third examines files for known code found in previous viruses.

Within these three basic types of antiviral software, implementation details vary greatly. Some systems are meant only for use on standalone systems, whereas others provide support for centralized operation on a network. With Internet connections being so important now, many packages can be run in conjunction with content scanning gateways or firewalls.

String Search (Signature-Based)

Scanners examine files, boot sectors, and memory for evidence of viral infection. They generally look for viral signatures, sections of program code that are known to be in specific viral programs but not in most other programs. Because of this, scanning software will generally detect only known viruses and must be updated regularly. Some scanning software has resident versions that check each file as it is run.

Scanners have generally been the most popular form of antiviral software, probably because they make a specific identification. In fact, scanners offer somewhat weak protection, because they require regular updating. Scanner identification of a virus may not always be dependable: a number of scanner products have been known to identify viruses based on common families rather than definitive signatures.

Change Detection (Integrity Checking)

Change detection software examines system and program files and configuration, stores the information, and compares it against the actual configuration at a later time. Most of these programs perform a checksum or cyclic redundancy check that will detect changes to a file even if the length is unchanged. Some programs will even use sophisticated encryption techniques to generate a signature that is, if not absolutely immune to malicious attack, prohibitively expensive, in processing terms, from the point of view of a piece of malware.

Change detection software should also note the addition of completely new entities to a system. It has been noted that some programs have not done this and allowed the addition of virus infections or malware.

Change detection software is also often referred to as integrity-checking software, but this term may be somewhat misleading. The integrity of a system may have been compromised before the establishment of the initial baseline of comparison.

A sufficiently advanced change-detection system, which takes all factors including system areas of the disk and the computer memory into account, has the best chance of detecting all current and future viral strains. However, change detection also has the highest probability of false alarms, because it will not know whether a change is viral or valid. The addition of intelligent analysis of the changes detected may assist with this failing.

Real-Time Scanning

Real-time, or on-access, scanning is not really a separate type of antivirus technology. It uses standard signature scanning, but attempts to deal with each file of object as it is accessed or comes into the machine. Because on-access scanning can affect the performance of the machine, vendors generally try to take shortcuts to reduce the delay when a file is read. Therefore, real-time scanning is significantly less effective at identifying virus infections than a normal signature scan of all files.

Real-time scanning is one way to protect against viruses on an ongoing basis, but it should be backed up with regular full scans.

Heuristic Scanning

A recent addition to scanners is intelligent analysis of unknown code, currently referred to as heuristic scanning. It should be noted that heuristic scanning does not represent a new type of antiviral software. More closely akin to activity monitoring functions than traditional signature scanning, this looks for suspicious sections of code that are generally found in viral programs. Although it is possible for normal programs to want to "go resident," look for other program files, or even modify their own code, such activities are telltale signs that can help an informed user come to some decision about the advisability of running or installing a given new and unknown program. Heuristics, however, may generate a lot of false alarms and may either scare novice users or give them a false sense of security after wolf has been cried too often.

Permanent Protection

The ultimate objective, for computer users, is to find some kind of antiviral system that you can set and forget: that will take care of the problem without further work or attention on your part. Unfortunately, as previously noted, it has been proved that such protection is impossible. On a more practical level, every new advance in computer technology brings more opportunity for viruses and malicious software. As it has been said in political and social terms, so too the price of safe computing is constant vigilance.

Vaccination

In the early days of antiviral technologies, some programs attempted to add change detection to every program on the disk. Unfortunately, these packages, frequently called vaccines, sometimes ran afoul of different functions within normal programs that were designed to detect accidental corruption on disks. No program has been found that can fully protect a computer system in more recent operating environments.

Some vendors have experimented with an autoimmune system, whereby an unknown program can be sent for assessment, and, if found to be malicious, a new set of signatures created and distributed automatically. This type of activity does show promise, but there are significant problems to be overcome.

Activity Monitoring (Behavior-Based)

An activity monitor performs a task very similar to an automated form of traditional auditing: it watches for suspicious activity. It may, for example, check for any calls to format a disk or attempts to alter or delete a program file while a program other than the operating system is in

control. It may be more sophisticated and check for any program that performs direct activities with hardware, without using the standard system calls.

Activity monitors represent some of the oldest examples of antiviral software and are usually effective against more than just viruses. Generally speaking, such programs followed in the footsteps of the earlier anti-Trojan software, such as BOMBSQAD and WORMCHEK in the MS-DOS arena, which used the same "check what the program tries to do" approach. This tactic can be startlingly effective, particularly given the fact that so much malware is slavishly derivative and tends to use the same functions over and over again.

It is, however, very hard to tell the difference between a word processor updating a file and a virus infecting a file. Activity monitoring programs may be more trouble than they are worth because they can continually ask for confirmation of valid activities. The annals of computer virus research are littered with suggestions for virus-proof computers and systems that basically all boil down to the same thing: if the operations that a computer can perform are restricted, viral programs can be eliminated. Unfortunately, so is most of the usefulness of the computer.

PREVENTION AND PROTECTION TECHNIQUES

In regard to protection against viruses, it is germane to mention the legal situation with regard to viruses. Note that a virus may be created in one place and still spread worldwide, so issues of legal jurisdiction may be confused. In addition, specific activity may have a bearing: in the United States it may be legal to write a virus, but illegal to release it. However, in the first 16 years of the existence of viruses as a serious occurrence in the computing environment, only five people have been convicted in court of writing computer viruses, and in all five cases the defendants entered guilty pleas. Therefore, it is as well not to rely on criminal prosecutions as a defense against viruses.

The converse, however, is not true. If you are infected with a virus, and it can be demonstrated that your system subsequently sent a message that infected someone else, you may be legally liable. Thus, it is important to protect yourself from infection, even if the infection will not inconvenience you or cause loss to your business.

Training and some basic policies can greatly reduce the danger of infection. The following are a few guidelines that can really help in the current environment:

- Do not double-click on attachments.
- When sending attachments, be really specific when describing them.
- Do not blindly use Microsoft products as a company standard.
- Disable Windows Script Host. Disable ActiveX. Disable VBScript.
- Disable JavaScript. Do not send HTML formatted e-mail.
- Use more than one scanner and scan everything.

There are now companies that will provide insurance against virus attacks. This insurance is generally an extension of business loss-of-use insurance, and potential buyers would do well to examine the policies very closely to see the requirements for making a claim against it and also conditions that may invalidate payment.

Unfortunately, the price of safe computing is constant vigilance. Until 1995 it was believed that data files could not be used to transport a virus. Until 1998 it was believed that e-mail could not be used to automatically infect a machine. Advances in technology are providing new viruses with new means of reproduction and spread. Two online virus encyclopedias are listed in the Further Reading section and information about new viruses can be reliably determined at these sites.

NON-PC PLATFORM VIRUSES

As noted, many see viruses only in terms of DOS or Windows-based programs on the Intel platform. Although there are many more PC viruses than on other platforms (primarily because there are more PCs in use than other computers), other platforms have many examples of viruses. Indeed, I pointed out earlier that the first successful viruses were probably created on the Apple II computer.

CHRISTMA exec, the Christmas Tree Virus/Worm, sometimes referred to as the BITNET chain letter, was probably the first major malware attack across networks. It was launched on December 9, 1987, and spread widely on BITNET, EARN, and IBM's internal network (VNet). It has a number of claims to a small place in history. It was written, unusually, in Restructured Extended Executor (REXX), a scripting system used to aid with automating simple user processes. It was mainframe-hosted (on Virtual Machine/Conversational Monitor System [VM/CMS] systems) rather than microcomputer-hosted, quaint though that distinction sounds nowadays when the humblest PC can run UNIX.

CHRISTMA presented itself as a chain letter inviting the recipient to execute its code. This involvement of the user leads to the definition of the first e-mail virus, rather than a worm. When it was executed, the program drew a Christmas tree and mailed a copy of itself to everyone in the account holder's equivalent to an address book, the user files NAMES and NETLOG. Conceptually, there is a direct line of succession from this worm to the social engineering worm/Trojan hybrids of today.

In the beginning of the existence of computer viruses actually proliferating in the wild, the Macintosh computer seemed to have as many interesting viruses as those in the DOS world. The Brandau, or "Peace" virus, became the first to infect commercially distributed software, and the nVIR virus sometimes infected as many as 30% of the computers in a given area. However, over time it has become evident that any computer can be made to spread a virus, and the fact that certain systems have more than others seems to be simply a factor of the number of computers of a given type in use.

CONCLUSION

Malware is a problem that is not going away. Unless systems are designed with security as an explicit business requirement, which current businesses are not supporting through their purchasing decisions, malware will be an increasingly significant problem for networked systems.

It is the nature of networks that what is a problem for a neighboring machine may well become a problem for local systems. To prevent this, it is critical that the information security professional help business leaders recognize the risks incurred by their decisions and help to mitigate those risks as effectively and economically as possible. With computer viruses and similar phenomena, each system that is inadequately protected increases the risk to all systems to which it is connected. Each system that is compromised can become a system that infects others. If you are not part of the solution, in the world of malware, you are most definitely part of the problem.

GLOSSARY

Terms derived from the "Glossary of Communications, Computer, Data, and Information Security Terms" posted online at http://victoria.tc.ca/techrev/secgloss.htm and http://sun.soci.niu. edu/~rslade/secgloss.htm.

Activity Monitor A type of antiviral software that checks for signs of suspicious activity, such as attempts to rewrite program files, format disks, and so forth. Some versions of activity monitor will generate an alert for such operations, whereas others will block the behavior.

Change Detection Antiviral software that looks for changes in the computer system. A virus must change something, and it is assumed that program files, disk system areas, and certain areas of memory should not change. This software is very often referred to as integrity-checking software, but it does not necessarily protect the integrity of data, nor does it always assess the reasons for a possibly valid change. Change detection using strong encryption is sometimes also known as authentication software.

False Negative There are two types of false reports from antiviral software: false negatives and false positives. A false negative report is when an antiviral reports no viral activity or presence when there is a virus present. References to false negatives are usually only made in technical reports. Most people simply refer to an antiviral missing a virus. In general security terms, a false negative is called a false acceptance, or Type II error.

False Positive The second kind of false report that an antiviral can make is to report the activity or presence of a virus when there is, in fact, no virus. False positive has come to be very widely used among those who know about viral and antiviral programs. Very few use the analogous term, *false alarm*. In general security terms, a false positive is known as a false rejection, or Type I error.

Heuristic in general, heuristics refer to trial-and-error or seat-of-the-pants thinking rather than formal rules. In antiviral jargon, however, the term has developed a specific meaning regarding the examination of program code for functions or opcode strings known to be associated with viral activity. In most cases, this is similar to activity monitoring but without actually executing the program; in other cases, code is run under some type of emulation. Recently the meaning has expanded to include generic signature scanning meant to catch a group of viruses without making definite identifications.

Macro Virus A macro is a small piece of programming in a simple language used to perform a simple, repetitive function. Microsoft's Word Basic and VBA macro languages can include macros in data files and have sufficient functionality to write complete viruses.

Malware A general term used to refer to all forms of malicious or damaging software, including viral programs, Trojans, logic bombs, and the like.

Multipartite Formerly a viral program that would infect both boot sectors and files, the term now refers to a virus that will infect multiple types of objects or that reproduces in multiple ways.

Payload This term is used to describe the code in a viral program that is not concerned with reproduction or detection avoidance. The payload is often a message but is sometimes code to corrupt or erase data.

Polymorphism Techniques that use some system of changing the form of the virus on each infection to try and avoid detection by signature scanning software. Less sophisticated systems are referred to as self-encrypting.

Scanner A program that reads the contents of a file looking for code known to exist in specific viral programs. Also known as a signature scanner.

Stealth Various technologies used by viral programs to avoid detection on disk. The term properly refers to the technology and not a particular virus.

Trojan Horse A program that either pretends to have or is described as having a (beneficial) set of features but that, either instead or in addition, contains a damaging payload. Most frequently the usage is shortened to Trojan.

Virus A final definition has not yet been agreed upon by all researchers. A common definition is, "a program which modifies other programs to contain a possibly altered version of itself." This definition is generally attributed to Fred Cohen, although Cohen's actual definition is in mathematical form. Another possible definition is "an entity which uses the resources of the host (system or computer) to reproduce itself and spread, without informed operator action."

Wild, in the A jargon reference to those viral programs that have been released into, and successfully spread in, the normal computer user community and environment. It is used to distinguish those viral programs that are written and tested in a controlled research environment, without escaping, from those which are uncontrolled "in the wild."

Worm A self-reproducing program that is distinguished from a virus by copying itself without being attached to a program file or that spreads over computer networks, particularly via e-mail. A recent refinement is the definition of a worm as spreading without user action, for example by taking advantage of loopholes and trapdoors in software.

CROSS REFERENCES

See *Hackers, Crackers, and Computer Criminals; Hoax Viruses and Virus Alerts; Hostile Java Applets; Spyware; Trojan Horse Programs.*

FURTHER READING

Are good viruses still a bad idea? Retrieved March 2004, from http://www.frisk.is/~bontchev/papers/goodvir.html.

Bidgoli, H. (Ed.). (2002). *Encyclopedia of information systems*. San Diego, CA: Academic Press.

Cohen, F. (1994). *A short course on computer viruses* (2nd ed.). New York: Wiley.

Ferbrache, D. (1992). *A pathology of computer viruses*. London: Springer-Verlag.

F-Secure/Data fellows virus encyclopedia. Retrieved March 2004, from http://www.f-secure.com/v-descs/.

Gattiker, U., Harley, D., & Slade, R. (2001). *Viruses revealed*. McGraw-Hill, New York

Highland, H. J. (1990). *Computer virus handbook*. New York: Elsevier Advanced Technology.

Hruska, J. (1992). Computer viruses and anti-virus warfare (2nd ed.). London: Ellis Horwood.

IBM Research Papers. Retreived March 2004, from http://www.research.ibm.com/antivirus/

Kane, P. (1994). *PC security and virus protection handbook*. New York: M&T Books.

Lammer, V. (1993). *Survivor's guide to computer viruses*. Abingdon, UK: Virus Bulletin.

Shoch, J.F., & Hupp, J.A., (1982, March). The "worm" programs—early experience with a distributed computation of the ACM, 25 (3), 172-180.

Slade, R. M. (1996). *Robert Slade's guide to computer viruses* (2nd ed.). New York: Springer-Verlag.

Solomon, A. (1991). *PC viruses: Detection, analysis and cure*. London: Springer-Verlag.

Solomon, A. (1995). *Dr. Solomon's virus encyclopedia*. Aylesbury, UK: S&S International PLC.

Sophos virus encyclopedia. Retrieved March 2004, from http://www.sophos.com/virusinfo/analyses/.

Tipton, H., & Krause, M. (Eds.). (2003). *Information security management handbook* (4th ed., vol. 4). Auerbach: Malware.

Vibert, R. S. (2000). *The enterprise anti-virus book*. Braeside, Canada: Segura Solutions.

Trojan Horse Programs

Adam L. Young, *Cigital, Inc.*

INTRODUCTION

In computer security, a *Trojan horse* is defined as a segment of executable code that performs some function that the user does not expect and that resides in a program. A Trojan can be placed in the program when the program is compiled or can be added to the program after it is compiled.

The term *Trojan horse* carries with it a very negative connotation due to the abundance of deployed Trojan horses that have been designed to subvert computer systems. At the very least, a Trojan horse may be nothing more than a nuisance, and at worst a Trojan horse can completely undermine the integrity of the machine that it resides on. An example of a Trojan that is merely an annoyance is the cookie monster Trojan that prompts the user to enter the word "cookie" periodically. An example of a rather common form of malicious Trojan is *spyware* (which may be integrated into a program or may be stand-alone) that is deployed by a software vendor that sends private information pertaining to the user back to the vendor for marketing and development purposes. Some malicious Trojans nefariously log the keystrokes of users to a hidden file and are referred to as keyboard loggers or password snatchers. These Trojans allow the perpetrator to impersonate other users when the hidden file is later obtained.

This chapter covers the history of Trojan horse programs and also describes several classes of Trojan horse attacks. The chapter concludes with several defenses that can be used to help mitigate the risk of Trojan horse attacks.

Laying Siege to Troy

The term *Trojan horse* is a fitting one for describing malicious software and is based on a Greek myth. According to legend, the Greeks were unable to penetrate the city

of Troy using siege machines and other weapons of war. So, they devised a plan. They built a huge wooden horse with a hollow belly and filled it with Greek warriors that were poised for attack. The Greeks pushed the horse to the outskirts of Troy and then sailed away. The Trojans assumed that it was a peace offering and brought the horse inside the city to celebrate the presumed departure of the Achaeans. The citizens rejoiced and drank heavily throughout the evening and much of the night. The Greek warriors took the city by surprise under cover of dark.

One often hears the term *logic bomb* within the context of malicious software attacks. A logic bomb is a portion of code in an application or operating system that remains dormant for a specified period of time or until a particular event occurs that causes it to perform some predefined action. This action is often referred to as the payload of the malware. As a result, certain Trojan horses are logic bombs and vice versa. However, a Trojan can cause perpetual damage such as wasting central processing unit (CPU) cycles by performing useless computations on a regular basis. Such a Trojan is not a logic bomb.

How Trojans Differ from Viruses and Worms

Trojan horses differ from computer viruses and worms because they do not replicate. A computer virus is a program that replicates by infecting programs and requires some form of user action to propagate. A worm, however, may or may not infect programs and often does not require any explicit user intervention to replicate. Worms typically replicate and spread much faster than computer viruses. Slightly different definitions of a virus and a worm have appeared over the years, but no one would argue that a Trojan horse does not replicate.

Trojan horse programs can be roughly divided into those that are deployed by modifying source code and those that are deployed by manually infecting the host executable in much the same way that an executable is infected with a virus. The former deployment method assumes that the Trojan author has the luxury of modifying the original source code to contain the Trojan horse program and that the Trojan author can then compile and deploy the apparently innocent program. This option is not always possible, and so malware authors sometimes resort to modifying preexisting binary executables. The programs that are modified in this way are typically popular programs that are subsequently made available for download or operating system programs that reside on a machine that is under attack.

HISTORY OF TROJAN HORSES
Early Investigations into Abnormal Finite Automata

The notion of unusual or abnormal finite automata can be traced back to 1949 when John von Neumann presented lectures that encompassed the theory and organization of complicated automata (von Neumann, 1949). The notes corresponding to these lectures were later reprinted (von Neumann, 1966). In these lectures, Neumann postulated that a computer program could reproduce itself. In retrospect, it is remarkable how soon after the notion of the stored program concept the notion of self-replicating programs was investigated. Neumann is credited for promoting the notion of storing programs in memory (as opposed to using punch cards).

Bell Laboratories employees eventually gave life to Neumann's notion of self-replicating machines in the 1950s in a game dubbed *core wars*. In this game, two programmers would unleash software organisms and watch as the programs attempted to lay claim to the address space in which they fought. The core wars were described in a May 1984 issue of *Scientific American* (Dewdney, 1984).

The core wars were a way to model and observe highly simplistic forms of artificial life. These life forms would fight for resources, namely processor time and memory, within the core. The programs that were unleashed were written in a very simple assembly language for an equally simple virtual machine. Some programs fared better against some programs yet were vulnerable to others. It may well be that the earliest analog to a Trojan horse was evident as a program in core wars. There were programs that replicated in an attempt to overwrite the other hostile program in the core. There were also bomber programs that did not replicate at all but rather bombed locations outside of the bomber program. The bombing operation could be as simple as overwriting a memory location with binary zeros. Many of the ingredients for a Trojan were present since, at least with respect to the enemy program, the bomber was a malicious program that did not replicate.

Early Military Awareness Due to Shared-Resource Machines

The notion of a Trojan horse as we know it today can be traced back to the late 1960s. The concept of multiuser operating systems grew out of the need to make efficient use of expensive computing machinery. Prior to this, physical controls were used to maintain the security of batch processing machines, yet the effectiveness of such controls began to wane as soon as programs from different users began sharing memory on a single computer.

When the military began utilizing multiuser and networked operating systems, security issues surrounding these systems came to a head. Petersen and Turn addressed computer subversion in an article that was published in the proceedings of the AFIPS Conference (Peterson & Turn, 1967). The question of security control in resource-sharing systems was the focus of series of events in 1967. The Advanced Research Projects Agency (ARPA) was asked to form a task force to study and recommend hardware and software safeguards to protect classified information in multiaccess resource-sharing computer systems. This would be used to protect information from the lowest to the highest security levels—for example, unclassified, classified, secret, and top secret where top secret is the highest security level. The task force contained a technical panel that included, among others, James P. Anderson and Daniel J. Edwards. RAND published the report of the task force under ARPA sponsorship (Ware, 1970).

The RAND report defines *deliberate penetration* to be a deliberate and covert attempt to (a) obtain information contained in the system, (b) cause the system to operate to the advantage of the threatening party, or (c) manipulate the system to make it unreliable or unusable by the legitimate operator. The report notes that deliberate efforts to penetrate secure systems can either be active or passive: *passive* methods include monitoring electromagnetic emanations and wiretapping, whereas *active* methods involve attempting to enter the system to obtain data files or to interfere with files or the system. The discussion of subversion cites the AFIPS paper (Peterson & Turn, 1967).

A class of active infiltration that is identified in the report is the exploitation of *trapdoor* entry points into the system to bypass the security facilities to permit direct access to data. A trapdoor entry point is often created deliberately during the design and development stage to simplify the insertion of authorized program changes by legitimate system programmers and is closed prior to operational use. The report also notes the risk of implicit trapdoors that may result from improper system design. Finally, the report notes the possibility of an agent operating within a secure organization. It is noted that such an agent may attempt to create a trapdoor that can be exploited at a later date.

The actual phrase *Trojan horse* appeared in a computer security technology planning study that was prepared for the U.S. Air Force (USAF) by James P. Anderson (1972). The report addressed the growing security concerns of the USAF and suggested ways that the Air Force could prepare for attacks, from both inside and outside, against the USAF computing infrastructure. The report cited several issues that fueled the need for the study.

The first concern was that there was a growing requirement to provide shared use of computer systems that contained different classification levels and need-to-know requirements in a user population that was not uniformly cleared. In some systems, particularly those found in the

USAF Data Services Center at the Pentagon, users were permitted and encouraged to directly program the system for their applications. It is due to this kind of use that weaknesses in the technical foundation of security were most acutely felt.

An issue that compounded the security risk was the growing pressure to interconnect separate but related computer systems into increasingly complex computer networks. At that time the security issues surrounding multiuser systems and interconnected computers received nowhere near the amount of attention that it gets from the open research community today. In the same vein as the RAND study, the Anderson report identifies the threat of a single user that operates as a hostile agent. It is noted that such an agent can simply modify an operating system to bypass or suspend security controls. This fact, coupled with the fact that the implementation of the operating system was outside USAF control, contributed strongly to the reluctance to certify the security of the systems that were used at the time.

A number of specific threats are articulated in an appendix of the Anderson report titled, "Security Threats and Penetration Techniques." The section titled "Trojan Horse" identifies a trapdoor that is embedded in a program that appears to be so useful that the user will use it even though it may not have been produced under the user's control. A hypothetical Trojan is detailed that records the user ID and passwords to a file and it is noted that this file may be accessible to the perpetrator. A footnote attributes the Trojan horse attack to D. J. Edwards (from the National Security Administration [NSA]).

The Anderson report also describes the notion of a *clandestine code change* in which code that contains trapdoors is injected into the system for exploitation by the perpetrator. Section 1.3 describes a trapdoor that can be installed when the implementers are not cleared and that is activated by some unique string of input characters that is presented by a collaborating user. The report foreshadowed much of the computer security threats that we face today and was of paramount importance in shedding light on the issue of malicious software.

The Bell and LaPadula model (BLP) was devised to control access of a set of active entities to a set of passive (i.e., protected) entities based on some security policy (Bell & LaPadula, 1976). Active entities are called subjects (e.g., programs) and passive entities are called objects (e.g., data files). The two effects that an access can have on an object are the extraction of information (observing) and the insertion of information (altering).

The BLP *-property (pronounced "star-property") was devised primarily to counter the Trojan horse threat for high-assurance, military systems. A simplified version of the Bell and LaPadula *-property is as follows. The *-property holds if: in any state, if a subject has simultaneous observe access to object o_1 and alter access to object o_2 then the security level of o_2 is greater than or equal to the security level of o_1. The reader is referred to the original technical report for the complete version of this definition.

The discussion thus far has focused on the theoretical notion of a Trojan horse. In the early 1970s, an actual Trojan horse was inserted into Multics binary code and was distributed to all sites. Paul Karger and Roger Schell (1974) give a description of this Trojan. The paper details a penetration exercise of Multics on a HIS 6180 computer. The range of possible Trojan horse attacks was expanded in the work of Gus Simmons, which is the subject of the next section.

The Trojan Threat to Nuclear Arms Control Verification Systems

Gus Simmons investigated a highly specialized form of Trojan horse attack in the 1970s. The attack constituted a Trojan horse that resided within a cryptographic algorithm and deviated significantly from the Trojans that had been foreseen at the time. The Trojan was number theoretic in nature and was designed for the sole purpose of covertly transmitting information outside of its host.

Simmons' research grew out his analysis of cryptographic protocols that were designed to verify the compliance of the Strategic Arms Limitation Treaty II (SALT II), a treaty that was intended to control the nuclear arms race. This work forms the cornerstone for the theory of subliminal channels and is regarded as seminal with respect to cryptographic protocol failures and trust-related issues for black-box (e.g., microchip) cryptosystems. It is instructional to cover the origin of this interesting cryptographic phenomenon (Simmons, 1994).

In 1978, the Carter administration was seriously considering the adoption of a national security protocol that was designed to allow Russia to verify how many nuclear missiles the United States had fielded in the 1,000 U.S. silos without exposing which silos were actually armed. To constitute an acceptable solution to Russia, the compliance messages would have to be digitally signed in a way that would not be possible for the United States to forge. At any given time the United States was permitted to have 100 missiles residing in randomly chosen silos. Any more than this would be a violation of the SALT II treaty (Simmons, 1998).

The scheme that the Carter administration was endorsing was often referred to in the press as the missile shell game. This is because the 100 missiles would be shuttled randomly using trucks among the 1,000 Minuteman silos on a continual basis. It was envisioned that these trucks would even haul fake payloads, such as water, to conceal whether a given payload actually contained a live missile. This was necessary because the trucks could be observed via spy satellites. However, simply hauling fake loads would of course not be enough. The trucks would all have to exhibit the same acceleration, lest they be distinguished using elementary kinematics.

The proposed solution, one that would allow Russia to verify the number of missiles that the United States had placed afield, utilized both sensors and cryptographic devices. The sensors were to be placed in the silos. The data acquired by the sensors would indicate the presence or absence of a missile in a given silo, thus constituting a single bit of information. This bit had to be protected so that it could not be forged or falsely attributed. Both countries agreed that the sensor technology was acceptable. Gravimetric sensors could be used to detect underground features versus voids, tilt sensors could also be used, and so forth. In the proposed solution, each country would provide its own cryptographic algorithm.

This problem was being solved at about the same time that the Diffie-Hellman key exchange was devised. Symmetric ciphers were the norm at that time. The basic idea was to have the cipher use a secret key to encrypt a message. Both the ciphertext and plaintext would be output by the device. Signature verification amounted to decrypting the ciphertext and comparing the result to the plaintext. Implicit in this approach was that it should not be possible to leak information in each ciphertext. The ability to do so could potentially compromise the identity of the silo and give the enemy the opportunity to launch a devastating first strike.

As the story goes, the NSA viewed the SALT II treaty as an opportunity to learn more about the state of cryptography in Russia. It was suggested that the Russians devise their own cipher to place inside the device. Simmons saw the peril in this approach. He called for a meeting with the NSA, armed with the fact that the recently discovered Rabin cipher could be used inside the device to leak a single bit to the Russians. To sign a message in Rabin, the message is transformed into a square modulo the public key. A square root of the message is then computed using the two prime factors of the public key. Four square roots exist and so any of the four square roots can be used as the signature on the message. This was an incredibly important discovery. It implied that for certain appropriately designed algorithms that could be placed in the device, elbowroom exists to leak information unbeknownst to the United States. Exactly two of these roots can safely be used to leak a single bit. These two roots are the ones that have a Jacobi symbol of 1. Had this channel actually been exploited, the code to do so would constitute a Trojan horse program.

This was conveyed to the NSA and the response was largely that of disinterest. They indicated that they would never approve of such a cipher and said that a 1-bit channel is insignificant. Ten bits would allow the unambiguous identification of a given silo because $2^{10} = 1024 > 1000$. Ultimately, it was the projected cost of the solution and not this channel that caused the whole idea to be abandoned.

The cryptographic Trojan that Simmons envisioned was sound in design and constituted a plausibility result: namely that by carefully crafting a backdoor into a cryptographic treaty compliance algorithm, the enemy could learn the location of the missiles to enable a devastating first strike. This type of Trojan horse was far off the beaten path from the Trojans that were envisioned at the time. It involved a carefully selected cryptographic algorithm to subliminally leak information and was nontrivial in every respect, especially considering the fact that ad hoc symmetric ciphers were the bread and butter of the cryptographic research community at that time.

Simmons continued to explore the implications of subliminal channels with respect to computer security. He proposed what is now known as the *prisoner's problem* (Simmons, 1984). This problem is not to be confused with the prisoner's dilemma from game theory. In the prisoner's problem, Alice and Bob are in prison and they want to coordinate an escape plan. They are permitted to digitally sign messages to each other but are not allowed to give each other ciphertexts. The warden actively monitors the messages that they send to one another and verifies the signatures. A message is not forwarded unless the corresponding signature is valid. The problem is to devise a way for Alice and Bob to communicate privately without the warden knowing about it by sending signed messages to one another, where the subliminal message is contained in the signature. This eliminates the use of trivial encodings in the actual messages that are signed. As it turns out, the prisoner's problem can be solved for quite a number of digital signature algorithms including ElGamal and the digital signature algorithm (DSA).

The solution to the prisoner's problem can be applied to carry out rather devastating Trojan horse attacks against smart cards. The purpose of this attack is to leak the private signing key of the user to the manufacturer of the smart card. The algorithm that transmits information over the subliminal channel can be embedded within a digital signing algorithm, which in turn is implemented within a smart card. So, code within the smart card can be regarded as Alice, the manufacturer can be regarded as Bob, and the unwary user of the smart card can be regarded as the warden. Simmons described an attack in which the smart card transmits the bits of the user's DSA private key to the manufacturer through the signatures that the card produces. The manufacturer can obtain these signed messages if and when they become public (Simmons, 1993).

The idea that advanced and customized Trojan horses can be devised specifically for attacking certain cryptographic algorithms contributed heavily to the development of other types of Trojan horses and viruses. It became apparent that cryptography itself could be employed by Trojan horses to strengthen the attacks that they mounted against their hosts. The areas that explore this possibility have been dubbed cryptovirology (Young & Yung, 1996a) and kleptography (Young & Yung, 1996b). Asymmetric cryptography is the central enabling technology for such Trojan horse attacks.

A cryptotrojan is a Trojan horse that contains and uses the public key of its author. The private key is kept private by the author and is not included in the Trojan. This makes it possible for the Trojan to perform trapdoor one-way operations as part of its payload using the public key. Only the author can reverse these trapdoor one-way operations because only the author knows the private key. No matter how carefully the Trojan is analyzed, the private key will not be revealed. Cryptovirology attacks are interesting because it is not enough to be the world's greatest antiviral expert to reverse their effects. It is necessary to be the world's greatest cryptanalyst.

TYPES OF TROJAN HORSE ATTACKS

It is difficult at best to devise a strict hierarchy of Trojan horse attacks that is organized according to what the Trojan horses do. By definition, a Trojan horse program is *already inside* the system in question, so its capabilities are bounded only by the access controls placed on its host. This is the primary restriction that is placed on the capabilities of a Trojan horse program. In the most general sense, a Trojan can do *anything* to the system that its host is permitted to do.

However, the ability to do anything to the host system by no means implies that Trojans can be safely designed (from the attacker's perspective) to do anything. A secondary design-level restriction that is placed on a Trojan horse is the fact that the host program may be under constant surveillance. This occurs when heuristic activity monitors that, for example, execute from within the safety of the operating system kernel attempt to identify if the program misbehaves. Activity monitors observe, record, and attempt to interpret the actions of the host program on a regular basis (some even have automated response systems). A Trojan horse program that causes the host to behave in a noticeably suspicious way may reveal the presence of the Trojan.

Malicious versus Benign Trojan Horses

Many databases on computer viruses, worms, and Trojan horses categorize malware as being malicious or benign. A benign Trojan is one that, for instance, presents a modal dialog box saying "Happy Halloween" every October 31. Whereas it may be argued that such a Trojan is benign in many respects, it is perhaps safest to say that it is malicious. Such a Trojan demands the user's attention and should not be in the system in the first place.

The view that is adopted here is that any Trojan horse is malicious because by definition it has a payload that does something that the user does not expect. This implies that, for example, the insertion into a program of a dummy variable that is never used constitutes a Trojan. After all, an unused variable may end up wasting space on the stack in random access memory (RAM).

In this study, Trojan horses are identified as being either overt or covert in their operation. The hierarchy that is given in the next section is not meant to supersede any existing formal characterizations of Trojan horses. Rather, it is intended to convey the types of Trojans that are employed time and time again by computer assailants.

An Attempt to Categorize Trojans

Depending on the attacker's goal, it may be possible to carry out a Trojan horse attack covertly. This type of attack is ideal from the attacker's perspective, especially when the attack is a perpetual one, because the Trojan attracts little attention and is therefore more likely to survive. Examples of covert attacks include information theft, subtle information alteration, and subtle resource usage.

In a covert information theft attack, the Trojan transmits stolen information from the host system to the author of the Trojan. This can be the login/password pair of a user, for instance. In an information alteration attack, the state of the host machine is changed in a way that is likely to go unnoticed for a prolonged period of time. For instance, fractions of a cent may be siphoned off from the payroll accounts of employees and moved into a secret account that the Trojan author has access to (*salami slicing* attack). Also, the Trojan may attempt to utilize the resources to which the host machine has access. For instance, the Trojan horse author may try to get several host machines

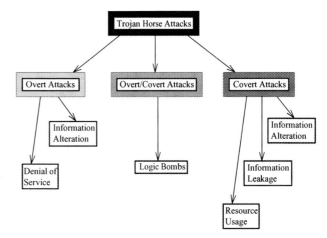

Figure 1:   Hierarchy of Trojan horse attacks.

to solve an instance of a hard problem, such as breaking a password by brute force, and later send the broken password to the author if it is found. These computations would utilize the CPU in small increments to go unnoticed. In this particular attack, the Trojan horse steals CPU time to solve a problem that would be difficult, if not impossible, to solve on a single machine.

Some types of Trojan horses are unavoidably overt in nature. For example, a purely destructive Trojan that deletes the hard drive would hardly go unnoticed once the deletion occurs. This is a form of overt information alteration. Another form of overt attacks is a denial of service (DoS) attack. A DoS attack denies users or processes access to a service. Overt Trojan horse attacks often (but not always) lead to the discovery of the Trojan soon after the attack is carried out. In contrast, a Trojan with a covert payload may carry out the attack for months or even years without notice.

Given these two extremes, it makes sense to divide Trojans into those that operate in secret and those that by design will not go unnoticed (see Figure 1). There are, however, some discrepancies between the covert attacks on the right and the overt attacks on the left that bear mentioning. A parallel can be drawn between DoS attacks and covert resource usage. From the perspective of the operating system kernel, peripheral devices provide a service to user processes. A line printer lets a process print data out on paper. A hard disk lets processes store data in nonvolatile memory. A form of denial of service against a process is denying network access, preventing writes to disk, and so on. So, overt DoS attacks and covert resource usage both affect services, yet they do so in fundamentally different ways. In a DoS attack, users and user processes are denied access to a service, whereas in a covert resource usage, a service is utilized slowly over time by the Trojan horse program.

Another aspect to note is the absence of information leakage in the overt attacks category. The reason for this is that there is often little reason for a Trojan horse to attract attention when all it has to do is leak information to the attacker.

There are a variety of ways to covertly transmit information. In some cases, it may be possible to establish a network connection and simply transmit the sensitive information to the attacker. Yet subtler methods exist to do this. For example, the data can be *steganographically* encoded into images or sound files that are normally sent out. When cryptosystems are involved, the data can be sent via a subliminal channel, and so on.

Observe that there is a generic heading for overt/covert attacks utilizing a *logic bomb*. This category is intended to encompass any attack that does not directly fall under the previously mentioned categories. Almost all Trojan horse payloads activate under a prescribed set of conditions and so a category encompassing overt/covert logic bombs addresses most of these other forms of attack.

A good example of a logic bomb is the cookie monster Trojan that ran on PDP machines (Harley, Slade, & Gattiker, 2001). Its name derives from the Cookie Monster on the television show *Sesame Street*. This Trojan would flash the message "I want a cookie" to the user on the monitor. The word "cookie" had to be fed to the program to keep it quiet. This type of Trojan horse payload is clearly overt in nature. A cookie monster virus was also reported (McAfee & Haynes, 1989).

This middle category is also meant to encompass Trojan horses that may or may not be covert in nature. For example, the Trojan called *Trojan.Download.Revird* (Symantec, 2003a) may be covert or overt depending upon the savvy of the computer user. This Trojan terminates processes belonging to security and monitoring applications. The Trojan horse titled *Backdoor.Gaster* terminates predefined processes as well (Symantec, 2003b). The act of terminating processes may be overlooked by the average user yet be detected by more observant users. These Trojans also contain backdoor functionality that is designed to permit the author to perform functions on the host machine. In this case, whether the Trojan is overt is at the discretion of the attacker that executes commands remotely via the Trojan.

COVERT TROJAN HORSE ATTACKS

A covert Trojan horse attempts to perform some function on the host machine in such a way that the operation of its payload is overlooked by the human user and by processes on the machine. Some defensive actions, such as killing security processes and deleting security-related files, might be overt enough to be noticed. However, this category may be loosely defined as encompassing those Trojan horses that are intended to go unnoticed.

Covert Information Alteration

There are a great number of possible covert information alteration attacks. An offensive tactic against military simulation systems is to introduce small errors into the experimental simulations to produce erroneous outputs. Other less spine-chilling and more nefarious attacks include remapping two keys on the keyboard. For example, a Trojan could with some small probability register a Y as the received keystroke instead of T when the user presses the T key. The desired effect is to frustrate the user into thinking that the letter T was mistyped. Such an attack is covert if the probability of remapping is so small that the user dismisses it as a random yet irritating occurrence.

An interesting example of covert information alteration is a salami-slicing Trojan that steals from the payroll accounts of employees. The first case of this may well be an urban legend. However, there do exist concrete sources that at least pinpoint when the attack allegedly occurred. A brief description of this attack appeared in an article dated November 3, 1987 (Makin, 1987). The article described a talk given by Sergeant Ted Green of the Ontario Provincial Police. Green described several logic-bomb attacks and other attacks against systems.

One attack was a Trojan horse that was clearly intended to achieve financial gain. An employee of a bank is said to have carried out an attack in which $70,000 was accumulated by funneling a few cents out of every account into his own (Neumann, 1987). This type of attack is called a salami-slicing attack (Parker, 1976) since small portions of money are purloined from numerous accounts. Stealing in small increments is necessary to prevent employees from noticing that their paychecks are a tiny bit less than they should be.

Covert Information Leakage

A covert information leakage attack is one in which malware transmits sensitive information outside the host system in an inconspicuous fashion. Early examples of covert information transmission include the password-pilfering Trojan mentioned in the Anderson report and the findings of Gus Simmons. However, in this section a bit more light is shed on the subject.

A well-known measure to protect against Trojan horses is to encapsulate programs into small domains that are given the minimal amount of rights necessary to perform their tasks. However, even when encapsulated, a program may have access to secret parameters that are passed to it by a caller. A Trojan in the program may retain the information for later use or transmit the data to the Trojan horse author. A program that is not able to transmit or store its parameters is said to be *confined*. The *confinement problem* is the problem of confining a program as such to eliminate the possibility of subversion. Lampson (1973) first explored the intricacies of this problem.

An inconspicuous way of leaking information via a Trojan horse is through the use of a *covert channel*. A covert channel is a channel that was not originally designed to transfer information at all. A concrete example will go a long way to explain what a covert channel is. Suppose that Alice and Bob are connected to a computer that is running a multiuser operating system. In a secure operating system that can be used for sensitive (e.g., military) applications, it should not be possible for a process that Alice is running to transmit information covertly to a process that Bob is running. But, suppose that a printer is connected to this machine. Each process can make an operating system call to print data. This call will return a result code indicating success or failure. The result code will also indicate if the printer is busy printing out a document. Alice's process can utilize a special communication protocol to speak with a process that Bob is running. For example, printing out two short documents with a brief pause in between could correspond to a binary "1" and printing out one document could be a binary "0." Bob's process calls the operating system routine in a busy waiting fashion to receive bits from Alice's process.

A *timing channel* is a special type of covert channel. For example, a Trojan may execute in such a way that its running time is proportional to some confidential value x, which it reads. By measuring the running time on a clock that operates independent of the system, the Trojan horse author can determine the value of x (D. E. Denning, 1983).

A channel that is related to a covert channel is a *subliminal channel* (Simmons, 1984). Typically, the term *subliminal channel* is used to refer to an information transmission channel that can be used to send information out of (or potentially into) a cryptosystem. A covert channel, on the other hand, is somewhat broader in scope. It has been shown that subliminal channels can be used to securely and subliminally leak private keys outside of cryptosystems in a way that is very robust against reverse engineering and that cannot, under reasonable intractability assumptions, be detected (Young & Yung, 1996b). This area of research has been dubbed *kleptography*.

Finally, *steganography* is the study of encoding data in other forms in a way that is not detectable. For instance, steganographic techniques allow a particular binary string to be encoded into certain graphics and sound files when there exists some leeway in terms of how the multimedia information is encoded. Steganography differs from cryptography because it does not provide for confidentiality; if the adversary knows which bits correspond to the steganographically encoded message, then the plaintext will be revealed. The challenge is to make these bits indistinguishable from bits that are normally present. The secure use of steganographic techniques usually involves encrypting the plaintext message and then steganographically encoding the resulting ciphertext.

Entire volumes could be written on the subject of covert information leakage, and the notions presented here are merely the tip of the iceberg. The bottom line is that it is very difficult to prevent information leakage (proactive) and to detect information leakage when it occurs (reactive). Research is ongoing in this area, and it encompasses both new ways to covertly leak information as well as new ways to counter clandestine information leakage.

Covert Resource Usage

Covert resource usage is loosely defined as the use of the host machine and associated peripherals in a way that is likely to go unnoticed. This includes but is not limited to the CPU, RAM, disk space, and so on. A general-purpose computing machine is a resource all by itself and has value to an attacker irrespective of the data that it processes and contains.

A good example of covert resource usage is a Trojan horse program that tries to solve an instance of an intractable problem. For example, it could try to solve an instance of the traveling salesman problem or some type of optimization problem. It could also be used for the purposes of breaching security by doing a brute-force key search, and so forth.

Steve White investigated the possibility of using viruses to conduct key searches. In particular, he observed that

a virus could try to determine the Data Encryption Standard (DES) key that was used to produce a particular symmetric encryption (White, 1990). Trojans can be used to steal CPU time to try to factor composites, compute discrete logarithms, and so on. In general, this type of Trojan needs to salami-slice the CPU usage so that the attack can be carried out for a prolonged period of time without notice.

OVERT TROJAN HORSE ATTACKS

Overt Trojan horses carry out attacks that will more than likely be noticed when they occur. The distinction is often subtle, because some Trojans delete files belonging to antiviral programs, which is an offensive tactic, but the overall rationale is defensive in nature. Overt Trojan horse attacks are offensive attacks, for the most part.

Overt Information Alteration

A classic overt information alteration attack is the deletion of data, although many other forms of malicious information alteration exist. The business of deleting data on a hard disk is subtle because a single write to disk will not necessarily destroy all traces of the previously stored binary digits. If not done properly, people that specialize in digital forensics may be able to recover the original data. The standard approach to deleting information on silicon platters is to overwrite with zeros, then overwrite with ones, then overwrite with zeros, and so on. Usually more than five iterations of this are performed to ensure that the ions on the surface of the disk do not reveal their original orientations.

The ChinaTalk Trojan is an Apple Macintosh Trojan that mounts an overt information alteration attack. The system extension containing the Trojan is advertised as being a sound driver for a female voice that is compatible with the MacInTalk program (Wilding & Skulason, 1992). However, the Trojan erases the hard disk.

Denial of Service

The subject of DoS attacks is not treated in detail here because a chapter in this *Handbook* is dedicated to this subject. Trojans can carry out DoS attacks, so the subject must be addressed here.

The notion of a DoS attack within the context of application programs was originally defined as follows (Needham, 1993). A contractor uses a client, the network, and a server to provide a service to a given customer. In a DoS attack, service is denied to the customer, not to the client. DoS attacks may consist of destroying or disabling the client. They may also involve interfering with the network traffic or with the server. Needham was the first researcher to investigate the effects of DoS attacks in the application layer. He focused mainly on end-to-end solutions for a given application.

DoS attacks have been carried out on the Internet to bring down various Internet and Web services. A particular type of DoS attack, called a *distributed denial of service attack*, is geared toward disrupting a service by overloading servers with packet requests and the like. Multiple machines located at multiple locations typically carry out these types of attacks. The machines submit packet requests (or some similar disruptive function) simultaneously to the target machine to disrupt service. A challenge in defending against this type of attack is distinguishing legitimate packet requests from the packets involved in the attack (e.g., packets that originate from Trojans residing on the machines). There has been a significant amount of research into countering this threat.

A cryptovirus attack can be regarded as a form of DoS attack (Young & Yung, 1996a). The payload of a cryptovirus (or cryptotrojan) encrypts critical data files on the host machine using the public key of the virus author. This public key is contained within the virus. If the critical data files are not backed up, then the host data files are effectively lost to the victim. This is due to the fact that an analysis of the virus will only reveal the public encryption key and not the needed private decryption key. The author of the virus can therefore hold these data ransom in return for the private decryption key.

Although there is no "service" involved in this scenario, the attack is nonetheless reminiscent of a DoS attack. For example, in a DoS attack that involves making packet requests, service can be restored when the bogus requests cease. In a cryptovirus extortion attack, the author can restore the critical data by revealing the private decryption key. This differs greatly from an overt information alteration attack that simply destroys data.

DEFENSES AGAINST TROJAN HORSE PROGRAMS

There are several challenges surrounding the design of robust Trojan horse programs and designing algorithms to detect Trojans wherever present. The first part of this section covers the issue of string matching. Antivirus programs often use string matching to positively identify viruses and Trojan horse programs. The development of antiviral string-matching programs led to the development of polymorphic viruses, which are viruses that are specifically designed to foil string-matching programs. The notion of polymorphism is a very general one and has been applied to the design of Trojan horses. For example, the Trojan horse program *Backdoor.Smorph* uses polymorphic techniques (Lancaster University, 2001).

Scanners

Consider a case in which a moderately sized Trojan horse has been discovered and analyzed by antivirus experts. When some or all of its binary code stays the same when the infected program is run, then there exists a simple way to detect the Trojan whenever it appears in plaintext form. The basic method for doing so is called *pattern matching* (Cohen, 1986). The idea is to take a string of bytes from the malware that is invariant across invocations of the malware and use it to find other instances of the malware. By checking an executable for the presence of this substring, it can be determined whether the executable is infected. Antiviral programs called *scanners* perform this scanning process. If the string is sufficiently long and the pattern it contains is unique, this method will detect the presence of the malware in infected programs. This approach is not

flawless since the string may appear naturally in certain programs. As a result, this method sometimes produces false positives.

However, this method can never produce a false negative when used to identify known Trojans. Stealth techniques are an exception to this rule because they have the potential to alter the scanner's perception of the true binary data in the program. This is due to the fact that a stealthy Trojan horse (or virus) reroutes operating systems calls so that a disk read will reveal an image of the original uninfected sectors of the disk to the caller. So, with the exception of stealth techniques and the like, string matching is performed correctly every time and an invariant string from the malware will never be missed.

A countermeasure to scanners is to design a Trojan horse program so that it does not contain any of the strings contained in the database. This is incredibly easy for an attacker to do: the attacker inserts the Trojan into a host program and then subjects the program to all available antivirus tools to see if the Trojan is found. A scanner is capable of detecting a deployed Trojan only after the needed search string is included in the list of search strings. It is often the case that a new Trojan is detected only after it mounts a successful attack against a host. Consequently, scanners are not very proactive in identifying Trojan horse programs and viruses. The measure is occasionally proactive because a new Trojan sometimes reuses the code of other Trojans or contains trivial modifications and as a result succumbs to an existing search string.

Polymorphic Code

A straightforward countermeasure to scanners is designing malware that modifies its own coding sequence. In laboratory experiments, Fred Cohen produced viruses that had no common sequences of over 3 bytes between each subsequent generation by using encryption (Cohen, 1986, 1987). Cohen referred to such viruses as *evolutionary viruses*, but they are more commonly referred to as *polymorphic viruses*.

Numerous polymorphs have appeared in the wild. For example, the Tremor virus is a polymorphic virus that has almost 6 trillion forms (Slade, 1994). A polymorphic program typically consists of two parts: a header and a body. When dormant, the body remains in encrypted form. When activated, the header decrypts the body of the malware. Once the body is decrypted, the header transfers control to the body. The body then performs the normal malware operations. When the body is finished, it sends control to the host program.

The header stores the symmetric key needed to decrypt the body. At periodic intervals, the malware can choose a new symmetric key randomly, replace the key in the header with it, and make sure that the body of the malware is encrypted under the new key. The problem now, from the perspective of the malware author, is that scanners can successfully search for the decryption header.

Malware authors have a variety of methods for changing the appearance of the decryption header as well. Some approaches for this are more effective than others. One obvious method is to employ several different ciphers and randomly select among them. This is a good approach but may in some cases lead to unacceptably large viruses.

Another common approach is to weave dummy instructions between the instructions that constitute the decryption algorithm. Most processors support a NOP instruction that literally does nothing. It is shorthand for no-operation and has many uses. On reduced instruction set computing (RISC) machines, these instructions cause the program to wait until all pending bus activity is completed. This allows synchronization of the pipeline and prevents instruction overlap. It is not uncommon on complex instruction set computing (CISC) machines to see NOP instructions woven within the sections of a switch statement to improve the performance of the instruction cache by aligning each section on a new cache line.

There are also a number of arithmetic dummy instructions. For instance, the additive identity element 0 can be used in an *add* instruction. The multiplicative identity element 1 can be used in a *multiply* instruction, and so on. There are dummy instructions for logical operations such as *or* as well.

Another type of dummy instruction is any instruction that operates on registers that are not used in the underlying algorithm. For example, many algorithms do not require the use of all of the data registers at once on the target microprocessor. In this case, the addition, multiplication, and so forth of any number in that register has a null effect. All of these dummy instructions have the potential to foil string-matching scanners.

There exist a number of tools that antiviral analysts use that specifically search for such dummy instructions. These tools typically have false positive rates that are very high and as a result make them unsuitable for use by the average user. They nonetheless greatly minimize the time needed for skilled analysts to find polymorphic code.

A better way to obfuscate the decryption header is to replace instructions with other instructions that perform the same operation and to exploit the fact that many instructions can be reordered without affecting the overall correctness of the algorithm (Skardhamar, 1996). Register usage is another aspect that is easily randomized. On the Motorola 68000 processor, there are eight general-purpose data registers. A given decryption algorithm may only require the use of four data registers. There are 8 choose 4 ways of selecting four distinct registers from the set of eight registers.

It has been observed that, because many viruses execute before the host, it is often possible to positively identify polymorphic viruses by letting them decrypt themselves (Nachenberg, 1997). The general idea behind this heuristic is to emulate the operation of the host program for the first few thousand or so instructions and then scan the resulting executable for the presence of known polymorphic viruses. The method is called *generic decryption* and involves three components: a CPU emulator, an emulation control module, and a scanner. The CPU emulator is designed to emulate a particular CPU such as a Pentium IV processor. The emulation control module determines such things as how many instructions will be emulated and is also responsible for making sure that no damage is done to the underlying machine as a result of the presence of malware. For example, writes to the disk may be prevented or otherwise contained. The scanner is applied to the code at regular intervals during the emulation to attempt to detect malicious software. Generic decryption can be performed on the fly along with traditional scanning methods to help identify polymorphic malware that is present at the beginning of programs.

Using generic decryption to scan the first several thousand instructions in a program is particularly useful in finding polymorphic Trojans that gain control soon after the program is executed. This applies to Trojans that have been appended to the host program after it was compiled and to Trojans that are inserted into the source code near the beginning of the program.

A countermeasure to generic decryption is to make the malware decrypt its body with some fixed probability. The malware could generate a random number and with some probability not decrypt its main body at all. For example, when the malware gains control in a given invocation of the host program, it could roll a six-sided die. If the result is "1" then the malware could decrypt itself and then go about its normal activity. If the result is not "1" then it could simply send control back to the host.

Another countermeasure to generic decryption is to make the malware gain control at a randomly determined offset within the host program. Implementing this countermeasure is more complicated than it seems because simply overwriting portions of the host will likely lead to crashes. When a Trojan is appended to a preexisting program, the bulk of the Trojan can be stored at the end of the host program. The problem then remains to modify the host to send control to the Trojan. One approach to accomplishing this is to choose an offset within the host randomly and overwrite the code at that location with a jump instruction. The original code would need to be stored within the Trojan, and the overlaid jump instruction would send control to the Trojan unconditionally. When the Trojan finishes executing, it repairs the host by overwriting the jump instruction with the original host code and then sends control back to where it normally would have been.

This approach is not without its risks, however. The jump instruction and the Trojan code that follows it should preserve the state of the program. Register values should be pushed onto the stack, and so on, and popped when the Trojan completes. Also, if the jump instruction is too long, it might overwrite code that forms an entry point for another jump instruction within the host. This could cause the host program to crash as a result of the inserted jump instruction. The Trojan would have to heuristically analyze the host to make certain that this cannot occur. If the host were naturally polymorphic, this analysis would be just as hard as the problem faced by antiviral programs. Finally, race conditions could cause faulty behavior within the host. If the jump instruction were written over an atomic action that operates on a semaphore and if the Trojan's code exacerbates the race condition, then the infected host could crash or produce erroneous results. There are numerous other problems that could result as well. For example, the inserted jump could cause a digital signature verification to fail, cause a checksum to fail, and so on.

Another general heuristic for detecting polymorphic malware is to look for changes in memory where the code for the currently running executable resides (Symantec, 1999). Symantec developed a tool that interprets the program one instruction at a time and takes note of every byte in the program's code space that changes. This method is a solid countermeasure, but has certain weaknesses. For example, it is possible to make the Trojan utilize multiple encryption layers with decryption headers in the host. These small headers can decipher the rest of the binary executable and therefore almost every byte of the program in memory can be changed. Another issue to deal with is programs that spawn child programs. For example, processes could *fork* and *exec* (e.g., in the UNIX operating system), thereby creating more heap zones that need to be analyzed.

Heuristic Activity Monitors

The ability to patch operating-system routines provides a good approach to assessing abnormal program behavior. An interrupt activity monitor works by loading antiviral interrupt handlers soon after the computer is booted. These handlers are collectively managed and typically span several different operating system routines. When they gain control from an operating system call, they analyze the circumstances surrounding the call and often maintain state information across calls. Heuristic activity monitors are useful for proactively detecting new Trojans and viruses that have been released. To address the threat of viruses, they have been designed to look for attempts to write to any sector containing executable code such as device drivers, boot sectors, and so on (McAfee & Haynes, 1989; Spafford, Heaphy, & Ferbrache, 1990). Monitors are equally useful in detecting certain actions that are characteristic of Trojans. They take note of such things as suspicious network activity, attempts to delete sectors, and attempts to reformat mounted volumes.

Activity monitors typically create audit trails of certain events that occur in the system. Users and system administrators can later analyze these audit trails to look for security breaches. Audit trails often have the potential to reveal the sequences of events leading up to an attack. When a suspicious event is about to occur (e.g., by intercepting a system call), some activity monitors will proactively display a message to the user that implicates the calling program. The monitor may request permission from the user to allow the suspicious event to occur. This way, users have a chance to stop a Trojan or virus before it adversely affects the underlying system.

The alerts from an activity monitor are very effective at identifying self-replicating code. However, the alerts often arise when a software patch is applied or when a new program is compiled. Another case is when a program utilizes a copy protection scheme that causes the program to write to itself. This happened in an old version of WordPerfect (McAfee & Haynes, 1989).

One of the dangers in using activity monitors is that if the alerts occur too frequently, the user may become desensitized to them. Too many alerts create a situation akin to crying wolf. This makes it more likely that users will allow a Trojan or virus to attack the system down the road because agitated users may eventually disable or ignore the alerts altogether. Unlike scanners, activity monitors are designed to identify both existing and future malware and, as a result, activity monitors are prone to yield false negative results.

Code Signing and Security Kernels

Although heuristic activity monitors provide a solid line of defense, they are after all only heuristic in nature. Another measure that can be taken to minimize the Trojan horse threat is to utilize strong authentication techniques. This approach combines the notion of a secure kernel with digital signatures (P. J. Denning, 1988). In this method, the kernel stores the root and certificate authority digital certificates of the public key infrastructure (PKI) used to certify the application that is to be run. The manufacturer digitally signs the application and releases it along with the digital signature and certificate that are needed to verify the signature. When the user runs the application, the certificate and signature are given to the kernel. The kernel verifies the authenticity of the certificate using the internally stored certificate authority certificate and also checks a certificate revocation list if necessary. Once the certificate is deemed valid, it is used to verify the signature on the application. The application is run if and only if the certificate and signature are valid (D. E. Denning, 1983). When a signature is valid, it is overwhelmingly certain that a Trojan (or virus) was not placed within the program after the software manufacturer released it.

This form of integrity checking, if implemented properly, will never produce false positive results. If the digital signature is invalid, then without a doubt the application has been changed. However, there is a negligible chance that a false negative will result. A malicious user or program can change an application and still have the signature verify correctly with negligible probability. This type of defense is likely to be utilized more and more as time goes on and as PKIs become more widespread.

CONCLUSION

A study of Trojan horses was presented that is based on how inconspicuous a given Trojan horse is. Insomuch as possible, the set of Trojan horses was partitioned into those that are intended to act covertly and those that are unavoidably overt in their actions. This contrasts with typical classifications that identify Trojans as being malicious or benign, for some (arguably vague) definition of benign. Several types of covert attacks and overt attacks were identified. Some of these attacks are advanced because they utilize modern concepts in cryptography and steganography. It is essential to understand how attackers think, what they seek, and what tools they have at their disposal to minimize the Trojan horse threat.

GLOSSARY

Certificate Revocation List (CRL) A CRL is used by a certification authority to publicly disclose key pairs that have been revoked. It lists revoked key pairs and is digitally signed by the certification authority. A CRL is typically updated on a regular basis (e.g., every day or two).

Cryptotrojan   A Trojan horse program that contains and uses the public key of its author (or more generally any public key).

Cryptovirus   A computer virus that contains and uses the public key of its author (or more generally any public key).

Data Encryption Standard (DES)   A standardized symmetric cipher with a 64-bit block size. It has been replaced by the Advanced Encryption Standard.

Intractable Problem   A problem is intractable if in general it cannot be solved efficiently. A problem cannot be solved efficiently if there does not exist a probabilistic poly-time Turing machine that solves it.

Logic Bomb   Code surreptitiously inserted into a program that causes it to perform some destructive or security-compromising activity whenever a specified condition is met.

Malware (Malicious Software)   Examples of malware include computer viruses, worms, and Trojan horses.

Public Key Infrastructure (PKI)   An infrastructure that is designed to distribute the public keys of users securely, thereby avoiding man-in-the-middle attacks.

Subliminal Channel   A communications channel, usually within cryptosystems, that when utilized allows information to be transferred in secret without hindering the normal operation of the cryptosystem.

Trojan Horse   A code segment that is appended, designed, or integrated into another program that does something that the user does not expect.

CROSS REFERENCES

See *Computer Viruses and Worms; Hackers, Crackers and Computer Criminals; Hoax Viruses and Virus Alerts; Hostile Java Applets; Spyware.*

REFERENCES

Anderson, J. P. (1972). *Computer security technology planning study* (ESD-TR-73-51, vol. 2). Hanscom Air Force Base, MA: HQ Electronic Systems Division.

Bell, D. E., & LaPadula, L. J. (1976). Secure computer system: Unified exposition and multics interpretation (MTR-2997). MITRE Corporation.

Cohen, F. (1986). *Computer viruses*. Ph.D. thesis, University of Southern California, ASP Press.

Cohen, F. (1987). Computer Viruses: Theory and experiments (IFIP-TC11). *Computers and Security, 6,* 22–35.

Denning, D. E. (1983). *Cryptography and data security*. Reading, MA: Addison-Wesley.

Denning, P. J. (1988). The science of computing: Computer viruses. *American Scientist, 76,* 236–238.

Dewdney, A. K. (1984). Computer recreations: In the game called Core War hostile programs engage in a battle of bits. *Scientific American, 250*(5), 14–22.

Harley, D., Slade, R., & Gattiker, U. E. (2001). *Viruses revealed*. New York: Osborne/McGraw-Hill.

Karger, P. A., & Schell, R. R. (1974). *Multics security evaluation: Vulnerability analysis*. (ESD-TR-74-193, vol. 2).

Hanscom Air Force Base, MA: HQ Electronic Systems Division.

Lampson, B. W. (1973). A note on the confinement problem. *Communications of the ACM, 16*(10), 613–615.

Lancaster University. (2001). *Backdoor.Smorph, Trojan found at Lancaster University*. Retrieved from http://www.lancs.ac.uk/iss/a-virus/v-smorph.htm.

Makin, K. (1987, November 3). *Globe and Mail*.

McAfee, J., & Haynes, C. (1989). *Computer viruses, worms, data diddlers, killer programs, and other threats to your system*. St. Martin's Press.

Nachenberg, C. (1997). Computer virus-antivirus coevolution. *Communications of the ACM, 40,* 46–51.

Needham, R. M. (1993). Denial of service. *Proceedings of the First ACM Conference on Computer and Communications Security*, pp. 151–153. ACM Press.

Neumann, P. G. (1987). Logic bombs and other system attacks—in Canada. *The Risks Digest, 5*(63).

Parker, D. B. (1976). *Crime by computer*. Charles Scribner's Sons.

Petersen, H. E., & Turn, R. (1967). System implications of information privacy. *Proceedings of the AFIPS Spring Joint Computer Conference*, vol. 30, pp. 291–300. AFIPS Press.

Simmons, G. J. (1984). The prisoners' problem and the subliminal channel. *Advances in Cryptology—Crypto '83*, pp. 51–67. New York: Plenum Press.

Simmons, G. J. (1993). Subliminal communication is easy using the DSA. *Advances in Cryptology—Eurocrypt '93*. Lecture Notes in Computer Science, vol. 765, pp. 218–232. New York: Springer-Verlag.

Simmons, G. J. (1994). Subliminal channels: Past and present. *IEEE European Transactions on Telecommunication, 5,* 459–473.

Simmons, G. J. (1998). The history of subliminal channels. *IEEE Journal on Selected Areas in Communication, 16,* 452–462.

Skardhamar, R. (1996). *Virus detection and elimination*. San Diego, CA: Academic Press.

Slade, R. (1994). *Robert Slade's guide to computer viruses*. New York: Springer-Verlag.

Spafford, E. H., Heaphy, K. A., & Ferbrache, D. J. (1990). A computer virus primer. In P. J. Denning (Ed.), *Computers under attack: Intruders, worms, and viruses*. New York: Addison-Wesley.

Symantec Corporation. (1999). Understanding and managing polymorphic viruses. *The Symantec Enterprise Papers*.

Symantec Corporation. (2003a). *Security response: Trojan.download.revird*. Retrieved December 27, 2003, from http://securityresponse.symantec.com/avcenter/venc/data/trojan.download.revird.html

Symantec Corporation. (2003b). Security response: Backdoor.Gaster. Retrieved December 29, 2003, from http://securityresponse.symantec.com/avcenter/venc/data/backdoor.gaster.html

Von Neumann, J. (1949). *Theory and organization of complicated automata*. Unpublished manuscript (lecture notes).

Von Neumann, J. (1966). Transcripts of lectures given at the University of Illinois (A. W. Burks, Ed.). Part 1, pp. 29–87.

Ware, W. H. (Ed.). (1970). *Security controls for computer systems* (R-609). Santa Monica, CA: RAND.

White, S. R. (1990). Covert distributed processing with computer viruses. *Advances in Cryptology—Crypto '89.* Lecture Notes in Computer Science, vol. 435, pp. 616–619. New York: Springer-Verlag.

Wilding, E. (Ed.), & Skulason, F. (Tech. Ed.). (1992, August). [Entire issue]. *Virus Bulletin.*

Young, A. L., & Yung, M. M. (1996a). Cryptovirology: Extortion-based security threats and countermeasures. *Proceedings of the IEEE Symposium on Security and Privacy,* pp. 129–141. Los Alamitos, CA: IEEE Press.

Young, A. L., & Yung, M. M. (1996b). The dark side of black-box cryptography, or: Should we trust Capstone? *Advances in Cryptology—Crypto '96.* Lecture Notes in Computer Science, vol. 1109, pp. 89–103. New York: Springer-Verlag.

FURTHER READING

Grimes, R. A. (2001). *Malicious Mobile Code.* O'Reilly & Associates, Inc.

Harley, D. Slade, R., Gattiker, U. E. (2001). *Viruses Revealed.* Osborne/McGraw-Hill.

Slade, R. (1994). *Robert Slade's Guide to Computer Viruses.* Springer-Verlag.

Young, A., Yung, M. (2004). *Malicious Cryptography: Exposing Cryptovirology.* John Wiley & Sons.

Operating System Security

William Stallings, *Independent Consultant*

INFORMATION PROTECTION AND SECURITY

The growth in the use of time-sharing systems and, more recently, computer networks has brought with it a growth in concern for the protection of information.

A publication of the National Bureau of Standards (Bransted, 1978) identified some of the threats that need to be addressed in the area of security:

1. Organized and intentional attempts to obtain economic or market information from competitive organizations in the private sector.
2. Organized and intentional attempts to obtain economic information from government agencies.
3. Inadvertent acquisition of economic or market information.
4. Inadvertent acquisition of information about individuals.
5. Intentional fraud through illegal access to computer data banks with emphasis, in decreasing order of importance, on acquisition of funding data, economic data, law enforcement data, and data about individuals.
6. Government intrusion on the rights of individuals.
7. Invasion of individual rights by the intelligence community.

These are examples of specific threats that an organization or an individual (or an organization on behalf of its employees) may feel the need to counter. The nature of the threat that concerns an organization will vary greatly from one set of circumstances to another. However, there are some general-purpose tools that can be built into computers and operating systems that support a variety of protection and security mechanisms. In general, the concern is with the problem of controlling access to computer systems and the information stored in them. Four types of overall protection policies, of increasing order of difficulty, have been identified (Denning, and Brown 1984):

- **No sharing:** In this case, processes are completely isolated from each other, and each process has exclusive control over the resources statically or dynamically assigned to it. With this policy, processes often "share" a program or data file by making a copy of it and transferring the copy into their own virtual memory.
- **Sharing originals of program or data files:** With the use of reentrant code, a single physical realization of a program can appear in multiple virtual address spaces, as can read-only data files. Special locking mechanisms are required for the sharing of writable data files, to prevent simultaneous users from interfering with each other.
- **Confined, or memoryless, subsystems:** In this case, processes are grouped into subsystems to enforce a particular protection policy. For example, a "client" process calls a "server" process to perform some task on data. The server is to be protected against the client discovering the algorithm by which it performs the task, while the client is to be protected against the server's retaining any information about the task being performed.
- **Controlled information dissemination:** In some systems, security classes are defined to enforce a particular dissemination policy. Users and applications are given security clearances of a certain level, whereas data and other resources (e.g., I/O devices) are given security classifications. The security policy enforces restrictions concerning which users have access to which classifications. This model is useful not only in the military context but in commercial applications as well.

Much of the work in security and protection as it relates to operating systems can be roughly grouped into three categories.

- **Access control:** Concerned with regulating user access to the total system, subsystems, and data, and regulating process access to various resources and objects within the system.
- **Information flow control:** Regulates the flow of data within the system and its delivery to users.

- **Certification:** Relates to proving that access and flow control mechanisms perform according to their specifications and that they enforce desired protection and security policies.

This chapter looks at some of the key mechanisms for providing operating system (OS) security.

REQUIREMENTS FOR OPERATING SYSTEM SECURITY

Requirements

An understanding of the types of threats to OS security that exist requires a definition of security requirements. Computer and network security address four requirements:

- **Confidentiality:** Requires that the information in a computer system only be accessible for reading by authorized parties. This type of access includes printing, displaying, and other forms of disclosure, including simply revealing the existence of an object.
- **Integrity:** Requires that computer system assets can be modified only by authorized parties. Modification includes writing, changing, changing status, deleting, and creating.
- **Availability:** Requires that computer system assets are available to authorized parties.
- **Authenticity:** Requires that a computer system be able to verify the identity of a user.

Computer System Assets

The assets of a computer system can be categorized as hardware, software, and data. Let us consider each of these in turn.

The main threat to computer system **hardware** is in the area of availability. Hardware is the most vulnerable to attack and the least amenable to automated controls. Threats include accidental and deliberate damage to equipment as well as theft. The proliferation of personal computers and workstations and the increasing use of local area networks increase the potential for losses in this area. Physical and administrative security measures are needed to deal with these threats.

The operating system, utilities, and application programs are the **software** that makes computer system hardware useful to businesses and individuals. Several distinct threats need to be considered.

A key threat to software is an attack on availability. Software, especially application software, is surprisingly easy to delete. Software can also be altered or damaged to render it useless. Careful software configuration management, which includes making backups of the most recent version of software, can maintain high availability. A more difficult problem to deal with is software modification that results in a program that still functions but that behaves differently than before. A final problem is software secrecy. Although certain countermeasures are available, by and large the problem of unauthorized copying of software has not been solved.

Hardware and software security are typi
of computing center professionals or indivi
of personal computer users. A much more wide
problem is **data** security, which involves files and other
forms of data controlled by individuals, groups, and business organizations.

Security concerns with respect to data are broad, encompassing availability, secrecy, and integrity. In the case of availability, the concern is with the destruction of data files, which can occur either accidentally or maliciously.

The obvious concern with secrecy, of course, is the unauthorized reading of data files or databases, and this area has been the subject of perhaps more research and effort than any other area of computer security. A less obvious secrecy threat involves the analysis of data and manifests itself in the use of so-called statistical databases, which provide summary or aggregate information. Presumably, the existence of aggregate information does not threaten the privacy of the individuals involved. However, as the use of statistical databases grows, there is an increasing potential for disclosure of personal information. In essence, characteristics of constituent individuals may be identified through careful analysis. To take a simple-minded example, if one table records the aggregate of the incomes of respondents A, B, C, and D and another records the aggregate of the incomes of A, B, C, D, and E, the difference between the two aggregates would be the income of E. This problem is exacerbated by the increasing desire to combine data sets. In many cases, matching several sets of data for consistency at levels of aggregation appropriate to the problem requires a retreat to elemental units in the process of constructing the necessary aggregates. Thus, the elemental units, which are the subject of privacy concerns, are available at various stages in the processing of data sets.

Finally, data integrity is a major concern in most installations. Modifications to data files can have consequences ranging from minor to disastrous.

Design Principles

Saltzer and Schroeder (1975) identify a number of principles for the design of security measures for the various threats to computer systems. These include the following:

- **Least privilege:** Every program and every user of the system should operate using the least set of privileges necessary to complete the job. Access rights should be acquired by explicit permission only; the default should be "no access."
- **Economy of mechanisms:** Security mechanisms should be as small and simple as possible, aiding in their verification. This usually means that they must be an integral part of the design rather than add-on mechanisms to existing designs.
- **Acceptability:** Security mechanisms should not interfere unduly with the work of users, while at the same time meeting the needs of those who authorize access. If the mechanisms are not easy to use, they are likely to be unused or incorrectly used.
- **Complete mediation:** Every access must be checked against the access-control information, including those

accesses occurring outside normal operation, as in recovery or maintenance.
- **Open design:** The security of the system should not depend on keeping the design of its mechanisms secret. Thus, the mechanisms can be reviewed by many experts, and users can therefore have high confidence in them.

PROTECTION MECHANISMS

The introduction of multiprogramming brought about the ability to share resources among users. This sharing involves not just the processor but also the following:

- memory;
- I/O devices, such as disks and printers;
- programs; and
- data.

The ability to share these resources introduced the need for protection. Pfleeger (1997) points out that an operating system may offer protection along the following spectrum:

- **No protection:** This is appropriate when sensitive procedures are being run at separate times.
- **Isolation:** This approach implies that each process operates separately from other processes, with no sharing or communication. Each process has its own address space, files, and other objects.
- **Share all or share nothing:** The owner of an object (e.g., a file or memory segment) declares it to be public or private. In the former case, any process may access the object; in the latter, only the owner's processes may access the object.
- **Share via access limitation:** The operating system checks the permissibility of each access by a specific user to a specific object. The operating system therefore acts as a guard, or gatekeeper, between users and objects, ensuring that only authorized accesses occur.
- **Share via dynamic capabilities:** This extends the concept of access control to allow dynamic creation of sharing rights for objects.
- **Limit use of an object:** This form of protection limits not just access to an object but the use to which that object may be put. For example, a user may be allowed to view a sensitive document, but not print it. Another example is that a user may be allowed access to a database to derive statistical summaries but not to determine specific data values.

The preceding items are listed roughly in increasing order of difficulty to implement, but also in increasing order of fineness of protection that they provide. A given operating system may provide different degrees of protection for different objects, users, or applications.

The operating system needs to balance the need to allow sharing, which enhances the utility of the computer system, with the need to protect the resources of individual users. This section considers some of the mechanisms by which operating systems have enforced protection for these objects.

Protection of Memory

In a multiprogramming environment, protection of main memory is essential. The concern here is not just security, but the correct functioning of the various processes that are active. If one process can inadvertently write into the memory space of another process, then the latter process may not execute properly.

The separation of the memory space of various processes is easily accomplished with a virtual memory scheme. Either segmentation or paging, or the two in combination, provides an effective means of managing main memory. If complete isolation is sought, then the operating system must simply assure that each segment or page is accessible only by the process to which it is assigned. This is easily accomplished by requiring that there be no duplicate entries in page and/or segment tables.

If sharing is to be allowed, then the same segment or page may appear in more than one table. This type of sharing is most easily accomplished in a system that supports segmentation or a combination of segmentation and paging. In this case, the segment structure is visible to the application, and the application can declare individual segments to be sharable or nonsharable. In a pure paging environment, it becomes more difficult to discriminate between the two types of memory, because the memory structure is transparent to the application.

Segmentation especially lends itself to the implementation of protection and sharing policies. Because each segment table entry includes a length as well as a base address, a program cannot inadvertently access a main memory location beyond the limits of a segment. To achieve sharing, it is possible for a segment to be referenced in the segment tables of more than one process. The same mechanisms are, of course, available in a paging system. However, in this case the page structure of programs and data is not visible to the programmer, making the specification of protection and sharing requirements more awkward. Figure 1 illustrates the types of protection relationships that can be enforced in such a system.

An example of the hardware support that can be provided for memory protection is that of the IBM System/370 family of machines, on which OS/390 runs. Associated with each page frame in main memory is a 7-bit storage control key, which may be set by the operating system. Two of the bits indicate whether the page occupying this frame has been referenced and changed; these are used by the page replacement algorithm. The remaining bits are used by the protection mechanism: a 4-bit access control key and a fetch-protection bit. Processor references to memory and direct memory access (DMA) I/O memory references must use a matching key to gain permission to access that page. The fetch-protection bit indicates whether the access control key applies to writes or to both reads and writes. In the processor, there is a program status word (PSW), which contains control information relating to the process that is currently executing. Included in this word is a 4-bit PSW key. When a process attempts to access a page or to initiate a DMA operation on a page, the current PSW key is compared to the access code. A write operation is permitted only if the codes

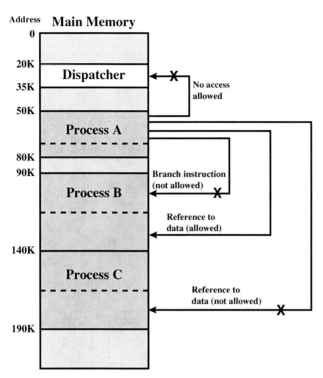

Figure 1: Protection relationships between segments.

match. If the fetch bit is set, then the PSW key must match the access code for read operations.

User-Oriented Access Control

The measures taken to control access in a data processing system fall into two categories: those associated with the user and those associated with the data.

The control of access by user is, unfortunately, sometimes referred to as authentication. Because this term is now widely used in the sense of message authentication, it is not applied here. The reader is warned, however, that this usage may be encountered in the literature.

The most common technique for user access control on a shared system or server is the user logon, which requires both a user identifier (ID) and a password. The system will allow a user to log on only if that user's ID is known to the system and if the user knows the password associated by the system with that ID. This ID/password system is a notoriously unreliable method of user access control. Users can forget their passwords and accidentally or intentionally reveal their password. Hackers have become very skillful at guessing IDs for special users, such as system control and system management personnel. Finally, the ID/password file is subject to penetration attempts.

User access control in a distributed environment can be either centralized or decentralized. In a centralized approach, the network provides a logon service that determines who is allowed to use the network and to what the user is allowed to connect.

Decentralized user access control treats the network as a transparent communication link, and the usual logon procedure is carried out by the destination host. Of course, the security concerns for transmitting passwords via the network must still be addressed.

In many networks, two levels of access control may be used. Individual hosts may be provided with a logon facility to protect host-specific resources and application. In addition, the network as a whole may provide protection to restrict network access to authorized users. This two-level facility is desirable for the common case, currently, in which the network connects disparate hosts and simply provides a convenient means of terminal-host access. In a more uniform network of hosts, some centralized access policy could be enforced in a network control center.

Data-Oriented Access Control

Following successful logon, the user has been granted access to one or a set of hosts and applications. This is generally not sufficient for a system that includes sensitive data in its database. Through the user access control procedure, a user can be identified to the system. Associated with each user, there can be a profile that specifies permissible operations and file accesses. The operating system can then enforce rules based on the user profile. The database management system, however, must control access to specific records or even portions of records. For example, it may be permissible for anyone in administration to obtain a list of company personnel, but only selected individuals may have access to salary information. The issue is more than just one of level of detail. Whereas the operating system may grant a user permission to access a file or use an application, following which there are no further security checks, the database management system must make a decision on each individual access attempt. That decision will depend not only on the user's identity but also on the specific parts of the data being accessed and even on the information already divulged to the user.

A general model of access control as exercised by a file or database management system is that of an **access matrix**, illustrated in Figure 2a, based on a figure in Sandhu and Samarati (1994). The basic elements of the model are as follows:

- **Subject:** An entity capable of accessing objects. Generally, the concept of subject equates with that of process. Any user or application actually gains access to an object by means of a process that represents that user or application.
- **Object:** Anything to which access is controlled. Examples include files, portions of files, programs, and segments of memory.
- **Access right:** The way in which an object is accessed by a subject. Examples are read, write, and execute.

One dimension of the matrix consists of identified subjects that may attempt data access. Typically, this list will consist of individual users or user groups, although access could be controlled for terminals, hosts, or applications instead of or in addition to users. The other dimension lists the objects that may be accessed. At the greatest level of detail, objects may be individual data fields. More aggregate groupings, such as records, files, or even the entire database, may also be objects in the matrix. Each entry in the matrix indicates the access rights of that subject for that object.

157

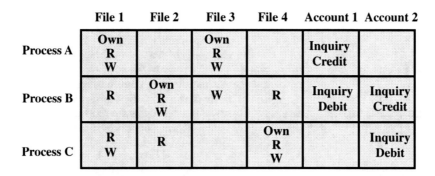

(a) Access matrix

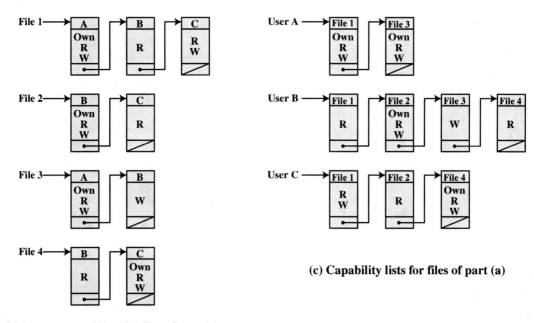

(b) Access control lists for files of part (a)

(c) Capability lists for files of part (a)

Figure 2:   Example of access control structures.

In practice, an access matrix is usually sparse and is implemented by decomposition in one of two ways. The matrix may be decomposed by columns, yielding **access control lists** (Figure 2b). Thus for each object, an access control list lists users and their permitted access rights. The access control list may contain a default, or public, entry. This allows users who are not explicitly listed as having special rights to have a default set of rights. Elements of the list may include individual users as well as groups of users.

Decomposition by rows yields **capability tickets** (Figure 2c). A capability ticket specifies authorized objects and operations for a user. Each user has a number of tickets and may be authorized to loan or give them to others. Because tickets may be dispersed around the system, they present a greater security problem than access control lists. In particular, the ticket must be unable to be forged. One way to accomplish this is to have the operating system hold all tickets on behalf of users. These tickets would have to be held in a region of memory inaccessible to users.

Network considerations for data-oriented access control parallel those for user-oriented access control. If only

certain users are permitted to access certain items of data, then encryption may be needed to protect those items during transmission to authorized users. Typically, data access control is decentralized, that is, controlled by host-based database management systems. If a network database server exists on a network, then data access control becomes a network function.

Protection Based on Operating System Mode

One technique used in all operating systems to provide protection is based on the mode of processor execution. Most processors support at least two modes of execution: the mode normally associated with the operating system and that normally associated with user programs. Certain instructions can only be executed in the more privileged mode. These would include reading or altering a control register, such as the program status word; primitive I/O instructions; and instructions that relate to memory management. In addition, certain regions of memory can only be accessed in the more privileged mode.

The less privileged mode is often referred to as the **user** mode, because user programs typically would execute in

Table 1 Typical Kernel Mode Operating System Functions

> **Process Management**
>
> - Process creation and termination
> - Process scheduling and dispatching
> - Process switching
> - Process synchronization and support for interprocess communication
> - Management of process control blocks
>
> **Memory Management**
>
> - Allocation of address space to processes
> - Swapping
> - Page and segment management
>
> **I/O Management**
>
> - Buffer management
> - Allocation of I/O channels and devices to processes
>
> **Support Functions**
>
> - Interrupt handling
> - Accounting
> - Monitoring

this mode. The more privileged mode is referred to as the **system mode**, **control mode**, or **kernel mode**. This last term refers to the kernel of the operating system, which is that portion of the operating system that encompasses the important system functions. Table 1 lists the functions typically found in the kernel of an operating system.

The reason for using two modes should be clear. It is necessary to protect the operating system and key operating system tables, such as process control blocks, from interference by user programs. In the kernel mode, the software has complete control of the processor and all its instructions, registers, and memory. This level of control is not necessary, and for safety is not desirable for user programs.

Two questions arise: How does the processor know in which mode it is to be executing and how is the mode changed? Regarding the first question, typically there is a bit in the program status word (PSW) that indicates the mode of execution. This bit is changed in response to certain events. For example, when a user makes a call to an operating system service, the mode is set to the kernel mode. Typically, this is done by executing an instruction that changes the mode. When the user makes a system service call or when an interrupt transfers control to a system routine, the routine executes the change-mode instruction to enter a more privileged mode and executes it again to enter a less privileged mode before returning control to the user process. If a user program attempts to execute a change-mode instruction, it will simply result in a call to the operating system, which will return an error unless the mode change is to be allowed.

More sophisticated mechanisms can also be provided. A common scheme is to use a ring-protection structure. In this scheme, lower numbered, or inner, rings enjoy greater privilege than higher numbered, or outer, rings. Typically, ring 0 is reserved for kernel functions of the operating system, with applications at a higher level. Some utilities or operating system services may occupy an intermediate ring. Basic principles of the ring system are as follows:

1. A program may access only data that reside on the same ring or a less privileged ring.
2. A program may call services residing on the same or a more privileged ring.

An example of the ring protection approach is found on the VAX/VMS operating system, which uses four modes:

- **Kernel:** Executes the kernel of the VMS operating system, which includes memory management, interrupt handling, and I/O operations.
- **Executive:** Executes many of the operating system service calls, including file and record (disk and tape) management routines.
- **Supervisor:** Executes other operating system services, such as responses to user commands.
- **User:** Executes user programs, plus utilities such as compilers, editors, linkers, and debuggers.

A process executing in a less privileged mode often needs to call a procedure that executes in a more privileged mode; for example, a user program requires an operating system service. This call is achieved by using a change-mode (CHM) instruction, which causes an interrupt that transfers control to a routine at the new access mode. A return is made by executing the REI (return from exception or interrupt) instruction.

FILE SHARING

In a multiuser system, there is almost always a requirement for allowing files to be shared among a number of users. Two issues arise: access rights and the management of simultaneous access.

Access Rights

The file system should provide a flexible tool for allowing extensive file sharing among users. The file system should provide a number of options so that the way in which a particular file is accessed can be controlled. Typically, users or groups of users are granted certain access rights to a file. A wide range of access rights has been used. The following list is representative of access rights that can be assigned to a particular user for a particular file:

- **None:** The user may not even learn of the existence of the file, much less have access to it. To enforce this restriction, the user would not be allowed to read the user directory that includes this file.
- **Knowledge:** The user can determine that the file exists and who its owner is. The user is then able to petition the owner for additional access rights.

- **Execution:** The user can load and execute a program but cannot copy it. Proprietary programs are often made accessible with this restriction.
- **Reading:** The user can read the file for any purpose, including copying and execution. Some systems are able to enforce a distinction between viewing and copying. In the former case, the contents of the file can be displayed to the user, but the user has no means for making a copy.
- **Appending:** The user can add data to the file, often only at the end, but cannot modify or delete any of the file's contents. This right is useful in collecting data from a number of sources.
- **Updating:** The user can modify, delete, and add to the file's data. This normally includes writing the file initially, rewriting it completely or in part, and removing all or a portion of the data. Some systems distinguish among different degrees of updating.
- **Changing protection:** The user can change the access rights granted to other users. Typically, only the owner of the file holds this right. In some systems, the owner can extend this right to others. To prevent abuse of this mechanism, the file owner will typically be able to specify which rights can be changed by the holder of this right.
- **Deletion:** The user can delete the file from the file system.

These rights can be considered to constitute a hierarchy, with each right implying those that precede it. Thus, if a particular user is granted the updating right for a particular file, then that user is also granted the following rights: knowledge, execution, reading, and appending.

One user is designated as owner of a given file, usually the person who initially created a file. The owner has all of the access rights listed previously and may grant rights to others. Access can be provided to different classes of users:

- **Specific user:** Individual users who are designated by user ID.
- **User groups:** A set of users who are not individually defined. The system must have some way of keeping track of the membership of user groups.
- **All:** All users who have access to this system. These are public files.

Simultaneous Access

When access is granted to append or update a file to more than one user, the operating system or file management system must enforce discipline. A brute-force approach is to allow a user to lock the entire file when it is to be updated. A finer grain of control is to lock individual records during update. Issues of mutual exclusion and deadlock must be addressed in designing the shared access capability.

TRUSTED SYSTEMS

Much of what has been discussed so far has been concerned with protecting a given message or item from passive or active attack by a given user. A somewhat different

but widely applicable requirement is to protect data or resources on the basis of levels of security. This is commonly found in the military, where information is categorized as unclassified (U), confidential (C), secret (S), top secret (TS), or beyond. This concept is equally applicable in other areas, where information can be organized into gross categories and users can be granted clearances to access certain categories of data. For example, the highest level of security might be for strategic corporate planning documents and data, accessible by only corporate officers and their staff; next might come sensitive financial and personnel data, accessible only by administration personnel, corporate officers, and so on.

When multiple categories or levels of data are defined, the requirement is referred to as **multilevel security**. The general statement of the requirement for multilevel security is that a subject at a high level may not convey information to a subject at a lower or noncomparable level unless that flow accurately reflects the will of an authorized user. For implementation purposes, this requirement is in two parts and is simply stated. A multilevel secure system must enforce the following:

- **No read up:** A subject can only read an object of less or equal security level. This is referred to in the literature as the **simple security property**.
- **No write down:** A subject can only write into an object of greater or equal security level. This is referred to in the literature as the ∗-**property** (pronounced *star property*).

These two rules, if properly enforced, provide multilevel security. For a data processing system, the approach that has been taken, and has been the object of much research and development, is based on the *reference monitor* concept. This approach is depicted in Figure 3. The reference monitor is a controlling element in the hardware and operating system of a computer that regulates the access of subjects to objects on the basis of security parameters of the subject and object. The reference monitor has access to a file, known as the *security kernel database*, that lists the access privileges (security clearance) of each subject and the protection attributes (classification level) of each object. The reference monitor enforces the security rules (no read up, no write down) and has the following properties:

- **Complete mediation:** The security rules are enforced on every access, not just, for example, when a file is opened.
- **Isolation:** The reference monitor and database are protected from unauthorized modification.
- **Verifiability:** The reference monitor's correctness must be provable. That is, it must be possible to demonstrate mathematically that the reference monitor enforces the security rules and provides complete mediation and isolation.

These are stiff requirements. The requirement for complete mediation means that every access to data within main memory and on disk and tape must be mediated. Pure software implementations impose too high a performance penalty to be practical; the solution must be at least

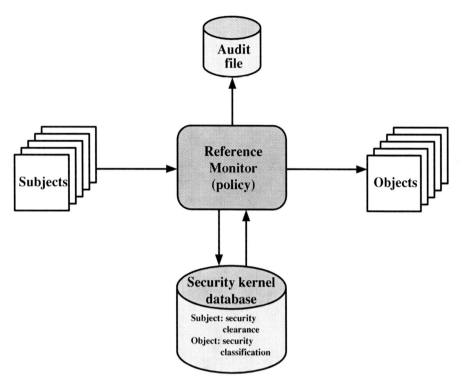

Figure 3: Reference monitor concept.

partly in hardware. The requirement for isolation means that it must not be possible for an attacker, no matter how clever, to change the logic of the reference monitor or the contents of the security kernel database. Finally, the requirement for mathematical proof is formidable for something as complex as a general purpose computer. A system that can provide such verification is referred to as a **trusted system**.

A final element illustrated in Figure 3 is an audit file. Important security events, such as detected security violations and authorized changes to the security kernel database, are stored in the audit file.

To encourage the widespread availability of trusted systems, standards bodies and interested government agencies worldwide have worked to define architectural principals and evaluation criteria. The goal is to be able to validate products that are designed to meet a range of security requirements. These product validations can serve as guidance to commercial customers for the purchase of commercially available, off-the-shelf equipment. Key to this effort is ISO (International Standards Organization) Standard 15408, known as the Common Criteria for Information Technology Security Evaluation. Based on this standard, there is a multinational effort, known as the Common Criteria Project, to further develop requirements, evaluation criteria, and product validations. The U.S. effort is conducted jointly by the National Security Agency and the National Institute of Standards and Technology.

Trojan Horse Defense

A Trojan horse is a computer program with an apparently or actually useful function that contains additional (hidden) functions that surreptitiously exploit the legitimate authorizations of the invoking process to the detriment of security. One way to secure against Trojan horse attacks is the use of a secure, trusted operating system. Figure 4 illustrates an example (Boebert, Kain, & Young, 1985). In this case, a Trojan horse is used to get around the standard security mechanism used by most file management and operating systems: the access control list. In this example, a user named Bob interacts through a program with a data file containing the critically sensitive character string "CPE170KS." User Bob has created the file with read/write permission provided only to programs executing on his own behalf: that is, only processes that are owned by Bob may access the file.

The Trojan horse attack begins when a hostile user, named Alice, gains legitimate access to the system and installs both a Trojan horse program and a private file to be used in the attack as a "back pocket." Alice gives read/write permission to herself for this file and gives Bob write-only permission (Figure 4a). Alice now induces Bob to invoke the Trojan horse program, perhaps by advertising it as a useful utility. When the program detects that it is being executed by Bob, it reads the sensitive character string from Bob's file and copies it into Alice's back-pocket file (Figure 4b). Both the read and write operations satisfy the constraints imposed by access control lists. Alice then has only to access the back-pocket file at a later time to learn the value of the string.

Now consider the use of a secure operating system in this scenario (Figure 4c). Security levels are assigned to subjects at logon on the basis of criteria such as the terminal from which the computer is being accessed and the user involved, as identified by password/ID. In this example, there are two security levels, sensitive (gray) and

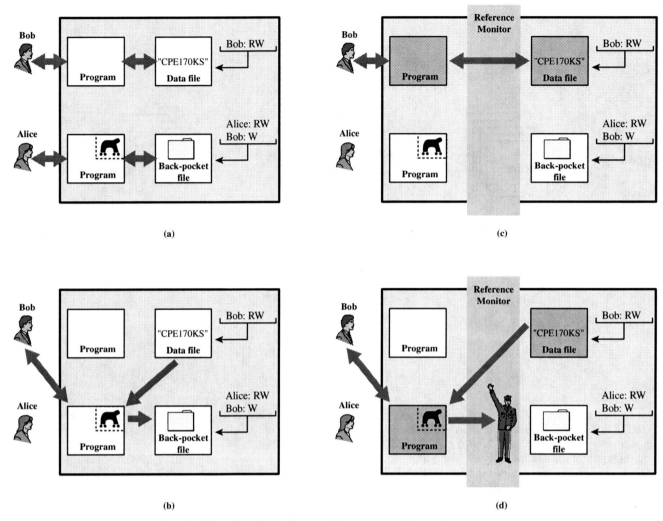

Figure 4: Trojan horse and secure operating system.

public (white), ordered so that sensitive is higher than public. Processes owned by Bob and Bob's data file are assigned the security level sensitive. Alice's file and processes are restricted to public. If Bob invokes the Trojan horse program (Figure 4d), that program acquires Bob's security level. It is therefore able, under the simple security property, to observe the sensitive character string. When the program attempts to store the string in a public file (the back-pocket file), however, the *-property is violated and the attempt is disallowed by the reference monitor. Thus, the attempt to write into the back-pocket file is denied even though the access control list permits it: The security policy takes precedence over the access control list mechanism.

GLOSSARY

Access Control Techniques and mechanisms that ensure that only authorized users have access to a particular system and its individual resources and that access to and modification of particular portions of data are limited to authorized individuals and programs.

Authenticity The requirement that a computer system be able to verify the identity of a user.

Availability The requirement that computer system assets are available to authorized parties when needed.

Confidentiality The requirement that the information in a computer system only be accessible for reading by authorized parties.

Integrity The requirement that computer system assets can be modified only by authorized parties. Modification includes writing, changing, changing status, deleting, and creating.

Password A character string used to authenticate an identity. Knowledge of the password and its associated user ID is considered proof of authorization to use the capabilities associated with that user ID.

Trojan Horse A computer program with an apparently or actually useful function that contains additional (hidden) functions that surreptitiously exploit the legitimate authorizations of the invoking process to the detriment of security.

Trusted System A computer and operating system that can be verified to implement a given security policy.

CROSS REFERENCES

See *Linux Security; OpenVMS Security; Unix Security; Windows 2000 Security.*

REFERENCES

Boebert, W., Kain, R., & Young, W. (1985, July). Secure computing: The secure ada target approach, *Scientific Honeyweller*. Reprinted in Abrams, M., & Podell, H. (1987). *Computer and Network Security.* Los Alamitos, CA: IEEE Computer Society Press.

Bransted, D., ed. (1978, February). *Computer security and the data encryption standard.* Gaitheisburg, MD: National Bureau of Standards, Special Publication No. 500–27.

Denning, P., & Brown, R. (1984, September). Operating systems. *Scientific American.*

Pfleeger, C. (1997). *Security in computing.* Upper Saddle River, NJ: Prentice Hall PTR.

Saltzer, J., & Schroeder, M. (1975, September). The protection of information in computer systems. *Proceedings of the IEEE.* 63, 9, 1278–1308.

Sandhu, R., & Samarati, P. (1994, September). Access control: Principles and practice. *IEEE Communications.*32, 9, 40–48.

FURTHER READING

Computer and Network Security Reference Index. Retrieved May 25, 2005 from http://www.vtcif.telstra.com.au/ info/security.html

Computer Security Resource Center. Retrieved May 25, 2005 from http://csrc.nist.gov/

Gasser, M. (1988). *Building a secure computer system.* New York: Van Nostrand Reinhold.

Gollmann, D. (1999). *Computer security.* New York: Wiley.

Stallings, W. (2003). *Cryptography and network security: Principles and practice* (3rd ed.). Upper Saddle River, NJ: Prentice Hall.

Trusted Computing Platform Alliance. Retrieved May 25, 2005 from http://www.trustedcomputing.org/home

Database Security

Michael Gertz, *University of California, Davis*
Arnon Rosenthal, *The MITRE Corporation*

INTRODUCTION

In the past three decades, database systems have evolved from specialized applications to fundamental components of today's computing infrastructures. Many organizations in industry, government, and research sectors rely on database systems to manage, share, and disseminate various forms of data in an effective and reliable manner. In fact, the most valuable assets of many organizations are their data, and the loss of hardware or software is often easier to overcome than the loss of data that have been collected and maintained over many years. As our society becomes increasingly dependent on information, the protection of data against various security threats becomes an important mission for database designers, developers, and administrators. Threats to database security typically concern the integrity, secrecy, and availability of data. They are characterized as follows:

- *Data integrity* refers to the requirement that the data residing in a database system are protected from improper modifications. The integrity is violated if unauthorized changes are made to the data through either intentional or accidental operations, including the insertion, deletion, and modification of data. Violations of database integrity, if not corrected, can result in erroneous or inaccurate decisions that are based on the improperly modified data.
- *Data secrecy* refers to the protection of sensitive data from unauthorized disclosure. An unauthorized, accidental, or unanticipated disclosure of confidential data can result in the loss of confidence in the data provider or even in legal actions against the organization maintaining the data.
- *Data availability* refers to the requirement that data are available to users and applications that have the legitimate right and authorization to access or modify the data. Loss of data availability can result in the unavailability of services and applications that operate on the database.

Database systems offer several countermeasures to protect data against these types of security threats. Countermeasures include (1) access controls that ensure that all accesses to data occur exclusively according to the rules described by security policies specifying certain security goals; (2) flow controls that regulate the distribution and flow of information among accessible objects; (3) inference control that aims at protecting data from indirect detection; and (4) encryption of data. The effective realization of countermeasures is driven by security policies and data security principles. A *security policy* is a (formal) statement or rule that partitions the states of a system into secure and nonsecure states. *Data security principles* guide the design and realization of database security policies. In particular, these principles include the following:

- *Least privilege.* Users and applications should be given those privileges they need to complete their tasks. That is, if an entity does not need to operate on some data managed by the database, this entity should not have the right or authorization to operate on that data.
- *Reconstruction of events.* Improper behavior of a user or application that leads to a violation of database security should be detected, thus preventing future (accidental or intentional) misuse of privileges and making individuals accountable for their operations on the data. In an ideal setting, events should be monitored and a misuse of privileges should be prevented rather than only detected after the event(s) happened.

These principles, among others, equally apply to the more general context of computer security (see, e.g., Bishop, 2003; Landwehr, 2001), in particular to operating systems security and network security.

In this chapter, we give an overview of the database security aspects that address the preceding security threats and principles, and we discuss how security aspects are realized in current database technology. Our focus is on relational database management systems (RDBMSs) because these are (and will be for the foreseeable future) the major type of database system used in the industry, government, and research sectors. In the section entitled Database Security Models and Mechanisms, we present the principles and components of database security models. We discuss in detail discretionary access control, which is supported by all major relational RDBMSs and included in the structured query language (SQL). We then discuss the main usage of role-based access control and outline mandatory access control as it is realized in some RDBMSs. We conclude this section with a discussion of security mechanisms that support the different access controls.

In the section entitled Database Security Design, we focus on security design aspects of databases. Too often, database security mechanisms are implemented in an ad-hoc fashion, without well-defined security design guidelines and security policies on hand. In this section, we also compare the security design for databases with the design of secure systems and outline database security design tasks, with a particular focus on nonidealized settings.

Finally, in the section entitled Database Security Evaluation and Reconfiguration, we approach the different aspects of database security at a more practical level. In today's world, data, applications, and security requirements change while a system is in service. Thus, database systems require continuous monitoring for vulnerabilities, misuse, and other types of system weaknesses security threats can expose. We outline several approaches to evaluate the security of a database system and to restore security.

As indicated earlier, in this chapter, we exclusively focus on security aspects in relational databases. A more comprehensive framework detailing security aspects related to other types of database systems, including object-oriented databases and statistical databases, can be found in the textbook by Castano, Fugini, Martella, and Samarati (1995).

DATABASE SECURITY MODELS AND MECHANISMS
Overview

A security model provides a semantically rich set of concepts and tools to (formally) specify and analyze security policies. Security models for database systems are not that different from general computer security models except that they place more emphasis on the modeling of access controls and less emphasis on user identification, authorization, and data encryption. In general, *access controls* are concerned with security policies that describe the principles on which access to objects is granted or denied (see also Access Controls: Principles and Solutions, chapter 168). There are several reasons for the importance of access controls in database systems. First, database systems manage many different types of objects (relations, views, stored procedures, and so forth) and at different levels of granularity (relation, tuple, attribute value). Second, database objects can be composed of other objects. For example, database views can refer to relations and other views. Third, standard read/write operations assumed in many security models translate into operations to create, delete, update, alter, and read database objects at different levels of granularity.

For database management systems, one can distinguish among three approaches to access controls: *discretionary access control*, *mandatory access control*, and *role-based access control*. Discretionary access control (DAC) is based on the concept of object ownership and mechanisms with which object owners can assign privileges to users, including policies on the administration of privileges. Almost all of today's RDBMSs provide means to specify and enforce security policies through discretionary access control. We focus on the basic concepts of DAC and in particular its realization in SQL in the section entitled Discretionary Access Control.

Mandatory access control (MAC), on the other hand, is based on labeling data objects with security classes and assigning security clearances to users. System-wide policies, which cannot be changed by individual users, then specify whether a user with a given clearance can read and/or write an object that has a given security label. The objective of the policies is to ensure that a user who does not have the necessary clearance can never obtain sensitive data, an important security requirement typically found in data management scenarios in the military. Mandatory access control is discussed in the section entitled Mandatory Access Control.

Role-based access control (RBAC), the third type of access control relevant to database systems, is concerned with aggregating access privileges into named entities (called roles) and assigning such entities to individual users, groups of users, and other roles. Although RBAC can be used to simulate DAC and MAC, in practice it is primarily used to manage effectively access privileges in RDBMSs comprising large amounts of objects and users and applications operating on these objects. In the section entitled Role-Based Access Control, we give a brief overview of RBAC and outline how RBAC is typically used to administer privileges.

No matter which type of access control is used, one must eventually map access policies to database security mechanisms that implement the policies to prevent and detect improper accesses. In the section entitled Database Security Mechanisms, we give an outline of the mechanisms available in RDBMSs and discuss how such mechanisms are used to enforce access control.

Discretionary Access Control

In the DAC model, access control is based on object ownership. Privileges on objects are granted to other entities at the discretion of the object owner. Formally, a discretionary access policy consists of a set of policy assertions. An assertion is a Six-tuple $<u, o, t, s, p, f>$, stating that user u (grantor) has granted operation o on object t to user s (grantee). The optional component p is a predicate and can define conditions on system or environmental variables to enable the specification of context-dependent access control. For example, Bertino, Bettini, Ferrari, and Samarati (1996) describe how such predicates can formulate temporal conditions and how such conditions can be embedded into access control mechanisms for database systems. Beznosov (2002) proposes a CORBA-like architecture in which various attribute providers can be called to provide information the policies need. f is a Boolean value and states whether user s can further transfer $<o, t, p, f>$ to other users, and thus enables the specification of access administration.

In the context of relational databases, a few aspects of a discretionary access policy are worth mentioning. First, underlying access control in general and DAC in particular is the notion of *authorization identifier (AuthID)*, which is either the identifier of a database user or a role name. According to the SQL:1999 standard (Melton & Simon, 2001), when an SQL session is initiated (e.g., an application connects to the database), the authorization identifier is determined in an implementation-defined manner. For the previous form of access policy, this means that the grantor is a database user and the grantee is an AuthID; that is, either a database user or a role. Second, in addition to object privileges, there are also *system privileges* for operations on a database as a whole or on objects of a particular type. For example, to create an AuthID, table, database file, or role, or to start up or shut down the database, the AuthID performing the operation must have respective system privileges. Typically, only administrative personnel possess such system privileges. As an example, Oracle 9i supports more than 100 system privileges.

Discretionary access control is included in the current SQL standard (SQL:1999) and is supported by all major commercial and public domain RDBMSs that offer security. The SQL GRANT command has the following syntax:

object-relational database management systems, such as Oracle or DB2, support more object privileges than RDBMSs that do not provide any object-relational features, such as user-defined data types or methods. In the following, we concentrate on the discussion of privileges related to tables and views because these object types are supported by all RDBMSs.

The following object privileges can be specified for a table using a GRANT statement:

- select [{columns}]. The grantee has the privilege to read the specified columns. If no column is given, the grantee is allowed to read all columns, even those added later through an ALTER TABLE statement.
- insert [{columns}]. The grantee is allowed to insert rows with values for the named columns into the table. If no column is specified, values for all columns can be inserted.
- update [{columns}]. The semantics of this privilege is analogous to the insert [{columns}] privilege.
- delete. The grantee has the privilege to delete rows from the table.
- references [{columns}]. The grantee is allowed to define foreign keys (in another table) that refer to the specified columns.

In SQL terminology, a view is a table that is derivable from other tables, which can be previously defined views

---

GRANT <PRIVILEGES> TO <GRANTEE>[{,<GRANTEE>}] [WITH GRANT OPTION]

A GRANT statement specifies which AuthID(s) are allowed to execute which SQL commands. If the WITH GRANT OPTION is specified, each AuthID different from a role is allowed to further grant the privilege(s) to other AuthIDs. If the privileges to be granted are all system privileges, these privileges are enumerated (e.g., create user, create table, alter database). Because system privileges are often related to administrative tasks, some RDBMSs, such as Oracle, use the clause WITH ADMIN OPTION if a grantee is allowed to further grant the privileges. If the GRANT statement specifies object privileges to be granted, these are numerated in the form of comma-separated <OBJECT PRIVILEGE> ON <OBJECT NAME> clauses.

Only AuthIDs with the following certain privileges can execute a GRANT statement: (1) the grantor has created (hence owns) the database object; (2) the grantor has received the privilege(s) with respective administrative options; or (3) the grantor has received the privileges GRANT ANY PRIVILEGE (for system privileges) or GRANT ANY OBJECT PRIVILEGE (for object privileges). Thus, the semantics of the SQL GRANT statement clearly resembles the semantics of the $<u, o, t, p, f>$ components of a discretionary access policy, as introduced earlier. We should mention, however, that neither the SQL standard nor any existing RDBMS supports the specification of a predicate p as part of a discretionary access policy.

The object privileges available in existing RDBMSs vary from system to system, depending on the types of objects supported in the different systems. For example,

or base tables. Views are either implemented by (1) query modification, in which the defining view query is translated into a query on the underlying base tables, or (2) view materialization, which involves physically storing the result when the view is first queried (see, e.g., Ramakrishnan & Gehrke, 2003; Elmasri & Navathe, 2004). Privileges on views can be granted in the same way as privileges on tables can be. A user creating a view must have the system privilege CREATE VIEW and at least the select privilege on all base tables and views referred to in the view query. If a user grants the privilege to insert, update, or delete rows from a view to another AuthID, this AuthID must have respective privileges on the base tables underlying the view. We talk more about views as important security mechanisms in the following sections.

There are some interesting aspects worth mentioning regarding granting privileges on database objects. If a user wants to grant all privileges on an object to an AuthID, instead of enumerating all these object privileges, the user can simply specify ALL PRIVILEGES ON <OBJECT NAME> in the <PRIVILEGES> clause. Different RDBMSs, however, associate different sets of privileges with the ALL PRIVILEGES clause. For example, in Oracle, granting all privileges on a table to an AuthID not only includes the object privileges listed earlier, but also the privileges to create an index on that table and to alter the table definition (i.e., column definitions, integrity constraints). If a set of privileges needs to be granted to all AuthIDs known to a database system, the keyword PUBLIC can be specified. Of course, this type of GRANT statement has to be used with care.

Another type of object supported by many RDBMSs is stored procedures as programming language extensions to SQL. Stored procedures are typically used for the development of database applications and functionality within the RDBMS. They enable bundling logically related procedures and functions in the form of packages. Triggers are stored procedures that execute program code whenever some specified database action occurs. A user defining a stored procedure must have the system privilege CREATE PROCEDURE. If a procedure operates on database objects, such as tables or views, or it invokes other procedures and functions, the user must have respective privileges on these objects. Some systems, such as Oracle, require that such privileges be explicitly granted to the user and not through a role. A user can grant access to a procedure to other users using the object privilege EXECUTE. This is the only privilege a grantee needs to invoke a procedure defined by another user.

To revoke system, object, or administrative privileges from users and roles, SQL provides the REVOKE statement, which has the following form:

The precise semantics associated with revoking administrative, object, and system privileges heavily depends on the type of object, nature of the authorizer (role or user), and RDBMS used. For example, if a user holds the privilege to create an index on a table and then this privilege is revoked, what happens to the index? Another scenario is when a user has been granted the REFERENCES privilege and has used this privilege to define a foreign key constraint on one of the user's tables. In Oracle, for example, this constraint is deleted if the privilege is revoked from the user. The SQL:1999 standard and several other works describe a precise semantics for the revocation of privileges in different settings (e.g., Bertino, Jajodia, & Samarati, 1995; Bertino, Jajodia, & Samarati, 1999). However, it is good practice to consult the documentation accompanying individual RDBMSs for the precise semantics of the REVOKE statement.

We conclude this subsection with a final remark on DAC in RDBMSs. In principle, DAC is based on the concept of *ownership-based administration*. That is, the creator (and thus owner) of an object has all privileges on that object and can grant such privileges to other users. Only when all objects in a database system are owned by

---

REVOKE [GRANT OPTION FOR | ADMIN OPTION FOR] <PRIVILEGES> FROM <GRANTEE> [CASCADE]

The command is used to (1) revoke grant options on system or object privileges (i.e., the grantee received the privileges with a grant or admin option) and (2) revoke system or object privileges from the grantee. Recall that a user who has received a privilege with a grant or admin option can further grant this privilege to other users. This is a case in which the CASCADE option can be used. When this clause is specified in a REVOKE statement, the listed privileges are revoked from all users who currently possess these privileges based on a GRANT command previously issued by the user who now issues the REVOKE command. If a user has been granted the same privilege from different users, no single REVOKE command is sufficient to revoke the privilege from that user. Figure 1 illustrates the behavior of the CASCADE option.

Assume user John has granted a privilege P with grant option to both Paul and Peter, who, in turn, both granted privilege P with grant option to Mary. The edge numbers indicate the points in time the respective grant statements have been issued. Mary has granted privilege P to Tom at time point 40. If John revokes P from Peter using the CASCADE option, Mary still possesses the privilege P; so does Tom because his privilege P is based on a grant Mary got at time point 30. Tom, however, would lose privilege P if John (or Paul) would revoke P from Mary using the CASCADE option.

a single user and this user grants privileges to other users (without allowing them to further grant these privileges) can we talk about *centralized access administration*. The latter scenario is typical for most database settings in practice where all applications operate on a schema owned by a single user. Such a setting naturally requires that authorization identifiers and privileges associated with these applications are properly managed, an aspect we discuss next.

Role-Based Access Control

Database systems that serve as the back end to large-scale information system infrastructures, for example, those used in supply chain management or customer relationship management, typically support dozens, sometimes more than a hundred, different applications. Administration of the database privileges the numerous applications users need to perform all the activities corresponding to their job descriptions can be a daunting task. This holds in particular for database environments where the same user is supposed to have access to different applications and the tasks associated with the applications require different privileges. Clearly, it is not a good strategy to simply grant users all the database privileges they need to use all applications with which they are supposed to work.

Roles provide an effective means to administer database privileges in such settings. Conceptually, a *role* is a named collection of privileges and can be granted to AuthIDs, optionally with the permission to grant this role to other users. Because roles can be granted to roles as well, it is possible to specify role hierarchies. But roles provide further important functionality in administering AuthIDs and the jobs and tasks that are associated with AuthIDs.

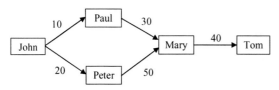

Figure 1: (Cascading) revocation of privileges.

In a database system, there are typically different types of users. One can broadly classify database users as (1) application owners, that is, users who own database objects as part of an application, (2) end users who operate on application objects but do not own any object in the database, and (3) administrators. With a given application, different tasks are associated, each task requiring the execution of specific operations and accesses to application objects. Based on these tasks, roles are defined that precisely describe the privileges necessary and are sufficient for an end user to execute a task. Roles determined by an application owner are then assigned to end users by the application owner. Roles associated with administrators primarily contain system privileges to manage physical and logical database components, such as data files, users, and security mechanisms. In summary, roles provide an important means to define application-specific security and to manage privileges dynamically based on application-specific tasks.

In the past decade, there have been several developments and advancement in role-based access control (RBAC) models. RBAC models are not specifically aimed at database systems but provide a general type of access model that can be used in combination with discretionary or mandatory access controls. In fact, based on a seminal paper published by Sandhu, Coyne, Feinstein, and Youman (1996) proposing a family of models known as RBAC96, Osborn, Sandhu, and Munawer (2000) show that RBAC96 can be configured to model DAC or MAC. One of the recent developments in RBAC is the adoption of a consensus standard model by the U.S. National Institute of Standards and Technology (NIST) (Ferraiolo, Sandhu, Gavrila, Kuhn, & Chandramouli, 2001; Sandhu, 2001). In the following, we outline some properties of RBACs in RDBMSs. Though somewhat outdated, Ramaswamy and Sandhu (1998) give a more detailed overview of how major commercial RDBMSs support different features of RBACs.

The concept of roles has also been adopted for the SQL:1999 standard. There, the CREATE ROLE statement is used to define a role. Some systems allow adding an authentication clause to the definition of a role. This authentication can be based on passwords users give if they want to assume that role, or the identification can occur externally, for example, through the operating system. As illustrated in the section entitled Discretionary Access Control, the GRANT command is used to assign privileges to roles. Because roles can be granted to other roles, role hierarchies can be built in which roles with more (powerful) privileges form the upper part of such a hierarchy. The concepts underlying role hierarchies and the administration of such hierarchies are discussed in detail by Ferraiolo et al. (2001) and Sandhu (1998).

In an RDBMS, there are typically several predefined roles. Many of them concern administrative tasks. A set of default roles can be assigned to a database user when the user is created using the CREATE USER statement. Other roles that have been created and granted to a user can be enabled by the user on demand through the SQL statement SET ROLE <role name>. Although several roles can be accessible to a user, according to the SQL:1999 standard, a user can hold exactly one role at a time. Given that a user can enable or disable roles, an important security design aspect is that only those roles are enabled that are necessary and sufficient to perform the operations in the current application context. Such a design is typically guided by higher level security policies that precisely describe which roles (and thus privileges) are required for which application-specific tasks and who is allowed to activate which roles at which times.

This aspect is also related to the security principle of *separation of duties*, which states that no single user should be able to tamper with the integrity of the data, but several users must collude to violate the integrity of data. To support this principle in the context of RBAC, it thus must be possible to impose constraints on role relationships and role activations. Although neither the SQL standard nor existing commercial RDBMSs support this principle, in practice, it can be realized by using stored procedures for enabling and disabling roles. Such procedures then can be called from within applications, and database users are prevented from issuing SET ROLE statements during sessions. In respective procedures, the current role setting and constraints implementing the previously mentioned higher level policies on role relationships are then checked and enforced.

Mandatory Access Control

Mandatory access control (MAC) is based on system-wide policies that cannot be changed by individual users. MAC, first introduced by Bell and LaPadula (1976), plays an important role in environments where data can be classified (e.g., based on its sensitivity) and users are cleared (e.g., based on their trustworthiness not to disclose sensitive information). In the following, we give a brief overview of MAC and outline how it is supported by commercial RDBMSs. We refer readers interested in the details of MAC to Castano et al. (1995). Bertino et al. (1995) give an excellent overview of MAC and the underlying multilevel relational data model. Several comprehensive articles addressing multilevel secure databases can be found in Abrams, Jajodia, and Podell (1995).

In MAC, each database object is assigned a security class, and each subject is assigned a clearance for a security class; subjects are active entities, for example, users, which operate on the objects. The policies specify whether a subject with a given clearance can read or write an object that has a given security class. The objective of the policies is to prevent the flow of information from sensitive objects to less sensitive objects.

In MAC, policies are based on *access classes*, each of which is a class comprising a *security level* and a set of *categories*. Security levels build a hierarchically ordered set. For example, in the military domain, security levels often include Top Secret (TS), Secret (S), Confidential (C), and Unclassified (U), forming a hierarchy with TS > S > C > U. A set of categories is simply a subset of an unordered set of named entities that represent, for example, application domains or departments of an organization and depend on the considered environment.

In a military environment, such categories can include NATO, Air Force, Army, and so forth. An access class AC_1 = (L_1, C_1) with security level L_1 and set of categories C_1 is said to *dominate* an access class AC_2 = (L_2, C_2) with security level L_2 and set of categories C_2, denoted $AC_1 > AC_2$, if and only if $L_1 \geq L_2$ and $C_1 \supseteq C_2$. Two access classes AC_1 and AC_2 are said to be incomparable if neither $AC_1 \geq AC_2$ nor $AC_2 \geq AC_1$ holds. Thus, access classes are partially ordered. Based on the concept of access classes, the following two principles are employed by all security models that enforce MAC policies.

No read-up (also known as the *Simple Security Property*), meaning a subject can read only those objects whose access class is dominated by the access class of the subject. For example, a subject with security level TS can read a table that has security level C, but a subject with security level C is not allowed to read a table with security level TS.

No write-down (also known as the **-Property*), meaning a subject can only write those objects whose access class dominates the access class of the subject. For example, a subject with security level S is allowed to write only objects with security level equal to or greater than S.

For a RDBMS to support MAC, a security class must be assigned to each database object, which can be a table, a row, or even individual column values, depending on the policy employed. In general, the application of MAC to relational data leads to the concept of *multilevel relations*, which are tables in which users with different security levels see different collections of rows when they access the same table. We refer the reader interested in the concepts (and problems) of multilevel relational databases to Abrams et al. (1995). In the following, we outline how a flavor of MAC is supported in some commercial RDBMSs, here Oracle9i. Before we do so, we should mention that no major RDBMS fully supports MAC mainly because MAC needs to be applied to a complete computing infrastructure from the top to the bottom. That is, mandatory access control and multilevel security must be realized at all layers, including the operating system, network components, and application components. For example, in military environments, security levels are generally physically isolated. MAC policies specified at the RDBMS level thus must be applied appropriately at the operating system layer as well, physically separating data that have different security classes. Trusted operating system infrastructures are essential in this context.

In practice, the realization of MACs at all levels is not only very costly but also requires substantial system administration skills and sophisticated security management tools for MAC; the latter is almost nonexistent. However, to provide customers with some flavor of MAC (and some of its functionality), some RDBMS vendors provide additions to traditional DAC. For example, in Oracle9i, row-level access control is supported with the virtual private database (VPD) technology. VPD provides fine-grained access control that is context dependent and row based (Levinger, 2002; Nanda, 2004). This technique is known as *Oracle Label Security* (*OLS*), first introduced in Oracle8i Release 3.

OLS is a set of procedures and constraints that are built into the database engine, and it enforces row-level access control on a single table. Following is a brief summary of how an OLS policy is realized.

First, after initializing (naming) a security policy, the administrator defines security levels. Each level is associated with a policy and has a name; security levels describe the sensitivity of table data, such as "Confidential" or "Public." Then, compartments can be defined. Compartments correspond to categories and enable a refined access to rows of a table within a level. The purpose of compartments is the same as that of categories introduced earlier in the context of access classes. OLS also allows defining user groups as another way to restrict access within a level, in particular when there are hierarchies of users. After this, labels are defined. Labels are a combination of security levels, compartments, and groups. Whereas a label must contain one security level, compartments and groups are optional. A label thus can be viewed as an access class that determines the types of access required for users to the table data. Each label is assigned a number, which must be unique among all the security policies in the database.

In the next step, the label policy is applied to a given table, realizing read and write control for users. This step adds an extra column to the table. Attribute values correspond to the labels introduced earlier; this extra attribute can be hidden from users. Figure 2 is an example of a table that manages information about projects. Two levels have been specified: Public and Confidential, and each row has a label (attribute ProjectLabel). Now one needs to define which users have which types of access within the policy. This is done by assigning labels to database users; a label specifies a maximum read level and maximum/minimum write levels. Respective levels refer to the security levels introduced previously and can be refined by adding compartments. For example, a maximum read level "Internal:Finance" specifies that the user is allowed to read documents (rows) whose label is equal or less than the security level "Internal" and that belong to the compartment "Finance." Finally, once all users have been assigned labels, these users then are granted discretionary access privileges (select, insert, update, delete) to that table.

As indicated earlier, OLS works in combination with regular discretionary access control. Within the Oracle database engine, security enforcement works as follows. If a user issues an SQL statement, this statement is first processed as in standard DAC, as outlined in the following section, Database Security Mechanisms. After this,

ProjectID	ProjectName	Level	ProjectLabel
1	WideStreets	Public	100
2	HighWalls	Confidential	200
3	LargeSUVs	Confidential	200
4	OilDrill	Confidential	200

Figure 2: Example of a table to which a row-level security policy has been applied.

a so-called VPD SQL modification occurs in which the SQL statement is refined in a way such that only those rows whose row label satisfies the read/write label specified for the user are retrieved. The latter step thus realizes fine-grained access control. We refer the reader interested in all the details of Oracle's Label Security to Levinger (2002).

Database Security Mechanisms

To support an access control model, an RDBMS has to provide database mechanisms implementing the access policies specified in that model. The purpose of a security mechanism is to enforce one or more security policies. Current database technology provides several types of security mechanisms that differ in functionality, efficiency, and flexibility. In the following paragraphs, we outline the basic properties of the mechanisms available in database systems with a focus on authentication and in particular access control mechanisms.

The process used to determine that a user is who he or she claims to be is called *authentication* (see, e.g., chapter 169, Password Authentication, and chapter 170, Computer and Network Authentication in this handbook). All RDBMSs provide authentication mechanisms that prevent unauthorized users from using the database system and specific application components realized in the database. Authentication can even be applied to the enabling of roles, as discussed in the section entitled Role-Based Access Control. One can broadly distinguish between three authentication mechanisms for database systems: internal authentication, application-based authentication, and operating system (OS)–based authentication. Internal authentication mechanisms are part of the RDBMS functionality for which a user has to give a user name and password to connect to the database. Only if the user is known to the database (i.e., the authentication information is stored in the RDBMS system catalog) is the user authorized to use the database. OS-based authentication is a combination of an authentication mechanism provided by the OS that hosts the RDBMS and the authentication mechanism provided by the RDBMS. Once a user is authenticated by the OS, the user can connect to the database. In the context of large-scale database systems that manage several applications, application-based authentication is the most prominent approach in which authentication is accomplished at the application level using third-party mechanisms external to the RDBMS. Kerberos-based authentication is a popular technique of that type (see chapter 63, Kerberos). We refer the reader interested in a detailed discussion of the different authentication models supported by some of today's commercial RDBMSs to respective system documentation such as for Oracle Advanced Security and Microsoft SQL Server.

Once a user has been authenticated, the RDBMS authorization mechanisms govern the user's database operations and accesses. In the section entitled Discretionary Access Control, we discussed the realization of DAC in databases using the GRANT command. The specification of an access policy using the GRANT statement and subsequent access controls are realized by mechanisms as follows.

All system and object privileges a user (or more generally, an AuthID) has received are recorded in the system catalog. That is, whenever a valid GRANT or REVOKE statement is issued, modifications to system catalog tables are performed. Now consider the scenario in which a database user submits an SQL statement in a database session, for example, through an application. Note that in a session an AuthID is associated with the user and that an active role is associated with that AuthID. The SQL statement is passed to the query compiler component of the RDBMS, which verifies the syntax and semantics of the statement for correctness. In particular, it verifies whether the AuthID that issued the SQL statement has the privilege to execute the statement and to perform accesses to database objects (tables, attributes, views) referred to in the statement. For this, the query compiler uses the parse tree for the SQL statement, and it queries the system catalog to check for respective permissions associated with the AuthID. Thus, the GRANT command results in a *compile-time* approach for access control. That is, authorization occurs during the verification of an SQL statement. A REVOKE statement results in the deletion of respective entries from the system catalog.

Views provide another important mechanism to prevent users from accessing data they are not supposed to access. The usage of views as access control mechanisms was first suggested in the 1970s by Stonebraker (1975). Recall that a view definition is a named query and that the view definition as well as object privileges on views that have been granted to AuthIDs are recorded in the system catalog. If an AuthID submits an SQL statement that refers to a view, checking proper object privileges on the view occurs in the same manner as described previously, that is, during the compilation of the SQL statement. Views provide for much finer access control to tables and other views because one can precisely specify rows and columns to select in the query by using a WHERE clause and subqueries in the view definition. Thus, views provide a *data-dependent access control mechanism* in which the data an AuthID can access are determined based on the data stored in base tables.

Many of today's RDBMSs provide programming language extensions to SQL, such as stored procedures or embedded SQL. These extensions can be used to realize sophisticated security and access control mechanisms. Although these mechanisms provide for more functionality, their design and usage is nontrivial and requires a very good knowledge about the security requirements of applications and the RDBMS's environment. Stored procedures can realize security mechanisms that are not possible through using only GRANT/REVOKE statements and views. Because stored procedures offer programming language constructs, such a loops, if-then-else blocks, and calls to other procedures, they are in particular useful for implementing *context-dependent* access controls. Recall that context-dependent access uses information about the context in which a data access or an operation on the database occurs. This can include time information, that is, when an SQL statement has been issued, information about previous statements the AuthID has issued, or information about other current activities in the database system. Stored procedures can be used to realize many features of access control that are not supported by current RDBMS access control models, including negative authorizations, separation of duty in the context of role-based access control, and context-, resource-, and data-dependent access control policies. The drawbacks of more expressive and flexible mechanisms, of course, are higher design and maintenance costs and difficulty in understanding the system behavior, as well as some performance impact on the database.

All mechanisms discussed previously are *preventive mechanisms* in that they check at the compile time of an SQL statement whether an AuthID is authorized to execute the statement. Most RDBMSs also support *detection mechanisms* that are realized through *auditing*. Although auditing can occur at many places in an information system infrastructure, that is, at the application, network, and database layers, in this chapter we are mainly concerned with auditing database activities. An RDBMS naturally supports the logging of all database operations and activities in the form of database logs (Weikum & Vossen, 2002; Gray & Reuter, 1993). Although such logs, which record database activities in typically proprietary data formats, are mainly used for database recovery purposes, several federal and government regulations require the archiving of such logs for reporting purposes (see, e.g., Nanda & Burleson, 2003). Database logs can be analyzed using tools (e.g., Oracle's LogMiner; Rich, 2003) to check for possible access violations and other types of potential security breaches. In addition to database logs, some RDBMSs also provide for recording information in audit tables. That is, the database administrator (DBA) can specify users or types of accesses on database objects that are to be audited, and respective audit information is recorded in audit tables. Audit information can readily be queried and analyzed using SQL and thus provides another useful setting for realizing detection mechanisms in a database.

DATABASE SECURITY DESIGN

Database design is concerned with accurately modeling an organization's information needs, and then implementing the model as a high-performance relational database. Numerous textbooks concentrate on the various database design approaches, concepts, and techniques (e.g., Batini, Ceri, & Navathe, 1992; Ramakrishnan & Gehrke, 2003; Elmasri & Navathe, 2004), but very few include database security design aspects. Only Castano et al. (1995) give a very detailed, though idealized, description of the different steps and approaches in database security design. In the following sections, we give an overview of the different practical database security design aspects, how they relate to system security design approaches, and how database and security design tasks interact with each other.

The enterprise's security administration goal is to find an optimal mix of benefit (convenient operation) and risk. They might configure jobs so that few people have access

to sensitive data. For example, commercial processes deliberately minimize the number of people able to change payment information, whereas military processes split tasks to execute at a single security level. At the level of privilege administration, job redesign is rarely an option. In this case, the ideal is to allow each user exactly the accesses needed for legitimate tasks. This ideal cannot be attained, for several reasons:

- It is normally too difficult to determine *exactly* which actions are appropriate for a job.
- The policy might not have access to context information (e.g., location of the user, which middleware-resident function made the request, which stage of the task the user is currently executing) or might be unable to express subtle choices even for the context it does have.
- Administrators are overburdened and often choose coarse granule privileges on database objects, such as table rather than column. Even when they have been conscientious, they will rarely bother to revoke privileges that are no longer needed.
- The cost to the administrator or the organization of improper denial is high, so the administrators grant extra privileges. For example, as new applications are added, the administrator does not want repeated calls that development has stopped because of lack of access privileges.

The following section, Protecting the RDBMS, discusses some practical aspects of protecting an RDBMS. The section entitled Designing Security Policies examines the design of access policies on data, at successively greater levels of detail. The section Security Policy Implementation outlines the steps of implementing security policies on a given RDBMS.

Protecting the RDBMS

Despite some marketing claims, RDBMS products can be hacked or bypassed. This section briefly discusses attacks that cause unexpected behavior. Following are some considerations one has to keep in mind when protecting an RDBMS:

- *With any complex software system, poor configuration practices cause vulnerability* (see, e.g., Newman, 2004; Theriault & Newman, 2001). Passwords might be unchanged from vendor defaults or database tables are left accessible to Public. The sheer complexity of RDBMS configuration parameters exacerbates the problem. Security configuration and management software can help administrators in analyzing and keeping track of security settings.
- *The database administrator has excessive privileges.* Administrators' actions require auditing in a trail not under their control.
- *By penetrating the underlying operating system, an attacker can copy, change, or delete database files.* Significant skill is required to execute such types of attacks.

Penetrating a system in ways that keep applications working to hide the penetration can be particularly difficult. To avoid tampering with files, data, and query results, several products offer encryption techniques, and researchers have proposed schemes for digital signatures to authenticate query results (e.g., Devanbu, Gertz, Martel, & Stubblebine, 2003). However, the performance effect might be serious.

• *Applications that construct queries on the fly can be fooled into constructing improper requests.* "SQL injection" techniques apply when an application constructs an SQL query on the fly, for example, by inserting a user-supplied value into a query string (Anley, 2002; Boyd & Keromytis, 2004). A malicious user can manipulate quotation marks to insert additional SQL statements. This problem can be addressed by coding standards on query builders or (more secure but less flexible) by having the user supply parameters to a precompiled query.

A strategy of defense in depth is appropriate, for example, placing the RDBMS server behind a firewall or limiting the number of accounts authorized to submit SQL statements. In system terms, RDBMSs provide a layer of protection even after the operating system has been penetrated. The reader might also wish to examine general advice on using security software systems and components residing at the network, operating, or application layer of a computing system discussed in detail elsewhere in this handbook.

Also note that several security standards (though not specific to RDBMSs) help customers and vendors focus on protection requirements and provide design and implementation strategies for a secure (database) system. These include the DoD criteria (U.S. Department of Defense, 1985); various documents published by the NIST Computer Security Resource Center (CSRC; http://csrc.nist.gov/), which are also available as part of the NCSC & DoD Rainbow series through the Network Security Library (NSL) at http://secinf.net/; the *Site Security Handbook* (Fraser, 1997); and the Common Criteria for Information Technology Security Evaluation (*Common Criteria*, 2004). Most database vendors furthermore provide extensive documentation on how to secure system components that interact with a database system and database applications, including application servers and network components.

Designing Security Policies

Today's RDBMSs offer considerable flexibility in protecting data from inappropriate access by authorized users. To harness this power, one must first *model the data to be protected*; then *define what access is permissible*. Thus, data administration practices and artifacts must be understood to practice security design, implementation, and administration.

There is a vast body of data administration literature in the context of database systems (see references given at the beginning of the section entitled Database Security Design), with many proposed methodologies. A typical idealized story goes like this: an idealized picture of an enterprise assumes that system development begins with comprehensive analyses of available technologies and user requirements. Requirements are then elaborated to functional requirements, architectures, descriptions of business processes, and lists of individual transactions. Based on all this knowledge, one derives a conceptual design for a database and then an implementation design, which is carefully mapped to the process descriptions. At the same time, one examines security requirements, including both organizational needs and applicable laws and regulations, carefully mapping them to all the preceding information.

From this, one gets a security policy expressed in terms of a *conceptual model*, a model that models the problem domain. An *implementation model* tells about the implementation in a given computing system, for example, which data are physically stored, what is the interface to a service. Concepts useful for categorizing information are also defined (e.g., Financial, Medical) and carefully mapped to individual data elements. One further assumes that these models and mappings are kept in well-managed repositories, and whenever a change is desired, the various models are changed, too. Unfortunately, we are unaware of any large organization that conforms to this ideal. Few organizations capture and maintain all the artifacts formally, but they still guide designers. In the following paragraphs, we describe a simple picture that seems to capture the essence, without proposing a specific formalism.

Most data systems are designed or understood using a series of models, each an elaboration of higher level ones. For example, many approaches suggest having an external layer, a conceptual layer, and a physical implementation layer. By looking at any layer, one gets a specification (possibly very vague) covering the data in the system. There is a mapping of objects in each layer L_i to objects at the next most detailed level L_{i+1}. A security policy defined in terms of objects at layer L_i needs to be implemented by a policy on L_{i+1}. Furthermore, if L_{i+1} identifies more detailed granules of data (e.g., attributes as well as entities), more detailed policies can be written. Layers can also elaborate sets of information that are not intended as structural units. For example, one layer can require auditing of access to "sensitive medical information," deferring to the next layer the definition of what information is medical and what is sensitive. The relationships of entities and attributes to "sensitive" and "medical" are important metadata and capture the mappings between levels.

Data administration often begins with naming large categories of data that a system is to manage, with later layers identifying entities and attributes that constitute, for example, medical or financial information. The policy front is similar. An organization is likely to have policies driven by upper management statements, phrased in terms of a high-level model. Lower-level models add flesh to the concepts used by upper management. In addition to categorizing data, it is also important to categorize users and privileges, for example, in the form of user groups and roles (see the section entitled Role-Based Access Control). In both cases, the category is given a name and a human-understandable membership criterion, for example, a group of DrugResearchers (scientists or statisticians engaged in drug research) or Check-Out role (privileges needed to check a patient out of the hospital). A policy then delegates a role to a group, that is, asserts that it is appropriate for its members to have those rights. Our formulation is intended to maximize the amount that can be handled by routine judgments and minimize the policy decisions that need careful consideration. It also guides maintenance decisions as the system evolves. It is crucial to set up a process by which user needs are learned, groups and roles designed, and policy decisions made. Some approaches to designing roles and groups appear in the literature. For example, an extension of Entity-Relationship (ER) modeling concepts to address security and authorization features has been proposed by Oh and Navathe (1995). Approaches to modeling roles and role relationships have been proposed by Neumann and Strembeck (2002) and Epstein and Sandhu (1999, 2001). In general, important (application-specific) tasks should be identified and described—the privileges needed for a task are assigned to a role. Some roles might correspond to "natural" groups of resources, such as Medical Records, and new kinds of records need to be appropriately characterized. It is essential that the *meaning* of each group and role be explained, in human-understandable form, independent of its current membership. This explanation is particularly important for evolution as new job titles, tasks, and data are created.

For each substantive policy determined during the previously described steps, one also needs a policy on required strength of implementation. Such a specification is likely to be done by categorizing policies and having a treatment for each category, which might include default treatments. For example, some U.S. government agencies require various degrees of physical and logical separation between classified data and systems accessed by users with low or no security clearances. The next section discusses the core issues in actually implementing policies in terms of the mechanisms provided by an RDBMS.

Security Policy Implementation

The final step in database security design is the actual implementation of the database using a particular RDBMS. That is, the database schema and security policies (specified at the finest level of granularity) are transformed into the implementation data model, which in the context of this chapter is the relational model. Several tools exist that automate this process at least for a conceptual database schema formulated as an ER or Unified Modeling Language (UML) diagram. The transformation of a database schema results in a set of tables and views. Furthermore, the roles determined during the policy design phase are specified using the CREATE ROLE command (see the section entitled Role-Based Access Control), individual database users are created (including appropriate user authentication mechanisms), and privileges and roles, including the administration of privileges, are assigned to users using the GRANT command. For security policies that include predicates, either views or procedural security mechanisms (see the section entitled Database

Security Mechanisms) are created. If security policies furthermore include accountability aspects, such as what users issued what operation on objects at what time, auditing mechanisms are initialized as well. In cases in which procedural security mechanisms, such as stored procedures and triggers are used, the performance impact of these mechanisms on the operation of the database system should be verified and compared with the performance and functional requirements of the database stated during the requirements analysis.

Once all security mechanisms have been created, it is important to verify (at least partially) the security mechanisms for correctness and completeness. That is, based on the security threats identified prior to the policy design phase, privileges assigned to users and roles that operate on sensitive data should be verified to determine whether they correctly reflect all the requirements stated (at all model levels). For this, documents that focus on the security design and evaluation of systems provide important and useful guidelines in verifying the correct mapping and realization of requirement and policies using the different levels of abstraction employed during policy design and implementation (see references at the end of the section entitled Protecting the RDBMS).

DATABASE SECURITY EVALUATION AND RECONFIGURATION

From a security point of view, in an ideal setting (1) database applications and users have precisely all the privileges to perform their tasks and (2) all operations on the database and objects can be traced back to users. In practice, however, this is rarely the case. There are several reasons for this. Many database settings are dynamic; new applications and middleware components are added, underlying database structures are changed, or security settings are modified to accommodate new or changing requirements (e.g., to address performance). Even if a database has been designed and implemented following the security design steps outlined in the previous section, security requirements, policies, and mechanisms can become outdated. Thus, the security settings of the database might not correctly reflect current (now implicit) security policies and requirements.

Assume a setting where a database serves as the back end to several applications. One might want to ask the following security-related questions: What are the potential vulnerabilities of the database? Are there database users who misuse their privileges and thus might cause a threat to the security of the database? If the answer to either of the two questions is positive, a follow-up question then is: How can the current database security mechanisms be reconfigured to exclude these vulnerabilities? A brute force approach, as often suggested in the literature, is to perform an extensive auditing of all database actions and to analyze audit logs for possible vulnerabilities and insider misuse. Without further guidance, such an approach is unrealistic and impractical for databases that mange hundreds of tables, views, and stored procedures, and a high volume of transactions is constantly executed against the database.

In the following sections, we outline an approach for the evaluation and reengineering of the security of a database. The approach is based on a data-centric view to database security and employs a technique called focused auditing.

Database Security Evaluation

The first phase in evaluating the security of a database for possible vulnerabilities and insider misuse is the inspection of the current database security mechanisms. All database users, including their database privileges, are verified against current security requirements and expectations. Information about database users, their privileges, and association with database roles can easily be obtained from the database's data dictionary. This simple inspection, which resembles a reverse engineering of security policies in a database system, not only leads to valuable insights into the current security setting of a database, but it also provides an up-to-date picture of the state of access controls in a database. Results of this analysis include (1) database user accounts (AuthIDs) that have been associated with applications and that are not needed anymore (e.g., they have been used during some test phase), and (2) privileges and role associations that do not reflect current information needs for users or applications. For example, several commercial RDBMSs come with preinstalled database accounts. If these accounts (AuthIDs) are not used, they should be deleted (or deactivated) in order to not cause a possible entry point for attacks. In general, the outcome of this evaluation phase should be a revised (conceptual) security design that formulates current access policies and roles and associates privileges and roles with users (AuthIDs).

Now assume that the privileges associated with AuthIDs have been verified to be sound and complete; that is, they reflect all the accepted information needs of users and applications. Consider the scenario in which a database user has been granted the privilege to select rows from a table, say, a table with customer information. If this table contains millions of rows and the application in which the user is operating on this table serves a specific task, the access privilege might be too coarse grained. That is, the user is supposed to retrieve only data about specific customers but has been granted the privilege to perform selections on all customers. Such a discrepancy between the granularity of privileges assigned to a user and operations supposed to be executed by the user can result in insider misuse. Ideally, one would like to know what users are executing what types of operations on what database objects based on the privileges they have been assigned.

To address the issue of possible insider misuse, in the following, we outline the concept of *focused auditing* (see also Gertz & Csaba, 2003, for more details). In this approach, auditing of database events is tailored to a few tables that contain sensitive data (e.g., as determined during policy design). That is, initially auditing focuses on data and not that much on users. Respective audit logs are analyzed to determine which users operate on the tables

using which types of operations. Note that we specifically refer to audit logs and not general database logs that are used for transaction management and recovery purposes. Audit logs contain only information about specified database events of interest and they can easily be queried. Database logs, on the other hand, contain information about all database events, and the analysis of log data requires separate data extraction and analysis tools. All major RDBMS provide tools and SQL commands to manage the auditing of operations on tables. Through these tools, access frequencies and other temporal properties of accesses to a table can be determined, for example, during what time period(s) what accesses (insert, update, delete, select) occurred. Although most RDBMS tools provide for statement-level auditing, that is, they record what AuthIDs executed what operation at what time, in most systems, fine-grained access audit information can be obtained only using triggers. Fine-grained audit information includes information about individual tuples that have been inserted, deleted, and updated.

In the focused auditing approach, fine-grained access information to tables of interest is recorded in extra tables. The data are accumulated over a period of time and are analyzed using SQL queries and reporting tools. Results include access frequencies of operations (grouped by AuthIDs), average and median values of attributes being updated, and aggregated properties of tuples inserted and deleted. Different grouping criteria of access data recorded in these tables enable administrators to inspect different aspects of accesses to the underlying table; such aspects include AuthID-specific aspects, that is, what AuthID performed what types of operations, and data-specific aspects, that is, how did tuples and attribute values evolve over time. This information then again is compared to the security requirements formulated during the security policy design phase. Administrators can easily expand the focus of the auditing to other (semantically related) tables and AuthIDs.

In summary, the idea of the security evaluation approach is first to establish a focus that consists of one or more sensitive tables, perform a fine-grained auditing of operations on these tables using triggers, and use the obtained audit data to further explore the behavior of AuthIDs with respect to other database objects. Such focused auditing can naturally be used to investigate possible or potential scenarios for insider misuse (see, e.g., Chung, Gertz, & Levitt, 1999).

Security Reconfiguration Through User and Data Profiling

Security reconfiguration of a database encompasses the definition of views, roles, and procedural access control mechanisms that provide for access control that is more fine-grained than simple object privileges assigned to users and roles using the GRANT command. In addition to deleting or deactivating unused AuthIDs and revoking unused privileges from users and roles, security reconfiguration tries to adhere to the least privilege principles.

That is, although an AuthID has been granted privileges to perform insert, update, delete, or select operations on a table, based on the information obtained through fine-grained auditing, these operations should be applied only to certain rows in a table or in a specific context.

Audit information about accesses is used in two ways: to create *data profiles* and *user profiles*. A data profile describes the current state of attribute values in a table and includes information about the distribution of attribute values, minimum and maximum values for attributes, and occurrences of null values (if permitted by the table specification). It also includes information about how attribute values evolve over time, for example, in the context of update operations. The information can be presented to the administrator based on different grouping criteria on access measures, and it can be appropriately visualized to provide the administrator with a complete picture of the data in a table. What role does a data profile play in the context of database security? First, if data values are observed that clearly represent outliers (e.g., a value for a salary attribute that is 10 times the maximum of the other salary values), integrity constraints can be added to the audited table to prevent such erroneous data values in the future. Obviously, removing existing erroneous table entries and attribute values requires "cleaning" the data, a typical activity in data quality frameworks (Johnson & Dasu, 2003). Second, even if no outliers are observed, integrity constraints that might have been neglected or not known during the design of the database can be added; these then better describe admissible values or further restrict admissible values. In both cases, additional integrity constraints, which are either added to the table specification or specified in the form of triggers, prevent future data entries that might be caused by accidental or malicious modifications of table data.

User profiles are much harder to derive from audit data. The goal of a user profile is to describe the behavior of a database user (or more generally, an AuthID) in terms of insert, update, delete, and select operations against one or more tables. The area of profiling users operating on database objects is relatively unexplored, and we thus give only some ideas of how profiles can be obtained. If audit data includes information about the user performing the operation, frequencies and time windows for the different operations can be established. For example, a profile might include the statement that a user executes between 70 and 100 select operations between 9 a.m. and 2 p.m. If this behavior corresponds to the expected behavior, a respective security mechanism can be implemented that detects deviations from this behavior. The mechanism can be a stored procedure or function through which the select operation occurs (see the section entitled Database Security Mechanisms). A user profile can include statements at different levels of granularity, for example, the user behavior on a daily basis or an hourly basis. It can simply include access frequencies or might include profiles of the data accessed by the user, as described earlier. A user profile can include statements about accesses to one or more tables and might even include information about which accesses occur together, for example, in the context of user transactions. There is no limit to what a user profile can

contain. However, based on the audit data available, different levels of granularity can be established and an increasing set of tables can be audited through the focused auditing approach, thus providing an administrator with a means to verify the behavior of a user incrementally and to configure security mechanisms that guard against deviations from the behavior determined by profiles. Eventually, user profiles can be compared and similarity measures can be established, thus providing a means to discover roles from individual user behaviors. Similar profiles indicate similar necessary privileges, which thus can be specified in the form of roles.

In general, although all the preceding analysis and profiling tasks can be done using the functionality supported by today's RDBMSs, tools are needed that provide administrators with a comprehensive and flexible way to configure, manage, and analyze audit data and to (semi-)automatically translate audit results, such as data and user profiles, into respective security mechanisms.

CONCLUSIONS AND FUTURE DIRECTIONS

Today's computing systems are not secure. This holds for network components, operating systems, and database systems. A significant amount of work on securing networks and operating systems has been done, for example, in the context of intrusion detection systems (Intrusion Detection Systems Basics, chapter 191) or code analysis. Security for relational database systems, on the other hand, has mainly focused on providing access control mechanisms, which in today's relational database systems are primarily realized through granting privileges to users, specifying roles, and occasionally through using stored procedures. This is despite the fact that there has been a tremendous amount of research and proposals on more sophisticated security mechanisms and access controls for database systems. We therefore envision the following future directions in database security research and development.

First, in addition to security products at the network and operating system layer that try to detect security breaches, an intrusion and misuse detection system *within* an RDBMS might add another layer of defense against security threats. Such a system would monitor the behavior of users and their operations on sensitive data and establish user and data profiles from which security mechanisms are automatically derived. Such a system would be a significant step toward dealing with insider misuse. Note that insider misuse is a type of security breach that is most frequently observed in existing systems (Anderson, 1999; Neumann, 1999; Power, 2002).

Second, most of the existing commercial database products provide means to manage application logic within the database. For example, Java programs can be called from within SQL queries and stored procedures; such programs can even call functions and procedures external to the RDBMS. As RDBMSs are able to manage more and more types of objects and become programming platforms, richer access control and information flow models are needed that go beyond operations on just database tables and views.

Third, although current RDBMSs provide database designers and developers with several types of security mechanisms, there is a lack of support for security design, administration, and management tools. Tools are needed to support all database security design tasks and furthermore help and guide administrators in maintaining the security of the database through monitoring, auditing, and analyzing the collected data.

In summary, we envision several opportunities for tool developers to provide (database) administrators and security personnel with comprehensive and flexible database security configuration, management, and analysis tools that help these users to better deal with the complexity and diversity of security aspects in today's large-scale and mission-critical database systems.

ACKNOWLEDGMENTS

The work by Michael Gertz was partially supported by the National Science Foundation under Grant No. IIS-0242414.

GLOSSARY

Access Control A framework to specify and reason about security policies that describe the principles on which access to objects is granted or denied.

Auditing The process of analyzing a (database) system to determine which actions took place and who performed them.

AuthID The authorization identifier uniquely identifies a database user or a role name in a database system. It is determined by a system in an implementation-dependent manner.

DAC Discretionary access control (DAC) is based on the concept of object ownership and mechanisms that allow owners to assign privileges to users, including policies on the administration of privileges.

Data Dictionary A relational database management system maintains all information (metadata) about logical and physical database objects in a data dictionary (also called system catalog).

Least Privilege The principle of least privilege states that a subject should be given only those privileges that it needs to complete its tasks.

MAC When a system mechanism controls access to an object and an individual user cannot alter that access, the control is mandatory access control (MAC). This type of access control is typically based on system-wide security policies.

Policy A (security) policy describes constraints placed on entities and actions in a system; a policy is independent of the system mechanisms that enforce the policy.

RBAC Role-based access control (RBAC) is concerned with aggregating access privileges into named entities (roles) and assigning such entities to individual users, groups of users, or other roles.

Security Mechanism A security mechanism implements a security policy to prevent and/or detect improper accesses that violate the policy.

Separation of Duties The principle of separation of duties (or privileges) states that a system should not grant permission based on a single condition.

Stored Procedure A stored procedure is a program that is executed through a single SQL statement that can be locally executed and completed within the process space of the database server.

Trigger A trigger is a type of stored procedure that describes database actions to be executed when certain database events occur.

View A view is a table that is derivable from other database tables, which can be previously defined views or base tables. A view is specified through an SQL query.

CROSS REFERENCES

See *Access Control: Principles and Solutions; Auditing Information Systems Security; Security Policy Guidelines.*

REFERENCES

Abrams, M. D., Jajodia, S., & Podell, H. J. (Eds.). (1995). *Information security: An integrated collection of essays*. New York: Wiley-IEEE Computer Society Press.

Anderson, R. (1999). RAND Corporation: Research and development initiatives focused on preventing, detecting, and responding to insider misuse of critical information systems. *Conference Proceedings* CF-151-OSD.

Anley, C. (2002). *Advanced SQL injection in SQL Server applications*. Next Generation Security Software Ltd. Retrieved June 30, 2005 from http://www.ngssoftware.com/papers/advanced_sql_injection.pdf

Batini, C., Ceri, S., & Navathe, S. B. (1992). *Conceptual database design: An entity-relationship approach*. Redwood City: Benjamin/Cummings.

Bell, D. E., & LaPadula, L. J. (1976). *Secure computer systems: Unified exposition and multics interpretation* (Technical Report). Bedford, MA: MITRE Corporation.

Bertino, E., Bettini, C., Ferrari, E., & Samarati, P. (1996). A temporal access control mechanism for database systems. *IEEE Transactions on Knowledge and Data Engineering, 8*(1), 67–80.

Bertino, E., Jajodia, S., & Samarati, P. (1995). Database security: Research and practice. *Information Systems, 20,*(7), 537–556.

Bertino, E., Jajodia, S., & Samarati, P. (1999). A flexible authorization mechanism for relational database systems. *ACM Transactions on Information Systems, 17*(2), 101–140.

Beznosov, K. (2002). Object security attributes: Enabling application-specific access control In middleware. R. Meersman and Z. Tari (Eds.) *4th International Symposium on Distributed Objects and Applications (DOA),*

Lecture Notes in Computer Science 2519, (693–710), Springer.

Bishop, M. (2003). *Computer security: Art and science.* Boston: Addison-Wesley.

Boyd, S. W., & Keromytis, A. D. (2004). SQLrand: Preventing SQL injection attacks. In *Proceedings of Applied Cryptography and Network Security, Second International Conference, ACNS 2004, Lecture Notes in Computer Science 3089*, Springer.

Castano, S., Fugini, M., Martella, G., & Samarati, P. (1995). *Database security.* Boston: Addison-Wesley.

Chung, C., Gertz, M., & Levitt, K. (1999). A misuse detection system for database systems (pp. 159–178). In M. E. van Biene-Hershey and Strous (Eds.) *integrity and internal control, IFIP TC11 working group 11.5, Third working conference an integrity and internal control in information system.* Kluwer Academic Publishers.

Common Criteria for Information Technology Security Evaluation (Version 2.2). (2004). Retrieved June 30, 2005 from http://niap.nist.gov/cc-scheme/cc_docs/cc_v2_part1.pdf

Devanbu, P., Gertz, M., Martel, M., & Stubblebine, S. G. (2003). Authentic data publication over the Internet. *Journal of Computer Security, 11*(3) 291–314.

Elmasri, R., & Navathe, S. B. (2004). *Fundamentals of database systems* (4th ed.). Addison-Wesley.

Epstein, P., & Sandhu, R. (1999). A UML-based approach to role engineering. *Proceedings of the Fourth Workshop on Role-Based Access Control. 135–143, NewYork: ACM.*

Epstein, P., & Sandhu, R. (2001). Engineering of role/permission assignments. *Proceedings of the 17th Annual Computer Security Applications Conference (ACSAC)* 127–136 IEEE Computer Society.

Ferraiolo, D. F., Sandhu, R., Gavrila, S., Kuhn, D. R., & Chandramouli, R. (2001). Proposed NIST standard for role-based access control. *ACM Transactions on Information and System Security, 4*(3), 224–274.

Fraser, B. (1997). *Site Security Handbook* (Request for Comments (RFC) 2196). Network Working Group, Internet Engineering Task Force. Retrieved June 30, 2005 from http://www.ietf.org/rfc/rfc2196.txt

Gertz, M., & Csaba, G. (2003). Monitoring mission critical data for integrity and availability In *5th International IFIP TC-11 WG 11.5 Working Conference on Integrity and Internal Control* (pp. 189–201). Kluwer Academic Publishers.

Gray, J., & Reuter, A. (1993). *Transaction processing: concepts and techniques.* San Francisco: Morgan Kaufman.

Johnson, T., & Dasu, T. (2003). Data quality and data cleaning: An overview. *Proceedings of the ACM SIGMOD International Conference on Management of Data.* p. 681, NewYork: ACM.

Landwehr, K. (2001). Computer security. *International Journal of Information Security, 1,* 3–13.

Levinger, J. (2002). *Oracle label security administrator's guide, release 2 (9.2), part number A96578-01.* Redwood Shores, CA: Oracle Corporation.

Melton J., & Simon, A. R. (2001). SQL 1999-Understanding Relational Language Components, (2nd Edition) San Francisco: Morgan Kaufman.

Nanda, A. (2004, March/April). Oracle's row-level security gives users their own virtual private databases. *Oracle Magazine.*

Nanda, A., & Burleson, D. (2003). *Oracle privacy security auditing (includes Federal Law Compliance with HIPAA, Sarbanes-Oxley and the Gramm-Leach-Bliley Act GLB).* Kittrell, NC: Rampant TechPress.

Neumann, P. G. (1999). *The challenges of insider misuse.* Paper prepared for the Workshop on Preventing, Detecting, and Responding to Malicious Insider Misuse, August 16–18, 1999, at RAND, Santa Monica, CA. Retrieved from http://www.csl.sri.com/users/neumann/pgn-misuse.html

Neumann, G., & Strembeck, M. (2002). A scenario-driven role engineering process for functional RBAC roles. *Proceedings of the 7th ACM Symposium on Access Control Models and Technologies,* 33–42. NewYork: ACM

Newman, A. (2004). Six security secrets attackers don't want you to know. *DB2 Magazine 9*(2).

Oh, Y., & Navathe, S. (1995). SEER: Security enhanced entity-relationship model for modeling and integrating secure database environments. In M. Papazoglou (Ed.), *OOER'95: Object-Oriented and Entity-Relationship Modeling, 14th International Conference, Lecture Notes in Computer Science, 1021* (pp. 170–180). Springer.

Osborn, S., Sandhu, R., & Munawer, Q. (2000). Configuring role-based access control to enforce mandatory and discretionary access control policies. *ACM Transactions on Information and Systems Security, 3*(2), 85–106.

Power, R. (2002). 2002 CSI/FBI computer crime and security survey. Computer Security Institute.

Ramakrishnan, R., & Gehrke, J. (2003). *Database management systems* (3rd ed.). New York: McGraw-Hill.

Ramaswamy, C., & Sandhu, R. (1998). Role-based access control features in commercial database management systems. In *21st National Information Systems Security Proceedings: Papers.* Retrieved June 30, 2005, from http://csrc.nist.gov/nissc/1998/papers.html

Rich, K. (2003). Oracle Database Utilities. Part No. B10825. Oracle Corporation, Redwood City.

Sandhu, R. (1998). Role activation hierarchies. In *Proceedings of the 3rd ACM Workshop on Role-Based Access Controls,* 33–40. NewYork: ACM

Sandhu, R. (2001). Future directions in role-based access control models. Keynote lecture at 2nd International Workshop on Mathematical Methods, Models, and Architectures for Computer Network Security, *Lecture Notes in Computer Science 2776,* Springer. Retrieved June 16, 2005, from http://www.list.gmu.edu/confrnc/misconf/mms01-rbac-future.pdf

Sandhu, R., Coyne, E. J., Feinstein, H. L., & Youman, C. E. (1996). Role-based access control models. *IEEE Computer, 29*(2), 38–47.

Sandhu, R., & Samarati, P. (1994, September). Access control: Principles and practice. *IEEE Communications Magazine,* 40–48.

Stonebraker, M. (1975). Implementation of integrity constraints and views by query modification. *Proceedings of the 1975 ACM SIGMOD International Conference on Management of Data,* 65–78. NewYork: ACM

Theriault, M. L., & Newman, A. (2001). *Oracle security handbook: Implement a sound security plan in your Oracle environment.* New York: McGraw-Hill Osborne.

U.S. Department of Defense. (1985). *Trusted computer system evaluation criteria* (DoD 5200.28 - STD). Retrived June 30, 2005, from http://www.radium.ncsc.mail/tpep/library/rainbow/5200.28-STD.html.

Weikum, G., & Vossen, G. (2002). *Transactional information systems.* Morgan Kaufman.

Client-Side Security

Charles Border, *Rochester Institute of Technology*

INTRODUCTION

Although large organizations spend millions of dollars every year to secure the periphery of their networks through the use of firewalls, a technological solution that controls the actions of insiders has thus far proved elusive. According to Thompson and Ford (2004), "The issue is trust. Insiders must be trusted to do their jobs; applications must be trusted to perform their tasks. The problem occurs when insiders—be they users or applications—intentionally, or unintentionally, extend trust inappropriately." Client-side security involves finding ways to control the ability of insiders to extend the trust relationship that they acquire as insiders in ways that are detrimental to the overall security of the network. Because a wholly technological solution has remained beyond the reach of developers, managers of both information technology professionals and other employees must work together to develop a solution that involves not only technology but also improving user awareness through policies, procedures, and user education.

Client-side security is a particularly important topic now. Many of the most damaging attacks to hit organizational networks have succeeded based on the exploitation of attack vectors that circumvent firewalls placed on the periphery of networks. Malicious code arrives either as attachments to routine e-mail messages or by being released inside the periphery of protected networks by infected laptop computers or mobile devices. It is particularly difficult to apply a technological solution to these types of attack vectors because they rely on the assistance of naïve or malicious users with direct access to the inside of organizational networks.

Although technology can be our most valuable aid to secure networks from many attacks, managerial solutions such as the promulgation of acceptable use policies and user education programs can be the most effective solution to these types of attacks.

This chapter provides a rationale for maintaining the security of client computers and outlines some of the most important precautions that can be taken to protect networks from attacks based on exploitation of insecure clients. This is accomplished first by discussing some of the characteristics of recent client-based attacks followed by a discussion of the relevant characteristics of clients and how this affects the techniques that must be used to protect them. Securing clients on an organizational network from attack involves tools and techniques that can be grouped in four areas:

- *Deployment.* The deployment of known and well-understood operating systems and applications in a managed and secure fashion
- *Management.* Management and maintenance of the currency of applications and operating systems through the secure and organized deployment of patches and updates to organizational computing resources
- *Monitoring.* The development and implementation of tools and techniques to monitor application and resource use to ensure that the consistency of configuration and exposure to vulnerability are within organizational guidelines
- *Improving user awareness.* Making users aware of their rights and responsibilities as they relate to the security of the network

Securing the client side of a network involves more than securing all the operating systems on all the clients on that network. The goal of a client-side security program is a general hardening of the interior of a network that, when combined with a strong perimeter, is part of a layered approach to overall network security. Client-side security is a process that involves the entire life cycle of network resources.

Many of the tools and techniques mentioned in this chapter are more thoroughly discussed in other chapters of this book. When possible, this chapter contains cross-references to both other chapters and Web sites that the reader might find useful.

WHY WORRY ABOUT THE SECURITY OF CLIENTS?

According to the F-Secure Corporation (2004), on January 25, 2003, around 4:31 UTC, the importance of controlling

342

the configuration of clients on large organizational networks was driven home by the onset of the Slammer worm. The Slammer worm exploited a vulnerability in a common component in many Microsoft products, the Microsoft Desktop Engine (MSDE), which caused compromised clients to put all their considerable resources to work trying to contact other MSDE engines. The resulting surge in traffic was the biggest attack up to that date and spread around the globe in about 15 minutes. The net result of this surge in traffic was a denial of service that slowed down Internet-based communications worldwide. The reason this attack was so problematic had nothing to do with the attack itself; rather, that it affected far more machines than most administrators expected it to affect was of significance. Most administrators knew and in many cases had patched the most important of the SQL Server servers (the most well known of the MSDE-based applications) on their networks. (A patch had been available for 26 days.) But the small clients, desktop and laptop computers—the configuration of which administrators had long ago lost control of— brought down many networks. In an era of trusting the security of a network to server-side security and controlling the perimeter through firewalling, this attack forced administrators to rethink their previous strategies and to attempt to regain control of the configuration of clients.

The basic techniques used to maintain the security of a large network of clients and servers are not very different from those used to maintain strictly server-side security. Client-side security is not about technical revolutions; it is about cultural revolutions. It requires the same thinking that goes into securing servers against crackers applied to securing clients, with one huge exception. When maintaining the security of servers from attack, we have three important assets on our side: a relatively small number of hosts to worry about, a better trained user at the console, and a tradition of concern to fall back on. This is not the case with client-side security. The main difference between server-side security and client-side security is that when we attempt to secure clients from attack, we must attempt to deal with our history of relations with the users at the keyboard. An educated and responsible user community is our best and last hope for securing our networks from client-based attacks. And it is here where our collective history of neglecting user concerns and not investing in user training comes home to roost.

RFC 2196 *Site Security Handbook*

Before an effective client-side security plan can be developed, some very basic and very fundamental questions need to be addressed. These questions relate primarily to the role of information in the organization and the types of security exposures that are most relevant for a given network. RFC 2196 edited by B. Fraser (1997) from the Internet Engineering Task Force (IETF) outlines the following as the more important questions that must be addressed in a site security handbook.

1. *Identify what you are trying to protect.* Client-side security is primarily about protecting the ability of users to use technology to accomplish their jobs. Users who must stop working while a virus is being cleaned off their computer or a group of users who are unable to access a server because a workstation in their workgroup is infected with a virus are not able to do their jobs, and the huge investment their organization has made in technology is not returning anything to the organization. Users who lose all the important files on their computer and do not have backup copies might have permanently damaged their careers. As organizations integrate technology more closely into their business process, the ability of users to access technology becomes crucial for them to do their jobs and for the organization as a whole to accomplish its goals and objectives.

2. *Determine what you are trying to protect it from.* Client-side security has many aspects. You might be trying to protect users of the network from the malicious attempts of others within or outside the organization to access personal or sensitive files. You also might be trying to protect users from a virus that they might unknowingly download from malicious Web sites. Although these are two very different goals, they are not mutually exclusive and are both part of a comprehensive client-side security program.

3. *Determine how likely the threats are.* Information technology (IT) managers and security administrators must be cognizant of both technical and societal indicators that might have a bearing on the likelihood of an attack. Threats to an organizational network can originate from either inside or outside the network. The likelihood of malicious outsiders targeting your organization for exploitation can have more to do with random chance, or the perceptions of activists on the other side of the globe, than it does with anything you can control. Some of the factors that should be included in the process of identifying the likelihood of attacks from outsiders include the organization's current level of security, the ease with which the organization has been attacked in the past, the type of transactions for which the organization uses the Internet (information only versus online transactions), and the history of the organization's involvement in activities that might be considered controversial by the hacking community.

Threats from users inside an organization can be either malicious or accidental in nature and far more damaging in extent. Insider users are granted much more access to organizational resources and have a better understanding of the role of specific information sources in the organization. IT managers and security administrators must be cognizant of the relationship between the organization and its insiders and the effect that any changes might have on the motivation of insiders either to damage information resources maliciously or accidentally.

For detailed information on this topic, please consult Chapter 81, Hackers, Crackers, and Computer Criminals, and Chapter 82, Hacktivism.

4. *Implement measures that will protect your assets in a cost-effective manner.* A balance must be found between the cost of protecting information assets and the value of those assets to the organization. This balance must be informed by a thorough understanding of the role of information technology in the organization and the public's perception of the organization.

5. *Review the process continuously and make improvements each time a weakness is found.* The current

paradigm for client-side security is a continual battle between malicious crackers and system administrators. The results of the battle thus far have been a draw, with system administrators frantically blocking ports and upgrading software and crackers honing their techniques in search of the elusive zero-day attack (an attack on a vulnerability that has not previously been realized). This paradigm requires that system administrators continuously review the processes by which they secure their networks and continuously improve those processes that are found lacking.

TYPES OF ATTACKS

Before you can gain an adequate understanding of how to secure clients from attack, you need to have a conceptual understanding of the different types of attacks that might be executed.

In the most general terms, the goal of any client-side security program is to protect client computers from being used as the platform for launching two general types of attacks: those that attempt to gain inappropriate access to resources located directly on the local host and those that attempt to use the trust relationship of the local host to attack other resources either within or outside the network. When we look at the security architecture common to most networks, the two most relevant design elements we see are a reliance on securing the network by securing the perimeter through the use of firewalls at all points of connection with the Internet, and the reliance on the idea that requests for resources originating from within the network can be trusted more than requests for resources originating from outside the network (see Figure 1). This architecture falls apart in the face of attacks that either originate on the inside from a malicious user or are released on the inside of the network by a naïve user who uses a mobile computing device as both an office workstation during the day and a home workstation in the evening.

HOW CAN CRACKERS ACCOMPLISH THEIR GOALS?

The technique that crackers rely on revolves around finding a way to escalate the permissions at which their processes are run. This can be accomplished in only two ways: either users of trusted computers are somehow induced to extend the trust relationship they have as insiders to a cracker's program by running that program, or the cracker exploits software vulnerabilities that exist in the operating system or application software on the computer to do

other things. John Pescatore (2003) of the Gartner Group has developed what he refers to as "a taxonomy of software vulnerabilities" that divides vulnerabilities into two broad groups and two subcategories:

1. *Software defects*.
   a. *Coding flaws*. Vulnerabilities can be incorporated into well-designed programs through the accidental inclusion of coding mistakes.
   b. *Design flaws*. Vulnerabilities can be designed into applications as the applications iterate through the design process.
2. *Configuration errors*.
   a. *Dangerous/unnecessary services*. Ease of administration and security can come into conflict and result in the deployment of additional services that then can be used as part of an exploit.
   b. *Access administration errors*. Although the deployment of permission structures sounds like a simplistic operation, it can become very complex as the size of a user community grows in both geographic and temporal diversity.

Protecting client computers from these two groups of software vulnerabilities requires two very different approaches. Software defects are very difficult for individual users to find out about and hence to protect themselves from. Commercially developed and open-source software is conventionally tested for usability long before it is released to the general public. The problem with the software defects that crackers exploit is that such defects do not affect the general use of the software (those defects are usually caught in testing). They involve the internal workings of the software with which users seldom if ever interact. From the user's perspective, the software appears to work fine, in spite of the presence of design or coding flaws.

Configuration errors are much more common and potentially much more dangerous because they provide a means for the normal operating procedures of the computer to be turned against the user or organization. One reason configuration errors are common revolves around the conflict between the incentives developers have to make their software as flexible as possible as soon as it is installed and the needs of system administrators for a secure deployment. This leads to an initial installed configuration that has more available services running than is strictly necessary—exactly the wrong scenario for a secure configuration. (The ideal for a secure configuration is that only those services required for users to accomplish their specific jobs be running at any given time.)

CLASSES OF CLIENTS

One of the more recent trends that makes securing all clients more important is the growing number of always-on connections to the Internet. Always-on connections are provided as part of an organizational network, a Small Office/Home Office (SOHO) setup, or a home computer connected to the Internet through a high-speed cable modem or Digital Subscriber Line (DSL). The first class of client computers that must be secured encompasses those

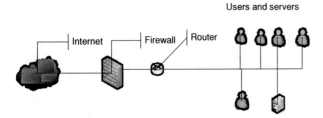

Users and servers

Figure 1: Common network architecture.

that are physically connected to the Internet through their connection to a parent organization network. As members of a larger network, they are nominally protected from attack by firewall devices located at the perimeter of the network, and, more important, they are protected by having access to a group of IT personnel who are responsible for seeing that the client operating systems and application software are kept up-to-date and can be relied on to intervene when problems arise.

The second class of clients are those that are owned by individuals and are used to connect SOHO computers directly to the Internet through DSL or cable modem systems. In the past, most of these computers connected to the Internet through an Internet service provider (ISP) by using dial-up modems and actively disconnected when the connection was no longer needed so that the phone line could be used for voice connections. When these computers connect to the Internet through DSL or cable modems, they are frequently left on and are connected to the Internet all the time. According to a study by the National Cyber Security Alliance by America Online, Inc., the owners of these always-on computers are not well educated about the perils of viruses and worms and do little to prevent their computers from becoming vehicles for attacking others computers. "The vast majority of subjects (86%) said they felt their computer was very or somewhat safe from online threats, however only 11% had a safe broadband connection—with a properly and safely configured firewall, recently upgraded anti-virus protection, and, if children were present in the household, parental controls" (National Cyber Security Alliance, 2003, p. 4). This class of computers presents a very different set of problems when it comes to client security. The reason relates to the lack of support users have from any IT personnel.

Although securing SOHO-based computers from exploitation by crackers might seem irrelevant to an organizational client-side security program, this is not the case for two very important reasons: many of the computers that connect to the Internet through unfiltered DSL or cable modem connections are in reality laptops owned by large organizations that are brought home at night by members of the organization, or they are exploited as e-mail relay agents to generate spam, which then floods organizational e-mail systems.

ACTIVE CONTENT AND CLIENT-SIDE SECURITY

Much of what is considered cool on the Internet is a new class of content called *active content*. Active content consists of small applications or applets that users actively download from Web sites or that are downloaded automatically when a Web site is first accessed. These small applications then generate dancing hippos (for example) by running a small program on the client computer rather than on the server that provides the content. The problem with active content is that users have little if any idea what the active content actually will do before they run these applications or programs. The only effective security that exists between the client computer and the arbitrary application developed by someone the user doesn't know and

whose code the user has not evaluated in any fashion is that provided by the security settings of the browser in which the processes will execute or the language in which the application is written.

Rolf Oppliger (2003) of eSECURITY.com has developed a list of the types of active content that are designed to interact with client workstations: binary mail attachments, helper applications and plug-ins, scripting languages, Java applets, and ActiveX controls. He points out that one of the most dangerous things that a user can do on a networked computer is download an unknown piece of software and execute it locally. Most operating system software places little restraint on an authenticated user's ability to execute programs. Although this is the desired situation in most circumstances (it enables users to run the applications they need to do their jobs), when users download and execute programs from unknown sources, they are placing themselves, and all the systems that they are attached to them by their network, in the hands of a stranger.

For detailed information on this topic, please consult Volume III, Part 1 of this handbook: Threats and Vulnerabilities to Information and Computing Infrastructures. Also, see chapter 145, Computer Viruses and Worms, chapter 146, Trojan Horse Programs, chapter 148, Hostile Java Applets, and chapter 149, Spyware.

Binary Mail Attachments

It has become standard procedure for users to rely on e-mail attachments to send small programs to friends and coworkers over the Internet. These programs are usually attached to ordinary e-mail messages and enter the destination network as binary files. These binary files can be images or formatted text messages, and they can be based on the multipurpose Internet mail extension (MIME) standard or be basically anything the sender wants to attach. The problem is that hackers can send executable files that, when clicked by the recipient, automatically execute with the same rights as the recipient. In effect, recipients are then running a program whose source they may or may not know and whose purpose and the ways in which it interacts with the client workstation and others on the users' network are not understood. For some time, this has been one of the main means of transmitting Trojan horse viruses. Browsers and e-mail clients can easily be configured to open a message box asking the user for confirmation to run the file instead of automatically executing files like this, but many users have determined for themselves that the convenience of automatic execution outweighs the potential risk. Although many users have received extensive instruction not to execute attachments sent to them from unknown sources, the trick for the hacker is to find a way to increase the probability that some users will execute the file. Crackers have become very adept at preying on people's natural curiosity and baser instincts to induce users to execute binary attachments. Some of the more intriguing means through which this has been attempted in the past include using a subject line message of "I love you," "pictures of Anna Kournikova attached," or "an urgent message from the University Registrar."

Helper Applications and Plug-Ins

In the early days of browser development, browsers were able to work with only a few types of files (basically, American Standard Code for Information Interchange [ASCII], Hypertext Markup Language [HTML], graphics interchange format [GIF], and Joint Photographic Experts Group [JPEG] files), but users wanted to do more with their browsers. The natural solution was to develop helper applications that had their own address space. When a specific type of file was called, the helper apps automatically ran and processed the file. Although this provided a fairly extensible workaround, Netscape developed a different version of the same idea called plug-ins. Plug-ins do the same thing as helper applications, but they share the address space of the browser. To make it easier for users to obtain and use the correct plug-in or helper application, browsers were configured to prompt the user for a specific plug-in when they encountered a new file type. This opened a huge security hole that was quickly exploited by crackers. Crackers discovered that users who were prompted to download and install a new plug-in would do it with very little consideration of the developer of the plug-in or the veracity of the code. Crackers developed Web sites to exploit the gullibility of users and to prompt them to install plug-ins developed by the crackers that allowed the crackers to gain control over client workstations.

The problem of unauthenticated plug-ins remains. And although users have become somewhat more sophisticated about installing plug-ins from companies they do not know, crackers continue to use this technique successfully.

Scripting Languages

Another way to extend the functionality of browsers is to configure them to support the execution of scripting languages on the client. Although several powerful scripting languages can be supported by browsers (JavaScript, Jscript, VBScript), the security of each of these languages can be gauged, in its most basic form, by the existence of capabilities that allow them to operate outside their own "sandbox" (the operating environment of the browser), such as the ability to open other files or establish network connections that can be exploited by crackers to accomplish their goals. The problem with this idea is that the intentionally limited capabilities of a scripting language need not be used to attack a client machine directly; instead, they can be used to increase the sophistication of a social engineering attack and therefore the likelihood that the cracker can trick the user into doing something that the scripting language by itself cannot do.

JavaScript, when run in a Netscape Navigator browser, has the following security-related restrictions placed on it:

- It is unable to read or write files.
- There is no access to file system information.
- It can't execute programs or system commands.
- It is able to make network connections only to the computer from which the code was downloaded.
- There are restrictions to the access of <form> data.

Wagner and Wyke (2000) also point out that while JavaScript is somewhat secure, as outlined earlier, it is still subject to many of the same issues as any other programming language, such as infinite loops, stack overflows, infinite modal dialogs, and use of all available memory. Even though a JavaScript program that runs into these problems could be dismissed as poorly coded, the net result to a user is a denial of service that incapacitates the browser and requires that it be manually shut down. In the early days, the preceding security restrictions were sufficient to prevent many of the hacks that had surfaced, but this has not continued to be the case. The reason for this is twofold: the browsers in which the applets are run have proved to be less secure than they should be, and the ability of the JavaScript to create cute and enticing applets has been used as part of social engineering schemes to lure unsuspecting users to Web sites containing malicious code.

Java Applets

The Java programming language and Java applets (small Java programs that can be run only within a Java-enabled Web browser) were designed with a dynamic, extensible security architecture. The boundary between untrusted source code and the resources of the host system is contained by three distinct layers: the Security Manager, the Class Loader, and the Verifier. Included in the Java language are such useful technologies as cryptography, authentication, authorization, and support for public key infrastructures.

ActiveX Controls

ActiveX controls are essentially Component Object Model (COM) objects that support the IUnknown interface. They can be used to enhance the usability of Web pages and can be made to be relatively secure. The problem arises in that they can, either through malice or by accident, be made extremely insecure. According to Microsoft (2004a), ActiveX controls must be designed from the beginning to be secure, and the onus is on the programmer to make them secure. Once a control is initiated, it can be repurposed (used in ways that you did not intend) by any application that can gain the control's class identifier (CLSID). Because all ActiveX controls are Microsoft Win32 components, they are not limited to any sandboxing limitations and can be made to run without any restrictions. They therefore can be made to modify any of the settings in the local registry or the file system.

SECURING CLIENTS

This section discusses some of the tools and techniques used to enhance the security of clients in an organizational network. To effectively secure a network of clients from attack requires attention to be paid to those clients throughout their effective life. They should be deployed with a well-known operating system, antivirus program, personal firewall, and applications properly installed and configured. They need to be maintained and managed throughout their effective lifetime with patches and upgrades automatically installed. And their configuration, access to the network, and exposure to vulnerabilities need to be monitored through periodic host scans and a program of vulnerability management.

Julia H. Allen and the Computer Emergency Response Team Coordination Center (CERT/CC) at Carnegie Mellon University have developed a list of practices to be followed to enhance client security (Allen, 2001). The list of practices are not specific to any one operating system but represent generic good practices that should be followed at any installation where client-side security is an issue. Their goal in developing these practices was to secure clients in the following ways:

- To provide a backup to the failure of perimeter defenses as well as provide a first line of defense against internal threats
- To assist in the early recognition of security incidents and thereby enhance the ability to respond to those incidents and prevent their occurrence in the future
- To promote consistency of configuration and deployment across clients and thereby make it easier to identify behavior that is outside the norm and potentially indicative of an attack

Their recommendations are based on the premise that client-side security is not only about technology. The approach that CERT/CC advocates for effective client-side security is a holistic approach that recognizes the vital role that users play in the securing of computer networks, and it can be divided into four separate areas: planning, configuring, maintaining, and improving user awareness.

Initial Deployment

The initial deployment of clients to a network is a very important time because it is the only time when system administrators can feel entirely comfortable with their configuration. To make the initial deployment as effective and secure as possible, the following areas need to be covered.

Planning

Security cannot be added onto a deployment of user workstations. For security to be effective, it must be planned in from the onset. Many questions need to be asked regarding the deployment of individual computers, but they revolve around gaining an understanding of exactly what the purpose of each computer is and deploying that computer with only the required services enabled to support that purpose. The following questions can be helpful in the planning phase:

- What will the computer be used for?
- What types of information will be stored on the computer?
- What types of information will be processed on the computer?
- What are the security requirements for the information to be processed on the computer?
- How will the computer interact with other computers on the network?

- What users will have access to the computer, what configuration changes will they be able to make to the computer, and how are the users related?
- What trust relationship will this computer have with other computers on the network?

The answers to these questions will help determine the operating system and application software configuration that a computer will require. Having a thorough, well-documented deployment plan enables you to make the correct decisions in balancing usability and security.

Configuring

It is vitally important that new clients not be released onto the network without a tested and thoroughly understood initial operating system and application software configuration. The initial configuration should have all vendor updates installed and browsers configured with only those services required to enable users to perform their tasks. Many client-side security problems can be avoided by deploying computers with secure configurations, including encrypted authentication, virus protection, and personnel firewalls.

Virus Protection

Virus protection software must be a part of every client configuration. It should be installed with an up-to-date signature file prior to placing the device on the network, and new updates must be implemented as soon as they become available. Because new virus signatures cannot be developed prior to a virus appearing on the Internet, virus protection software is always somewhat out of date. There are, however, enough old viruses on the Internet at any given time that virus protection software is a requirement for every client connection.

For detailed information on this topic, please consult the chapter titled Antivirus Technology.

Personal Firewalls

The traditional model of deploying firewalls at the periphery of networks is not effective in the face of attacks that crackers send into the interior of networks as e-mail attachments and those that are released on the internal side of networks by malicious or naïve users. To safeguard client workstations more fully requires the deployment of firewalls on all computing devices that can be monitored and configured centrally.

For detailed information on this topic, please consult Volume III, Chapter 175, Firewall Basics, Chapter 176 Firewall Architectures, Chapter 177, Packet Filtering and Stateful Firewalls, and Chapter 178 Proxy Firewalls.

Intrusion Detection

Although intrusion detection systems have been likened to dashboard indicators on cars, which go on only after the damage is done, they still have a valuable role to play in the overall securing of computer networks. As more work is done on the actual means by which attacks occur, intrusion detection systems will become more reliable in their ability to analyze network traffic and system configuration information and therefore better able to apply that baseline information against the current conditions to judge if an attack is actually occurring.

For detailed information on this topic, please consult Volume III, chapter 183, Intrusion Detection Systems Basics, chapter 184, Host-Based Intrusion Detection Systems, chapter 185, Network-Based Intrusion Detection Systems, chapter 186, The Use of Agent Technology for Intrusion Detection, and chapter 194, Use of Data Mining for Intrusion Detection.

User Authentication

User authentication is the basis for all security in a networked environment. There are four processes involved in securely granting access to network resources. Users must *identify* themselves to the system. This is usually accomplished through the use of a user name but might also be accomplished through something that the user has, such as an identification card. Users must then *authenticate*, or prove their asserted identity, to the system. Although this is usually accomplished through a password, the use of biometrics such as hand geometry or fingerprint or retinal scans is becoming more common. Linked to a valid account are all the *authorizations* or privileges that accrue to an identity. Once a user's identity has been proved and the privileges ascertained, the final step in the process is the granting of *access* to actual resources. There are a number of variations or extensions to the preceding general scheme. Two-factor authentication requires that users have both a user name and password as well as an access token to authenticate. One of the problems with two-factor authentication is that it can be difficult and expensive to equip all the potential access points to a network with hardware that can authenticate the access token as a legitimate access token. One of the ways around this is the use of time-based authentication codes that are recalculated every minute on both the host and a credit-card-sized authenticator that the user must possess.

For detailed information on this topic, please consult Volume III, chapter 164, Password Authentication, and chapter 165, Computer and Network Authentication. For more information on biometrics and their use, please see Volume III, chapter 167, Biometric Basics and Biometric Authentication, chapter 168, Issues and Concerns in Biometric IT Security, and chapter 174, Applications of Biometrics in Financial Security Transactions.

Client-side Security in a Microsoft Environment

The means and the extent of security settings available in a Microsoft Windows environment are very much dependent on the type of network involved and the relationship of the client to that network. Although it is beyond the scope of this chapter to discuss the specifics of the many Microsoft Windows client operating systems and the different types of domains to which they can be joined, the following subsections outline some of the issues involved with Microsoft Windows XP clients, Microsoft Windows 2000 and Windows 2003 Server servers, and Active Directory domains.

Microsoft Windows XP Clients in Active Directory Domains

Windows XP clients in Active Directory domains are the typical configuration in a Microsoft enterprise environment. Windows XP is the current release of the Microsoft Windows client operating system, and it provides a very sophisticated interface between the user and the network. The Active Directory is a database of user information that uses an implementation of the Lightweight Directory Access Protocol (LDAP) to access a centralized store of information and configuration settings that is replicated to computers called *domain controllers*. Domain controllers not only store this database but also handle such administrative tasks as user authentication and authorization services.

One of the many other interesting functions that domain controllers provide as part of the logon process is to push out to clients a series of user and environment configuration settings called Group Policy Objects (GPOs). GPOs can be used to apply and maintain a consistent set of security settings or policies across a network of clients and servers from a central location. Recognizing that many people are ambivalent about the role that Microsoft products have played in many of the security problems that have plagued the Internet recently, Microsoft has developed a set of recommendations for securing Windows XP in an Active Directory environment (Microsoft, 2004b). These security settings can be imported into GPOs by using templates and applied to all or some of the clients on a Microsoft network. Although most of the settings have to do with fairly esoteric areas of securing network communications, many have to do with more basic ideas.

Microsoft recommends evaluating whether to implement security settings through GPOs in more than 200 areas. Some of those areas include the following:

- *Password settings*. How often should passwords be changed? When changing passwords, what restrictions are placed on these changes?
- *Account lockout policy*. What should the computer do when a user tries unsuccessfully to log on? Should it allow the user another try, and if so, how many?
- *Audit policy*. What events should the computer record and save to log files? What should happen when the log files become full? How often should the log files be reviewed and analyzed?
- *User rights*. What rights should the local user have on the local computer? Should users have the right to install new software? The right to change the system time? The right to back up or restore files?
- *Login messages*. What message should be displayed at login (for example: "This system is restricted to authorized users. Individuals attempting unauthorized access will be prosecuted.")?

Microsoft Windows XP Clients in Stand-Alone Environments

Without the network infrastructure that an Active Directory environment provides, the options for implementing security settings on Windows XP clients are much more limited. Each Windows XP client, however, has at least one Local Group Policy Object (LGPO) that can be used to implement some security-related settings. The limitations relate to the ways in which the client interacts with the network and Active Directory. All of the previously referenced settings are still possible.

For detailed information on this topic, please consult Volume II, chapter 130, Operating System Security, chapter 135, Windows 2000 Security; very good sources on the Web include http://www.windowsecurity.com/ and http://www.microsoft.com/security/default.mspx.

Client-side Security in a UNIX/Linux Environment

Although most of the more serious worms and viruses have had the greatest impact on Microsoft Windows–based clients, it is important for users and administrators responsible for the security of UNIX/Linux-based clients to be concerned with the security of their computers. This is particularly the case as more mature, higher quality, graphical user interfaces have made more practicable the deployment of UNIX/Linux-based computers as clients for less experienced users.

Many of the basic ideas behind securing a UNIX/Linux computer are the same as securing any other: use strong passwords and authentication, keep installed applications revisions up-to-date, only deploy those services that are necessary for users to accomplish their tasks, use personal firewalls, and use antivirus software. The most significant difference between securing Microsoft Windows and Apple Macintosh computers and securing UNIX/Linux computers is the lack of a single, centralized company that can be expected to provide many of the software updates for the UNIX/Linux operating system and applications. To maintain the security of applications with UNIX/Linux clients, users must have a deeper understanding of their computer and the applications that are running on it. They also must be aware of security warnings from many more organizations. A user running an Apache Web server as a personal Web server on an Intel-based computer using Mandrake as an operating system needs to pay attention to security warnings from both Apache and Mandrake, and it might not be the case that Mandrake would warn the user of problems with the Apache Web server.

Because of the long history of UNIX/Linux as an enterprise operating system, many Web-based resources provide information on securing UNIX/Linux clients. Some of the better ones include the following: the Computer Emergency Response Team (CERT) Coordination Center of Carnegie Mellon University in conjunction with the Australian Computer Emergency Response Team (AusCERT) has published a UNIX Security Checklist with an extensive set of potential vulnerabilities, scripts, and white papers that detail both the vulnerabilities and steps that can be taken to remediate them (http://www.cert.org/tech_tips/usc20_full.html). A very good place to learn the latest in Linux security advisories and to find out about new open-source and proprietary security applications is http://www.linuxsecurity.com/. A Linux Security Quick Reference guide and a Quick Start guide also can quickly get you organized (http://www. linuxsecurity.com/docs/).

For detailed information on this topic, please consult Volume II, chapter 130, Operating System Security, chapter 132, UNIX Operating System Security, and chapter 133, Linux Operating System Security.

Client-side Security in a Mac OS X Environment

Mac OS X is a version of UNIX originally developed based on the BSD UNIX family, and it provides users with a very stable and reliable platform. Mac OS X is well supported with both printed and online resources to help users better secure their computers. Some of the better online resources related to Mac OS X security include the following: *An Introduction to Mac OS X Security* (http://developer.apple.com/internet/security/ securityintro.html), *A Security Primer for Mac OS X* (http:// www.macdevcenter.com/pub/a/mac/2004/02/20/security. html), and *Macintosh OS X Security: Understanding the Platform and Usage* (http://www.securemac.com/ macosxsecurity.php). As originally installed, Mac OS X is a very secure operating system that Apple does a very good job maintaining by releasing timely patches as needed. There are, however, certain practices that must be implemented to maintain the security of most Mac OS X computers. The most important security practice that can be applied to any computer, including a Macintosh, is the use of strong passwords. The default configuration of Mac OS X has the root account disabled and instead utilizes a very sophisticated graphical user interface (GUI) that assumes the capabilities of root (by invoking SUDO) when root access is required. Although access to the root account can be accomplished without much technical sophistication, this is actively discouraged by Apple based on the fear that users might then use the root account as their normal account and expose themselves to hacks based on processes being run as root. As initially installed, very few services operate in Mac OS X. Although it is relatively easy to enable additional services, such as Windows file sharing and remote access, it is very important for users to understand how the services work and the implications of the additional services before they enable them. Mac OS X comes with a personal firewall that enables users to limit the ports through which their Mac is listening for connections. The firewall is called ipfw (IP firewall) and can be enabled from the Sharing Preferences pane in the System Preferences application. Finally, as with other operating systems, it is vitally important that the user install and keep current antivirus software. Although traditionally most antivirus software was written for MS Windows operating systems, the attack vectors used by crackers now are beginning to span platforms, and vendors are now developing antivirus software specifically for Mac OS X.

For detailed information on this topic, please consult Volume II, chapter 130, Operating System Security, chapter 132, UNIX Operating System Security, and chapter 133, Linux Operating System Security.

Maintenance

Computer operating systems, software applications, and hardware are very complex systems with substantial

Table 1

Company	Product Name	Product URL
Ecora	Patch Manager	http://www.ecora.com/ecora/
Shavlik	HFNetChkPro	http://www.shavlik.com/
St. Bernard	UpDate Expert	http://www.stbernard.com/
Patchlink	Update	http://www.patchlink.com/
Configuresoft	ECM	http://www.configuresoft.com/

market incentives for vendors to get a product released quickly to market. The combination of complexity of configuration and market incentive for early release creates a situation in which many of the defects in hardware and software are not discovered until after release. Vendors usually respond to this by releasing updates for newly discovered flaws that must be installed with administrator or superuser access permissions. Although several systems attempt to make this process as automated as possible, they are not infallible and can introduce new problems in the process of resolving others.

According to Allen (2001), some of the more common problems with the current update/patch deployment process relate to the following:

- It is impossible for all clients on a network to receive and install the update at exactly the same time; therefore, there will be a period during which different machines are operating with different configurations. This can lead to data corruption (depending on the nature of the update/patch), inconsistent operation, or worse.
- Some of the vendors, and many of the users, do not know how to use authentication via encryption appropriately to deploy updates/patches to users. This leaves users wide open to crackers deploying Trojan horses and viruses through the social engineering practice of sending them to users disguised as updates/patches deployed by a vendor they know and trust.
- To install some updates, it is necessary that the host be taken offline or restarted before the update can take effect. The unavailability of the host during this time can cause problems depending on the services it provides to other members of the network.
- With the plethora of updates/patches that have been released recently, it is virtually impossible for network administrators to evaluate them effectively before they are installed. The time pressure that this has induced for system and network administrators can force them to violate good practice for update deployment and install

updates without properly researching and testing them in their own environment.

Automated Patch and Update Management

Passive patch management techniques might not be as effective as required in dealing with the large-scale deployment of necessary patches. According to a survey done by Theo Forbath of the Product Strategies and Architecture Practice of WiPro Technologies (2005), enterprises spent on average $297 on each Windows client and $343 on each Open Source System per year to apply patches in 2004. Although the tidal wave of patches has not let up since then, the use of automated patch management tools has greatly increased. Several products are available that automate the patching process either as stand-alone tools or as part of asset and configuration tool sets. The key functionality of these systems is the ability to analyze systems remotely for installed patches and to push required patches out to individual computers. There are several closed-source automated patch management products available. Table 1 provides only a short list.

Automated Application Deployment

Another topic of importance during the maintenance phase of client-side security is the automated deployment of new and modified applications. As with patch and update management, the goal is to deploy applications in a secure, manageable, and consistent fashion to groups and subgroups within an organization with little if any user involvement. A valuable resource in both understanding the available technology and finding vendors for closed- and open-source products is AppDeploy.com (http://www.appdeploy.com/).

This site does not sell products but instead serves as a central point for information dissemination. Other companies that sell products that provide application deployment and client management functionality include those listed in Table 2.

Table 2

Company	Product Name	Product URL
Altiris	Client Management	http://www.altiris.com/
BMC Software	Marimba Client Management	http://www.bmc.com/
Tally Systems	Cenergy Client Management Suite	http://www.tallysystems.com/
Hewlett-Packard	Client Manager Suite	http://www.hp.com/

Monitoring

One of the maxims of computer security is that if a cracker gains physical access to the console, that cracker owns the computer. With client-side security, that is the situation we face everyday. With that in mind, an important part of a comprehensive client-side security program is the monitoring of clients and the users that use them. Monitoring in this case involves several activities, some technological and others more managerial in nature.

Vulnerability Management

The incredible proliferation of vulnerabilities and the speed at which exploits have been developed have created a situation in which it is no longer possible to deploy all patches as soon as they are available. Administrators are forced to prioritize and accept a certain degree of exposure to vulnerabilities at any given time. Determining which vulnerabilities to patch immediately and which can be safely ignored until several patches can be deployed at once is a managerial decision that should be made based on a thorough knowledge of the degree of exposure and the risk that putting off deploying a patch incurs.

Host Scanning

Given the degree of physical access that users have to the clients that are to be secured, it is crucial that the currency of configuration be monitored on a periodic basis. This can take the form of the deployment of a closed-source hardware-based tool such as Foundstone's Enterprise Manager (http://www.foundstone.com/). This tool continually scans the devices on a network and compares any vulnerabilities it finds to a vulnerability database that prioritizes vulnerabilities based on their potential impact to the specific network and automatically takes remedial actions. Although this degree of sophistication comes at a significant price, less sophisticated but still effective host scanners can either be developed in-house based on such tools as SuperScan (also from Foundstone, but freely downloadable), Nmap (freely downloadable from http://www.insecure.org/tools.html), or Nessus (also freely downloadable from http://www.insecure.org/tools.html).

Host-Based Intrusion Detection Systems

No matter how secure a network of clients is, crackers will attempt to search for and exploit vulnerabilities. Although it is possible to manage your direct exposure to vulnerabilities and attempt to keep that exposure within a set of guidelines, it is becoming impossible to be impervious to exploits and still remain connected to the Internet. With this in mind, the deployment of host-based intrusion detection systems should be part of a client-side security program. Host-based intrusion detection systems enable network and system administrators to develop historic baseline information regarding the expected use or configuration of resources on a network when the resource is in a known state. This baseline can then be compared to a current state to determine whether there is cause to suspect an ongoing cracking incident. The problem with these systems is that they have the potential to overwhelm network and system administrators with false positives and false negatives. Although this should not obviate

their use, administrators need to be aware of this limitation as they begin to determine the configuration of the devices.

Many closed-source host-based intrusion detection systems are currently on the market either as stand-alone programs or as part of an enterprise security service. Also, many open-source programs are available that can provide an acceptable level of security, including Snort (available at http://www.snort.org/) and Tripwire (available at http://www.tripwire.com/).

For detailed information on this topic, please consult Volume III, chapter 190, Intrusion Detection Basics, chapter 191, Host-Based Intrusion Detection Systems, chapter 192, Network-Based Intrusion Detection Systems, chapter 193, Use of Agent Technology for Intrusion Detection, and chapter 194, Use of Data Mining for Intrusion Detection.

Procedures

As the complexity of computer networks and individual computers grows, it is ever more important that they be managed according to a set of procedures that are well understood by those affected by them. Although it might have been possible in the past for a group of system administrators and desktop support personnel to keep track of the individual configuration of each client workstation on their network, the growing complexity of operating systems and the ubiquity of computing across the enterprise obviates this practice. One of the keys to the securing of a network of computers is to develop and then securely deploy standardized configurations to all the devices on the network. Although this cold, hard rule can be softened somewhat by the development of several different configurations for different user groups, the proliferation of active content and the reliance on social engineering and adeptness at getting past perimeter defenses of the current crop of viruses and worms require that greater control be exercised over client configurations. This can be accomplished only by regularizing the means through which we interact with users, and client configurations, through the use of procedures.

The software engineering community has long worked to improve the processes that organizations use as a way to enhance the products that those organizations produce. From their efforts, a Capability Maturity Model (CMM) has been developed and refined (Carnegie Mellon Software Engineering Institute, n.d.). This same thinking is now being applied to the deployment of many information technology–related processes by Frank Niessink and his associates (Niessink, Clerc, & van Vliet, 2004). They are in the process of developing an IT service CMM that is designed to aid organizations in both gauging the current maturity of their IT services and in understanding how to improve the way that IT services are provided. The IT service CMM is composed of five levels, only three of which are currently defined. An organization that scores high on the IT service CMM will be able to deliver reliable IT services tailored to the needs of their customers in a reliable and consistent fashion as well as continuously improve those services over time.

Level 1 of the IT service CMM is the ad hoc level where services are delivered as well as possible with little thought to consistency or learning from past mistakes. Level 2 is the repeatable level. Basic service management policies are in place and attempts are made to build on past successes to deliver services more effectively in a repeatable fashion. Level 3 involves the development of documentation and service definitions to enhance the organization's ability to deliver consistent services. In level 4, the focus shifts to the development of quantitative measures of service delivery process and quality. The final level involves the development of feedback loops that build upon the efforts of the previous level to improve the quality of service delivery continuously.

For detailed information on this topic, please consult Volume III, chapter 205, Managing a Network Environment, chapter 210, Multilevel Security, and chapter 211, Multilevel Security Models.

Improving User Awareness

At the end of the day, there is no way that the security of client workstations with access to the Internet can be maintained from a central location. It is ultimately the responsibility of the users of a system to keep that system secure. One of the most important and most easily ignored aspects of client-side security relates to training users to both maintain their systems and to avoid doing things that could put their systems and, by extension, the entire network in jeopardy. Many IT organizations have a continuing relationship with the users of their systems to help them to utilize their IT systems more effectively. Part of any IT training program needs to include a discussion of the user's responsibility to maintain the security of clients used on a daily basis. This discussion can take place as a face-to-face discussion, and it can also be a mediated discussion that takes place through mailings, Intranet Web sites, or newsletters. Because the threats to which clients are exposed change every day, provisions should be made for an ongoing training and education program designed to keep users up-to-date on ways in which technology can be used to make them more productive and to alert them to new threats and hacking techniques.

For detailed information on this topic, please consult Volume III, chapter 197, Implementing a Security Awareness Program.

Policies

The front line in this effort is the development and promulgation of an acceptable use policy (AUP) for all users. It is unreasonable to expect users to "just know" what their rights and responsibilities are as they relate to client-side security. What is expected of the users of a workstation and their role in securing a network from malicious code must be spelled out in detail, and users must be asked to acknowledge having read and understood the policy. Policies developed for this purpose should not take the form of commandments from on high; instead, they should emphasize the "we're all in this together" aspect of security and provide users with available means for asking legitimate questions when they arise. According to CERT (2003), the following practices are very important in the development of an AUP:

- *Gain management-level support.* In many cases, the detection of violations of the provisions of an AUP falls under the aegis of the IT department, whereas the enforcement falls under the aegis of management or human resources. This situation requires that management be brought in early in the development of the AUP.
- *Designate an individual with responsibility for the development, maintenance, and enforcement of the AUP.* In many cases, a chief information officer (CIO), rather than a system administrator, is given the responsibility for developing, maintaining, and enforcing the AUP. A CIO is better positioned to have the organization-wide perspective that makes a more effective AUP and also has the authority to better enforce it across organizational lines.
- *Develop the policy with participation from all stakeholders.* A policy developed with input from those it affects is both more likely to prevent those actions it seeks to prevent and allow users the freedom they need to accomplish their tasks.
- *Explain the policy to users and train them to follow it.* The introduction of an AUP to an existing organization can force changes in user behavior that might initially be challenged. An organization that both explains a new AUP to users and trains them periodically to work within its guidelines is much more likely to have a successful implementation.
- *Document user acceptance of the policy.* Documenting the acceptance by users of a new AUP enables the organization to enforce the AUP with less chance of litigation. Documenting acceptance of the AUP on an ongoing basis further bolsters the importance of the AUP in the organization's standing.
- *Provide explicit reminders at each login.* At each login, a banner should be displayed that reminds the user of the existence of the AUP and the function, ownership, and consequences of unauthorized access that are used to monitor user compliance.
- *Maintain the policy to reflect changes in your business and the technologies that you utilize.* Because businesses and their use of technology evolve over time, the AUP should also evolve to reflect any changes. This is particularly important now as more organizations implement mobile and wireless networking devices.

Lawrence (2002) discusses the cross-functional aspect of AUP development and points out that the following groups should be involved: human resource and legal departments to cover liability issues, marketing and strategic planning groups to ensure positive use of the tools, and information technology and information security to ensure security and the efficient use of the technological tools.

The AUP should outline for users what is and what is not allowed for them to do with their computers, the consequences of violating the policy, and the means by which their actions will be monitored to ensure that they are not violating the policy. It should outline what maintenance procedures are the responsibility of the user and the types of applications that can be used on the computer. It should also inform users of their rights and responsibilities in relation to e-mail attachments and active content. The AUP should be reviewed on a periodic basis, and users should acknowledge the policy as part of their periodic review process. There are many sources of information available on the Web for templates and guides to aid in the construction of an AUP.

For detailed information on this topic, please consult Volume III, chapter 206, E-Mail and Internet Use Policies, chapter 208, Security Policy Guidelines, and chapter 213, Security Policy Enforcement.

CONCLUSION

Client-side security is an overarching term that covers the tools and techniques used to secure client computers on organizational networks from attacks originating on the inside or outside of the network. Rather than a single technology, client-side security is a process that involves the deployment of several different technologies, managerial policies, and procedures. The client-side security tools and techniques can be grouped into four different areas:

- *Deployment.* The deployment of known and well-understood operating systems and applications in a managed and secure fashion
- *Management.* Management and maintenance of the currency of applications and operating systems through the secure and organized deployment of patches and updates to organizational computing resources
- *Monitoring.* The development and implementation of tools and techniques to monitor application and resource use to ensure that the consistency of configuration and exposure to vulnerability are within organizational guidelines
- *Ensuring user awareness.* Making users aware of their rights and responsibilities as they relate to the security of the network

Securing the client side of a network involves more than securing all the operating systems on all the clients on that network. The goal of a client-side security program is a general hardening of the interior of a network that, when combined with a strong perimeter, is part of a layered approach to overall network security.

GLOSSARY

Acceptable Use Policy (AUP) A document that outlines the rights and responsibilities of computer users for organizational assets. Some questions to answer in an AUP include: Are e-mail communications considered private, or are they subject to monitoring by managers? Can users freely browse the Internet, or are they restricted in the sites that they may visit? What are the responsibilities of users for maintaining their own workstations?
Active Content Portions of Web sites that are either interactive or dynamic. Usually, active content is downloaded as a small program from the Web site and executed on the client computer.
Application A program designed to perform a specific function.

Authentication The process of ascertaining whether someone or something is who they assert that they are. Many times this is done through the use of a combination of a user name and password for a computer user.
Client-Side Security A combination of the tools and techniques used to control access to and the configuration of client computers in a network environment.
Firewall Usually located between a network and the Internet, a firewall is a set of programs that examines each packet of information being sent out or coming in and compares it to a set of rules. A firewall is used to prevent users from sending unauthorized information out from a network and to prevent unauthorized packets from coming into a network.
Host-Based Security A synonym for *client-side security*.
Host Scanning An automated process used to check individual computers for configuration problems and available services.
Internet Service Provider (ISP) An organization that provides access to the Internet for computer users.
Intrusion When an unauthorized user gains access to computing resources either inside or outside a network.
Information Technology Capability Maturity Model (IT CMM) A set of best practices for the delivery of information technology services.
Patch Management The processes (both managerial and technological) used to aid in the deployment of software upgrades.
Personal Firewall A firewall that is installed on an individual workstation that is designed to halt the spread of unwanted programs.
Services A general term used to refer to capabilities a server computer offers to other computers.
Small Office/Home Office (SOHO) Many people now work out of their homes or from offices not located at the home location of their employers. These offices are usually connected to their parent office by either a DSL or cable modem connection to the Internet.
Virus An unwanted self-replicating program that attempts to spread from one computer to others.
Vulnerability A weakness in a process or program that could be exploited by attackers to do damage.
Vulnerability Management The processes (both managerial and technological) used to aid in the management of weaknesses in organizations. Although primarily used to discuss avenues of attack that exist in computing systems, this term could also refer to physical facilities.
Worm A self-replicating virus that does not alter files.

CROSS REFERENCES

See *Computer Viruses and Worms; Denial of Service Attacks; Hostile Java Applets; Intrusion Detection Systems Basics; Protecting Web Sites; Trojan Horse Programs.*

REFERENCES

Aberdeen Group. (2003). *Patch management*. Retrieved July 31, 2004, from http://www.aberdeen.com/2001/research/06030015.asp.

Allen, J. H. (2001). *The CERT guide to system and network security practices*. Indianapolis, IN: Addison-Wesley.

Apple Computer Corporation. (2004). *An introduction to Mac OS X security for Web developers*. Retrieved January 3, 2005, from http://developer.apple.com/internet/security/securityintro.html.

AusCERT. (2001). *UNIX security checklist V2.0*. Retrieved January 3, 2005, from http://www.cert.org/tech_tips/usc20_full.html.

Carnegie Mellon Software Engineering Institute. (n.d.). *Getting started with CMMI adoption*. Retrieved January 3, 2005, from http://www.sei.cmu.edu/cmmi/adoption/cmmi-start.html.

CERT. (2003). *Develop and promulgate an acceptable use policy for workstations*. Retrieved January 3, 2005, from http://www.cert.org/security-improvement/practices/p034.html.

Fraser, B. (Ed.). (1997). *Site security handbook IETF 2196*. Retrieved January 3, 2005, from http://www.ietf.org/rfc/rfc2196.txt?number=2196.

F-Secure Corporation. (2004). *F-Secure Corporation's data security summary for 2004: The year of phishing, professional virus writing, and arrests*. Retrieved January 3, 2005, from http://www.f-secure.com/2004/.

Forbath, Theo, Patrick Kalaher, and Thomas O'Grady (2005). *The total cost of security patch management: A comparison of Microsoft Windows and Open Source Software*. Retrieved June 25, 2005, from http://download.microsoft.com/download/1/7/b/17b54d06-1550-4011-9253-9484f769fe9f/TCO_SPM_Wipro.pdf.

Fraser, B. ed. (1997). *Site Security Handbook*. Internet Engineering Task Force. Retrieved June 25, 2005, from http://www.ietf.org/rfc/rfc2196.txt?number=2196.

Kermadec, F. J. (2004, February 20). *A security primer for Mac OS X*. Retrieved January 3, 2005, from http://www.macdevcenter.com/pub/a/mac/2004/02/20/security.html.

Lawrence, P. (2002, March). *Acceptable use: Whose responsibility is it?* Retrieved January 3, 2005, from http://www.sans.org/rr/papers/2/3.pdf.

Microsoft Corporation. (2004a). *Designing secure ActiveX controls*. Retrieved January 3, 2005, from http://msdn.microsoft.com/library/default.asp?url=/workshop/components/activex/security.asp.

Microsoft Corporation. (2004b). *Windows XP security guide*. Retrieved January 3, 2005, from http://www. microsoft.com/downloads/details.aspx?FamilyID=2d3e25bc-f434-4cc6-a5a7-09a8a229f118&displaylang=en.

Morrison, J. (2004, June). Blaster revisited. *ACM Queue*, 2(4). Retrieved January 3, 2005, from http://www.acmqueue.org/modules.php?name=Content&pa=showpage&pid=159.

National Cyber Security Alliance (2004). AOL/NCSA Online Safety Study. Retrieved June 25, 2005, from http://www.staysafeonline.info/news/safety_study_v04.pdf

Niessink, F., Clerc, V., & van Vliet, H. (2004, June 24). *The IT service capability maturity model*. Retrieved January 3, 2005, from http://www.itservicecmm.org/doc/itscmm-0.4.pdf.

Oppliger, R. (2003). *Client-side security*. Retrieved January 3, 2005, from http://www.ifi.unizh.ch/~oppliger/Presentations/WWWSecurity2e/sld160.htm.

Pescatore, J. (2003). *Taxonomy of software vulnerabilities*. Gartner Group, Stamford, CT.

Russell, R., et al. (2002). *Hack proofing your network* (2nd ed.). Rockland, MA: Syngress Publishing.

SecureMac.com. (n.d.). *Macintosh OS X security: Understanding the platform and usage*. Retrieved January 3, 2005, from http://www.securemac.com/macosxsecurity.php.

Thompson, H. H., & Ford, R. (2004, June). The insider, naivety, and hostility: Security perfect storm? *ACM Queue*, 2(4). Retrieved January 3, 2005, from http://www.acmqueue.org/modules.php?name=Content&pa=showpage&pid=164.

Wagner, R. & Wyke, R. A. (2000). *Javascript unleashed* (3rd ed.). Indianapolis, IN: Sams.

FURTHER READING

For further information on concentrating security devices on the periphery of networks, please see Lindquist, C. (2004). *The world is your perimeter*. Retrieved January 3, 2005, from http://www.csoonline.com/read/020104/perimeter.html.

For more information on firewalls and their deployment, please see Robinson, C. (2002). *Best practices for firewall deployments*. Retrieved January 3, 2005, from http://www.csoonline.com/analyst/report563.html.

For more information on the importance of involving employees at all levels in the securing of organizations, please see CIO, Inc. (2002). The Security Revolution. Retrieved June 25, 2005, from http://www.csoonline.com/whitepapers/061502security.

OpenVMS Security

Robert Gezelter, *Software Consultant*

INTRODUCTION

OpenVMS is a system with a unique history. It has a system architecture designed to produce a high-efficiency, high-integrity environment. High-security operation is a direct consequence of these goals. Philosophically, this has been crucial to its success. Thus, OpenVMS avoids the vulnerabilities plaguing systems that do not have security and integrity as part of their initial design. This chapter begins with a full examination of OpenVMS architecture, followed by a detailed examination of its integral security-specific design and related features.

The original OpenVMS design was a combined hardware/software architecture project. The protection modes, memory management, and privileged instruction set of the VAX processor were designed with the collaboration of the operating system's engineering team.

This coengineering process produced an operating system with a unique character. The design blends the knowledge and experiences gained from earlier operating systems together with the supporting hardware elements. The design provides a rich collection of facilities with an unusual degree of consistency and reliability.

These hardware elements are not legacies of the original VAX processor but are the echoes of the coengineering process and reflect the fact that the original VAX architecture was specifically engineered to support VAX/VMS.

Today, OpenVMS is fully supported on three processor architectures: VAX, Alpha, and Intel's IA-64 Itanium. There are almost no differences between them at the applications level. The differences between the versions are limited to

- differences between the hardware environments (such as subroutine calling standards),
- low-level trap/interrupt handling, and
- 64-bit memory support (which is only available on Alpha and IA-64).

This multiple hardware architecture environment is achieved through common code and well-defined interfaces. The overwhelming majority of the 10 million lines of code are common to all three processor platforms. In the case of Alpha and IA-64, the commonality is greater than 95%. The multiple platforms are released on the same schedule and use a common documentation kit, supplemented by manuals specific to each of the hardware architectures. OpenVMS Clusters are frequently constructed with all combinations of the supported architectures interoperating with a fully shared file system.

Configured as recommended, OpenVMS provides an extremely well-protected environment for the user, with fine control over access rights and privileges. It is also the first system to use a common run-time library with a consistent calling standard across all supported languages, from MACRO-32 (the VAX assembler language) to higher-level languages including FORTRAN, BASIC, PL/I, C/C++, and others.

The design emphasizes correctness, completeness, and fine levels of detail in privileges and access rights, together with an overall refusal to specify issues that need not be decided at the operating system level. The combination of detail and deferral of unneeded decisions makes OpenVMS able to support a high degree of nuance. Nuance is the ability of an operating system to be sculpted to express the subtleties of an end user's requirements without losing its essential form or character.

History

The initial design, in 1977, was a combined hardware/software effort at Digital Equipment Corporation (since merged with Hewlett-Packard), comprising both the VAX hardware architecture and the VAX/VMS operating system. The VAX reflected a trend in 1970s technology toward higher-level language support directly in hardware, particularly in the areas of bounds checking, flow control, and common operations. In 1991, reflecting the breadth of industry standards supported by VAX/VMS, the operating system was renamed OpenVMS.

Semiconductor technology changes in the late 1980s favored processors with simplified instruction sets. Earlier limits in memory bandwidth had favored more complex instructions. Later VAX processors were simplified and their implementations pruned to remove functions from central processor microcode. Program compatibility was maintained through emulation of these rarely used instructions.

This trend toward processor simplification resulted in the design of Digital's 64-bit RISC Alpha, unveiled in 1992. The Alpha architecture combined support for larger memory spaces with a reduced instruction set designed for high-speed implementations in CMOS technologies.

In 2001 the decision was made to adopt Intel's IA-64 architecture, referred to as Itanium, as the follow-on architecture to Alpha. The first bootstrap of OpenVMS Itanium occurred on January 31, 2003.

BASIS IN ARCHITECTURE

Philosophically and structurally, OpenVMS is the descendant of two streams of operating system evolution within Digital Equipment Corporation:

- The RSX-family operating systems for the 16-bit PDP-11 processors and
- TOPS-20, the operating system for the 36-bit DECsystem-20 series.

Each of these antecedents contributed thoughts and philosophies to OpenVMS, including internal structures, file systems, and command languages. Problems and shortcomings in earlier designs were also considered in the new design. The OpenVMS architecture is a particularly impressive achievement when one considers that few operating systems running today were in existence 25 years ago, much less in a form that allows many programs to continue to run without recompilation or change.

OpenVMS exemplifies that it is possible to significantly characterize the architectural requirements of applications in many areas, including file formats. It is then possible to provide operating system layers to implement those characterizations as an enabling technology. The OpenVMS Run-Time Library (known as *VMSRTL*) is, in many respects, an object-oriented toolkit, although its design predates the popularity of that paradigm by a decade. This is in contrast to other operating systems, which have entirely omitted this software level of abstraction.

Implementation Techniques

OpenVMS is characterized by an embracive architectural approach, coupled with an emphasis on quality and performance. The architectural focus is on providing the user/developer with a complete toolkit for the implementation of both software and environments for users to build and employ a wide range of applications. The security aspects of the operating system follow naturally from the focus on robustness, integrity, and efficiency. There is also an overall emphasis on ensuring that system components interoperate reliably through supported building blocks.

Multiple CPU/Memory Access Modes

The design uses four access modes, each with its own access rights. From least privileged to most privileged, these are *User, Supervisor, Executive*, and *Kernel*. The overwhelming majority of users (and their applications) are restricted to *User* mode, which does not allow the execution of machine instructions or memory accesses that can affect the operation of the machine as a whole.

Access to inner (more privileged) access modes is provided through appropriate system services, subject to privilege controls. Elevating privileges requires a hardware trap and validation of the request for execution at a more privileged level (see Figure 1).

Memory Protection Model

The memory protection model provides for accesses to be controlled on a page-by-page basis. Access is controlled on a Read, Write, or Execute basis. Each access mode can have different access rights, a capability fundamental to maintaining the integrity of the operating system's internal functions. This contrasts with other operating systems that store information in areas readable and writeable by user programs, rendering them vulnerable to compromise.

The OpenVMS memory protection model permits operating system components to store process-specific information on behalf of a user process securely within the process's own address space. However, such pages are protected to only permit access to the inner access modes and are invisible and unmodifiable from User mode access (Figure 2). This secures information within a process, avoiding security breaches caused by commingling structures in a shared area maintained by the system kernel.

Command line interpreters, such as DCL (Digital Command Language), execute in Supervisor mode but within the context of each user's process.

System components requiring access to higher levels of privilege execute in Executive mode. The Record Management System (RMS) has some components that execute in User mode and some components that execute in Executive mode. For example, global buffering and cluster-wide locking would not be directly available to a nonprivileged User mode process.

The system kernel, device drivers, and similar components execute in Kernel mode, which allows access to all of the hardware of the host machine.

Fine Granularity of Privilege

Fine gradations of privilege are also characteristic of OpenVMS. Where some operating systems are distinguished by a binary approach to privilege (a user or process is either fully privileged or fully not privileged), OpenVMS from the outset has had a more nuanced approach. Presently, basic OpenVMS has 36 different privileges (three additional privileges are only available under SEVMS, the OpenVMS version with mandatory access controls). In many instances, an OpenVMS application or user can perform very powerful system

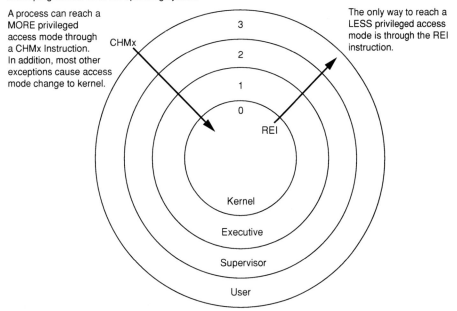

Access mode fields in the PSL are not directly accessible to the programmer or to the operating system.

A process can reach a MORE privileged access mode through a CHMx Instruction. In addition, most other exceptions cause access mode change to kernel.

The only way to reach a LESS privileged access mode is through the REI instruction.

The boundaries between the access modes are nearly identical to the layer boundaries pictured in Figure 5.
Nearly all system services execute in kernel mode. RMS and some system services execute in executive mode.

Command language interpreters normally execute in supervisor mode.
Utilities, application programs, run-time Library procedures, and so on normally execute in user mode. Privileged utilities sometimes execute in kernel or executive mode.

Figure 1: OpenVMS memory/processor access modes (from *VAX/VMS Internals and Data Structures, Version 5.2 [1991]*, p. 16).

management functions, such as managing print queues or storage volumes, with a single or a small number of relatively innocuous privileges, rather than full system management functions.

String Descriptors

The programmer's interface to OpenVMS uses descriptors for references to most data types (see Figure 3). The overwhelming majority of internal interfaces also use descriptors. The exception to the use of descriptors is simple parameter references of the call-by-value (familiar to C/C++ programmers) and simple call-by-reference (familiar to FORTRAN/C programmers).

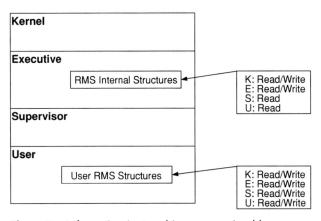

Figure 2: Information is stored in a process's address space but is not modifiable by the *User* mode program.

The pervasive parameter checking enabled by the use of descriptors has rendered native OpenVMS code relatively immune from string overflow and similar errors. String and buffer overflows have plagued other systems, particularly systems written in C, which have used C's ubiquitous 0x00 (null) terminated strings.

Descriptors allow system library functions to completely check their input and output arguments before processing. System library routines check the validity of input and output parameters, returning errors if they are not in appropriate locations.

Embracive Architecture

From the outset, OpenVMS has had a substantial focus on well-reasoned architecture, which provides a solid basis for the implementation of robust software. OpenVMS's architecture strikes a balance between specification as needed to ensure correctness and specification that leaves enough open space within the architecture to ensure sufficient room for growth.

This approach has proved successful in that it has ensured compatibility for a huge corpus of code, consisting of OpenVMS itself, layered products, and third party and user code over a 25-year period. Incompatible changes from the original specification have been rare.

Scaling

OpenVMS, in its latest releases, is officially qualified to run on a wide range of hardware, from the MicroVAX 3300 (2.5 MIPS) to Alpha and Itanium systems well into

32-Bit Form (DSC)

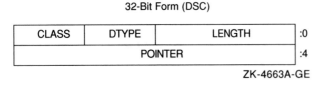

ZK-4663A-GE

64-Bit Form (DSC64)

ZK-7656A-GE

Figure 3: OpenVMS string/other descriptors were extended to include 64–bit lengths and addresses with the 1992 advent of the 64–bit Alpha processor (diagram from *OpenVMS Calling Standard, 2001*, p. 5–3).

the billions of instructions per second (1000+MIPS). Only within the last few years has official support for the original VAX-11/780 been withdrawn, as main memory requirements have increased beyond its capabilities.

Systems supported on OpenVMS range from uniprocessors to 32-way processors. The minimum supported memory configuration is 14 Mbytes on a VAX, 64 Mbytes on an Alpha. Alpha systems are able to efficiently exploit gigabytes of memory.

Platform Independence

Most users have been unaware that translated and interpreted images have been part of the base OpenVMS system since its original release in 1977. The original VAX/VMS contained numerous 16-bit PDP-11 images that were hardware interpreted. To this day, certain commonly used programs have been translated rather than recompiled. The TECO text editor and the MONITOR utility (pre–OpenVMS release 7.3-2) are the products of binary translation from VAX to Alpha.

There is little doubt that recompilation is the most effective way to make use of the power of a new processor architecture. The availability of image translation represents a viable trade-off between the costs of rebuilding applications and lost processor performance against schedule and engineering costs.

The interpretation/translation/recompilation approach on a system with a common API is both viable and effective. It is another case, where OpenVMS provides a nuanced approach, allowing project managers to take advantage of system facilities to shorten schedules in ways that are functionally transparent to users.

Environment Portability

OpenVMS is designed for use in a data center because it provides the mechanisms for implementing a tightly controlled environment. It is always simpler and less error prone to relax tightly controlled environments than it is to impose stricter controls on relaxed environments. Adding

security and integrity controls after the fact is often an underlying source of security problems.

OpenVMS Clusters

OpenVMS clusters, announced in 1983, remain a unique concept. An OpenVMS cluster is composed of multiple, independent CPUs, each running an independent copy of the operating system, with the cluster members coordinating access to a shared file system, down to the record level in individual files. By contrast, a conventional multiprocessing system comprises multiple CPUs with common memory sharing a single memory-resident copy of the operating system. Individual cluster members are often themselves multiprocessors. Although the individual cluster members are running separate copies of OpenVMS, the cluster itself operates as a single security domain (see Figure 4).

In an OpenVMS cluster, the CPUs and mass storage controllers communicate via a high-speed local area interconnect, originally the CI (Computer Interconnect, a proprietary dual 70 Mbit/sec CSMA/CD LAN). Today, IEEE 802.3/Ethernet (10 M/100 M/1 Gbit/sec) is often used. Usually, the entire file system is shared, with access to file system structures, files, and even byte ranges or records within files controlled via the Distributed Lock Manager.

The Distributed Lock Manager implements a shared locking domain. This unique characteristic of OpenVMS clusters allows the entire cluster to act as one system for the purpose of file-based applications. Each OpenVMS system has a copy of the Distributed Lock Manager. In an OpenVMS cluster, the Distributed Lock Managers on each cluster member exchange information about which system holds locks on which resources. Architecturally more important, the Distributed Lock Manager only deals with resource names. Thus, the Distributed Lock Manager represents a fundamental building block for end-user developers to implement synchronization tasks other than those envisioned by the OpenVMS engineering team.

File locking is controlled by the file structure support component, known as the *XQP* (extended QIO Processor). Record Management Services, known as RMS, supplements the file-level access provided by the XQP with facilities used to access the contents of files and is responsible for locking on granularities smaller than entire files. RMS supports a wide range of file contents, including simple sequential files, byte stream files, relative files, and indexed files.

Officially, an OpenVMS cluster is limited to 96 nodes with a maximum radius of 500 miles (800 km). Customers have configured OpenVMS clusters that exceed these limits in one or more ways, primarily in terms of the number of nodes in the cluster. This is a wider and more flexible scope than other products. When extreme emergencies and catastrophes occur, OpenVMS clusters, configured in a disaster-tolerant mode with multiple sites separated geographically, have continued IT operations unscathed. Even the 9/11 destruction of the World Trade Center complex in New York City did not stop several disaster-tolerant OpenVMS cluster systems that had cluster members within the Twin Towers or surrounding buildings. The other sites continued operating with an imperceptible pause.

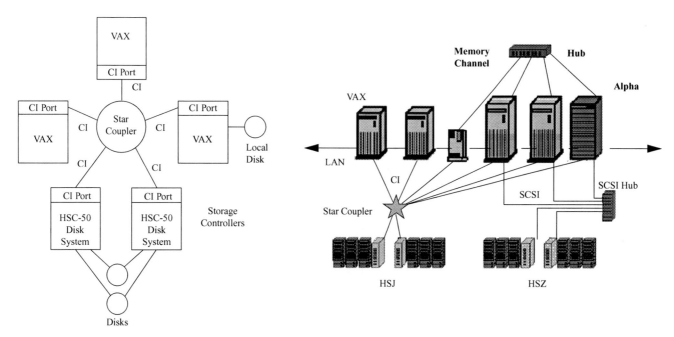

Figure 4: Unchanging fundamentals of OpenVMS cluster: 1983–2004 (diagrams from Kronenberg, Levy, & Strecker, 1986 and *HP OpenVMS: The World's Leader in Clustering,* 2003).

Software Basis

Architecturally, the approach is a classic, layered approach in the spirit of Dijkstra's classic paper on THE (1968). There are few special-purpose components in the system. The approach is one of conceptual and implementation uniformity. The libraries and supporting infrastructure used to implement the operating system are the same tools available to support user development (see Figure 5).

Processes

OpenVMS processes consist of page tables, logical name tables, thread contexts (including register states), stacks, mapping to common shared memory regions, and process-private memory regions.

Historically, OpenVMS processes had single-register contexts, and therefore a single thread of execution associated with each process. On the 64-bit platforms, beginning with version 7.0, support for multiple threads per process was added, allowing a single process to simultaneously use multiple processors in a multiprocessor system.

Privileges

OpenVMS implements a fine-granularity privilege model. There are a number of different privileges, and many of them permit operations personnel to do their jobs without giving them unrestricted management access to the system.

Some privileges, such as **NETMBX** (the ability to create network mailboxes; which is needed to use DECnet or TCP/IP) and **TMPMBX** (the ability to create temporary mailboxes) are innocuous and can be routinely issued to students in a college course without cause for worry.

Some privileges, although less innocuous, only affect members of an individual group but are not dangerous to the system as a whole. These can be issued in safety in a properly configured system.

Other privileges have potentially greater side effects. Privileges classed as DEVOUR can, in the words of the *HP OpenVMS Guide to System Security* (2003), "consume noncritical systemwide resources." Privileges classed as SYSTEM can similarly "interfere with system operation." Those classed as OBJECTS can "compromise the protection of protected objects." Class ALL privileges have the "potential to control the system."

Assigning privileges is important in the context of security but is inevitably a compromise. A common trade-off is to provide certain privileges, particularly **OPER**, **READALL**, and sometimes **MOUNT**, to operators to permit normal operations such as managing queues and performing backups.

The privileges categorized as DEVOUR, SYSTEM, OBJECT, and ALL have the ability to affect system operation, whether it is merely resource starvation (as in a runaway program with **EXQUOTA**, the ability to ignore disk space quotas) or crash the system (through the misuse of the **WORLD** privilege). Others, such as those classified as SYSTEM, can totally compromise the security of the system.

Some privileges fall into barely safer categories, such as **SYSPRV**, which allows a variety of system management functions, including modifications to the SYSUAF file. The danger here is subtler. Because access to the SYSUAF permits the changes to the list of authorized users, as well as changes to the authorized and default privilege masks for an account, it effectively permits a user to give themselves (or a confederate) full privileges.

Implications of Privileges—Security Issues

When planning a security environment, it is important to consider the security implications of routine tasks. System backups are an interesting case in point. Backup operators frequently are issued the **READALL** privilege to ensure

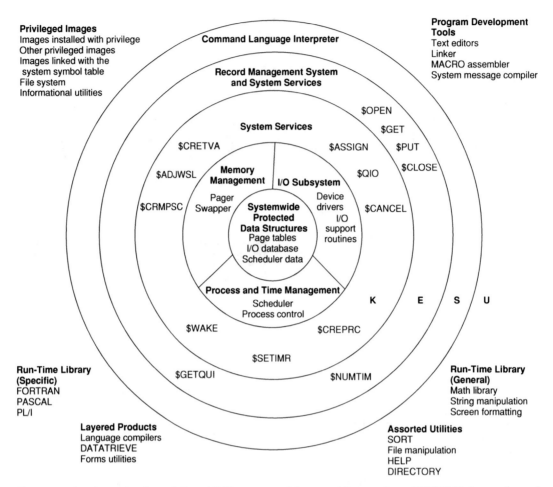

Figure 5: A schematic view of OpenVMS system architecture (diagram from *VAX/VMS Internals and Data Structures, Version 5.2, 1991*, p. 10).

that the backups are able to read all the files on mass storage when producing backup tapes. Thus, they must inherently be trustworthy.

Some files, however, may need to be omitted from the routine backups. The reasons for this omission are varied. Some or all of the reasons for omissions may apply to particular installations. For example,

- some files may be both large of size and transitory in nature. It may be substantially easier to recreate the file in the event of a problem than it is to allocate sufficient time and archive space for the backups.
- some information is sufficiently sensitive that it should not be part of the normal backup process. In this case, the information can be located on different disks or marked in a way that it will be omitted from the normal backup process.
- some files may be subject to retention or archiving restrictions that are different from the overall backup and retention policies of the installation. For example, a file may be subject to a court protective order requiring that all copies be destroyed as part of the proceedings. Such files should not be included in routine backups. They should, however, be part of a project or activity backup.

OpenVMS, through its file system and **BACKUP** utility provide mechanisms to manage file migration and backup for all of these possibilities. The **BACKUP** utility is designed specifically to seamlessly incorporate all of these needs without requiring external, special-purpose utilities.

Quotas

OpenVMS has extensive facilities for the management of system resources by processes, whether they are privileged processes belonging to the system or conventional user processes. These limits are known as *quotas*. Used properly, they prevent an individual process from impairing system operation by causing a depletion of significant system resources, such as system dynamic memory or disk space. Other quotas, such as the quotas on aggregate buffered and direct IO operations, serve to prevent a single process or job from monopolizing the overall system.

Disk quotas allow system managers to control the amount of disk space on each volume used by an individual. Quotas may be associated with UICs or Rights Identifiers. Rights Identifier-specific quotas allow space to be allocated on a project basis. These mechanisms are complementary, not exclusive.

Threading and Asynchronous System Traps (ASTs)

Hierarchically preemptible processing is central to the OpenVMS architecture. Fundamental to its structure, OpenVMS supports a single-threaded environment, with support for a very lightweight FIFO (first in, first out) event-processing thread for each access mode. These event-processing threads, which preempt the main thread of processing, are called *Asynchronous System Traps* (*ASTs*).

Speaking in terms of evolution, ASTs are descended from the RSX family of operating systems. They have proved to be a highly efficient mechanism for processing asynchronous events (such as timers and IO completions) without excessive overhead. ASTs are extremely lightweight because they do not have any context of their own but preempt the main thread of execution. Their inherent synchronization is one of their simplest yet most powerful features. Within a particular access mode, AST processing is FIFO and nonpreemptible. This implicit synchronization makes it unnecessary to explicitly synchronize different ASTs in the same access mode within a particular process. Inner access mode ASTs can preempt outer mode ASTs.

They can be used with few limitations, other than quotas, by any process. OpenVMS makes extensive use of AST processing in system libraries and the file system. The importance of the AST mechanism can be seen from the ongoing attention paid to AST implementation on the VAX, Alpha, and Itanium processors.

This is in contrast to the signal model used in UNIX-style operating systems, which are structured in a less modular, less general basis and where blocking of signals is commonplace (to prevent preemption), with the resulting synchronization issues.

Common Run-Time Library

From the outset, OpenVMS was designed to be programming language agnostic. It was the first operating system with a defined, cross-programming language run-time library. From its origin on the VAX architecture, routines written in one programming language have been effortlessly able to invoke other routines written in different languages. It is common to encounter individual programs written using a variety of languages, particularly so in cases where one language has a clear advantage in clarity of expression or functionality over the other (e.g., BAS-BOL: BASIC with COBOL subroutines and COB-FOR: COBOL with FORTRAN subroutines). This feature is used within OpenVMS itself, where components have been written in VAX MACRO-32, BLISS, BASIC, FORTRAN, PASCAL, PL/I, and C/C++.

The run-time library also provides a rich underpinning of functionality for user and third-party programs. Seemingly complex mechanisms in system-provided utilities are nothing more than calls to run-time library routines, accessible to all users.

System Services

The lowest-level, user-visible interfaces to OpenVMS are referred to as system services. These services are a diverse group, including:

- very simple building blocks, such as those which format ASCII output, $FAO and $FAOL (which run in User mode),
- functions that perform extensive processing in privileged modes (e.g., $QIO and $QIOW) to make a system capability available to a user program in a safe manner, and
- gateways (e.g., $CHKPRO, $CHMKRNL and $CMEXEC) to the rare programs that need inner access modes.

The $QIO and $QIOW system services (Queue IO Operation and Queue IO Operation Wait) act as gatekeepers to IO resources for all system components. $QIO is an excellent example of the OpenVMS philosophy, in that it provides a rich set of functions and common processing for IO requests, including:

- parameter checking,
- common device driver initiation and completion processing, and
- definitions for operations, based upon common models of device functionality (e.g., file systems) without imposing inappropriate demands at the interface level. For example, the 16-bit IO function codes have defined meanings for file opens (read-only, read-write, and read-write-extend), file attributes (read/write attributes), and various values for control of communications channels (see Table 1).

$QIO does not attempt to specify all possible operations so much as it annunciates a framework for expressing the possibilities for interfacing to an external (or pseudo) device. It also provides an intermediation between requesting programs and the actual details of managing a physical device.

Device Drivers

In common usage, the term *device driver* has become overloaded, acquiring multiple meanings. Originally, a device driver was a software component that formed the privileged interface between a particular IO device and the

Table 1 OpenVMS IO Function Codes by Category

Function	Symbolic Value	Value (hexadecimal)
Create file	IO$_CREATE	0x0051
Access file	IO$_ACCESS	0x0050
Read virtual	IO$_READVBLK	0x0049
Write virtual	IO$_WRITEVBLK	0x0048
Deaccess file	IO$_DEACCESS	0x0052
Delete file	IO$_DELETE	0x0053
Modify file	IO$_MODIFY	0x0054
Read with prompt	IO$_READPROMPT	0x0055
ACP control	IO$_ACPCONTROL	0x0056
Mount volume	IO$_MOUNT	0x0057

Source: *HP OpenVMS I/O User's Reference Manual* (2003), additional detail extracted from libraries
SYS$LIBRARY: STARLET.MLB and SYS$LIBRARY: SYS$STARLET_C.TLB module IODEF.

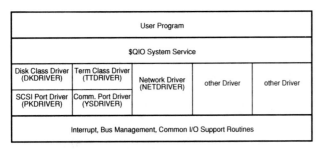

Figure 6: OpenVMS device drivers in relation to the kernel and the QIO system service. An OpenVMS *device driver* does not operate in a vacuum, but in the context of the User Process and the overall direction, policies, and scaffolding provided by the system kernel.

operating system kernel. Some operating systems and applications have muddied the definition by using device driver to refer to nonprivileged components that address device idiosyncrasies, such as printer escape codes.

OpenVMS uses the term device driver in the original meaning of the phrase. Device drivers are the components that actually manage the operation of specific devices. In OpenVMS, device drivers are loadable kernel subroutines that interface between the kernel, particularly the program accessible $QIO system service, and the actual hardware (see Figure 6). Although device drivers do not have a full context, they do not exist in a vacuum. Device drivers are subroutines of the kernel, and, in the case of IO initiation, operate in the mapping context of the requesting process. OpenVMS device drivers do not form the lowest layer of the software architecture but are an intermediate layer between the routines that actually perform hardware accesses and the QIO layer providing generic IO services. Architecturally, the lowest layer is populated by the an extensive collection of routines that allow device drivers to perform common functions, from managing the mapping of transfers to interrupt management.

As an example of OpenVMS's flexibility, adding storage volumes to OpenVMS does not require a reboot but merely a command to bring the new device online.

OpenVMS device drivers have substantial capabilities and act as more than mere filters or funnels of information between the generic IO services provided by the kernel and the device. Device drivers do significant processing, perform transformations of data, and are solely responsible for dealing with the idiosyncrasies of the different devices. However, some operations, such as managing the disk file structure, looking up files, and locating file segments on the disk, require additional operations that are beyond the capabilities and context of an OpenVMS device driver.

Ancillary Control Processes

File structure management is one such class of operations. Structurally, IO operations must belong to a process. Device drivers, being kernel subroutines, do not have a process context of their own. If the IO request requires more than straightforward processing, a helper process with a full process context is used. These helper processes are referred to as an *Ancillary Control Processes* (*ACPs*) and are associated with the device used. ACPs are privileged OpenVMS processes whose function is an intermediate level of device-specific management. An ACP effectively extends the conceptual IO model supported by the device (see Figure 7).

An ACP is associated with a particular device or a class of devices. ACPs are employed where IO related tasks, such as file system management or network connection management, require more extensive processing.

Often, as in the cases of mass storage devices, an ACP will create and manage driver-accessible data structures that permit the driver to directly map or translate future requests without the need to invoke ACP processing. This eliminates the context switches to and from the ACP.

In the case of conventional file processing, even this efficiency was deemed insufficient, and the FILES-11

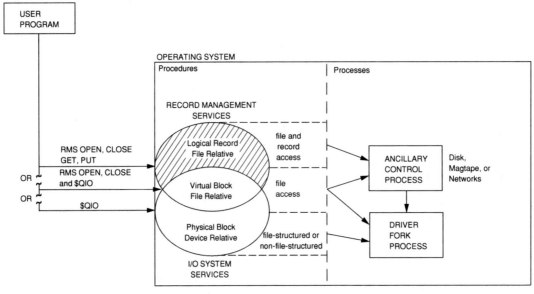

Figure 7: Record Management Services as an example of the multiple exposed steps of OpenVMS interface (from VAX-11 Software Handbook, 1979, Digital Equipment Corporation, 1979).

Level 2 ACP was reimplemented as a kernel-mode library, invoked by the driver in the calling process's context, without the need for additional context changes (Goldstein, 1987).

Shared Libraries

OpenVMS makes extensive use of shared libraries. In most cases, a user image will contain few, if any, actual run-time library routines. The majority of the references are to shareable libraries. Qualitatively speaking, this means that updates to run-time environments rarely require recompilation or relinking of user applications but merely an exit and reinitiation of the running image. Nor is a system restart needed. Applications need only be recompiled or relinked on the rare occasions when the interface between a run-time library and its callers change.

As with most OpenVMS features, there is nothing structurally special about a shareable library. Users, organizations, and software providers frequently use shareable libraries as the preferred mechanism to access executable code referenced by a program.

Privileged Shareable Libraries

Shareable libraries can be created with inherent privilege. Although this capability has a potential for abuse, it is a source of significant strength.

Privileged libraries permit the construction of services to provide particular functions that require privilege without requiring the entire requesting application to be privileged. This allows the OpenVMS mail facility to be implemented as a very small "mail delivery" privileged library, with very limited capabilities, thereby reducing the risk that the privileges needed to deliver mail are misused for other purposes.

By way of comparison, making the entire mail-delivery process privileged, as is done in UNIX sendmail, is an ongoing source of security holes. The OpenVMS philosophy, separately implementing only that small portion of the facility that requires elevated privileges, is a far safer alternative.

Command Language Support

The standard command language on OpenVMS is known as DCL (Digital Command Language). It is intended to be somewhat English-like, with commands consisting of a verb, qualifiers, and operands. (See Table 2.)

Command and file name parsing is performed by a set of standard utility subroutines, which, together with tools for expressing the syntax of a command, allow a high degree of consistency without restricting the capability to the original development team.

Used properly, these tools permit OpenVMS to make extensions (as were made to support filenames with lowercase and special characters) without requiring extensive modifications to every program.

Command qualifiers permit the same verb to activate different programs depending on the qualifier specified. For example, the default editor is known as TPU (Text Processing Utility). The older, but still popular, EDT editor is still accessible through the use of a qualifier (EDIT/EDT). Wrappers, based on the TPU editor, are used to edit Access Control Lists and file definitions.

SECURITY-SPECIFIC ARCHITECTURE

OpenVMS security functionality is based on a UIC (User Identification Code), rights list, and privilege list associated with each user login. Although OpenVMS does not directly enforce a requirement that UICs be uniquely associated with a user, it is the recommended practice.

A UIC is a 28-bit code broken into two elements:

- a 12-bit Group number
- a 16-bit User number

Each process has an associated UIC, privilege mask, and rights identifier list. These form the foundation for all subsequent security-related checking, whether it is the basic traditional set of OpenVMS protections or the more versatile rights identifier–based protections.

The traditional OpenVMS access checks are first based on the UIC, with privileged access (BYPASS, READALL) only used if the requested access is denied. System accesses are available to those processes whose group does not exceed MAXSYSGROUP (a system parameter whose normal value is 10_8) or whose SYSPRV bit is enabled in the process's privilege mask.

Traditional Protection/Ownership Hierarchy

The basic and most efficient resource access control mechanism in OpenVMS is the traditional System/Owner/Group/World protection scheme based upon these factors:

- the UIC and privilege mask of the accessing process; and
- the protection mask of the target resource, which

Table 2 Common Example of OpenVMS Commands

DCL Command	Meaning
DIRECTORY	List files in current directory
DIRECTORY *.FOR	List all files in current directory of filetype FOR (Fortran-77 source files)
SET DEFAULT [.FOX]	Set current directory to the FOX subdirectory
TYPE X.TMP	Type (on the standard output, SYS$OUTPUT) the contents of the file X.TMP
CREATE X.TMP	Create a sequential file X.TMP (from the standard input, SYS$INPUT)

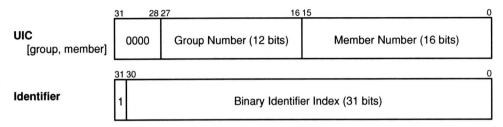

Figure 8: User identification codes and identifiers from the basis of OpenVMS security facilities.

specifies which accesses, Read, Write, Execute, or Delete, are permitted for each category of user.

The traditional UIC-based identification works by categorizing users into four categories:

- Owner: Processes whose UIC is the owner of the object.
- System: Processes whose UIC is in the System range.
- Group: Processes whose UIC is in the same Group as the owner of the object.
- World: Processes whose UIC is not in one of the previous categories.

Rights Identifiers

Rights identifiers are the basic building block of the non-UIC based security and auditing mechanisms. Externally, identifiers are represented by ASCII strings of 1–31 characters. Internally, these strings are mapped to 31-bit binary values. Non-UIC-based identifiers all have the 32nd [high-order] bit set; identifiers referring to UICs are equal to the UIC and have the high-order four bits clear (see Figure 8). This allows UICs to be used as identifiers in their own right. The mapping between printable and binary forms are stored in a file known as the RIGHTSLIST, generally SYS$SYSTEM:RIGHTLIST.DAT.

Most references to rights identifiers refer to the conceptual identifier externally represented by the printable identifier. In any event, these identifiers are the mechanism used to resolve access to resources.

System services ($ASCTOID and $IDTOASC) and the DCL lexical function F$IDENTIFIER (with subfunctions for both sets of conversions) are available to convert identifiers from the ASCII string form to the 32-bit binary form and vice versa, respectively.

Identifier-Based Access

The mechanism used to allow access to a protected resource under OpenVMS with discretionary access controls is a matching undertaken between a the set of access rights (called "identifiers") held by a process and the Access Control List (ACL) associated with the resource.

Reference Monitor Concept

The conceptual framework of OpenVMS access control is that of a reference monitor, a central entity responsible for the monitoring of all accesses by processes (and hence by users) to system objects (see Figure 9).

A reference monitor creates a single point of responsibility for access control and auditing. In OpenVMS, it

is implemented as a small number of gatekeepers for different resource classes, generically known as *objects* (see Table 3). Reference monitor terminology refers to all entities that act as initiators of security-related requests as *subjects*. In the OpenVMS context, a *subject* normally represents a process (or thread of a process). There is no loss of generality, as users cannot make requests for access to objects without in some way going through a process (or thread of a process).

It should be remembered that access control through identifiers and ACLs operate in the absence of access through other means, such as the System/Owner/Group/World protection mask, and the privilege mask. If a resource is to be protected based on ACLs and identifiers, then care must be taken to ensure that access is not available through the other mechanisms.

Access to SYSPRV and other so-called ALL-class privileges should be carefully controlled. Systems programming and systems management staffs routinely need these privileges to maintain the operating system. Applications development, testing, and most production activities do not require privileges.

The identifier/ACL mechanism provides an excellent tool to permit the delegation of management activities and privileges to users without the need to grant DEVOUR-class privileges to a wide circle of individuals.

Resources

The OpenVMS reference monitor model controls access to 11 different classes of objects (see Table 3).

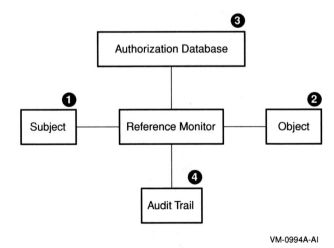

Figure 9: Reference monitor model used by OpenVMS to implement security related facilities (from *OpenVMS Guide to System Security*, 2003, Figure 2-1, p. 28).

Table 3 Classes of Objects Subject to Protection by the Reference Monitor

Capability	A capability of the host system, presently the only such capability is the vector processor on certain VAX CPUs.
Common Event Flag Cluster	A named set of 32 event flags that are shared between collections of different processes.
Device	A hardware or pseudodevice connected to the system.
File	A file on a file structured mass storage medium (e.g., disk).
Group Global Section	A shared memory section available to a collection of processes.
Logical Name Table	A table of logical names accessible to a collection of processes.
Queue	A set of jobs to be processed in a batch, print, or other queue.
Resource Domain	A namespace controlling access to the lock manager's resources.
Security Class	A data structure containing the elements and management routines for all members of the security class.
System Global Section	A shareable memory region potentially available to all processes in the system.
Volume	A volume mounted on a device (e.g., tape, disk).

Source: *OpenVMS Guide to System Security*, 2003, Table 2-1.

References to resources are controlled according to the ownership, protection masks, and ACLs associated with each object. The checking is performed in a defined order and eliminates the need for many, if not all, applications-based security checks (see Figure 10).

Access Control Lists

Each object with the potential for restricted access has provisions for an optional ACL. The ACL contains a list of identifiers and the types of access to be granted to the holder of the identifier. Although they may be associated with any file, other Access Control Elements (ACEs) generally have meaning only when attached to directory files, providing for the propagation of ownership, protection masks, and access control lists to new files.

Order of appearance of the ACEs in an ACL has significance. The matching of identifiers to rights enumerated in the ACL proceeds one ACE at a time until a match is detected. Thus, if a process holds multiple rights identifiers, as is typical, the ACL must be ranked as follows:

- Denials of access (ACEs with the **ACCESS=NONE** term)
- High-grade access (ACEs with the most access). For example:
  ACCESS=READ+WRITE+EXECUTE+DELETE+CONTROL)
- Lesser degrees of access
- Minimal access (ACEs that solely contain **ACCESS=READ** or **ACCESS=EXECUTE** terms)

To summarize, the first ACE whose rights identifier matches a rights identifier held by the process (or thread) will be used to determine whether the access is permissible.

Audit Server

Significant security-related events are reported to the audit server, a process which writes those events to an audit log (by default, **SYS$MANAGER: AUDIT_SERVER.DAT**). Operator messages are also written to those terminals that have been set to display operator messages of class **AUDIT**.

If there is insufficient space for the audit log file, system operation will be suspended, with no log-ins permitted (with the exception of the physical system console).

U.S. Government Security Certification

VAX/VMS version 4.3 was the first (1986) system certified to support the requirements of the Department of Defense's *Trusted Computer System Evaluation Criteria*, colloquially referred to as the *Orange Book*. This standard, originally developed by the National Computer Security Center and now administered through NIST, divides systems into a variety of categories. The lowest useful category is C2, described as "Discretionary Access Controls." Systems that provide mechanisms for security managers to mandate the use of security controls are categorized as level B systems.

In 1987 and again in 1993, OpenVMS was reevaluated against both the C2 and B1 levels of trust. The OpenVMS variant with the facilities required for operation at the B levels is referred to as SEVMS. SEVMS was first released, unevaluated, in 1987. The next release, corresponding to OpenVMS 6.0, was released in 1993. The security rating is maintained by a process supervised by the National Center for Secure Computing, with the bulk of the effort undertaken by the OpenVMS engineering team.

IMPLEMENTING SECURE USER ENVIRONMENTS

Implementing a secure user environment requires utilizing the facilities to maximum advantage. The implicit security facilities provided through inheritance and the user authentication mechanisms are both efficient and auditable.

Implicit Security

It is less complex than it would first appear to implement a large-scale, secure OpenVMS environment. The key to building an environment that works is to leverage the strengths of the system.

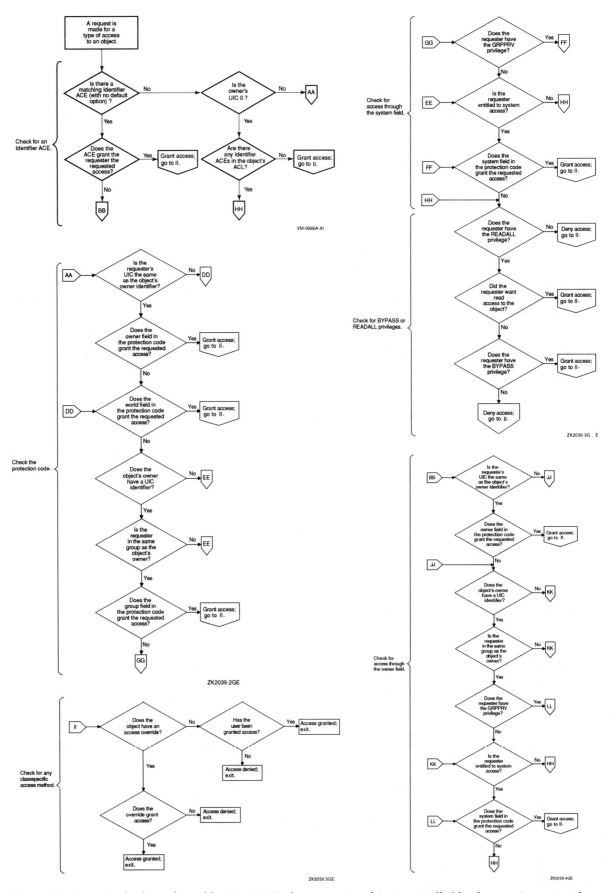

Figure 10: Security checks performed by OpenVMS when accessing objects controlled by the security system (from *OpenVMS Guide to System Security*, pages 71, et seq.). These checks, performed by OpenVMS, eliminate the need for applications-based security checks.

Table 4 Different Classes of Users for a Typical Application

Maintainer	An individual responsible for maintaining the files.
Operator	An individual responsible for day-to-day maintenance (e.g., backups).
User	Normal user authorized to access and modify records in the file.
Query Clerk	Low-level user authorized to only access (not modify) data within the file.

Although it may seem complex, the recommended technique of creating categories of personnel and assigning access rights to those categories is straightforward, secure, auditable, and efficient.

Identifiers are created to refer to collections of users. These collections are often based upon departments or applications (e.g., Accounting, Payables, Human Resources) and level of personnel (e.g., Supervisor, Clerk, Inquiry Clerk; see Table 4). These identifiers are then granted to individual users using the **AUTHORIZE** utility (**AUTHORIZE** can also be used to display the identifiers held by a given user). When the user logs onto the system, their process will be granted the identifiers associated with their username.

Beginners often try to add ACLs with ACEs for every individual user. Putting individual access rights onto each and every resource is a poor approach for many reasons, including:

- It is not maintainable. As users come and go, each and every ACL will have to reviewed and updated accordingly.
- As job responsibilities ebb and flow, each and every ACL will have to be reviewed and updated accordingly.
- When access controls are audited, as is common in larger companies, each and every ACL and each and every ACE will have to be verified.
- The resulting large ACLs will require excessive time to evaluate, compromising system performance.

The role-based approach is far more efficient, maintainable, and auditable. In a role-based approach, files have ACLs composed of ACEs referencing a set of defined roles. In effect, the system dynamically constructs the matrix of individual user's access rights based upon their identifiers and the ACLs, eliminating the need for special access checking code in programs, privileges, or other cumbersome mechanisms.

Users will hold a list of identifiers as a form of electronic badge endorsement. In effect, the rights identifiers provide management the tools to separate user validation from user clearances.

If job responsibilities change, or if a user's access must be suspended because of an investigation, it is a simple matter to remove critical rights identifiers from the authorization profile, while still permitting access to the system for other matters (e.g., electronic mail, time sheet filing, benefits filing). If the access environment is properly implemented, security and audit managers can be confident that the prohibitions will be effective.

File Protection

Properly categorized, the same program, running on the same machine at the same time, can operate on different files with dramatically different protection regimes. The security mechanisms and logical name environment provide a framework to control access. The degree of access available is implicit in the individual user (or the group with whom the user is associated), from wide open to strictly controlled.

The different permutations of the elements, and their inherent flexibility, permit a wide range of choices as to degree of security, even within an organization. This is especially important for organizations and systems that have differing security needs in different units or departments. There is no need for separate systems and variant applications when a proper security regime is implemented.

Limited Accounts

OpenVMS also has provisions for limited user log-ins, known as CAPTIVE accounts. Users whose accounts are CAPTIVE are restricted in several ways:

- no ability to specify options at login,
- no access to the DCL command prompt, and
- if the command script ever exits, the session is automatically terminated.

These restrictions, which allow a user access to specified command procedure or an application menu with controlled choices, are a good security measure for non-IT applications users. Such an account, together with the other security controls, enables the construction of user environments with multiple levels of protection and control, with no corresponding need to develop and maintain special-purpose code.

Secure Subsystems

The OpenVMS security mechanisms are powerful; yet, there are situations where controlled access to an object is desired beyond the constraints expressible in the basic security model. OpenVMS has a facility for addressing these exceptions called *protected subsystems*. Protected subsystems work because the user holds the identifier(s) needed to access the application, whereas the applications image itself holds the identifiers needed to access the object.

Results of Security Violations

The action taken when a security violation occurs has important implications. Merely preventing the inappropriate (or undesired) reference is essential but, generally speaking, an insufficient response. Auditors and security personnel need to know that an unauthorized attempt to access resources has occurred. The realities of large-scale systems operations complicate this task. Protecting resources too tightly can result in voluminous alarm indications, which serve no purpose other than making it harder to identify true security violations.

OpenVMS, through the combination of its integrity-based design, resource monitor, and audit server, provides good mechanisms to tailor security reporting to those security-related events that are desired, without reporting false alarms, and still protect the overall system from misuse.

Damage Limitation

The central goal of the implicit security-related mechanisms is to limit damage to other system users and the overall system. In a direct sense, as mentioned earlier, it is a consequence of the integrity, robustness, and safety aspects of the design philosophy.

The initial provision of System, Owner, Group, and World categories of access represent a good first approximation as to the structure of many organizations. The brick wall protection, and resulting near total encapsulation of system internal details, renders it simpler for application programs to ignore the specifics of the configuration and the environment than to delve into them.

Ease of Programming Model

The programming model for using ACLs and rights identifiers is straightforward. In most cases, the presence of the security system is implicit, yielding the same results as the implicit security provided by the original, traditional OpenVMS security model.

There is full support for defining default ACLs, file protections, and ownership of new files on a directory-by-directory basis. This reduces security-related issues to a management issue, irrelevant to the applications programmer. Removing the security-related issues from applications programming also allows security issues to be driven by the data being managed, rather than the applications program being used. As an example, consider that the same applications can be used to process data subject to HIPAA (Health Insurance Portability and Accountability Act of 1996, Public Law 104–191; the applicable Department of Health and Human Services Privacy regulations may be found at 45 CFR Parts 160 and 164) as data that is not subject to such restrictions.

The integrity of the security-related environment is also assured by using a resource monitor implementation for enforcing security not code embedded in the applications program. In fact, the application itself is subject to protection. For example, restricting access to executable images represents a mechanism to ensure compliance with training standards in an auditable manner subject to documentation.

The security and access checking facilities are fully available to the programmer. The $CHKPRO system service provides the developer with full access to the access checks used throughout OpenVMS. The list of identifiers held by a process is also available, both within executable images and within command procedures (using the $GETJPI system service and the F$GETJPI lexical function, respectively).

APPLICATION PROGRAMMING INTERFACES

Outside of areas that virtually obligate replication, mostly because of the different higher-level language-formatting models, there are few examples of parallel functionality that serendipitously differ. Interfaces that can execute completely in user mode do so; functions, such as system services requiring privileged processing, do

Table 5 DECent Phase IV/V Protocols

DDCMP	Digital Data Communications Message Protocol
NSP	Network Services Protocol
DAP	Data Access Protocol
CTERM	Remote Terminal Protocol
MOP	Maintenance Operations Protocol

so below the user's visibility, albeit using documented interfaces.

Access to system services is via conventional CALL-type interfaces; if the system service requires supporting processing from system components operating in inner (more privileged) access modes, the system service is responsible for generating all requests of lower level system functions.

File System Access

The normal user and programmer access files using Record Management Services (RMS). RMS provides a toolkit of functionality to create, delete, and manipulate files and records within files. Within files, RMS provides support for fixed and variable record files, relative files, indexed files, and byte-stream files.

When files are being shared between processes and between different machines in an OpenVMS cluster, RMS is the system component responsible for requesting locks on the files and the records within files to ensure orderly access.

RMS also provides for buffering on a per-process and global basis for the different types of files. Buffering is controlled by a variety of parameters.

Network Access

Network access in OpenVMS occurs in two modes: transparent and nontransparent. Transparent access is a facility provided by cooperating elements of RMS and DECnet to allow access to files over the network using the same semantics that would be available were the files located on local storage. Sequential, direct, relative, and indexed files can be accessed at the record or block level. A demonstration of the transparency of this facility is that one can run assemblies and compilations of files located on different network-accessible machines by setting one's default to a remote directory and running the compiler.

DECnet

The DECnet protocol suite has its origins in the late 1970s, predating the widespread use of local area network (LAN) technology. DECnet implements point-to-point and multipoint links and, since the mid-1980s, has included IEEE 802.3 LAN connections. DECnet is based on a series of protocol specifications developed by Digital (see Table 5).

DECnet Phase V, released in 1991, incorporated support for the ISO-developed OSI protocols in addition to those defined by Digital. Support has also been included to tunnel DECnet connections over Internet protocol (IP) infrastructure.

A significant architectural difference between the TCP/IP protocol stack and the DECnet protocol stack is the presence in the DECnet stack of a Session Control layer, including authentication as part of the network-provided functionality.

TCP/IP

Although the definition of TCP/IP occurred at approximately the same time as the design of OpenVMS, TCP/IP remained an essentially educational and research network until the mid-1990s. Digital did not develop a TCP/IP stack until 1988.

There are, at the time of this writing, three TCP/IP implementations actively available for the OpenVMS platform:

• TCP/IP Services for OpenVMS (HP),
• Multinet (Process Software Corporation), and
• TCPware (Process Software Corporation).

Multinet and TCPware have been growing closer in functionality since Process Software's acquisition of Multinet.

OPEN SOURCE SOFTWARE

There is a wealth of open source and other low-cost software for OpenVMS. Some of this software is shipped with the operating system distribution on the freeware and open source tools disks. Other programs are available from their authors.

Some standard components provided by HP are open source or closely based on industry widely available sources. Tools such as Kerberos, SSH (secure shell), SSL (Secure Session Layer), and Apache are fully supported (see Table 6).

There is, however, a duality to the use of open source software. Open source software is, by definition, implemented across a variety of different platforms, with a wide range of engineering practices. Some of these practices are state of the art in software engineering, and some of them are less robust.

It is the less-robust software engineering practices that represent a challenge to the OpenVMS community. Widely adopted technologies are a highly valued form of leverage for quickly developing applications to address business needs. On the other hand, some of these technologies have come with preexisting security weaknesses that undermine OpenVMS's longstanding record of security and integrity.

As an example, consider software with two different types of shortcomings, one at the implementation level and one at the architectural level.

At the implementation level, programs written in C are often victim to buffer overflows, caused by the failure to check requests for situations that can overflow buffers.

At the architectural level, more than a few programs have been designed in a manner that presumes an all-or-nothing security environment, often exemplified by UNIX's setuid. The ubiquitous sendmail program fits into this category. Modifying sendmail to operate with a more nuanced approach to security is possible, but it represents a major engineering undertaking, which is often as complex, if not more complex, than reengineering the entire application from the beginning.

Software that does not invoke privileges in its operation, except for the implicit ability to access files through the normal mechanisms, poses a far lesser threat to the integrity and security of the OpenVMS system.

The challenge is to find ways to assimilate the leverage represented by open source software while not sacrificing the bulletproof security and integrity that are OpenVMS's strengths.

SUMMARY

OpenVMS is a world-class operating system, with a long history of solid, reliable operation and is considered to be the "Gold Standard in clustering," as eloquently stated by David Freund in his 2002 paper on UNIX clusters.

The OpenVMS architecture and approach have proved to be a strong, viable foundation, with many impressive achievements over a quarter century. Long-lived is not legacy. OpenVMS, starting on the original VAX-11/780, has gone on to manage systems more than a thousand times larger with a high degree of efficiency and reliability and with little to change in its fundamental structure or architecture.

OpenVMS presents a reliable, solid system with unlimited growth potential.

Table 6 Low-Cost/Freeware/Open Source Software Available for OpenVMS

INFO-ZIP	File compression utility, file compatible with PKZIP on Windows
UNZIP	File decompression utility, file compatible with PKZIP on Windows
APACHE	Web server developed by the Apache Software Foundation
TCL/TK	Tool Command Language/Tool Kit, and interpretive scriping language, by John Ousterhout
PERL	Practical Extraction and Report Language, by Larry Wall
PHP	Personal Home Page, originally by Rasmus Lerdorf
TOMCAT	A Java servlet and Java Server Pages implementation for Apache
XML	Extensible Markup Language
SOAP	Simple Object Access Protocol
NetBeans	Modular, standards-based IDE for Java
BISON	A parser-generator, developed by the GNU Project
GHOSTSCRIPT	A freeware (under the GPL) PostScript® interpreter

ACKNOWLEDGMENTS

I thank the numerous people who generously took the time to speak with me about their roles and recollections of events. I thank members of OpenVMS Engineering, including Leo Demers, Susan Skonetski, Andrew Goldstein, Stephen Hoffman, and others, who contributed recollections and pointers to information. I also thank John Streiff, James Gursha, Jerrold Leichter, and others who read drafts and contributed their comments. I also thank Fern Hertzberg for her assistance in organizing and copyediting this chapter.

GLOSSARY

Asynchronous System Trap (AST) A lightweight thread of execution within a processes context. ASTs are queued on a first-in, first-out basis by Access mode, with Kernel mode ASTs executed first, and User mode ASTs executed last. Although a higher-priority (inner mode) AST may preempt a lower-priority (outer mode) AST, ASTs are not otherwise preemptible within a process. This preemption is an intraprocess issue; ASTs have no effect on interrupt servicing or scheduling interaction between different processes.

DECnet A proprietary networking scheme architected and implemented by then–Digital Equipment Corporation in the late 1970s. DECnet provides most of the services identified in the ISO's Open System Interconnect model of networks. On OpenVMS, DECnet is used as a basis for several tools, including transparent remote file access, system management, and remote terminal handling.

Object An entity belonging to the classes of objects that can be subject to access controls.

Queue IO (QIO) The user-accessible system service that serves as the gatekeeper for all IO operations on OpenVMS.

Reference Monitor The software component responsible for checking a subject's degree of access to an object.

Subject An OpenVMS user process.

User Identification Code (UIC) A 28-bit binary number, split into a 12-bit Group number and a 16-bit Member number which uniquely identifies a user for access purposes on an OpenVMS system.

CROSS REFERENCES

See *Linux Security; Operating System Security; Unix Security; Windows 2000 Security.*

REFERENCES

Digital Equipment Corporation. (1977). *VAX11 software handbook 1977–78.* (Vol. 3). Order Number EB 08126.

Digital Equipment Corporation. (1979). *VAX11 architecture handbook.* Order Number EB 17580.

Dijkstra, E. (1968). The structure of "THE"—Multiprogramming system. *Communications of the Association for Computing Machinery, 11*(5), 341–346.

Freund, D. (2002, August 9). Disaster tolerant Unix: *Removing the last single point of failure.* Illuminata, Inc.

Goldenberg, R., Kenah, L., et al. (1991). *VAX/VMS version 5.2 internals and data structures.* Digital Press.

Goldstein, A. (1987). The design and implementation of a distributed file system. *Digital Technical Journal, 1*(7), 45–55.

HP OpenVMS guide to system security, OpenVMS version 7.3-2. (2003, September). Order Number AA-Q2HLG-TE.

HP OpenVMS I/O user's reference manual, OpenVMS 7.3-2. (2003, September). Order Number AA-PV6SF-TK.

Kronenberg, N., Levy, H., & Strecker, W. (1986). VAXcluster: A closely-coupled distributed system. *ACM Transactions on Computer Systems, 4*(2), 130–146.

OpenVMS calling ststandard. (2001, April). Order Number AA-QSBBD-TE.

FURTHER READING

Manuals

HP OpenVMS Alpha Version 7.3-2 release notes. (2003, September). Order Number AA-RV8YA-TE.

HP OpenVMS DCL dictionary: A–M. (2003, September). Order Number AA-PV5KJ-TK.

HP OpenVMS DCL dictionary: N–Z. (2003, September). Order Number AA-PV5LJ-TK.

HP OpenVMS system manager's manual. Vol. 1: Essentials. (2003, September). Order Number AA-PV5M H-TK.

HP OpenVMS system manager's manual. Vol. 2: Tuning, monitoring, and complex systems. (2003, September). Order Number AA-PV5NH-TK.

HP OpenVMS system services reference manual: A—GETUAI. (2003, September). Order Number AA-QSBMF-TE.

HP OpenVMS system services reference manual: GETUTC—Z. (2003, September). Order Number AA-QSBNF-TE.

OpenVMS calling standard. (2003, April 14). [Draft including IA-64 additions].

OpenVMS programming concepts manual. Vol. 1. (2002, June). Order Number AAS-RNSHB-TE.

OpenVMS record management services reference manual. (2002, June). Order Number AA-PV6RE-TK.

OpenVMS version 7.2 new features manual. (1999, January). Order Number AA-QSBFC-TE.

VMS/Ultrix Connection system managers guide. (1988–1990). Order Number AA-LU49C-TE.

Books and Papers

Bell, C. G., Mudge, C., & McNamara, J. (1978). *Computer engineering: A DEC view of hardware systems design.* Boston, MA: Digital Press.

Brooks, F. (1975). *The mythical man-month: Essays on software engineering.* Addison-Wesley.

Callander, M. A., Sr., Carlson, L., Ladd, A., & Norcross, M. (1992). The VAXstation 4000 model 90. *Digital Technical Journal, 4*(3), 82–91.

Chisvin, L., Bouchard, G., & Wenners, T. (1992). The VAX 6000 model 600 processor. *Digital Technical Journal, 4*(3), 47–59.

Crowell, J., & Maruska, D. (1992a). Design of the VAX 4000 model 100 and MicroVAX 3100 model 90. *Digital Technical Journal, 4*(3), 73–81.

Crowell, J., Kwong-Tak, A., Kopec, T., Nadkarni, S., & Sovie, D. (1992b). Design of the VAX 4000 model 400, 500, 600. *Digital Technical Journal, 4*(3), 60–72.

Davis, S. (1991). Design of VMS volume shadowing phase II: Host-based shadowing. *Digital Technical Journal, 3*(3), 7–15.

Digital Equipment Corporation. (1978). *VAX11 software handbook 1978–79*. Order Number EB 15485.

Digital Equipment Corporation. (1980). *VAX software handbook 1980–81*. Order Number EB 18057.

Digital Equipment Corporation. (1981, April). *VAX/VMS internals and data structures, version 2.2*. Order Number AA-K785A-TE.

Digital Equipment Corporation. (1997). *OpenVMS at 20: Nothing stops it!*

Donchin, D., Fischer, T., Fox, T., Peng, V., Preston, R. & Wheeler, W. (1992). The NVAX CPU chip: Design challenges, methods, and CAD tools. *Digital Technical Journal, 4*(3), 24–37.

Duffy, D. The System Communication Architecture, *Digital Technical Journal, 1*(5) 22–28.

Durdan, W., Bowhill, W., Brown, J., Herrick, W., Marcello, R., Samudrala, S., Uhler, G, & Wade N., (1990). An overview of the VAX 6000 model 400 chip set. *Digital Technical Journal, 2*(2) 36–51.

Fox, M., & Twoskus, J. (1987) Local area VAXcluster systems, *Digital Technical Journal, 1*(5) 56–68.

Fox, T., Gronowski, P., Jain, A., Leary, M., & Miner, D. (1988). The CVAX 78034 chip, a 32-bit second-generation VAX microprocessor. *Digital Technical Journal, 1*(7) 95–108.

Gamache, R., & Morse, K. (1988) VMS symmetric multiprocessing, *Digital Technical Journal, 1*(7) 57–63.

Gezelter, R. (1989, November). *Your key to efficient event driven systems under VAX/VMS: Asynchronous system traps*. Paper presented at the DECUS Pre-symposium Seminar, Anaheim, CA.

Gezelter, R. (2000a, October 6). *Building secure OpenVMS applications*. Paper presented at the Compaq Enterprise Technology Symposium, Los Angeles, CA.

Gezelter, R. (2000b, October 6). *Introduction to OpenVMS AST programming*. Paper presented at the Compaq Enterprise Technology Symposium, Los Angeles, CA.

Gezelter, R. (2000c, October 6). *OpenVMS shareable libraries: An implementer's guide*. Paper presented at the Compaq Enterprise Technology Symposium, Los Angeles, CA.

Gezelter, R. (2004). Inheritance based environments in stand-alone OpenVMS systems and OpenVMS clusters. *HP OpenVMS Technical Journal, 3*.

Goldenberg, R., Dumas, D., & Saravanan, S. (1997). *OpenVMS Alpha internals: Scheduling and process control, version 7.0*. Boston, MA: Digital Press.

Goldstein, A. (1977). *Files-11 on disk specification, level 2.*, private communication

Gursha, J. (1997). *High performance cluster configuration system management*. Boston, MA: Digital Press.

Harvard Research Group. (2001). *OpenVMS: When continuous availability really matters*.

Hayes, F. (1994). Design of the AlphaServer multiprocessor server systems. *Digital Technical Journal, 6*(3), 8–19.

Intel. (2002a). *Intel Itanium architecture software developer's manual. Vol. 1: Application architecture, revision 2.1*. Order Number 245317-004.

Intel. (2002b). *Intel Itanium architecture software developer's manual. Vol. 2: System architecture, revision 2.1*. Order Number 245318-004.

Intel. (2002c). *Intel Itanium architecture software developer's manual. Vol. 3: Instruction set reference, revision 2.1*. Order Number 245319-004.

Lauck, A., Oran, D., & Perlman, R. (1986) A Digital Network Architecture overview. *Digital Technical Journal, 1*(3) 11–24.

Leahy, L. (1991). New availability features of local area VAXcluster systems. *Digital Technical Journal, 3*(3), 27–35.

McCoy, K. (1990). *VMS file system internals*. Digital Press, Boston, MA.

National Computer Security Center. (1996, October 24). *Final evaluation report, digital evaluation report: OpenVMS and SEVMS, version 6.1, with VAX or Alpha*. National Security Agency, Fort George G. Meade, Maryland, NCSC-FER-93/001.B, NCSC-FER-93/002.B.

Russo, A. (1994). The Alphaserver 2100 I/O subsystem. *Digital Technical Journal, 6*(3), 20–28.

Sites, R. (Ed.). (1992). *Alpha architecture reference manual*. Boston, MA: Digital Press.

Snaman, W.E., Jr. (1987). The VAX/VMS Distributed Lock Manager, *Digital Technical Journal, 1*(5), 29–44.

Snaman, W.E., Jr. (1991). Application design in a VAXcluster system. *Digital Technical Journal, 3*(3), 16–26.

TechWise Research. (2000, June). *Quantifying the value of availability: A detailed comparison of four different RISC-based cluster solutions designed to provide high availability*. Version 1.1a.

TechWise Research. (2004, February). *Total cost of ownership for entry-level and mid-range clusters: A detailed analysis of the total cost of ownership of three different RISC-based server clusters including HP OpenVMS, IBM AIX, and Sun Solaris*. Version 1.0.

TechWise Research. (2004, May). *Are some RISC-based clusters easier to manage than others? A detailed comparison of the resources required to manage HP OpenVMS and IBM AIX server clusters*. Version 1.0.

TechWise Research. (2004, June). *Are some RISC-based clusters more secure than others? A detailed comparison of potential vulnerabilities and security-related crashes for HP OpenVMS, IBM AIX, and Sun Solaris*. Version 1.0.

Uhler, G. M., Bernstein, D., Biro, L., Brown, J., III, Edmondson, J., Pickholtz, J., & Stamm, R. (1992). The NVAX and NVAX+ high performance VAX microprocessors. *Digital Technical Journal, 4*(3), 11–23.

Weiner, H. (1973, February). *An analysis of computer software security at Cornell*, unpublished.

Server-Side Security

Slim Rekhis and Noureddine Boudriga, *National Digital Certification Agency and University of Carthage, Tunisia*
M. S. Obaidat, *Monmouth University*

SERVER VULNERABILITIES

Securing a server is a difficult and challenging task that cannot be fully accomplished. Introducing an additional solution to enhance a server's security can increase vulnerability and exposure to further threats. One answer to the problem is to understand server vulnerabilities and start implementing a risk-mitigation approach. In general, server security vulnerabilities might exist in three main areas: installed software, defined and enforced security policies, and used protocols.

Software Vulnerabilities

Operating systems, services, and applications are all subject to specification, configuration, or implementation flaws that can generate embedded security vulnerabilities. The latter, when exploited, can grant intruders the opportunity to gain the privileges under which the related programs are running, thus reducing the security of the server and the entire network. Examples of software vulnerabilities include *buffer overflow, race conditions*, and *special character processing* (Cowan, et al., 2000). Whereas the first type of vulnerability is caused by poor bounds checking on the user input, the second represents an undesirable situation that can occur when a program attempts to perform operations that should be done in a proper order, and the last mainly affects the scripts that can be subverted by passing arbitrary inputs to yield the control of the system to intruders.

Examples of buffer overflow vulnerability involve the one found in the WebDAV component in Microsoft IIS Web Server 5.0 (Wood, 2003), which allows remote intruders to execute arbitrary commands under the server security context of the Internet Information Server (IIS) service. An example of a race condition is present in the Samba daemon (Vulnerability Information Center, 2004), which allows local attackers to overwrite files on the server when writing REG files (i.e., text files that contain registry information and have the file extension .reg). Security administrators should be aware of the potential vulnerabilities, particularly when they are deploying their own developed tools.

The most reliable way for security administrators to react against the preceding weaknesses is to keep the server up-to-date with software suppliers' fixes and patches. Careful consideration should be made, particularly when a deployed software component is developed by the company itself without security awareness. Meanwhile, tools such as Cqual (Foster, 2002), MOPS (Chen & Wagner, 2002), Flawfinder, and ELF Finder (DaCosta, Dahn, Mancoridis, & Prevelakis, 2003) are useful to scan (usually during program compiling) source code for patterns of known flaws such as buffer overflow or format string problems. Other vulnerabilities (e.g., general logic errors) are more tedious to identify during program compilation. Therefore, server vulnerabilities represent a hard challenge to address. A good way to ensure their mitigation is provided through complementing the automated verification of software with manual extensive testing and continuous monitoring.

Server Security Policies

Even if security solutions such as antivirus software (AV) and intrusion detection systems (IDSs) are deployed, security breaches remain persistent because system owners and operators might misuse the system and security standards. To ensure that a system is used in an effective and productive way without exposing it to the realm of intruders, a security policy should be defined, including a strategy to protect and maintain the availability of the organizational resources. An example of writing an information security policy that is compliant with the BS7799 standard is provided in NHSnet (2004). The use of a security policy helps considerably in preventing configuration inconsistencies and can shorten reaction time to incidents. However, defining a security policy is not sufficient for good protection. The policy should also be valid, consistent, well understood, and correctly enforced by server operators. A simple modification in the configuration of a security component without an understanding of the organizational security objectives can expose the whole network to harmful security weaknesses.

In practice, security specialists have noticed that a high percentage of server security vulnerabilities are caused by problems related to security policy. For instance, testing new software components on a public online server can add a temporary privileged user with a weak password. Obviously, this can temporarily introduce a flaw that exposes the server to attacks. Another example is a vulnerability found in Windows NT Server Service Pack 6 (Syed, 2002). It enables a valid user, whose permission for changing passwords is revoked (here, the administrator is supposed to apply the local policy, "User cannot change password"), to still change his or her password through IIS 4.0 Web service by using the following uniform resource locator (URL): http://iisserver/iisadmpwd/aexp3.htr. Therefore, defining a security policy should be done carefully to prevent the introduction of inconsistencies that can alter the protection policy and strategy.

Protocol Vulnerabilities

Protocols are extremely hard to design in a correct and secure manner, even if the goal is straightforward. Any design flaw that has a relationship with security can lead to damaging impact on the protocol usage. Often, during the design phase of a security solution, administrators select the security technology required to implement the organizational policy but neglect to consider the protocol features. Consequently, if security administrators rely on vulnerable protocols, they might see their network resources, including servers, become victims of attacks.

In practice, a lot of powerful security attacks have emerged because of vulnerabilities in protocols; particularly for those protocols developed with no security features. Transmission control protocol/Internet protocol (TCP/IP) represents a common example of such protocols. One of its most fascinating security holes is based on a sequence-number prediction used to construct TCP/IP packets without the need for any response from the server (Bellovin, 1989). Such a weakness enables an intruder to spoof a trusted host and perform malicious actions on the server. Another way to compromise servers is through routing protocols. Routing Information Protocol (RIP), for instance, propagates routing information and updates the gateways routing tables without checking the received information. An intruder can send erroneous routing information to the gateways on a given path and induce them to build incorrect routing paths with the purpose of deviating all packets issued from the server (and addressed to a legitimate host) to the intruder's machine.

Cryptographic protocols are widely used to guarantee security properties, such as authentication or secrecy in the information exchange between servers and their users. Despite the fact that they use secure cryptographic primitives, several protocols have been declared insecure because of design flaws. For instance, servers that rely on an authentication protocol such as the *Needham-Schroeder public key authentication protocol* (Needham & Schroeder, 1978) can easily be compromised using the *Lowe's attack* (Lowe, 1995), where an intruder can start a legitimate session with user A and impersonates it to mislead user B in a second session.

SERVER SECURITY ISSUES

It is obvious from the previous section that securing a server requires significant effort because the weakest neglected point can be a source of access. In fact, protecting a server from attacks implies considering issues including security policy, user management, security auditing, system configuration, and log management. An overview of these issues is discussed in this section.

Server Security Policies

The use of a security policy helps prevent configuration inconsistencies and helps administrators react efficiently to security incidents. A security policy is a progressive document that aims to protect an organization's information security systems, delimit acceptable uses, elaborate on personnel training plans for security policy enforcement, and enforce security measures. Because organizations are facing different types of threats, server security policies should be customized to the organization's need to cope with its business activity, information infrastructure, and resource sensitivity. Consider the case of remote-server administration. For instance, say organization A could prohibit a given activity after identifying the relevant need and consequent risk, whereas organization B could allow the activity but constrain it to strong requirements (e.g., restricting access to specific source IP domains or defining access timetables). Organization C could allow such activity using a weak authentication with user name and password. Canavan (2003) presents a guide to develop organizational security policies and describes the elements to be considered during its design and maintenance.

Security policies need to be reviewed on a regular basis and also on the occurrence of situations when new vulnerabilities are of concern. Such occurrences can require changing security rules, developing new plans, modifying practices, or restructuring security information services. For example, a vulnerability revealed in Cisco switch and router IOS (ITSS Information Security Services, 2003) leads these devices to be victims of denial of service attacks, if exploited. It can be dealt with through the upgrade or the acquisition of a new IOS. A more straightforward solution is to modify the organization's security policy by implementing appropriate ingress filtering.

Finally, it is worth mentioning that ideally a security policy should be sufficiently clear and comprehensive. It should come with a set of procedures for maintaining and evaluating its effectiveness. Similar to a software specification, it should satisfy a set of properties and requirements (e.g., validation, verification, modularity, completeness, and consistency). However, because of the occurrence of threats and unpredicted vulnerabilities, modifications and monitoring represent serious challenges.

Management of Users

Users are the most active participants in server activity. Locally and remotely, they can abuse, misuse, or compromise server security. To prevent damages and reduce the consequent risk of their uses, users should be managed effectively. Default configurations of services and applications often include default accounts with known passwords, as well as active guest accounts. These are commonly known and widely used by the intruder community. They can be worked out using tools that make it easier to penetrate a system (e.g., the Default Account Database as provided by Swordsoft, which includes approximately 1,500 default passwords), if configured by default. Moreover, some users such as e-mail server subscribers can be granted access to the system to perform a very restrictive activity (e.g., sending and receiving e-mails). Because their number is large, an administrator should be aware of the potential risks that such users can generate and should not allow them to get interactive shells. More common user-management issues are related to how account passwords are set. Weak parameters in the choice of password should be avoided, particularly when these parameters correspond to length, complexity, aging, reuse possibility, number of failed attempts accepted, and change authority. Thus, password-checking software could be used to reject all passwords that do not satisfy a predefined password policy.

Granting full trust to a server user who has been authenticated can cause major concerns because an unauthorized user can, for example, take control of an active session while its legitimate user is away. To reduce this risk, the server operating system can be configured to lock any user session after an idle period. Such a solution can be insufficient in highly sensitive contexts. More elaborate solutions can be provided, including smart cards and hardware tokens, which can be used to lock the system when the owners extract them from the computer device. User passwords can be replaced or complemented with more secure solutions such as a private key stored inside cryptographic tokens, one-time password systems, and biometric solutions (Obaidat & Sadoun, 1999). Even though these solutions are expensive and require significant effort to be integrated, they can be justified in many situations.

Auditing Server Security

From the moment a server risk-mitigation plan is enforced in an organization and a security policy including procedures and configuration settings is established, a security audit needs to be begun and continuously conducted on the server because it remains necessary to verify whether the security policy is being enforced correctly. Auditing aims to check that no breaches in the server configuration have been introduced during system operation and that the server is sufficiently protected. Depending on the practices and activities affecting the server, a security audit needs to be performed on a regular basis and whenever undesired conditions are observed.

During the audit procedures, the system configuration, operating system, services, and applications need to be examined carefully with an understanding of the impact of each component on the security of others.

Verifying software vulnerabilities is very important, and any neglected vulnerability can call into question the overall server security. A remote vulnerability that grants unprivileged access to a server can enable an intruder to exploit a local vulnerability on that server to gain privileged access and affect its neighborhoods, especially if sniffed data can reveal relevant information (e.g., clear passwords or a trusted relation is established between the server and its neighbors). Multiple software tools can help considerably in checking the security of a server under audit against the presence of known vulnerabilities, as they are described in general information sources, such as National Institute of Standards and Technology (NIST), Computer Emergency Response Team (CERT), Australian CERT (AusCERT), Bugtraq, and Security Focus. Some of these sources (e.g., NIST) maintain a security vulnerabilities metabase that can be interrogated online, allows the download of supporting new software, and provides flexible search capabilities and links for patch information.

To check whether security measures taken to protect a server have really protected the server, the security audit should try to identify whether the server has been targeted or subverted by intruders. To this aim, the set of available logs (these should cover network logs because an intruder might have cleaned the server log content before leaving the machine) have to be examined, statistical analysis performed, anomalies detected, and alerts correlated to identify attack scenarios and decide the appropriate countermeasures. Remote penetration testing complements the local vulnerability auditing. A series of remote attacks can be conducted against the server by a trusted user that behaves exactly like an intruder. Methods, techniques, and tools used for penetration testing are described in McClure, Scambray, and Kurtz (2003), where the authors demonstrate how to defend against a large number of security attacks.

However, because most security threats are generated by insiders, penetration testing is insufficient to defend against vulnerabilities. Therefore, a security audit should also cover personnel misuse and hardware failures. International security standards such as ISO 19977 identify the range of controls to be performed on the information systems.

System Configurations

Protecting the server from attacks caused by poor or wrong configuration is a challenging task. A system configuration involves setting file and program ownerships and permissions, activating and deactivating software components and add-ons, restricting access to the system, and so forth. A security administrator needs to implement an accurate configuration to prevent attacks. Thus, only minimal software functionalities are activated, minimal effort is spent in administering security, and minimal risk is assumed. Vulnerabilities could flow out from bugs in the software components, the related programs, or the used libraries. Consequently, any component (e.g., add-on, add-in, and script) that is not needed should be de-activated, if not uninstalled. Program privileges also play an important role because the program might grant its privileges to an intruder, if subverted or exploited. An example of such a problem occurs when an administrator configures a Web server to run under the root user. In that case, any subversion of the Web daemon (e.g., PHF attack; NMRC 2003) can lead to the execution of the intruder's commands under root privileges. Guidelines for securing and hardening these are widely available on the Internet. Some tools were developed to make the process easy and to automate the set of tasks to be used for such purposes. The tool XPLizer, for instance, is a front-end tool designed to provide a graphical user interface (GUI) for fixing some of the most common security problems in Microsoft Windows, whereas Languard Network Security Scanner helps considerably in auditing the configuration part of Windows systems.

Management of Logs

Log files represent the most common source for detecting suspicious behaviors and intrusion attempts. The efficiency of these files is strictly affected by any failure or attack on the related data collection mechanisms and any weakness in protecting their output. Log protection is very important in that intruders can access these files or the utilities that manage them to remove information, alter signs of malicious activity, or even add erroneous information to these files.

Log file protection can be altered because of badly configured access permissions, storage in public areas, and insecure transfer to remote hosts, in addition to any successful penetration of the system that hosts the log files. Logging data locally is easy to configure; it allows instantaneous access, although it is less secure because the log content can be lost whenever the server is compromised. On the other hand, remote log storage protects against this threat, but requires strengthening the communication security medium, using, for example, a separate subnet path or an encryption mechanism. The logging mechanism is also subject to denial of service attacks. In Linux systems, for example, an intruder could fill the Syslog output files until the logging partition becomes overloaded. This forces the logging process to stop. In Windows NT systems, the logging process starts to overwrite old files when the available storage is filled. Solutions to avoid this include compression, periodic remote transfer, and a warning report if logs reach their size limits.

Choosing the kind of information to log is an important issue. A security administrator should be aware of the resources required to store the generated files and must read, understand, and interpret log-file contents without being swamped with data. In fact, mechanical interpretation of log content can become boring, requiring

a look into a lexicon to understand the meaning of the records. Windows Server 2003, for instance, uses failure code 3221225578 with event ID 680 to denote that a wrong NTLM authentication occurred, where the user name is correct but the password is wrong. To enhance the significance of the generated log files, a security administrator should consider using log-dedicated tools that automate some operations, including content aggregation, automated interpretation, and statistics generation. GFI's LANGuard SELM, for instance, is a tool specialized in monitoring Windows security event logs, with centralization of alerts and reporting capabilities.

When deciding how long a log file is kept available, first consider the file's category and content. An error or a warning log generated a month ago, for example, is irrelevant today because errors that are faced today can be completely different from past errors or because system components might have been updated.

It is worthwhile to complement the log management with a verification mechanism to ensure that log content is consistent, meaningful, and useful when trying to conduct a forensic examination following a security incident.

PROTECTING SERVERS FROM OVERLOAD

One important challenge that server-security administrators face is the guarantee of server availability, especially when servers are very much in demand. Server overload should be correctly managed to avoid being a victim of worsening quality of service (QoS), where client response time is increasing and the target begins reaching a denial of service. To protect servers from overload, simply bounding the flow rate is inefficient, but different actions should be taken, including traffic shaping, load controlling, and policy management.

Traffic Shaping

Because server overload is generally caused by uncontrolled reception of client requests, controlling the overload can start at the network entry to the server. Shape the traffic flow to meet server performance by delaying excess traffic using buffering, queuing mechanisms, and request rejection. Such mechanisms are currently available in different networks such as Asynchronous Transfer Mode (ATM) networks, where in addition to resource management techniques that include virtual paths and connections admission control, traffic shaping has been implemented through two main traffic-shaping algorithms: the *leaky bucket algorithm* and *token bucket* (Li & Stol, 2002). The token bucket, for example, is a formal definition of the transfer rate using a formula involving three components: burst size, mean rate, and a time interval. The burst size denotes the traffic quantity that can be sent within a given unit of time without scheduling.

Incoming network traffic to a server can be arranged into different classes, where incoming packets are mapped to their corresponding classes. Various types of parameters can be used to define the set of classes depending on the granularity of the classification. These include the server-side IP addresses or services (user datagram protocol [UDP] and transmission control protocol [TCP] ports), client IP addresses, DiffServ bits, client socket connections, and processes that will be generated on servers when processing packet content. Traffic classification plays an important role in reducing the complexity of eliminating malicious activity. For example, to protect a server from a SYN flood attack (Kargl, Maier, & Weber, 2001), a traffic class should be defined based on TCP SYN packets. For example, an e-commerce firm that wants the company Web site to be continually available to high-paying customers even under heavy loads might define traffic classes based on ordering requests. This is a high-gain criterion that imposes costly traffic processing to differentiate between classes.

Load Controlling

Classifying traffic is not enough to reduce or avoid overload on the supervised server. It should be complemented by a load-controlling mechanism based on well-defined and reliable traffic metrics. Once a packet is mapped to its corresponding class, the set of load metrics associated with that class are assessed to decide which action should be taken against that packet. Load indicators and metrics can be defined based on static or dynamic observations of the system capacity. With static controlling, a priori resource bounds are generally imposed (e.g., maximum number of client socket connections, maximum incoming packet rate). These metrics should be carefully defined to compromise between resource underuse and resource exhaustion. A particular static metric can be expressed in the form of *processing packet X gets Y% of the CPU* (Welsh & Culler, 2002). These metrics are based on resources accounting and assume that the controller has an exact and up-to-date idea of the server's resource status. Static metrics definition seems to work well with services that have an a priori knowledge of the resources required.

In dynamic controlling, a load controller is aware of the server's capacity and adjusts the used metrics actively based on the observed system's behavior and performance. To use dynamic controlling effectively, appropriate parameters should be taken into consideration to provide system stability and reduce false interpretations. For example, a minimal amount of time may be imposed on the load controller between metrics changes. Another load-controlling parameter can be defined by the minimal variation of the observed metric value that should be noticed before switching metrics.

Policy Management

Policy management is partly the administratively configurable part of the overload protection component. It defines the metrics values, describes the server reactions, and specifies whether specific measures should be taken when the load controller metrics reach their limits. Policy management can, for example, state to refuse additional SYN packets when the number of service-connection attempts has reached its throughput limit Y within an observed Z seconds. This is a straightforward and naive policy rule that can be associated with static load controlling. Another policy can specify that the system should begin trying to adjust the priorities of a traffic class under a heavy load from a value X to value Y if the server resource Z has reached its limit value W. When the system becomes overloaded, the set of new connections corresponding to the assigned traffic class can then be refused.

QGuard (Jamjoom & Reumann, 2000) provides a differentiation treatment for incoming traffic based on the adjustment of the priority or admission control parameters. It divides the system capacity to grant more importance than preferred server clients and enables protection against SYN floods and the ping of death.

Protecting from Denial of Service

Denial of service (DoS) attacks attempt to deprive systems and applications from needed resources to prevent them from providing their services. Consequently, a server that is a victim of such an attack will appear unreachable to its users. Recently, DoS attacks have evolved into more intense and damaging attacks, including distributed DoS (DDoS) attacks that use many compromised servers to launch coordinated DoS attacks against single or multiple targets. The most famous event illustrating such attacks occurred in February 2000, when a variant of the Smurf and DoS attacks was conducted against Yahoo!, Buy.com, and Amazon.com. A DDoS attack starts by installing a master program on a compromised server to hide the intruder. At a later time, the master program initiates a coordinated attack performed by a set of agents (called zombies) installed on a set of compromised distributed sites. Intermediate systems/nodes called reflectors can be used to hide the identity of the intruder or to amplify the attack.

DDoS attacks have become easier to conduct. Many variants of DDoS attack tools exist today such as the Triple Flood Network (TFN) tool that supports Internet Control Message Protocol (ICMP) floods, SYN floods, UDP floods, and Smurf-style attacks. A more complex variant, called TFN2K, makes its recognition more difficult by using encryption and by communicating over multiple transport protocols, including TCP and UDP.

To protect servers against DoS attacks, many proposals have been made, but they don't completely solve the issue. Protection mechanisms include packet filtering, automated attack detection, and security vulnerability fixing. With packet filtering, end routers apply ingress packet filtering to allow only server-supported protocols and to deny security-critical services, suspicious identified source IP domains and services, directed broadcasts (RFC 2644), and forged IP addresses (RFC 2267). Routers should be monitored to update their filtering rules because intruders' techniques and behaviors evolve.

Automated attack detection is benefited by the fact that DoS attacks disrupt server resources (e.g., memory occupancy, processor utilization, network buffer) conspicuously. Therefore, end system resources should be continuously monitored and alerts should be instantaneously issued to enable a very quick reaction.

Security vulnerability fixing is achieved through the following actions: (1) servers should be configured carefully and securely; (2) unnecessary network services should be permanently deactivated; and (3) highly available services should be patched with all available security fixes.

Protection from DoS is sometimes insufficient, especially in cases where packets are spoofed. Many research proposals are making considerable effort to identify the real sources of packets. Savage and associates (Savage, Wetherall, Karlin, & Anderson, 2000) have used a probabilistic packet-marking scheme to enable tracing packets back to their source after an attack has occurred. Song and Perrig (2001) have enhanced the marking scheme and provided an efficient mechanism to authenticate the packet marking such that a compromised router cannot forge markings of other routers on the path connecting the intruder to the target server. Bellovin (2000) enabled ICMP messaging to be emitted randomly by routers along the path to a destination. This reduces the computation complexity but increases the overall network traffic. Finally, Snoeren et al. (2002) enabled single traceback IP packets by generating audit trails for traffic within the network.

SERVER SCRIPTING ISSUES

A script is generally referred to as an external program component used to create dynamic content without modifying the server code. Its use is of great importance in Web development. Perl, PHP, Active Server Pages (ASP), and JavaServer Pages (JSP) are examples of server-side scripting languages. Common gateway interface (CGI) represents another way to achieve this end (see Figure 1). A CGI defines an interface between the server and external programs and enables a Web page to call programs written in any language. Because security vulnerabilities can be easily introduced in any step during the life cycle of a script (e.g., design, encoding, configuration), enabling the running of insecure programs on the server can increase the risk of attacks. There is no denying that the content of this section is extremely suitable for Web servers; nevertheless, it can be applied to any server that uses scripts.

Risk Mitigation in the Use of Scripts

The installation and use of scripts and external programs should be done with maximum attention to reduce their potential damage risk. To do so, the script should be checked against poor programming practices that can lead to known vulnerabilities such as buffer overflow or misuse of characters input (e.g., metadata that can involve the execution of unexpected system commands).

Server-side include (SSI), which is Perl-based coding that enables dynamic information to be gathered from servers at the time the Web pages are generated (i.e., at the last modification time), can be the root of potential vulnerabilities that intruders can easily exploit. A buffer overrun in Microsoft FrontPage server extensions, for instance, allows code execution (Microsoft Corporation, 2004). The key idea for protection is to disable SSI whenever possible

as well as any other external program or script kept available for remote use on the server.

Server administrators need to keep track of all the scripts installed on the server. A single directory such as cgi-bin can be set, for example, for serving all the scripts. The access to this directory should then be controlled to detect any malicious creation or nonpermissible execution attempts. Integrity-checking tools can also be used to track any unauthorized changes. All users should be prohibited from seeing the directory's contents, and none of the script backups (e.g., *.cgi.bak, *.cgi~) should be left in that directory.

Another issue related to scripts is granting privileges. Requested script permissions should be restricted to allow the execution of scripts only by the user under which the process is invoked. Moreover, the user IDs granted to these scripts and programs should be different from those under which the service software that accommodates the scripts runs.

In cases in which a script needs to grant supplementary privilege to its users without allowing them much more than required, the script can be made *suid* (a practice specific to UNIX systems). This should be used only if necessary, and the need for it ought to be carefully evaluated. A weakness in making a script *suid* allows an intruder to access not only the set of files of the script owner but also any other file that could be accessed by the user on whose behalf the script is running.

Writing Safe CGI Scripts

A CGI script works as follows. First, it processes the client input taken from the Web server while the script is invoked. Then, it executes and returns the related results to the Web server, which combines this result with the requested HTML page and returns it to the client. Despite its power, a CGI script can introduce security holes on the server. Such holes can be grouped into three categories: system information leaking, access grant to internal and undesirable system commands, and system resource exhaustion. To overcome these holes, security measures should be taken both when configuring the server to accommodate the scripts and during the CGI script encoding.

When encoding a script, the script developer must be aware of the security issues related to the selected language. CGI scripts can be written using compiled languages such as C or interpreted languages such as Perl. Interpreted languages make it easy to pass data to the system shell and wait for the output. Unfortunately, they might introduce a risky security hole because an intruder can pass arbitrary string commands as input to be executed by the shell. Moreover, because the source

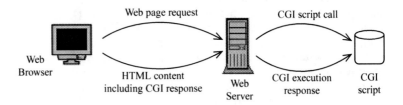

Figure 1:　Common gateway interface operation.

code for interpreted scripts is accessible, this makes it easier to find a bug to exploit. In this context, compiled languages are more difficult to subvert. The complexity of the compiled languages makes it also more difficult to find an embedded bug to exploit.

Once the coding language is chosen, the script developer should be aware of the possible unexpected user input that can contain shell metacharacters. To illustrate this issue, let's discuss the following Perl script, which can be used to send an e-mail after filling out a form.

```
$mail_to = $input{email_address};
open (MAIL, "|/path_to/sendmail $mail_to");
print MAIL "To: $mailto\n FROM: The Web user\n\n";
close MAIL;
```

The first instruction affects the variable $mail\_to$, an e-mail address that the user of the form inserts in the appropriate field. Then, the command $sendmail$ followed by variable $mail\ to$ is started and the body of the mail is printed. Finally, the $sendmail$ command is closed.

The developer here assumes that the user will always input an e-mail address. Such a statement can easily introduce a security weakness because an intruder can, for example, introduce the following string:

myname@mailserver.com; mail myname@mailserver.com < /etc/passwd"

When appended to the $sendmail$ command, this input will also e-mail the content of the /etc/passwd file. To avoid such a situation, it is, in general, inappropriate to pass commands through a shell; rather, it is recommended to pass arguments directly to external programs as separate elements in a list. In all cases, the pattern of the user input should be matched against the set of undesirable shell metacharacters (see Kamthan, 1999) and removed or corrected, if necessary. The first instruction of the previous example can be complemented as follows to ensure that the user has entered a valid e-mail address:

```
$mail_to = $input{email_address};
if ($mail_to = ~/[;<>\*\|\'&\$!#\(\)\[\]\{\}:"'\n\r])}{
    &return_error (500, "Invalid Address", "invalid email characters");
    }
else {...}
```

Reducing CGI Risk Using Wrappers

Reducing these risks requires an administrator to be familiar with coding languages and to be able to spend a long period of time analyzing them. In some circumstances, when a provider allows its customers to upload their own scripts, checking scripts against security weaknesses is difficult.

A common solution to this problem is the use of wrappers on the server. Wrappers allow changing the user under which the script is running to prevent damages if the script is broken. Wrappers perform additional security checks before they allow scripts to be executed. They can also put restrictions on scripts to access limited parts of the file.

CGIWrap is a popular CGI wrapper. It runs any CGI script as its file owner, performs a set of security checks, and blocks the script execution if any of the checks fail. But it cannot guarantee that no misuse of the resources was done (e.g., a script is generating e-mails or introducing errors in the server logs), and it does not prevent a subverted CGI script from manipulation of the user's home directory under which it is running. It also cannot check whether scripts running with the same user permission are interfering with each other (e.g., a script is deleting another script's database entries). Another popular wrapper is suEXEC, which allows users to run scripts as the owner mentioned in the Apache server's configuration file. It also runs a series of approximately 20 security checks.

ACCESS CONTROL

Apart from security efforts that aim at providing the needed protection of the delivered content, there must be requirements regarding the assurance of interacting principals' identities. Obviously, access control is of great importance to prevent unauthorized operations and malicious uses of server resources. After describing the types of access control, we discuss the set of widely used methods in practice.

Types of Access Control

The literature distinguishes three types of access control mechanisms that are used to protect systems from unauthorized access (Kraft, 2002; Weber, 2003; Obaidat & Sadoun, 1997). They are called discretionary access control (DAC), mandatory access control (MAC), and role-based access control (RBAC). The first class works by assigning privileges on objects to subjects. The access is based on the identity of the involved user, the access mode, and the requested object. Because DAC allows an object's owner to grant or revoke a privilege to another subject, it requires that all operations be set only by the administrator. To this limitation, one can add that DAC is also limited by the cascade of positive and negative rules that can lead to contradictions. Nevertheless, DAC is widely used because of its effectiveness and simplicity. Access control lists (ACLs) represent the most popular implementation of DAC.

MAC bases its decision on the sensitivity level relating to the information content of the objects and the formal authorization of subjects to access information. A lattice of information sensitivity is first established and a security level is then assigned to each object and subject, called classification and clearance, respectively. A subject is typically authorized to read classified information, which is lower or equal to its clearance and is disallowed to introduce modifications on the classified information only if its clearance is equal or higher. MAC policy is well suited for rigid environments with a centralized information owner; but, on the other hand, it is unsuited for services that are processing unclassified information and presents a problem when there are multiple instances of objects that are classified differently despite their same meaning.

RBAC techniques have shown their effectiveness in managing security in dynamic environments, such as commercial contexts. RBAC works by defining roles and assigning the appropriate users to them. The roles are created based on the user activity on the system, and they are updated by granting or revoking new permissions as new system components are added or removed. Typically, a role can hold many users, and a user can be assigned many roles. Similarly, a role can hold several permissions, and a permission can be allocated to many roles. Roles introduce great simplicity in managing server security, and users can be reassigned easily to new roles as their responsibilities or categories change. With RBAC, an administrator can grant the minimal necessary privileges to a system's users. In contrast with MAC policy, RBAC can support abstract permissions (e.g., cipher, decipher, generate key, recover key) rather than generic read and write permissions.

Other models of access control have emerged, including the Clark-Wilson model for the preservation of integrity and the Chinese Wall model for the preservation of confidentiality by preventing conflict of interest in commercial activities. Details on these models can be found in Yao (2003).

IP-Based Control

Various fields and traffic characteristics within the TCP/IP protocol can serve as a basis for access control. A server inspects the traffic received to extract the subject's information. Examples of subject IDs involve the requested service (TCP or UDP port number), protocol identifier at the transport layer, and IP source address. Once the subject ID is extracted, a list is used to deduce whether the client is allowed to use the local resource. This access control is widely implemented in basic solutions, terminal servers, and routers. It is simple, easy to implement, and can cope with the possibility of managing the whole network identity. Nevertheless, the level of user-identity assurance is low (e.g., users that connect from the same machine look the same) and the server administrator may be brought to manage a huge amount of meaningless subject identities. The reasons for this include the use of proxies and Network Address Translation, which allows a great number of users to share the same IP address. In addition, the lack of security in the TCP/IP protocol suite can misrepresent identification results. An intruder can forge an IP address to gain unauthorized access to the server or can substitute an identity for a legitimate user and behave maliciously to induce the server administrator to deny the corresponding IP address. Doing so is a form of DoS. Some access control solutions rely on, in addition to TCP/IP identifiers, the use of the host name (e.g., domain name system [DNS] name, NetBIOS name), which is being used by the user

that connects to the server. This is also inefficient because it does not point out which user is accessing the server.

Although the discussed solution is the easiest access control method, it is better to use it only in situations where the level of security requirements is reasonably low or when the security is handled jointly with other solutions (e.g., firewall, authentication server). The Linux TCP Wrapper is an example that provides an efficient IP-based access control mechanism in addition to its capability of logging requests. Its daemon *tcpd* checks the *hosts.allow* file and the *hosts.deny* file before granting or denying access. The two files mark which hosts are allowed to access which network services and keep the list of which hosts are denied.

Name-Based Control

With the previous control scheme, the server was able to identify the host initiating connections and not the users themselves. With *name-based* access control, subjects should provide valid information (e.g., user names and passwords) on their IDs to the server so the server can decide whether the subject is authorized to access its resources. On the server side, a naming scheme such as uniform resource names (URNs; RFC 1737) should be used to map subject IDs to the real users efficiently. The notion of groups, which can be a set of users granted the same privilege, is used to reduce administration efforts in allocating authorizations. Permission for users with similar privileges is granted or denied to the entire group, instead of applying it separately to each user. Nevertheless, administrators should be aware of the potential weaknesses that can be introduced if a user is included simultaneously in groups having different privileges. Name-based access control can become a hard task to manage, especially when the number of clients is high or growing at a fast rate. Moreover, users are forced to manage a lot of IDs, especially when every server they are connecting to uses its own ID database.

To overcome these shortcomings, some solutions that rely on centralized authorities to verify user identity have been developed. Microsoft Passport represents such a solution. It allows a user to access sites that have implemented the Passport Single Sign-In using a single sign-in (SSI) name and password. Other solutions such as Terminal Access Controller Access Control System Plus (TACACS+) and Remote Authentication Dial-In User Service (RADIUS) rely on the use of authentication services. They receive the user ID from the server and send it back to make the authorization decision (e.g., accept, reject, or change password).

Separate management of user IDs requires that each site that stores user IDs deploy efficient security mechanisms. However, although such approaches are more practical than the distributed approaches, they can lead to damages in the case where a user gained access to the user IDs database.

Access Control and Scripts

The use of scripts is a suitable solution to strengthen and customize the access-control mechanism previously presented. Suppose a server provides name-based access control to its users, and the users have specified at the time of their subscription whether they are connecting from a laptop or a desktop computer. To enforce the reliability of the access-control mechanism, a script can be implemented to record the IP addresses of the machines from which the connections are initiated. After verifying the user login and password, the script checks the stored mobility attribute of the user and its current IP address. If the attribute is set to false information, this could mean that an intruder has stolen the user account and used it to connect with a spoofed source IP address. Therefore, the script can initiate countermeasures such as sending an e-mail to the system administrator, logging the observation, or locking the account. Obviously, these measures are commonly implemented in reactive intrusion-detection systems, but they can be used to provide efficient access control. Scripts play an important role in enriching the authorization rules needed to maintain access control.

Certificate-Based Access Control

X.509 certificates provide support for access control because they bind the owner identity, a private key, and the related public key (the private key is kept secret by its owner). A trusted certificate authority digitally signs each issued certificate after appending a set of attributes, including the user identity. The access control is then performed by first ensuring that the user mentioned in the certificate owns the corresponding private key. This is done typically by asking the user to digitally sign a message with its private key. Once the message is received, the server accesses the user certificate and starts signature verification. This includes validation of the certificate, decryption of the signature, and computation of the message hash. To test the validity of a user's certificate, a set of checks has to be performed, including the certificate integrity (using the public key of the certificate issuer), the chain of trust (i.e., if the signature really has been issued by the certificate authority, and if the certificate authority is trusted), and the certificate's expiration time.

Even if all the quoted tests have succeeded, the certificate can be meaningless if the certificate issuer has revoked it (for reasons that are described in RFC 3280). To determine the certificate status, the server typically downloads a certificate revocation list (CRL) that has a list containing the serial numbers of all revoked certificates. This list is issued periodically to enable clients to access up-to-date information. All the certificates and the CRL are made available through public directories, generally using Lightweight Directory Access Protocol (LDAP) or Web servers.

Despite its high level of subject identity assurance, certificate usage requires the availability of a whole infrastructure (LDAP server, certificate authority, revocation lists) to guarantee the availability of the publication service. The use of CRL technology implies that there is always a short period between revocation requests and CRL publication during which the certificate holder might still use its private key and temper access control. Also, processing a CRL generates problems in terms of server resources and traffic usage because CRLs can become very large. To overcome this limitation, the use of Online

Certificate Status Protocol (OCSP) has emerged. A user sends a request for certificate status to the OCSP server to receive the certificate status instantaneously. Another security issue regarding the use of public-key infrastructure is that a certificate's validity is dependent on all its parents' issuers, including intermediate certificate authorities and the root certificate authority.

Certificate-based access control is useful to authenticate users. It also can be used to authorize the execution of actions within the server. To state whether a user has the required rights to perform an action, one idea is to append the user rights, roles, and authorization information to the certificate based on the X.509 version 3 extensions. But this is quite undesirable because the authorization information, user identity, and user public key do not have the same life duration. Furthermore, the certificate issuer might not have enough information on the authorizations accorded to users. Another solution to this problem proposes a role-based access-control infrastructure using X.509 public-key certificates and attributes certificates that can be used to store users' roles and authorizations (Zhou & Meinel, 2004).

GUIDELINES FOR IMPROVING SERVER SECURITY

As outlined previously, securing servers is subject to many challenges. Thus, administrators need a set of guidelines to follow to simplify their tasks and reduce the likelihood of introducing potential security weaknesses. The content of this section is written with the help of many references available on Web sites belonging to CERT, the SANS Institute, and the University of Minnesota.

Server-Side Security Practices

Effective security practices involve managing accounts, hardening installations, fixing vulnerabilities, configuring files and directories access permissions, managing logs, and performing backups.

Account Management

Unauthorized users can put the security of the server's information in danger if they successfully access it. To avoid such circumstances, administrators should carefully consider account management, including the following points:

- Because the security policy states that only authorized users can access server resources, the server should be configured to authenticate all users who attempt to access it.
- The security policy should describe under what conditions user accounts are created, modified, and deleted. Refer to a set of administrative practices to specify requirements regarding users' usage of passwords. For example, they should be prohibited from exposing their passwords.
- A password policy should be stated and enforced. It includes rules related to password length, complexity (generally, alphanumeric and special characters are recommended), aging, possibility of reuse, and timetables

access. Such parameters depend heavily on the context and frequency of the server use, account types (e.g., administrator accounts have different lifetimes than user accounts), and risk associated with password compromise.

- Default accounts and groups should be renamed or disabled whenever possible to avoid their use by intruders. Moreover, old, unused, and unnecessary accounts should be disabled, if not deleted.
- Accounts that do not require an interactive login (e.g., user mail accounts) should not be permitted to get a command shell.
- Assembling users into appropriate groups and assigning group-based privileges should be used whenever possible, particularly when the number of users per group is important. Particular attention should be paid to users who belong to distinct groups.
- Server administrators should be ensured that the password policy is followed by users when they change their passwords. Password auditing tools or cracks can be used by administrators if it is permitted by the security policy to ensure password robustness.
- Whenever possible, system account settings should be configured to reject passwords that are not in accordance with the password policy and deny login and lock the account after a predefined number of failed attempts.
- Users should be requested through formal procedures to lock access to the system whenever they leave it and configure their system to be locked after an idle period of time.
- An administrator account should be used only if necessary. In the case where different administrative accounts are used, they should be named differently to better distinguish each administrator activity. Moreover, default administrator accounts should be renamed whenever possible.
- Anonymous access should be restricted whenever possible. Guest accounts should be renamed and, if possible, disabled.

Secure Installation and Vulnerability Fixing
To cope with the occurrence of new vulnerabilities on operating systems and applications, vendors and security groups release patches, fixes, and updates. The following practices can help secure servers:

- Security updates on production servers should follow a policy that defines their periodicity, the required testing phases, the documentation of these operations, and the required user privileges.
- Administrators should install and run up-to-date versions of operating systems and applications. They should use packages that are actively supported by their providers for security updates and vulnerability fixing.
- Only needed services should be installed on servers; unnecessary features must be disabled, and configurations should respond to security constraints. Moreover, any required feature should be limited, and all recommended patches have to be applied.

- Applications and services should run with the lowest required privileges to reduce potential damages if they are compromised.
- Necessary and unsecured services such as file transfer protocol (FTP), telnet, and simple network management protocol (SNMP) should be replaced by more secure services. For example, *SSH* can be used instead of *rlogin* and *ftps* instead of *ftp*.
- Often, vendors provide update utilities that automatically connect, download, and install packages. Because these utilities do not usually cope with administrator privileges, they should be disabled whenever it is possible to download and install updates manually. Such prevention reduces potential damages if a server is compromised.
- Up-to-date scanners of vulnerabilities should be actively used to find the latest common and most critical vulnerabilities. Examples of scanners include IIS Internet Scanner and Nessus.
- A risk-mitigation strategy is highly recommended to implement to study the possible attack scenarios and reduce the cost relative to the security measures that can be applied against threats.
- In the case where a trust relationship is defined between servers, configurations should be reviewed carefully. An intruder can use the trust relationship to access another host from a compromised host.

Files and Directories Access Permission
The following practices help set the most accurate file and directory permissions to reduce security breaches and maintain integrity and secrecy:

- The installed operating system (OS) should be provided with a secure file system, and the disk partitions should be formatted using the most secure available file formats (e.g., NTFS for Windows systems and EXT3 for Linux).
- File and folder permissions as well as access should be configured with the lowest required rights (e.g., public scripts should be configured to be modified by their owner only, and the log files permissions should be set to append only whenever possible).
- Access to files and directories storing OS configurations should be restricted to administrators only, with even the read privilege revoked from others.
- Attention should be given to access-control inheritance when creating or appending new files and directories. The best way is to let access-control propagate down directory hierarchies.
- When the relationship between users is complex or when secrecy must be maintained, encryption should be used to protect sensitive data.
- File-sharing services should be disabled whenever possible. File and folder shares should be reduced whenever unneeded, and access permissions should be configured to maximum security levels. File owners should know how the system should behave to satisfy local-access and shared-access permissions.
- Remote registry access should be minimized, restricted, and generally allowed only for administration purposes.

- In UNIX and Linux file systems, the use of *suid* files should be refused, unless required. An audit of these files should be periodically performed.

Logging Configuration

Managing logs effectively should help administrators detect signs of intrusion, evaluate system performance, and detect faults. The following practices are recommended:

- Security policy should define explicitly the use of logs, their period of availability (depending on their category), and the relevant responsibilities. Logged activities should include administrative operations (e.g., account creations), successful and unsuccessful connections, remote and local connections information (e.g., IP address, requested service), authentication information (e.g., used account name, failed or successful attempts), and unsuccessful file accesses.
- If permitted by the logging mechanism, the level of detail should be set so that only useful information is recorded. Log files as well as their locations should be protected by defining the most restrictive access permissions to prevent them from being illegitimately modified. The access to the utilities that can modify these logs should be restricted.
- Public servers such as Web and FTP servers should maintain logs relative to user activities, including the rejected and dropped requests.
- Server logs should be rotated periodically to avoid the saturation or the alteration of system resources. If permitted by the logging mechanism, the log file content should be split into many fragments in a way that makes it easy to find any record inside the log.
- Whenever required, log files can be compressed to save storage space.
- Log files should be stored into a secure location. Keeping logs locally is not secure because they can be altered whenever the server is compromised. It is worthwhile to transfer them securely to a more secure place. The use of remote logging (e.g., *Syslog* service) is very helpful.
- Security personnel should be trained to review server logs on a regular basis and ensure that logs are recorded in accordance with the security policy and any time it is needed (e.g., in cases where an anomaly is perceived).
- The system clock should provide the correct time to ensure accurate results when correlating the different log outputs issued from different network sources. Protocols such as Network Time Protocol (NTP) can be used to synchronize server clocks.
- Procedures to handle situations where breaches are detected should be prepared in advance. Moreover, security personnel should be trained to use forensic-data-collection mechanisms and extract evidences and preserve them from being altered.
- Server security administrators should periodically conduct a security audit to evaluate the security practices and locate potential weaknesses in configurations. To do so, administrators can use software to correlate and analyze server logs and should rely on their intuition and skills to find anomalies.

Performing Backups

Providing a service without developing backup and restoration plans can be inappropriate. The following practices enable administrators to perform efficient backups and help them restore the system state after the occurrence of critical incidents:

- Administrators should create a backup and restoration plan based on the following queries: what (file identification), where (backup media), when (backup periodicity), and how (type of backup) to backup.
- Scheduled backup creation should be constrained by the required time to perform the backup, the storage space needed, and the complexity of restoring files from backups.
- Server administrators should be informed about their responsibility regarding backups and restoration activities.
- Backups should be performed periodically in accordance with the defined schedule.
- Performing backups locally on the server does not require additional security mechanisms to protect data that traverse the network. But it increases the needed effort because it requires managing different storage media at each workstation. If backups are centralized, secrecy and integrity of the transferred files should be guaranteed. Appropriate tools (e.g., Amanda and Arkeia) should be used to help implement the defined backup scheme.
- After the creation of backup files on given media, the files should remain encrypted and the media should be documented along with the restoration guidelines.
- A copy of the backup tools should be stored offline because they cannot be trusted after the server that stores them is targeted by security attacks.
- The set of media as well as backup and recovery processes should be tested periodically to enhance the restoration ability and detect potential backup deficiencies.
- Servers that provide highly available services and whose content changes often should be fully replicated on a backup machine that can be plugged into the network directly in case an incident occurs.
- Reuse of backup media outside the backup activity should be done prior to their secure deletion.

Effective Use of Security Software

Relying on the set of built-in system tools and services is insufficient to guarantee an acceptable system security level. Supplementing the protection mechanisms with additional security solutions as described here is essential:

- It is highly recommended to install up-to-date antivirus software with filtering capabilities on servers that are used to store user data content (e.g., public FTP servers, e-mail servers, and Web servers with personal user directories). In cases where the security policy allows the server to initiate connections, the server should be configured to periodically look up updates on virus signatures and detection algorithms. In other cases, a security administrator should perform this role.

- The real-time capturing of state features (e.g., system performance, processes, and files) and the monitoring of any potential deviation of the expected behavior should be implemented. This includes the use of host-based or application-based intrusion detection systems (IDSs). Moreover, network-based IDSs should be installed on the most sensitive network segments to monitor the network traffic for suspicious events. It should generate alerts and take a snapshot of any suspicious activity as soon as it happens.

- Because network firewalls are not able to prevent local attacks (those issued from internal users or from compromised neighborhood servers), the deployment of local server firewalls is recommended. These firewalls should be configured with a total understanding of legitimate server traffic.

- Reactive IDSs (e.g., snort-inline) can complement the set of protection mechanisms because they can take countermeasures on the detection of intrusions (e.g., active connections killing and router ACL updating). They should be used carefully to prevent DoS attacks. In all cases, the set of countermeasures should follow an a priori response policy (e.g., when, what, and how long a countermeasure is applied).

- The use of integrity-checking software should complement the intrusion-detection effort because it can be applied to static content (e.g., configuration files, administrative binary commands) to detect changes. Use integrity-checking software carefully to avoid confusing legitimate and malicious file modification.

- Remote privileged access to the server should be reduced as much as possible. When used, the access should be strictly controlled using IP filtering tools, utilities, and encryption. Secure Shell (SSH) and virtual private networks (VPNs) can be used to encrypt the user session traffic (including login and password) and provide lower-level traffic encryption, respectively.

- Authentication techniques should be used on the server based on server activity. For example, usually a public Web server does not require the same level of authentication as a remote administration server does. Virtual local area networks should be used whenever possible because they represent another type of efficient access control that can be implemented in networks.

- Servers should implement data encryption for sensitive data to avoid illegal reading and retrieving if the server is compromised. For example, a Web server that uses X.509 certificates should store its corresponding private key privately in a ciphered form (e.g., PKCS#1).

Infrastructure Countermeasures

Protecting an information system by applying the strongest security measures can be insufficient to guarantee that once the security policy is violated, an efficient and accurate incident response can be undertaken

quickly. Mandia and Prosise (2003) defined an incident-response methodology and described a set of goals. We describe a series of considerations to be made prior to a server incident occurrence so that administrators can minimize the impact of the incident, determine the relevant causes and effects, track intruders, provide accurate reports, and finally promote prevention and detection:

- The first consideration relates to host security. The set of used applications, services, and operating systems should have been well patched and verified against potential security exploits. All supplementary security functions such as logging, filtering, wrapping, and controlling access need to be implemented even if they are repetitive. It is also important to decide from the beginning which protocols and activity to log.

- The second consideration relates to the network. Some network-based security schemes measure the adequacy of countermeasures when they are installed. The network architecture and topology configured should be favorable to monitoring. For example, it is better to install a Linux Syslog server in the internal network stub to avoid the destruction of log content if an intruder takes control of the public network.

- The third consideration relates to network protocols. Protocols that are more secure, in the sense that they provide an accurate representation of participant identity and activity, should be used because they present more meaningful proof of intruder activity and identity.

- The fourth consideration relates to the expert team qualified to perform incident response and forensic investigation. Preparing the team should involve considering the needed hardware and software, appropriate policies, operating procedures, and staff training.

- Finally, the fifth consideration relates to the legal environment. Any security measure should be governed by law because any omission can expose the person responsible for server security to legal repercussions. This is important because it is essential to find the proof for law-enforcement agencies to track intruders. For example, if the country laws state that a lawful electronic certificate involves only X.509 certificates, an authentication server that uses SPKI certificates will be unable to prove the identity of the user that has been accepted by the system.

ADVANCED ISSUES

Various advanced issues present challenges for server-side security, including remote authoring, transaction security, and server protection from user-side holes. Because the latter issue can be considered as part of the former issues, we describe in the following subsection the remote authoring and transaction security challenges.

Remote Authoring and Administration

Remote authoring is the ability to write and store a resource (e.g., HTML file, database entry) in the storage area of a remote server. This process can initiate a distributed interactivity between users and servers. Distributed authoring on the Web requires scaling the content across the resources, users, and transaction rates. Supporting these requirements can demand a decentralized repository with an easy-to-use, standard, multiuser, and multiversion interface. Access is required based on open and non-proprietary document formats. Hypertext transfer protocol (HTTP) fulfills some of these goals and requirements as a remote procedure call protocol. It is stateless and relatively secure. However, HTTP is not sufficient to support remote authoring on the Web. One important limitation is the HTTP POST method, which can be used to invoke any operation on the server. The POST method ends up being a security hole through which any operation can be executed. Trying to analyze POST message bodies to determine which operations are being performed is extremely difficult.

Therefore, HTTP provides no means for organizing the complex content that is typical of a Web server supporting multiple applications. It does not provide any way to link multilevel security documents. The solution is to improve HTTP to satisfy remote authoring needs. Web-distributed authoring and versioning (Web-DAV) is an example of a solution that provides new methods to extend HTTP functionality. Despite its advantages, HTTP does not accommodate easily adding new methods because interactions between headers and methods should be explicitly defined. However, server security and access control benefit from adding new methods.

Server-Side Transactions Security

To process transactions securely, a server might need to be able to evaluate credentials and set up credential acceptance policies; it should also be able to export parts of its acceptance policies to users who ask for explanations. In addition, the server administrator needs to have a clear understanding of the services the server provides and the roles a user could assume when accessing the services. The response to a transaction depends on the role of the user, who is initiating the transaction.

When a set of credentials is submitted with a transaction (or request for a service), the server might need to decrypt, parse, and determine whether a credential has been revoked by its issuer before processing the related transaction. This can induce a translation of the credential formats into the internal language used for reasoning by the server.

The translated credentials along with the classification of a transaction under process might need to be submitted to a knowledge base describing the server's credential acceptance policy. Often, the set of eligible roles can be passed because it is to the server's application. It is beyond the scope of this chapter to discuss several important issues, including the authentication of a transaction initiator to one of the individuals mentioned in the credential, role conflict, credential translation, and policy explanation.

GLOSSARY

CGI Wrapper A script that prevents users of common gateway interface (CGI) scripts from compromising the security of the Web server. This is usually achieved by running a series of security checks on the invoked script, restricting the script access, or even denying the script access to the user's home directory.
Common Gateway Interface (CGI) An interface between the Web server and external programs called gateways. It enables a server to return dynamic Web content by calling programs written in any language and sending their output back to the browser.
EXT3 A file system common to Linux that adds speed, reliability, and support for large drives in comparison to old UNIX file systems. It adds journaling to enhance recovery after crashes or data loss.
Network Address Translation (NAT) A protocol that enables networking resources to use a set of Internet Protocol (IP) addresses for internal traffic and a second set for external traffic.
Server-Side Include (SSI) Enables dynamic Web pages to be created by inserting hypertext markup language (HTML) comment commands within static HTML files. Theses commands are processed by the server when Web pages are requested by the client. Can be used to call external programs such as common gateway interface (CGI) scripts.
Simple Network Management Protocol (SNMP) It provides information exchange between two SNMP entities about configuration and resource status.
Traffic Shaping A mechanism that adjusts the network-flow characteristics to guarantee performance and quality of service (e.g., avoid overload) while meeting the requirements of the server, network, and resources.
Uniform Resource Name (URN) It represents a name assigned to an Internet resource. URNs are maintained using naming services and are designed to have a long lifetime.
Virtual Local Area Network (VLAN) This concept is defined in RFC 3069. It represents a subgroup of network computers (including any network hardware) that behaves as if they are connected to the same wire, although in fact they belong to different physical networks.

CROSS REFERENCES

See *Access Control: Principles and Solutions; Client-Side Security; Computer Security Incident Response Teams (CSIRTs); Protecting Web Sites; Security and Web Quality of Service.*

REFERENCES

Bellovin, S. M. (1989). Security problems in the TCP/IP protocol suite. *Computer Communications Review,* 2(19), 32–48.
Bellovin, S. M. (2000). *ICMP traceback messages—Internet draft.* Retrieved June 8, 2004, from http://www.research.att.com/~smb/papers/draft-bellovin-itrace-00.txt

Burke, J. (2003). *Windows forensic how-to: Incident response plan for abuse of corporate assets*. Retrieved June 2005, from http://www.giac.org/practical/GSEC/Joe_Burke_GSEC.pdf

Canavan, S. (2003). An information security policy development guide for large companies. *Information Security Reading Room*.

CERT. (2000). *Configure computers for file backups*. Retrieved June 10, 2004, from http://www.cert.org/security-improvement/practices/p071.html

CERT. (2001a). *Configure computers for user authentication*. Retrieved June 10, 2004, from http://www.cert.org/security-improvement/practices/p069.html

CERT. (2001b). *Keep operating systems and applications software up to date*. Retrieved June 10, 2004, from http://www.cert.org/security-improvement/practices/p067.html

CERT. (2001c). *Manage logging and other data collection mechanisms*. Retrieved June 10, 2004, from http://www.cert.org/security-improvement/practices/p092.html

Chen, H., & Wagner, D. (2002, November 18–22). MOPS: An infrastructure for examining security properties of software. *ACM Conference on Computer and Communications Security (CCS '02)*.

Cowan, C., Beattie, S., Kroah-Hartman, G., Pu, C., Wagle, P., & Gligor, V. (2000). SubDomain: Parsimonious server security. *14th USENIX Systems Administration*.

DaCosta, D., Dahn, C., Mancoridis, S., & Prevelakis, V. (2003). Characterizing the "security vulnerability likelihood" of software functions. *International Conference on Software Maintenance (ICSM '03)*.

Foster, J. F. (2002). *Type qualifiers: Lightweight specifications to improve software quality*. Unpublished doctoral dissertation, University of California, Berkeley.

ITSS Information Security Services. (2003). Denial of service in Cisco IOS caused by IPv4 packets. Retrieved June 5, 2004, from http://securecomputing.stanford.edu/alerts/cisco-ios-17jul2003.html

Jamjoom, H., & Reumann, J. (2000). *QGuard: Protecting Internet servers from overload* (Tech. Rep. No. CSE-TR-427-00). University of Michigan.

Kamthan, P. (1999). CGI security: Better safe than sorry. Retrieved June 5, 2004, from http://tech.irt.org/articles/js184/

Kargl, F., Maier, J., & Weber, F. (2000). Protecting Web servers from distributed denial of service attacks. *International World Wide Web Conference*, 514–524.

Kraft, R. (2002). Research and design issues in access control for network services on the Web. *The 3rd International Conference on Internet Computing, 3,* 542–548.

Li, F. Y., & Stol, N. (2002). QoS provisioning using traffic shaping and policing in 3rd-generation wireless networks. *IEEE Wireless Communications and Networking Conference (WCNC), 17*(21), 139–143.

Lowe, G. (1995). An attack on the Needham-Schroeder public-key authentication protocol. *Information Processing Letters, 56*(3), 131–133.

Mandia, K., & Prosise, C. (2003). Introduction to the incident response process. In *Incident Response and Computer Forensics* (2nd ed., pp. 11–32). New York: McGraw-Hill Osborne Media.

McClure, S., Scambray, J., & Kurtz, G. (2003). *Hacking exposed: Network security secrets and solutions* (4th ed.). New York: McGraw-Hill Osborne Media.

Microsoft Corporation. (2004). *Microsoft Security Bulletin MS03-051. Buffer overrun in Microsoft FrontPage Server Extensions could allow code execution*. Retrieved June 8, 2004, from http://www.microsoft.com/technet/security/bulletin/MS03-051.mspx

Needham, R. M., & Schroeder, M. D. (1978). Using encryption for authentication in large networks of computers. *Communications of the ACM, 21*(12), 993–999.

NHSnet. (2004). Information security policy. Retrieved June 5, 2004, from http://www.nhsia.nhs.uk/nhsnet/pages/connecting/hospices/High_Level_InfoPolicy_PCT.pdf.

NMRC. (2003). The hack FAQ: Web browser as attack tool. Retrieved June 7, 2004, from http://www.nmrc.org/pub/faq/hackfaq/hackfaq-09.html

Obaidat, M. S., & Sadoun, B. (1997). Verification of computer users using keystroke dynamics (Part B). *IEEE Transactions on Systems, Man, and Cybernetics, 27*(2), 261–269.

Obaidat, M. S., & Sadoun, B. (1999). Keystroke dynamics based identification. In Anil Jain et al. (Eds.), *Biometrics: Personal identification in networked society* (pp. 213–229). MA: Kluwer Academic Publishers.

Savage, S., Wetherall, D., Karlin, A., & Anderson, T. (2000). Practical network support for IP traceback. *2000 ACM SIGCOMM Conference*, 295–306.

Snoeren, A. C., Partridge, C., Sanchez, L. A., Jones, C. E., Tchakountio, F., Schwartz, B., Kent, S. T., & Strayer, W. T. (2002). Single-packet IP traceback. *IEEE/ACM Transactions on Networking (ToN), 10*(6), 721–734.

Song, D. X., & Perrig, A. (2001). Advanced and authenticated marking schemes for IP traceback. *IEEE Infocomm*, 878–886.

Syed, M. A. (2002). NT users can bypass password changing policy via IIS. Retrieved June 6, 2004, from http://www.securiteam.com/windowsntfocus/5NP082A6KM.html.

Thiagarajan, V. (2003). *Information security management—BS 7799.2:2002—audit check list*. Retrieved June 11, 2004, from http://www.sans.org/score/checklists/ISO_17799_checklist.pdf

University of Minnesota, Office of Information Technology. (2003). *Server installation security guidelines*. Retrieved June 10, 2004, from http://www1.umn.edu/oit/security/ServerInstall.pdf

Vulnerability Information Center. (2004). *Samba smbd buffer overflow and race condition vulnerabilities*. Retrieved June 5, 2004, from http://www3.ca.com/securityadvisor/vulninfo/Vuln.aspx?ID=7286

Weber, H. A. (2003). Role-based access control: The NIST solution. Retrieved June 9, 2004, from http://www.giac.org/practical/GSEC/Hazen_Weber_GSEC.pdf

Welsh, M., & Culler, D. (2002). Overload management as a fundamental service design primitive. *Tenth ACM SIGOPS European Workshop*.

Wood, M. (2003). *WebDAV buffer overflow vulnerability revisited*. Retrieved June 5, 2004, from http://www.frame4.com/php/modules.php?name=News&file=printpdf&sid=468

Yao, W. T. (2003). *Trust management for widely distributed systems*. Unpublished doctoral dissertation, Jesus College, University of Cambridge, England.

Zhou, W., & Meinel, C. (2004). Implement role based access control with attribute certificates. *IEEE International Conference on Advanced Communication Technology (ICACT2004)*, 536–541.

Security Policy Guidelines

Mohamed Hamdi, *National Digital Certification Agency, Tunisia*
Noureddine Boudriga, *National Digital Certification Agency, Tunisia*
Mohammad S. Obaidat, *Monmouth University, NJ, USA*

INTRODUCTION

Because computer system technologies are rapidly spreading from academic research to industrial applications, many security issues have been raised. This need for security is driven by the increasingly large proportion of losses caused to the enterprises by various security incidents. Security attacks may disturb the operation of the system, entail loss of secrets and privacy, and become a risk to the national security and economy. Several studies, such as the CSI/FBI survey (2004) and Campbell, Gordon, Loeb, & Zhou (2003) have analyzed the consequences of digital attacks on representative sets of organizations. It has been shown that, in most cases, severe economic losses result from these adverse events. Many organizations already had some protection mechanisms at the moment they were attacked. However, they are not 100% immune from possible damages caused by such attacks. Effectively, most security threats are not due to the lack of security equipments, but instead are due to breaches at the planning level. Clearly, there should be a strategic security plan for each organization. In fact, security controls are rarely acquired within the frame of a global security program.

To alleviate this problem, enterprises should consider computer system security as a means to achieve their business objectives. Hence, it should be subjected to a documentation activity just as is done for normal production processes. Strategies, policies, procedures, and guidelines should regulate the security management program.

Obviously, to reduce the security risks that threaten the communication infrastructure, the aforementioned documentation should be based on a set of security principles. This chapter attempts to cover various aspects related to security policy (SP), which is the kernel of security documentation.

Security Policy Fundamentals

The purpose of this section is to provide the basic concepts of several key considerations related to the SP. More precisely, we define the SP from the perspective that security rules can apply at many levels of the information system. Then, the objectives and the requirements that an SP should fulfill are presented. Finally, various key considerations and practical guidelines related to the SP components and the development process are discussed.

Security Policy Definition

Finding a precise meaning for this term turns out to be a very arduous task because it is used to refer to numerous disparate aspects of information systems' security. The following examples give an idea of the different ways an SP can be defined depending on the context. The quoted sentences have been taken verbatim from the source documents so that the reader can concretely note this ambiguity.

1. Information system SP: For an organization that owns a set of networked assets, the SP constitutes the core of the security plan, which entails the design and the implementation of security measures as well as documentation of security incidents. The SP is the foundation for a security program that addresses the business needs of the organization. It should reflect the enterprise's strategic approach to coping with the security risks that characterize the environment. In Hare

(2002, pp. 353), the SP has been defined as a "high level statement that reflects organization's belief related to information security." The major purpose of the SP is to select the appropriate security solutions to face those threat events while ensuring that the cost of protecting the infrastructure does not exceed the benefit it provides. In business jargon, the rules of the SP should guarantee a return on investment (ROI).

2. Operating system (OS) SP: Because of the numerous security threats that exploit weaknesses at the OS level, a set of protection mechanisms should be implemented to plug up such vulnerabilities. The totality of the protection mechanisms related to an OS is called the trusted computing base (TCB). They concern the various resources of the computer system (e.g., hardware, software, processes). The most relevant example consists of the access control policy, which is enforced by secure OSs to protect the objects they handle. Obviously, for consistency and completeness purposes, those mechanisms should abide by a set of rules, which form the SP. The reference monitor is an entity that mediates accesses to objects by subjects. Among those accesses, only those that conform to the SP are allowed. The reference monitor basically guarantees that the OS respects several predefined security principles such as least privilege and continuous protection.

3. Key management SP: To establish a secure tunnel using the IPSec protocol suite, two end points should agree upon a set of mutually acceptable cryptographic parameters called security associations (SA). These security parameters are managed according to local security policies, which are set in each end node. For example, when creating a new SA in order to modify an older one, "deletion of the old SA is dependent on local security policy." Besides, a standard has been recently developed to administrate IPSec security policies; it defined the concept of IP security policy (IPSP).

These examples lead us to discuss the various SP types. It is noteworthy that rather than being conflicting, these definitions present the same concept from different angles. The attentive reader would have remarked that the first definition, related to information systems security, provides the broadest view in the sense that both OS security and the usage of secure protocols can be seen as specific components of the global security program. In our sense, the difficulty of defining an SP stems from the basic fact that security is related to many organizational aspects. For example, from a human resource perspective, the SP serves "to inform all individuals operating within an organization on how they should behave related to a specific topic" (Tudor, 2001). From a risk management point of view, "policies should be concerned with what assets to protect and why they need to be protected" (Canavan, 2001, pp. 239).

To unify all of these views, the SP can be defined as a set of rules that determines how a particular set of assets should be secured. This definition can in fact be applied to represent all SPs without delving into details concerning the context and the language to adopt (natural language or machine language).

Therefore, the SP is a multifaceted concept that can effectively be defined in various manners. Security specialists who addressed SPs mentioned this aspect. Most of them have agreed that "a suite of policy documents rather than a single policy document works better in a large corporate environment" (Canavan, 2003, p. 5). In fact, splitting the SP into fragments has multiple advantages:

1. All SP audiences can be addressed efficiently.
2. All security requirements can be addressed.
3. The security properties (e.g., confidentiality, integrity) of the various SP portions can be preserved more easily.

More concretely, a classification scheme should be considered to ensure that multiple policies are developed to address the same security context.

SP Classes

Many SP classifications have been proposed in the literature. The most relevant ones are discussed in this subsection. As it has been pointed out, SPs can be classified according to their target audience, the security issues they treat, or their sensitivity (from a security point of view). Examples of such classifications are given here to highlight the importance, or even the necessity, of SP fragmentation.

1. Audience-based classification: Canavan (2003) argued that policies should be structured according to a hierarchical system with respect to the structure of roles. He proposed three policy types, which are governing policy, technical policy, and end-user policy.
2. Issue-based classification: Ensuring the security of a system is proportionally difficult to its complexity. Requirements related to security are defined with respect to the functionalities that the system provides. Depending on the assets to protect, some issues can be emphasized more than others. For example, an Internet service provider's (ISP) major need is to guarantee access to network services and to respect contracts, laws, and ethics. For this reason, ISPs concentrate their SPs on access control, authentication, and availability. However, because the data structures they handle are simple (compared with other types of organizations), developing an information classification policy (ICP) requires less effort. On the opposite end of the scale, a certification authority (CA) manages a richer data set. Cryptographic keys, digital certificates, and revocation lists are just examples of these data. Consequently, information classification becomes more complex than in the former case (ISPs). In the following, we attempt to list some of the security issues that would need a separate policy. The information security policy and the access control policy are discussed in particular detail. The remaining policies are discussed in later sections.
   a. Information classification policy (ICP): The amount of data managed by a typical organization is so large that security controls cannot be applied on a per-object basis. Consequently, the data to be handled should be divided into a finite set of classes so that the security measures can affect a whole class of

objects instead of being applied to each individual piece of information. This classification can be performed according to many criteria, such as critical level and usage. Determining the critical level of a piece of information consists of assessing the amount of loss that could result from the violation of one of its security properties (i.e., confidentiality, integrity, and availability). For example, the documentation of a product, which is under development, is of utmost importance because if accessed by a competitor, the position of the organization would be affected. At this stage, it is important to point out that classification should not depend solely on the content of a piece of data, but also on the type of the enterprise. Effectively, sensitivity levels must be assigned on the basis of organization's requirements against the needs for confidentiality, integrity, or availability. This means that two identical records may have distinct classifications in two different environments. For instance, personal information (e.g., name, address) pertaining to employee X does not require specific controls when stored in the database of his employer. Nonetheless, if X is client of bank Y, its records must be classified as private because they are protected by laws.

b. Access control policy (ACP): Once the sensitive objects have been determined and classified, measures to ensure a convenient protection should be defined. To this purpose, an ACP is created. An ACP is generally built around three basic activities: (a) identifying and authenticating users, (b) managing credentials (e.g., passwords, cryptographic keys), and (c) enforcing the application of good practices (such as least privileges and dual control). Of course, the ACP is strong related to the ICP. The nature of authentication credentials required to access a particular object is in fact determined by the object's classification. Authentication mechanisms customary are grouped into three types: (a) knowledge-based authentication, (b) token-based authentication, and (c) characteristic-based authentication. For example, a password may be sufficient to protect ordinary files on a user machine. However, private keys used to sign digital documents should be kept on smart cards or cryptographic tokens to prevent those keys from being stolen. Practically, two main approaches can be followed to build an ACP: (a) discretionary access control, where the owner of data determines the objects that are allowed to access the data and the privileges they possess, (b) mandatory access control, where both the owner and the system define the access policy on the basis of subject privilege (or clearance) and subject sensitivity (or classification).

3. Sensitivity-based classification: Gaining knowledge about how a system is protected is often one of the primary goals for an attacker. Thus, the SP itself should be secured in the sense that it should not be accessed by unauthorized entities. This presumes that SP content is divided into pieces, each corresponding to a security level. The most trivial sensitivity-based classification consists of separating internal policies from external policies (Purser, 2004). Policies that address the secure functioning of the production process are internal. Their content should not be published outside the organization. Conversely, external policies are those that are intended to be published to an external audience. This classification can be improved by being more granular. For example, internal policies themselves can be split into many categories depending on the sensitivity of the concerned department.

Security Policy Objectives

An enterprise's for a SP can be driven by various reasons, which depend essentially on the organization's nature and on the context in which it operates. As is outlined in this section, SPs can be directed toward the panoply of need. Thus, fixing a set of objectives to the SP development process would be very hard. However, what would be interesting at this level is to describe a spectrum of potential objectives and show how these can be ranked according to the enterprise characteristics. The objectives that we consider are listed here. They have been divided into two major categories: business-oriented objectives and regulatory objectives.

1. Business-oriented objectives: The reasons for developing and implementing SPs should align with the basic organizational objectives. The benefits of having an SP can be either direct or indirect. Some can be easily assessed in monetary terms (e.g., preventing critical assets from being attacked) whereas the others are abstract (e.g., preserving the reputation of the enterprise). The most important among the business-oriented objectives are as follows:

a. Performing risk management: The measures of the SP should maintain the security of critical components at an acceptable level. In other terms, the SP should help the organization reduce the likelihood or the effects of harmful adverse events. Because perfect security cannot be actually reached, the organization should evaluate the risks that it faces and select the appropriate countermeasures. According to Swanson (1998), some of the main purposes of security plans are to "provide an overview of the security requirements of the system and describe the controls in place or planned for meeting those requirements," which constitute the essence of the risk management process. The SP is then one of the most important deliverables of the risk management cycle.

b. Handling security incidents: The SP should outline the specific actions that would preserve the business activities when a devastating event occurs. This means that the key activities of the organization should not be disrupted by such events. In addition, the critical attacked components should be totally recovered once the event has passed. To this purpose, three SP components should be particularly focused upon: the monitoring policy, the recovery policy, and the forensics policy. These policies address the principal phases of the incident-response process, which are detection, reaction, and investigation. The monitoring policy primarily fixes the metrics used to define the system state. In addition, it defines the mechanisms that differentiate between normal and abnormal states. Attack signatures are also used in this context to detect the occurrence of security threats. The appropriate policy must describe how these signatures are handled (i.e., built, modified, and detected). It is noteworthy that the monitoring policy interferes with some other policies such as the data classification policy and the access control policy. Indeed a high proportion of the information needed to control the system state is sensitive. Consequently, the two policies must be considered when thinking about the means to gather the required data. Log files are among the most relevant examples because they constitute a rich source that provides views on the actions targeting the monitored system. Their integrity (and often confidentiality) should be strictly preserved. Moreover, administrators have to be authenticated conveniently when accessing these files. The recovery policy specifies how responses to security incidents should be conducted. These responses generally break into two categories: automated responses and manual responses. The former class concerns reactions that are mechanically executed by some components of the attacked system to stop the effect of a harmful event or to simply prevent it from happening. The latter category encompasses responses that cannot be triggered without the intervention of a human expert team. The interaction among the different members, including task scheduling and documentation handling, should be addressed in this context. Finally, the forensics policy should set the rules to determine the origin of a specific incident based on rigorous proofs. This requires procedures to gather, analyze, protect, store, and archive digital evidence.

c. Ensuring information integrity, confidentiality, and availability: Information is a crucial concern for successful enterprises. The SP should define the controls that protect appropriately the information assets. The three basic properties that must be preserved to avoid losses are integrity, confidentiality, and availability. Hare (2000) describes the SP as designed around two principal security goals, which are confidentiality and integrity. According to Hare, availability is generally not addressed by SPs. The main reason for this point of view is that only mathematical models of SPs have been studied in this reference. In our sense, none of those properties should be privileged. On one hand, if the integrity of critical business information is altered, several strategic organizational decisions could be seriously biased. On the other hand, if some piece of confidential information is divulged to competitors, the enterprise benefits might be considerably affected. Finally, availability is also a special concern to organizations that provide services through the means of their communication infrastructure. As it has been pointed out previously (handling security incidents), any disruption tackling a component of the information system can result in important losses.

d. Fixing individual responsibilities: The SP is designed so that all individuals operating within the target context know how they are intended to behave when interacting with the information system components. According to RFC 2196 (IETF, 1997), "the main purpose of a security policy is to inform users, staff and managers of their obligatory requirements for protecting technology and information assets." Likewise, according to Swanson (1998), SPs "delineate responsibilities and expected behavior of all individuals who access the system." Employees are asked to conform their actions to the content of the SP. Defining user responsibilities precisely is often useful to protect the enterprise's reputation. For example, if an employee does not act in conformance with the security rules, the organization can easily demonstrate that it did not approve the malicious actions.

2. Regulatory objectives: The security measures of the SP are often developed as a regulatory obligation. Organizations that operate in sensitive sectors are particularly concerned with this issue. In the following, we illustrate our reasoning by using two significant examples: banks and CAs. The former category is accountable for the operations it carries whereas the latter handles various types of critical information (e.g., key pairs, private user information). The following principles have to be respected, among others:

a. Duty of loyalty: When carrying his charges, an employee must place the employer's interest above his own. The relationship between the enterprise and the employee should be based on honesty and faith.

b. Conflict of interest: A conflict of interest corresponds to a situation where the effect of a given action is positive for a category of employees and negative for others. The SP should guarantee that the security rules do not include such discriminatory clauses.

c. Duty of care: The employees should proceed with caution when performing critical tasks. For example, the internal security auditing team should protect adequately the resources to which it has access (e.g., log files, personal information) to avoid divulgating confidential information.

d. Accountability: For accountability, the employees should be uniquely identified and authenticated. When the responsibility of an employee has a legal aspect, which is often the case, the identification and authentication have to be compliant with regulations. More precisely, credentials used for authentication purposes must conform to legislation. For instance, when asymmetric cryptographic keys are of use in this context, SP developers should verify that protocols (e.g., generation protocols, encryption protocols), format, and key lengths do not conflict with the regulatory framework.

Generally, the most important goals that might be achieved by a SP are these:

1. The measures of the SP should maintain the security of critical components at an acceptable level. In other

terms, the SP helps enterprises in reducing the amount of risk related to harmful adverse events.

2. The SP must include some response schemes that make the system recover if an incident occurs (e.g., security attack, natural disaster).

3. The SP must ensure the continuity of the critical processes conducted by an enterprise whenever an incident occurs.

4. Individual responsibilities and consequences must be defined.

Achieving these objectives instills a set of requirements that is presented in the next section.

Policy Requirements

Following the discussion of the previous section, a SP must possess several properties to conform to the aforementioned objectives. The essence of these properties is given in the following.

1. Accountability: Every action performed on the system should leave a trace that can be monitored. This guideline is tightly related to the continuous control of the IT infrastructure. Practically, the most common accountability mechanism consists simply of recording traces into log files. Nonetheless, as resources dedicated to this activity are generally limited (in the sense that they do not allow the capture of all the attributes defining a system state), the security policy should clearly treat the following issues:
   a. Generation: What should be logged? Which are the relevant data with regard to the intrinsic characteristics of the system under analysis?
   b. Analysis: How should the captured information be analyzed to state whether the policy has been violated?
   c. Archiving and storage: The information that accounts for the interaction of various components of the system often has important security levels. Furthermore, archiving is a key consideration because of the fact that traces might be needed a long time after they were captured. Therefore, the security policy must discuss storage procedures, while stressing access control issues.

2. Awareness: Every user of the system should possess the appropriate knowledge to interact with the system in a secure manner. This principle is particularly important because most of the security attacks originate from the inside of the system or exploit vulnerabilities that exist in internal components (e.g., misconfigurations). In addition, awareness considerably reduces unintentional harmful actions. Training programs are often mentioned as a solution that fulfills these needs. However, we believe that a strong involvement of the human resources department is the best alternative for an enterprise to reach an acceptable security level. For instance, some investigations should be conducted to gather if the candidate caused security problems in his past jobs. Likewise, procedures that should apply when an employee leaves an organization have to be included

in the security policy to ensure that the employee no longer possesses his security privileges.

3. Proportionality: Security measures defined in the security policy must match the risks that threaten the system. In other terms, the value of critical information as well as the probability of security attacks (deduced from studying the environment of the system) should be taken into consideration when developing security policy. Obviously, overlooking these aspects would lead to grave consequences because of unrealistic views.

Some other requirements can also be added to the aforementioned ones. The most important, from a security point of view, are completeness and cost-effectiveness. In fact, for a SP to adequately protect a set of resources, all the adverse events that may decrease the security level of the system should be considered and thwarted. On the other hand, the rules of the SP should guarantee cost-effectiveness, meaning that the money and effort spent to reach an acceptable security level should not outweigh the benefit resulting from the application of those rules.

An intriguing point that might have been noticed by the reader is that the two latter objectives are, in some sense, conflicting. A complete SP is rarely cost-effective because the attacks corresponding to a generic environment are so numerous that mitigating all of them cannot be achieved with a reasonable budget. Another problem may arise from the fact that completeness is a utopia that can never be objectively reached. Effectively, the SP development team can never build a zero-uncertainty representation of the environment.

Consequently, the dependency between the SP requirements should be considered when fulfilling the objectives highlighted in the previous subsection. The major requirement for a SP is that it should be flexible enough by partially supporting all the elementary requirements that have been mentioned.

SP Components

To fulfill these objectives and the requirements, the SP should cover some basic security elements. Canavan (2001) cited seven topics that should be addressed by a typical security policy: identification, authentication, access control, availability, confidentiality, integrity, and accountability.

Throughout the foregoing discussion, we found that the three first items can be merged into a single one called access control. Availability is addressed by the BCP and DRP whereas confidentiality and integrity are treated by both the DCP and ACP. Finally, accountability requires a backup policy for audit trails that constitute the output of the ACP.

The constituency of the SP is also a fundamental issue that is closely related to both objectives and requirements. The major components of a good SP should include the following:

1. An access policy: This defines privileges that are granted to system users to protect assets from loss or misuse. It should specify guidelines for external connections and adding new devices or software components to the information system.

2. An *accountability policy:* It defines the responsibilities of users, operation staff, and management. It should specify the audit coverage, operations, and the incident-handling guidelines.

3. An *authentication policy:* It addresses different authentication issues such as the use of operating system (OS) passwords, authentication devices, or digital certificates. It should provide guidelines for use of remote authentication and authentication devices.

4. An *availability policy:* It states a set of users' expectations for the availability of resources. It should describe recovery issues and redundancy of operations during downtime periods.

5. A *maintenance policy:* It describes how the maintenance people are allowed to handle the information technology systems and networks. It should specify how remote maintenance can be performed, if any.

6. A *violations reporting policy:* This describes all types of violations that must be reported and how reports are handled.

RFC 2196 proposes three other components that should be included in the SP (IETF, 1997):

1. A set of *computer technology purchasing guidelines:* These specify required or preferred security features.

2. A *privacy policy:* It defines the barrier that separates the security objectives from the privacy requirements. Ideally, this barrier must not be crossed in either direction.

3. A set of *supporting information:* It provides system users and managers with useful information for each type of policy violation.

Clearly, each of these points corresponds to a category of security services. We believe that this categorization is not the most appropriate scheme mainly because the SP should not necessarily include all of these categories. Therefore, a better approach consists of considering a dynamic set of components that differ from one environment to another. This ensures a better adaptation of the SP constituency to the enterprise needs. More concretely, the SP should be split into sections that represent the categories of the available assets (e.g., Web server, mail server, desktop workstation, private network). Then, a set of security requirements is associated with each asset category depending essentially on its nature. Hence, this reasoning can be seen as a mapping between the asset categories and the security requirements. These requirements can be ranked by order of importance for each asset category. For example, integrity is much more important than privacy and authentication when thinking about the security of a Web server. On the opposite, for a mail server, privacy should be carefully considered to ensure that the selected security measures preserve the secrecy of some private messages (or some message portions) while they are monitored. Moreover, authentication becomes essential in this case to avoid mail-spoofing attacks. To have a more concrete idea about the different security mechanisms that correspond to the most important resource categories, the reader is recommended to refer to the Computer Emergency Response Team (CERT) collection.

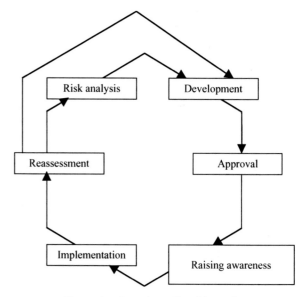

Figure 1: Security policy life cycle.

Obviously, more sophisticated approaches to determine the SP constituency can be evolved. However, the main point to retain from this discussion is that the SP components should be dynamically determined according to a sound methodology rather than being statically defined.

SECURITY POLICY LIFE CYCLE

Developing a security policy should be done according to several steps that constitute a life cycle as represented in Figure 1.

These main steps are briefly explained:

1. Risk analysis: It includes essentially a mission statement, asset evaluation, and threat assessment. It is worth mentioning that some parts of the SP can be written in this step. In fact, the risk analyst needs some rules to assign a security level to each resource, meaning that the data classification policy should have already been constructed at this level.

2. Development: This step consists of selecting the security rules that best fit the requirements of the organization. The SP development team must use convenient languages to model and validate the SP. The main characteristic of this step is that it is performed progressively to move from an abstract representation toward a more concrete one.

3. Approval: It relies on a multidisciplinary committee that validates the security policy. At every layer (i.e., abstraction degree) of the development process, the SP should be validated against (a) the upper layer and (b) the security objectives.

4. Raising awareness: This ensures that the security policy is accessible to everyone who is authorized to access it. Thus, the SP is published correctly and every user of the secured system must possess the skills that are suitable to his or her responsibilities.

5. Implementation: It enforces the application of the security policy. During this step, operational and technical

controls are put in place. Operational controls are security mechanisms that are essentially implemented and executed by the users themselves, whereas technical controls include the automated security countermeasures.

6. Reassessment: It guarantees a continuous monitoring of the security policy through scheduled revisions and analyses. This process is essential to practically test the efficiency of the SP because new threats can occur.

Nevertheless, even if this life cycle is generic enough to represent the development steps of most SP types, it fails to model several specific cases. In fact, it is sometimes impossible to follow it rigorously. The life cycle architecture must change to adapt to system development. It should then be "flexible" enough to support such modifications. As for traditional systems, a security system life cycle consists of two principal phases: the acquisition phase and the utilization phase. Theoretically, the SP life cycle can be initiated at any point of the system development life cycle, even if it is always preferred that the SP evolve in parallel with the system (ISS, 2000; Grance, Stevens, 2003). As a result, some processes of the SP life cycle can be deleted, added, or modified. For example, when the information system is still in the acquisition phase, the implementation of the security controls cannot take place because some of the needed components are not available yet. Similarly, a cost-estimation activity should be performed initially to estimate the security budget and the human resources that would be necessary to apply the SP program. This task becomes unnecessary when doing a periodical review of the security policy.

Achieving the fixed security goals at the end of each step of the system's life cycle is crucial. If some SP components are not developed or not implemented during the appropriate phase, some security breaches might be left that would be hard to seal. This simply stems from the fact that the later a mistake is detected, the more difficult it is to repair.

COST-EFFECTIVENESS: THE RISK ANALYSIS PROCESS

Security risk analysis is the process of identifying assets and threats, prioritizing the related vulnerabilities, and identifying appropriate measures and protections. A risk analysis activity has to be performed prior to the security policy development. It should take into account many factors such as the environment (e.g., existing assets, potential threats), the cost considerations, and the type of the security documents (BSI, 2000; Peltier, 2001). This section shows how risk analysis can be integrated in to the security policy life cycle.

Integrating Risk Analysis Process into the SP Life Cycle

In this context, risk analysis is viewed as an activity generating data sets that will be used during the development of an SP. However, risk analysis itself is a discipline that has attracted great interest in the research community. Many models and methods have been built to support it.

Actually, risk analysis cannot be reduced to a preparatory step for the development of the SP because it has much more influence on the security process. It is generally conducted within the frame of the risk management cycle. The reader should be aware that in the present chapter, our discussion is focused on those aspects that are closely related to the SP development process.

Performing risk analysis allows us to (a) identify the important components of the system; (b) recognize the potential threats, risks, or issues related to the assets; (c) assess the risk degree related to each critical asset; (d) implement, for each risk, corrective countermeasures and controls, or accept the risk; and (e) measure the effectiveness of the countermeasures and controls. This assessment can be based on either a quantitative or a qualitative evaluation. The former assigns numerical values to the identified risks whereas the latter uses scales.

More simply, going through a risk assessment process allows the SP development team to determine what should be protected, how to protect it, and from what to protect it. Even more, this process ensures that the protection mechanisms are compliant with the available security budget, on one hand, and feasible, on the other hand. In fact, feasibility should be considered a major factor to enhance the efficiency of the resulting SP. For instance, requiring access codes (to a physical facility) to be changed daily is a security measure that cannot be concretely applied. Although it allows achieving a high protection level, the number of codes to be managed would be overwhelming. More generally, if a security process is difficult to apply, most of the employees will simply ignore it.

The advantages of performing risk analysis before constructing the SP stem from two major points:

1. Existing risk analysis methods can be often automated to a great degree through the use of software tools that considerably facilitate key tasks. Automation becomes very important, even necessary, in the case of large systems that have complex topologies. For a system including thousands of computers, which are also segmented into networks and subnetworks, the risk analyst would face substantial difficulties when trying to manually determine the threats related to each asset. Moreover, given that most of the available risk analysis methods are probabilistic, threat frequencies have to be kept up to date. This obviously requires the use of a learning mechanism. Thus, the use of databases, expert systems, and learning mechanisms are helpful to reduce decision time by mechanizing resource-demanding computations.

2. Including measures in the SP is equivalent to a decision-making process that might be affected by potential errors at the input stage. Risk analysis (RA), if conducted properly, should minimize these errors by providing a view that reflects accurately the security state of the system to be protected. Therefore, risk analysis makes the SP respect at least one of its major requirements, which is proportionality.

There are two types of security risk analysis: quantitative analysis and qualitative analysis. Quantitative RA attempts to assign independently objective numeric values to the elements of the risk analysis and to the level of potential losses. Even though it requires large amounts of preliminary work, quantitative RA generates efficient results that are expressed in management-based language.

Qualitative RA is subjective in nature and is based on scenarios and "what if" questions. Qualitative RA provides flexibility in the processing and reporting activities,;ut presents no basis for cost-benefit analysis of risk mitigation. Deciding which risk analysis process is appropriate for an enterprise is an important issue. Hybrid approaches are often used to combine the advantages of both approaches.

Risk Analysis Steps

To be efficient, the risk analysis process should consist of the following steps:

1) Mission statement: Identifying the context is among the important tasks when developing a security policy. In fact, the content of the security policy depends essentially on two factors: (a) the objective of the security policy, which can be regulatory, informative, or advisory, and (b) the structure of the organization. (It has been stated previously that the SP content depends heavily on this factor.) Existing standards, regulatory policies, and guidelines should also be taken into account to ensure the compliance of the security policy with those documents. Moreover, the security objectives to be fulfilled by the potential countermeasures should be determined at this level. These should be balanced with the available human and monetary resources to schedule adequately the development, implementation, and review of the SP.
2) Asset analysis: This process consists essentially of gathering information about the different resources to classify them according to their criticality. The interdependency among the identified resources should be taken into consideration.
3) Threat analysis: The most important threats will be identified through a detailed analysis of the environment of the analyzed system.

Absolute security is unachievable and unrealistic. Nevertheless, potential losses must be weighed against risk factors, the value of the information, and its accessibility to the mission of the agency. In doing this, an enterprise must develop a risk mitigation plan through the use of risk analysis.

A risk analysis, when done by qualified evaluators and involving the application/data owners, is imperative to properly assess overall risk and determine a course of action to alleviate or minimize those risks identified.

Overall risk analysis considers (a) the likelihood that a threat will breach a vulnerability and (b) the value of the asset, that is, a quantification of the loss, possibly in dollars, resulting from that breach in terms of lost worker productivity (wages), cost of recovery from the problem, and even nonmonetary cost such as political exposure and other ramifications. Potential losses must be weighed, and the expenditure on security controls must be balanced against the value of the information resource and the consequences that could result from its loss or inaccessibility.

The information security officer should conduct periodic risk analyses to address any change in the organization's priorities and threats to information. The analyses should be conducted with sufficient regularity to ensure realistic responses to current risks (e.g., agencies with sensitive data should do this quarterly or semiannually, and agencies with minimal sensitive data may find annual reviews sufficient).

Results of risk analysis should be documented, and that documentation should be included as part of the enterprise's documented information security program. The documentation should be considered sensitive and potentially confidential and be treated accordingly.

The risk analysis may vary from an informal, but documented, review of a microcomputer or terminal installation to a formal, fully quantified risk analysis for a large computing environment.

At a minimum, risk analysis should involve consideration of the following factors:

- the nature of the information and systems,
- business purpose for which the information is used,
- environment in which the system is used and operated,
- protection provided by the controls in place,
- organizational consequences that would likely result from a significant breach of security,
- realistic likelihood of such a breach occurring in light of prevailing threats and controls, and
- determination of which information resources are to be protected and to what extent.

WRITING EFFICIENCY: THE DEVELOPMENT PROCESS

After determining the major points that define the security needs of the target enterprise, a set of security rules have to be built to prevent the system from being jeopardized. To this end, a multidisciplinary team should be involved in the development process to reach an agreed-upon version of the SP. Development is, perhaps, the most critical task in the SP life cycle because it encompasses many seemingly unrelated aspects. The SP is certainly the cornerstone of the development of an efficient security program; however, it is not the only document that should be considered. It is a single component of a complex documentation hierarchy that should be developed in conjunction with the hierarchy. This section explores the concerns related to all of the security documentation and addresses particularly the following issues: (a) What are the documents that should accompany the development of the SP? (b) What are the steps that should be followed in the SP development process? (c) How to choose the appropriate language to express and validate the SP? (d) What is the role played by the security models in the SP development task? (e) What are the writing techniques that should be respected to ensure SP effectiveness? (f) What are the roles and the responsibilities that should be considered to develop the security documentation?

SP and the Documentation Hierarchy

Before beginning to write the SP, the development team should carefully analyze the output of the risk analysis step to identify the documents that must be defined. This allows the team to build a global unified view about system security by taking into account the relationship among documents. To address this need, the classifications proposed in the first section are useful.

The problem at this stage is to organize the countermeasures selected throughout the risk analysis process into a complete and coherent documentation, which should be easy to use, easy to maintain, accurate and up to date, appropriate for target audiences, and self-contained. Raw security decisions must then be refined to have the appropriate format required for integratration into the SP. To respect the uniformity of the organization's approach to potential threats, the SP must be closely related to the whole security documentation. In the following, we outline the main document categories that should be used to build effective security architecture.

1. Standards: A standard is a document that defines how a specific task should be performed. It can concern, for instance, the development of a product or a protocol related to a secure process. Generally, standards are developed so that the community using the target system knows what should be done to interact with it securely.
2. Procedures: Procedures describe exactly how to use the standards and guidelines to implement the countermeasures that support the policy. These procedures can be used to describe everything from the configuration of operating systems, databases, and network hardware to how to add new users, systems, and software.
3. Baselines: Baselines are used to create a minimum level of security necessary to meet policy requirements. Baselines can be configurations, architectures, or procedures that might or might not reflect the business process, but that can be adapted to meet these requirements. They can be used as an abstraction to develop standards.
4. Guidelines: Sometimes security cannot be described as a standard or set as a baseline, but some guidance is necessary. These are areas where recommendations are created as guidelines to the user community as a reference to proper security. For example, your policy might require a risk analysis every year. Rather than requiring specific procedures to perform this audit, a guideline can specify the methodology that is to be used, leaving the audit team to work with management to fill in the details.

The SP classes defined in the first section can be hierarchically covered to cluster the security decisions (that will later become security rules). The SP development team must first determine the audience concerned by the countermeasure, then the issue it treats, and finally the sensitive data it might enclose.

Language and Validation

From the previous discussion, we know that two important issues should be addressed: the SP language and the SP validation. Effectively, the SP is customarily written in a human natural language. When it is applied, the SP is translated into another language that is suitable to the secured process. To illustrate this idea, consider a policy describing the security of a networked system. To implement it, the administrator should configure the firewall, using its proper command set, in such a way that it will apply the SP. Even if the original SP substantially achieves its objectives, an error made by the administrator might make it deviate from these goals. Henceforth, the main problem at this stage is to prove that an expression of a SP in a given language conforms to another expression of the same SP in a different language. This issue is analogous to the software development process where many specifications corresponding to different levels of abstraction can be considered. These specifications that deal with the same problem are derived from each other by decreasing the abstraction level at each refinement. A key consideration is to test the conformance of each specification to the one it was derived from. On the other hand, an SP expressed through the use of a language must be validated to state whether it allows reaching the predefined security objectives (Cholvy & Cuppens, 1997; Siewe, Cau, & Zedan, 2003)

Many specification languages can be used to validate two key properties of the SP: consistency and completeness. Analyzing the SP consistency allows one to check whether the application of some security rules lead to conflicting situations. For example, in the case of an access control policy, an employee may have access to an object according to a specific measure, whereas another rule forbids this access. Completeness permits one to verify that the SP has covered all the environment of the organization.

In addition to this, the choice of the specification language often depends on the enterprise context, and more precisely, on the characteristic of the sensitive resources. For instance, the temporal aspect has not been investigated in early research activities that treated information access control. Nonetheless, recent works dealing with network security access control give great importance to this factor.

Consistency and completeness can be achieved while observing the following rules:

- The SP should be kept flexible. An SP should be made independent from specific hardware and software details. Mechanisms for updating the SP should be provided and be easy to use.
- Security services should be completely defined. This property can be achieved through the establishment of a complete list of the network services to be provided to the users who will be authorized to access the services and to the administrators of the services.
- Provided services should be separated and their real needs identified. Services should be isolated on dedicated hosts and filters be defined to cope with the services need.

SP Development Phases

Throughout this discussion, it appears that the SP development can be viewed, from a certain angle, as an iterative process where two functions are repeatedly executed:

Table 1 Example of Abstraction Levels

Abstraction level	Target population	Security rule
High	SP validator	Each subject is allowed read access to objects that are less sensitive than it.
Medium	Security administrator	The financial and the production network must be put on two separate virtual local area networks (VLANs).
Low	High managerial	The employees of the financial department do not have read access to the production data.

specification and validation. From one step to another, the specification used to model the SP becomes less abstract and closer to the reality. The process is stopped if a sufficient abstraction level is reached. This level may be adjusted according to the target population. In fact, the heterogeneity of the enterprise staff requires the development of different versions of the same SP. Each employee will have access to the version that fits with his or her position. Table 1 gives an illustrative example where the same security is expressed in three different manners. It shows how the same security statement can be expressed according to the audience. The last security rule (corresponding to low abstraction level) may seem close to the first one (corresponding to high abstraction level), but they exhibit important differences. The use of the term "each" confers an abstract aspect to the first rule. The last rule appears as an instantiation of the high-level one because abstract variables ("subject" and "object") have been substituted by concrete entities ("employees of the financial department" and "the production data").

The ITSEC defines three main abstraction levels for a SP:

- Corporate SP: Includes standards that apply to all the information systems of the enterprise as well as the relationship between these systems and the external ones.
- System SP: Defines the countermeasures that guarantee, for each category of sensitive resources, the respect of the corresponding security requirements.
- Technical SP: Defines the hardware and software mechanisms that should be used for a secure implementation of the system SP.

Using the documents issued at the RA analysis phase, the specification step applies the following guidelines to achieve a complete specification of an asset to protect:

- Identify all possible problems of the asset including misconfigurations, access points, and software bugs.
- Choose controls to protect the asset from the detected problems to reduce the related risk. Mulitple strategies should be used.
- Define appropriate procedures to identify unauthorized activity. These procedures should be based on an efficient monitoring of the system.
- Define the actions to be taken when a malicious activity is performed on the asset. Business activity and law enforcement should be involved in actions definition.

SP validation integrates several issues including formal validation, auditing, and testing. Formal validation should be achieved using formal models that allow proving ad hoc properties and checking whether the SP is consistent. Auditing process should be used to enhance system security, locate abuses, and control security procedures through logs and traces. Finally, testing can be realized in two phases: the first step generates case tests, and the second phase executes (or checks) the SP on the test cases.

In addition, SP validation may involve various departments in the company through a reviewing process. An SP may need to be reviewed by the legal department to provide advice on current relevant laws that may require certain types of information to be protected in specific ways. The human resources department also may need to review and approve or reject part of the SP depending on how it will relate to existing company policies. Finally, the internal audit department (IAD) in the company is likely to be involved in the SP validation. For instance, the IAD should conduct a companywide compliance of the SP with other policies, when implemented.

Mathematical Models

The main advantage of representing an SP formally is to discard some relatively insignificant details. A mathematical model corresponds to an abstraction degree, giving an idea about the amount of the withdrawn details. A highly abstract formal framework provides a coarse view of the analyzed system. Actually, fixing this abstraction degree is often a delicate task. It should not drastically eliminate relevant details and it must simultaneously avoid rendering the SP development more complex by considering superfluous entities. Furthermore, mathematical modeling allows, through the application of a sequence of decreasing abstraction levels, the building of a set of views that represent the system in a fashion that is increasingly close to the reality. The language used at a given level can be enriched to refine the granularity of the representation. The model resulting from this process would clearly be more realistic. According to this reasoning, the development process can start with an abstract model and be refined gradually until it reaches an "acceptable" representation.

Generally, a formal modeling framework consists of (a) a set of entities that represent the elements of the analysis, (b) a logic allowing clauses and formulas, (c) a set of axioms that define the main properties of the system, and

(d) a set of deduction rules that show how logical formulas can be inferred ones from the others.

In the following, the concept of multilevel security (MLS) is defined. Particular importance is given to MLS because it is the basis of a wide range of policy models such as the Bell–La Padula (Bell & La Padula, 1976) model and the Biba (Biba, 1977) model. For space limitations, several more recent formalisms are not be treated in this chapter. The interested reader should refer to Ryan (2000) for more details.

Multilevel Security Policies

These models consider a set of subjects S, objects O, and access modes A. A state of the system is represented by a matrix M whose rows, columns, and entries correspond to the subjects, objects, and the access granted to the subject on the object, respectively. These access privileges belong to the set A^*, meaning that they are subsets of A. The matrix M is often modeled by the following function $M: S \times O \to A$. Each element e of $S\ UO$ possesses a clearance (or a security level) denoted $C(e)$. The mapping C is then defined as function $C: S\ U\ O \to L$, where L is the set of security levels, which is presumed to possess a lattice structure.

For instance, at the organization level, the set L could be composed of *TopSecret, AD-Secret* (for administration department SECRET), *TD-Secret* (for technical department SECRET), *AD-confidential, TD-confidential,* and *Public*. The corresponding lattice is illustrated by Figure 2. This shows that *AD-Secret* dominates *AD-confidential* and *TD-confidential*. However, *AD-Secret* and *TD-Secret* cannot be compared and neither can *AD-confidential* and *TD-confidential*.

Multilevel security policies began to be used at the end of the 1970s to state what must and must not be done to guarantee the security of information flows. The most famous multilevel security models are Bell–La Padula (BPL) and Biba, which focus on confidentiality and integrity, respectively.

SECURITY AWARENESS PROGRAM: THE PUBLICATION PROCESS

Hare (2002) argued that "the success of a given policy is based on the level of knowledge that the employees have

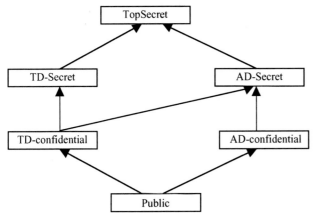

Figure 2: Organization security lattice.

about it." In fact, an awareness program has to be associated with the development of the security policy to ensure its efficiency. All the staff should understand (and apply) the directives of the security policy. To this purpose, the organization must communicate appropriately the content of the policy. To have an optimal efficiency to the awareness process, four main points should be addressed:

1. Which documentation should be developed to support the publication of the SP?
2. Which components of the SP should be communicated to each employee?
3. How to train accurately the organizations' staff?
4. How to ensure the cost-effectiveness of the awareness process?

Awareness programs should concentrate on all the organization's user population to achieve a successful IT security program. The program should focus on informing users of their responsibilities as documented in the SP.

Documenting the SP

A set of documents should be created to allow all the staff to understand the SP. In the previous section, the problem of extracting procedures and guidelines from the SP has been highlighted. In fact, this seems to be the most relevant issue at this level because users of a given system often do not have access to the SP itself but only to some of its ramifications.

The issuing organization should therefore establish priorities to rank these documents according to their importance. Effectively, even several security plans can be extracted from the SP such as the BCP and the DRP. More practical documents, such as the code of conduct (CoC), can also be based on the SP. It is noteworthy that these documents should fulfill the same conditions as the SP. Recall that an SP must be

- *Simple and clear.* This can be attained by (a) ensuring that the documents writers have a consistent style, (b) using concrete rather than abstract language, (c) using easy-to-understand language, and (d) applying effective rules such as avoiding the use of very negative statements (Canavan, 2004).
- *Known to employees.* For this, documents should be published in such a way that they remain available to all company employees. The documents should be easily accessible for download and printing. Various tools can be used to inform employees about the SP (e.g., e-mail).
- *Supported and adhered to by top management.* SP documents include a single document called *governing policy*, which should cover information security concepts at a high level, to be read by managers. Governing policy should be closely aligned with existing and future human resource strategies and other company policies.

Moreover, SP updates need to be carefully undertaken by the personnel. Old versions must be correctly withdrawn and simple procedures have to be set for identifying the latest versions.

Distributing the SP

The SP often includes some critical data about the security of the organization that has issued it. Therefore, the awareness process should be role-dependent in the sense that distinction should be considered among the components that should be made accessible to various employee categories. Because of their diversity, managing the SP and the related security documents is a hard task. Documents should be stored in such a way that they can easily be retrieved by authorized people. Similarly, access should be denied to unauthorized entities. To illustrate this reasoning, consider the case where an information security policy is about to be published. The different roles that are customarily considered to categorize the people who handle classified data are given in the following:

- Originator: the person who creates the information.
- Authorizer: the person who manages access to the information.
- Owner: the person who might manage or have created the information.
- Custodian: the person who executes the rules fixed by the authorizer.
- User: the person who has access to the information in order to fulfill some job responsibilities.

It can be easily remarked that interferences between the policies concerning each of these roles would affect the overall system security. For instance, if an originator has a precise idea about how the authorizer and the custodian communicate, he would have more opportunities to build a successful attack strategy. The rules related to this communication would be indeed very helpful when an entity tries to substitute itself for the authorizer.

More generally, the content of the policy should be split into a number of fragments, each having a different security level. Every employee should have access only to the fragments that fit with his position in the organization. Furthermore, employees should acknowledge and accept the organization's defined security policies, procedures, and responsibilities.

Training the Staff

Security awareness, including the training of information resource custodians, users, providers, and management, is one of the most effective means of reducing vulnerability to error and fraud and must be continually emphasized and reinforced. The training programs should suit the needs of the organization. In, three levels of complexity have been associated with training materials:

- Beginning level: for people who do not have any important technical knowledge.
- Intermediate level: for more experienced employees who have wider responsibilities.
- Advanced level: For experts whose jobs incorporate the highest level of trust. Security administrators, security officers, and network administrators are examples of people belonging to this category.

Security awareness and training programs can be described as a four-phase process (Wilson & Hash, 2003):

- Program design. During this phase, an assessment of the enterprise is conducted and a training strategy is developed and approved. Awareness and training program design must address the following main tasks: (a) how to structure the training activity, (b) how to conduct an assessment, (c) how to develop a training plan, (d) how to establish priorities, and (e) how to fund the program.
- Program development. This phase focuses on the availability of training resources, scope, content, and development of training material. The awareness and training program should develop material and identify the audiences and resources for each training course. It also should integrate useful tools to develop security training courses including methodologies such as those provided in. The first step in determining sources of training material to build a course is to decide if the material will be developed in-house or contracted out.
- Program implementation. This phase addresses effective communication for delivery of awareness and training program (ATP) material. Once the plan for implementing the ATP has been explained, the awareness material and messages can be presented and disseminated through the organization using messages, newsletters, computer-based sessions, and so forth. Techniques for effective delivery of training material should take advantage of technologies that support ease of use, scalability, and accountability.
- Program postimplementation. This step develops guidelines to keep the awareness and training program current and monitor its effectiveness. Continuous improvements should always be the theme for security ATP. Processes must be put into place to monitor compliance and effectiveness. An automated tracking system should be designed to capture key information regarding the program.

The ATP should include mechanisms for managing a security training function based on an understanding and assessment of budget and other resource-allocation mechanisms.

Cost-Effectiveness of the Awareness Process

The needs related to awareness and training should be assessed to ensure the cost-effectiveness of the ATP. Determining these needs is very important because it must be shown that (a) the resources used in the frame of the awareness process have an *acceptable* cost and (b) the awareness process will have an *acceptable* efficiency. Obviously, part of these tasks should be conducted at the risk analysis step. However, some residual tasks can be achieved only after the SP has been developed. NIST guidelines for building the information technology security ATPs gave great importance to this topic. NIST requested that many roles be involved in the needed assessment. Executive managers, security personnel, system owners, system administrators, and operational managers should participate to this task, among others.

SECURITY POLICY REASSESSMENT: THE AUDITING PROCESS

In the previous sections, we have described how to validate the SP during the different phases of its development. Meanwhile, such a priori validation is not sufficient. In fact, the starting point of the SP development often consists of a formal specification, which is gradually refined. The main shortcoming of this approach is that the specification, by nature, abstracts away some details that could turn out to be relevant. Even the refinement process does not allow a complete description of the environment. As a result, it is necessary to perform a postimplementation validation to verify whether the SP effectively achieves its objectives. This section discusses the SP reassessment by addressing the following key considerations:

- Which data are necessary for the SP assessment?
- How to scan the collected data?
- How to update the SP?

Collecting Relevant Data

RFC 2196 states that "audit data should include any attempt to achieve a different security level by any person, process, or other entity in the network" (IETF, 1997). This document focuses on the login/logout procedure and does not discuss several important features that are highlighted in the following points:

- The auditing mechanisms, which are integrated in the OSs, do not offer the capability to gather sufficient information about the activity of different entities. For instance, log files containing login attempts are often corrupted by the attacker. Hence, more advanced monitoring tools are needed to give a clearer idea about the behavior of the system.
- When choosing the appropriate monitoring strategy, the following considerations should be thought of:
1. Privacy: The monitoring process should not divulge private information to the security analysts. For example, the use of a file integrity checker should not give access to the content of the sensitive files to unauthorized users. This issue requires special attention because auditors generally have a lower security level than information owners.
2. Cost: Information used during the monitoring process may become very voluminous if a high granularity is targeted. The auditors should take into consideration the available storage and processing capabilities before setting the monitoring infrastructure. For example, logging the activity of a firewall might require a dedicated log server. It must be checked whether the cost of this server is proportional to the importance of the information it generates.
3. Efficiency: Each monitoring tool or procedure must substantially enhance the auditing capabilities. Potential redundancies should be removed.
4. Security: The collected data includes sensitive information that should be maintained at a high security level. Audit trails must be secured to guarantee their integrity as well as their secrecy.
5. Quality of service (QoS): Many data collection tools may have a negative effect on the production system of the enterprise. For instance, the sensors used by an IDS can slow the network activity when transmitting the collected data to the corresponding analyzers. Similarly, logging activity may require storage capabilities that cannot be offered by the available resources. Therefore, monitoring should not overwhelm the system with the data it generates.

Assessing the SP Efficiency

Testing of the SP can be performed through the use of numerous mechanisms that vary according to the tested component. For instance, when testing an authentication policy, the security analyst should first see if an attacker did get through the access control system by spoofing the identity of an authorized user. This can be achieved by using data generated during the collection process. In addition, some penetration tests can serve to fulfill this goal. Many automated tools can be used by auditors in this context. A more interesting topic is the contingency plan.

A contingency plan should be tested periodically because there will undoubtedly be flaws in the plan and in its implementation. The plan will become dated as time passes and as the resources used to support critical functions change. Responsibility for keeping the contingency plan current should be specifically assigned. The extent and frequency of testing will vary among organizations and systems. There are several types of testing, including reviews, analysis, and simulations of disasters.

A *review* can be a simple test to check the accuracy of contingency plan documentation. For instance, a reviewer could check if individuals listed are still in the organization and still have the responsibilities that caused them to be included in the plan. This test can check home and work telephone numbers, organizational codes, and building and room numbers. The review can determine if files can be restored from backup tapes or if employees know emergency procedures.

An *analysis* may be performed on the entire plan or portions of it, such as emergency response procedures. It is advantageous if the analysis is performed by someone who did *not* help develop the contingency plan, but has a good working knowledge of the critical function and supporting resources. The analyst(s) may mentally follow the strategies in the contingency plan, looking for flaws in the logic or process used by the plan's developers. The analyst may also interview functional managers, resource managers, and their staff to uncover missing or unworkable pieces of the plan.

Organizations may also arrange *disaster simulations*. These tests provide valuable information about flaws in the contingency plan and provide practice for a real emergency. Although they can be expensive, these tests can also provide critical information that can be used to ensure the continuity of important functions. In general, the more critical the functions and the resources addressed in the contingency plan, the more cost-beneficial it is to perform a disaster simulation.

The ISO 17799 (BSI, 2000) provides a set of guidelines that can be used to evaluate the security documentation. It addresses a wide spectrum of security aspects including access control, backup and recovery, disaster recovery, risk management, physical security, security monitoring, and security awareness.

Updating the SP

Several mechanisms must be subordinated to the policy itself to allow detecting events that require several changes in the policy. Also, the lifetime of the security policy is an important issue because it depends heavily on the type of the policy and on the context of the organization. Essentially, SP auditing should occur periodically to keep up with potential changes that may affect the system environment. Moreover, the update process should be triggered by the occurrence of security incidents. This stems from the fact that these incidents are often caused by weaknesses at the SP level.

Updating the SP often follows the same steps as its development (i.e., specification, validation). However, because the modifications are usually partial, in the sense that they touch only some fragments of the original SP, the process should take less time than the original development. Once it has been revised, the SP is then redistributed to the staff in a way that conforms to the awareness strategy.

LEGAL ASPECTS

A strong interaction between the security policy and the regulatory framework must be considered. Some legal constraints can affect aspects of the security policy. The more important ones are highlighted here.

To take into account these considerations, the responsibilities that are incumbent upon each individual should be clearly defined. Moreover, the SP should be compliant with various laws related, for example, to digital investigation and digital crime penalties. In fact, one of the major benefits of structuring the security activity within the enterprise is to fix the appropriate penalties for someone who violates the SP. These penalties are often considered at the internal level. Administrative and disciplinary measures are defined proportionally to the security fault that has been committed. Nevertheless, some legal procedures can also be conducted to instill a criminal aspect to such faults if they have been previewed by the law of the corresponding country. In the United States, several legal acts (Electronic Confidentiality Act, Electronic Espionage Act, 1996) can illustrate this interaction between the SP and the legal framework. According to the Electronic Espionage Act, stealing sensitive data from an organization is a federal crime that may lead to fines and imprisonment. This Act encourages organizations to put in place the necessary mechanisms to appropriately protect their resources.

GLOSSARY

Cost-Effectiveness The security rules that constitute the policy should contain measures that require an *acceptable* cost. Often, this cost is acceptable if it does not exceed the estimated benefit that would result from the implementation of those measures. Nonetheless, more sophisticated criteria can also be considered.

Development Lifecycle The process that should be followed during the development of several assets (e.g., pieces of software, network segments). Achieving the canonical security objectives requires the integration of the security policy within the development lifecycle.

Formal Model A mathematical framework that represents rigorously the security requirements and models the rules of a security policy. It allows verification of the consistency of the policy and checks whether it fulfills the security objectives.

Policy Assessment Because of the changes that affect the security of the target system, the security policy should be continuously monitored and updated. A periodical assessment of the security rules allows the detection of potential breaches. Moreover, the security policy should be evaluated every time it is violated.

Risk Analysis (RA) A process that aims at evaluating (either quantitatively or qualitatively) the threats corresponding to a specific system. It basically consists of determining the critical assets, listing the existing vulnerabilities, and deducing the potential threats. The main interest of risk analysis is that it guarantees cost-effectiveness. Others define RA as the process for measuring the relationship among frequency of attack, cost of attack, and cost of the asset involved.

Security Awareness The success of a security program heavily depends upon the level of knowledge that the employees have about it. An awareness program should therefore be conducted. More precisely, the security policy should be documented, distributed, and the staff should be appropriately trained.

Security Policy A set of rules that define how a process should be secured. These rules can be applied to a software development process, management of information systems, or communication protocols.

Validation The security policy has to be validated at more than one step. During the different phases of its development, every version of the policy should be proven to conform to the regulatory framework, the upper-level version, and the business objectives of the organization.

CROSS REFERENCES

See *Contingency Planning Management; Implementing a Security Awareness Program; Risk Management for IT Security; The Legal Implications of Information Security: Regulatory Compliance and Liability.*

REFERENCES

Bell, D. E., & La Padula, L. J. (1976). *Secure computer systems: Unified exposition and Multics interpretation* (Tech. Rep. ESD-TR-75-306). Bedford: MITRE Corporation.

Biba, K. J. (1977). *Integrity considerations for secure computer systems*. Technical Report MTR 3143. Bedford, MA: MITRE Corporation.

British Standard Institute (BSI). (2000). *ISO 17799 toolkit: Policy templates*. Retrieved September 13, 2004, from http://www.iso17799software.com

Campbell, K., Gordon, L. A., Loeb, M. P., & Zhou, L. (2003). The economic cost of publicly announced information security breaches: Empirical evidence from the stock market. *Journal of Computer Security, 11*, 431–448.

Canavan, J. E. (2001). *Fundamentals of network security* (pp. 239–259). Norwood, MA: Artech House.

Canavan, J. E. (2003). *An information security policy: Development guides for large companies*. Bethesda, MD: SANS Institute.

Cholvy, L., & Cuppens, F. (1997, July). *Analyzing consistency of security policies*. Paper presented at the IEEE Symposium on Security and Privacy, Oakland, CA.

CSI/FBI. (2004). *Computer crime and security survey*. Retrieved January 24, 2005, from http://www.gocsi.com

Hare, C. (2000). Policy development. In H. F. Tipton & M. Krause (Eds.), *Handbook of information security* (Vol. 3, Chap. 20, pp. 353–389). New York: Auerbach.

Internet Engineering Task Force (IETF). (1997). *Site security handbook* (RFC 2196). IETF Network Working Group. Retrieved August 24, 2004, from http://www.ietf.org/rfc/rfc2196.txt

Internet Security Systems (ISS). (2000). *Creating, implementing and managing the information security lifecycle*. Retrieved August 24, 2004, from http://documents.iss.net/whitepapers/securitycycle.pdf

Peltier, T. R. (2001). *Information security risk analysis*. New York: Auerbach.

Purser, C. (2004). *A practical guide to managing information security*. Norwood, MA: Artech House.

Ryan, P. Y. A. (2000). *Mathematical models of computer security* (pp. 1–62). Lecture Notes in Computer Science, 2171. Berlin: Springer-Verlag.

Siewe, F., Cau, A., & Zedan, H. (2003, October). *A compositional framework for access control policies enforcement*. Paper presented at the ACM Conference on Computer Security, FMSE '03, Washington, DC.

Swanson, M. (1998). *Guide for developing security plans for information technology systems* (NIST Special Publication 800-18). Retrieved September 4, 2004, from http://www.csrc.nist.gov/publications/nistpubs/800-18/Planguide.pdf

Tudor, J. K. (2001). Security policies, standards, and procedures. *In Information security architecture: An integrated approach to security in the organization* (pp. 79–100). New York: Auerbach.

Wilson, M., & Hash, J. (2003). *Building an information technology security awareness and training program* (NIST Special Publication 800-50). Retrieved September 4, 2004, from http://www.csrc.nist.gov/publications/nistpubs/800-50/NIST-SP800-50.pdf

FURTHER READING

Swanson, M., Wohl, A., Pope, L., Grance, T., Hash, J., & Thomas, R. (2002). *Contingency planning guide for information technology systems* (NIST Special Publication 800-34). Retrieved September 4, 2004, from http://www.csrc.nist.gov/publications/nistpubs/800-34/op800-34.pdf

U.S. Department of Defense (DoD). (1985). *DoD trusted computer security system evaluation criteria* (*The Orange Book*; DoD 5200.28-STD). Retrieved September 13, 2004, from http://www.boran.com/security/tcsec.html

Access Control: Principles and Solutions

S. De Capitani di Vimercati and S. Paraboschi, *DTI–Università di Milano, Italy*
Pierangela Samarati, *DIGI–Università di Bergamo, Italy*

INTRODUCTION

An important requirement of any system is to protect its *data* and *resources* against unauthorized disclosure (*secrecy* or *confidentiality*) and unauthorized or improper modifications (*integrity*), while at the same time ensuring their availability to legitimate users (*no denial-of-service* or *availability*) (Samarati & De Capitani di Vimercati, 2001). The problem of ensuring protection has existed since information has been managed. However, as technology advances and information management systems become more and more powerful, the problem of enforcing information security also becomes more critical. The increasing development of information and communication technology has led to the widespread use of computer systems to store and transmit information of every kind, offering concrete advantages in terms of availability and flexibility but at the same time posing new serious security threats and increasing the potential damage that violations may cause. Today more than ever organizations depend on the information they manage. A violation to the security of the information may jeopardize the whole system and cause serious damage. Hospitals, banks, public administrations, and private organizations all depend on the accuracy, availability, and confidentiality of the information they manage. Just imagine what could happen, for example, if an organization's data were improperly modified, were not available to the legitimate users because of a violation blocking access to the resources, or were disclosed to the public domain.

A fundamental component in enforcing protection is represented by the *access control* service, whose task is *to control every access to a computer system and its resources and ensure that all authorized and only authorized accesses can take place*. To this purpose, every management system usually includes an access control service that establishes the kinds of rules that can be stated, through an appropriate specification language, and then enforced by the access control mechanism enforcing the service. By using the provided interface, security administrators can specify the access control policy (or policies) that should be obeyed in controlling access to the managed resources.

The definition of access control policies to be fed into the access control system is far from a trivial process.

One of the major difficulties lies in the interpretation of real-world security policies, which are often complex and sometimes ambiguous, and in their translation in well-defined unambiguous rules enforceable by the computer system. Many real-world situations have complex policies, where access decisions depend on the application of different rules coming, for example, from laws, practices and organizational regulations. A security policy must capture all the different regulations to be enforced and, in addition, must consider all possible additional threats because of the use of computer systems. Given the complexity of the scenario, it is therefore important that the access control service provided by the computer system be expressive and flexible enough to accommodate the different requirements that may need to be expressed, while at the same time be simple both in terms of use (so that specifications can be kept under control) and implementation (so to allow for its verification).

An access control system should include support for the following concepts/features:

Accountability and reliable input. Access control must rely on proper input. This simple principle is not always obeyed by systems allowing access control rules to be evaluated on the basis of possibly unreliable information. This is, for example, the case of *location-based* access control restrictions, where the access decision may depend on the IP from which a request originates, a piece of information that can be easily faked in a local network, thus fooling access control (allowing nonlegitimate users to acquire access despite the proper rule enforcement). This observation has been traditionally at the basis of requiring proper user authentication as a prerequisite for access control enforcement (Sandhu & Samarati, 1997). Although more recent approaches may remove the assumption that every user is authenticated (e.g., by allowing credential-based access control), still the assumption that the information on which access decision is taken must be correct indeed continues to hold.

Support for fine and coarse specifications. The access control system should allow rules to be referred to specific accesses, providing fine-grained reference to the subjects and objects in the system. However,

406

fine-grained specifications should be supported but not forced. In fact, requiring the specification of access rules with reference to every single user and object in the system would make the administration task a heavy burden. Besides, groups of users and collections of objects often share the same access control requirements. The access control system should then provide support for authorizations specified for groups of users, groups of objects, and possibly even groups of actions (Jajodia, Samarati, Sapino, & Subrahmanian, 2001). Also, in many organizational scenarios, access needs may be naturally associated with *organizational activities*; the access control system should then support authorizations referred to organizational roles (Sandhu, Coyne, Feinstein, & Youman, 1996).

Conditional authorizations. Protection requirements may need to depend on the evaluation of some conditions (Samarati & De Capitani di Vimercati, 2001). Conditions can be in the simple form of system's predicates, such as the date or the location of an access (e.g., "Employees can access the system *from 9 a.m. to 5 p.m.*"). Conditions can also make access dependent on the information being accessed (e.g., "Managers can read payroll data of *the employees they manage*").

Least privilege. The least privilege principle mandates that every subject (active entity operating in the system) should always operate with the least possible set of privileges needed to perform its task. Obedience to the least privilege requires both static (policy specification) and dynamic (policy enforcement) support from the access control system. At a static level, least privilege requires support of *fine-grained authorizations*, granting each specific subject only those specific accesses it needs. At a dynamic level, least privilege requires restricting processes to operate within a *confined set of privileges*. Least privilege is partially supported within the context of *roles*, which are essentially privileged hats that users can take and leave (Sandhu et al., 1996). Authorizations granted to a role apply only when the role is active for a user (i.e., when needed to perform the tasks associated with the role). Hence, users authorized for powerful roles do not need to exercise them until those privileges are actually needed. This minimizes the danger of damage because of inadvertent errors or by intruders masquerading as legitimate users. Least privilege also requires the access control system to discriminate between different processes, even if executed by the same user, for example, by supporting authorizations referred to specific applications or *applicable only during the execution of specific programs*.

Separation of duty. Separation of duty refers to the principle that no user should be given enough privileges to misuse the system (Sandhu, 1990). Although separation of duty is better classified as a policy specification constraint (i.e., a guideline to be followed by those in charge of specifying access control rules), support of separation of duty requires the security system to be expressive and flexible enough to enforce the constraints. At a minimum, fine-grained specifications and least privilege should be supported; *history-based authorizations*, making one's ability to access a system

dependent on previously executed accesses, are also a convenient means to support separation of duty.

Multiple policies and exceptions. Traditionally, discretionary policies have been seen as distinguished into two classes: *closed* and *open* (Samarati & De Capitani di Vimercati, 2001). In the more popular closed policy, only accesses to be authorized are specified; each request is controlled against the authorizations and allowed only if an authorization exists for it. By contrast, in the open policy (negative), authorizations specify the accesses that should not be allowed. All access requests for which no negative authorization is specified are allowed by default.

Policy combination and conflict resolution. If multiple modules (e.g., for different authorities or different domains) exist for the specification of access control rules, the access control system should provide a means for users to specify how the different modules should interact, for example, if their union (maximum privilege) or their intersection (minimum privilege) should be considered. Also, when both permissions and denials can be specified, the problem naturally arises of how to deal with *incompleteness*, that is, existence of accesses for which no rule is specified, and *inconsistency*, that is, the existence of accesses for which both a denial and a permission are specified. Dealing with incompleteness—requiring the authorizations to be complete would be very impractical—requires support of a *default* policy either imposed by the system or specified by the users. Dealing with inconsistencies requires support for *conflict resolution* policies. Different conflict resolution approaches can be taken, such as the simple *denials take precedence* (in the case of doubt access is denied) or *most specific* criteria that make the authorization referred to the more specific element (e.g., a user is more specific than a group, and a file is more specific than a directory). Although among the different conflict resolution policies that can be thought of (see Samarati & De Capitani di Vimercati, 2001, for a deeper treatment) some solutions may appear more natural than others, none of them represents "the perfect solution." Whichever approach we take, we will always find one situation for which the approach does not fit. Therefore any conflict resolution policy imposed by the access control mechanism itself will always be limiting. Conversely, support of negative authorizations is not free, and there is a price to pay in terms of authorization management and less clarity of the specifications. However, the complications brought by negative authorizations are not because of negative authorizations themselves but rather the different semantics that the presence of permissions and denials can have in the different real-world scenarios and requirements that may need to be captured. There is therefore a trade-off between expressiveness and simplicity. Consequently, current systems try to keep it simple by adopting negative authorizations for exception support, imposing specific conflict resolution policies, or supporting a limited form of conflict resolution.

Administrative policies. As access control systems are based on access rules defining which ones are (or are not) to be allowed, an administrative policy is needed to regulate the specification of such rules, that is, define who can add, delete, or modify them. Administrative policies are one of the most important, though less understood, aspects in access control. Indeed, they have usually received little consideration, and, although it is true that a simple administrative policy would suffice for many applications, it is also true that new applications (and organizational environments) would benefit from the enrichment of administrative policies. In theory, discretionary systems can support different kinds of administrative policies: *centralized*, where a privileged user or group of them is reserved the privilege of granting and revoking authorizations; *hierarchical/cooperative*, where a set of authorized users is reserved the privilege of granting and revoking authorizations; *ownership*, where each object is associated with an owner (generally the object's creator) who can grant to and revoke from others the authorizations on its objects; and *decentralized*, where, extending the previous approaches, the owner of an object (or its administrators) can delegate other users the privilege of specifying authorizations, possibly with the ability of further delegating it. For its simplicity and large applicability the ownership policy is the most popular choice in today's systems (see Access Control in Operating Systems). Decentralized administration approaches can be instead found in the database management system contexts (see Access Control in Database Management Systems). Decentralized administration is convenient because it allows users to delegate administrative privileges to others. Delegation, however, complicates the authorization management. In particular, it becomes more difficult for users to keep track of who can access their objects. Furthermore, revocation of authorizations becomes more complex.

In the remainder of this chapter, after a brief overview of the basic concepts about access control policies (Access Control Policies), we survey the access control services provided by some of the most popular operating systems (Access Control in Operating Systems), database management systems (Access Control in Database Management Systems), and network solutions (Access Control for Internet-Based Solutions). Although clearly their characteristics will vary from one class to the other as their focus is different (e.g., database management systems focus on the data and rely on the operating systems for low level support), it will be interesting to see how they accommodate (or do not accommodate) the features introduced above. Also, it will be noticed how, while covering a feature in some way, some systems take unclean solutions that may have side effects in terms of security or applicability, aspects that then should be taken into account when using the systems.

ACCESS CONTROL POLICIES

An access control policy must capture all the different regulations to be enforced and, in addition, must also consider possible additional threats because of the use of a computer system. Traditionally, access control policies can be grouped into three main classes:

Discretionary (DAC) (authorization-based) policies control access based on the identity of the requestor and on access rules (authorizations) stating what requestors are (or are not) allowed to do.

Mandatory (MAC) policies control access based on mandated regulations determined by a central authority.

Role-based (RBAC) policies control access depending on the roles that users have within the system and on rules stating what accesses are allowed to users in given roles.

Discretionary and role-based policies are usually coupled with (or include) an *administrative policy* that defines who can specify authorizations/rules governing access control. Because the access control services described in the following sections are based on discretionary policies, we now focus on such a kind of policies.

A simple way to represent a set of authorizations for their enforcement consists in using an access *control matrix*. First proposed by Lampson (1974) for the protection of resources within the context of operating systems, and later refined by Graham and Denning (1972), the model was subsequently formalized by Harrison, Ruzzo, and Ullmann (HRU model) (1976), who developed the access control model proposed by Lampson to the goal of analyzing the complexity of determining an access control policy. The name access matrix derives from the fact that the authorizations holding at a given time in the system are represented as a matrix. The matrix therefore gives an abstract representation of protection systems. In particular, the state of the system is represented by a triple (S, O, A), where S is the set of subjects, O is the set of objects (often the set S is considered as a subset of O), and A is a matrix whose rows correspond to subjects, columns corresponds to objects, and the entry $A[s,o]$ includes the privileges (i.e., read, write, own, and execute) that s can exercise on o. By simply providing a framework where authorizations can be specified, the model can accommodate different privileges. For instance, in addition to the traditional read, write, and execute actions, *ownership* (i.e., property of objects by subjects), and *control* (to model father–children relationships between processes) can be considered.

Figure 1 illustrates a simple example of access matrix. Because the access matrix is usually large and sparse, its storage implies a waste of memory space. There are three basic approaches of implementing the access matrix in a practical way:

Authorization table. Store a table of nonnull triples of the form (s,a,o). It is especially used in database management systems (DBMSs), where authorizations are stored as catalogs.

	fileA	fileB	programC
Alice	own write read	write	execute
Bob	read	read	execute read write
Eve	read	read	

Figure 1: An example of access matrix.

Access control lists (ACLs). Each object is associated with an ACL that specifies which users have which access modes on it.

Capability lists (tickets). Each user is associated with a capability list that specifies the objects that the user can access and the access modes the user can exercise on them.

Intuitively, an entry in the authorization table corresponds to a cell in the matrix, an ACL corresponds to a column of the matrix, and a capability corresponds to a row of the matrix.

Figure 2 illustrates the authorization table, ACLs, and capability lists corresponding to the access matrix in Figure 1. ACLs and capabilities have dual advantages and disadvantages: the ACL approach provides efficient per-object access, whereas the capability approach provides efficient per-subject access. In particular, in the ACL approach, by looking at an object's ACL, it is easy to determine which actions subjects are currently authorized for that object. Determining all accesses for which a subject is authorized would require instead the examination of all the ACLs. Conversely, in a capability-based approach it is easy to review all accesses that a subject is authorized to perform by simply examining the subject's capability list. However, determination of all subjects who can access a particular object requires examination of each and every subject's capability list. A number of capability-based computer systems were developed in the 1970s but did not prove to be commercially successful. As we will see, modern operating systems typically take the ACL-based approach.

ACCESS CONTROL IN OPERATING SYSTEMS

We describe access control services in two of the most popular operating systems: Linux (e.g., www.redhat.com, www.linux-mandrake.com, www.suse.com) and Microsoft Windows 2000/XP (www.microsoft.com).

Access Control in Linux

We use Linux as a modern representative of the large family of operating systems deriving from Unix. We signal the features of Linux that are absent in other operating systems of the same family.

Apart from specific privileges such as access to protected TCP ports, the most significant access control services in Linux are the ones offered by the file system. The file system has a central role in all the operating systems of the Unix family, as files are used as an abstraction for most of the system resources.

User Identifiers and Group Identifiers

Access control is based on a user identifier (UID) and group identifier (GID) associated with each process. A UID is an integer value unique for each username (login name), where the association between usernames and UIDs is described in file /etc/passwd. A user connecting to a Linux system is typically authenticated by the login process, invoked by the program managing the communication line used to connect to the system (getty for serial lines, telnetd for remote telnet sessions). The login process asks the user for a username and a password and checks the password with its hash stored in read-protected file /etc/shadow; a less secure and older alternative stores hashed password in the readable-by-all file /etc/passwd. When authentication is successful, the login process sets the UID to that of the authenticated user, before starting an instance of the program described in the user entry in /etc/passwd (typically a shell, like /bin/bash). Users in Linux are members of groups. Every time a user connects to the system, together with the UID, a primary GID is set. The primary GID value to use at login is defined in file /etc/passwd. Group names and additional memberships in groups are defined in file /etc/group. Command *newgrp* allows users to switch to a new primary GID. If a user is listed in /etc/group as belonging to the new group, the request is immediately executed; otherwise, for groups having a hashed password in /etc/group, the primary GID can be changed after the password has been correctly

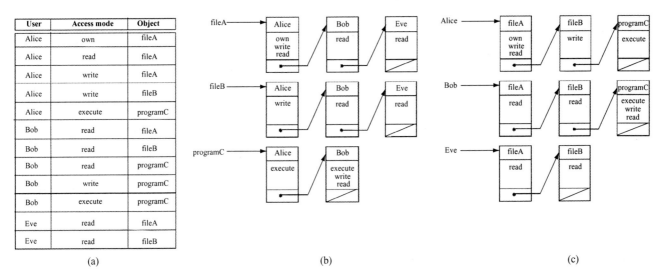

User	Access mode	Object
Alice	own	fileA
Alice	read	fileA
Alice	write	fileA
Alice	write	fileB
Alice	execute	programC
Bob	read	fileA
Bob	read	fileB
Bob	read	programC
Bob	write	programC
Bob	execute	programC
Eve	read	fileA
Eve	read	fileB

(a)   (b)   (c)

Figure 2: Authorization table (a), ACLs (b), and capabilities (c) for the matrix in Figure 1.

returned. However, group passwords are deprecated, as they easily lead to lapses in password management.

Processes are usually assigned the UIDs and GIDs of the parent processes, which implies that processes acquire the UIDs and GIDs associated with the login names with which sessions have been started. The process UID is the central piece of information for the evaluation of the permitted actions. There are many operations in the system that are allowed only to a user that has zero as the value of its UID. By convention, user *root* is associated with UID value zero and represents the owner of the system, who supervises all the activities. For instance, the TCP implementation allows only user *root* to open ports below 1024.

Files and Privileges

In the Linux file system, each file is associated with a UID and a GID, which typically represent the UID and primary GID of the process that created the file. UID and GID associated with a file can be changed by commands *chown* and *chgrp*. Each file has associated a list of nine privileges: *read*, *write*, and *execute*, each defined three times, at the level of *user*, *group*, and *other*. The privileges defined at the level of *user* are the actions that will be permitted to processes having the same UID as the file; the privileges defined at the level of *group* are granted to processes having the same GID as the file; the privileges at the level of *other* are for processes that share neither UID nor GID with the file. The privileges are commonly represented by the *ls -l* command as a string of nine characters (preceded by a character representing the file type). Each privilege is characterized by a single letter: r for *read*; w for *write*; x for *execute*; the absence of the privilege is represented by character -. The string presents first the *user* privileges and then *group* and finally *other*. For instance, rwxr-xr-- means that a process having as UID the same UID as the file has all the three privileges, a process with the same GID can read and execute (but not write) the file, and remaining processes can only read the file. When a user belongs to many groups, all the corresponding GIDs are stored in a list in the process descriptor beside the primary GID; other operating systems of the Unix family stored only the primary GID within the process descriptor. All the groups in the list are then considered: if the GID of the file is the primary GID, or appears anywhere in the list, group access privileges apply.

The semantics of privileges may be different depending on the type of the file on which they are specified. In particular, for directories, the *execute* privilege represents the privilege to access the directory; *read* and *write* privileges permit respectively to read the directory content and to modify it (adding, removing, and renaming files). Privileges associated with a file can be updated via the *chmod* command, which is usable by the file owner and by user *root*.

Additional Security Specifications

The file system offers three other file privileges: *save text image* (sticky bit), *set user ID* (*setuid*), and *set group ID* (*setgid*). The *sticky bit* privilege is useful only for directories, where it allows only the owner of the file, owner of the directory, and root to remove or rename the files contained in the directory, even if the directory is writable

by all. The *setuid* and *setgid* privileges are particularly useful for executable files, where they permit to set the UID or GID of the process that executes the file to that of the file itself. These privileges are often used for applications that require a higher level of privileges to accomplish their task (e.g., users change their passwords with the *passwd* program, which needs read and write access on file /etc/shadow). Without the use of these bits, enabling a process started by a normal user to change the user's password would require explicitly granting the user the write privilege on the file /etc/shadow. Such a privilege could, however, be misused by users who could access the file through different programs and tamper with it. The *setuid* and *setgid* bits, by allowing the *passwd* program to run with root privilege, avoid such security exposure. It is worth noticing that, although providing a necessary security feature, the *setuid* and *setgid* solutions are themselves vulnerable as the specified programs run with root privileges—in contrast to the least privilege principle, they are not confined to the accesses needed to execute their task—and it is therefore important that these programs be *trusted* (Samarati & De Capitani di Vimercati, 2001).

The *ext2* and *ext3* file systems, the most common in Linux implementations, offer additional boolean attributes on files. Among them, there are attributes focused on low-level optimizations (e.g., a bit requiring a compressed representation of the file on the disk) and two privileges that extend access control services: *immutable* and *append-only*. The *immutable* bit specifies that no change be allowed on the file; only the user *root* can set or clear this attribute. The *append-only* bit specifies that the file can be extended only by additions at the end; this attribute can also be set only by *root*. Attributes are listed by command *lsattr* and are modified by command *chattr*.

IP-Based Security

Linux offers several utilities that base authentication on IP addresses. All of these solutions should be used with care, as IP addresses can be easily spoofed in a local network (Bellovin, 1989) and therefore fool the access control system. For this reason, they are not enabled by default. Among these utilities, *rsh* executes remote shells on behalf of users; *rcp* executes copies involving the file systems of machines in a network; NFS permits to share portions of the file system on the network. For these applications, access control typically is based on a few relatively simple textual files, which describe the computers that can use the service and the scope of the service; patterns can be used to identify ranges of names or addresses, and groups may be defined, but overall the access control features are basic. Secure solutions of the above applications (such as the *ssh* application and the *scp* program offered within the same package) offer a greater degree of security, at the expense of computational resources, configuration effort, and in general less availability.

Evaluation of Linux Access Control

We briefly evaluate the access control features of Linux in terms of the principles presented in the introduction.

Accountability and reliable input: the operating system allows the use of reliable and strong authentication solutions; some of the access control mechanisms, like those based on IP security, show limited protection. The various Linux distributions have evolved on this respect and the standard configuration typically does not activate the weak solutions (indeed, for a relatively inexperienced Linux user, the activation of insecure services may require a significant effort).

Support for fine-grained and coarse-grained specifications: the Linux operating system essentially offers access control only at the level of files/directories; protection privileges (like setuid/setgid and access to network resources) also suffer of a limited granularity. It is possible to introduce applications within the Linux operating system that protect their resources with a finer granularity, but the native operating system support is limited.

Conditional authorizations: it is possible to specify in a declarative way protection, specifying, for example, patterns of IP addresses and DNS identifiers; protection of files does not permit the use of conditions or declarative mechanisms.

Least privilege: because fine-grained authorizations are not supported, Linux can offer a limited support to the least privilege principle; theoretically, the use of groups can be used to approximate the presence of many different access requirements for different users, but in practice this strategy does not work very well and is not scalable.

Separation of duty: the presence of an all-powerful *root* user represents the approach against which this principle is directed.

Multiple polices and exceptions: the access control services offered by Linux do not support this requirement.

Policy combination and conflict resolution: conflicts may arise when privileges represent conflicting requirements; for instance, a user may not have the privilege to access a directory, but it may be the owner of a file contained within it. In Linux, the user is not allowed to access the file, unless she has the *execute* privilege on all the directories present in the path. The presence of symbolic links complicates the matter, because a single resource can be identified by different paths. The path used to identify the resource has to be completely accessible by the user to permit access to the resource. The conflict resolution mechanism is ad hoc and is not flexible.

Administrative polices: administration is based on the identification of a resource owner, together with the presence of an all-powerful root user.

Overall, Linux shows its lineages and represents a modern version of an operating system that was created when security was not as important as it is today. A lot of effort is currently being directed at designing Linux components that are able to overcome these limits and to let it become the core of complex computer architectures (e.g., the Security Enhanced Linux initiative and many others). For a role as a specialized server, the limitations of the design are probably under control; for Linux to be an effective solution for the construction of multiuser information systems, the development of novel access control services is probably required.

Access Control in Windows

We now describe the characteristics of the access control model of the Microsoft Windows 2000/XP operating system (msdn.microsoft.com). Most of the features we present were already part of the design of Microsoft Windows NT; we will clarify the features that were not present in Windows NT and were introduced in Windows 2000. We use the term Windows to refer to this family of operating systems. We do not consider the family of Windows 95/98/ME operating systems.

Security Descriptor

One of the most important characteristics of the Windows operating system is its object-oriented design. Every component of the system is represented as an object, with attributes and methods. In this scheme, it is natural to base access control on the notion that objects can be *securable*; that is, they can be characterized by a *security descriptor* that specifies the security requirements of the object (this corresponds to implementing access control with an access control list approach [Samarati & De Capitani di Vimercati, 2001], equivalent to the nine-character string in Unix). Almost all of the system objects are *securable*: files, processes, threads, named pipes, shared memory areas, registry entries, and so on. The same access control mechanism applies to all of them.

Any subject that can operate on an object (user, group, logon session, etc.) is represented in Windows by a *Security Identifier* (SID), with a rich structure that manages the variety of active entities. The main components of the *security descriptor* are the SIDs of the owner and of the primary group of the object and two access control lists: a *Discretionary Access Control List* (DACL) and a *System Access Control List* (SACL).

Access Control Element

Each access control list consists of a sequence of *Access Control Elements* (ACEs). An ACE is an elementary authorization on the object, with which it is associated by way of the ACL; the ACE describes the subject to which the authorization applies, the action (operation) that the subject can execute on the object, the type (allow, deny, or audit), and several flags (to specify the propagation and other ACE properties). The subject (called *trustee* in Windows) is represented by a SID. The action is specified by an *access mask*, a 32-bit vector (only part of the bits are currently used; many bits are left unspecified for future extensions). Half of the bits are associated with access rights valid for every object type; these access rights can be divided into three families as follows:

Generic: *read*, *write*, *execute*, and the union of all of them.

Standard: *delete*, *read_control* (to read the security descriptor), *synchronize* (to wait on the object until a signal is generated on it), *write_dac* (to change the DACL), and *write_owner* (to change the object's owner).

SACL: *access_system_security* (a single access right to modify the SACL; the right is not sufficient, as the subject must also have the SE_SECURITY_NAME privilege). It cannot appear in a DACL.

The remaining 16 bits are used to represent access rights specific to the object type (directory, file, process, thread, etc.). For instance, for directories access rights *open*, *create_child*, *delete_child*, *list*, *read_prop*, and *write_prop* apply. Active directory services, described under "Fine Granularity Access Control," are the base for the introduction of object-specific ACEs.

Access Token

Each process or thread executing in the system is associated with an *Access Token*, an object that describes the security context. An access token describing the user is created after the user has been authenticated and is then associated with every process executing on behalf of the user. The access token contains the SID of the user's account, SIDs of the groups that have the user as a member, a *logon* SID identifying the current logon session, a list of the privileges held by the user or the groups, an owner SID, the SID of the primary group, and the default DACL to use when a process creates a new object without specifying a security descriptor. In addition, there are other components that are used for changing the identifiers associated with a process (called *impersonation* in Windows) and to apply restrictions.

Evaluation of ACLs

When a thread makes a request to access an object, its access token is compared with the DACL in the security descriptor. If the DACL is not present in the security descriptor, the system assumes that the object is accessible without restrictions. Otherwise, the ACEs in the DACL are considered one after the other, and for each one the user and group SIDs in the access token are compared with the SID in the ACE. If there is a match, the ACE is applied. Order in the DACL is extremely important. The first ACE that matches will apply or deny the access rights in it. The following matching ACEs will only be able to allow or deny the remaining access rights. If the analysis of the DACL terminates and no allow/deny has been obtained for a given access right, the system assumes that the right is denied (closed policy). As an example, with reference to Figure 3, for user Bob the second ACE will apply (as it matches the group in the thread's access token) denying Bob the execute and write accesses on object1. The approach of applying the first ACE encountered corresponds to the use of a "position-based" criterion for resolving possible conflicts (Samarati & De Capitani di Vimercati, 2001). Although simple, this solution is quite limiting. First, it gives the users specifying the policy the complete burden of solving each specific conflict that may arise (not allowing them to specify generic high level rules for that). Second, it is not suitable if a decentralized administration (where several users can specify authorizations) should be accommodated. Also, users should have explicit direct write privilege on the DACL to properly order the ACEs. However, doing so it would be possible for them to abuse the privilege and set the ACL in an uncontrolled way.

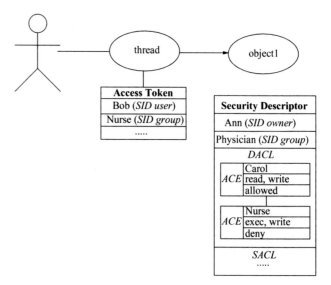

Figure 3: Access control in Windows.

It is worth noting how an empty DACL (which returns no permissions) will deny all users the access to the object, whereas a null DACL (which returns no restrictions) would grant them all. Then, attention must be paid to the difference between the two.

The object creator sets the DACL. When no DACL is specified, the default DACL in the access token is used by the system. The SACL is a sequence of ACEs like the DACL, but it can only be modified by a user having the administrative privilege SE_SECURITY_NAME and describes the actions that have to be logged by the system (if the ACE for a given access right and SID is positive, the corresponding action must be logged; if it is negative, no trace will be kept); the access control system records access requests that have been successful, rejected, or both, depending on the value of the flags in the ACE elements in the SACL. Each monitored access request produces a new entry in the *security event log*.

System Privileges

A system privilege in Windows is the right to execute privileged operations, such as making a backup, debugging a process, increasing the priority of a process, increasing the quota, and creating accounts. All these operations are not directly associated with a specific system object, and ACEs cannot conveniently represent them in an object security descriptor. System privileges can be considered as authorizations without an explicit object. System privileges can be associated with user and group accounts. When a user is authenticated by the system, the access token is created; the access token contains the system privileges of the user and of the groups in which the user is a member. Every time a user tries to execute a system privileged operation, the system checks if the access token contains the adequate system privilege. System privileges are evaluated locally; a user can then have different system privileges on different nodes of the network.

Impersonation and Restricted Tokens

Impersonation is a mechanism that permits threads to acquire the access rights of a different user. This feature is similar to the *setuid* and *setgid* services of Linux, where the change in user and group identifier permits programs invoked by a user to access protected resources. In Windows, impersonation is also an important tool for client–server architectures. The server uses impersonation to acquire the security context of the client when a request arrives. The advantage is that, in a network environment, a user will be able to consistently access the resources for which the user is authorized, and the system will be better protected from errors in the protocol used for service invocation or in the server application.

Each process has an access token (created at logon) built from the profile of the authenticated user. An impersonating thread has two access tokens, the primary access token that describes the access token of the parent process and the impersonation access token that represents the security context of a different user. Obviously, impersonation requires an adequate system privilege.

Windows 2000 introduced primitives for the creation of restricted tokens. A restricted token is an access token where some privileges have been removed or restricting SIDs have been added. A restricting SID is used to limit the capabilities of an access token. When an access request is made and the access token is compared with the ACEs in the ACL, each time there is a match between the restricting SID in the token and the SID in an ACE, the ACE is considered only if it denies access rights on the object.

Inheritance

Some important securable objects contain other securable objects. As an example, folders in the NTFS file system contain files and other folders; registry keys contain subkeys. This containment hierarchy puts in the same containers objects that are often characterized by the same security requirements. Then, it is extremely convenient to permit an automatic propagation of security descriptions from an object to all the objects contained within it (cf. Introduction, support of abstractions). This feature is realized in Windows by access control *inheritance*.

A difference exists between Windows NT and Windows 2000 and later with respect to inheritance. In Windows NT there was no distinction between direct and inherited ACEs; in addition, ACEs were inherited by an object only when the object was created or when a new ACL was applied onto an object. The result was that a change in an ACE was not propagated down the hierarchy to the object that had inherited it. In Windows 2000 and later, propagation is automatic (as users would probably expect). In addition, Windows 2000 gives higher priority to ACEs directly defined on the specific objects by putting the inherited ACEs at the end of the DACL.

In Windows 2000 and later, three flags characterize every ACE. The first flag is active if the ACE has to be propagated to descendant objects. The second and third flag are active only if the first flag is active. The second flag is active when the ACE is propagated to child objects without activating the first flag, thus blocking propagation to the first level. The third flag is active when the ACE is not applied to the object itself. In addition, in the security descriptor of a securable object there is a flag that permits disabling the application of inherited ACEs to the object.

Fine Granularity Access Control

Another innovation of Windows 2000 is the introduction of a fine-grained access model, which supports the Windows object model. There are two different solutions. The first solution is applicable to directory services objects and uses new ACE types defining access rights on specific object properties. These ACEs are based on an object structure that extends the regular ACE with two GUID parameters (a GUID is the general object identifier). The first GUID represents the specific property, property set, or child object for which the ACE is defined. The second represents the object that can inherit the ACE.

The second solution is the one offered within Active Directory services by the *controlAccessRight* object. The object specifies access rights on object properties or on user-defined actions. The object is then referenced within an ACE inserted in the DACL of the object itself.

Evaluation of Windows Access Control

As we did with Linux, we evaluate Windows access control services along the principles presented in the Introduction.

Accountability and reliable input: the operating system allows the use of reliable and strong authentication solutions. Because of its dominance of the desktop platform, many providers of authentication mechanisms focus their products on the Windows platform. Because of the need to avoid obstacles to its use by inexperienced users, the standard configuration of the Windows platform presents choices that are questionable from a security perspective, but it is possible to create resilient solutions with a careful configuration.

Support for fine-grained and coarse-grained specifications: the security model permits the definition of authorizations at different granularities.

Conditional authorizations: the Windows security model is based on the construction or inheritance of a concrete ACL for every resource that needs to be protected. Conditions are not supported.

Least privilege: to realize this principle, the security administrator has to carefully design the security policy.

Separation of duty: the separation between the DACL and SACL is the basis for the construction of a system where the administrator actions are monitored. Nonetheless, the system administrator has complete control over the local system.

Multiple policies and exceptions: the Windows security model supports exceptions, in the form of positive and negative authorizations. There is no explicit support for multiple policies, except the combination that may occur because of authorization inheritance.

Policy combination and conflict resolution: when there is the need to combine policies, for example, when for an object there are explicit and inherited authorizations, Windows considers the position in the ACL (between two conflicting authorizations, the first one wins). Because inherited authorizations are considered after the locally specified ones, the inherited policies are dominated by those specified on the object or nearer to the object.

Administrative polices: administration is based on the ownership of resources, together with the presence of an administrator able to define policies for all the resources of the system.

Overall, the Windows security model is quite powerful, but given its reliance on the position of authorizations within the ACL to solve conflicts, it is more adequate as an enforcement mechanism rather than a policy definition language; it appears an interesting opportunity that is the design of tools that is able to represent policies at an abstract level and then to map the defined policy in the terms that are adequate for the Windows mechanism.

ACCESS CONTROL IN DATABASE MANAGEMENT SYSTEMS

Database management systems (DBMSs) usually provide access control services in addition to those provided by the underlying operating systems (Castano, Fugini, Martella, & Samarati, 1995). DBMS access control allows references to the data model concepts and the consequent specification of authorizations dependent on the data and on the applications. Most of the existing DBMSs (e.g., Oracle Server, SQL Server, and Postgres) are based on the relational data model and on the use of Structured Query Language (SQL) as the data definition and manipulation language (Atzeni, Ceri, Paraboschi, & Torlone, 1999). The SQL standard provides commands for the specification of access restrictions on the objects managed by the DBMS. We here illustrate the main SQL facilities with reference to the latest version of the language, namely SQL:1999 (ISO International Standard, 1999).

Security Features of SQL

SQL access control is based on *user* and *role* identifiers. User identifiers correspond to login names with which users open the DBMS sessions. DBMS users are defined by the DMBS in an implementation-dependent way and are usually independent of the usernames managed by the operating system; SQL does not define how OS users are mapped to SQL users. Roles, introduced in SQL:1999, are "named collections of privileges" (Sandhu, Ferraiolo, & Kuhn, 2000), that is, named virtual entities to which privileges are assigned; by activating a role, users are enabled to execute the privileges associated with the role.

Users and roles can be granted authorizations on any object managed by the DBMS, namely tables, views, columns of tables and views, domains, assertions, and user-defined constructs such as user-defined types, triggers, and SQL-invoked routines. Authorizations can also be granted to public, meaning that they apply to all the user and role identifiers in the SQL environment. Apart from the drop and alter statements—which permit deletion and modification of the schema of an object and whose execution is reserved to the object's owner—authorizations can be specified for any of the commands supported by SQL, namely *select*, *insert*, *update*, and *delete* for tables and views (where the first three can refer to specific columns) and *execute* for SQL-invoked routines. In addition, other actions allow controlling references to re-

sources; they are as follows: *reference, usage, under*, and *trigger*. The *reference* privilege, associated with tables or attributes within, allows reference to tables/attributes in an integrity constraint: a constraint cannot be checked unless the owner of the schema in which the constraint appears has the *reference* privilege on all the objects involved in the constraint. The reason for this is that constraints may affect the availability of the objects on which they are defined, and therefore their specification should be reserved to those explicitly authorized. The *usage* privilege, which can be applied to domains, user-defined types, character sets, collations, or translations, allows the use of the object in one's own declarations. The *under* privilege can be applied to a user-defined type and allows subjects to define a subtype of the specified type. The *trigger* privilege, referred to a table, allows the definition of a trigger on the table.

In addition to authorizations to execute privileges on the different objects of the database management system, SQL also supports authorizations on roles. In particular, roles can be granted to other users and roles. Granting a role to a user means allowing the user to activate the role. Granting a role r' to another role r means permitting r to enjoy the privileges granted to r'. Intuitively, authorizations of roles granted to roles introduce chains of roles through which privileges can flow. For instance, consider the case in Figure 4 where the rightmost three nodes are users, the remaining three nodes are roles and an arc corresponds to an authorization of the incident node on the role source of the arc (e.g., Ann has an authorization for the Admin_Supervisor role). Although each of the users will be allowed to activate the role for which it has the authorization (directly connected in our graph) it will enjoy the privileges of all the roles reachable through a chain. For instance, when activating role Admin_Supervisor, Ann will also enjoy, in addition to the privileges granted to this role, the privileges granted to roles Secretary and Accountant.

Access Control Enforcement

A pair <uid, rid> always identifies the subject making a request, where *uid* is the SQL session user identifier (which can never be null) and *rid* is a role name, whose value is initially null. Both the user identifier and the role identifier can be changed via commands set session authorization and set role, respectively, whose successful execution depends on the specified authorizations. In particular, enabling a role requires the current user to have the authorization for the role. The current pair <*uid, rid*> can also change upon execution of an SQL-invoked routine, where it is set to the owner of the routine (cf. "Views and Invoked Routines"). An *authorization stack* (maintained using a "last-in, first-out" strategy) keeps track of

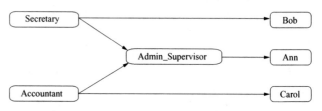

Figure 4:   An example of role chains in SQL.

the sequence of pairs *<uid, rid>* for a session. Every request is controlled against the authorizations of the top element of the stack. Although the subject is a pair, like for authorizations and ownership, access control always refers to either a user or a role identifier in mutual exclusion: it is performed against the authorizations for *uid* if the *rid* is null; it is performed against the authorizations for *rid*, otherwise. In other words, by activating a role a user can enjoy the privileges of the role while disabling her own. Moreover, at most one role at a time can be active: the setting to a new role rewrites the *rid* element to be the new role specified.

Administration

Every object in SQL has an owner, typically its creator (which can be set to either the current_user or current_role). The owner of an object can execute all privileges on it or a subset of them in case of views and SQL-invoked routines (cf. "Views and Invoked Routines"). The owner is also reserved the privilege to drop the object and to alter (i.e., modify) it. Apart for the drop and alter privileges, whose execution is reserved to the object's owner, the owner can grant authorizations for any privilege on its objects, together with the ability to pass such authorizations to others (grant option).

A grant command, whose syntax is illustrated in Figure 5, allows granting new authorizations for roles (enabling their activation) or for privileges on objects. Successful execution of the command requires the grantor to be the owner of the object on which the privilege is granted or to hold the grant option for it. The specification of all privileges, instead of an explicit privilege list, is equivalent to the specification of all the privileges, on the object, for which the grantor has the grant option. The with hierarchy option (possible only for the *select* privilege on tables) automatically implies granting the grantee the *select* privilege on all the (either existing or future) subtables of the table on which the privilege is granted. The with grant option clause (called with admin option for roles) allows the grantee to grant others the received authorization (as well as the grant option on it). No cycles of role grants are allowed.

The revoke statement allows revocation of (administrative or access) privileges previously granted by the revoker (which can be set to the current_user or current_role). Because of the use of the grant option and the existence of derived objects (see "Views and Invoked Routines"), revocation of a privilege can possibly have side effects, because there may be other authorizations that depend on the one being revoked. Options cascade and restrict dictate how the revocation procedure should behave in such a case: cascade recursively revokes all those authorizations that should no longer exist if the requested privilege is revoked; restrict rejects the execution of the revoke operation if other authorizations depend on it. To illustrate, consider the case where user Ann creates a table and grants the select privilege, and the grant option on it, to Bob and Carol. Bob grants it to David, who grants it to Ellen, and to Frank, who grants it to Gary. Carol also grants the authorization to Frank. Assume for simplicity that all these grant statements include the grant option. Figure 6(a) illustrates the resulting authorizations and their dependencies via a graph reporting a node for every user and an arc from the grantor to the grantee for every authorization. Consider now a request by Ann to revoke the privilege from Bob. If the revoke is requested with option cascade, the authorizations granted by Bob (who would not hold anymore the grant option for the privilege) will be revoked, causing the revocation of David's authorization, which will recursively cause the revocation of the authorization David granted to Ellen. The resulting authorizations (and their dependencies) are illustrated in Figure 6(b). Note that no recursive revocation is activated for Frank as, even if the authorization he

```
grant all privileges|<action>
on[table]|domain|collation|character set|translation|type <object name>
to <grantee>[{<comma> <grantee>}...]
[with hierarchy option]
[with grant option]
[granted by <grantor>]
```

```
grant <role granted> [{ <comma> <role granted>}...]
TO <grantee>[{ <comma> <grantee>}...]
[with admin option]
[granted by <grantor>]
```

```
revoke [grant option for|hierarchy option for]<action>
on[table]|domain|collation|character set|translation|type <object name>
from <grantee>[{ <comma> <grantee> }...]
[granted by <grantor>]
cascade|restrict
```

```
revoke[admin option for]
<role revoked>[{ <comma> <role revoked> }...]
from <grantee>[{ <comma> <grantee> }...]
[granted by <grantor>]
cascade | restrict
```

Figure 5: Syntax of the grant and revoke SQL statements.

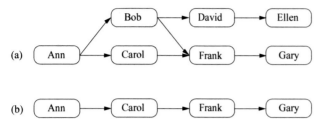

Figure 6: A graphical representation of authorizations before (a) and after (b) a cascade revocation.

received from Bob is deleted, Frank still holds the privilege with the grant option (received from Carol). By contrast, if Ann were to request the revoke operation with the `restrict` option, the operation would be refused because of the authorizations dependent on it (those which would be revoked with the `cascade` option).

Views and Invoked Routines

A special consideration must be devoted to authorizations for derived objects (views) and SQL-invoked routines, where the case can be that the owner creating them does not own the underlying objects used in their definition.

A view is a *virtual* table derived from base tables and/or other views. A view definition is a SQL statement whose result defines the content of the view. The view is virtual because its content is not explicitly stored but it is derived, at the time the view is accessed, by executing the corresponding SQL statement on the underlying tables. A user/role can create a view only if it has the necessary privilege on all the views, or base tables, directly referenced by the view. The creator receives on the view the privileges that it holds on all the tables directly referenced by the view. Also, it receives the grant option for a privilege only if it has the grant option for the privilege on all the tables directly referenced by the view. If it holds a privilege on the view with the grant option, the creator can grant the privilege (and the grant option) to others. The grantees of such privileges need not hold the privileges on the underlying tables to access the view; access to the view requires only the existence of privileges on the view. Intuitively, the execution of the query computing the view is controlled against the authorizations of the view's owner (similar to what the *suid* bit does in Unix). Also, views provide a way to enforce finer grained access (on specific tuples). For instance, a user can define a view `EU_Employees` on table `Employees` containing only those rows for which the value of attribute `nationality` is equal to `EU`. She can then grant other users the *select* privilege on the view, thus allowing (and restricting) them access to information on employees within the European Union. Views are the only means to bypass an *all tuples* or *no tuple* access on tables. Although convenient, views are, however, simply a trick for enforcing content-dependent fine-grained access control (which is not the main reason why they were developed) and as such result are limiting for this purpose: a different view should be defined for any possible content-dependent access restriction that should be enforced.

A SQL-invoked routine is an SQL-invoked procedure, or a SQL-invoked function, characterized by a header and a body. The header consists of a name and a possibly empty list of parameters. The body may be specified in SQL or, in the case of external routines, written in a host programming language. At object creation time, a user is designated as the *owner* of the routine. Analogous to what is required for views, to create a SQL-invoked routine, the owner needs to have the necessary privileges for the successful execution of the routine. The routine is dropped if at any time the owner loses any of the privileges necessary to execute the body of the routine. When a routine is created, the creator receives the *execute* privilege on it, with the grant option if it has the grant option for all the privileges necessary for the routine to run. If the creator of a routine has the *execute* privilege with the grant option, she can grant such a privilege, and the grant option on it, to other users/roles. The *execute* privilege on a SQL routine is sufficient for these other users/roles to run the routine (they need not have the privileges necessary for the routine to run; only the creator does). Intuitively, SQL routines provide a service similar to the *setuid/setgid* privileges in Linux and impersonation in Windows (controlling privileges with respect to the owner instead of the caller of a procedure).

Evaluation

We now evaluate SQL access control services along the principles presented in the Introduction.

Accountability and reliable input: DBMSs typically employ an authentication mechanism separate from that of the operating system on which the system executes. This permits a greater flexibility and independence from the specific operating system. Authentication usually is based on the use of passwords, but the model is compatible with other approaches and it is quite common to protect access to the database from the outside, allowing access only from specified network nodes.

Support for fine-grained and coarse-grained specifications: views and stored procedures are powerful tools that permit representation of the security policy with fine granularity.

Conditional authorizations: views permit the introduction of authorizations on table portions specified by a query, fully satisfying this principle.

Least privilege: the SQL access model satisfies this principle with roles, which are acquired dynamically before accessing a protected resource and should be immediately released.

Separation of duty: the database administrator has complete control over the DBMS.

Multiple policies and exceptions: the current access control model only envisions positive authorizations.

Policy combination and conflict resolution: policy combination may arise because of the presence of many users able to give privileges for access to their resources. Because there are no negative authorizations, policy combination is trivial, as it only requires for each user to add all the privileges obtained from any user in the system.

Administrative policies: the SQL access control model clearly identifies the possibility to grant the privilege to pass to other users the authorization that a user has received, implementing a delegation model.

Overall, the SQL access model presents several features that characterize it as a modern access control solution.

ACCESS CONTROL FOR INTERNET-BASED SOLUTIONS

We here survey the most common security features for Internet-based solutions. Again, we illustrate the most popular representative of the different families. We therefore look at TCPD for Internet service access, at Apache for Web-based solutions, and at the Java 2 security model.

```
#hosts.allow
in.ftpd: ALL: mail -s "remote ftp attempt from %h" admin)
#hosts.deny
ALL: ALL
```

TCPD

The `tcpd` program (`www.porcupine.org/wietse`) is a wrapper program that is normally used in Unix-like operating systems to monitor incoming requests for Internet services such as `telnet`, `finger`, and `ftp`, among others. `tcpd` is activated by the `inetd` process every time a request for service is received on a port. Upon activation, `tcpd` logs the request (recording the timestamp, the client host name, and the name of the requested service) as specified in `etc/syslog.conf` and evaluates files `/etc/hosts.allow` and `/etc/hosts.deny` (which are the files where access control rules are specified) to determine whether the request should be granted or denied. Each of these files include zero or more *access rules* of the form

service_list: *client_list* [: *shell_command*],

where *service_list* is a list of service daemons (e.g., `ftpd`, `telnetd`, and `fingerd`); *client_list* is a list of host names, host addresses, or patterns; and *shell_command* is an optional shell command that must be executed every time the rule is matched. Wildcards can be used in place of a specific service/client to denote a set of them. For instance, wildcard `ALL` matches with any service/client, whereas `LOCAL` matches any host whose name does not contain a dot character. Patterns are partial host/address specification and are used to refer, in a convenient way, to groups of hosts or addresses (all those matching with the pattern). Typically a pattern specifies only the most generic part of a host/address identifier (namely the rightmost elements for symbolic addresses and the leftmost elements for numeric IPs), thus denoting a whole subnetwork of machines. In other words, a symbolic pattern begins with a dot character and matches all host names whose rightmost components equal those specified. For instance, patterns `.it` or `.acme.com` will match all machines in the `it` domains or within the `acme.com`

subnetwork, respectively. Conversely, a numeric pattern ends with a dot character and matches all host addresses whose leftmost fields equal those specified. For instance, pattern `159.155.` will match all machines in the `159.155.` subnetwork.

The difference between files `hosts.allow` and `hosts.deny` is that `hosts.allow` expresses permissions (i.e., which hosts should be allowed access to the mentioned services), whereas `hosts.deny` expresses denials.

The access control process performs first an evaluation of `hosts.allow`. If a matching rule is found access is granted (and the shell command executed, if any). Otherwise, `hosts.deny` is evaluated and, if a matching rule is found, access is denied (and the shell command executed, if any). The fact that the evaluation order is established by the mechanism implies that only this single predefined conflict resolution policy is supported. If no rule is found in either file, the access is granted (open policy by default). As an example, we consider the specification in Figure 7, which denies all accesses but `ftp`. The shell command in the permission, executed in correspondence of `ftp` requests, sends an e-mail message to the system administrator signaling the ftp request from client `%h`, where the symbolic name `%h` is expanded to the client host name or IP address.

Overall, the access control model is relatively simple and all its features are present in the host-based access control of Apache. For this reason, we omit the evaluation on the principles.

Apache Access Control

The Apache HTTP server (www.apache.org) allows the specification of access control rules via a per-directory configuration file usually called `.htaccess` (Apache, 2005). The `.htaccess` file is a text file including access control rules (called *directives* in Apache) that affect the directory in which the `.htaccess` file is placed and, recursively, directories below it. See Evaluation of .htaccess

```
SetEnvIf Referer www.mydomain.org internal_site
AuthName "user-based restriction"
AuthType Basic
AuthUserFile /home/mylogin/.htpasswd
AuthGroupFile /home/mylogin/.htgroup
Order Deny,Allow
Deny from all
Allow from acme.com
Allow from env= internal_site
Require valid-user
Satisfy any
<FilesMatch public_access.html>
 Allow from all
</FilesMatch>
```

Figure 7: A simple example of the TCPD configuration files.

253

files. Figure 7 illustrates a simple example of the .htaccess file.

Access control directives, whose specification is enabled via module mod access, can be either *host based* (they can refer to the client's host name and IP address, or other characteristics of the request) or *user based* (they can refer to usernames and groups thereof). We start by describing such directives and then illustrate how the .htaccess files that include them are evaluated.

Host-Based Access Control

Host-based directives resemble and enrich the security specifications of the tcpd solution examined earlier. Both permissions and denials can be specified, by using the Allow (for permissions) and Deny (for denials) directives, which can refer to location properties or environment variables of the request. *Location-based* specifications have the following form:

    Allow from *host-or-network*/all
    Deny from *host-or-network*/all,

where *host-or-network* can be a domain name (e.g., acme.com), an IP address or IP pattern (e.g., 155.50.), a network/netmask pair (e.g., 10.0.0.0/255.0.0.0), or a network/*n* mask size, where *n* is a number between 1 and 32 specifying the number of high-order 1 bits in the netmask. For instance, all the following definitions are equivalent: 10.0.0.0/8 and 10.0.0.0/255.0.0.0. Alternatively, value all denotes all hosts on the network.

Variable-based specifications have the following form:

    Allow from env = *env-variable*
    Deny from env = *env-variable*,

where *env-variable* denotes an environment variable. The semantics is that the directive (allow or deny) applies if *env-variable* exists. Apache sets environment variables based on different attributes of the HTTP client request, using the directives provided by module mod_setenvif. The attributes may correspond to various HTTP request header fields (see RFC 2616; Fielding et al., 1999) or to other aspects of the request. The most commonly used request header field names include User-Agent (typically the browser originating the request) and Referer (the URI of the document from which the URI in the request was obtained). For instance, in Figure 7 directive SetEnvIf sets "internal_site" if the referring page was in the www.mydomain.org Web site. The "Allow from env = internalsite" directive, then, permits access if the referring page matches the given URI.

Access control evaluates the content of file .htaccess to determine whether a request should be granted or denied. The Order directive controls the order in which the Deny and Allow directives must be evaluated (thus allowing users to dictate the conflict resolution policy to be applied) and defines the default access state. There are three possible orderings:

Deny, Allow: the deny directives are evaluated first, and access is allowed by default (open policy). Any client that does not match a deny directive *or* matches an allow directive is granted access.

Allow, Deny: the allow directives are evaluated first and access is denied by default (closed policy). Any client that does not match an allow directive *or* matches a deny directive is denied access.

Mutual-failure: only clients that do not match any Deny directive *and* match an Allow directive are allowed access.

For instance, the .htaccess file in Figure 7 states that all hosts in the acme.com domain and requests with a referring page in the www.mydomain.org Web site are allowed access; all other hosts are denied access.

User-Based Access Control

In additions to host-based access control rules, Apache includes a module, called mod_auth, that enables user authentication (based on usernames and passwords) and enforcement of user-based access control rules. Usernames and associated passwords are stored in a text *user file*, reporting pairs of the form "*username:MD5-encrypted password*." Command htpasswd is used to modify the file (i.e., add new users or change passwords) as well as to create/rewrite it (a -c flag rewrites the file as new). The command has the following form:

    htpasswd [-c] *filename username*,

where *filename* is the full path name of the user file and *username* is the name of the created user. Upon entering the command, the system will ask to specify the password (as usual, asking its input twice to avoid insertion errors). An alternative to the text user file provided by module mod_auth is given by modules mod_auth_db and mod_auth_dbm. With these modules, the usernames and passwords are stored in Berkeley DB files and DBM type database files, respectively.

To define user-based restrictions, a name can be given to the portion of the file system that requires authentication. This portion, called *realm*, corresponds to the subtree rooted at the directory containing the .htaccess file.

The main directives to create realms are as follows:

AuthName, to give a name to the realm. The realm name will be communicated to users when prompted for the login dialog (e.g., as in Figure 8).

AuthType, to specify the type of authentication to be used. The most common method implemented by mod_auth is Basic, which sends the password from the client to the server unencrypted (with a base64 encoding). A more secure, but less common, alternative is the Digest authentication method, implemented by module mod_auth_digest, which sends the server a one-way hash (MD5 digest) of the username:password pair. This Digest authentication method is supported only by relatively recent versions of browsers (e.g., Opera, MS Internet Explorer, Amaya, Mozilla, and Netscape since version 7).

AuthUserFile, to specify the absolute path of the file that contains usernames and passwords. Note that the user file containing names and passwords does not need to be in the same directory as the .htaccess file.

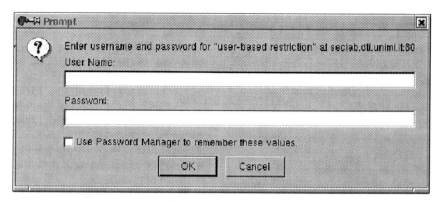

Figure 8: An example of dialog box that prompts for username and password.

`AuthGroupFile`, to specify the location of a *group file*, and therefore provide support for access rules specified for groups. The group file is a list of entries of the form `group-name: username1 username2 username3...` where *group-name* is the name associated with the group to which the specified usernames are declared to belong, and each of the usernames appearing in the list must be in the user file (i.e., be an existing username).

The four directives above allow the server to know where to find the usernames and passwords and what authentication protocol has to be used. User-based access rules are specified with a directive require that can take the following three forms:

`require user` *username1 username2...usernameN*
  Only usernames "*username1 username2...usernameN*" are allowed access.

`require group` *group1 group2...groupM*
  Only usernames in groups "*group1 group2...groupM*" are allowed access.

`require valid-user`
  Any username in the user file is allowed access

Host-Based and User-Based Interactions and Finer-Grained Specifications

Host- and user-based access directives are not mutually exclusive and they can both be used to control access to the same resources. Directive `Satisfy` allows the specification of how the two sets of directives should interact. `Satisfy` takes one argument whose value can be either `all` or `any`. Value `all` requires both user-based and host-based directives to be satisfied for access to be granted, whereas for value `any`, it is sufficient that either one is satisfied for access to be granted.

As already said, all the directives specified in .htaccess apply to the file system subtree rooted at the directory that contains the specific .htaccess file unless overridden. In other words, a .htaccess file in a directory applies to all the files directly contained in the directory and recursively propagates to all its subdirectories unless a .htaccess has been specified for them (*most specific takes precedence*). Apache 1.2 and later support finer-grained rules allowing the specification of access directives on a per-file basis by including `FilesMatch` section of the form "`<FilesMatch reg-exp>directives</FilesMatch>`," with the semantics that the directives included in the `FilesMatch` section apply only to the files with a name matching the regular expression specified. Also, directives can be specified on a per-method basis by use of a `Limit` section of the form "`<Limit` *list of access methods>directives*`</Limit>`," with the semantics that the directives included in the `Limit` section apply only to the accesses listed (again overriding the directives specified in the .htaccess file). As an example, directive

```
<Limit get post put>
  require valid-user
</Limit>
```

would allow any authenticated user to execute methods `get`, `post`, and `put`. The directive does not apply to other operations.

Evaluation of .htaccess Files

As mentioned previously, file .htaccess is used to control accesses to the files in a directory. Therefore, whenever an access request to a file is submitted, the Apache HTTP server starts checking in the top directory for a .htaccess file and then checks each subdirectory down to and including the directory where the requested file is stored. All .htaccess files found during this process (called *directory walk*) are processed and merged, thus resulting in a set of directives that apply to the requested file. More precisely, the directives specified in the .htaccess files have to be processed if they belong to the categories (`AuthConfig`, `FileInfo`, `Indexes`, `Limit`, and `Options`) listed in the `AllowOverride` list specified in a server configuration file. These directives are then merged according to the most specific principle; that is, directives within .htaccess files in subdirectories may change or nullify the effects of the directives within .htaccess files of parent directories. As an example, suppose that the access request for `http://acme.com/Department1/welcome.html` resolves to the file`/home/myaccount/www/Department1/welcome.html` and that statement `AllowOverride All` has been specified. In this case, the Apache HTTP server merges *all* directives included in the .htaccess files of directories: `/`; `/home`; `/home/myaccount`; `/home/myaccount/www`; and `/home/myaccount/www/Department1`.

Evaluation of the Apache Model

We now evaluate the Apache access control model along the principles presented in the Introduction.

Accountability and reliable input: the Apache server supports a few alternatives for authentication; an issue that often has to be faced is the inadequate support that often Internet browsers provide and that may require use of a weak solution in order not to penalize a portion of users.

Support for fine-grained and coarse-grained specifications: as was shown, the model permits use of a flexible granularity in the specification of authorizations.

Conditional authorizations: patterns may be used for addresses, host names, and resource identifiers.

Least privilege: the flexibility in the specification of authorizations permits identification of the specific resource portions that a user should access.

Separation of duty: the environment where the system is configured is completely separated from the HTTP requests that represent the way the system is accessed. The use of privileges on the file system may permit the construction of a partitioned system, with well-identified responsibilities for the different owners of resources exported by the server.

Multiple policies and exceptions: the Apache model contains positive and negative authorizations, and it also allows the specification of multiple policies.

Policy combination and conflict resolution: the Apache model offers flexibility in the choice of the policy combination that has to be used.

Administrative polices: an administrative policy may be realized using the access control services of the file system where the resources are stored together with the .htaccess file representing the security policy. Within the Apache model it is possible to specify which is the domain of options that a more specific policy can override.

Overall, the access control model of Apache presents many interesting features and is a powerful solution that has aimed to satisfy the requirements of modern access control solutions.

Java 2 Security Model

Java is both a modern object-oriented programming language and a complex software architecture. Java has been developed by Sun Microsystems and is currently one of the most important solutions for the construction of applications in a network environment. Java offers sophisticated solutions for the design of distributed and mobile applications, where the software can be partitioned on distinct nodes and downloaded from one node to be executed on another.

Since its introduction, Java designers have carefully considered the security implications of an architecture where executable code could be downloaded from the network, possibly from untrusted hosts. The first security model of Java, the one associated with Java Development Kit version 1.0 (JDK 1.0), was based on the construction of a *sandbox*, a restricted environment for the execution of downloaded code, with rigid restrictions on the set of local resources that could be used (e.g., with no access to the file system and with limits on network access).

The main problem of JDK 1.0 security model was the limited granularity and the availability of a single policy for all downloaded code. JDK 1.0 would let programmers revise the access control services and implement their own version, but the implementation of access control services is complex, expensive and delicate, making it unfeasible for most applications.

The evolution of Java to version 2 gave the opportunity to revise the security model and significantly improve it. We describe the Java 2 security architecture. A full and authoritative description of the architecture appears in Gong (1999).

We observe that the security services of Java are not related to the access control system of the host operating system. This design choice derives from the requirement to make Java a fully portable execution environment that does not depend on the services of the underlying system. The Java environment will have to be properly protected on the host system, as write access to the implementation of the Java Virtual Machine, or to its configuration, would permit bypassing of any security mechanism within the Java environment.

We focus the presentation on the security model that associates permissions with pieces of Java code. This code-centric model adequately supports the security of mobile code. We do not describe the *Java Authentication and Authorization Service* (JAAS, since Java 2 v. 1.4 integrated with the JDK), a set of Java packages that offers services for user authentication and management of access control rights. JAAS extends the native Java 2 security model, using all the mechanisms presented here.

Security Policy

The security policy describes the behavior that a Java program should exhibit. Each security policy is composed of a list of entries (an access control list) that define the permissions associated with Java classes and applications. There is a standard security policy defined for the whole Java installation, and each user can personalize it, extending the ACL in several ways, for example, writing a specific file in the personal home directory. A policy object represents the security policy.

Each entry in the security policy describes a piece of Java code and the permissions that are granted to it. Each piece of Java code is described by a URL and a list of signatures (represented in Java by a CodeSource object). The URL can be used to identify both local and remote code; with a single URL it is also possible to characterize single classes or complete collections (packages, JAR files, directory trees). The signatures may be applied on the complete URL or on a single class within a collection. Because URLs may identify collections, it is important to support implication among CodeSource objects (e.g., http://www.xmlsec.org/classes/ implies http://www.xmlsec.org/classes/xml.jar).

Permissions

Permissions describe the access rights that are granted to pieces of Java code. Each permission is represented by an instance of the abstract class `Permission`. Permissions are typically represented by a target and an action (e.g., file target `/tmp/javaAppl/buffer` and action `write`). There are permissions that are characterized only by the target, with no action (e.g., target `exitVM` for the execution of `System.exit`). The `Permission` class is specialized by many concrete classes, which define a hierarchy. Direct descendants of `Permission` are `FilePermission` (used to represent access rights on files), `SocketPermission` (used to control access to network ports), `AllPermission` (used to represent with a single permission the collection of all permissions), and `BasicPermission` (typically used as the base class for permissions with no action).

The current security model considers only positive permissions. The rationale is that the evaluation is more efficient and the model is clearer for the programmer. However, no fundamental restriction has been introduced and the model could evolve to support negative authorizations (in a future version of Java, or in an ad hoc security mechanism built for a specific application).

It is also interesting to note that permissions refer to classes and not to instance objects. A model granting permissions to objects would have offered finer granularity, but it would have also been more difficult to manage. Specifically, objects exist only at run-time, whereas the security policy is static and it is not convenient to specify in it permissions at the level of objects.

To manage sets of permission, the Java model offers class `PermissionCollection`, which groups permissions of the same category (e.g., file permissions). Class `Permissions` represents collections of `PermissionCollection` objects, that is, collections of collections of `Permission` objects.

Access Control

In the Java 2 architecture, permissions are not directly associated with classes. Class `ProtectionDomain` realizes the link between classes and permissions. The security policy specifies permissions for a URL, which may correspond to many classes; all the classes refer to the same protection domain. There is a predefined *system* domain that associates permission `AllPermissions` with all the classes in the core of the Java architecture.

In Java 2, access control is realized at two levels: `SecurityManager` and `AccessController`. At the higher level, class `SecurityManager` is responsible for evaluating access restrictions and is invoked whenever permissions have to be verified. In JDK 1.0 the class was abstract, forcing each Java implementation to provide its own realization. In Java 2 the class is concrete and a standard implementation is part of the run-time environment. The main method of class `SecurityManager` is `checkPermission`. In JDK 1.0 the check on permissions was realized by ad hoc methods (e.g., to check for read permission on a file, method `checkRead` was used). Java 2 maintains all the previous methods for backward compatibility, but it uses a single method `checkPermission` for every permission type. This increases the flexibility of the security

model, as the introduction of novel permissions can be managed with relative ease, without the need to modify the implementation of the `SecurityManager`.

Method `checkPermission` determines whether the permission that appears as first parameter of the method is granted. If the check is successful, the method returns the control to the caller; otherwise it generates a security exception.

Method `checkPermission` in the standard `SecurityManager` immediately calls method `checkPermission` of class `AccessController`. Class `AccessController` is a final (i.e., unmodifiable) class that represents the security policy that Java 2 supports by default. This distinction into two levels is motivated by two conflicting requirements, each managed at a separate level. On the one hand, there is the need for flexibility, for applications that may need a different security policy; for these applications it would be possible to realize a specialized implementation of the `SecurityManager` class that would then be automatically invoked for security checks by Java classes (which call the services of the `SecurityManager`). On the other hand, applications may prefer to have a guarantee that the security model used is the default one for Java 2; in this case, applications may opt to refer directly to the services of the `AccessController` class.

Access control is evaluated in the execution environment, which is characterized by an array of `ProtectionDomain` objects. There may be more than one `ProtectionDomain` object as Java classes may invoke the services of classes that belong to different domains. The problem is then to decide how to consider the permissions of different domains in the execution environment. The solution used in Java 2 is to consider as applicable only those permissions that belong to the intersection of all the domains. Consequently, when `checkPermission` runs, it considers all the `ProtectionDomain` objects and if there is at least one domain that has not been granted the permission being checked, a security exception is generated. The rationale for this policy is that this is the safest approach, realizing the least privilege principle.

There is an exception to the above behavior, which requires the use of method `doPrivileged` of class `AccessController`. Method `doPrivileged` creates a separate execution environment, which considers only the permissions of the `ProtectionDomain` associated with the code itself. The goal of this method is analogous to that of the *setuid* mechanism in Linux, where the privileges of the owner of the code are granted to the user executing it. For instance, a `changePassword` method that requires write permission on a password file can be realized within a `doPrivileged` method. The advantage of this mechanism with respect to the *setuid* mechanism is that in Java it is possible to restrict with a very fine granularity the Java statements that have to be executed in a privileged mode, whereas in Linux the privileges of the owner are available to the executor for the complete run of the program (in contrast to the *least privilege* principle). Finally, we consider how the security model integrates with the inheritance mechanism that characterizes the Java object model. Two classes where one is a specialization of the other may belong to distinct domains. When a method of a subclass is invoked, the effective `ProtectionDomain` is the one where the method is implemented; if the method is simply inherited from the superclass, with no redefinition, the domain of the superclass is considered; if the method is redefined in the subclass, the domain of the subclass is instead used by the `checkPermission` method.

Evaluation of Java Access Control Model

We now evaluate the Java access control model along the principles presented in the Introduction.

Accountability and reliable input: the Java environment supports many alternatives for authentication, with a rich collection of solutions that include support for PKI, hardware access control devices (e.g., smart cards and cryptographic tokens), and biometrics.

Support for fine-grained and coarse-grained specifications: privileges can be defined at several levels, depending on the needs of the application.

Conditional authorizations: patterns can be used to identify resources; resources are organized in hierarchies and it is possible to specify the privilege at an arbitrary level of the hierarchy.

Least privilege: the flexibility in the specification of authorizations permits identification of the specific resource portions that a user has to access, satisfying this principle. The mechanism of impersonation has also been introduced to satisfy this principle.

Separation of duty: this principle is applied in many contexts, for example, in the identification of the protection domains that characterize the access profiles needed for distinct activities.

Multiple policies and exceptions: the current security model allows only the definition of positive authorizations, for efficiency reasons. It is possible to implement several policy evaluation mechanisms, depending on the requirements of the application, with a considerable degree of flexibility.

Policy combination and conflict resolution: the combination of policies occurs when combining the protection domains of separate classes or when considering the policies defined at distinct levels of the class hierarchy. Because of the absence of negative authorizations, the combination of policies is relatively simple to manage.

Administrative polices: the owner of the Java execution environment is able to specify the policy that the system will have to follow.

Overall, the access control model of Java is a modern and complex solution that considers all previous research and implementation experience of previous systems and adapts the access control principles to the needs of a sophisticated execution environment. This adaptation has produced a flexible system that requires a significant learning effort to be exploited at its full potential. Current Java applications do not typically use all the features presented above, and the definition of a complex policy is a task that requires careful analysis, but in this way the Java environment is ready to be used for the construction of modern applications, possibly using additional support tools able to provide a higher level description of the access control policy.

CONCLUSIONS

In this chapter we have discussed the basic concepts of access control and illustrated the main features of the access control services provided by some of the most popular operating systems, database management systems, and network-based solutions. Hinting at the principles and how they are (or are not) satisfied by current approaches, the chapter can be useful to both those interested in access control development, who may get an overview of a wide array of solutions in many different contexts, and to those end users who need to represent their protection requirements in their systems and, by knowing their strengths and weaknesses, can make more proper and secure use of it.

ACKNOWLEDGMENTS

We thank the anonymous referees for helpful comments and suggestions. This work was supported in part by the European Union within the PRIME Project in the FP6/IST Programme under contract IST-2002-507591 and by the Italian MIUR within the KIWI and MAPS projects.

GLOSSARY

Authentication   Means of establishing the validity of a claimed identity.

Authorization   The right granted to a user to exercise an action (e.g., read, write, create, delete, and execute) on certain objects.

Availability   A requirement intended to guarantee that information and system resources are accessible to authorized users when needed.

Confidentiality   The assurance that private or confidential information not be disclosed to unauthorized users.

Data Integrity   A requirement that information is not modified improperly.

Discretionary Access Control   Policies control access based on the identity of the requestor and on access rules stating what requestors are (or are not) allowed to do.

Group   A set of users.

Integrity   Information has integrity when it is accurate, complete, and consistent. (See *data integrity* and *system integrity*).

Mandatory Access Control   Policies control access based on mandated regulations determined by a central authority.

Role   A job function within an organization that describes the authority and responsibility related to the execution of an activity.

Role-Based Access Control   Policies control access depending on the roles that users have within the system and on rules stating what accesses are allowed to users in given roles.

Secrecy   A requirement that released information be protected from improper or unauthorized release.

Security   The combination of integrity, availability, and secrecy.

Security Mechanism Low-level software and/or hardware functions that implement security policies.
Security Policy High-level guidelines establishing rules that regulate access to resources.
Subject An active entity that can exercise access to the resources of the system.
User A person who interacts directly with a system.

CROSS REFERENCES

See *Computer and Network Authentication; Database Security; Linux Security; Password Authentication; Unix Security; Windows 2000 Security.*

REFERENCES

Apache (2005). *HTTP server version 2.0.* http://httpd.apache.org/docs-2.0/en.
Atzeni, P., Ceri, S., Paraboschi, S., & Torlone, R. (1999). *Database systems—Concepts, languages and architectures.* New York: McGraw-Hill.
Bellovin, S. M. (1989). Security problems in the TCP/IP protocol suite. *Communication Review, 19*(2), 32–48.
Castano, S., Fugini, M. G., Martella, G., & Samarati, P. (1995). *Database security.* Boston: Addison-Wesley.
Coar, K. (2000). *Using .htaccess files with apache.* http://apache-server.com/tutorials/ATusing-htaccess.html
Fielding, R., Gettys, J., Mogul, J., Frystyk, H., Masinter, L., Leach, P., & Berners-Lee, T. (1999). *Hypertext Transfer Protocol—HTTP/1.1.* http://www.rfc-editor.org/rfc/rfc2616.txt
Gong, L. (1999). *Inside Java 2 platform security.* Boston: Addison-Wesley.
Graham, G. S., & Denning, P. J. (1972). Protection principles and practice. In *Proceedings of the Spring Jt. Computer Conference* (Vol. 40, pp. 417–429). Montvale, NJ: American Federation of Information Processing Societies Press.
Harrison, M. H., Ruzzo, W. L., & Ullman, J. D. (1976). Protection in operating systems. *Communications of the ACM, 19*(8), 461–471.
ISO International Standard. (1999). Database Language SQL—Parts 1–5. ISO/IEC 9075.
Jajodia, S., Samarati, P., Sapino, M. L., & Subrahmanian, V. S. (2001). Flexible support for multiple access control policies. *ACM Transactions on Database Systems, 26*(2), 18–28.
Lampson, B. W. (1974). Protection. In *5th Princeton Symposium on Information Science and Systems* (pp. 437–443). *ACM Operating Systems Review, 8*(1):18–24.
Samarati, P., & De Capitani di Vimercati, S. (2001). Access control: Policies, models, and mechanisms. In R. Focardi & R. Gorrieri (Eds.), *Lecture notes in computer science: Vol. 2171: Foundations of security analysis and design.* New York: Springer-Verlag.
Sandhu, R. (1990). Separation of duties in computerized information systems. In *Proceedings of the IFIP WG11.3 Workshop on Database Security.* The Netherlands: North-Holland.
Sandhu, R., Coyne, E. J., Feinstein, H. L., &Youman, C. E. (1996). Role-based access control models. *IEEE Computer, 29*(2), 38–47.
Sandhu, R., Ferraiolo, D., & Kuhn, R. (2000). The NIST model for role-based access control: Towards a unified standard. In *Proceedings of the Fifth ACM Workshop on Role-Based Access Control* (pp. 47–63). New York: ACM Press.
Sandhu, R., & Samarati, P. (1997). *CRC handbook of computer science and engineering* (pp. 1929–1948). Boca Raton, FL: CRC Press.